Programming for Parks, Recreation, and Leisure Services: A Servant Leadership Approach

Third Edition

Programming for Parks, Recreation, and Leisure Services: A Servant Leadership Approach

Third Edition

by

Donald G. DeGraaf, Ph.D.
Calvin College

Debra J. Jordan, Re.D.
East Carolina University

Kathy H. DeGraaf

Venture Publishing, Inc.
State College, Pennsylvania

Production Manager: Richard Yocum
Manuscript Editing: Richard Yocum, George Lauer, Andrea Puzycki
Cover by StepUp Communications, Inc.

Library of Congress Catalogue Card Number 2009942722
ISBN-10 1-892132-87-7
ISBN-13 978-1-892132-87-1

Dedication

To those striving to be their best, to live a life of servant leadership, and to make a positive contribution to the world in which we live.

Table of Contents

Chapter Five ~~Old Chap 6~~

Chapter Six ~~Old Chap 7~~

Chapter Seven ~~Old Chap 8~~

Chapter Eight ~~Old Chap 9~~

Chapter Nine *old ch 10*

Chapter Ten *old ch 11*

Chapter Eleven *old ch 12*

Preface

Dynamic programming is a must if parks, recreation, and leisure services organizations are going to thrive in the twenty-first century. Programming is the one common, tangible, visible medium through which parks, recreation and leisure services professionals touch people's lives. Yet we all know that quality programs do not just happen; they require careful planning and development. This book is about the art and science of the complete programming process. We strive to go beyond merely presenting the knowledge and skills needed to provide quality programs; we suggest the integration of values into this process. We do this from a servant leadership perspective.

In previous editions of *Programming for Parks, Recreation, and Leisure Services: A Servant Leadership Approach,* we noted the findings of the 1997 National Curriculum on Parks and Recreation (2005). In examining undergraduate education, skills, technical competencies, and values were identified as important components for a quality undergraduate degree in parks and recreation. The emphasis on values is noteworthy as the conference proceedings identified the need for students to have a clear sense of purpose and a vision for the field. "This vision should emphasize the contributions of recreation and parks to human well being and the quality of community life. There must be a realization that the field, and therefore personal action, are parts of the larger social system . . . Part of this involves sensitivity to human circumstances, compassion and a commitment to help others" (Sessoms, 1997, p. 8).

In completing the revision process for this edition of *Programming for Parks, Recreation, and Leisure Services: A Servant Leadership Approach*, we are even more convinced that the servant leadership approach offers our profession a model that makes serving and leading through programs possible. As recreation programmers, we see the world changing around us and must respond to those changes in the ways people live, work, and recreate. These can create

a sense of uneasiness in terms of how we serve and lead others in order to improve the quality of life of those involved in our programs. In response to this balancing act we often seek to take the easy route of selecting either serving or leading, but not both. Yet, the concept of servant leadership presented throughout this book challenges this approach and encourages us to disregard the *either* serving *or* leading option and instead live in the paradox of serving *and* leading.

The concept of servant leadership offers a solid foundation on which the knowledge and skills of programming can be developed. We feel it is a powerful model to guide the recreation programming process for it encourages leaders to listen and empower rather than dominate and dictate. It is our hope that even if you do not agree with our values orientation of servant leadership that the book will be a catalyst for discussing the types of values that professionals in park, recreation, and leisure services should emulate.

The book is organized into three parts. Part One lays the foundation for the book and is about the art of programming. It lays the foundation on which programs can be developed by introducing the concept of servant leadership, helping readers understand the planning processes necessary for effective programming, and examining the relationship between service and quality in the programming process. Parts Two and Three of the book are more about the science of programming— examining the process of designing, implementing, and evaluating leisure programs. New to this third edition:

- An instructor/student CD with supplemental information and exercises for each chapter. The CD is designed to encourage an active learning environment where students are challenged to think for themselves and to integrate theory with practice. The chapters noted on the CD correlate to each chapter in the text and include learning objectives, identification of key concepts and terms, questions for reflection and study, and suggested applications and practice. Other resources included on this CD are practice exams, case studies, and program highlights on many different organizations and/or programs.

- Further integration of the concept of servant leadership into every aspect of the programming cycle.

- Expanded information on such topics as social capital, the experience economy, and developmental assets, as well as biographies on such leaders as Robert Greenleaf and Jane Addams.

- Added Programmer Profiles that highlight real people working in the parks, recreation, and leisure services profession as programmers.

- A reorganization of the book, including reordering some chapters, removing one chapter, and integrating this content into the rest of the book.

- Including 'theory sidebars' throughout the text to illustrate how particular theories of programming are implemented in various agencies.

- Updating facts and figures throughout the text.

In undertaking a project such as this there are a number of people to whom we are indebted. We would like to thank the many people who have assisted us (both directly and indirectly) in the completion of this text. Richard Yocum, George Lauer, and Andrea Puzycki at Venture Publishing worked long hours to pull our material together to form a quality product. In addition, the cover designer, Sigrid Albert, always gives us her best work and we are most appreciative.

The evolution of knowledge in a profession is an ongoing process; with this in mind we would like to thank the many authors of programming-related texts who have preceded us. They are numerous and have helped us to think and reflect on the many meanings of programming and its importance to our profession. Those individuals we profiled in the text provide a sense of grounding in the workforce for the ideas we present in the text. In addition, colleagues and students throughout the country have been supportive and willing to critique ideas and offer suggestions.

We also owe a debt of gratitude to the many leisure services professionals and organizations that shared program ideas, promotional pieces, and other pertinent material to the programming process for the book. We would be remiss if we did not also recognize both Calvin College and East Carolina University for supporting this writing endeavor over the last year. Last, but certainly not least, we would like to thank our families and loved ones who continue to offer their enduring support, love and encouragement throughout the writing process.

—DGD, DJJ, KHD (2010)

Reference

Sessoms, D. (1997, October). *Proceedings of the National Curriculum Conference on Parks and Recreation*. National Recreation and Park Association Congress, Salt Lake City, UT.

About the Authors

Don DeGraaf has been involved with camps and other youth serving programs for over 20 years. In addition, Don has served as a U.S. Peace Corps volunteer in the Philippines, and he and his wife Kathy have lived overseas in Korea and Hong Kong. These international adventures have fostered a strong interest in cross-cultural experiences and a global perspective on a wide variety of issues. Don enjoys writing and has co-authored several textbooks and over 90 articles and book chapters on a variety of youth leadership, environmental, and management concerns; he has also presented almost 100 workshops in the areas of programming, leadership, and management. Don earned a B.S. from Calvin College, his M.S. from Indiana University and his Ph.D. from the University of Oregon. Currently, Don is a professor and the Director of Off-Campus Programs at Calvin College in Grand Rapids, Michigan.

Deb Jordan has been involved in recreation leadership and programming for over 30 years. She has experience in outdoor recreation, special events, camps, military recreation, nonprofit organizations, public parks and recreation, and international settings, and has worked with a wide diversity of people in these settings. Deb has made over 120 presentations to local, state, national, and international groups, and written books and articles about programming, leadership, diversity, inclusion, risk management, and outdoor recreation. Deb earned her B.S. from Slippery Rock State College in Pennsylvania, her M.S. from Western Illinois University, and her Re.D. from Indiana University. For fun, Deb reads, travels, and tries to kayak as often as she can. Deb is currently serving as Professor and Chair of the Recreation and Leisure Studies Department at East Carolina University in North Carolina.

Kathy DeGraaf has been involved with camps, schools and social service agencies for over 25 years. Currently, Kathy works for New Branches Public Academy in Grand Rapids, Michigan. She enjoys writing and has written a number of articles and books related to working with children in a variety of settings. Kathy earned her B.S.W. from Valparaiso University and has taken classes toward a Master's Degree in Education from Northern Illinois University. For fun, both Kathy and Don are avid and safe (not to be confused with good) outdoor enthusiasts, love to travel, as well as read about future adventures. Together they have two children, Isaac and Rochelle, and one dog, Lantau.

About the Cover

The cover uses a variety of visual elements to express the many different concepts discussed in this book. The central row of five paper cutout figures reaching out to each other symbolizes the concept of community and mutual support. The dominant green color represents the outdoors, parks, and nature. The textures represent personal expression and artistry, which are important components and possible positive outcomes of leisure services, but also acknowledge the increasingly urban environment in which many leisure activities now take place. The spiral-shaped graph in the center contains a heart shape which symbolizes the caring, social aspect, as well as the scientific side of programming, which has to take data and statistics into account. The overall effect is meant to be that of a rich visual tapestry symbolizing human interactions and recreational endeavors.

Photo courtesy of the Greenleaf Center for Servant Leadership

Programmer Profile

Robert Greenleaf and the Beginnings of Servant Leadership

Welcome to *Programming for Parks Recreation and Leisure Services: A Servant Leadership Approach*! We are excited that you will be joining us as we explore the process of delivering meaningful recreation programs. As you begin each chapter you will find a Programmer Profile of a parks, recreation, or leisure services professional working in one of the many diverse organizations offering recreation programs. The purpose of these profiles is to introduce you to *real people* who are planning, implementing, and evaluating actual recreation programs. In the profiles, the programmers will share a bit about themselves, where they work, how they use programs to achieve specific outcomes, and how they are putting into practice the principles of servant leadership in their work.

Our first profile is about Robert Greenleaf and, although he was not a leisure services professional, he was the driving force behind the concept of servant leadership that serves as the philosophical base of this book.

▶ **What was Greenleaf's career path?**

- Greenleaf was born in 1904; he attended college and joined the American Telephone and Telegraph Company (AT&T) in the mid 1920s. At the time AT&T employed more people than any other business in the world.
- In part, his decision to take a position at AT&T was influenced by a college professor who challenged his students during their senior year with the following:

  > *there is a new problem in our country. We are becoming a nation that is dominated by large institutions—churches, businesses, governments, labor unions, universities—and these institutions are not serving us well. I hope that all of you will be concerned about this. Now you can do as I do, stand outside and criticize, bring pressure if you can, write and argue about it. All of this may do some good, but nothing of substance will happen unless there are people inside these institutions who are able to (and want to) lead them into better performance for the public good. Some of you ought to make careers inside these big institutions and become a force for good—from the inside.* (Greenleaf, 1977, pp 1–2)

- He worked at AT&T for over forty years; during his time at AT&T he worked in a variety of human resources and management positions.
- After retirement, Greenleaf began a second career teaching and consulting at institutions ranging from Harvard Business School to the Ford Foundation, to scores of churches and nonprofit institutions. During the tumultuous 1960s, Greenleaf tried to understand why so many young people were in rebellion against America's institutions, especially universities. He concluded that the fault lay with the institutions: they weren't doing a good job of serving, therefore, they were doing a poor job of leading.

▶ **What book had a big impact on Greenleaf's life?**

- His quest for understanding young people in the 1960s led Greenleaf to begin to read Hermann Hesse's short novel, *Journey to the East*—a mythical account of a group of people on a spiritual journey. The central figure of the story is Leo who accompanies the party as the servant who does the menial chores, and who sustains the group with his spirit and song. He is a person of extraordinary presence. All goes well until Leo disappears. Then the group falls into disarray and the journey is abandoned; they cannot make it without their servant Leo. The narrator, one of the party, after some years of wandering finds Leo and is taken into the Order that had sponsored the journey. There he discovers that Leo, whom he had known first as servant, was in fact the titular head of the Order, its guiding light, and a great and noble leader. After reading the book, Greenleaf concluded that its central meaning was that a great leader is first experienced as a servant to others, and this simple fact is central to his or her greatness. "True leadership emerges from those whose primary motivation is a deep desire to help others" (Spears, 2002, p. 3).

▶ **Greenleaf's accomplishments and thoughts on servant leadership:**

- He wrote several books including: *The Servant as Leader* (1970), *The Institution as Servant* (1972), *Trustees as Servant* (1974). Many of his writings describe some of the characteristics and activities of servant-leaders, which show that individual efforts, inspired by vision and a servant ethic, can make a substantial difference in the quality of society. Greenleaf advocated that followers choose their leaders. He discussed the skills necessary to be a servant-leader; the importance of awareness, foresight and listening; and the contrasts between coercive, manipulative, and persuasive power.
- Until his death in 1990, Robert Greenleaf kept writing on the themes of management, servanthood, organizations, power, and spirituality. The Greenleaf Center for Servant Leadership (http://www.greenleaf.org) has become a worldwide resource for those interested in applying the principles of servant leadership in their own work environment.
- Today, the ideas of Robert Greenleaf continue to gain importance, influencing leaders in business, education, ministry, and medicine. Servant leadership crosses all boundaries and is being applied by a wide variety of people working with businesses, nonprofit corporations, and churches, universities, health care institutions, and foundations. Perhaps the greatest contribution made by Greenleaf is the timeliness and universality of servant leadership.

Basic Concepts | 1

Why are you interested in pursuing a degree in parks, recreation, and leisure services? What are you hoping to get from taking a class in recreation programming? Why did you choose a career in this field? How do you see yourself making a difference in this world through your choice of a major or career in parks, recreation, leisure services, and related fields? We begin this book with these questions because we feel that leisure services professionals can make a difference through the programs they offer. Programs are one of the primary means by which leisure services professionals provide value to people and make a difference for individuals, communities, and society at large.

Over 20 years ago, two professionals in our field defined programming; the definition still stands today. Carpenter and Howe characterized programming as a *continual process of planning, implementing, and evaluating leisure experiences for an individual or a group of individuals* (1985). Thus, programming is an important concept for all leisure services professionals to grasp and understand. Whether you are working for a municipal recreation department providing sport leagues for adults, for a nonprofit organization providing day camp programs for children with disabilities, as a commercial tour operator offering wilderness backpacking trips for inner-city youth, or an event coordinator planning a festival, programming is a central part of your job.

Most are well aware that quality leisure programming does not just happen—it is hard work. And, to complicate things a bit, programming can be viewed as both an art and a science. The art aspect of programming comes from experience and creativity while the scientific aspect of programming includes

the systematic study of preparing, delivering, and evaluating programs. The purpose of the early part of this book is to examine the philosophical and scientific aspects of programming to provide a strong foundation on which the intuitive (art) aspect of programming can be developed, nourished, and encouraged (see Figure 1.1 below).

Our goal is to explore both the art and science of programming, and to integrate a servant leadership perspective throughout the text (see the Programmer Profile at the beginning of this chapter). The importance of servant leadership is based on the premise that all parks, recreation, and leisure professionals serve their constituents through programs. Thus, a servant

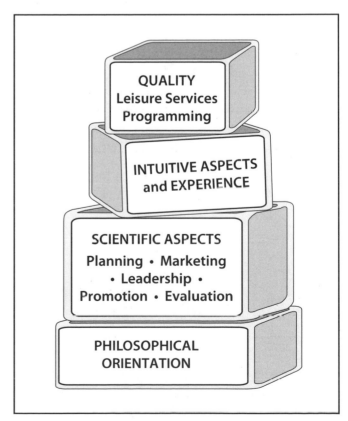

Figure 1.1 The building blocks of programming

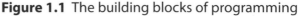

leadership perspective is an integral aspect of programming. In describing the importance of servant leadership, Greenleaf (1977, p. 49) stated:

> …if a better society is to be built, one that is more just and more loving, one that provides greater creative opportunity for its people, then the most open course is to raise both the capacity to serve and the very performance as servant of existing major institutions by new regenerative forces operating within them.

This chapter begins to lay the foundation for the remainder of this text. Operational definitions of leisure and recreation are presented along with a glimpse of the history of recreation programming and the relevance of programming in today's world. Individual and societal benefits of recreation programming are examined with an emphasis on helping the reader understand an outcomes-based management approach to programming. In addition, this chapter examines the role of the parks, recreation, and leisure services professional in the programming process, with special emphasis placed on helping the reader gain an understanding of the relevance and importance of servant leadership to programming. As the story about Leo and servant leadership in Greenleaf's Programmer Profile at the beginning of this chapter suggests, parks, recreation, and leisure professionals are often the *spirit and song* of society.

Definitions

An important starting point for understanding leisure programming is understanding the meaning of the

Figure 1.2 Leisure means different things to different people—variety is important in programs.

terms, *leisure* and *recreation*. Defining these terms is a complex task due to the individual nature of the leisure experience. In fact, semester-long courses in the history and philosophy of leisure are spent trying to understand these elusive concepts. Part of the difficulty is that what one person considers a leisure experience (e.g., gardening, jogging, reading) another might view as work. Although there is a danger of oversimplifying the concepts, we can see that throughout history, leisure has been identified in a number of different ways. These explanations have included leisure as time, a state of mind, activity, a symbol of social class, and as a holistic concept. Brief descriptions of these conceptualizations follow.

Leisure as Time

The easiest and most popular way economists and laypeople define leisure is by describing it as discretionary time; that is, time left over from work and other life maintenance activities. Discretionary time implies that individuals have choice, autonomy, and freedom to exercise their will to experience leisure.

Leisure as State of Mind

Defining leisure as a state of mind suggests the leisure experience is a function of one's subjective understanding of leisure. In this case, leisure is an attitude based on an individual's own perspective, feelings, values, and past life experiences.

Leisure as Activity

This definition pays no attention to the concept of leisure as it relates to what happens within an individual's mind; rather, leisure is defined by categories of activity such as sports, social activities, travel, and outdoor activities. This view is most closely aligned with the term *recreation*.

Leisure as a Symbol of Social Status

The evolution of a "leisure class" where people use leisure as a way of claiming or demonstrating social status in society by virtue of the products and services they consume or purchase can be seen throughout history. For example, the brand of athletic shoe and type of recreational equipment a person buys can express their desire to be aligned with a particular social group.

Leisure as a Holistic Concept

The holistic perspective suggests that leisure has the potential to be present in many forms of human endeavor. This focus of leisure is on an individual's ability to shape an integrated lifestyle in which opportunities to operate creatively, expressively, physically, and intellectually exist. Leisure as a holistic concept considers all aspects of one's life.

◆◆◆

As can be seen from these explanations, no one definition of leisure can capture all that leisure represents. We do know, however, that leisure is a societally based phenomenon and is heavily influenced by culture. This means that there is no such thing as one universal definition that explains what leisure is in every society or in every situation. As can be imagined, this can present a challenge to those of us who program leisure experiences.

Whereas little consensus exists in defining the term *leisure*, the term *recreation* has commonly been viewed as an activity that is freely chosen and has the potential of many desirable outcomes. Further, most agree that recreation is an activity that takes place during one's free time, is enjoyable, freely chosen, and benefits the individual emotionally, socially, physically, cognitively, and/or spiritually.

Because these terms are closely related (and for ease of reading), we will use the terms *leisure* and *recreation* interchangeably throughout this text. Both terms will represent experiences that include the five factors explained in the following section. These factors have been shown to relate to satisfying leisure experiences (Neulinger, 1974; Samdahl, 1991), and are often achieved through recreation.

Freedom

To be free means to be able to act without interference or control from another, or to choose or act in accordance with one's own will. If we are free, no one else forces us do something. We are free to choose to do anything. In order for a successful leisure experience to occur, participants must exercise some element of choice (freedom).

Perceived Competence

The perception of having skills and abilities necessary for successful participation leads to a satisfying leisure experience. Thus, in order for a successful leisure experience to occur, individuals must perceive themselves to have a degree of competence equal to the challenges of the intended leisure experience. If not, they must freely choose to "stretch" themselves. Generally, people match their skill levels to their choice of participation in a particular game, activity, or experience.

Intrinsic Motivation

Beyond having the element of choice in leisure activities, participants must choose their involvement because they are moved from within and not because they are influenced by external factors. This means that the drive for leisure comes from within each person; the activity itself motivates an individual to act (rather than the motivation coming from a desire to lose weight, be with friends, and so forth).

Locus of Control

The concept of locus of control refers to the need to exert influence within the context of the leisure

Figure 1.3 Freedom is an important component in exploring leisure interests.

experience. Individuals need to have some control or influence within the leisure process in order for a successful leisure experience to occur. This does not mean that participants need to be involved in the planning of every aspect of every event, but they should feel some degree of control as the experience unfolds. For instance, participants might choose their teammates; influence the day, time, or place an activity occurs; or decide to modify rules.

Positive Affect

The remaining factor that relates to a satisfying leisure experience is that of positive affect. This refers to enjoyment—people who have positive affect are happy, up-beat, and pleasant. Recreation and leisure experiences offer inherent affect, and if they are truly recreation and leisure, result in positive affect for the participants.

◆◆◆

Understanding these five factors as they relate to satisfying leisure experiences is very important if leisure services programmers are going to design and implement leisure programs and services to meet the needs and demands of a variety of people. When leisure professionals plan programs to help individuals experience these elements, they can facilitate a positive leisure experience.

Recreation Programs

Recreation programs are found in all areas of work and life in the public, nonprofit, and commercial sectors, which include the following types of leisure services organizations:

1. Public or governmental agencies at the federal, state, and local levels (e.g., National Park Service, City of Tucson Parks and Recreation Department, Mecklenberg County Parks and Recreation Department)

2. Voluntary nonprofit organizations, both nonsectarian and sectarian (e.g., Jewish Community Center, Boys & Girls Club of America)

3. Private membership associations (e.g., The Dunes Golf and Country Club, Green Valley Recreation, Inc.)

4. Commercial, profit-oriented recreation businesses (e.g., Schlitterbahn Waterpark Resort, Bar W Guest Ranch)

5. Armed Forces (although these are components of government, they constitute a distinct form of recreation programming) (e.g., Coast Guard Morale, Welfare and Recreation, Air Force Child Development Centers)

6. Campus recreation programs serving college and university students and staff members (e.g., University of California—Davis Campus Recreation and Intramurals, Boise State University Outdoor Program)

7. Corporate recreation programs serving company employees (USAA Insurance Employee Recreation and Fitness Centers, Yellowstone Co-Op Employee Recreation Program)

8. Therapeutic recreation services for people with special needs—both in clinical and community settings (e.g., Inclusion Programs, County of Maui Recreation and Support Division; Cincinnati Children's Hospital Therapeutic Recreation Division)

The scope and breadth of recreation programs in all of these settings continue to expand to meet the needs and demands of a variety of participants. For example, it is not uncommon to find senior citizens demanding high-risk activities like alpine skiing, adolescents wanting opportunities to travel, blended families who are looking for bonding opportunities, and singles flocking to wine tasting travel programs. The common tie between all these groups and activities is programming.

In addition to these types of organizations we have seen a continuous increase in partnerships between organizations to better meet the needs of participants. For instance, across the United States new programs are appearing as a result of collaboration between therapeutic recreation services and campus recreation programs. As an example, consider STRIVE, a nonprofit organization established 2004 with a mission to:

> Enhanc[e] the quality of life for all our clients through the provision of world-class, enjoyable, and accessible recreational opportunities unlike any other available throughout Michigan. Through our dedication to professional development and advocacy for individuals with disabilities and the Americans with Disabilities Act (ADA), we strive to

offer unique and excellent services through our programs, recreational therapy, consulting services and the rental, purchase, and construction of adaptive equipment. (STRIVE, 2007)

STRIVE partners with a wide range of individuals and organizations to provide leisure programs for people with disabilities (see Figure 1.4). They work with individuals as part of post-accident rehabilitation and assist in finding accessible recreation opportunities in a community. STRIVE also works with public parks and recreation departments to enhance programming for people with disabilities as well as with businesses and community organizations. They offer in-service trainings across the state of Michigan related to the ADA and working with individuals with disabilities.

Recreation programs have long been the lifeblood of leisure services organizations in that programs are the vehicle professionals use to deliver leisure benefits to both individuals and society. Programs are where people and parks, recreation, and leisure services organizations meet. *Recreation programs are purposeful interventions deliberately designed and constructed to produce certain behavioral outcomes (e.g., having fun with family and friends, meeting new people, learning new skills, increasing fitness levels) in an individual and/or group.* A key element to remember is that programs are not ends in themselves; rather, people (and the outcomes they desire) are the true reasons for the existence of leisure services organizations. This commitment to people through leisure can be seen throughout the history of the organized parks, recreation, and leisure movement in the United States, which dates back to the late 1800s. It is also the reason we call for a servant leadership approach to programming.

The Beginnings of Leisure Programming

Formal recreation organizations emerged during the late 1800s to address the tremendous social, psychological, and general welfare needs that grew out of the Industrial Revolution. Social reformers saw the potential of using play and recreation to improve people's quality of life. For instance, the Boston Sand Gardens (considered to be the first playground) were established to meet the play needs of disadvantaged children and give them a safe place to play. Also, many of the first organized camps were designed for and targeted at "sickly boys." Large city parks (e.g., Central Park in

New York) were designed in an attempt to regain the rural countryside in the middle of an urban area and give people who lived in crowded slum tenements a place to relax and "get away from it all." Further, the settlement house movement used recreation as a means to ease the transition of immigrants to living in large urban American cities (see the Programmer Profile for Jane Addams in Chapter Two). Sessoms and Stevenson have written that

Adult education, recreation, and social group work all have a common heritage. Each is a product of the social welfare reforms that occurred in our cities and industries at the turn of the nineteenth century. Their founders shared a belief—they were concerned with the quality of life and believed that through the "proper" use of leisure it could be achieved. (1981, p. 2)

Initially, many aspects of the recreation movement were focused on providing *places* for leisure—parks,

Photo courtesy of STRIVE RTS

Figure 1.4 A STRIVE program expanding the opportunities for people with disabilities.

playgrounds, and recreation centers. As the movement progressed the importance of organized programs was acknowledged. Curtis (1915) wrote, "the playground that has no program achieves little" (p. 163). Boden and Mitchell (1923) suggested that, "programs are necessary to make playgrounds more interesting and efficient" (p. 264). The expansion of leisure services programs has been a major factor in the growth and development of public recreation departments. As the profession matured and diversified, most public recreation agencies across the country adopted a philosophy that views leisure as an end in itself. In other words, public recreation drifted away from a social welfare model (with specific social service goals) and adopted a model of providing services to all.

Beginning in the last half of the twentieth century we have seen tremendous growth in all sectors of parks, recreation, leisure services, and other aspects of what is known as "the experience industry." Public, private nonprofit, and commercial leisure services organizations continue to grow at a rapid rate. In addition, leisure services organizations have dealt with phenomenal social and economic changes. On one hand, the demand for leisure experiences has skyrocketed. People from all walks of life are seeking and demanding leisure experiences in their lives. At the same time, the environment in which these experiences can be created has also been changing. For example, both public and private nonprofit organizations are being asked to be more financially accountable and do more with less. Commercial organizations are being asked to be more ethically responsible (fuel/energy conscious) in the programs they offer (e.g., ecotourism). All organizations are being asked to respond to greater diversity in potential customer groups.

In examining the wide range of leisure services organizations that developed over the last 120 years, Godbey (1997) noted that three factors have shaped all forms of leisure services: the desire to help people; an entrepreneurial spirit; and changes in technology which facilitate or necessitate such intentions.

The Desire to Help People

Whether it be public agencies responding to the play needs of children by creating playgrounds, private nonprofit organizations developing summer camps to help children experience the great outdoors, or Thomas Cook (a commercial tour operator) creating traveler's checks to help people feel secure when they travel, leisure services professionals have always demonstrated a desire to make people's lives better. This is a vital element of the servant leadership philosophy that is even more important today.

Increasingly, leisure services organizations are being called upon to address a wide range of societal issues such as building community, encouraging healthier lifestyles, and preparing young people to be successful adults.

An Entrepreneurial Spirit

The entrepreneurial spirit may be defined as a belief in innovative ideas that result in quality products or services that will benefit both those who use the product and those who developed it. It also implies creativity, a willingness to take risks, and innovation. Putnam (2000) recognized this entrepreneurial spirit in the early social reformers who were instrumental in developing parks, playgrounds, and community centers. He said:

> We desperately need an era of civic inventiveness to create a renewed set of institutions and channels for reinvigorating our civic life that fits the way we have come to live. Our challenge now is to reinvent the twenty-first century equivalent of the Boy Scouts or the Settlement House or the playground.... What we create may well look nothing like the institutions Progressives invented a century ago, just as their inventions were not carbon copies of the earlier small town folkways whose passing they mourned. We need to be as ready to experiment as the Progressives were. Willingness to err—and then correct our aim—is the price of success in social reform. (p. 401)

Changes in Technology

Successful parks, recreation, and leisure services organizations have always been able to respond to societal changes that are going on around them as evidenced by their entrepreneurial spirit. For example, in 1893, Jane Addams wrote, "the one thing to be dreaded in the settlement [house movement] is that it lose its flexibility, its power of quick adaptation, its readiness to change its methods as its environment may demand." The environmental changes we have been experiencing in recent years include the technology boom. Technology has been (and is) growing and changing at an astonishing rate; it has been increasing in usability and accessibility for the masses, and because of this, it impacts leisure and leisure programming. Economist Jeremy Rifkin, in his book *The Age of Access* (2001), noted that we are headed for a new economic era where people will shift from a paradigm of ownership to one of experience. As experiences become more important, implications for leisure services organizations will become increasingly visible.

To be successful, leisure services programmers must build upon their past—by going forward—to meet and create the future. Recreation programmers will need to continue to respond to societal changes in innovative ways to empower individuals and communities to grow and develop through leisure programs.

Beneficial Outcomes of Leisure Programs

Today's complex world demands that parks, recreation, and leisure services providers understand societal changes as well as the specific beneficial outcomes customers expect from recreational programs and experiences. This knowledge is vital when planning and developing programs to meet constituent needs. In an attempt to accomplish this task, many leisure services organizations (especially public leisure services organizations) embrace a beneficial outcomes-based approach to providing services.

A beneficial outcomes approach to leisure has evolved from outcomes-focused management theory (Driver, 2008). This theory encourages recreation providers to consider a broad model for explaining outcomes in such a way that funders and managers understand the positive and negative outcomes of participating in leisure and recreation programs. Within such a model, benefits are defined as:

- an improved change in a condition. Individuals, communities, as well as biophysical and heritage resources can all experience these types of benefits. The gains can be psychological, physiological, social, economic, and/or environmental.

- maintenance of a desired condition, prevention of an undesired condition, or reduction of an undesired condition. These benefits include maintaining facilities, structures, and spaces; preventing social ills; and decreasing negative impacts on the natural environment.

- the realization of a satisfying recreation experience. Benefits one can accrue from participating in satisfying recreation experiences include a reduction in stress, increased physical fitness, and spiritual renewal. (Driver, 2008, p. 4–5)

In this regard, outcomes-focused management has become a major catalyst in helping to dispel a popular myth: that parks, recreation, and leisure agencies provide something of value, but only as long as the pleasurable experience lasts. Outcomes-focused management, particularly the focus on beneficial outcomes, moves the leisure profession forward by integrating the concept that value is added to people's lives (and the environment) following on-site recreation participation. For example, Figure 1.5 (see p. 10) identifies a variety of immediate benefits and potential long-term benefits of a couple hiking together in a natural area.

According to Driver and Bruns (1999) the fundamental question raised by a benefits approach to leisure is

…[W]hy should a particular leisure service be provided? The answer to this question is formulated in terms of clearly defined positive and negative consequences of delivering that service with the objective being to optimize net benefits—or to add as much value as possible. To do this, leisure policy analysts and managers must understand what values would be added by each leisure service provided, articulate those values, and understand how to capture them. (p. 4)

Thus, it is important for programmers and managers to understand the immediate and potential long-term beneficial outcomes connected to their programs and work to maximize those outcomes. The National Recreation and Park Association (NRPA) has embraced the concept of outcomes-focused management starting in the 1990s with "The Benefits Are Endless" campaign. Although NRPA has moved on to other marketing campaigns, the message of these new promotions is consistent with an outcomes-focused management approach to providing services. Consider the recent efforts of the Florida Recreation and Park Association, which began the "It Starts in Parks" initiative to better position park and recreation in the future and to bring attention to the important beneficial outcomes and services provided by the profession. Through this campaign the following beneficial outcomes have been associated with recreation programs and facilities (see Figure 1.6, p. 11):

- Achievement: Big achievements in life start with small successes. Like learning how to be part of a team. Or figuring out that excellence comes from a daily commitment of time and hard work. Florida's parks give children a chance to learn those life lessons, to experience success early, and to dream big. Parks build future leaders by giving youth the opportunity to lead. Personal achievement. It starts in parks.

- Community: What transforms a crowd into a community? A chance for people to connect. Parks provide that chance. Florida's parks are where lifetime friendships are formed, where the gap between generations is bridged, where people discover what they have in common. How do you grow a hometown with a sense of community? It starts in parks.

- Conservation: Air. Water. Land. These are our greatest natural treasures. Yet, a growing population threatens the quantity and quality of these vital resources. Conserving green spaces and waterways

for the generations to come is crucial for our very survival. Florida's parks hold a key. Preserving what's precious. It starts in parks.

- Economic Development: Parks offer the perfect venue for community and regional events— tournaments, concerts, exhibitions, food festivals—that draw visitors and new dollars into our backyard. A vibrant, growing community. It starts in parks.

- Health: Good Health—Physical activity is the key to maintaining a healthy body weight,

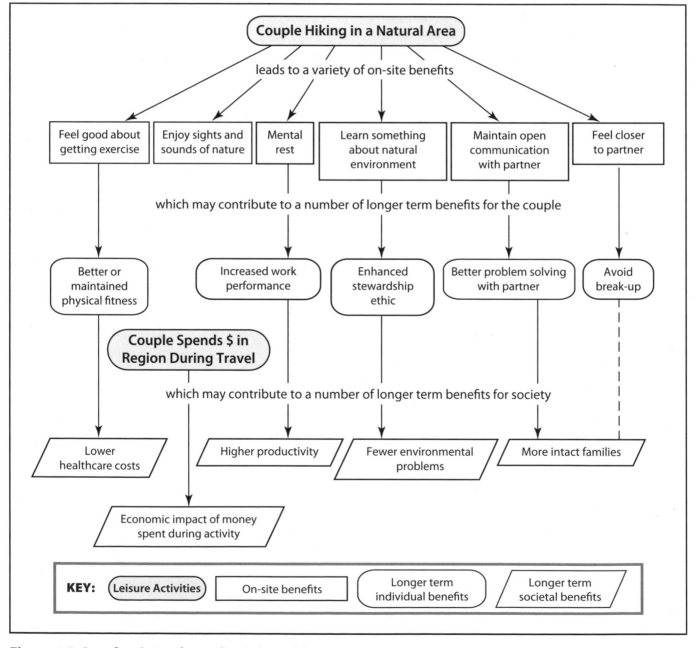

Figure 1.5 Benefits chain of causality (adapted from Driver & Bruns, 1999)

preventing disease and feeling better. A growing body of research shows that physically active adults and children are less prone to obesity, diabetes, heart disease—even depression. Florida's parks offer a wide range of free and low-cost opportunities to get out and play. Physical activity and good health. It starts in parks.

- Heritage: Ties to our Heritage…One step brings you back in time to the days of European exploration (Spanish Conquistadors) and the Seminole Indians. Tour a reconstructed Seminole chickee, or a fort that has seen two wars and still stands today. Whether we were born and raised on the Florida peninsula, or just moved in yesterday, our rich heritage shapes who we are as Floridians and makes us proud to call Florida our home. Finding our shared heritage. It starts in parks.

- Nature: Respect for Nature… Whether it's feeling the sun on your face, learning how things grow, or enjoying the awe-inspiring beauty of a summer's day, nature's innovation sustains us from the inside

out. Spending time outside reminds us of our unique place in the world. A connection to nature. It starts in parks.

- Florida's Future: 1,000 new residents a day. With that kind of relentless population growth, people need a place to connect and form new relationships, to learn about Florida's heritage and its natural treasures—a place to become Floridians. Florida's parks are the place where it all comes together—a sense of community, an appreciation of history and place, respect for nature. How do you weave strangers into citizens? It starts in parks.

As one can see, the benefits of leisure are far reaching and can impact the well-being of both individuals and communities. With this in mind we now turn to examining each of these types of beneficial outcomes.

Figure 1.6 Example of a poster from the "It starts in parks" campaign

Beneficial Outcomes of Leisure for Individuals

Signs exist everywhere that people are concerned with improving the quality of their lives. We want a higher degree of life satisfaction—typically defined as a stronger sense of well-being and more happiness. Understanding people's subjective level of happiness or well-being has drawn a lot of attention over the last twenty years (Weimer, 2008). Drawing from a wide range of research on happiness, Meyer has noted that

Table 1.1 Specific types and general categories of benefits (Moore & Driver, 2005)

Personal Benefits — Psychological

Better Mental Health and Health Maintenance
- Holistic sense of wellness
- Catharsis
- Positive changes in mood and emotion
- Stress management (i.e., prevention, mediation, and restoration)
- Prevention of, or reduced, depression/anxiety/anger

Personal Development and Growth
- Self-confidence
- Self-competence
- Values clarification
- Leadership
- Adaptability
- Spiritual growth
- Problem solving
- Tolerance
- Self-reliance
- Self-assurance
- Humility
- Aesthetic enhancement
- Creativity enhancement
- Cognitive efficiency
- Nature learning
- Balanced living
- Environmental awareness/understanding
- Balanced competitiveness
- Independence/autonomy
- Improved academic/cognitive performance
- Sense of control over one's life
- Prevention of problems to at-risk youth
- Acceptance of one's responsibility
- Cultural/historic awareness/learning/appreciation

Personal Appreciation and Satisfaction
- Sense of freedom
- Flow/absorption
- Stimulation
- Challenge
- Creative expression
- Nature appreciation
- Quality of life/Life satisfaction
- Positive change in mood and/or emotion
- Self-actualization
- Exhilaration
- Sense of adventure
- Nostalgia
- Aesthetic appreciation
- Spirituality

Environmental Benefits
- Environmental ethic
- Maintenance of physical facilities
- Stewardship/preservation of options
- Public involvement in environmental issues
- Maintenance of natural scientific laboratories
- Preservation of particular natural sites and areas
- Improved relationships with natural world
- Understanding of human dependency on the natural world
- Preservation of cultural/heritage/historic sites and areas
- Environmental protection—ecosystem sustainability and species diversity

Personal Benefits — Psychophysiological
- Improved control and prevention of diabetes
- Increased bone mass and strength
- Reduced spinal problems
- Decreased body fat/obesity/weight control
- Improved neuropsychological functioning
- Reduced incidence of disease
- Increased life expectancy
- Management of menstrual cycles
- Management of arthritis
- Improved functioning of the immune system
- Reduced or prevented hypertension
- Reduced serum cholesterol and triglycerides
- Reduced consumption of alcohol and use of tobacco
- Increased muscle strength and healthier connective tissue
- Cardiovascular benefits (including prevention of strokes)
- Respiratory benefits (increased lung capacity, benefits to people with asthma)

Social and Cultural Benefits
- Ethnic identity
- Social support
- Reciprocity/sharing
- Cultural identity
- Enhanced worldview
- Reduced social alienation
- Community satisfaction
- Family bonding
- Social mobility
- Cultural continuity
- Community integration
- Nurturance of others
- Pride in community/nation (pride in place)
- Community/political involvement
- Social bonding/cohesion/cooperation
- Conflict resolution/harmony
- Support democratic ideal of freedom
- Understanding and tolerance of others
- Environmental awareness, sensitivity
- Socialization/acculturation
- Prevention of social problems by at-risk youth
- Developmental benefits for children
- Cultural/historical awareness and appreciation
- Greater community involvement in environmental decision making

Economic Benefits
- Reduced health costs
- Decreased job turnover
- Reduced on the job accidents
- Local and regional economic growth
- Contribution to net national economic development
- International balance of payments (from tourism)
- Increased productivity
- Less work absenteeism

Happiness depends less on exterior things than most suppose. Better clues come from knowing people's personality traits and the quality of their work and leisure experiences, knowing whether they enjoy a supportive network of close relationships, and knowing whether the person has a faith that encompasses social support, purpose, and hope. (2000, p. 65)

Weimer reported that "social scientists estimate that about 70% of our happiness stems from our relationships, both quantity and quality, with friends, family, coworkers, and neighbors. During life's difficult patches, camaraderie blunts our misery; during the good times, it boosts our happiness" (2008, p. 114). As a recreation programmer, it is important to note the role leisure plays in promoting a sense of well-being and happiness, and understand the role that recreation programs can play in promoting close relationships, social support, purpose, and hope.

In examining the benefits of leisure participation, Moore and Driver (2005) identified five categories of both individual (e.g., psychological, psychophysiological) and social benefits of leisure (e.g., sociological, economic, environmental). Table 1.1 (previous page) presents a few examples of specific benefits in each category. What additional benefits would you identify, and into which category would those benefits fall? In recent years parks and recreation professionals have worked hard to document many of these benefits through research and evaluation. The following are a few examples of studies documenting the role that recreation programs play in a person's well-being:

- Organized camping has had a positive impact on youth development. Reports from groups of children and young people, parents, and camp counselors indicate significant growth from pre-camp to post-camp in each of the following four domains: social skills, physical and thinking skills, positive identity, positive values, and spiritual growth. According to campers' self-reports at the six-month follow-up the gains realized at camp were maintained, particularly in the domains of positive identity (Henderson, Thurber, Scanlin, & Bialeschki, 2007).

- Physical benefits have been documented through evaluation results from the Heart N' Parks program. From eating more heart-healthy foods to being more physically active, participants in Hearts N' Parks programs across the country reported significant improvements in what they know, think, and do about heart-healthy eating and physical activity. A collaboration between the National Recreation and Park Association and the National Heart, Lung, and Blood Institute of the National Institutes of Health, Hearts N' Parks is a community-based program designed to reduce the growing trend of obesity and to lower the risk of coronary heart disease in the United States. (Hearts N' Parks, 2004)

- In a literature review of leisure and subjective well-being, Estes and Henderson (2003) remind us of the central role that recreation and leisure play in fostering enjoyment for people in their day to day lives. They conclude: "with its focus on individual, community, environmental and economic outcomes, the 'benefits' movement has served the profession well as a foundation for documenting important extrinsic benefits of parks and recreation. Professionals shouldn't forget, however, that the outcomes related to enjoyment are still at the core of what makes our profession unique and valuable among other human service areas—we facilitate fun and intrinsically motivating experiences. Although the values of our profession go beyond 'fun and games,' enjoyment is, at all times, central to our work. Therefore, parks and recreation professionals would do well to remember the unique thing they do best—providing people opportunities for enjoyment" (p. 27).

Despite the many positive benefits of leisure, many individuals find obtaining them difficult—constraints interfere with experiences. Thus, leisure services programs are needed to help people experience leisure. Jackson (2005) have suggested that constraints are multidimensional, and noted that there is "...a stable range of categories of restraints to leisure, typically consisting of 1) cost of participating; 2) time and other constraints; 3) problems with facilities; 4) isolation (sometimes subdivided into social isolation and geographical isolation); and 5) lack of skill and abilities" (p. 7). Some of these factors can be addressed on an individual level, while others require collective action for an overall community or region. For instance, lack of time is often cited as one of the major constraints for individuals in experiencing leisure (Jackson, 1994; Jackson & Henderson, 1995). This seems to be related to what many sociologists have identified as time famine for many Americans. Although some express disagreement over the extent of time famine for individuals, there is consensus that, real or not, people perceive that they are more rushed and believe they have less free time now than in the past. Many attribute this to the rapid pace of contemporary society. Regardless of the cause, people are feeling a time crunch, and this has led to a paradox inherent in leisure. In the past it may have been possible to allow leisure experiences to "just happen"; today individuals need to intentionally make time for leisure.

The implications of time famine for leisure services programs are diverse and include helping individuals create time for leisure, as well as preparing and educating individuals to use discretionary time wisely. According to Robinson and Godbey (1997), leisure services programmers can create programs that help individuals "back up and see what they have missed, accepting the gift of time" (p. 318). Likewise, Henry Ward Beecher's advice over a century ago to "multiply picnics" by reconnecting with our friends and neighbors is still relevant today. "We should do this, ironically not because it will be good for America— though it will be—but because it will be good for us" (Putnam, 2000, p. 414).

Beneficial Outcomes of Leisure to Society

Leisure settings such as parks and community centers, and recreation programs such as sports leagues and art classes offer people the opportunity to connect with others and to build friendships. This is important because relationships play an essential role in our overall well-being. Weimer (2008) recently reiterated this in his book, *The Geography of Bliss: One Grump's Search for the Happiest Place on the Planet*. Weimer reviewed the data on subjective happiness in countries around the world and concluded that,

> Money matters, but less than we think and not in the way that we think. Family is important. So are friends. Envy is toxic. So is excessive thinking. Beaches are optional. Trust is not. Neither is gratitude…[Ultimately he concluded that] happiness is relationships and trustworthiness. Trust is a prerequisite for happiness. Trust not only of your government, of institutions, but trust of neighbors. Several studies, in fact, have found that trust—more than income or even health—is the biggest factor in determining happiness. (p. 92)

In documenting the importance of creating places where trust can develop, Oldenburg (2000) coined the term *third place*. Third places are public places where people can gather and interact informally. In contrast to first places (home) and second places (work/school), third places allow people to put aside their concerns and simply enjoy the company and conversation around them. Third places include such places as parks, organized camps, sports fields, basketball courts, main streets, community centers, senior centers, fitness centers, pubs, cafes, coffeehouses, post offices, and other places that are the heart of a community's social vitality and the foundation of a functioning democracy. They promote social equality by leveling the status of those present, provide a setting for grassroots politics, create habits of public association, and offer psychological support to individuals and communities.

An example of a third place that has incorporated recreation programs into their operations is the Green Bean, a nonprofit coffee shop in Seattle. The guiding philosophy of the Green Bean is simple hospitality:

> When coffee beans arrive from their country of origin, they are jade green in color. As they are roasted a transformation occurs which brings them to their full potential and aroma. Just like the bean itself, the Green Bean Coffeehouse is here to promote positive transformation in the lives of those who share their time with us. It's our hope to exist as a community center as much as a café; here you can expect a mean cup of coffee, a fantastically inviting atmosphere and programs that both encourage individuals and foster connections between all who enter here. (greenbeancoffee.org, 2009)

The owners say, "we want to provide a space where people can feel loved and accepted and have their gifts appreciated no matter who they are." That means that besides serving up a great cup of coffee and fantastic treats and sandwiches, they also offer a wide variety of programs such as children's story time, summer backpacking trips, concerts, community festivals, and classes that range from knitting to women's self defense to hip-hop dance. They focus their programming on building relationships with customers and as one of the co-founders puts it, "saying yes to them. Yes to the homeless people who want to contribute something and offer to sweep or wash windows. Yes to the lonely students who offer to help do the baking. Yes to the artists who want to display their work and the activists who want to publicize events" ("Serving up Yes!," 2006).

Social Capital

Understanding and advocating for the societal beneficial outcomes of leisure demands that leisure services professionals are able to articulate these outcomes in contemporary terms. One such term that has been receiving increasing attention is social capital, defined as "features of social life—networks, norms, and trust—that enable participants to act together more effectively to pursue shared objectives" (Putnam, 1995 cited in Robinson & Godbey, 1997, p. 168). This is a critical element to the success of democracy. Yet, Putnam, in his book *Bowling Alone* (2000), documents the decline of social capital in the U.S. as reflected by decreasing membership in voluntary organizations such as the Boy Scouts, the League of Women Voters, and Parent Teacher Associations. Putnam (2000) also recognizes leisure services professionals and the programs they offer as important elements in rebuilding the social capital needed for us to move forward as communities.

L. Judson Hanifan, a young educator, first identified the idea of social capital in 1916 when he returned to his native West Virginia to work in the rural school system after being gone for several years. He observed that older customs, general neighborliness, and civic engagement (e.g., debating societies, barn raisings, apple cuttings) had been neglected and people had become less considerate of their neighbors. As a result, families were isolated and the community stagnated (Putnam & Goss, 2002). As the theory of social capital has developed, various distinctions of social capital have emerged; they include:

Formal versus informal social capital. Formal social capital refers to organizations that have recognized officers, membership requirements, dues, and regular meetings, like clubs and associations. Informal social capital refers to nonformal gatherings, like pickup games of basketball or people who gather at a pub or coffeehouse.

Thick versus thin social capital. Thick social capital is closely interwoven and multistranded such as a group of steelworkers who work, play, and worship together. Such strong ties are defined in terms of frequency of contact and closeness, while a weak or thin tie is someone with whom an individual has a passing acquaintance and shares few common friends.

Inward-looking versus outward-looking social capital. Some social capital is inward-looking and tends to promote the material, social, or political interests of its members, while other social capital is outward-looking and concerns itself with public goods such as seeking the common good (i.e., what is in the best interest of all).

Bridging versus bonding social capital. These types of social capital are similar to the inward and outward-looking forms of social capital. Specifically, bridging social capital refers to the social networks that bring people together who are unlike one another. Bonding social capital usually brings together people who are like one another in some respect (e.g., ethnicity/race, sex/gender, religion; Putnam & Goss, 2002).

It is interesting to note the multidimensional nature of social capital as well as the connection between the various forms of social capital. For example, informal, thin, outward-looking, and bridging social capital all share some common characteristics; likewise the formal, thick, inward-looking, and bonding types of social capital appear connected. Although all types of social capital are important, Florida (2002) notes that

> where strong ties among people were once important, weak ties are now more effective. Where old social structures were once nurturing, now they are restricting... our evolving communities and emerging society are marked by a greater diversity of friendships, more individualistic pursuits and weaker ties within the community. People want diversity, low entry barriers, and the ability to be themselves. (p. 269)

This type of informal social capital can be generated through recreation programs and may be best suited for knitting a society together and for building broad norms of generalized reciprocity. Hanifan, himself, documented the connection between social capital and recreation programs.

> The community as a whole will benefit by the cooperation of all its parts, while the individual will find in his [sic] associations the advantages

of the help, the sympathy, and the fellowship of his neighbors....When the people of a given community have become acquainted with one another and have formed a habit of coming together occasionally for entertainment, social intercourse, and personal enjoyment, then by skilled leadership this social capital may easily be directed towards the general improvement of the community well-being. (cited by Putnam, 2002, p. 5)

The recent attention being paid to social capital has generated much debate over whether social capital has declined or is changing into new ways for people to connect. Certainly, technology has influenced the way people connect in the 21st century. As this debate plays out, many believe that significant attention in the United States needs to "be devoted to creating social capital that does a better job of bridging between the privileged and the marginalized" (Wuthnow, 2002, p. 102).

Likewise, it is important to understand the kinds of support that individuals and families will need in the future. We cannot be bound by the past and we must be willing to consider that "the life we think about as uniquely American—close families and friends, tight neighborhoods, civic clubs, vibrant electoral politics, strong faith-based institutions and a reliance on civic leadership—is giving way to something new" (Florida, 2002, p. 269).

From the context of an outcomes approach to leisure, the connection between social capital and recreation programs is an important one to explore. Early research on leisure and social capital is mixed and some caution must be used in directly correlating social capital and leisure. Hemingway (2000), in examining the role of leisure in building social capital, noted that the importance of social capital to a democratic society cannot be overlooked; in addition, research is needed to examine the role leisure can play in reinventing and encouraging social capital. The Viata program in Romania, an outreach of the New Horizons Foundation, is one example of a recreation program that is working on "developing caring citizens who feel empowered to act" (check the web at http://www.new-horizons.ro).

In an effort to document the benefits of its program, Viata initiated a study of 327 Romanian youth to see if there was a significant difference in social capital between campers entering and exiting one of their one-week programs. Social capital was measured by asking questions on four dimensions: interpersonal trust, teambuilding, participant perception of their own qualities and abilities, and empowerment.

In their study Colyn, DeGraaf, and Certan (2008) found a significant difference in social capital between pre- and post-test scores for those who had participated in the one-week camp. This change in social capital could be a result of the interpersonal trust dimension, which has been identified as one of the most important components of social capital as it contributes to the development of other values and abilities (e.g., empowerment, teambuilding, cooperation). In this specific study, data indicated that interpersonal trust increased in campers by 23% following the experience. The other three dimensions (team building, self perception of their own qualities and abilities, and empowerment) also showed some increase over the course of a one-week camp experience.

A second finding by Colyn, DeGraaf, and Certan (2008) indicated that youth who had participated in previous experiences emphasizing cooperation among group members had a higher level of trust entering the camp experience than youth who had never participated in such activities. This suggests that the more youth are exposed to camp experiences like this one, the greater the opportunity to develop interpersonal trust with others.

Building social capital may be one of the major ways in which all parks, recreation, and leisure organizations whatever the service orientation—private, public, or commercial—serve society (Russell, 2002). Commercial leisure services organizations may be involved on an individual level, assisting individuals in building bonding social capital with family and friends. Public organizations, on the other hand, might be more involved at a community level, encouraging the development of bridging social capital. Strengthening the social fabric of communities through leisure experiences can help build neighborhood ties and strengthen intergroup and intergenerational relations. The American Planning Association has developed a series of briefing papers highlighting the community benefits of parks (2002). In one of their papers, staff

Figure 1.7 The New Horizons Foundation is working to develop social capital.

make three key points: "1) parks are one of the quickest and most effective ways to build a sense of community and improve quality of life; 2) parks provide places for people to connect and interact in a shared

environment; and 3) parks channel positive community participation by getting diverse people to work together toward a shared vision" (p. 1).

In addition to social capital, Russell (2002) identified the importance of leisure in building the cultural capital that people need to be successful in life. The more cultural capital an individual has, the greater her or his potential to succeed in school and occupations. In many ways, leisure pastimes and recreation experiences provide individuals the shared experiences they need to succeed in society. Russell cited the research of Downey and Powell (1993) as an example of the power of recreation to help children succeed in school. The researchers found that eighth graders who were most successful in school participated in scouting, hobby clubs, neighborhood clubs, Boys and Girls Clubs, nonschool team sports, 4-H, YMCA/YWCA activities, and summer and other recreation programs.

Crompton (2008) has also identified the importance of recognizing the community benefits of recreation programs, especially for public and nonprofit organizations, which compete strongly for tax dollars as well as grants and donations (Figure 1.8). Crompton argues that if recreation programs simply look to provide on-site benefits to those who participate in our programs (individual benefits), we run the risk of losing the support of the larger public who may not participate in these programs. "To gain the support of nonusers, an agency has to provide a convincing answer to the question, 'what is in it for them?' Broader community support is likely to be dependent on an agency being able to demonstrate in easily recognized, preferably quantifiable terms that tax payers and elected officials understand that park and recreation services are effectively and efficiently addressing issues of importance to the community. Widespread community support will be based primarily on the off-site benefits that accrue to nonusers, rather than on on-site benefits that accrue to users" (p. 192).

As a result of the emphasis placed on the beneficial outcomes of leisure over the last twenty years, the profession has quantifiable evidence of the impact of recreation facilities and programs. Crompton (2008) organized these beneficial outcomes into the following three areas: 1) economic prosperity, 2) environmental sustainability, and 3) alleviating social problems. Understanding the community benefits as well as such important concepts as social and cultural capital, provide a strong argument for more public support of recreation facilities and programs in the future. Yet, we cannot stop at simply

---

Each of the benefits listed in this figure are a result of research studies that demonstrate the role that recreation programs, services, and facilities play in the community.

Economic Prosperity: Recreation programs and services generate additional tax revenues, create jobs, and enhance economic development; these benefits can take the form of:

> Attracting tourists
> Attracting businesses
> Attracting retirees
> Enhancing real estate values
> Reducing taxes
> Stimulating equipment sales

Environmental Sustainability: Parks, open spaces, and other natural areas provide environments where natural resources can function as intended, and cost effectively. These services include:

> Protecting drinking water
> Controlling flooding
> Cleaning air
> Reducing traffic congestion
> Decreasing energy costs
> Preserving biological diversity

Alleviating Social Problems: A failure to invest resources in delivering services today often creates bigger issues for the overall community at a later date. Recreation programs, services, and facilities are a strong vehicle for facilitating the social process of enhanced social connectedness (social capital). These benefits include:

> Moderating environmental stress
> Regenerating communities
> Preserving cultural and historical resources
> Facilitating healthy lifestyles
> Reducing deviant behavior
> Raising levels of educational achievement
> Alleviating unemployment distress

Figure 1.8 Community benefits of leisure (Crompton, 2008) understanding the community benefits of recreation programs and facilities; the key to sustaining this support is for public and nonprofit organizations to continually reposition themselves so they are perceived to contribute to alleviating a community's most pressing problems. According to Crompton, the key question is, "What can leisure services deliver more effectively and efficiently than other agencies or organizations, which contributes to resolving important community problems?" (p. 201). As discussed earlier in this chapter, the "It Starts in Parks" campaign is one attempt to connect recreation programs and facilities to many contemporary issues in our communities.

Leisure Services Professionals

Many people feel that the increasing number of leisure choices for participants, the concern about the lack of social capital in communities, and the growing time famine are just some of the challenges that must be overcome in planning, implementing, and evaluating leisure services programs. Addressing problems such as these takes a tremendous commitment on the part of leisure services organizations. In addition to organizational commitment, energetic and skilled professionals who desire to serve others and live with a servant leadership orientation are needed.

Leisure services programmers may be found working in a variety of agencies and organizations including public agencies (e.g., city, county, state, and federal governments), private, nonprofit agencies (e.g., religious sponsored organizations, youth serving organizations, organizations serving special populations [hospitals, treatment centers], relief organizations, social service organizations, conservation organizations, service clubs), and commercial organizations (e.g., travel tour operators, entertainment services, theme parks). Because of leisure programmers' widespread impact, our role as leisure services professionals is to understand the power and potential of leisure services experiences to meet desired ends (outcomes) of constituents. Whether we are involved in direct leadership, organizing a specific aspect of a program or event, or managing a leisure facility, programmers are pivotal to the success of leisure services organization.

Characteristics and Skills of Leisure Services Professionals

First and foremost, the leisure services programmer is a professional. This is true to the extent that we are members of a profession that has a statement or code of ethics, an accreditation process for practitioner preparation programs, a professional association that seeks to provide continuing education and establish standards (e.g., ACA, NRPA, AEE), and individual certification (e.g., CPRP, CTRS, CRSS). We also exhibit various qualities that reflect our professionalism, including taking initiative, having integrity, and following through with tasks related to programs and services.

According to Edginton, Hudson, Dieser, and Edginton (2004) the efforts of a professional are directed toward service rather than simply financial remuneration. The professional is concerned about the overall well-being of participants and works for their growth and development. In addition to serving constituents, programmers provide services to their communities, their organization, and work colleagues. In these capacities, programmers use a variety of skills. These skills are often grouped into three areas: technical skills, human relation skills, and conceptual skills (Jordan, 2007). Technical skills are those that are specific to accomplishing tasks. They enable a person to do a particular job or task. Examples include managing a pool at an aquatics center, leading a game, and recording a city festival on videotape. Human relation skills are those skills and techniques that involve relationships with people. Understanding group dynamics, facilitating cooperation and trust, and communicating with participants all fit within the human relations realm of leadership. Conceptual skills include the ability to analyze, anticipate, and see the big picture of programs and activities. Critical thinking, problem solving, creativity, and being able to handle ambiguity are commonly considered conceptual skills.

In looking at the kind of experiences that foster job skills in recreation organizations, Knapp (as cited by Knapp & McLean, 2002) identified five categories of developmental career experiences: 1) exposure to challenges, 2) networking, 3) involvement in professional organizations, 4) building a sense of community, and 5) interaction with mentors. Job-related experiences have long been a powerful source of learning for programmers and it is important for recreation organizations to develop strategies to help young professionals grow and develop. To ensure a meaningful and successful future, established parks, recreation, and leisure services professionals must move toward enriching jobs and empowering new professionals. This will take some planning, but will pay dividends as the next generation of qualified practitioners grow and develop. In developing these skills on an individual level, Godbey (1997) identified a number of strategies for those who will work in leisure services in the twenty-first century. Similar to the factors that have shaped our field identified earlier in this chapter, the strategies center on being adaptable and innovative in serving others. These strategies include serving others, becoming an entrepreneur, seeking continuous learning opportunities, being flexible, and calling attention to the importance of what we do.

Serving Others

An ethic of service will continue to distinguish leisure services in the public, private nonprofit, and commercial sectors. A leisure services programmer emphasizes the people served and the beneficial outcomes provided rather than the program itself. Thus, leisure programs are not thought of as an end, but rather

> …a means to an end—a higher quality of life, increased learning, better health, improved physical fitness, more appreciation and understanding of nature, improved morale, and less crime are among the many benefits….The worth of the profession (and the professional) is not linked to recreation, but to the benefits recreation, under some conditions and in some circumstances, can provide. (Godbey, 1997, p. 228)

Becoming an Entrepreneur

Peter Drucker, a noted management theorist, believes that entrepreneurship involves systematic innovation. According to Drucker (1985), systematic innovation consists of the purposeful and organized search for changes and systematic analysis of the opportunities such changes might offer for economic or social innovation. A new entrepreneurial spirit has emerged in the United States and Canada, reflected by the number of unique new jobs that emerged over the past few decades. These new jobs result from entrepreneurial ventures in the service and information sectors of society, with many in the leisure services area. "Entrepreneurs serve as pace-setters of opportunity, a challenging and demanding role. Their work is dynamic, diverse, inventive, and creative. Entrepreneurs produce new ways of meeting needs, work to improve existing products and services, and respond to changing demographic conditions" (Edginton, Jordan, DeGraaf & Edginton, 2002, p. 311).

Seeking Continuous Learning Opportunities

As the primary basis of the economy becomes knowledge (rather than manufacturing, for instance) parks, recreation, and leisure services professionals will need to remain current with the world around them through lifelong learning. Professionals seek out these experiences at professional meetings, workshops, and conferences, as well as through opportunities provided by university extension programs and self-education (e.g., reading, watching training videos, webinars, and podcasts).

Becoming More Flexible

In a world of rapid and continuing change, the ability to adapt to changing circumstances is critical. One of the worst ways that professionals in leisure services sometimes lose flexibility is to assume that an issue does not concern them because "leisure" is not a central theme.

> Leisure is among the more diverse and complex ideas in the world and, perhaps unfortunately, it relates to myriad issues that concern freedom, pleasure, human growth and understanding, health, nature, spirit, learning and other huge ideas. Becoming more flexible means the boundaries of what is relevant to you must become more flexible. (Godbey, 1997)

Calling Attention to the Importance of What We Do

Leisure services professionals must believe in the power and potential of leisure programs to affect change in the lives of individuals and society. We must be strong and vocal advocates, stressing the notion that leisure (and related) services are critical components of society, not just "frosting on the cake." Leisure services can contribute to the creation of an environment that nourishes the human potential. Leisure services professionals must also believe in their own ability to make a difference in the world. Little things do matter.

In a wide variety of settings, leisure programmers blend these skills and strategies to design programs that facilitate leisure experiences for participants. In the programming process, programmers manipulate a variety of variables in the physical, natural, and social environments that help participants experience the conditions needed to produce a leisure experience (e.g., freedom, perceived competence, intrinsic motivation, locus of control, and positive affect). Within this framework it is important to remember that programmers do not produce recreation experiences and outcomes, but instead produce *opportunities* for recreationists to produce these experiences and benefits for themselves. Thus, leisure services managers produce recreation opportunities, just as teachers produce learning opportunities and doctors produce health-restoring opportunities. Identifying the process of creating, implementing, and evaluating programs, and understanding how programmers can manipulate the variables associated with this process is a recurring theme throughout this text.

Programming: A Servant Leadership Approach

In designing opportunities for leisure, we believe there is a need for a new type of leadership and programming model, a model that puts serving others—including customers, employees, and the community—as the number one priority. As a result, we advocate a servant leadership approach as the foundation upon which leisure and recreation programming should be based for all types of recreation and leisure organizations. We believe this emphasis on serving others stresses the similarities between various commercial, private nonprofit, and public organizations rather than their differences. Although the philosophy of each of these types of organizations will impact programming decisions, the underlying desire to serve will remain constant.

In some ways the term *servant leadership* is an oxymoron, since people commonly view a leader as one who leads and a servant as ones who follows. Yet, this is part of the inherent value of the concept of servant leadership; the importance of both leadership and followership are emphasized. All of us both lead and follow. One is not better than the other; in the course of our lives we are called to do both.

Leisure professionals must learn to be good leaders by learning to be good followers, by listening to participants and by helping them lead so we (as leisure professionals) can follow. This holds true in programming. We must truly listen to our constituents and follow their lead before we make global statements about appropriate programming. Thus, servant leadership offers a powerful foundation to guide the recreation programming process. Throughout the remainder of this book, we will examine how the characteristics of servant leaders fit into the overall planning process to help recreation professionals co-create programs. In this way, we feel the reader will be prepared to follow in the footsteps of the early pioneers like Jane Addams (see the Programmer Profile at the beginning of Chapter Two), to improve the quality of life of individuals, and contribute to the common good of society.

Characteristics and Skills of Servant Leaders

Spears (1995) identified servant leadership as an approach that

> …attempts to simultaneously enhance the personal growth of workers and improve the quality and caring of our many institutions through a combination of teamwork and community, personal involvement in decision making and ethical and caring behavior. (p. 4)

The power of the servant-leadership model lies in the ability of its ideas to inspire us to be collectively more than the sum of our individual parts. According to Greenleaf, leadership should call us to serve something or someone beyond ourselves, a higher purpose. Thus, one of the most important aspects of leadership is helping organizations and staff identify their higher purpose. It is worth restating that the best test of servant-leadership is…

> …do those served, grow as persons; do they, while being served, become healthier, wiser, freer, more autonomous, more likely themselves to become servants? And, what is the effect on the least privileged in society: Will he [or she] benefit; or at least will he [or she] not be further deprived? (Greenleaf, 2002, p. 24)

To achieve this higher purpose in our leisure services organizations, we must be passionate about our desire to improve our communities and ourselves. The process of becoming a servant leader demands that we understand our own strengths and shortcomings. To guide individuals in this process, we present ten characteristics of servant leaders in Table 1.2 (Spears, 1995).

When considering the ten characteristics of servant leaders, it is important to look at them in relationship to one another rather than as individual elements. Rather than a ladder or a cyclical process, where characteristics build upon each other or lead one to the other, it is more appropriate to view these characteristics as a weaving, with each strand supporting and shaping each other. As with any good weaving, the servant leader draws greater strength from the combination of these characteristics rather than their application in isolation. The servant leader who is able to combine these ten characteristics in a dynamic process when dealing with people and the environment will fulfill the potential of servant leadership to make a difference in the lives of the people they serve. DeGraaf, Tilley, and Neal (2004) have identified three key themes that run through the ten characteristics and form the foundation on which they are built. These three themes are reflection, integrity, and passion.

Reflection

To commit to being a servant leader, one must create time to reflect in order to understand who he or she is and how he or she relates to staff, customers, and the larger community. This is referred to as being reflexive. Being reflexive provides the opportunity to step back and understand the big picture of the organization while not forgetting the small integral parts that must come together to help achieve the mission. Self-reflection helps one to rejuvenate and find the inner confidence to move forward in dealing with staff and customers, as well as practice such characteristics as listening, empathy, healing, conceptualization, and foresight.

Table 1.2 The ten characteristics of servant leaders (Spears & Lawrence, 2002)

The ability to listen.

Listening is the first characteristic of servant leadership, for it is through listening that many of the other characteristics can be nurtured. When we listen, not just to others but also to our own internal voice we create a mindset that fosters such characteristics as empathy, awareness, foresight, and commitment to others.

The ability to empathize with others.

Empathy is the capacity for participation in another's feelings or ideas; it is important in dealing with staff and customers. People need to be accepted and recognized for their special and unique spirits.

The ability to offer healing.

Being a healer within our organizations starts with understanding the "matters of the heart." Learning to heal is a powerful force for transformation and integration. The desire to foster the healing process in our organizations comes to us as we listen and empathize with those with whom we serve and work.

The ability to be self-aware.

In our ever-changing world, the need for leaders to be aware of their customers, their staff, and their organizations is well-documented. Yet, servant leaders are asked to take an additional step, to develop self-awareness. This entails making time for self-reflection, to understand the big picture. This type of general awareness, and especially self-awareness, aids in understanding issues involving ethics and values. It enables one to view most situations from a more integrated position.

The ability to build consensus.

Servant leadership offers a scenario whereby leaders encourage workers to build consensus around the true purpose of the organization as well as the means of achieving this purpose. Within this type of environment, staff are encouraged to use persuasion rather than coercion in influencing others to their point of view.

The ability to conceptualize "what might be."

From an early age, we are taught to deal with complexity by breaking things down into their separate parts. The flip side of this approach is to see the big picture, or to see things whole, we need to put the pieces back together. The ability to see things whole and offer a preferred vision for programs or the organization as a whole is critical to the success of any program or organization.

The ability to foresee issues and plot the course of the organization.

Foresight is closely related to the ability to the conceptualize the future, yet still distinct. Conceptual skills allow us to see the big picture, the *where* we want to go. Foresight allows us to map out how we are going to get there by anticipating the various consequences of our actions and then picking the action that will best serve the organization.

The ability to be a good steward.

In today's society, stewardship is often seen in association with environmental or financial responsibility, yet it can be so much more if we are willing to be accountable for something larger than ourselves. Peter Block, in his book *Stewardship: Choosing Service Over Self-Interest*, defines stewardship as "the willingness to be accountable for the well-being of the larger organization by operating service, rather than control, of those around us. Stated simply, it is accountability without control or compliance."

The ability to be committed to the growth of others.

By committing to the growth and development of staff and customers, servant leaders can adopt a benefits-based approach to delivering services and recognizing the inherent power of our programs and services to make a difference. Consider how the definition of a benefit parallels the ultimate test of a servant leader. A benefit is defined as a realization of desired and satisfying on-site experience, changes that are viewed to be advantageous as a result of an experience, or the prevention of a worse condition. Now reconsider Greenleaf's ultimate test of a servant leader. "Do those served grow as persons; do they, while being served, become healthier, wiser, freer, more autonomous, more likely themselves to become servants (the realization of desired and satisfying on-site experiences)? What is the effect on the least privileged in society: Will they benefit (improvement in condition) or, at least, will they not be further deprived (prevention of a worse condition)?"

The ability to build community.

Servant leaders are committed to contributing to the bigger picture, constantly looking for ways in which their programs and organizations can contribute to the "common good." This can be accomplished in many ways. For example, building community through programs, encouraging virtuous behavior in staff, and encouraging customers to take responsibility for themselves and their actions lead to the common good.

Integrity

One definition of integrity is completeness, the ability to live out one's values and vision as well as dealing with others in a straightforward manner. By being reflexive and thinking before acting, servant leaders can deal with people and programs with integrity. When a leader is perceived as acting with integrity, it enables her or him to be a healing force within the organization and to persuade others to her or his point of view. Leaders who are perceived to act with integrity are well on the way to earning the trust and support of staff and customers, which is needed to harness the synergistic power that is inherent in servant leadership.

Passion

Passion goes beyond simply being dramatic, powerful, and emotional; it is more accurately characterized as an unfailing dedication to an ideal. Thus, intensity and duration often demonstrate passion. Seeing things through over the long haul, whether it be a program or the way a department functions, and not being deflected requires passion. When servant leaders can demonstrate their passion for many of the core values of their organization, they reaffirm their organization's commitment to the growth of people and building social capital within their communities. As a result, we must continue to develop the "inner fire within ourselves." This allows us to continue to deliver programs and services at a high level over the long-term, as well as encouraging a passion for services within our staff to meet the needs of customers.

◆◆◆

In following through on these themes of reflection, integrity, and passion, servant leaders can begin to weave many of the characteristics presented in Table 1.2 (p. 21) with the characteristics and skills of leisure services professionals presented in the preceding section. Through this integration process, we can create the blend of compassion and effectiveness that is the mark of a servant leader. However, it is also important to stress that there are no easy answers presented in this model and that the concept of the servant leader is a paradox. The real strength of the concept is in remembering the process of balancing the concept of servant and leader is not *either/or;* it is *and*. In the end, being a servant leader is not something we do, but rather something we are. It is about creating the right environment to get the best out of people and unleash their true potential.

Summary

All parks, recreation, and leisure services organizations are concerned with programming. After all, programs are the vehicle professionals use to deliver leisure benefits to both individuals and society. In this chapter we have laid the foundation for understanding the recreation programming process by presenting definitions, a very brief history, and a number of important concepts. First and foremost, recreation programmers must understand the five prevailing factors that characterize the leisure experience—freedom, perceived competence, intrinsic motivation, locus of control, and positive affect. Freedom implies choice, spontaneity, and being free from constraints that inhibit participation. Perceived competence refers to the skills that an individual believes she or he possesses that will contribute to successful participation. Intrinsic motivation refers to an individual's desire to participate in leisure experiences based on personal needs and desires, rather than external motivation. Locus of control refers to the need of an individual to control elements of the leisure experience once she or he is engaged in the process, and positive affect refers to a sense of enjoyment. Understanding these factors as they relate to satisfying leisure experiences is imperative if parks, recreation, and leisure services programmers are going to design and implement programs and services to meet the needs and demands of a variety of people.

A second important consideration in delivering leisure experiences is the concept of outcomes-focused programming. An outcomes-focused approach to leisure encourages a broad understanding of the long-term and short-term beneficial outcomes provided by the leisure experience. Both individual and societal benefits exist. The development of social capital is one common outcome or benefit of parks, recreation, and leisure services programs. In many ways, benefits serve as the driving force behind programming approaches.

In addition to discussing the foundations of recreation programming, we also introduced the role of the programmer in planning, implementing, and evaluating programs. Important elements include understanding what it means to be a part of a profession as well as defining what makes a profession—a code of ethics, opportunities for accreditation and certification, taking advantage of ongoing educational opportunities, and behaving with integrity. Within the professional context, we presented servant leadership as a philosophical approach to programming leisure experiences. Servant leadership emphasizes increased service to others by encouraging shared decision making and a sense of community. Such an approach emphasizes the three factors that have shaped all forms of leisure services at their best: the desire to help people, an entrepreneurial spirit, and the ability to respond to societal changes.

Servant leaders exhibit a number of important charactcristics. Each subscqunet chapter of this book will highlight various characteristics from Table 1.2 that fit with the contents of that chapter. One characteristic—commitment to the growth of people—flows through every chapter in the book, and is profiled here. Edginton and Chen (2008) in their book, *Leisure as Transformation*, note that leisure provides an optimal environment for individuals to seek new experiences, experiment, and to learn and grow anew. Leisure provides an environment that enables individuals to change or to be transformed. They go on to note

> Increasingly, leisure service providers will be viewed as advocates, social entrepreneurs, community organizers, facilitators, as well as direct service providers. This new focus for assisting and facilitating the process of transformation; helping individuals, communities, and nations think differently about issues related to social justice, the environment, and in general their social development including how humans use their creative abilities to enhance their quality of life and well-being from multiple perspectives including social, cultural, and economic interests related to leisure. Because the properties of leisure not only assist people in the transformation or change process, but also help individuals maintain a link to their more stable roots, leisure service providers will be key agents in assisting individuals to cope with the ever increasing social, cultural and economic disruptions that will occur during this time of great transformation. (p. 127)

In fulfilling this role, leisure services programmers must not only help people grow and develop, but must also help them deal with the changing world. This is a tremendous responsibility, as well as an opportunity to fulfill the promise of leisure for both individuals and communities. It is our hope that this book will help you catch the vision of the possibilities of recreation programs to make a difference, while also giving you the tools and knowledge to create programs that help participants grow and develop.

Key points presented in this chapter that will serve as the foundation of this book include:

- All parks, recreation, leisure services, and related organizations are concerned with programming—it is the lifeblood of what we do.

- Recreation programs have the potential to make a positive difference in the lives of individuals and their communities if they are well-planned and implemented; programs must be purposeful interventions.

- Programs are not ends in themselves; they are the means by which leisure services professions produce beneficial outcomes—the benefits people seek in their leisure experiences (e.g. freedom, perceived competence, intrinsic motivation, locus of control, positive affect).

- Although leisure services programmers should always remember that fun and enjoyment are central to what we do, we must also remember the power of programs to address larger societal issues such as health and fostering active living, enhancing community and building relationships, environmental issues, and helping people connect to the world. We believe that this demands that we take a servant leadership approach to offering programs.

- Servant leadership will serve as the philosophical foundation for designing, implementing, and evaluating recreation programs. Servant leadership emphasizes increased service to others by encouraging shared decision making and a sense of community. Such an approach emphasizes the three factors that have shaped all forms of leisure services at their best: the desire to help people, an entrepreneurial spirit, and the ability to respond to societal changes.

Programming from Here to There

This section will end each chapter and will offer thought-provoking concepts, stories, and programs that embody many of the principles discussed. In this chapter, we present an innovative program that exemplifies taking a benefits (or outcomes) approach to programming by centering on contributing to the growth of participants. This program originates from the city of Albany, Oregon where the Parks and

Recreation department partnered with local business leaders to offer the "Rosie the Riveter" program. Katie Nooshazar, Recreation Program Manager for the city of Albany, outlines how the department uses a form of benefits to determine a community need. "We begin by identifying a community challenge or issue, for this particular program the department focused on the decline in most girls' level of self-esteem and sense of self-worth as they reach middle school. The community partners wanted to create a program to build self-esteem, improve problem-solving skills, and assist girls in developing an image that is strong, confident, capable, and ready to meet life's challenges. In addressing these issues, we focused on what experience we wanted girls to have, from anticipation and participation to reflection." Once the staff had a clear picture of these desired outcomes, they were able to design the program.

In this case the program was a day camp for middle school-aged girls that offered the opportunity to learn nontraditional skills. The girls learned trade skills such as welding, carpentry, plumbing, window installation, and wiring from women in each trade. The female electrician taught them how to change a light fixture. The female welder helped them create metal yard art. The girls installed windows, built patios, changed plumbing fixtures, and did basic electrical work. At lunch, women in the community who held nontraditional jobs (e.g., firefighter, police officer, public works director, newspaper publisher) ate with the girls and provided mentoring. The female trades instructors worked hand in hand with male assistants so the girls saw strong men and women working together (Sjothun, 2008). As this program is replicated in the future, it will be important to evaluate the outcomes of the program to quantify its benefits. This program and thousands of others demonstrate the potential of recreation programs to intentionally make a difference in the lives of both individuals and communities.

References

Addams, J. (1893). The subjective necessity for social settlements: A new impulse to an old gospel. In Henry C. Adams (Ed.), *Philanthropy and social progress*. New York, NY: Thomas Y. Crowell and Co.

American Planning Association. (2002). *How cities can use parks for…Community engagement*. Chicago, IL: American Planning Association

Boden, W. P. & Mitchell, E. D. (1923). *The theory of organized play*. New York, NY: Barnes.

Colyn, L., DeGraaf, D., & Certan, D. (2008, March/April). Social capital and organized camping. *Camping Magazine, 81*(2), 30–36.

Crompton, J. (2008). Evolution and implications of a paradigm shift in the marketing of leisure services in the USA. *Leisure Studies 27*(2), 181–206.

Curtis, H. (1915). *The practical conduct of play*. New York, NY: Macmillan.

DeGraaf, D., Tilley, C., & Neal, L. (2004). Servant leadership characteristics in organizational life. In Spears, L. & M. Lawrence (Eds.). *Practicing servant leadership: Succeeding through trust, bravery, & forgiveness*. San Francisco, CA: Jossey-Bass.

Downey, D. & Powell, B. (1993). Do children in single-parent households fare better living with same-sex parents? *Journal of Marriage and the Family, 55*, 55–71.

Driver, B. L. (Ed.). (2008). *Managing to optimize the beneficial outcomes of recreation*. State College, PA: Venture Publishing, Inc.

Driver, B. L. & Bruns, D. H. (1999). Concepts and uses of the benefits approach to leisure. In E. L. Jackson and T. L. Burton (Eds.), *Leisure studies: Prospects for the twenty-first century* (pp. 349–369). State College, PA: Venture Publishing, Inc.

Drucker, P. (1985). *Innovation and entrepreneurship*. New York, NY: Harper and Row.

Edginton, C. R. & Chen, P. (2008). *Leisure as transformation*. Champaign, IL: Sagamore Publishing.

Edginton, C. R., Hudson, S., Dieser, R., & Edginton, S. (2004). *Leisure programming: A service centered and benefits approach* (4th ed.). Boston, MA: McGraw-Hill.

Edginton, C. R., Jordan, D., DeGraaf, D., & Edginton, S. (2002). *Leisure and life satisfaction: Foundational perspectives* (3rd Ed.). Dubuque, IA: McGraw-Hill.

Estes, C. & Henderson, K. (2003, February). Research Update: Enjoyment and the good life: The less advertised benefits of parks and recreation. *Parks & Recreation*.

Florida Parks and Recreation Association. (2008). *It starts in parks campaign.* Retrieved August 11, 2009, from http://web.frpa.org

Florida, R. (2002). *The rise of the creative class and how it's transforming work, leisure, community and everyday life.* New York, NY: Basic Books.

Godbey, G. (1997). *Leisure and leisure services in the 21st century.* State College, PA: Venture Publishing, Inc.

Greenbeancoffee.org (2009). *About Us.* Retrieved March 4, 2009, from www.greanbeancoffee.org/about.php

Greenleaf, R. (2002). Essentials of servant-leadership. In L. Spears and M. Lawrence (Eds.), *Focus on leadership: Servant leadership for the 21st century.* New York, NY: John Wiley.

Greenleaf, R. (1991). *The servant as leader.* Indianapolis, IN: The Robert Greenleaf Center

Greenleaf, R. (1977). *Servant leadership: A journey into the nature of legitimate power and greatness.* New York, NY: Paulist Press.

Hearts N' Parks program reports increase in physical activity, heart-healthy diets: June 10. (2004). *Physical Therapy* (August, 2004). Retrieved March 17, 2010, from http://findarticles.com/p/articles/mi_hb237/is_8_84/ai_n29112060/

Hemingway, J. (2000). *Conceptualizing social capital generation in leisure: Social networks and discussion patterns.* Paper presented at Leisure Research Symposium on Leisure Research, National Recreation and Park Association Annual Congress, Phoenix, AZ.

Henderson, K. A., Thurber, C. A., Scanlin, M., & Bialeschki, M. D., with assistance from Leslie Scheuler (Philliber Research Associates) and Michelle Gambone (Youth Development Strategies, Inc.). (2007). Deepening knowledge of the variables: Youth development findings from group camps. *Search Institute Insights & Evidence, 4*(1), 1-11.

Jackson, E. (1994). Activity specific constraints on leisure participation. *Journal of Park and Recreation Administration, 12*(2), 33–50.

Jackson, E. (2005). *Constraints to leisure.* State College, PA: Venture Publishing, Inc.

Jackson, E. & Henderson, K. (1995). Gender-based analysis of leisure constraints. *Leisure Sciences, 17,* 31–51.

Jordan, D. (2007). *Leadership in leisure services: Making a difference* (3rd ed.). State College, PA: Venture Publishing, Inc.

Knapp, J. & McLean, D. (2002). Help employers move to the top of your organization. *Parks and Recreation, 37*(8), 20–27.

Moore, R. L. & Driver, B. L. (2005). *Introduction to outdoor recreation: Providing and managing natural resource based opportunities.* State College, PA: Venture Publishing, Inc.

Neulinger, J. (1974). *The psychology of leisure.* Springfield, IL: Charles C. Thomas Publisher.

New Horizons Foundation. (2009). New Horizons Foundation: Social capital & capabilities development homepage. Retrieved January 9, 2010 from http:/www.new-horizons.ro/

Oldenburg, R. (2000). *Celebrating the third place: Inspiring stories about the "Great Good Places" at the heart of our communities.* New York, NY: Marlowe & Company.

Putnam, R. (2002, February 11). Bowling together. *The American Prospect, 13*(3). Retrieved on September 25, 2009, from http://www.prospect.org/cs/articles?article=bowling_together

Putnam, R. (2000). *Bowling alone: The collapse and revival of American community.* New York, NY: Simon & Schuster.

Putnam, R. (1995, January). Bowling alone: America's declining social capital. *Journal of Democracy, 6*(1), 65–78.

Putnam, R. & Goss, K. (2002). Introduction. In R. Putnam (Ed.), *Democracies in flux: The evolution of social capital in contemporary society* (pp. 3–21). New York, NY: Oxford Press.

Rifkin, J. (2001). *The age of access.* New York, NY: Jeremy P. Tarcher/Putnam

Robinson, J. & Godbey, G. (1997). *Time for life: The surprising ways Americans use their time.* University Park, PA: Penn State Press.

Russell, R. (2002). *Pastimes: The context of contemporary leisure* (2nd ed.). Champaign, IL: Sagamore Publishing.

Samdahl, D. (1991). Measuring leisure: Categorical or interval? *Journal of Leisure Research, 12*(1), 1–24.

Serving up Yes! An alunmi profile of Lisa and Hayden. (2006, Fall). *Calvin College Spark,* 61.

Sessoms, D. & Stevenson, J. (1981). *Leadership and group dynamics in recreation services.* Boston, MA: Allyn & Bacon.

Sjothun, B. (2008). Benefits in action: Rosie the riveter. *Benefits and Partnership Success.* NRPA.

Spears, L. (1995). Servant leadership and the Greenleaf legacy. In L. Spear (Ed.), *Reflections on leadership: How Robert K. Greenleaf's Theory of Servant Leadership influenced today's top management thinkers* (pp. 1–16). New York, NY: John Wiley & Sons.

Spears, L. & Lawrence, M. (Eds.). (2002). *Focus on leadership: Servant-leadership for the 21st century*. New York, NY: John Wiley & Sons.

STRIVE RTS (2007). STRIVE RTS, Inc. *Mission Statement*. Retrieved on February 22, 2009, from http://striveonline.org/about.htm#mission

Weimer, E. (2008). *The geography of bliss: One grump's search for the happiest places in the world*. New York, NY: Twelve.

Wuthnow, R. (2002). United States: Bridging the privileged and the marginalized. In R. Putnam (Ed.), *Democracies in flux: The evolution of social capital in contemporary society* (pp. 59–103). New York, NY: Oxford Press.

Programmer Profile

Jane Addams

Photo courtesy of the University of Illinois at Chicago, Special Collections and University Archives (JAMC_0000_0030_0855)

In Chapter Two we turn to another historical figure, Jane Addams, for our programmer profile. She was a pioneer in the fields of social work, community and economic development, as well as parks and recreation. She was also one of the first women to graduate from college in the late 1800s and was the epitome of a servant leader. Addams lived during a time of great transition in America as large numbers of immigrants entered the United States. Many of the immigrants worked in low-paying and dangerous jobs created by the industrial revolution. She saw recreation programs as one way to address many of the social issues facing the United States as a result of large-scale immigration and industrialization.

▶ **What was Addam's career path?**

After graduating from Rockford College in 1881, Addams toured Europe. This trip lasted two years and was followed by a second trip in 1887. During this second trip she visited Toynbee Hall in London, which was a product of the settlement house movement. The settlement house movement began in industrial England in the mid 1800s and offered food, shelter, and educational opportunities to the urban poor. Toynbee Hall "offered something new in place of old-fashioned modes of relief to the poor; it provided mutual engagement across class lines and a broad education for working men and women" (Elshtain, 2002, p. 74).

Addams and her traveling companion, Ellen Gates Starr, were impressed by what they saw at Toynbee Hall and resolved to begin a similar endeavor among the working poor in the United States, not through charity, but by living and working together to make a better life for all. Thus, after returning home in 1889 Jane Addams and Ellen Gates Starr opened the doors of Hull House in the 19th ward of Chicago. Hull House quickly became a center of community life, attracting people who needed services. Residents (staff members) were often idealistic young middle class men and women who committed to live for an extended period of time in urban slums, seeking to bring education and other programs to the immigrant poor. What made Hull House unique was that Addams thought of those who came and went as citizens, or citizens in the making, not as clients or receivers of services (Elshtain, 2002). In the process, the residents of Hull House worked with the working class poor and created the following firsts (Elshtain):

- First social settlement in Chicago, and first social settlement to include both men and women residents
- First public baths and first public kitchen in Chicago
- First public playground and first public gymnasium in Chicago
- First little theater in the United States
- First citizenship preparation classes in the United States
- First painting loan program in Chicago
- First Fresh Air camps for children in Chicago
- First public swimming pool in Chicago
- First Boy Scout troop in Chicago

▶ **What roles did Addams fill at Hull House?**

- *Community Activist and Social Reformer.* Jacob Riis—as quoted in Elshtain (2002)—penned these words of praise for Jane Addams; "They have good sense in Chicago. Jane Addams is there." This sentiment, however, was not universally shared. In 1935, Elizabeth Dilling in her book, *The Red Network: A Who's Who and Handbook of Radicalism for Patriots*, described Addams as a "dangerous radical masquerading as a saintly champion of the poor" (p. 19).

- *Friend and Mentor.* Asked to sum up Hull House and Jane Addams, one member of the neighborhood stated: "she opened up a whole new world to us, is what she and the others did…I see her as a great lady. She had a way with children, a way with people. And she emphasized responsibility. You can do it, she would say. You can do it, and we did it partly because we didn't want to disappoint her. We did it out of respect… Hull House was the greatest experience of my life" (Elshtain, 2002, p. 13).

- *Sanitary Inspector for the City of Chicago.* This was the only paid position Jane Addams ever held and it grew out of her concern for children and youth playing close to the rotting garbage on Chicago streets. Through her efforts at Hull House, Addams and her staff educated local residents about the importance of garbage removal and treatment.

- *Advocate for Women's Suffrage.* Addams was a fearless campaigner for women's right to vote and became a political force on the national scene. She made the nominating speech for Theodore Roosevelt as the presidential candidate for the Progressive Party in 1912.

- *Anti-war Demonstrator, Peace Activist.* Her experience in the Hull House had shown her that people of different nationalities could live together peacefully; thus, Addams opposed the war. This opposition to the war lost her popular support among local politicians and residents, yet the support slowly returned and she was awarded the Nobel Peace Prize in 1931.

▶ **How did Jane Addams exemplify the characteristics of a servant leader?**

Addams was a woman of vision who also had the ability to work with people to co-create the future. Underlying all her efforts was the drive to build citizens and equip them with the social capital necessary to make a difference and, in the process, build up a social culture of democracy. In this endeavor, everyone contributed and became partners in working for the common good. "Addams was adamant throughout her life that Hull House should offer shelter from the storm and a new way of being in this world. It was a place of civic *education, a spirited enterprise that served as a vehicle for the creation of community and the sustaining of identities…[For Addams] there was no cure for the human condition, but there was a cure for the sense of purposelessness, and it lies in the forging of purposeful lives in and through community. One doesn't use community for self seeking purposes. One participates, and in fellowship and friendship, finds the self relocated*" (Elshtain, 2002, 153–155).

Addams saw the potential of recreation to promote fellowship and friendship, and through relationships was able to work together with others to improve the quality of life of many. Thus, Addams is a fine example for all recreation professionals, combining the ability to be an entrepreneur, to continually grow and develop to serve others, while practicing many of the virtues of servant leadership.

Service and Quality in Programming | 2

Programming leisure experiences for or with people can be done in a variety of ways and requires a holistic view of both the individual and the community. In this chapter we examine some of the overarching tenets to providing leisure services, as well as how recreation programs have been planned in the past. In addition, entrepreneurial and empowerment models are offered as approaches to delivering recreation programs.

Sharing the worldview of indigenous peoples, John Muir, the great American naturalist, once stated, "When we try to pick out anything by itself, we find it hitched to everything else in the universe" (Sierra Club Staff, 1992, p. 73), and so it is with programming leisure experiences. Parks, recreation, and leisure services programmers must be aware of a vast array of factors in planning recreation programs; these include demographic, political, economic, and societal factors. As was stated in Chapter One, one of the characteristics of successful leisure services organizations and professionals is the ability to respond to changes going on around them. For example, the National Recreation and Park Association (NRPA) is a professional membership organization that advocates for public parks and recreation on a national level. One of roles of NRPA is to identify critical issues and trends in society, and create a public parks and recreation agenda through their strategic planning process; these issues are articulated through organizational goal statements (see Table 2.1 on p. 30). This information is made available on the NRPA website and members are asked to provide input at several steps of the planning process. In this way, members become aware of, and help with, the NRPA's efforts to advance the public parks and recreation agenda.

In examining the list of critical issues and trends identified by NRPA, one that is especially applicable to all aspects of leisure services is the need to deliver quality services. As a result, this chapter will focus initially on examining the leisure experience as a service, considering the role of quality in providing leisure programs, and understanding the importance of serving both individuals and society through programs. It will also address various philosophical approaches to the delivery of leisure services and the need for organizations to take a social entrepreneurial approach to developing and implementing programs.

Understanding the Leisure Experience

The most marked change in the structure of developed economies over the past 50 years has been the societal transformation from a manufacturing economy to a service economy. In the United States alone, the percentage of workers employed in the service sector has risen from a mere 30% in 1900 to an estimated 75% in 2002. This trend will continue as the service sector of the economy has been projected to grow to almost 80% of the workforce by 2014 (Berman, 2005).

The service economy is also changing. In their groundbreaking book entitled, *The Experience Economy*, Pine and Gilmore (1999) noted that we have been moving beyond a service economy to an economy based on experiences.

> Experiences have always been around, but consumers, businesses, and economists lumped them together with such uneventful activities as dry cleaning, auto repair, wholesale distribution, and telephone access. When a person buys a service, he [sic] purchases a set of intangible activities carried out on his behalf. But when he buys an experience, he pays to spend time enjoying a series of memorable events that a company stages to engage him in a personal way.... Companies stage an experience when they engage customers in a memorable way. (p. 3)

In this way, consumers may be compared to tourists; they are "sensation seekers and collectors of experience; their relationship with this world is primarily aesthetic; they perceive the world as a food for sensibility—a matrix of possible experiences" (Bauman, 1998, p. 94). This movement from commodities and goods to services and, ultimately, experiences is presented in Table 2.2 on p.31.

To be prepared to give individual customers the experiences they seek, leisure providers must first understand the nature of delivering services. We must also understand the role we play in co-creating experiences with our constituents. To understand the process of delivering quality experiences, we will begin

Table 2.1 NRPA organizational goals and objectives (adapted from NRPA, 2009)

NRPA Goals	Selected Objectives
	Increase our capacity to implement a broad based advocacy program that affects funding, policy, and regulations at the national level to benefit public parks, recreation, conservation, and environmental stewardship at the local, state, and federal levels.
Advocacy NRPA's government relations and advocacy initiatives will result in policy-making, legislation, and funding that benefits public parks, recreation, and conservation.	Improve the association's ability to increase visibility and mobilize support around emerging issues and legislative initiatives of importance to NRPA.
Knowledge NRPA's portfolio of high-quality, diversified, and relevant education and training resources will provide the knowledge, competency, and skill base that both park and recreation professionals and citizen advocates need to lead the field effectively.	Increase our internal capacity to conduct research and our external access to relevant data from similar national organizations, state affiliates, universities, and other relevant sources.
	Develop and deliver relevant, affordable, and accessible learning resources and opportunities for citizen advocates and professionals.
Awareness The general public, as well as public officials, legislators, and the media, will be more aware of the critical role played by public parks, recreation, and conservation efforts in encouraging healthy lifestyles, promoting environmental stewardship, and supporting community livability.	Enhance NRPA's overall media relations effectiveness. Establish and expand programs with private and public sector organizations, both not-for-profit and for profit, whose interests complement those of NRPA.
Citizen/Professional Collaboration Working together, parks and recreation professionals and citizen advocates will be champions for public parks, recreation, and conservation initiatives.	Expand the interest of the general public through creative programs and consistent messages. Strengthen professional members' understandings of the value of engaging citizen board and commission members, volunteers, and other supporters in NRPA.
Organizational Excellence NRPA will be an effectively governed, well managed, fiscally sound organization positioned to deliver maximum value to its members and stakeholders.	Increase the relevance and value of programs, products, and services to better meet member and stakeholder needs. Use innovative technology solutions to enhance business operations and member services.

by examining the unique characteristics that differentiate services from goods or manufactured products. The four most commonly identified characteristics ascribed to services are intangibility, heterogeneity, inseparability of production and consumption, and perishability (see Figure 2.1 on p. 32).

Intangibility

In services what is actually purchased is the experience rather than a tangible thing. As a result, criteria on which to evaluate the experience can be complex and difficult to capture. For example, a participant involved in a tour of a museum takes nothing tangible home beyond the personal value she or he placed on the experience. Because it comes from within each person, measuring the satisfaction of that intangible experience can be challenging.

Heterogeneity

This refers to the potential for variability in service delivery. This is especially prominent when a large number of employees is involved. The quality of services is largely dependent upon the actions of people. Therefore, the quality of interactions between personnel and customers is likely to vary among staff members. In addition, for individual staff members the quality of interactions may differ from day to day. For example, within dance classes some instructors are more requested than others as a result of how participants perceive the class experience.

Inseparability of Production and Consumption

Services are often delivered and experienced simultaneously. This usually requires the presence of both the consumer and the provider during the delivery process, and the service cannot be taken back and exchanged if the customer is not satisfied. The provider can show various examples of the service, but the customer's own creation, for example, does not exist and cannot be shown.

Perishability

It is not possible to store services in inventory. For example, a camping experience (i.e., service) is not like a can of soup, which can be produced and stocked for later consumption. Services are consumed as they develop. These characteristics by no means fully describe the differences between leisure goods and services—some products have one or more of these characteristics and not all services display all of the characteristics. For example, in identifying the degree of intangibility of a service Kotler (1991) distinguished four categories along a continuum ranging from a pure good to a pure service.

- a pure tangible good such as sporting equipment (e.g., tennis rackets, golf clubs, sports shoes) where no services accompany the product.

- a tangible good (e.g., waterpark or hotel room) with accompanying services to enhance its consumer appeal.

Table 2.2 Economic distinctions (Pine & Gilmore, 1999)

	Economic Offering			
Characteristic	**Commodities**	**Goods**	**Services**	**Experiences**
Economy	Agrarian	Industrial	Service	Experience
Economic function	Extract	Make	Deliver	Stage
Nature of offering	Fungible	Tangible	Intangible	Memorable
Key attribute	Natural	Standardized	Customized	Personal
Method of supply	Stored in bulk	Inventoried after production	Delivered on demand	Revealed over time
Seller	Trader	Manufacturer	Provider	Stager
Buyer	Market	User	Client	Guest
Factors of demand	Characteristics	Features	Benefits	Sensations

- a major service with accompanying minor goods and services such as a week at camp or an adult sports league.

- a pure service such as a painting class, fitness membership, or childcare.

This categorization helps us to understand why it is difficult to define or generalize services. This distinction becomes less clear, however, when we realize that the ultimate purpose of both goods and services is to engage the individual in a personal way to create lasting value (Pine & Gilmore, 1999).

In making the leap from services to experiences, Pine and Gilmore (1999) distinguish the products of different economies in the following way: "while commodities are fungible [i.e., they are what they are], goods tangible, and services are intangible, experiences are memorable" (pp. 11–12). From this progression, customers want and expect to be positively, emotionally, and memorably impacted at every level of their interaction with recreation programs.

Thus, within experiences, recreation programs should seek to add emotional value to the experience of customers. In this way, services become the stage and goods become the props to engage the individual. To understand this concept, consider a family trip to Walt Disney World. In addition to the actual event, parents take their children to Disney World to make that shared experience part of everyday family conversations for months and even years to come.

The Characteristics of Experiences

Examining the early work of Pine and Gilmore (1999), we can begin to think about experiences across two dimensions: customer participation and customer connection. At one end of the spectrum of the customer participation dimension is passive participation in which customers have no impact on the event or program—they simply experience it (e.g., watching television at home). At the other end of the spectrum lies active participation in which participants play key roles in creating the event that yields the experience (e.g., flag football players in a campus recreation league).

The second dimension of experience describes the connection or relationship that unites customers with the event or performance. At one end of the connection spectrum lies absorption, at the other end, immersion. People viewing a flag football game from the bleachers may absorb the event taking place in front of them; at the same time, people playing in the game are immersed on another level.

These four broad categories of experiences create four different realms of experience (Pine & Gilmore, 1998, 1999; see Figure 2.2).

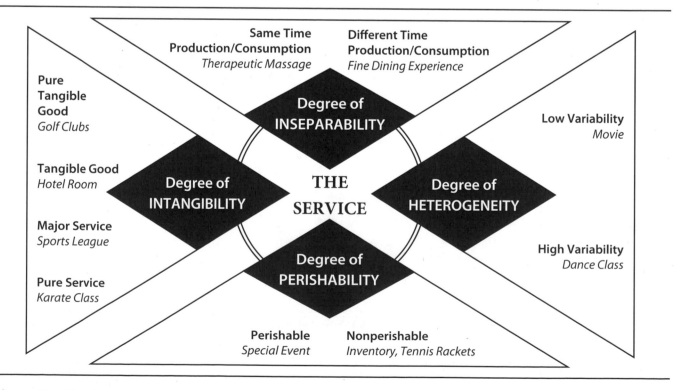

Figure 2.1 The four characteristics of a leisure service

- **Entertainment:** experiences where customers participate more passively than actively and their connection is more likely one of absorption than of immersion (e.g., watching a movie, sporting event, or theater production).

- **Esthetic:** experiences where customers are immersed in the event, but have little or no effect on it (e.g., attending a symphony concert or ballet, reading a book).

- **Escapist:** experiences where customers are actively involved and immersed and where the involvement of the participant greatly impacts the outcome of the experience (e.g., a camping trip, travel, creating something in a woodworking class).

- **Educational:** experiences where there is more active participation, but customers are still outside the event rather than immersed in the action (e.g., taking a skiing class, learning to paint, learning a second language).

Within each of these realms, leisure services professionals can begin to create programs that assist participants in connecting to the programs in ways that fit with the kind of experience they want at a specific time and place. What is important for parks, recreation, and leisure services professionals is recognizing that we should strive to move our programs beyond simply providing services to co-creating experiences with participants. Consider the following description of the positive emotions that Ari Weinzweig, cofounder of Zingerman's, a

$10 million a year delicatessen in Ann Arbor, MI, wants his employees to create for customers:

> I tell my people that you want the customer to think that they're the best thing that has happened to you all day. We're not here to sell a loaf of bread or a sandwich or an apple. We're selling them an experience. It's not enough to sell people a great bottle of olive oil. Who cares? You've got to give them a great experience. People are going to go where they have a great experience, where it's fun, where they feel appreciated. (as cited by Barlow & Maul, 2000, p. 6)

Creating memorable experiences and connecting with customers on a variety of levels is important and relates to the overall quality of the experience. Thus, the dimension of quality is an important part of meeting the needs of customers.

The Staging of Experiences

In an effort to create memorable experiences, Pine and Gilmore (1999) use the metaphor of theater to explain how experiences need to be staged in ways that tend to yield value for guests. In particular they identify five principles for staging encounters that draw guests into the experience. These principles are:

- Fully theme the encounter;

- Identify the appropriate "theatrical form" appropriate to the theme and ensure that employees stay in character consistent with the theme and theatrical form;

- Customize the encounter to the individual;

- Stimulate multiple senses during the encounter; and

- Provide (mix in) memorabilia.

We integrate many of these principles into later chapters and encourage programmers to think about how to address participants' needs as well as how to use facilities, staff, themes, and equipment to enhance the overall program experience. When taken together, these principles can be thought of as a "technology" recreation programmers can use to stage encounters that yield memorable experiences for guests. Building on the ideas of the experiential economy, Ellis and Rossman (2008) have taken the work of Pine and Gilmore (1999) and combined it with select literature

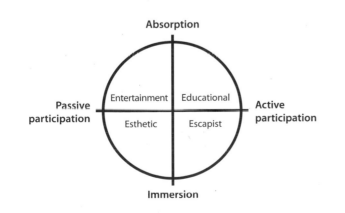

Figure 2.2 The four realms of an experience (Pine & Gilmore, 1998)

on customer service and quality management to create a model for staging experiences in recreation programs (see Figure 2.3). The model identifies both the artistic and technical expertise needed to deliver programs. Ellis and Rossman gathered the technical performance features from research on service quality and customer experience, much of which comes from the business world. The artistic performance features relate to many of the principles identified by Pine and Gilmore and include creating a theme; engaging multiple senses; and showing empathy for the unique perspectives, wants, and needs of guests as acts of personalizing the experience.

The technical performance and artistic performance elements of the model illustrate a focus on producing experiences in conjunction with the guest. Thus, the idea of co-creating programs is presented, recognizing that the programmer is not the only force involved in program or experience design. The guest also impacts each aspect of a program or experience. Ellis and Rossman state, "staging experiences facilitates the opportunity for the guest to have experiences that are of value. This notion of facilitating rather than fully providing the experience preserves the autonomy of the participant to help create the leisure experience as well as the freedom to do so" (2008, p. 13).

The Concept of Quality

As noted by Pine and Gilmore (1999), quality and value have become increasingly important elements in delivering services and experiences in the past twenty-five years. *Quality—a perception of excellence—is the extent to which the products and services received by the customer equal or exceed expectations.* As Albrecht (1992) noted "the most fundamental change in management's thinking going on today is the shift from managing the boxes on the organizational chart to managing customer outcomes" (p. 10). This quality revolution can be traced back to the years following World War II. This is when American quality control expert William Deming began sharing his approach with Japanese firms to focus on quality rather than focusing on cutting costs to increase profit margins. Deming

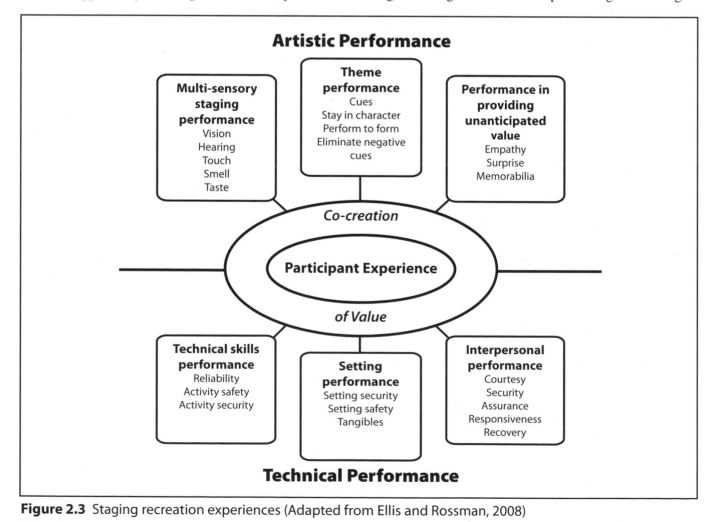

Figure 2.3 Staging recreation experiences (Adapted from Ellis and Rossman, 2008)

asserted that higher quality leads to lower costs and higher productivity, which in turn leads to higher profits, higher share price, the creation of more jobs, and more security for everyone involved (Aguayo, 1990). Deming presented 14 points for management to follow which concentrate on removing major roadblocks to quality improvement (see Table 2.3).

In his 14 points, Deming focuses on preventing errors before they appear by involving everyone in the organization. The aim is to have employees take pride in their work skills. The early work of Deming and others was focused on product quality and set the stage for the emergence of a revolution in the way organizations deliver goods and services.

> Call it the customer revolution, the quality revolution, the service revolution, or whatever you like. All of the various energies and lines of action that businesses are putting forth now are beginning to converge to a single focus: winning and keeping the customer's business by doing the right things outstandingly well. (Albrecht, 1992, p. ix)

As recreation programmers, we suggest taking this concept one step further by realizing the importance of delivering customer value, moving beyond customer satisfaction to customer delight, and producing a distinctive personal and emotional experience for each of our customers.

In this light, it becomes apparent that the old distinction between product and service is obsolete. Both the service and the product are incomplete pieces of the same element—delivering memorable experiences. Only when leisure services programmers combine them into a single, composite entity can we think about quality as a competitive advantage and a way of operating a business. What exists is total customer value—the combination of the tangible and the intangible experienced by the customer during all points of contact with the organization. These shape the participants' perceptions of doing business with that particular organization. The importance of understanding the perceptions of customers cannot be overstated. After all, perception of quality is crucial to the success of a service-oriented business. "It is not enough just to give good service; the customer must perceive the fact that he or she is getting good service" (Albrecht, 1985, p. 48).

Yet the quality story does not stop here. Pine and Gilmore (2007), in their new book, *Authenticity: What Consumers Really Want*, encourage organizations to move beyond quality to understand, manage, and excel at rendering authenticity. Consumers today are seeking meaning and organizations they can trust, products and services that resonate with integrity and transparency—in a word, authenticity. That quest for authenticity is a call to action for any organization or agency intending to be relevant in the 21st century (Vossoughi, 2008).

Being authentic demands that we know the benefits and outcomes we wish to offer our constituents while also paying attention to the process by which these benefits are delivered. This includes being intentional about inviting customers to help in co-creating

Table 2.3 Deming's 14 points of quality

1	Create consistency of purpose toward improvement of products and service.
2	Adopt a new philosophy. We can no longer live with commonly accepted levels of delays, mistakes, defective materials, and defective workmanship.
3	Cease dependence on mass inspection. Require instead statistical evidence that quality is built in.
4	End the practice of awarding business on the basis of price tag.
5	Find problems. It is management's job to work continually on the system.
6	Institute modern methods of training on the job.
7	Institute modern methods of supervision of production workers. The responsibility of foremen [sic] must be changed from numbers to quality.
8	Drive out fear, so that everyone may work effectively for the company.
9	Break down barriers between departments.
10	Eliminate numerical goals, posters, and slogans for the workforce; ask for new levels of productivity without providing methods.
11	Eliminate work standards that prescribe numerical quotas.
12	Remove barriers that stand between the hourly worker and his [sic] right to pride in workmanship.
13	Institute a vigorous program of education and retraining.
14	Create a structure in top management that will push every day on the above 13 points.

these outcomes. Many leisure services organizations already recognize the importance of providing quality programs that are consistent (authentic) with their values. As early as the 1990s, McCarville (1993) offered the following keys to quality programming:

- **Establish programming priorities.** Programmers must remember to serve constituents rather than simply operate programs. This is the core of servant leadership.

- **Discover customer needs.** Understand what customers want and expect from the recreation and leisure programs the organization provides. Leisure professionals do this through needs assessments and other forms of data gathering.

- **Develop programs from customer needs, wants, and expectations.** This requires that leisure professionals utilize the information they learn from data gathering and needs assessments in program planning and design.

- **Identify key program providers.** By making program staff and customers partners in the programming process, leisure professionals help identify key people, empower constituents, and enhance their responsiveness to constituents.

- **Identify key encounters with clients.** These key interaction points occur between customers and staff, customers and facilities, and between customers. They occur at all phases of program development.

- **Train staff for flexibility.** Adaptability is important, but when in doubt programmers should establish, maintain, and hold to standards.

- **Ask for help.** Successful programs result from endless innovation. As programmers, we should be open to opportunities to gather input from staff, customers, and other programs in an attempt to increase the quality of our programs.

According to McCarville (1993, p. 23), the "search for program excellence never ends. Excellent programs remain in a state of constant development. Once they cease to develop, they will cease to meet the changing needs of their clientele."

The Need for Social Responsibility

The importance of delivering quality leisure services within the emerging experience economy is clear; yet such a customer value paradigm is still not complete for several reasons. First and foremost may be the limits of excellence and the need for social responsibility. In examining the possible limits of excellence as well as the need for social responsibility we would like to encourage you to think about the following questions. Is the customer always right? What is the cost of excellence? What kind of excellence do we want to promote? How can leisure services programmers promote the common good?

Is The Customer Always Right?

Many businesses, nonprofit agencies, and other entities that serve others believe that "the customer is always right." This approach—that the customer is always right—is certainly a way to stress quality and guide staff behavior with customers. As a guide it is simple, easy to remember, and clear on what the staff should do. However, as Jandt (1995, p. 2) has noted

> [A]s an ideal it seems clear, but in practice it doesn't work…If a customer makes impossible demands…the customer leaves dissatisfied, may never return, and probably tells others about your failure.

Barlow and Maul (2000) concur with this notion saying the customer is not always right, but customers are always emotional. That is, they always have feelings, sometimes intense, other times barely perceptible, when they make purchases or engage in transactions connected with experiences. Thus, organizations must look to develop a win-win approach by using negotiation skills in the interaction between an experience provider and the customer. For interactions with customers to be successful for both parties over the long term, both the provider and the customer must feel that each has won. Customers must believe that they received the experience they expected at a price they accepted. Furthermore, the service provider must also feel good about providing the experience—and that often includes making a profit on the transaction.

What is the Cost of Excellence?

Kouzes and Posner provided another perspective on quality and excellence when they noted, "excellence is a noble goal…to surpass the average and to become superior is what makes for high quality services and products. But one can go too far. One can go beyond excellence to excess" (1993, p. 261). The result of such excessive emphasis may mean the short-term triumph of an organization, but at a costly long-term price for the individual, organization, and larger community. Wilkie (2008) describes this situation as being a trap of excellence noting that the more excellent we become, the higher the price we pay in terms of growing expectations.

To help understand this concept, think about the following example. One year staff operated a recreational youth sports program so efficiently that a budget surplus existed at the end of the season. Thus, the staff decided to host a surprise barbeque for the athletes and their families, free of charge. The barbeque was a huge success; it surpassed everyone's expectations because they were not expecting the "added value." The next year, however, costs were higher and no money was left over for an end-of-season barbeque. Having enjoyed the event the previous year, several people complained because their expectation (which was established the previous year) was not met. We must remember that as providers operate in ways that exceed expectations, constituents often anticipate the continuation of those markers of excellence. This results in a need to continually look for new ways to exceed increasing expectations, which can increase associated costs.

What is Excellence?

A third perspective on the limits of the customer value paradigm is based on how we might define excellence. In addressing the role of excellence in inter-collegiate athletes, DeGioia (2005) noted that people tend to define excellence for individual athletes in two different ways. The first is balance; a marker of excellence for an individual athlete is how well she or he balances the various dimensions of life (e.g., family, work, play). This view flows from Aristotle, who encouraged individuals to pursue the good life, developing all aspects of their beings in an attempt to flourish as balanced human beings. The second way to define excellence for individual athletes is the pursuit to be the best in one area of their lives at the expense of all other areas. Consider the parallel in how we offer recreation services and programs. We could distribute organizational resources in such a way as to offer a well-balanced set of well-run programs, which serve a wide range of interests in the arts, sports, outdoors, and educational pursuits. The other approach is to focus organizational resources on one very specific type of program and become known for excellence in that one aspect of the profession.

Likewise, we might explore our views on balancing the needs of individuals or meeting collective societal needs. As Machan (1986) pointed out

> [P]eople do not in fact automatically seek out what is best for them—if it were only so we would live in a wonderful world. Nor do they always know what is best for them—which too would be very helpful if it were so. Rather people must work very hard to learn what is best for them and then try hard to obtain it. (pp. 272–273)

Most strive to achieve some level of balance between the freedom of an individual to pursue her or his goals and the responsibility the individual has in living as a member of a common society. Thus, parks, recreation, and leisure services programmers (especially those seeking to be servant leaders in their communities) will want to achieve a balance of delivering quality leisure experiences and maximizing individual freedom, while at the same time being socially responsible to the local and global communities (see Figure 2.4 on p. 38).

This tension between promoting individual freedom and responsibility is found in all aspects of recreation programming. Assisting individuals to experience leisure is balanced by decisions about whom we serve, how we serve, what we provide, and so on. Different leisure services organizations will approach these questions differently as their basic values differ. Yet one constant remains—the desire to serve both the individual and society. For some organizations the emphasis may be on serving the individual rather than the community. For others the opposite may be true; still others will try to serve both individuals and the community equally. For instance, many nonprofit organizations try to provide programs with an educational component that also offers fun experiences. At the same time, the organization or agency advocates for what they feel is the common good. The Sea Life Safari is one example of such a program. This program is offered by the Clearwater Marine Aquarium (http://www.seewinter.com) as a way to provide a unique education experience that is fun and educational, while at the same time creating a level of awareness and memories that will remain in hearts and minds long after the experience ends (see Figure 2.5 on p. 38).

How Can Leisure Services Programmers Promote The Common Good?

Historically, the idea of serving society has been connected with the concept of the common good. Furthermore, serving the common good has been traditionally associated more with public (government) and private, nonprofit organizations than with commercial ventures. Consider that Aristotle's *Politics* begins with the following:

> Every community is established with a view to some good; for mankind [sic] always acts in order to obtain that which it thinks good. But, if all communities aim for the good, the city [polis] or political community, which is the highest of all, and which embraces the rest, aims at good in a greater degree than any other, and at the highest good… we assume the best life, both for individuals and for states, is the life of virtue. (as quoted in Bess, 1996)

Likewise, James Madison and other founders of the United States understood the need for pursuing the common good. In the *Federalist Papers*, Madison noted that, "…the public good, the real welfare of the great body of people, is the supreme object to pursue" (as cited in Wellman, Dustin, Henderson, & Moore, 2008, p. 7). Burns picks up this thread in his 2004 film about Thomas Jefferson. He interviewed historians and philosophers, asking them to explain what Jefferson meant by the words "life, liberty and the pursuit of happiness."

What he found was a profound sense that Jefferson connected both individual and societal happiness.

Today, the concept of the common good is an elusive one as a number of competing visions of the good life in contemporary society exist (Wellman et al., 2008) If, however, we view the common good as

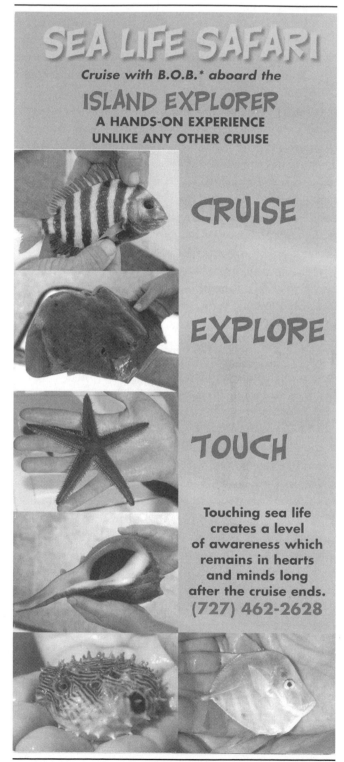

Figure 2.5 An example of opportunity to promote common good

Figure 2.4 Scales of balance

the conditions that promote human flourishing, it is an important goal for which to strive. Schultz, McAvoy, and Dustin (1988) have connected this desire to work for the common good by advocating a service ethic, especially with public recreation programs. They echo the spirit of Robert Greenleaf when they ask

> [S]houldn't public recreation be governed by a social service ethic that rises above the bottom-line thinking? How can we serve all people— not just those who are willing to pay? Who will look out for minorities, the environment, the poor, society's underprivileged? (p. 53)

In today's changing environment we see a blurring of the traditional lines between public, nonprofit, and commercial organizations. Public and nonprofit organizations are being asked to be increasingly innovative and entrepreneurial while commercial firms are being asked to be more socially responsible than in the past. As a result, society is seeing more collaboration and cooperation between all types of organizations to meet the demands of financial and social responsibility. As one CEO from a major Fortune 500 electronics firm stated

> [M]y philosophy is this; we don't run our business to earn profits. We earn profits to run our business. Our business has meaning and purpose—a reason to be here… People talk today about businesses needing to be socially responsible as if this is something new we need to do, on top of everything else we do. But social responsibility is not something that one should do as an extra benefit of the business. The whole essence of the business should be social responsibility. It must live for a purpose. Otherwise, why should it live at all? (Kiuchi, 1997)

The recreation movement in the United States has a rich history of building community and shared values, helping individuals and communities to act on what matters. Using a servant leadership perspective today continues to build on this tradition and recognizes that leisure services organizations are uniquely positioned to promote individual freedom, as well as encourage the common good in communities for a variety of reasons.

First, recreation programs offer communities opportunities for shared experiences through which common values can be developed. Figure 2.6, The Girls [*sic*] Think Tank flier depicts a community event that develops community and values. In Chapter One we discussed the opportunities that build social capital through shared experiences provided by recreation programs. When diverse members of the community gather on Saturday mornings for youth soccer games, the interactions and connections that are made can strengthen the social capital of that community. Community events and celebrations offer opportunities to build shared experiences as well as the fellowship necessary to begin to dialogue on other issues within the community.

Second, a key component to leisure and recreation is choice. People can choose to live differently based on the values and virtues that they hold. Juniu (2000) encourages people to slow down and not to rush during leisure as we do at work. She points to the phenomenon of downshifting, where people consciously choose to decrease their consumption of material goods in an effort to increase their quality of life as an example of an approach to balancing individual freedom and the common good.

The key for leisure services organizations to be successful in balancing the needs of the individual and society is to examine the benefits that people

Figure 2.6 An example of opportunity for shared experience

seek from programs and activities, and then find ways for participants to experience these benefits within a context of simultaneously demonstrating a caring attitude toward others, as well as the environment. This process involves two critical components: (1) listening to and understanding the needs of participants, and (2) assisting participants to understand and take responsibility for their actions. According to Edginton, DeGraaf, Dieser, and Edginton (2004), leisure professionals are in the life satisfaction business. When thought of in these terms, programs are not important. The focus is on the benefits that each program provides to increase the quality of life of participants. It is these benefits that are important.

Third, the diverse nature of recreation programming and the fact that programs are collective endeavors offers programmers a world of possibilities to contribute to the common good. In their book, *Service Living: Building Community through Public Parks and Recreation*, Wellman et al. (2008) put forth the idea of service living as a response to this opportunity. For these authors, "service living is distinguished by lifelong action that contributes to the health and well-being of all human things. It operationalizes an ecological worldview because through it we attend to the connections between our lives, other lives, and the systems and relationships that comprise the whole" (p. 1). The emphasis on the art and science of programming, leadership, and other aspects of the recreation profession uniquely prepares programmers to be aware of the whole. It also facilitates a desire to work toward delivering programs to be responsive to both individual wants and needs as well as community needs.

Strategies for Delivering Leisure Programs

In addressing the question of what is needed and feasible in delivering leisure experiences, we have focused on two overarching principles for leisure services organizations: (1) delivering quality experiences (that cater to an individual's freedom to choose what is best for her/him) while (2) responding to the collective needs of society. In addition to this, we need to examine the many approaches or strategies used in programming leisure experiences. These help us to understand the foundation from which programmers operate and can be used as frameworks to deliver quality programs.

A basic distinguishing characteristic between these strategies/approaches is the extent to which customers or constituents are involved in the planning process, and conversely the amount of planning and supervision provided by the leisure services programmer (see Figure 2.7). At one end of the continuum, leisure services professionals take on all the responsibility of planning leisure experiences. We serve as experts and develop leisure services programs based on what we think or believe is best for our constituents. Planning then becomes a task-oriented strategy directed toward solving problems. At the other end of the continuum, the leisure services programmer is more of a facilitator and collaborator empowering people to plan for their own leisure needs. In this context, planning utilizes a community development approach, a process-oriented strategy directed toward helping individuals identify their own needs and assisting them with resources necessary to address them (Edginton et al., 2004).

To further assist the reader in understanding the continuum presented in Figure 2.7, we will discuss each of the five general strategies found on the continuum: social advocacy, social planning, social marketing, marketing, and community development or grassroots empowerment. In discussing each of these strategies, we will present a general overview, a discussion about the role of the programmer, and an example of a leisure services program that might fit into each strategy for delivering services.

Social Advocacy

As a programming approach, social advocacy has a strong history in the parks, recreation, and leisure field. Social reformers advocated for the rights of disadvantaged populations and worked to right social injustices,

Social Advocacy	Social Planning	Social Marketing	Marketing Approach	Community Development

PROGRAMMER AS EXPERT → PROGRAMMER AS ENABLER

Figure 2.7 Continuum of program delivery strategies

forcing organizations to change the way they were distributing resources, hence services. Today, social advocacy continues to be important to serve underrepresented groups and entitle those who cannot speak for themselves (e.g., those with developmental or cognitive disabilities, children). Within a social advocacy framework, the leisure services programmer often works outside the established system to advocate for the rights of a specific group or issue.

Services and Advocacy for GLBT Elders (SAGE, 2010), established in 1978 in New York, is an excellent example of an organization that uses a variety of programming strategies, including a social advocacy approach, in serving constituents. This community-based organization has multiple purposes. It provides social services especially designed for seniors who are gay, lesbian, bisexual, or transgendered (GLBT). Services include medical services, legal services, bereavement counseling, and financial counseling. SAGE also provides social recreation and leisure opportunities designed for seniors (events include exercise, movies, antiquing, supper clubs, traveling, and book clubs). In addition, SAGE strives to educate participants and community members to act as advocates for the rights of individuals who are both seniors and either GLBT; to train new and existing professionals, and to develop innovative programs that meet the ever-changing leisure-related needs of this element of the population (see Figure 2.8 on p. 42).

Social Planning

Social planning is a task-oriented strategy directed toward rationally and logically distributing community resources. Participants are viewed as consumers of services that programmers create. It is a process of using the knowledge and expertise of professionals to plan, organize, and deliver services (Edginton, Hudson, Dieser, & Edginton, 2005). At its worst, social planning can mean simply providing programs based upon knowledge of past successes. When this happens, we do not respond well to social changes as they develop. At its best, social planning can be a systematic approach to identifying the needs of the individual, community, and organization and then creating recreation programs that the programmer believes will meet those needs.

An example of a program that uses a social planning approach is the *Opening Doors, Opening Minds* initiative developed by Hostelling International-USA (HI-USA). This program initiative was created in the aftermath of September 11, 2001 as a means by which HI-USA could use their existing hostels, staff, and re-

sources in an intentional push to break down barriers between nations and to promote cross-cultural understanding. The goal of the program is "to build a new generation of global citizens:

* unburdened by damaging stereotypes

* emboldened by open minds

* appreciative of their own heritage and understanding of others

* through the dialogue and education that comes through hostelling."

The program initiatives include a number of different components including travel scholar programs, international exchange programs, and community outreach programs (see Figure 2.9 on p. 43).

Social Marketing

Created as a way to produce social change, social marketing differs from other areas of marketing only with respect to the objectives of the marketers and their organizations. By this we mean that social marketing *seeks to influence social behavior not to benefit the marketer, but to benefit the target audience and general society.* Kotler and Lee (2008) note that social marketers often are selling behaviors that involve delayed self rewards (exercising) or doing something that benefits a third party (volunteering at the local recreation center), or that involves learning new skills (such as gardening or composting because it is good for the earth). For a variety of reasons social marketing is more difficult than commercial marking because it often involves changing the way people view the world.

At one time, social marketing was considered to be exclusively for public and nonprofit organizations. It was used for designing public awareness campaigns to promote social causes or to introduce behavior change. Social marketing, however, is also used by commercial organizations. For example, fitness clubs are often utilized not only as places to exercise, but also as opportunities for restoring balance to one's life. As another example, consider the work of Peace Games (www.peacegames.org). Peace Games believes in the power of young people to prevent violence. The organization partners with schools to increase knowledge, skills, relationships, and opportunities of young people, to help them work toward peace and justice issues. Peace Games provides resources and materials to schools and families, and teaches them to use games to empower

Services & Advocacy for GLBT Elders (SAGE)

Programs like SAGE become an important safety net for LGBT elders. Incorporated by lesbian and gay activists and aging service professionals in 1978 as Senior Action in a Gay Environment, SAGE (now Services & Advocacy for GLBT Elders) is the world's oldest and largest non-profit agency addressing the needs of lesbian, gay, bisexual, and transgender elders. SAGE works with LGBT elders to address and overcome the challenges of discrimination in senior service settings, while also being an essential component in the creation of informal caregiving support, and development of new "family" networks. SAGE's programs include:

- The nation's first Friendly Visiting program for frail and homebound LGBT seniors
- The country's first support group for LGBT seniors with HIV
- The nation's first program dedicated to caregiving services for LGBT seniors
- The nation's first LGBT Senior Drop-In Center
- The creation of the first national conferences devoted to LGBT aging concerns
- The only Robert Wood Johnson Foundation "Faith in Action" grantee (of more than 2,000 nation-wide) specifically targeting GLBT older people for supportive services

SAGE offers a wide variety of services and programs to LGBT seniors. The recreation and leisure services and programs include:

- Daily Drop-In gives seniors the chance to socialize in a relaxed and welcoming environment; monthly SAGE Walks and Brunches present opportunities to explore New York City and surrounding areas.
- Art & Culture Series is presented in the form of on-going groups and classes, like the Acting Class, the Art Studio, and the Opera-Lovers Group. This Series also includes special programming.
- Health & Wellness Series is an on-going program featuring guest professionals presenting on a range of medical and emotional health issues. We also offer a twice-weekly aerobic exercise class, SAGErcize, which takes place Tuesdays and Thursdays.
- Money & Finances Series includes regular meetings of the SAGE Savings & Investment Group as well as guest presenters discussing topics like estate planning, retirement planning, and Medicare.
- History & Heritage Series presents important community figures to SAGE members and the broader GLBT public. Recent speakers include Joan Nestle, David Carter, and Douglas Kimmel.
- Sex, Dating & Romance Series are special workshops designed to help GLBT seniors connect or stay connected to significant others of whatever stripe. Workshops are held for both men and women.

Figure 2.8 An example of social advocacy through leisure (http://www.sageusa.org/)

youth to create their own safe classrooms and communities. Partnerships with schools, families, and young adult volunteers support the aims of this organization.

Marketing

Marketing means many different things to different people. To some, the term is synonymous with sales and to others, advertising. Yet neither of these terms serve as accurate or complete definitions of marketing. For the purpose of this discussion, *marketing is defined as a process of human exchange whereby people exchange something of value for something they need.* Thus, marketing is the umbrella for all management functions that foster desired exchanges. Exchanges only take place when a target audience member takes an action, thus the ultimate goal of marketing is to influence behavior. An inherent component of marketing is determining what specific constituents (potential customers) or groups of constituents (i.e., a target market) need and then providing programs that meet those needs. Marketers do this by manipulating the price of the service, the place the service is delivered, and the ways in which the service is implemented and promoted to meet the expressed needs of constituents (see Figure 2.10 on p. 44).

As we move more fully into an experience economy, new methods of marketing are developing that speak to the increasingly diverse yet definitive nature of people's needs. This entails the need to manage the total experience, from identifying how participants wish to experience a program or event to communicating in such a way as to "inform them about their needs as it relates to a particular experience while simultaneously doing so in such a personalized manner that will move them to take action" (O'Sullivan and Spangler, 1998, p. 133). Thus, Ellis and Rossman's (2008) model of staging recreation experiences can be seen as an outgrowth of a marketing approach to delivering programs involving people not only in the planning of the experience, but also in the actual experience that take places during the program itself.

Consider American Girl, a commercial organization that was established as Pleasant Company in 1986. The mission of the organization is to "Celebrate Girls." In pursuit of this mission, American Girl provides products for each stage of a young girl's development. The American Girl brand educates and entertains girls with quality books, dolls, and toys that integrate learning and play experiences while emphasizing important values. These products are brought to life in the following experiences:

- American Girl Magazine delivers the message, "You're great—just the way you are!" to more than 700,000 girls every other month. The "Just Like You" line of dolls feature dolls that represent diverse groups, including those with disabilities.

- American Girl provides a website (http://www.americangirl.com/) where users can engage in interactive

OPENING DOORS
OPENING MINDS

Connecting youth worldwide through cross-cultural understanding and unique travel opportunities.

HOSTELLING INTERNATIONAL-USA
AMERICAN YOUTH HOSTELS

Figure 2.9 An example of social planning through leisure services: Hostelling International-USA experiences that stress history, fitness, time management, anti-bullying campaigns, and social skills; the site receives over 51 million visits per year.

• American Girl Place reflects the past and present of American girlhood, providing a place where girls can nourish their spirits, make lasting memories, and celebrate their interests in products and experiences designed just for them.

American Girl Place is the key component of turning a shopping event into an experience. At a number of flagship stores across the United States, the company offers "girls a chance to share unforgettable experiences with their family and friends." Each location offers boutiques filled with American Girl products and gifts as well as places where girls can treat their dolls to a new hairdo in the Doll Hair Salon, get repaired in the doll hospital, or have their pictures taken in photo studio. In addition to the boutiques, each location features an American Girl Theater and a café. In the American Girl Theater, one-hour shows are presented where "the voices of girls, past and present, ring strong and true" as performers brings to life the beloved characters of the American Girls Collection through song and dance.

One of the key benefits of American Girl as identified by Pine and Gilmore (2007) is its cross-generational appeal. "It is adept at fostering conversations between parent and daughters, and sometimes across three generations to include grandmother. In particular, the American Girl Places create numerous possibilities for bonding—from talking about the historical context of the company's dolls to discussing issues raised by table talk cards in each café" (p. 23).

Community Development/ Empowerment

Community development or grassroots empowerment is process-oriented and rests on the basic assumption that individuals should be partners in the process of determining their leisure destiny (Edginton et al., 2005; Rossman & Schlatter, 2008). It suggests that individuals are partners in the planning process. As partners, they can learn the processes and strategies necessary to plan, organize, and implement their own recreation services based on their perception of their own needs. The aim of community development is empowering communities and individuals to

(a) Stimulate local initiative by involving people in community participation, specifically the process of social and economic change;

(b) Build channels of communication that promote solidarity; and

(c) Improve the social, economic, and cultural well-being of community residents. (Christianson, Fendley & Robinson, 1989)

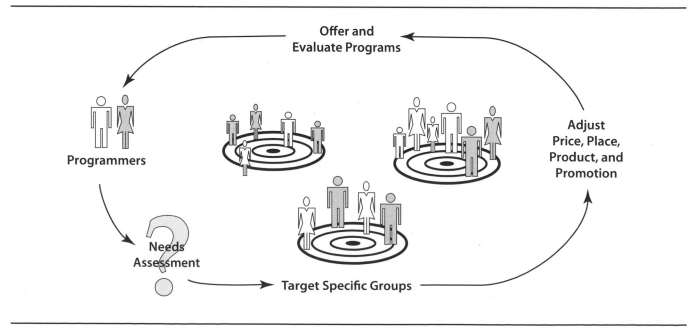

Figure 2.10 The marketing approach

Within a community development approach to providing services the leisure services programmer takes on the roles of facilitator, encourager, and cheerleader. Thus, the programmer listens to and assists individuals and communities in identifying their needs and assets, as well as planning and organizing programs to meet those needs. Within this framework, we de-emphasize leadership and invest more in citizenship. Block (2008) defines citizenship as

> our capacity to create for ourselves what we had sought from our leaders…agreeing to receive rights and privileges from the community and in so doing, to pay for them through our willingness to live within certain boundaries and act in the interest of the whole. At the core of citizenship is the desire to care for the well-being of the larger institution, be it an organization, a neighborhood, or a country. (pp. 89–90)

Thus, a community development approach to co-create leisure experiences with customers brings together many of the points of the first two chapters

of this book including building social capital and creating citizens to encourage all of us to act in socially responsible ways. Block (2008) challenges everyone to work to expand the social fabric of community by expanding our collective sense of belonging. This is a true benefit of recreation programs as we bring people from all walks of the community together for shared experiences.

Within the community development strategy for delivering human services is a move to a more holistic and integrated approach to solving problems. Table 2.4 (see p. 46) highlights many of the components of this changing model as it is being applied by Opportunity Works. This is a nonprofit organization in northeast Iowa committed to developing assets needed by individuals to make poverty temporary and infrequent in the region. What is interesting about this model is the role recreation plays in defining quality of life as well as the emphasis on such attributes as maintaining sustainability, being culturally relevant, focusing on assets, and working collaboratively. Figure 2.11 (below) presents a graphic model of what a community approach might look

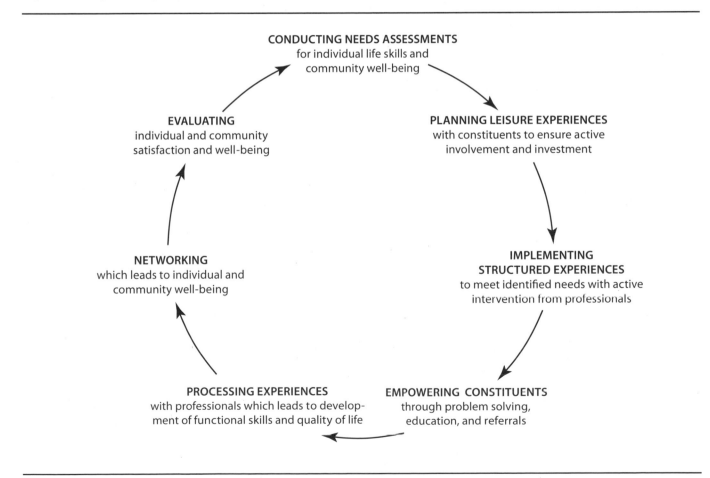

CONDUCTING NEEDS ASSESSMENTS
for individual life skills and community well-being

PLANNING LEISURE EXPERIENCES
with constituents to ensure active involvement and investment

IMPLEMENTING STRUCTURED EXPERIENCES
to meet identified needs with active intervention from professionals

EMPOWERING CONSTITUENTS
through problem solving, education, and referrals

PROCESSING EXPERIENCES
with professionals which leads to development of functional skills and quality of life

NETWORKING
which leads to individual and community well-being

EVALUATING
individual and community satisfaction and well-being

Figure 2.11 A model of community development (Adapted from Carter, Keller & Beck, 1996)

like. Notice that at every step the customer or constituents is included in the process.

Denver Urban Gardens (DUG) is a nonprofit organization that exemplifies the community empowerment model of programming. It was established in 1985 with three gardens in Northwest Denver; today, DUG's 80 active sites stretch beyond Denver into nine surrounding cities. DUG staff coordinate with other nonprofits as well as public parks and recreation departments to fulfill their mission of growing community—one urban garden at a time. Many of their garden sites are found in public parks. Critical to DUG's mission is to work with neighborhoods in a support role to facilitate the creation of local urban gardens. DUG seeks to enable, unite, and empower participants to reach out and build their community. The DUG program currently produces food, provides seeds, and plans special events and educational programs for over 25,000 individuals annually. An integral part of DUG success is the Healthy Neighborhood Network, which is a volunteer coalition of community gardeners and neighborhood leaders working together to cultivate the physical and social health benefits of gardens (Denver Urban Gardens, 2010; Needham, 2008).

The challenge inherent in a community development approach to planning programs is that it takes time to develop the relationships needed to build partnerships between programmers and participants, and time is a limited commodity. While a variety of strategies and approaches exists under the umbrella of community development, citizen participation is perhaps the approach that is most familiar in leisure services (Ari & Pedlar, 1997). Citizen participation is *a process in which individuals take part in decision making related to the organization and its programs and services that affect them in some manner*. Russell and Jamieson (2007) stressed the importance of customer participation in the planning process, yet acknowledged that there is no single technique to achieve this goal. It is up to leisure services programmers to identify the appropriate strategy that works with the other elements of the planning process.

Table 2.4 Paradigm shift: Toward a new model of community development (Stringer, Van Gorp & Scholl, 2003)

Focus	Traditional Community Development Model	Integrated Community Development Model
Paradigm/Lens		
Lens	Deficits/Need assessment	Assets/Assets mapping (see Chapter 5)
Typical focus	Economic development; private business	Integrated; multisector opportunities and amenities
Quality of life	Infrastructure = Roads, water, curbs, and gutters	Broad focus = Recreation, arts, education, and infrastructure (see Chapter 2)
Community livability	Jobs = Number of jobs and employment rates	Wages compared to costs and community benefits
Growth	All growth is good	Questioned: Sustainability, harmful consequences, and justice (see Chapter 2)
Coolness	Big, splashy, consumerism	Dynamic, affordable, family friendly, interesting
Design/Approach		
Focus	Isolated and linear action	Multifocused, portfolio asset approach
Dimensions	Simple/singular problems and solutions	Complex problems and solutions
Sources of ideas	Cookie-cutter	Culturally relevant/locally specific
How to grow	Recruit outside community/incentives	Grow your own/entrepreneurship (see Chapter 2)
Source of growth	Homogenization/franchising	Unique community attractions
Implementation		
Decision-makers	Only key leaders, exclusive	Critical mass; inclusive (see Chapter 6)
Implementers	Single entities	Collaborative, multisector
Funding	Single source	Multisource, sustainability focus (see Chapter 9)
Structure	Typical hierarchy	Chaordic (self-organizing); where chaos and order meet
Relationships	Competitive and parochial	Collaborative and regional (see Chapter 9)

Building a Strategy of Program Planning

Within the leisure services profession, we continue to debate which of the aforementioned strategies is the best. This debate can be seen throughout the history of the profession. In the late 1800s, social reformers used play and recreation to address the problems and needs that grew out of the Industrial Revolution. These early reformers used social advocacy and social planning approaches to programming. As public recreation continued to grow after World War II, most public recreation agencies across the country adopted the philosophy that views recreation as an end in itself (Gray, 1969). Public recreation drifted away from a social welfare model and moved to more of a social planning approach to providing services. Forerunners to current day therapeutic recreation professionals stepped into a social advocacy role.

In the mid-1970s, Gray and Greben (1974) authored a paper that urged the profession to stop simply providing activities and supervising facilities (a social planning approach to delivering services) and instead to think about the possibilities of the parks and recreation profession to transform people. "We should have discovered long ago the nature of the business we are in, but we have not…The critical questions are not, How many are there? Or who won? The critical question is: What happened to Jose, Mary, Sam, and Joan in this experience?" (pp. 49–50). This shift to a focus on participant benefits acknowledged that the field is not about the parks and facilities; it is about the experiences that people have in them (Crompton, 2008).

The shift to a marketing approach caused Dustin, McAvoy, and Schultz (1988) to question public organizations adopting business principles commonly found in marketing practices. They wrote, "the strategy of business is to convince customers that their desires are really needs and that they must have what is for sale. Business creates a dependency mindset disguised as customer loyalty. It is a strategy dictated by the bottom line" (p. 54). Others argued that when marketing is done 'right' it creates a partnership between constituents and the organization to build programs that respond to the needs of specific target markets.

More recently, we have seen discussions over Ellis and Rossman's (2008) work related to the experience economy. Sylvester (2008) laments the continued move to a business model over a public service approach to service delivery. He says, that in the past,

> the field of recreation has also sought to be included among those honorific group of service professionals regarded for what they give to the public, rather than what they gain for themselves…The pioneers of recreation were zealously committed to promoting and providing recreation as a medium that contributed to faith, health, virtue, justice, culture, education, community, citizenship, and the overall happiness of the public. They also wrote passionately about the importance of recreation for the public good. (pp. 28–29)

Sylvester contends that a shift to a business model (as expressed in the idea of the experience economy) takes us further from our social service roots.

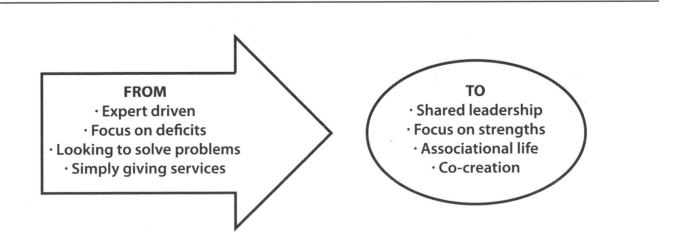

FROM
· Expert driven
· Focus on deficits
· Looking to solve problems
· Simply giving services

TO
· Shared leadership
· Focus on strengths
· Associational life
· Co-creation

Figure 2.12 Changing principles in human services (Lappe & Dubois, 1994, p. 146)

As can be seen by this historical snapshot, leisure services professionals have debated, and will continue to debate about the most appropriate strategies to employ in delivering recreation programs. While the debate is important and helps the various segments of the overall leisure profession clarify what is important, it is also important to remember that each of these strategies is a part of a toolbox for programmers to approach the complexity of delivering programs. At times it will be important to advocate for the rights of certain groups to experience leisure, at other times it may be necessary to plan and implement a program for others or convince people to engage in a specific behavior; other situations will encourage us to co-create programs through a marketing or community development strategy. Given this realization, we are beginning to see a move toward involving people as much as possible in the planning process for recreation programs and experiences.

Block (2008) suggests that human services (which includes recreation and leisure) are moving away from simply providing services to creating a living democracy model (see Figure 2.12 on p. 47). This model includes an expanding shared sense of belonging and caring. He notes that when people understand that they are connected and care for the well-being of the entire community, a civil and democratic society is created. Parks, recreation, and leisure services professionals are one group within local governments that is typically well-connected in the community. Thus, many professionals are reaching out to nontraditional partners to bring together different groups to focus on the greater good (Jarvi, 2001).

In this role, Jarvi (2001) advocates that parks and recreation programmers see themselves as "social entrepreneurs" rather than being "the ones in charge." In this light, leadership becomes

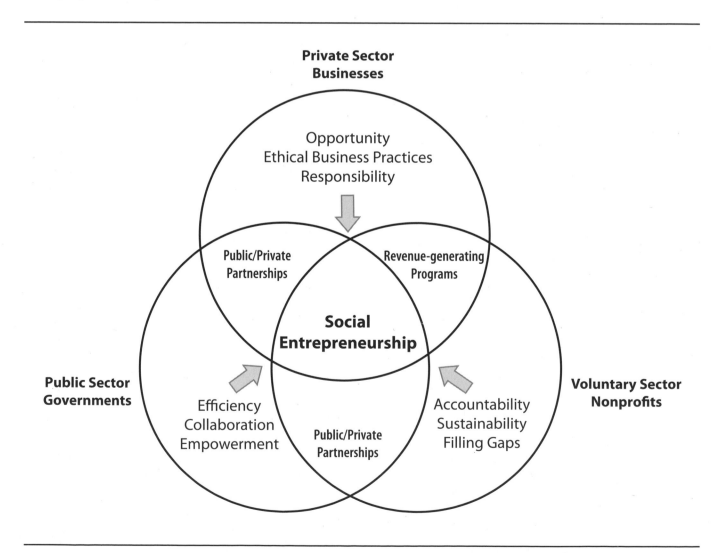

Figure 2.13 The blurring of sectors: Social entrepreneurship at the Nexus (adapted from Wolk, 2008)

a process of facilitating, mediating, mutual education, learning, mentoring, collaborating and cooperating with diverse groups and individuals. Leaders need to understand complexity, ambiguity and be able to work with power, not from above, but horizontally. Leaders must deal with both the social and physical infrastructures needed to make things happen, working with all groups to constantly assemble the social and capital infrastructure necessary to achieve their objectives. (p. 180)

The idea of encouraging recreation programmers to be social entrepreneurs is not confined to the public sector (see Figure 2.13), as anyone can be a social entrepreneur. Although the idea of social entrepreneurship is fairly new (starting in the late 1960s), history is full of people with big ideas who have addressed the social issues of their day. A social entrepreneur may be thought of as someone who uses entrepreneurial approaches to address social issues. Table 2.5 contrasts the core characteristics of an entrepreneur with those of a social entrepreneur. Whereas the typical entrepreneur looks to create new ways of doing things to create personal wealth, the social entrepreneur looks to create

new ways to address social issues. The goal is not to benefit one's self, but to improve systems, invent and disseminate new approaches, and advance sustainable solutions that create social value.

In many ways, the characteristics of a social entrepreneur are similar to the characteristics of a servant leader, as both seek to serve those they lead and to include as many people as possible in the creation process. Several organizations have emerged to support social entrepreneurs throughout the world. Table 2.6 (on p. 50) presents a number of these organizations as well as examples of recreation programs supported by these organizations that are making a difference. We encourage all parks, recreation, and leisure services programmers to create a vision for the power of programs to make a difference, and to work with others to co-create a preferred future. Table 2.7 (on pp. 51) provides an opportunity to apply the program cycle to developing recreation experiences.

Summary

Delivering quality leisure experiences should be the primary goal of all parks, recreation, and leisure services organizations. Committing to quality demands that parks,

Table 2.5 Characteristics of entrepreneurs and social entrepreneurs

Entrepreneurs	Social Entrepreneurs
Entrepreneurs work to create value for self or an organization by addressing a need of others. Entrepreneurs are change agents in society; they work to find new and better ways of doing things by challenging the ways things are done.	Social entrepreneurs are intelligent; have a compassionate heart and a service ethic.
	Social entrepreneurs know when to deal with risk; at the core of their actions is a sense of timing, a knowing when not to act, as well as when to act.
Entrepreneurs constantly search for change, respond to it, and exploit it as an opportunity. Entrepreneurs are resourceful; their reach exceeds their grasp. Entrepreneurs mobilize resources of others to achieve their objectives.	Social entrepreneurs are flexible; they adapt to change quickly.
	Social entrepreneurs look for connections; they have an ability to identify patterns and work with people from a wide range of experience. Social entrepreneurs are willing to share credit.
	Social entrepreneurs remember capacity is not fixed; they know they don't have to have all the skills or knowledge needed for a project. They are willing to learn along the way.
	Social entrepreneurs are reflective and aware of what is going on around them.

recreation, and leisure services organizations understand the dynamic nature of delivering experiences. A traditional starting place for defining experiences is understanding how services differ from products. The four most commonly identified characteristics ascribed to services are their intangibility and perishability, the potential variability inherent to service delivery, and the inseparability of production and consumption in delivering services.

Quality of service is an important concern of leisure services professionals. In delivering quality programs, the ability to meet the wants and desires of participants is extremely important, yet maximizing individual choice must be tempered with a sense of social responsibility for the collective community. In addition, we should focus on both the product and the process of programming. This requires an understanding of the various strategies available to planning recreation programs.

Historically, the parks, recreation, and leisure profession has used many different approaches and strategies to plan and deliver recreation programs. These may be visualized along a continuum of programmer and participant involvement. The five major approaches include social advocacy, social planning, social marketing, marketing, and community development. Little consensus exists about the proper way to plan because different situations demand different strategies. A movement toward encouraging involvement of participants in planning their own programs with programmers acting as enablers and resources to participants is emerging. Lastly, in this chapter we introduced the reader to the concept of parks and recreation professionals as social entrepreneurs.

Table 2.6 Organizations supporting social entrepreneurship

Ashoka (Global) – www.ashoka.org
Mission: Ashoka strives to shape a global, entrepreneurial, competitive citizen sector: one that allows social entrepreneurs to thrive and enables the world's citizens to think and act as changemakers.

Program Example: Program created by Jadwiga Lopata -- www.ashoka.org/fellow/2907
Jadwiga Lopata recognized that Poland's many small family-owned farms were ideally suited to convert to organic farming methods and thereby benefit from the emerging premium market for organic produce and livestock. To make this shift, however, supplemental income was required. To increase income Lopata suggested a steady stream of visitors (mostly urban families from Western Europe) who would pay for the opportunity to stay, eat, and work on the farms. Rural farmers learned that not only is organic farming viable, but so is their pastoral lifestyle.

Echoing Green (USA) – www.echoinggreen.org
Mission: Echoing Green strives to spark social change by identifying, investing, and supporting the world's most exceptional emerging leaders and their organizations. Through a two-year fellowship program, a network of visionaries develop new solutions to society's most difficult problems

Program Example: Peace Games – www.peacegames.org
Peace Games teaches young people tools to find creative solutions to the complex problems facing them through cooperation, communication, conflict resolution, and community. They learn the value of friends and teamwork, how to communicate in appropriate ways, how to resolve disagreements through talking rather than fighting, and how to utilize their community as a team that can change injustices around them.

Schwab Foundation for Social Entrepreneurs (Switzerland) -- www.schwabfound.org
Mission: The Schwab Foundation for Social Entrepreneurship provides unparalleled platforms at the national, regional, and global levels for leading social innovators that highlight social entrepreneurship as a key element to address social and ecological problems in an innovative, sustainable and effective way.

Program Example: Homeless World Cup – www.homelessworldcup.org
Mel Young founded the Homeless World Cup, which uses football (soccer) to energize people who are homeless to change their own lives. This is achieved with a world-class annual, international, football tournament uniting national teams of people who are homeless; and by triggering and supporting year-round grass roots football programs working with people who are homeless.

Programming from Here to There

We have raised the point that in today's changing environment we have seen a blurring of the traditional lines between public nonprofit and commercial organizations. Public and nonprofit organizations are being asked to be increasingly innovative and entrepreneurial, while commercial (for profit) organizations are being asked to be more socially responsible. This blurring of roles is evident in the Tampa Bay Club Sports organization, the largest provider of social sports leagues for adults in the Tampa Bay (FL) area. Tampa Bay Club Sports is a commercial (for profit) organization that offers a yearly membership (similar to non profit organizations) and works with a variety of area municipalities (using public parks and facilities) to offer its programs. Sports include football, soccer, softball, volleyball, kickball, dodgeball, golf, and others. The Club emphasizes meeting other people and the health benefits of involvement; thus, people of all skill levels can find a team to match their needs. The organization was established in the late 1980s and has been in continuous operation since 1995. For additional information on Tampa Bay Sports Club visit their website at www.tampabayclubsport.com/

Table 2.7 Practical theories: The cyclical programming process

Background

As we look to understanding the programming process it is important that we have a framework for action. For the purposes of this book, we have identified a cyclical programming process to serve as our framework for developing and implementing recreation programs. A cyclical process of programming presents the tasks to be accomplished as ongoing, without end. The process begins at one point, and returns to that same point, continuing in the cycle for as long as the organization continues to conduct and offer recreation and leisure programs. Farrell and Lundegren (1978) used this structure as the foundation for the parks, recreation, and leisure services programming process.

Practical applications of the theory

Typically, this process is characterized by identifying specific tasks to be done to put together a program or event, and following those tasks through. At the heart of this process is the organizational values, principles, philosophy, mission, and vision—these direct the focus of the other process components. Once we have identified the organization's values, principles, philosophy, mission, and vision we move outward to:

1. Assess participant needs
2. Plan or design a program/event
3. Engage in preprogram tasks such as pricing, promotion, and staffing
4. Implement the program/event
5. Conduct formative evaluations
6. Continue implementation with adjustments (based on the information gained from the formative evaluation)
7. Conduct the summative evaluation.

The last step then leads to a revisiting of the organization's mission, new participant assessments, improved program planning and design, new program implementation, revised program evaluation, and so on (see Figure 2.11). A graphic representation of the programming process might look like a stretched-out coil or spring. The process is moving forward, and not simply repeating itself. A key element of the program process is that it is not a start-and-stop type of activity. It is ongoing, and based on what has been learned from previous program efforts. The cyclical nature of this process enables practitioners to be responsive to social, cultural, and individual changes in needs and desires. Because of this, followed well, the process allows for continuous program improvement and innovation as well as the opportunity to deal with emerging societal trends and issues. Throughout this text, we will be basing our program examples on this cyclical program process.

Your turn

1. How does each program planning strategy (presented in this chapter) fit into this cyclical planning process?
2. How does this model relate to the community development model presented in Figure 2.11 on p. 45?
3. Brainstorm some different ways participants can be included in each of the stages presented in this model to co-create programs.

References

Aguayo, R. (1990). *Dr. Deming: The American who taught the Japanese about quality.* New York, NY: Carol Publishing Group.

Albrecht, K. (1992). *The only thing that matters: Bringing the power of the customer into the center of your business.* New York, NY: Harper Business.

Albrecht, K. (1985). *Service America.* Homewood, IL: Dow Jones–Irwin.

American Girl Magazine. (2010). Retrieved January 9, 2010, from http://www.americangirl.com/fun/agmg/

Ari, S. & Pedlar, A. (1997). Building communities through leisure: Citizen participation in a healthy communities initiative. *Journal of Leisure Research, 29*(2), 167–182.

Barlow, J. & Maul, D. (2000). *Emotional value.* San Francisco, CA: Berrett-Koehler Publishers.

Bauman, Z. (1998). *Globalization: The human consequences.* Cambridge, England: Polity.

Bellah, R., Madsen R., Sullivan, W., Swindler, A., and Tipton, S. (1985). *Habits of the heart: Individualism and commitment in American life.* Berkeley, CA: University of California Press.

Berman, J. (2005, November). Industry output and employment projections to 2014. *Monthly Labor Review, 128,* (11): 45–69.

Bess, P. (1996). Virtuous reality: Aristotle, critical realism, and the reconstruction of architectural and urban theology. *The Classicist, 3,* 6–18.

Block, P. (2008). *Community.* San Francisco, CA: Bartlett-Koshler Publishing.

Burns, K. (1996). Interview transcripts for the video *Thomas Jefferson.* Retrieved January 21, 2009, from http://www.pbs.org/jefferson/archives/interviews/frame.htm

Carter , M., Keller, M., & Beck, T. (1996). A vision for today: recreation and leisure services. *Parks and Recreation, 11*: 42–49.

Christianson, J., Fendley, K., & Robinson, J. (1989). Community development. In J. Christianson and J. Robinson (Eds.), *Community development in perspective* (pp. 3–25). Ames, IA: Iowa State University Press.

Crompton, J. (2008). Evolution and implications of a paradigm shift in the marketing of leisure services in the USA. *Leisure Studies, 27*(2), 181–206.

DeGioia, J. (2005). *Intercollegiate Athletics: Two compelling, competing logics of excellence.* Educause Forum Futures 2005. Available at: net. educause.edu/forum/ff05.asp?bhcp=1

Denver Urban Gardens. (2010). *Homepage.* Retrieved on January 27, 2010, from http://www.dug.org/home.asp

Dilling, E. (1935). *Red Network: A who's who and handbook of radicalism for patriots.* Ayer Company Publisher.

Dustin, D., McAvoy, L., & Schultz, J. (1988). *Stewards of access custodians of choice: A philosophical foundation for the park and recreation profession.* Champaign, IL: Sagamore Publishing.

Edginton, C., Hudson, S., Dieser, R., & Edginton, S. (2005). *Leisure programming: A service-centered and benefits approach* (4th ed.). Dubuque, IA: McGraw-Hill.

Edginton, C., DeGraaf, D., Dieser, R., & Edginton, S. (2004). *Leisure and life satisfaction: Foundational perspectives* (4th ed.). Boston, MA: WCB McGraw Hill.

Ellis, G. & Rossman, R. (J2008). Adding value for participants through experience staging: Parks, recreation and tourism in the experience economy. *Journal of Park and Recreation Administration, 26*(4): 1–20.

Elshtain, J. (2002). *Jane Addams and the dream of American democracy.* New York, NY: Basic Books.

Farrell, P. & Lundegren, H. (1978). *The process of recreation programming: Theory and technique.* New York, NY: John Wiley & Sons.

Gray, D. (1969). The case of compensatory recreation. *Parks and Recreation, 4*(4), 23–24.

Gray, D. & Greben, S. (1974, July). Future perspectives. *Parks and Recreation.* 26–56.

Jandt, F. (1995). *Contrary to what you've been told… What you know to be true! The customer is usually wrong.* Indianapolis, IN: Park Avenue Publishing.

Jarvi, C. (2001). Developing park and recreation professionals as social entrepreneurs. In D. Sessom and T. Mobley (Eds.), *Developing leadership for parks and recreation in the 21st century.* Myrtle Beach, SC: Leroy Springs and Co.

Juniu, S. (2000). Downshifting: Regaining the essence of leisure. *Journal of Leisure Research, 32*(1), 69–73.

Kiuchi, T. (1997, September 16). *What I learned from the rain forest.* Keynote from World Future Society, San Francisco, CA. The Future 500. Retrieved January 22, 2009, from http://www.newhorizons.org/future/kiuchi.htm

Kotler, P. (1991). *Marketing management: Analysis, planning and control* (7th ed.). Englewood Cliffs, NJ: Prentice Hall.

Kotler, P. & Lee, N. (2008). *Social marketing: Influencing behaviors for good*. Thousand Oaks, CA: Sage Publications, Inc.

Kouzes, J. & Posner, B. (2002). *The leadership challenge: How to keep getting extraordinary things done in organizations*. San Francisco, CA: Jossey-Bass.

Kouzes, J. & Posner, B. (1993). *Credibility: How leaders gain and lose it, why people demand it*. San Francisco, CA: Jossey-Bass.

Lappe, F. & Du Bois, P. (1994). *The quickening of America*. New York, NY: Jossey-Bass.

Machan, T. (1986, July). The ethics of privatization. *Freeman's Idea on Liberty, 36*(7), 270–273.

McCarville, R.E. (1993, October). Keys to quality leisure programming. *Journal of Physical Education, Recreation & Dance—Leisure Today*, 34–35, 46–47.

Needham, G. (2008, August). How does your garden grow? *Parks and Recreation, 43*(8), 32–37.

NRPA. (2009). *Strategic Planning Center, FY10-FY12 BOT Approved strategic plan*. Retrieved March 18, 2009, from http://nrpablog.typepad.com/nrpa_strategic_planning/

O'Sullivan, E. & Spangler, K. (1998). *Experience marketing*. State College, PA: Venture Publishing, Inc.

Pine J. & Gilmore, J. (1998, July/August). Welcome to the experience economy. *Harvard Business Review*. Retrieved September 25, 2009, from http://www.skowhegan.org/pdf/bids/200602edss/experience_economy.pdf

Pine, J. & Gilmore, J. (1999). *The experience economy: Work is theatre and every business a stage*. Boston, MA: Harvard Business School Press.

Pine, J. & Gilmore, J. (2007). *Authenticity: What consumers really want*. Boston, MA: Harvard Business School Press.

Rossman, R. & Schlatter, B. (2008). *Recreation programming: Designing leisure experiences* (5th ed.). Champaign, IL: Sagamore Publishing.

Russell, R. & Jamieson, L. (2007). *Leisure program planning and delivery*. Champaign, IL: Human Kinetics.

SAGE. (2010). Services and advocacy for gay, lesbian, bisexual and transgender elders. Retrieved January 9, 2010, from http://www.sageusa.org/index.cfm

Schultz, J., McAvoy, L., & Dustin, D. (1988). What are we in business for? *Parks and Recreation, 23*(1), 51–53.

Sierra Club Staff. (1992). Sierra Club centennial. *Sierra, 77*(3), 52–73.

Stringer, A., Van Gorp, S., & Scholl, K. (2003, October 25). *Enhancing Quality of Life: Innovative community development*. Session presented at the National Recreation and Park Association Congress, St. Louis, MO.

Sylvester, C. (2008). The ethics of experience in recreation and leisure services. *Journal of Park and Recreation Administration, 26*(4), 21–41.

Vossoughi, S. (2008, May 28). How to Stand Out? Authenticity. *Business Week*. Retrieved August 11, 2009, from http://www.businessweek.com/innovate/content/may2008/id20080528_503953.htm

Wellman, D., Dustin, D., Henderson, K., & Moore, R. (2008). *Service living: Building community through public parks and recreation*. State College, PA: Venture Publishing, Inc.

Wilkie, B. (2008). *Escape from excellence*. E-book available from www.charismadvisors.com/documents/scapefromExcellencebyBillWilkiePublishedToday.pdf

Wolk, A. (2008). *The blurring of sectors: Social entrepreneurship at the Nexus*. Retrieved August 11, 2009, from http://www.socialedge.org/blogs/government-engagement/the-blurring-of-sectors-social-entrepreneurship-emerges-at-the-nexus-1/?searchterm=The%20Blurring%20of%20sectors

Programmer Profile

Winnie Wong

Current Position: Co-founder and Executive Director, Play Infinity
Favorite Book: *Why People Play* by Mike Ellis (1973)
Favorite Recreation Activity: Water sports

▶ **Describe the path your career has taken.**

- I received my Diploma in Social Work from Hong Kong Polytechnic University
- After graduating I worked for TREATS, a youth serving organization in Hong Kong that strives to integrate children of different background and abilities in a recreation setting (e.g., camps) to help promote a better understanding of one another and to provide them with enjoyable ways of learning life skills.
- I established Play Infinity with my working partner, Bonita Kwok, in 1999. Play Infinity is a private, for-profit organization that offers programs to promote the value of play to a variety of populations in Hong Kong. Its mission is to
    …build up a platform for generating a play culture in Hong Kong and Macau,
    …build up a network with international play associations,
    …promote play as an art of uplifting human spirits and well-being, and
    …enhance holistic growth of participants.
- I completed my M.S. in Leisure, Youth, and Human Services at the University of Northern Iowa. I am working on an Ed.D. in Leisure, Youth, and Human Services at the University of Northern Iowa.

▶ **Describe the joys of working in your current position.**

As a play educator, the most joyful thing is to see the joyful expression and the enjoyment from my participants.

▶ **Do you have any advice for new programmers?**

Focus on customers' needs and listen to what participants want as they are the significant resources for your programs.

▶ **How has your organization's philosophy/vision/mission impacted the programs you offer?**

As a pioneer in play promotion in Hong Kong, one of the hopes of Play Infinity is to encourage a culture that believes in the power of play and brings joy and benefits of play to more people in Hong Kong. This philosophy is played out in many ways as we offer programs to a variety of groups in Hong Kong. In addition, we work to train play leaders throughout Hong Kong as we feel this is one of the best ways to advance our philosophy in educational institutions, social service organizations, churches, and corporations.

▶ **Share your ideas for developing creative programs.**

Join various creative workshops (e.g., drama and arts workshops) and adapt activities for your program. I also like to brainstorm new program ideas with colleagues a couple of times a month.

Principles, Philosophy, and Planning | 3

Principles serve as foundational centers of a person or entity (e.g., organization, agency, group). Often unstated, principles are important underlying assumptions that give structure to a belief system and a way of thinking—they are embedded in the way we look at the world, the way we think, and the way we act. Most dictionaries define the word principle as a basic or essential quality that determines one's intrinsic nature and/or characteristic behaviors. Thus, by determining our intrinsic nature (i.e., who we are inside), principles guide our behaviors and practices.

A *philosophy* is typically considered to be a set of beliefs or guiding principles. When we talk about our philosophy of leisure, for instance, we articulate several underlying principles that provide structure to our thoughts. Each individual, regardless of age, sex, or education has philosophy(ies) about life, love, leisure, and other abstract concepts. Factors that shape an individual's philosophy are the people, events, and circumstances that form her or his values and beliefs. These factors include family, teachers, friends, and coworkers; physical, mental, and emotional health; culture, history, and experiences. Philosophies provide us with a sense of direction and affect all aspects of individual behavior.

Organizations also have philosophies—the principal parties who guide the organization shape these ways of thinking. These people include members of advisory boards, boards of directors, executive directors, CEOs, presidents, administrative staff, treatment teams, service delivery staff, and service recipients or consumers. It is imperative that recreation programmers understand the underlying philosophy of the leisure services organization with which they work, and how the organization's philosophy impacts the creation and implementation of recreation programs. In so doing, programmers increase the clarity and continuity of programs and services provided, thereby increasing the likelihood of quality and a match with agency mission. Understood and shared philosophical positions benefit the agency, programmer, and participants.

Philosophies and principles help set the framework or structure for planning—which is the underlying element of all successful organizations and programs. Planning includes the necessary steps that lead up to the implementation and evaluation of programs and services. Typically, planning offers time-based logical actions that result in successful delivery of programs. This means that we anticipate what we need to do, in the order we need to do it (e.g., sequencing and progression), and by what times and dates to reach our goal (of providing a program or service), which we then evaluate.

In this chapter we introduce several key planning concepts by providing explanations and examples of terms related to the framework for programming in leisure services. The relationship between concepts is also addressed so that programmers will be able to determine where these ideas intersect within their own organizations. Lastly, we present and interpret these concepts from the perspective of servant leadership.

Foundation, Direction, and Reflection (FDR)

The ideas and terms presented in this chapter collectively serve several functions. The first is to provide a *foundation* for the work of the leisure services organization and recreation programmer. Specifically, principles (values and traditions) and philosophy combine to provide the building blocks for service delivery. The second function is to provide the leisure services organization and recreation programmer with *direction*. Most critical to this endeavor are organizational mission, vision, goals, and objectives. Finally, all of these concepts are *reflected* in the services provided to participants. In other words, the programs, facilities, and staff serve as mirrors that reflect the principles, philosophy, mission, vision, goals, and objectives of the organization. For the purposes of this text, these concepts, which are tied together by the functions of

Foundation, Direction and *Reflection*, will be referred to as FDR concepts (see Figure 3.1). The following definitions, examples, applications, and discussion of how FDR concepts interact, and implications for the recreation programmer as a servant leader should provide the reader with a thorough understanding of the meaning and importance of the foundational elements.

Principles, Values, and Traditions

Principles are those beliefs that we hold as important to our definition of who we are. They are standards, codes, or tenets that we value. Some think of principles as a series or amalgamation of connected values and traditions; typically they are related to how we view ourselves and the way we deal with others. For instance, the principles of social justice include beliefs such as nondiscrimination, open access, equitable application of policies, and an orientation toward the underserved. Related to principles are values, which may be defined as attributes or material items that we believe have worth. All of us have values and principles even though we may not be fully aware of them; they define us and are embedded in our philosophy of life. Examples of values include progress, conservation, service, equal opportunity, trust, self-discipline, competition, and freedom. Values are enduring—they are subject to change, but they are not fleeting whims or preferences. We see values in people's thoughts, words, and actions making them an inevitable component of our personal and professional lives. All decisions about programming—the distribution and use of facilities, staff, and equipment; as well as the application of policies, rules, and other program functions—reflect our principles and values.

Values help employees evaluate how well they fit within an agency and provide a sense of purpose and motivation for work. Understanding both stated and unstated values leads to values congruence—that is, both the employee and agency see "eye-to-eye" on important issues. In support of this idea, Atchinson (2007) found that 86 percent of study respondents believed that shared values between staff and the organization as a whole increased staff commitment to the agency and its goals. Consequently, a recreation programmer will want to be clear about her/his own values, as well as those of other colleagues and the overall agency or organization.

Because principles and values are apparent to others, it becomes important for programmers to pay attention to the fit between their intentions and the actual public perception of their behaviors. For instance, if we were to ask members of the community to identify our department or agency principles and values, could they do so? Would the values they name match the values we intended to express or demonstrate? How do our values relate to the way we treat people, utilize resources, enact policies and procedures, handle finances, interact with the environment, and engage with community members? What do we hope to demonstrate and does the public (and all our staff) understand what we are trying to accomplish?

Application of Values

The City of Manhattan Beach (CA) Parks and Recreation Department has identified ten core values that help to focus its provision of programs and services. The staff have also specified action steps to help them enact these values in their daily work (see Table 3.1). Many of these stated values directly relate to those embedded in servant leadership—consider the following:

Manhattan Beach values...

- Teamwork, respect, and support of others

- Encouraging, practicing, and active listening

- Integrity, fairness, respect, and a public service orientation

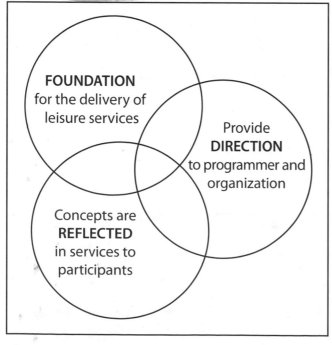

Figure 3.1 Functions of philosophical foundations

Table 3.1 City of Manhattan Beach core values

1. We will nurture and promote a spirit of teamwork. We will do this by:
   A. Feeling free to take an interest in others' work;
   B. Encouraging collaborative projects;
   C. Ensuring that our organizational structure, systems, and policies foster and promote teamwork.

2. We will contribute to and maintain an enjoyable work environment. We will do this by:
   A. Maintaining an objective and positive perspective about work and co-workers;
   B. Keeping a sense of humor;
   C. Practicing being friendly, courteous, and respectful;
   D. Finding joy in our works.

3. We will respect and support each other, as individuals and as employees occupying unique positions, and the organization as an entity. We will do this by:
   A. Acknowledging and appreciating the individual roles we all play for the benefit of the team, the organization, and the public.

4. We will recognize and celebrate the "good" qualities in each other. We will do this by:
   A. Making an effort to see the moon—the whole picture—in each person and situation: To find the balance in each personal encounter;
   B. Assuming the best intent is always in play and sticking to issues, not personalities.

5. We will encourage, practice, and value active listening. We will do this by:
   A. Not speaking while others are speaking;
   B. Practicing confirming what's been heard—"What I hear you saying is…is this correct?"
   C. Giving our focused and undivided attention and valuing what is said—and therefore the person saying it.

6. We will be fair, consistent, and detail oriented. We will do this by:
   A. Encouraging and promoting mutual respect;
   B. Standardizing methods to achieve consistent work practices;
   C. Measuring/reviewing twice and cutting/printing once.

7. We will maintain a "safe" work environment where thoughts and ideas can be shared openly and where effective communication will occur regularly. We will do this by:
   A. Avoiding condescending and judgmental behaviors;
   B. Promoting effective dialogue through regular communications.

8. We will promote the virtues that open space contributes to our quality of life. We will do this by:
   A. Developing appropriate public information materials;
   B. Being proactive in promoting virtues to the public;
   C. Sharing resource information and maintaining knowledgeable volunteers;
   D. Conducting special events which increase community awareness.

9. We will be fairly compensated and recognized for our work efforts. We will do this by:
   A. Expressing our appreciation to the department and general public;
   B. Promoting staff volunteer participation at district and community events;
   C. Developing appropriate department and public recognition programs.

10. We will conduct ourselves with integrity and nurture a work culture that values dedication to public service and organizational accomplishment. We will do this by:
   A. Taking pride in our job and professional work appearance;
   B. Focusing on the positive of our staff team and agency actions;
   C. Looking at problems as opportunities and being dedicated to get the job done;
   D. Making time to celebrate our individual and collective accomplishments.

- The recognition and celebration of the good qualities in one another

Servant Leadership values...

- Consensus building and community

- The ability to listen and a commitment to the growth of others

- The ability to be self-aware and to empathize with others; stewardship

- The ability to offer healing and build community

Because leisure programmers are in leadership roles, they are naturally in positions of influence, which provide the opportunity to model and share values. In fact, this will occur regardless of whether or not the programmer does so consciously. This dynamic is similar to the experience of professional athletes who find their behavior scrutinized because they are role models—whether they want to be or not. Likewise, by the very nature of the relationship between programmer and participant, and the value-laden society in which we live, programmers are in the business of modeling values every day.

As an example, suppose a parks, recreation, or leisure services organization receives a financial donation from a former participant: a message will be conveyed by how the organization chooses to allocate those funds. For example, if the money is used to build a ramp into a facility the organization demonstrates an emphasis on accessibility; if it is used to purchase a new treadmill, it may imply a priority for physical fitness; and if it is to be used to establish a scholarship fund for youth leadership training, community development is highlighted. Regardless of whether or not recreation professionals are thinking about the underlying values communicated with these types of decisions, through our actions we send a message upon which public perceptions are formed.

As mentioned earlier, human beings are not always aware of the values they hold or that they are expressing them through decisions and behaviors. As an example, a commercial tour operator who insists on adding registrants to an already full program at the expense of program quality might be demonstrating a higher value for making a profit than serving customers. On the other hand, if a program supervisor consistently challenges her staff to develop creative programs by involving local constituents, and repeatedly follows up

to see how and when constituents were involved in the planning process, she would be demonstrating a value of community involvement.

To stay focused and be sure leisure professionals are modeling the values as they intend, individuals and organizations will want to formally develop and publicly present their core values. Making these values public reflects and reinforces what the person or organization holds to be most important; it also provides direction to staff when developing programs. As an example, members and the staff of the public, nonprofit National Recreation and Park Association (NRPA) developed a set of core values to provide guidance for decision making and program development. The values include a focus on quality, fun, preservation, networking, transparency in decision making, services to members, and stewardship of the natural environment (see http://nrpablog.typepad.com/nrpa_strategic_planning/). Table 3.2 (on pp. 61-62) presents samples of core values from a variety of parks and recreation organizations.

Traditions

Many times when participants are asked to reflect on a particular leisure experience, they recall memories that may have occupied little of their actual time, but made a significant impact on them nonetheless. We tend to think that such recollections will undoubtedly reflect the unusual or exotic components of a program. However, many of these memories focus on what seem to be the opposite—traditions. *Traditions* are activities, interactions, or events that are repeated over time and convey something meaningful about the program or organization and its participants (including the program leaders). Participants often anticipate and expect traditions and become disappointed if they do not occur. This predictability illustrates some of the power and meaning that traditions hold for people.

When we think about traditions, we may think about patterns of behavior or customs in which our families engage during holidays and vacations. Many of us associate different holidays with an array of traditions such as turkey on Thanksgiving, candle lighting during Chanukah, and fireworks on Independence Day. We take many of these for granted until they are missing or changed for some reason. Such a change in a tradition often evokes an emotional response—somehow our feelings about the holiday are not quite the same. This is because traditions are a means of establishing bonds between those with whom we share the experiences. Traditions also are a way of building

Table 3.2 Examples of core values of selected parks, recreation, and leisure services agencies   Continued>>

University of Seattle Campus Recreation
Care: We put the good of students first.
Academic Excellence: We value excellence in learning with great teachers who are active scholars.
Diversity: We celebrate educational excellence achieved through diversity.
Faith: We treasure our Jesuit Catholic ethos and the enrichment from many faiths of our university community.
Justice: We foster a concern for justice and the competence to promote it.
Leadership: We seek to develop responsible leaders committed to the common good.
Source: http://www.seattleu.edu/recsports/page.aspx?ID=299

2003 San Francisco Strategic Plan
City of San Francisco Parks and Recreation Department
Working Well Together: Working well together embodies having respect for our co-workers, our community, and our environment; valuing each other's professional opinions, expertise, and collaboration, in order to deliver the best parks and programs.
Great Customer Service: Great customer service encompasses a caring and considerate attitude by Department staff. It reflects honest, professional, effective, and efficient communication to both co-workers and the community.
Always Dependable: Being consistently dependable allows the community and staff to count on the Department. This includes reliably accurate information, transparent communication, and unquestionable safety standards.
Inspiring Innovation: Inspiring innovation brings great riches to all we do. It encourages respect for the diverse creativity and dynamic environment in which we live and work, and it puts San Francisco at the forefront of many communities.
Excellence In Everything: In supporting our mission, values, vision, and the objectives that follow, we will bring excellence to everything that we do.
Source: http://www.parks.sfgov.org/wcm_recpark/Strategic/STP2003.pdf
----

Crystal Mountain Resort & Spa
• Strive to be a Customer Centered Company.
• Have Fun!
• Use teamwork to deliver high quality, value-priced services in a safe, clean, and environmentally sensitive manner.
• Maintain a wholesome and friendly environment.
• Promote a supportive work setting that includes high expectations, active participation, personal development and recognition, open communication, and trust.
• Earn a profit (it's like breathing).
• Give back to our community.
Source: http://www.crystalmountain.com/about/values

Comox Recreation Commission, BC, Canada
• We are dedicated to providing sustainable recreational activities that draw people together, are available to all and will benefit the community as a whole.
• We believe recreation includes physical, leisure, social, and cultural activities that promote wellness, are life-long and enrich the quality of life.
• We believe in being financially accountable to the community by operating in a prudent, transparent, and ethical manner.
• We value our members and provide a respectful and safe environment where individuals can achieve their goals.
• We encourage local partnerships and will seek to purchase supplies and services from local companies whenever possible.
• We take pride in providing buildings and equipment that are well maintained and strive to ensure that patrons feel safe when using our indoor facilities.
• We believe in working co-operatively with the Town of Comox to ensure that the needs of the community we serve are being met.
• We believe in providing a work environment that fosters growth, promotes teamwork, and provides development opportunities for staff, instructors and volunteers.
• We believe in recycling and utilizing materials and supplies that are in keeping with the protection of the environment.
Source: http://www.comoxrecreation.com/core_values.html

Table 3.2 Examples of core values of selected parks, recreation, and leisure services agencies (continued)

Blaze Sports

Integrity: We act with integrity in all that we do—with people with whom we work and the people whom we serve.

Teamwork: We believe teamwork incorporates respect, humor, communication, individual empowerment, and accountability.

Quality: We strive for quality through promoting excellence, fostering creativity, and nurturing a passion for learning in all that we do.

Commitment: We have a strong commitment to compassionately and tenaciously achieve our goals for the people we serve.

Stewardship: We take responsibility for being good stewards for all resources entrusted to our care.

Source: http://www.blazesports.org/DesktopDefault.aspx?tabindex=1&tabid=122&tablevel=2

MWR Germany • US Army Garrison Baden-Wurttemberg

Organization

Never say never

Empowerment

Team work

Excellence

Accountability

Mission first

(ONE TEAM)

Source: http://www.mwrgermany.com/HD/contentimages/on

Waukee (Iowa) Area Arts Council

Artistic quality: We pledge uncompromising adherence to the highest quality of professional artists, educational programming, and artistic presentations.

Education: Foster artistic expression through creative learning and entertainment opportunities in schools and public venues; thereby broadening community knowledge of the arts.

Diversity: Embrace diversity to serve the needs of the community through a variety of artistic opportunities.

Artistic support: Welcome a variety of forms of artistic expression and provide opportunities for those voices to be heard. Artists and arts organizations will be treated as professional and respected through support and compensation.

Personal impact: Touch and enrich individual lives through the arts in a multitude of ways including volunteerism, philanthropy, creativity, self-expression and appreciation.

Community impact: Enhance the quality of life by respecting the arts as a valuable asset in our community; impacting the economic, social, philanthropic and personal aspects of everyday life.

Source: http://www.waukeearts.org/aboutus/values.php

Leave No Trace Center for Outdoor Ethics

1. Is committed to the enjoyment, health, and protection of recreational resources on natural lands for all people;
2. Believes that education is the best means to protect natural lands from recreational impacts while helping maintain access for recreation and enjoyment;
3. Is founded on outdoor ethics whereby a sense of stewardship is gained through understanding and connecting with the natural world;
4. Believes that practicing the Leave No Trace principles is the most relevant and effective long-term solution to maintaining the beauty, health of, and access to natural lands;
5. Is science-based and builds ethical, pragmatic approaches to resource protection for varying types of outdoor recreation and enjoyment;
6. Strives to build key partnerships that support education programs, training and communities of volunteers, educators, land managers, organizations, and corporations committed to teaching and instilling the values of Leave No Trace;
7. Is inclusive, for all people, and focused on all non-motorized recreation activities occurring on natural lands;
8. Is apolitical and dedicated to education;
9. Does not discriminate on the basis of race, color, gender, sexual orientation, national origin, age, religion, marital status, military status or disability; and
10. Remains committed to its mission, core values, projects, and programs without deviation.

Source: http://www.lnt.org/aboutUs/index.php

a sense of community and loyalty within organizations and in neighborhoods.

Support for traditions is not to suggest that change is not a good thing; to the contrary, change and the resulting adaptations are necessary for any community or recreation program to survive and to thrive. Even traditions undergo change through the years, but the essence of each one continues. This knowledge calls us to simultaneously respect the value of tradition while responding to changes in society.

Application of Traditions

One example of a tradition that has changed significantly since its inception, but has survived the test of time is the *Rags* and *Leathers* programs offered at many YMCA camps. In 1914, in response to a camper who was acting out, a staff member introduced this program as a behavior management tool that focused on positive behaviors rather than undesirable behaviors. In contemporary times, all campers (not just those with behavior problems) can elect to earn rags (bandanas) or leathers (small pieces of leather) by participating in this program (YMCA Camp Oakes, 2009).

The *Rags* program is used to challenge youth ages 12 and older to focus on an area of self-improvement during the camp experience. The rags are colored coded (see Figure 3.2) and symbolize one attribute of character development. At the beginning of the camp session, counselors meet with each youth who decides to participate in the program to help them write goals in the area of development they have chosen. Throughout the camp session the participating campers meet regularly with their counselors to choose activities and behaviors to help them develop the chosen attribute. On the last night of camp, the "Raggers" (participating campers) are involved in a ceremony where they are blindfolded with their rag and led up a trail. Every 100 yards or so, a staff

member shares a reading or short story that pertains to the particular rag that individuals in the group have worked on; more readings are shared when they reach their destination. At the destination site, counselors share comments about each camper and her/his growth, and then the campers remove their rags—they emerge from a world of total darkness to find themselves in an area that is lit by candles arranged in patterns forming the YMCA symbols. Campers then have an opportunity to address the group and talk about their personal journey to develop this aspect of themselves.

The *Leathers* program was developed for campers aged 9 to 11 and is simpler, but similar to *Rags*. Each camper selects one area of self-improvement that corresponds to one of the three YMCA symbols (see Figure 3.3). During a closing ceremony, each participant is presented with a leather symbol that corresponds to the area she or he has worked on during the session. As might be imagined, these programs can be quite powerful and emotional for campers and staff members, alike. One former director of Camp Silver Creek recalled a particular evening when one of his "toughest kids broke down crying and told about how he had made his first real friend—his counselor."

This tradition is an example of being participant focused, an important aspect of servant leadership. In *Rags* and *Leathers*, campers are involved by choosing if they want to participate, selecting their challenge area, and developing their personal goals. Conscious of diversity issues and the rights of others, camp staff make provisions for non-Christian participants to adapt the challenge description to meet their own belief system. This demonstrates the value of developing and implementing a program that maintains the integrity of participants and protects their personal beliefs.

Philosophy and Programming

Principles, values, and traditions set the stage for being able to articulate a philosophy. Thus, a *philosophy* is a framework that reflects the principles, values, and

YMCA Rags Program

Color	Challenge Area
Blue	Loyalty to God, country and one's best self
Silver	Rededicate to Christian way of life and values
Brown	Service to others
Gold	Understanding, concern and acceptance of others
Red	Sacrifice of time, talents and personal will
Purple	To lead the best life possible
White	Life of full-time Christian service to youth

Figure 3.2 An example of traditions: The YMCA Rags Program

YMCA Leathers Program

Symbol	Challenge Area
Triangle	To grow in mind, body and Spirit
Square	To grow and become a better friend and keep good friends
Circle	To become close to God through the earth He created

Figure 3.3 An example of traditions: The YMCA Leathers Program

beliefs of an individual or organization. A philosophy is usually characterized by both breadth and depth as seen in the following examples:

- The purpose of leisure is pure fun and enjoyment; if it feels good, we should do it.

- Leisure is among our most basic needs and thus, an inherent right of all human beings.

- Leisure is laziness and selfish; it is the antithesis of work.

- Leisure is an ideal and leads to "the good life;" it is the disciplined use of free time.

- Culture depends for its very existence on leisure; leisure is the essence of culture.

- Leisure is physical activity that leads to personal and social well-being.

Each of these philosophy statements, which offer their own unique explanation of the concept of leisure, could serve as a foundation for organizations and individuals to develop corresponding mission and vision statements. As you consider each of these statements, identify the embedded principles and values within each. If a public parks and recreation department (or commercial, therapeutic, military, or other recreation setting) were to adhere to each of these positions, how might their programs and services differ? How would the type of programs offered differ? The timing of the programs? Who might be the target audience? What would be stressed within a particular program or service? How might staff interact and communicate with the public if they espoused each of these views?

As mentioned earlier, it is important for those working in parks, recreation, and leisure services to be able to articulate a personal professional philosophy as well as understand the philosophy of the organization in which they work. One of the best reasons for a recreation professional to invest time in identifying and developing one's philosophy is to remain grounded in her or his professional endeavors. The link between personal and organizational philosophies provides a sense of belonging for the recreation programmer and enhances commitment to the agency.

Application of Philosophy

Sacred Earth Travel is an eco-travel company that focuses its efforts on programming in eco-conscious ways (Sacred Earth, 2009). This includes treading lightly on the earth as well as maintaining the integrity of local cultures—the focus is on sustainable travel and local economic development. With concerns for conservation and maintaining the integrity of the indigenous people of a particular region of the world, the creator and owner of Sacred Earth Travel developed a comprehensive philosophy statement. Following is a portion of that philosophy statement; through it, we can see the strength of conviction of the company founder.

Culture and nature are the greatest treasures of our civilizations—they constitute our heritages. But both are in danger of disappearing under a flood of homogenizing corporate developments—nature has to give way to exploitation, which wreaks havoc in its wake. Formerly rich biodiversity hotspots are facing increasing pressures that threaten the once brimming life force of its flora and fauna. As we watch nature disappearing in front of our eyes we begin to realize its beauty and fragility—and its need for protection.

Sacred Earth Travel believes that all the earth is sacred—and that we must protect its fragile balance. I believe in treading softly on the earth—whether at home or travelling—for conscious living is a way of life. I believe that close contact with nature can heal the battle wounds of civilization that are inflicted on us by the stress of our busy daily lives. And I believe in the transformative power of travel—the journey within, as a way of reconnecting with the spirit and thus healing the soul.

I believe that eco-travel not only provides a superb way to become immersed in nature, but also offers great opportunities to help protect it for future generations. At its best, it can facilitate real, close-up encounters with the natural world as well as providing fascinating insights into the lives of people who continue to live in close relationship with their natural environment.

Eco-travel also provides a direct means of supporting conservation efforts at a local level. Eco-travel ventures often involve collaborative efforts between local communities and eco-travel companies, thus providing a sustainable source of income, which actively supports the conservation of nature and culture for communities that otherwise might be forced to move to the cities or earn their living from destructive exploitation of their homelands (e.g., cutting down the forests, cash crop agriculture, gold mining, etc). –Kat Morgenstern, Nov 2006

This philosophy statement (to read the full statement go to http://www.sacredearth-travel.com/philosophy.php) demonstrates the inseparability of personal and organizational principles, values, and traditions. These foundational elements are woven throughout the philosophy statement. Further, this statement makes clear the types of programs and services a potential participant might expect on a sponsored trip.

Agency Mission: Its Impact on Programming

A mission statement conveys the essence of an individual or organization and answers the question "What am I (or we) about?" The *mission* reflects an organization's essential reason for existence, its unique identity that sets it apart from others. It clarifies for all stakeholders (e.g., administrative boards, participants, employees, community members) what the organization considers important and in what areas they are likely to invest

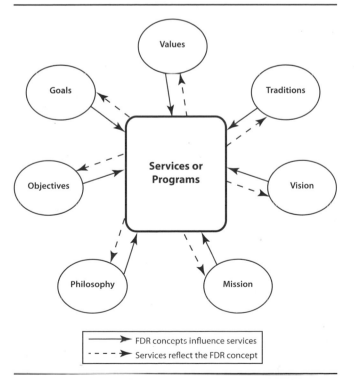

Figure 3.4 The relationships between FDR concepts and programs/services

energy and resources. A mission statement is generally a succinct, declarative statement of being that tends to be management oriented and focuses on what an agency will do for constituents.

Before an individual or organization can determine "where they want to go" in the future (their vision), they must have some understanding of where they are and what they are about in the present (i.e., What is the mission?). Imagine a scuba diver submerged in the ocean at an unknown depth. Perhaps she was very clear in her dive plan that she was going to descend to 15 meters and stay submerged for 40 minutes. But suppose in the process of descending the diver was so entranced in looking at marine life that she had no idea after 15 minutes how far she had descended. While the diver knows she wants to be at 15 meters, if she does not know her current depth, she does not know whether to swim up or down to achieve that depth. In this analogy, the diver's depth gauge serves the same function as a mission statement; it provides bearings so the goal can be pursued.

In a leisure services organization, a well-understood mission provides unity, focus, and a starting point for future endeavors. The bottom line is that without such a common purpose, recreation programmers are likely to find themselves simply scheduling activities rather than serving their communities through quality programs and services. Brown, Yoshioka, and Munoz (2004) found that employee attitudes toward an agency mission are influenced by: (1) awareness of the mission (i.e., do staff know what the mission is?); (2) their level of agreement with the expressed purpose and values of the agency (i.e., do staff believe in similar principles?); and (3) employees must see a connection between their work and fulfillment of the mission (i.e., can staff see how their work contributes to achieving the mission?). Thus, to be most effective in their roles, recreation programmers will want to strive to achieve awareness and understanding of the agency mission. See Table 3.3 (p. 66) for examples of parks, recreation, and leisure services agency mission statements.

Application of Mission

While the content of a mission statement may vary depending upon the type of leisure services organization (i.e., commercial, public, or nonprofit), the process of developing one is essentially the same for all. It is important to note that mission statements are not static — they should be reviewed and updated on a regular basis reflecting changes that occur as programs and agencies evolve. As an example, consider the evolution of the mission statement for Courage Center Camps (previously known as Courage Camps), a programmatic arm of a Minneapolis-based nonprofit rehabilitation and resource center serving adults and children from across the country. For several years Courage Center Camps published a comprehensive mission statement that reflected specific programmatic values. Recently, the staff revisited and rewrote the mission statement to address the essence of the organization's (rather than the program's) 'reason for being.' The camp-specific mission statement is now embedded in the general information describing the camp programs. In the mis-

Table 3.3 Mission statements of selected parks, recreation, and leisure services entities

Greensboro Parks & Recreation Department (NC)
The mission of the Greensboro Parks & Recreation Department (NC) is to provide diverse year-round leisure opportunities through the preservation of open space, park settings, recreational facilities and programs for residents of Greensboro. The benefits of leisure services are especially designed to meet the physical, mental, cultural and social needs of our residents and visitors to our community, while enhancing the overall quality of life in Greensboro.
Source: http://www.greensboro-nc.gov/departments/Parks/aboutus/

Native American Celebration in the Park (UT)
To educate and share the proud heritage of the Native American community to the world through music and dance, cultural displays, entertainment and the arts, both traditional and contemporary. To foster self-sufficiency and self-reliance for all Native Americans through entrepreneurship, sound financial practices and integrity. Lift Native Americans to a higher level of self-worth so that they will achieve their individual and community potential.
Source: http://www.nativeamericancelebration.com/native_american_celebration/about_native_american_celebration_park.html
----
Out of Africa Wildlife Park (AZ)
Out Of Africa Wildlife Park's purpose is to be your best family adventure. We invite people from around the world to experience and to appreciate animals in natural settings, and to share our peaceful interactive relationship with them in a physical and spiritual way that touches visitors' hearts. We aspire to be fun, friendly, and informative to all we meet.
Source: http://www.outofafricapark.com/mission.html

Lincolnway Special Recreation Association (IL)
The primary purpose of Lincolnway Special Recreation Association is to provide programs for people with special needs. These programs are developed with the intention of eliminating any recreational barriers and to facilitate the participants in developing a balance of leisure and socialization skills, recreation resources and opportunities, knowledge and independence, provided in a variety of settings. All of these will contribute to the participants' well-being in their recreational lifestyles.
Source: http://www.lwsra.org/programs/brochure.pdf

National Outdoor Leadership School (NOLS) (WY)
The mission of the National Outdoor Leadership School is to be the leading source and teacher of wilderness skills and leadership that serve people and the environment.
Source: http://www.nols.edu/about/values.shtml

The National Park Service (DC)
The National Park Service preserves unimpaired the natural and cultural resources and values of the national park system for the enjoyment, education, and inspiration of this and future generations. The Park Service cooperates with partners to extend the benefits of natural and cultural resource conservation and outdoor recreation throughout this country and the world.
Source: http://www.nps.gov/legacy/mission.html

Canyon Lake Senior Center (SD)
It is the mission of the Canyon Lake Senior Center to promote the physical, intellectual and social well-being of its members and the senior community. Thereby, enhancing the dignity, self-worth, independence and a wholesome life style for seniors in Rapid City.
Source: http://www.canyonlakecenter.com/mission.asp

sion statements noted below we have added the terms *camp* and *organization* to clearly distinguish the two versions.

Camp Mission Statement (pre 2009): Courage Camps offer safe, accessible, natural environments where children and adults with physical disabilities, sensory and language impairments, and other disabilities or illnesses discover abilities they never knew they had or they thought they had lost. Campers make new friends, and are often introduced to sports or hobbies they develop further at home or at school. Their self confidence grows and their attitudes improve.

Organization Mission Statement (post 2009): Courage Center empowers people with disabilities to realize their full potential in every aspect of life.

Examples of camp sessions: **"LIFE 101"**: A new session for adults who have Aspergers [syndrome]. This week long seminar offers morning classes and focuses on: understanding verbal and nonverbal communication, resume writing and mock interviews, and time management. Afternoons are filled with outdoor activities such as fishing, sailing, kayaking, photography, biking field trips, and more. After dinner, speakers and panel discussions allow informal networking and evening programs round out every day with fun social experiences. This session provides a nonclinical opportunity to learn social and life skills, and apply the lessons immediately in real-life situations.

Augmentative Alternative Communication (AAC) Camp: This session is for teens, ages 12–19, who use synthesized speech devices. This session is not designed for beginning AAC users, but for those users who need to learn more about the capabilities of their device and the importance of communication. Campers participate in all the fun camp activities, such as horseback riding and tubing behind a boat. Device use is encouraged before, during, and after each activity (except in the water!). Special night programs are designed to further encourage device use. During intake, camp pages and vocabulary as well as camp songs are loaded into each camper's device. Campers are able to meet other teens who use AAC devices as well as interact with a proficient AAC mentor. The session culminates in the production of an AAC play for family and friends. Our goal is to have campers learn the "power of communication" while having fun. (Camp Courage, 2008)

Agency Vision: Its Impact on Programming

Related to, yet distinct from, a mission statement which articulates an expression of what is (in the present), a vision statement addresses what an organization wants to become and where it wants to be in the future. A well-written vision statement will 'grab' the reader, and compel action and a desire to 'join up.' It also will empower others, inspire excitement and enthusiasm, and articulate an attractive and realistic future. A *practical vision* is one that serves as the hub or center of the program planning cycle; to be effective it should drive agency goals and objectives (see Table 3.4 on p. 68). In the words of an unknown individual, practical visions are "dreams and hopes that are available to us. They are what we deeply imagine and believe; they must be in place if there is to be a future." A vision statement reveals the direction that an organization or individual is heading and answers such questions as:

- Whom do we wish to serve?

- What values do we want to instill?

- What individual and community beneficial outcomes will we strive to achieve?

- How will we accomplish these benefits (what resources will we need)?

- What will the future look like? How does this future direction reflect our principles and philosophy?

- Why are these directions important to this agency/organization?

Characteristically, a vision statement inspires optimism and motivation to achieve high aspirations. To some it may seem idealistic and impractical, but by its very nature, a vision statement needs to focus on far reaching possibilities. In order to be truly effective, a vision statement (as well as the other foundational elements) must be evidenced in planning, programs, policies, personnel, participants, and how we use facilities and grounds.

Application of Vision

The Department of Campus Recreation at Texas State University in San Marcos (TX) presents a clear demonstration of how mission and vision statements are related to departmental (and programmatic) goals. This university enrolls almost 30,000 students in south-central Texas, and its campus recreation program offers programs and classes in aquatics, fitness, intramurals, club sports, outdoor recreation, golf, and open gym. They

Table 3.4 Vision statements from selected parks, recreation, and leisure services organizations

Dutch Wonderland Family Entertainment Complex (PA)
The Vision of Dutch Wonderland is to build upon its core competencies of family entertainment, campground management, and offsite retail operations. This mission-based growth will occur while maintaining the positive attributes of each existing operation. Dutch Wonderland strives to be the premier attraction in the Lancaster County destination and one that drives incremental tourism into the area.
Source: http://www.dutchwonderland.com/general/mission_statement.php

----

Alaska Divisions of Parks and Outdoor Recreation (AK)
The Alaska Division of Parks and Outdoor Recreation envisions an affordable and accessible system of parks that provide diverse, safe, year-round, high-quality, family-oriented, outdoor recreation experiences; statewide programs that enhance the enjoyment and stewardship of the state's outdoor recreation, natural, historic and cultural resources; and a dedicated, professional staff that fully meets the needs of the public.
Source: http://dnr.alaska.gov/parks/plans/strategicplan/mission_vision.pdf

----

The Museum of African American Music, Art & Culture (TN)
The Museum of African American Music, Art & Culture will be an educational facility, national tourist destination, and economic development engine for Nashville and the state of Tennessee. The Museum will tell the story of African American music nationally and internationally—including the important aspects of that story that occurred in history in Nashville—through the importance of the confluence of music, art, and culture.
Source: http://www.maamac.com/

Anderson Ranch Arts Center (CO)
Anderson Ranch strives to be a world leader in the growth and development of the visual arts, in the international dialogue that inspires common humanity through art making, and in the creation of a campus imbued with a spirit of community, challenge, support, exploration, innovation and discovery.
Source: http://www.andersonranch.org/about/index.php?page=mission-and-vision

----

Prince George's County Department of Parks and Recreation (MD)
The Department of Parks and Recreation pledges to:
• Provide stewardship of our county's natural, cultural, and historical resources.
• Foster the need of our citizens for recreational pursuits in a leisure environment.
• Provide the highest standard of excellence in public service through cooperative partnership with our diverse community.
Source: http://www.pgparks.com/info/about.html

The Marine Corps Community Services Division (USA)
The Marine Corps Community Services of 2025 is aligned to the Marine Corps mission offering innovative and expeditionary program and service delivers in its approach to taking care of Marines and their families. We are a progressive organization, focusing on creative expansion, wider technological capabilities, premier services and infrastructure, workforce development, and sound planning that is supported by flexible policies and fully automated executive information and decision-making systems. Marine Corps Community Services is valued by leadership as being a user-friendly and a responsive single portal that provides constant and unwavering support to Marines and their families throughout their entire service or affiliation with the United States Marine Corps.
Source: http://www.usmc-mccs.org/aboutmccs/downloads/Strategy%202025%20-%20FINAL.pdf

have a wide range of fields, facilities, and equipment to serve the students, faculty, and staff of the university.

Mission Statement

The Department of Campus Recreation serves as a vital and integral part of student life on campus. The mission of the department is to provide a broad spectrum of sports, recreation and leisure activities for students, staff and faculty, as well as members of the local community. The primary direction is to provide services and programs that stimulate growth, development, and retention of students in a contemporary and safe environment that develops fitness and wellness, social interaction, and leadership opportunities.

Vision Statement

During the next decade, Texas State Campus Recreation will continue to be recognized as a leader in recreational and leisure services on campus and in the state. We will develop a comprehensive program that supports student learning and life-long participation and wellness. We value student development, collaboration, and professionalism.

Goals

1. Enhance leadership, involvement, and social responsibility of Texas State students.

2. Improve the health and wellness of the campus community.

3. Develop and improve the Campus Recreation facilities.

4. Create outreach programs for targeted populations.

5. Improve knowledge and professional development of Campus Recreation staff.

6. Improve management of fiscal resources.

Responsibility

To effectively fulfill its mission and accomplish its goals, the Texas State Department of Campus Recreation provides, within the scope of its resources, the following:

- Opportunities for a variety of cooperative and competitive activities that will contribute to an individual's physical fitness;

- Access to quality, contemporary, and modern facilities and programs;

- A variety of programming including the major areas of informal/drop-in recreation, intramural sports, sport clubs, outdoor recreation, fitness, and golf operations;

- Coordination of the scheduling of events, promotion of activities, and maintenance of campus recreational facilities to maximize facility use to better serve the campus community;

- Development of a medium through which students can develop leadership, management, program planning, and communication skills;

- Extracurricular opportunities through participation and leadership roles designed to enhance social, psychological, and physiological development; and

- A resource center of outdoor program ideas, equipment, supplies, and rental materials.

(Texas State University, n.d.)

Embedded in these statements are the underlying principles and philosophy of the department. The mission statement clearly articulates the intent and purpose of the campus recreation unit. Their values include student development and retention, contemporary programs and facilities, safety, wellness, and leadership development. The vision statement is an outgrowth of the present focus—the department states a desire to be recognized as a leader, and to be engaged in learning and lifelong wellness. Values related to this vision are evident: student development, collaboration, and professionalism.

In addition to their mission and vision statements, the Texas State University Department of Campus Recreation articulates goals—note that these directly relate to its mission and vision statements. The connections are apparent and exist to guide staff efforts in all that they do. This department further explains its reason for being and future dreams by including a list of responsibilities to their constituents. This list serves as a basis for accountability as they go about the business of providing recreation and leisure opportunities to their various constituent groups.

◆◆◆

The title of this chapter is "Principles, Philosophy, and Planning"—all three are necessary to provide a framework around which we build programs and activities. The principles (including values and traditions) lead into the philosophy, which is made evident in mission and vision statements. From this bedrock we begin the planning process for parks, recreation, and leisure services. Planning first occurs at the organizational level and then into each aspect of our agency—particularly in programming.

Planning Processes

Committing to both quality leisure experiences for individuals as well as serving the needs of society is a challenging task requiring that leisure services professionals understand the basic planning process. Much of what recreation programmers know and use of planning theory comes from other disciplines such as social work, which sees planning as a means for problem solving; and from corporate or business fields, which see planning as a way of managing change. Over the past decade, interest in planning has increased as a result of a scarcity of resources (e.g., staff, economic, tangible goods) and by the belief that greater accountability comes with using a planning process. In this way the planning process becomes a mechanism for managing and controlling programs and services.

Planning must flow from an organization's underlying principles, philosophy, mission, and vision statements. Without these foundational building blocks, planning is prone to a lack of focus and direction. Policies and decisions can change quickly, and seemingly without a lot of forethought. Through effective planning, staff articulate the action steps needed to achieve the dream established through the FDR elements. At the agency or organization level, planning is often referred to as *strategic planning* or *long-term planning*. Generally, planning documents encompass a five- to ten-year period and include plans for the entire agency or organization. To ensure continued relevance and appropriateness of goals, staff review and update the plans on an annual basis.

Planning is often viewed as finding the "right fit" between the mission and vision of an organization, strengths and weaknesses within the organization, and opportunities and threats from outside the organization (see Figure 3.5).

It is important to remember that all people do not agree about the best way to plan. Agency or organizational culture, local politics, funding, and other internal and external forces will influence the process. Each plan has to be unique, tailored to the particular situation and planner(s), and use a blend of strategies and approaches. No matter the chosen approach, many find that involving constituents in the planning process tends to lead to increased programmatic success and participant satisfaction. Constituent participation is *a process in which individuals take part in decision making related to the organization and its programs and services that affect them in some manner*. It is up to leisure services programmers to identify the appropriate strategies that work with the other elements of the strategic planning process.

Constituent Involvement

As we have emphasized (and will continue to) throughout this text, involving constituents in the program planning process is an important element of a servant leadership approach to programming. Fortunately, we have several opportunities to solicit input into our program planning efforts. Many prefer to meet with constituent groups face-to-face, and in many instances this is the most appropriate mechanism to truly involve our various publics. We can go into the community to meet with constituents in their neighborhoods, or we can invite people to a common location. These types of meetings are often called town hall meetings and, when well-facilitated, can provide avenues for an open exchange of ideas and concerns. Focus groups are specific types of constituent meetings that can also yield excellent information to assist with planning.

We can also solicit ideas about types and formats of programs, policies and procedures, use of resources, and other programmatic elements through the use of comment cards (hard copy and/or computer-based) and formal asset and needs assessments. All of these techniques are more fully addressed in later chapters in this text. No matter our preferences or decisions related to involving the public in planning, once we have gathered input we can apply what we have learned to several different planning models.

Planning Models

If we think about the way a house is built, the foundation is laid and a framework is built on top of it. The sides and roof are then added, and finishing touches are applied. In programming the principles, philosophy, and other foundational pieces are first laid, and input is solicited. Then, a planning model is used to help define and provide a framework to the planning process. Planning occurs at the organizational level, as well as at the program level—planning models are often useful at both stages.

Logic Model

One common framework for agency and program planning is illustrated through a Logic Model (see Figure 3.6 on p. 72). A Logic Model is a systematic and visual representation of resources, activities, goals, and outcomes of a program (Kellogg Foundation, 2004; Wells & Arthur-Banning, 2008). This type of planning includes identifying and explaining several elements:

- **Factors or external influences:** These are policies, attitudes, norms, and politics of the local environment that can facilitate or inhibit effective programming. These factors are dependent upon the people who comprise our local constituency, and much can be discovered through asset mapping, which we present in the next chapter.

- **Resources and inputs:** These are the resources (e.g., finances, staffing, facilities, equipment) needed to operate a program.

- **Activities:** The processes, technology, policies, promotional tools, and tasks in which staff engage to deliver programs and services. This may include conducting needs assessments,

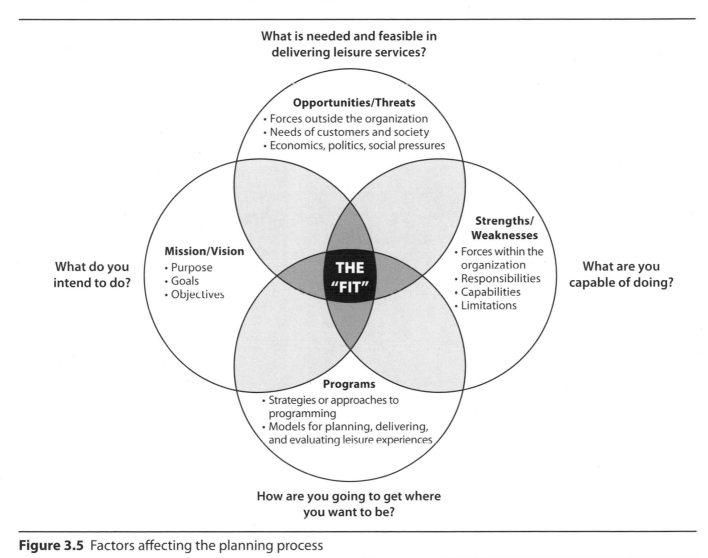

Figure 3.5 Factors affecting the planning process

choosing a target market, determining pricing, engaging in promotional activities, and other pre-implementation tasks.

- **Outputs:** A direct result of activities, outputs include services, programs, and products delivered by the agency to achieve outcomes. This involves who we reach through participation in our programs, as well as the larger society.

- **Outcomes:** These are desired changes in knowledge, attitudes, skills, and aspirations (KASA) for individuals involved in the programs or services. Outcomes may also be focused on the community-at-large.

- **Evaluation and impacts:** Planning always involves evaluation and an examination of the impacts that a program has had on the intended constituents. At this level, planners are looking for changes on an organizational or community level as a result of the program or service.

Through this model we must first define the external forces that might influence our approach to planning and program delivery. These influences can be subtle (e.g., political pressures) or overt (e.g., ordinances that prohibit certain activities); it can be helpful to talk with other staff and people in the community to get a solid sense of these factors. As will be seen in the following chapter, it will be very important to engage in asset mapping and needs assessments—in this way we determine the resources and inputs at our disposal. Once we have an awareness of the factors that might influence our choices and the resources available to us, we can then plan the various activities to help accomplish our goals.

The activities we undertake will lead to the provision and implementation of programs and services—these are considered outputs. The outputs involve not only what we offer, but also the people we reach through the delivery of programs and services. When well planned, outputs will lead to outcomes at both the individual and community levels. Outcomes might include such benefits as increased quality of life, enhanced social skills, and increased social capital. And,

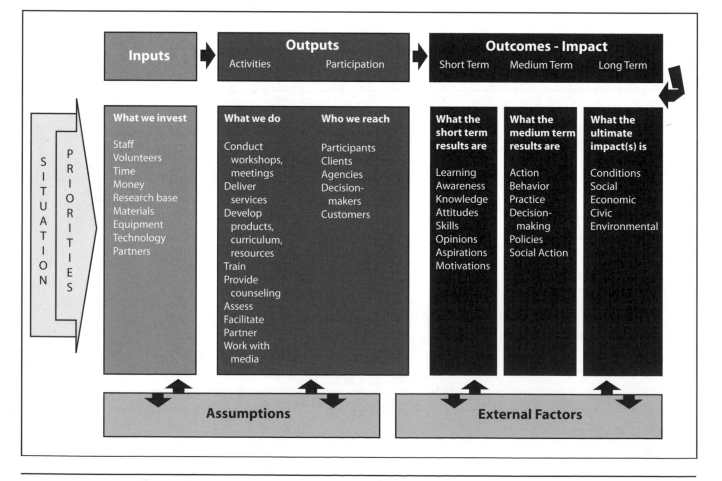

Figure 3.6 Logic model (Adapted from Kellogg Foundation, 2004)

of course, programming is incomplete until evaluations are conducted and we learn the actual impacts we had on the community—social, economic, civic, and environmental. Figure 3.7 (on pp. 74-75) presents an example of a program planning tool utilized by the City of Manhattan Beach (CA). By providing responses to the various items, they address the elements of the Logic Model.

Method of Eight Planning Cycle

Utilizing the basic logic model just described, The "Method of Eight Planning Cycle" is a five-year agency-wide planning process that articulates the various steps needed to ensure a fit within the community (Sabbach, 2009). Figure 3.8 (on p. 76) illustrates the various steps an agency or organization will follow as they go through the planning cycle. Initially, development or clarification of the organizational values, and the vision and mission statements sets the stage for what is to come. This is followed with time spent gathering data from the community. Identifying community concerns and issues involves area residents through surveys, focus groups, and town hall meetings. Gaining this type of input aids with local 'buy-in' and support of agency efforts. Step three involves identifying core services, which includes conducting needs and asset assessments. These two steps help to ensure that planning is relevant to the community and its concerns. Also important at this stage is clarifying the agency philosophy regarding resource allocation—this includes cost recovery expectations, how natural resources and facilities are utilized, and exploring related efficiencies. With this information in hand, the agency will then develop an operational plan that includes goals and objectives for moving ahead. Also at this point, planners begin to think about the evaluation component—what will we want to measure? What are alternative ways of gathering evaluative data? When will we want to conduct evaluations?

The sixth step in the Method of Eight involves articulating desirable and intended outcomes—results that will arise from following the operational plan. For example, if one of the program goals is to increase youth well being, an agency might offer programs such as a Walk in the Park program, Jump Rope for Heart, Just Say No to Drugs, nutrition classes, and other wellness-related programs and services. Logical outcomes from involvement in these programs might consist of increased cardio fitness levels among youth, decreased truancy from schools, lower rates of youth

smoking or substance abuse, increased engagement in active recreation and sports programs, and so on. Having identified intended outcomes, the next step in the planning cycle is to choose and implement appropriate programs based on the target audiences, the local culture, assets, and needs. We will want to measure those outcomes during and after implementation of the programs and services. This will include formative and summative evaluations, an examination of budget data, and other markers of achievement. Finally, in the Method of Eight Planning Cycle, the loop is closed through sharing the measurement information with the community; this provides accountability to the various constituent groups. Thus, the planning cycle begins in the community and ends in the community.

Gantt and PERT Planning Charts

Like goals and objectives (discussed in the following section), Gantt and PERT Charts are used for both planning and evaluation. In fact, most planning tools serve as bases for evaluation. As we plan what we want to accomplish and how we want to get there, we are identifying the very attributes that we will later want to measure. Thus, conversations about evaluation should be part of the planning process—before a program is implemented.

A Gantt chart (named after the person who developed the model) is essentially a bar chart that depicts a timeline of events that comprise the development, implementation, and evaluation of a program. To use this model, we first break down the program into the components that need to occur to make it happen (i.e., program task analysis). Once we have identified these elements, we place them on a calendar and the time for completion is noted by use of a bar chart. If all timelines are met, the program design process is said to be successful (see Figure 3.9 on p. 77).

The Program Evaluation Review Technique (PERT) process builds on the Gantt model. In addition to the timeline graphically represented by the Gantt chart, PERT includes a flow chart that depicts how a program will occur from the establishment of objectives through the evaluation process (see Figure 3.10 on p. 78). We identify time estimates to complete the event components and note the links between events on the flow chart. This model provides a very detailed look at the logistical elements and progression of a program. This type of system is particularly appropriate for process evaluation because it can tell us how we planned an event, and if that planning process was effective.

City of Manhattan Beach, CA * VIP Program Planning Form
(Adaptation. Original form by Mr. Idris Jassim al-Oboudi & Mr. Keith Fulthorp, 2004)

This programming tool will help you better formulate specific purposes for your program development. The form can be used in two strategic ways: 1) to align your current programs with our departmental Vision, Insight, Planning Framework (VIP) to help you better communciate our department's impact on community goals to decision makers; and 2) as an "end-in-mind" programming tool to help focus your programminig efforts toward specific purposes that can be better communicated to decision makers.

Community goal/current trend/issue:

Goal/issue/trend selected based upon the following criteria:

Data that drove this decision:

Program name and brief description:

Staff utilized or assigned to program:

Intended program outcomes:

VIP Mission Targeted:	VIP Strategy Utilized:
Strengthen community image and sense of place	Communicating the vision
Support economic development	Forming partnerships
Strengthen safety and security	Expanding professional competencies
Promote health and wellness	Strengthen the P&R ethic
Foster human development	Demonstrating results
Increase cultural unity	Documenting best practices
Protect environmental resources	Impacting public policy
Facilitate community problem solving	Expanding resources
Provide recreational experiences	

Resources Needed
* Funding * Training * Staff * Facilities * Supplies/Equipment * Volunteers * Technology * Registration
* Interdepartmental collaboration

Please Remember: Last year's recommendations/last year planning information, binder & evaluation/ planning meetings/tasks assignments and timelines/planning budget with projected revenue & expenditures/deposit of funds/receipts/vendors list/site map/location amenities/event map/back up location/set up map/directions to location/location information/rain date/plan of walking the site/special contracts list/vendor list & information/refund/registration total info/parking/electrical/PA/trash pick up/cleaning before & after event/safety & security needs, PD & fire/public work help needed/special printing needs/special PR & marketing needs photo, web, press release, product, & video needs/invite of special guest/proclamations etc./awards/volunteers/transportation/traffic control/communication/etc.

Other:

Program Delivery Method
* Special *Event * Class *Workshop * Marketing strategy * Council/Commission report * Staff training
* Meeting * Other (list or describe):

Program Timeline

Projected number of customers impacted	Targeted customer demographics

Program evaluation methods - Quantitative and Qualitative: How will you measure results?

Figure 3.7 Manhattan Beach planning form (http://www.ci.manhattan-beach.ca.us/Index.aspx?page=183) Continued>>

City of Manhattan Beach, CA * VIP Program Planning Form (continued) (Adaptation. Original form by Mr. Idris Jassim al-Oboudi & Mr. Keith Fulthorp, 2004)	
Budget items	**Projected costs**
1. Staffing — a. Coordinator's time: # of hours	
b. Coordinator's cost:	
c. # of staff:	
d. # of hours: total	
e. Cost of staff: total	
2. Facilities — Rental of meeting/reception rooms/rental of:	
a. Chairs	
b. Tables	
c. Props	
d. Lectern	
e. Tent/canopy	
f. Lighting	
g. Special electrical hookups	
h. Set-up charges	
i. Clean-up charges	
3. Food Service — Number of people/cost per person for:	
a. Coffee	
b. Luncheon/dinner	
c. Cocktails	
d. Other beverages	
e. Linens	
4. Equipment Rental — a. Flooring/carpeting	
b. Risers	
c. Ropes/stanchions	
d. Desks/tools	
e. Portable toilets	
f. Booths	
g. Backdrop	
h. Trash containers	
i. Fencing	
5. Decorations — a. Flowers	
b. Table decorations	
c. Extra plants	
d. Candles	
e. Direction signs	
f. Ribbons/balloons	
g. Food service linens	
6. Design & Printing — a. Fee for design concept	
b. Invitations	
c. Programs/flyers/posters	
d. Tickets	
e. Maps	
f. Place cards/name cards	
g. Other printed materials	
7. Postage & Shipping — a. Postage for invitations	
b. Bulk mailing	
c. Mailing house charges	
d. Shipping	
8. Recognition Items — a. Awards, plaques	
b. Engraving	
c. Calligraphy	
d. Framing	
e. Give-a-ways	
9. Miscellaneous — a. Gifts	
b. Mementos	
c. Insurance	
d. First aid station	
e. Water hookups	

Figure 3.7 Manhattan Beach planning form (continued from previous page)

Outcomes, Goals, and Objectives

Outcomes are measures of the ultimate impact of programs and services on individuals and society, while *goals* are broad-based statements of intent. They indicate what an individual or organization wishes to accomplish in the future. They may be short-term, to be accomplished within a few months, or long-term, to be accomplished in a few years. When writing goals, all entities to whom the programmer has some level of accountability should be considered. Consequently, the programmer's goals will likely reflect some benefit to, or involvement with, the leisure services organization, self, coworkers, participants, and community members.

Objectives are specific statements of intent that give focus to service delivery and provide a basis for subsequent evaluation. Consequently, they must be measurable. When writing objectives the programmer takes a general statement and puts it into language that reflects specific behaviors to be undertaken. Similar to a good journalistic article, each objective should answer the questions "Who?" "What?" "When?" "How?" "Where?" and "To what degree?" in a succinct manner. Each goal will have one or more corresponding objectives that will specify how it is going to be accomplished. Goals and objectives are discussed in detail in Chapter Eleven.

While the foundation, direction, and reflection (FDR) concepts all have a role in guiding individuals and organizations, one of the concrete tools that recreation professionals can actually "hang onto" are goals and objectives. It is the goals and objectives that highlight a path toward the organization's vision and dictate the actions needed to get there. They also serve as a foundation for evaluation. By ignoring this step in the chain of concepts, we run the risk of "spinning our wheels" in spite of having a well-developed mission and vision. Goals and objectives also provide accountability and, using a servant leadership model, ensure that services and programs are targeted to meet constituent needs.

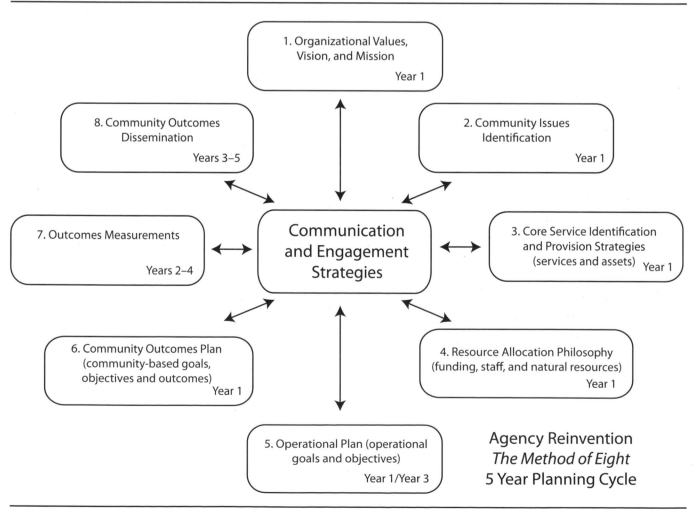

Figure 3.8 Method of Eight diagram (Sabbach, 2009)

Application of Outcomes, Goals, and Objectives

When writing outcomes it is important to remember that they should reflect the desired *ultimate* benefits to be achieved for individuals and the community. The following statements serve as examples of possible outcomes for a leisure services organization:

- To assist clients to achieve independence by successfully transitioning from a clinical therapeutic recreation setting into a community recreation setting.

- To decrease juvenile delinquency in the community.

- To enhance the professionalism of staff.

- To become the most visited resort in the region.

Each of these outcomes has a particular beneficiary, although there may be overlap since what benefits one entity is often beneficial to another. The first addresses the needs of participants, the second addresses the community, the third addresses staff members, and the fourth addresses the organization as a whole.

The next step in the process is to take each of the outcomes and write at least one goal that identifies an action statement, including the responsible person(s), and a target date to achieve the outcome. Using the outcomes listed in the previous paragraph, possible goals include:

- No later than one week prior to discharge, the CTRS will work with each client to develop an appropriate transition plan.

- The program supervisor will hold bimonthly leadership retreats at the Center for youth 12–15 years old.

- The program staff will attend one professional conference each year at the organization's expense.

- The marketing department will develop two 15-second television advertisements highlighting the resort features by March 30.

In actuality, most staff will write several goals for each outcome to increase the likelihood of success and utilize available resources to maximum benefit. Once the goals have been delineated, the programmer will develop even more specific action steps, or

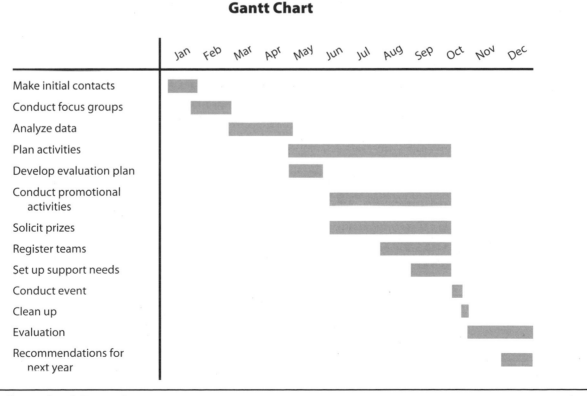

Figure 3.9 Example of Gantt chart

objectives, that will lead to accomplishing the goals and outcomes. Figure 3.11 illustrates the goals of a clinical therapeutic recreation program.

The Cyclical Programming Process

We presented the cyclical programming process in the previous chapter and reference it throughout the remainder of this text as a working framework for program planning. The cycle incorporates much of what we find in the other planning models, but it makes clear that programming is more than a start-and-stop activity. The model also reinforces the importance of gathering information before a program is designed (needs assessments and asset mapping) as well as during and after a program has been implemented (evaluation). Thus, a graphic representation of the programming process might look like a stretched-out coil or spring. The process is moving forward, and not simply repeating itself. A key element of the program process is that it is ongoing and based on what

has been learned from previous program efforts. The cyclical nature of this process enables practitioners to be responsive to social, cultural, and individual changes in needs and desires.

Interface of FDR Concepts

Principles (values and traditions), philosophy, and planning clearly support the FDR (Foundation, Direction, and Reflection) concepts that shape the decisions and actions of each recreation programmer as well as the organization in which she or he works. Likewise, programs and services reflect the philosophy, values, traditions, mission, vision, outcomes, goals, and objectives adopted by programmers and agencies.

As an example of this, let us look at a situation in which a consumer approaches a fitness trainer at a private health club pleading, "I can't stand myself anymore. I've tried everything to lose weight and get in shape and nothing works. Do something!" How the trainer responds to this request reveals a great deal about

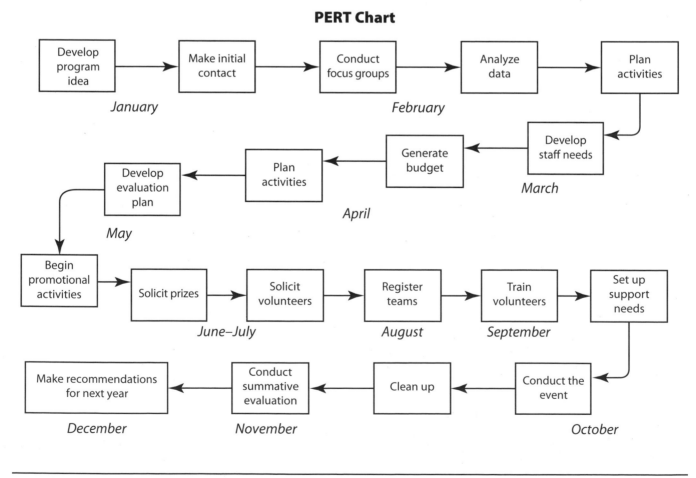

Figure 3.10 Example of PERT chart

her or his professional principles, values, philosophy, mission, vision, goals, and objectives. Suppose she or he responds saying, "You can be successful. I can support you, but within you is a trainer who can provide the motivation and discipline to make the changes you want." From such a statement we can extrapolate some of the driving beliefs and attitudes that influence this trainer. Values might include such things as empowerment of others, self-determination, and wellness. One philosophical statement we might attribute to the trainer is that human beings are incredibly resourceful and talented creatures. Her or his mission may be described as helping individuals feel better about themselves and enhance overall health. The trainer's vision might include something such as endeavoring to help each person reach her or his greatest potential and discover her or his inner resources. An example of a related goal would be to help the customer develop realistic objectives for weight loss and fitness improvement. Examples of objectives would be for the customer to read a particular motivational book within one week, and for the trainer and customer to cooperatively complete a fitness log to document details of activities as they are completed.

Compare the response of a different trainer who promises, "Don't worry about those other attempts. I'll shed those pounds and inches off you!" This trainer's FDR will be very different than the first trainer. Implied values might include authority and expertise; she or he might hold the philosophy that humans have little willpower or inner strength; and her or his mission might be to offer a carefully crafted training regimen that reflects her or his expertise and talents. Vision, goals, and objectives would reinforce

a similar message. Thus, it becomes very important for the recreation programmer to think through, design, develop, and evaluate a program plan with thoughtful consideration of the FDR concepts.

Implications for Recreation Programmers

When a parks, recreation, and leisure services professional applies and interviews for a job both the employer and employee share the responsibility to make a hiring decision that will result in a good fit between all parties. Thus, the employer will want to share organizational mission and vision statements with the applicant, and the applicant will want to share her or his views of the profession with the potential employer. Regardless of how creative and skilled the applicant is, an obvious incongruence between the organization and programmer will undoubtedly present problems.

Suppose the organization is an art museum located in a white-collar, urban neighborhood that perceives its mission is to provide a safe and aesthetic environment for working professionals to appreciate. In particular, the museum supports small area businesses by providing a convenient and pleasant environment for their employees to visit, thereby reducing stress and improving well-being. Furthermore, the art museum staff highly value the cultural benefits they provide to the local business community. In contrast, a job applicant to the museum indicates that she is committed to increasing the cultural and social skills of adolescents from low socioeconomic groups, particularly through hands-on discovery-based activities. In this case, while both parties may value what

---

Goals of the Therapeutic Recreation Program at the University of Iowa Hospitals & Clinics

- Educate patients in skills and resources to enhance stress management and contribute to personal growth
- Reduce anxiety, stress, and other effects of hospitalization through a spectrum of goal-directed activities
- Enable patients to meet challenges and overcome barriers in order to reinforce self-esteem
- Provide emotional support to patients and their family members
- Assist patients with adaptation of coping skills based on their cognitive, affective, physical, and psychosocial needs
- Afford patients opportunities for creative expression and other forms of communication
- Offer choices, giving patients more control over their environment
- Assist patients in planning for discharge needs

Source: http://www.uihcalthcare.com/depts/rehabilitationtherapies/therapeuticrecreation/goals.html

Figure 3.11 Goals for a clinical therapeutic recreation setting the other believes to be important, they will likely be incompatible due to differing priorities. However, a job applicant who expresses an interest in challenging local business executives by providing art appreciation classes shares priorities with the museum and demonstrates values congruent with the agency.

The Servant Leadership Perspective

The importance of the FDR concepts cannot be overstated as they address one of the greatest criticisms leveled at servant leaders. This criticism stems from the view that by waiting and empowering people, servant leaders abdicate their power and lose the opportunity to truly shape an organization by their vision of the agency's potential. Because of this, some view servant leadership as a "feel good" approach that results in pleasant sentiments and thoughts about the organization, but does not provide an energizing vision of the future (DeGraaf, Neal & Tilley, 2004)

We believe that this view of servant leadership overemphasizes the idea of the servant and ignores the power of the creative interface between these seemingly opposite ideas of servant leadership. In Chapter One, we identified a number of characteristics of servant leadership. Many of these characteristics lend themselves more to either being a servant or a leader. However, the true power (and the ultimate challenge) of servant leadership is blending the characteristics of being a servant and leader together. Remember, balance does not have to mean either/or (one or the other), it is but/and (inclusive of multiple views). In this light, the characteristics of conceptualization and foresight are particularly important as they relate to FDR. The challenge for servant leaders in terms of developing the concepts of FDR is to balance the need to empower others with the need to be strong, visionary, transformational leaders. Servant leadership demands that leaders are aware of their own values, that they listen to others, are able to conceptualize the big picture, and able to persuade and empower others to lend their own talents in fulfilling the mission of the organization. In this way, servant leaders are not victims of their organizations and the people they lead; they are the co-creators of the future. They must seek to find ways to create situations that ensure that all concerned—leader, staff, organization, and constituent—survive and thrive.

As we examine the FDR concepts from the perspective of servant leadership in more detail, let's first look at a diagram that captures some of the relationships between FDR concepts as defined by a servant leadership philosophy (see Figure 3.12). In this diagram, servant leadership serves as the core foundation of developing a program and leisure organization. It affects the values and vision that are developed as well as how other aspects of the organization are designed. We can see how participants are empowered, organizational structure is responsive to changes (i.e., agile), the community is utilized and supported through networking and partnerships, and leaders demonstrate empathy and compassion. The result of this is the delivery of quality services and energized staff, participants, and programs.

In the following section, we further illustrate how to apply this philosophy to parks, recreation, and leisure programming by describing several servant leadership values and attributes presented in Chapter One: accountability (reflected in the characteristic of stewardship), empathy, diversity, community, integrity, empowerment, and service (as related to the characteristic of commitment to the growth of people).

Accountability

One factor closely tied to the FDR concepts is organizational structure. For example, is the agency organized as a strict hierarchy or does it utilize a peer management structure? How does the structure reflect and influence the program philosophy? Are consumers part of the structure in any way? In 1997, Godbey proposed that all organizations become more "agile" in response to the rate of change we face in society. He characterized an agile organization as one that deals with customers' changing needs and desires; develops the knowledge, skills, and creativity of staff; distributes authority, decision-making expertise, initiative, and expertise throughout the organization; and fosters leadership, trust, and motivation rather than control and command.

If we apply the perspective of servant leadership to organizational structure, we may recognize that at times mission and vision need to start at the "top of the organizational pyramid." However, during implementation, it is essential that the pyramid be inverted. This ensures that energy and attention continue to flow toward constituents rather than agency administrators. If, for instance, in a traditional hierarchical structure staff perceive themselves working for the person above them, when we invert the pyramid, staff quickly realize they are now "working for" the constituent. Traditionally, administrators are perceived as *responsible* and staff are perceived as *responsive* to those at the top. By turning the pyramid upside down, the constituents or consumers become *responsible* and the staff are *responsive* to them. Creating this structure enables the servant leader to give constituent needs and desires primary consideration in all she or he does.

Empathy

In addition to conducting a formal needs assessment and asset mapping, one dimension of knowing consumer needs and desires is being able to empathize with them. Servant leaders must be willing to genuinely and actively listen and learn from all constituents. As servant leaders, when we listen, we should be asking ourselves reflective questions such as:

- Am I aware of the nonverbal messages I send and how they impact others?

- What cultural biases do I have that interfere with my ability to listen authentically?

- How am I responding to the nonverbal communication of those to whom I am listening?

- Do I understand the speaker's ideas; do I check my understanding with the person to whom I am listening?
- Am I listening for and aware of the feelings a person may experience when sharing her or his thoughts and feelings?

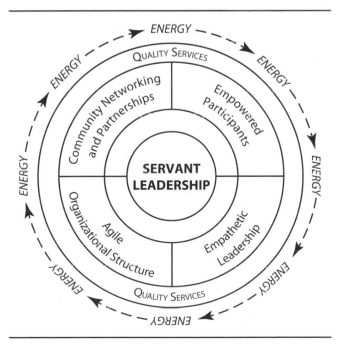

Figure 3.12 Servant leadership as applied to FDR concepts

- Do I have all the information I need to listen fully?

In addition, servant leaders need to be able to see issues from multiple perspectives. As the old adage states, "We should walk a mile in someone else's shoes before we judge them." These skills are important for our interactions with coworkers, as well as with customers and potential participants. Once we know what others want or need, we can then mobilize ourselves to act accordingly, including being prepared to get in the trenches and do what we ask of others. This can be quite a challenge as it involves identifying and understanding crosscultural issues and putting aside our own preconceived ideas about people, roles, biases, and prejudices.

Diversity

Since servant leadership is committed to the dignity and worth of all people and promotes diversity, recreation programmers with a servant leader orientation must search to find ways to accommodate participants who have a variety of abilities, varied backgrounds, and beliefs. This includes actions such as hiring a diverse staff that represents people of various ethnic backgrounds, utilizing graphics and terminology in marketing materials that demonstrate cultural competence, confronting participants and coworkers when they tell sexist jokes, offering mixed ability programs, scheduling programs at times and locations that are accessible to a variety of constituents, and other actions that protect the rights of all participants for equal access and participation in leisure programs.

Community

A leisure services organization that adopts a servant-leadership philosophy must consider beneficial outcomes of service to the community in addition to the organization and individual constituents. This responsibility to community reflects the servant leader's value for relationships and commitment to "a greater whole." This may take the form of networking with other leisure organizations, forming partnerships in all sectors of society, and referring constituents to the most appropriate organization to meet their needs—even competitors. By maximizing resources within the entire community, recreation programmers are able to provide variety and creativity in programs and services.

Integrity

In a world that seems to be increasingly bombarded with accusations of impropriety and challenges to standards of ethics, it is critical that servant leaders in the parks, recreation, and leisure services profession maintain a high level of integrity. Most importantly this involves being forthright, truthful, and responsible to constituents. Regardless of how dazzling a brochure, creative an idea, or exciting an event, a program is only as valuable as the leader's ability to be straightforward and honest with constituents. Furthermore, these types of behaviors reinforce participants' sense of dignity and being treated fairly. Integrity also relates to our financial dealings, actions that reflect stewardship of the environment, and equity in dealings with all people.

Empowerment

Programmers of leisure experiences can use a variety of techniques to empower participants. This may take the form of compiling customer opinions through surveys, interviews, and group meetings and using that information to make decisions. Participants may also be involved with governing committees and boards, such as city or county parks and recreation advisory boards. Even very young participants can be involved in the development and implementation of programs by offering suggestions about what they want to do and selecting programs from choices offered. When we involve participants through multiple avenues we help them to gain a sense of ownership; further, we provide services that are more responsive to customer needs.

Service

While the component of service to servant leadership may seem obvious, it is still helpful to examine this value and how it can be incorporated into leisure programs. Service involves a conscious effort to help those who are less privileged in our society. The less privileged frequently include the same people who are consistently underserved in parks, recreation, and leisure services. These are individuals who might not have transportation to program sites; people who have little (if any) discretionary income; those with mental health issues, and those who do not speak English (e.g., recent immigrants). Thus, programmers are challenged to be creative not only in the design of programs, but also in the delivery of programs and services—location, tim-

ing, staffing, and so on. Servant leadership reminds us that it is not just the public and nonprofit sectors that are called upon to serve all people. The leisure services programmer who works at a commercial amusement or theme park (for example) can serve others in such ways as establishing senior discounts, translating brochures and signs into multiple languages, and providing transportation to program sites.

Summary

Principles, values, traditions, and a philosophy are necessary for continued success of programs and organizations. They provide a foundation, direction, and something upon which staff reflect as they develop programs and services. To be most effective, a philosophy statement should reflect the values and beliefs that individuals deem important. When planning, implementing, and evaluating programs, staff will want to fully consider their personal philosophies and the agency philosophy with regard to resources, finances, staffing, participants, and organizational structure. If done consistently, programs based on these foundations will reflect not just attitudes about leisure, but also attitudes about time, communication, authority, diversity, and other social attributes, and will minimize conflict caused by incongruent philosophies. It is important to remember that programs and services that are *not* offered are often indicators of an individual and/or organization's philosophy, just as much as programs that *are* offered. Philosophy statements serve the foundation for developing mission and vision statements as well as goals and objectives. The servant leader-programmer is challenged to find ways to address the needs of all parties—organization, employees, and constituents—including those not represented on a day-to-day basis.

Many elements of an organization go into developing and working with a philosophy. Values, tradition, mission, vision, and goals and objectives are integral to a parks, recreation, and leisure services organization and the way it operates. We presented some basic planning models to aid in the design, implementation, and evaluation of programs and services. All programmers engage in the same tasks when designing and implementing programs. Those tasks include: being knowledgeable about the organizational mission and philosophy; conducting asset and needs assessments; planning and designing the program; engaging in pre-program activities such as pricing, promotion, and staffing; implementing the program; conducting formative evaluations;

making adjustments in the program based on those evaluations; and conducting a summative evaluation. The cycle is then continued by conducting additional needs assessments and continuing the programming process from there. Understanding how these concepts apply to planning and programming will facilitate programming from a servant leader perspective. That perspective directly relates to accountability through programming, as well as the values of empathy, diversity, community, integrity, empowerment, and service.

Programming from Here to There

The Washington State Parks and Recreation Commission created a Winter Recreation Strategic Plan 2008-2018, which may be found in its entirety online (Washington State Parks, 2009). Staff intend to use the plan to guide the management of the winter recreation program for the next seven years; public input was solicited at several stages during the planning process. Below is the executive summary from that plan—it provides an overview of the planning process and steps to come.

EXECUTIVE SUMMARY

Why a Strategic Plan?
- The last planning exercise completed by the Winter Recreation Program was in 1992.
- Program funding has stagnated, overcrowding is reported, and use conflicts are occurring.
- Staff, advisory committee members, and users alike recognize that it is time to do an evaluation, identify needs, and set clear and achievable goals for the future.
- To align the Winter Recreation Program with the Centennial 2013 Plan.

What the Plan seeks to accomplish.
- Clear expression of constituents' desires for the program in the years to come.
- Bolster program funding, with special attention to the nonmotorized program.
- Strengthen relationships with advisory committees and volunteers.
- Increase emphasis on customer service.
- Right-size the Sno-Park system.
- Better integrate the Winter Recreation Program into the agency.
- Review management and operational practices.
- Enhance local control of service deliver.

Plan Elements

Mission:
The mission of the Winter Recreation Program is to provide a variety of snow-based winter recreational opportunities to the public while protecting natural and cultural resources throughout the state.

Vision:
The Winter Recreation Program is a well-managed and respected program of the Washington State Parks and Recreation Commission providing effective and efficient service that: 1) is responsive to the recreational demands of the public; 2) facilitates public access to diverse snow-based recreational opportunities; 3) encourages responsible use and protection of natural and cultural resources; and 4) is closely integrated into the communities it serves through effective relationships with volunteers, local governments, and private property owners.

Upper Level Objectives and Supplementary Goals:

1. **Access to snow-based recreation will be our primary product.**
- Recreational access opportunities are responsive to user demands while reflecting sensitive environmental stewardship.
- The Program has viable planning functions.
- There is adequate separation of incompatible or conflicting recreational uses.
- Well-maintained, clearly signed and usable parking areas and trails, accurate maps.
- Effective, safe trail grooming is provided.

2. **We will build enduring partnerships.**
- A vigorous, organized, skilled, and respected volunteer program.
- Viable Advisory Committees that are regarded as full partners.

3. **We will maintain open and responsive communications with the public.**
- Safety, education, and resource stewardship are high priorities.
- We provide accurate and up to date information to the public.

- We respond to complaints and disputes in a timely and sensitive manner.

4. **We will exercise transparent decision making, with clear, understandable, and concisely written procedures, practices, grants, and contracts.**
- We actively involve people in decisions that affect them, and help people participate by providing them with credible, timely, and objective information.
- We employ effective contract management principles and techniques, and maintain high standards of financial accountability and management effectiveness, including responsive budgeting and clear financial reporting.

5. **We will manage public resources in a consistent and responsible manner.**
- Winter Recreation services are adequately and equitably funded.
- We plan ahead to compensate for variables that affect service delivery.

Implementation Strategies

The plan includes an extensive list of strategies to accomplish the above goals. The list is so extensive that there is no expectation that, by simply adopting the plan, the Commission will be able to implement each and every one of these strategies. The current funding problems and the state budget climates may preclude that possibility. However, the list should be considered a menu of desires and opportunities that could be pursued in the future. Certainly, not all of the strategies can be applied, even over the next ten years, and it is likely that, as plan implementation is underway, a number of the strategies will not be considered. New strategies will also be discovered and can be incorporated into the plan, which should remain flexible and be reviewed regularly. Evaluation and application of strategies should be incorporated into annual work plans for staff and advisory committees. Because of current funding limitations, those that can be engaged at little or no cost should be the first to be considered, and may result in revenue benefits to the program that will enable pursuit of more expensive strategies.

References

Atchinson, G. (2007). *Values congruency: A qualitative investigation into how first level managers view congruence between personal and corporate values*. Unpublished dissertation, Capella University, UMI Microform 3263174.

Brown, W., Yoshioka, C. & Munoz, P. (2004). Organizational mission as a core dimension in employee retention, *Journal of Park and Recreation Administration, 22*(2), 28–43.

Camp Courage. (2008). Retrieved March 4, 2009, from http://www.couragecamps.org/index.htm

City of Manhattan Beach (2008). *Core values*. Retrieved January 18, 209 from http://www.ci.manhattan-beach.ca.us/Index.aspx?page=183

DeGraaf, D., Neal, L. & Tilley, C. (2004). *Voices of servant leadership series—Essay 6*. Indianapolis, IN: Greenleaf Center for Servant Leadership.

Godbey, G. (1997). *Leisure and leisure services in the 21st century*. State College, PA: Venture Publishing, Inc.

Kellogg Foundation. (2004). *Logic model development guide*. Retrieved March 4, 2009, from www.wkkf.org/Pubs/Tools/Evaluation/Pub3669.pdf

Sabbach, J. (2009). *Method of Eight planning cycle*. Unpublished document.

Scared Earth. (2009). Retrieved January 9, 2010, from http://www.sacredearth-travel.com/philosophy.php

Texas State University. (n.d.). *Campus Recreation mission/vision statement*. Retrieved on March 4, 2009 from http://www.campusrecreation.txstate.edu/about/mission.html

Washington State Parks. (2009). *Winter recreation strategic planning process*. Retrieved March 4, 2009, from http://www.parks.wa.gov/winter/strategy/

Wells, M. & Arthur-Banning, S. (2008). The logic of youth development: Constructing a logic model of youth development through sport. *Journal of Park and Recreation Administration, 26*(2), 189–202.

YMCA Camp Oakes. (2009). Retrieved February 10, 2009, from http://www.campoakes.org/rags/

Programmer Profile

Photo provided by Carolyn Griffith

Carolyn Griffith

Current Position: Recreation Superintendent for the City of Casper, Wyoming
Favorite Recreation Activities: Golf and racquetball
Certifications: Certified Park and Recreation Professional (CPRP)

▶ **Describe the path your career has taken.**

- Graduated with a B.S. in Education in Health and Physical Education from Slippery Rock University in Pennsylvania
- Places I have worked include: City of Milford, Delaware Parks and Recreation Department; Holy Cross High School-Delaware; and the City of Dover, Delaware Parks and Recreation Department
- I currently work with youth and adults for the City of Casper, Wyoming Leisure Services Department. In my role of Recreation Superintendent I supervise, plan, and coordinate the activities and operations of the Recreation Division within the Leisure Services Department; coordinate assigned activities with other divisions, outside agencies, and the general public. A few examples of duties and responsibilities of the position include: coordinating the organization, staffing, and operational activities of the Recreation Division including the Casper Recreation Center, Casper Ice Arena, Casper Aquatics Center and Outdoor Pools, sports, and special programs; participating in the development, recommendation, and implementation of goals, objectives, policies, and priorities for the Recreation Division; identification of resource needs; the application of several aspects of Recreation Division staffing and personnel management; the identification of opportunities for improving service delivery methods and procedures; participation in the development and administration of the Recreation program budget; and the coordination of new construction and renovation projects.

▶ **Describe the joys of working in your current position.**

The most rewarding part of my job is when I have the opportunities to walk through our recreational facilities and see so many people participating in the variety of classes, programs, activities, events, or leagues that we offer. We are very fortunate in Casper to have so many wonderful recreational facilities.

▶ Do you have any advice for new programmers?

Prior to offering any class or activity, we evaluate the program for viability within the community. Once the legwork has been completed to determine that there is a need/want for a program or activity to be offered in the community, spend the time to develop a marketing strategy and carry it through. Even though citizens may wish to participate in a program, they still have to make the conscious choice of what to do with their leisure time. Grab their attention. Identify the values of participation and include those in the marketing message either directly or indirectly.

▶ What is the most creative program you have developed?

One Pitch Softball Tournament—The games are run just as a regular softball game except a batter only gets one pitch each time she or he is at the plate. The pitch results in either a hit, walk, strike-out/foul-out. Three games are guaranteed at a minimum for each team's entry in a tournament situation. Although seven innings are played, game time is minimized because it doesn't take long for each inning.

▶ What are the community benefits of recreation programs?

There are a number of different benefits that programs can provide. For example, the annual Casper Youth Basketball Tournament provides a great deal of economic benefit to the community. The event, annually held in Casper, Wyoming each March, is a fairly typical youth basketball tournament for girls and boys in grades 4-9. Over the past 17 years, an average of 135 teams have participated each year. Eighty-five percent of the teams that enter the tournament are out of town visitors. For a fairly isolated community of fewer than 50,000, the economic impact of 1,500+ visitors is significant. In addition, a small admission fee is charged at the entrances to the gyms and novelty items are sold at all sites. Proceeds generated from the tournament are turned over to the Community Recreation Foundation. The Community Recreation Foundation provides scholarships and free programs for youth 21 years and under, and adults 55 and over, to participate in recreation programs or to purchase recreation facility annual passes. So, although the event itself seems like the attraction, the local community benefits most positively through the economic impact of the visitors and the availability of scholarships and free programs for residents.

▶ Describe a program example that demonstrates a servant leadership philosophy.

A recent program that our agency has been developing is the Casper After School Program for Education and Recreation, C.A.S.P.E.R. for short. I feel that this program demonstrates a number of components that flow from a servant leadership philosophy. First, the program is addressing a number of needs in our community by offering free access for youth to a variety of recreational games and activities at the Casper Recreation Center after school hours. In addition, C.A.S.P.E.R. has developed several goals including: 1) engage C.A.S.P.E.R. participants in activities that are perhaps new to them, challenging, and fun; and 2) provide opportunities for employees and middle school students to lead while learning.

Second, the program has developed partnerships on many different levels. For example, local community college students are brought into the program as employees to plan, organize, and lead each day's activities. Professional recreation division staff provide resources for the C.A.S.P.E.R. staff to use in the organization and development of a course of activities for the youth who attend. In addition, staff are currently developing a mentoring program for middle school students to assist with C.A.S.P.E.R. activities while developing skills to lead group activities. Interested students from a nearby middle school are solicited for their interest in recreation leadership opportunities. These middle school students are then paired with C.A.S.P.E.R. employees to work together to introduce younger participants to new games and activities.

Lastly, the program has provided a model of stewardship by developing a shared model of funding for the program. Funding for C.A.S.P.E.R. is a cooperative effort between the City of Casper, the Natrona County School District, and the Community Recreation Foundation.

Asset Mapping and Needs Assessments | 4

In the program process cycle (which identifies the tasks to be undertaken in program development) the agency philosophy, mission, and vision are at the center, or heart, of all programming tasks. In addition, we take the approach that servant leadership and participant empowerment are important foundations upon which all parks, recreation, and leisure services entities build recreation and leisure programs. Thus, it becomes important to remind ourselves that potential participants and the community are the focus of our programs—not our organization or agency.

In this light, it becomes critically important that we involve participants and community members in the programming process. The first step in the program process cycle is designed just for this type of input. Asset mapping and conducting needs assessments enable leisure professionals to seek out community, citizen, and participant input about programming resources, ideas, desires, and needs of various constituent groups. These two processes (needs assessments and asset mapping) are *systematic inquiries into the skills, talents, experience levels, needs, attitudes, and behaviors of both participants and non-participants* (in this case, related to parks, recreation, and leisure services).

For many, the concept of *needs assessment* suggests a negative perspective—when we conduct a needs assessment we are looking for liabilities, deficiencies, or gaps in a community which we then try to "fix" or fill with programs. *Asset mapping,* on the other hand, is a process we undertake to learn about the positive attributes (skills, talents, resources) that exist within a community. Assets are "the positive strengths, qualities, merits, benefits, virtues, commodities, and character embedded in a community. They can be individual, organisational, and institutional" (Community Strengthening Branch, 2006). Assets also involve the relationships that exist among individuals, organizations, and institutions (Kretzman, McKnight, Dobrowolski, & Puntenney, 2005). Taken together,

asset mapping and needs assessments can provide a solid foundation on which to build programs.

Asset mapping, which was first conceptualized by Kretzman and McKnight (1993), is an effort we undertake to learn about the capacities, skills, and resources of individual citizens, informal community associations (such as a local garden club or homeowners' association), and formal institutions such as educational systems, medical service centers, local government, and human services agencies. Periodically assessing our community assets enables us to remain in touch with what is available to our citizenry and our agency, and highlights strengths upon which we can build.

Needs assessments and asset maps are conducted early in the programming cycle and are repeated often throughout the program process. The information we collect from both asset mapping and assessing needs should be used intentionally to help support individuals, groups, and the community as a whole. In addition to presenting several definitions of terms related to these processes, this chapter will discuss the importance of assessing assets and needs, and share a variety of ways in which information about assets and needs might be gathered.

Definitions

It is our firm belief that before beginning any effort to explain why and how something is done, it is important to come to an agreement on terminology. This section provides an overview of the meanings for common terms used in asset mapping and needs assessments as related to the field of parks, recreation, and leisure. These are the meanings used throughout the remainder of the text. In addition, they will set the stage for further explanation of the program process cycle.

Asset

An asset is the opposite of a liability—it is something we have, and includes positive attributes and strengths (skills, talents, resources) that exist within a person or community. These resources are valued by most and we often hold the expectation that making use of these assets will lead to future benefits. A fundamental component of community assets are the positive relationships between people, groups, and institutions. Common usage suggests that an asset is a useful or desirable thing or quality. Thus, in a particular parks, recreation, and leisure services organization/agency our assets could include our staff, facilities, equipment, policies, programs, partnerships, parks, and open spaces.

Conducting an asset inventory is one way to determine the strength of the assets in our community. In Chapter Five, we present a framework developed by the Search Institute to indentify important assets for youth. Through years of research, the Search Institute has identified 40 development assets—20 external to an individual and 20 internal to an individual—that make a difference in the positive growth of youth. Others have taken a broader approach to identifying assets, considering individual, group, and institutional assets.

Asset Mapping

Asset mapping is the process a programmer undertakes to identify and record the existence of assets throughout the community. A graphic map is sometimes used (along with Geographic Information Systems [GIS] and Global Positioning System [GPS]) data, but a detailed drawing of a community is not necessary to map assets. Asset mapping includes mapping/inventorying social capital (people and relationships), cultural resources (partnerships and networks), enterprising interests (local businesses and physical resources), and personal information (knowledge, expertise, experience) about our constituents (Beaulieu, 2002; Community Strengthening Branch, 2006). When placed on an actual map of the community, we can easily see the physical relationships and relative locations of the assets throughout the community. This can help in facilitating additional links and in deploying assets in needed areas of the community.

Comparative Need

It is very common for individuals from one community or geographic area to compare parks, recreation, and leisure opportunities available to them to those available to others living in nearby geographic areas. These are considered comparative needs. Comparative needs may exist due to differences in leisure opportunities because of geographic location, work shift differences, available facilities and spaces, finances, or due to social values (e.g., girls and boys are often offered different athletic opportunities). Through this comparison, an individual (or community) may discover that she or he is lacking in parks, recreation, and leisure opportunities, and thus, a comparative need is created.

Need

Most people probably think they know what a need is—they get a certain feeling when they are in need, and they tend to act in a particular way to satisfy that need. As examples, people believe that needs drive or motivate them to go running, buy something, call someone, or go on vacation. With the very complex society in which people live, however, and the wonderful marketing efforts of manufacturers and producers, people often think they *need* something when, in fact, that need is really a strong desire. Most people could live quite well, for instance, without that new pair of athletic shoes they saw on television that they think they "need."

A need is something that motivates or drives individuals to act in a certain way; and, once the need is met it no longer serves as a driving force for behavior. Furthermore, a need is born out of a physical, psychological, emotional, spiritual, or social deficiency an individual is currently experiencing. These are basic human need categories and affect all people in all cultures.

Normative Need

"Objective" needs that are established by experts in the field and relate to what humans require for good health and quality of life are known as normative needs. These needs are sometimes defined by a discrepancy analysis (i.e., what is needed minus what exists) based on expert opinion (Rossman & Schlatter, 2008). One example that relates directly to our field is the National Recreation and Park Association (NRPA) open space guidelines, which outline how much of a particular type of green space is needed for a specific number of people living in a community (e.g., a large park of five acres per 1,000 people serves citizens living within a one- to two-mile radius). These standards also recommend a certain number of swimming areas per capita (e.g., one pool with 8,000 to 10,000 square feet of surface water for every 20,000 persons), museums, golf courses, campgrounds, and other parks, recreation, and leisure amenities (Castleman, n.d.).

Normative needs are often used in city or community planning when issues of master planning arise. As different lands are zoned commercial, residential, or agricultural, these normative needs may be used to define the desire to preserve space for parks, recreation, and leisure services to enhance the population's quality of life. Normative needs are also used to justify changes in physical resources (e.g., new construction) for various leisure organizations.

Want/Desire

As mentioned earlier, many have difficulty in discerning the difference between a need and a want or desire. Part of the difficulty is that a want or desire is typically something that people perceive as being needed. However, it does not necessarily address the physical, psychological, emotional, spiritual, or social needs of being human. Wants and desires are culturally learned and are influenced by social fads and trends. In addition, they are often based on previous experience and knowledge. For example, people might experience a *need* for physical activity. Interests, experiences, skills, friends, existing social mores, and current trends influence whether an individual wants to go skateboarding or go for a walk to satisfy that need. Another example might be having a need for achievement. To meet that need one person might want to paint a picture while another prefers to engage in a competitive activity. One of the paradoxes of satisfying a want or desire is that satisfaction often leads to wanting more. This particularly becomes a dilemma when the desire is for a material thing and satisfying the need leads to wanting more.

◆ ◆ ◆

It is important for those who provide leisure services to understand the difference between assets, wants, and needs because they require different questions to be asked as part of the planning process. And, people will provide different types of responses depending upon the questions asked in the asset reviews and needs assessments. In addition, leisure services providers would want to be sure they learned about assets and needs in addition to learning about wants. Understanding these various characteristics of constituents will greatly influence programming efforts. Without knowing something about the constituent base leisure services professionals may be "programming in the dark."

Why Do Asset Mapping and Needs Assessments?

As mentioned at the beginning of this chapter, once leisure services professionals have a firm understanding of the organizational philosophy, conducting an asset review and needs assessment is the next step in the cyclical programming process. It is apparent, however, that many practitioners in the field begin the programming process without ever having conducted such assessments. This can be problematic because without the information gathered from these assessments, recreation and leisure services programmers are missing a vital aspect of providing appropriate programs and services for participants. For instance, programmers will not know if their

---

asset
(as´et), *n.* A useful or desirable thing or quality. In parks, recreation, and leisure service organizations assets include staff, facilities, equipment, policies, and programs

comparative need
(kəm par´ ə tiv nēd), *n.* To compare parks, recreation, and leisure opportunities available to oneself to those available to others living in nearby geographic areas.

created need
(krē āt´ id nēd), *n.* Determined by the agency or organization and accepted by participants without question. Clever marketing and promotion creates a need where none existed and is supported (and identified as a need) by constituents.

expressed need
(ik spres´ d nēd), *n.* These needs are defined by the activities in which people are currently participating.

felt need
(felt nēd), *n.* A felt need is an expressed need that hasn't happened yet. In other words, these are desires a person has, but has not yet actively expressed.

intention
(in ten´ shən), *n.* This has been described as the commitment to engage in specific actions that will address what a person wants under given market conditions.

interest
(in´ tər ist, –trist), *n.* This has been explained as an attraction to or identification with some type of experience.

need
(nēd), *n.* A need is something that drives us to act in a certain way; and, once the need is met it no longer serves as a driving force for behavior. Furthermore, a need is born out of a physical, psychological, emotional, spiritual, or social deficiency we are currently experiencing.

normative need
(nôr´ mə tiv nēd), *n.* "Objective" needs established by experts in the field and related to what humans require for good health and a modicum of quality of life.

want/desire
(wont, wônt; di zī° r´), *n.* Wants and desires are culturally learned and are influenced by social fads and trends.

Figure 4.1 Definitions of needs-related terms

efforts truly meet the needs and desires of constituents; thus, programmers will not know if programs and services contribute to the development of assets in the constituents and the community. Programs will be offered "because it's always been done that way" or out of convenience rather than based on any knowledge of constituent interests, wants, needs, or strengths. A parks, recreation, and leisure services professional has a duty to learn as much as possible about her or his community and constituents—both those who currently participate in activities and those who do not participate in activities—so the services provided are meaningful and result in benefits for all.

Asset reviews and needs assessments are conducted for a variety of reasons. All of the reasons should be reflective of a commitment on the part of the professional to best serve all of her or his constituents within the scope of the organizational mission or philosophy. This foundation helps to meet the goals of servant leadership. We provide several reasons for conducting asset inventories and needs assessments in the following section (see Figure 4.2).

Service Orientation/Participant Empowerment

We strongly believe that parks, recreation, and leisure services professionals have an opportunity to make a profound impact on people from all walks of life. From a position of servant leadership and with an attitude of empowering participants through leisure, asset inventories and needs assessments are the media through which leisure professionals begin to effectively and meaningfully engage others in dialogue. By empowering individuals to contribute to meeting their leisure needs, leisure programmers participate in the program process *with* them (rather than *for* them). This is true no matter an organization's profit orientation or leisure setting (e.g., commercial, military, therapeutic recreation). Several elements of empowerment are discussed in the following section.

To Build Interdependence and Collaboration

If providers act on their desire and belief in constituent empowerment as servant leadership demands, they will provide opportunities to learn about the community and for meaningful input by all of their constituents. Opportunities to co-create, collaborate, and coordinate with constituents can be beneficial to both the participant and the leisure professional. Asset reviews and needs assessments serve as opportunities for current

users and nonusers to influence the programming cycle. Leisure services professionals might solicit input regarding pricing (based on the economic asset information collected), promotion (based on the enterprising experience of the community), allocation of resources (based on understanding physical assets in the community), purchases, facilities, activities, and other elements of programming. All of this input, both as a part of the asset mapping process and the needs assessment process provide vital information to parks, recreation, and leisure services providers.

These two types of assessment are also used as a way to generate new program ideas. By asking the people who are in the service area about their skills, knowledge, and talents as well as ideas they have for enhancing, changing, or developing new programs, professionals can greatly enhance what they do. All individuals increase the breadth and diversity of ideas and viewpoints by asking people outside of one's agency or organization for ideas and thoughts. In addition, this question-asking process helps a professional to be culturally relevant.

The dialogue and focused conversations that arise out of exploring assets and asking about needs tends to enhance relationships with individuals and groups in the community. This can be crucial in times when an organization or agency needs support for a new endeavor, bond issue, or an increase in resources. One thing is certain in this dialogue effort—if professionals ask for input, they must demonstrate that they are utilizing that input. If the information gathered is not evident in the programming efforts, people will feel used and stop responding.

To Solicit Responses to New Ideas

Parks, recreation, and leisure services professionals tend to be creative people who desire to be innovative in their work. One way to do this is to develop and test new programming opportunities for various people in our communities. By trying out and asking for feedback about creative program ideas, professionals gain from the knowledge and experience of others. Asset mapping and needs assessments are tools that enable leisure services providers to do this. Programmers can solicit feedback about program ideas prior to implementation or conduct a pilot test of a program and then gather input about it. This is where the adage, "two (or more) heads are better than one" comes in to play.

To Ensure Inclusion

Serving people (i.e., delivering parks, recreation, and leisure services) is the crux of the profession, whether as part of a nonprofit, commercial, or community venture. In this respect, inclusion of all people is critical to meeting the goals of service and empowerment. By being inclusive of all people, regardless of sex, age, physical abilities and qualities, sexual orientation, race/ethnicity, religion, education level, socioeconomic status, and other aspects of diversity, leisure professionals promote inclusion and equality.

Inclusion can only occur once a programmer has determined the assets and needs of the many constituent groups in the community—this is accomplished by involving community members in the asset inventory and needs assessment processes. It is especially important for parks, recreation, and leisure services professionals to learn about various cultural groups (based on *all* the elements of diversity). Learning about others' values, beliefs, preferences, and cultural influences enables leisure services providers to be culturally responsive in a way that is meaningful to our entire constituent base.

For instance, it is too easy for an individual who is able-bodied and ambulatory to think that the reason there are never any people who use wheelchairs in the fitness/weight room facility is that they are not interested in lifting weights. It is not until an individual either puts her or himself in a chair to experience the facility, or has a guest who uses a wheelchair come in and try it, that he or she realizes that there may be no way to transfer out of a chair and onto the equipment. In this scenario, people who use wheelchairs may not use the facility because they cannot, not because they choose not to do so. This improved understanding, of course, could change one's entire view of programming in this area—there may very well be a need for an accessible fitness room. A needs assessment and asset review that solicits information from *all* constituents throughout the community can be quite revealing.

To Meet the Real Needs of Constituents

A servant leadership approach to programming requires that professionals be in tune with the real needs of people. Leisure services providers should strive to clearly identify the issues, skills, barriers, and desire for

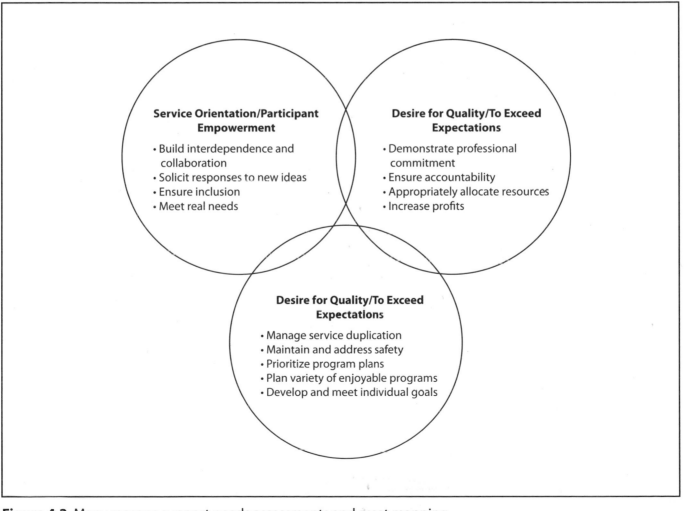

Figure 4.2 Many reasons support needs assessments and asset mapping

growth of their constituent base. These skills, needs, and concerns may include physiological needs such as food, water, and physical safety; psychological needs of achievement, self-esteem, and identity; socioemotional needs of belonging, love, and affection; and spiritual needs of knowing a power greater than us. Some of the needs such as health, economic standing, status, and personal skill development may easily be addressed through programming efforts. By orienting oneself toward the entire constituent base and using the information learned from the asset mapping process, one can be attentive to and responsive to the real needs of her or his community.

One aspect of the leisure services field in particular—therapeutic recreation—uses asset mapping and needs assessments (often at intake or initial screening) to identify client health status, strengths and opportunities, family and friend support structures, and interests to determine the appropriateness and use of selected activities in therapy. Inclusion specialists do something similar in working to meet the needs of community-based special needs clients. Assessments are also used to determine the specific tasks or activities needed for successful task intervention at various levels. In this capacity, assessments of assets and needs are extremely individualistic and recreation therapist responses to what is learned are client-specific; thus, individuals are helped to achieve their goals by utilizing important and valid information.

Desire for Quality and to Exceed Expectations

Dedicated professionals have a concern for quality in all that they do. Quality in interactions with customers, programming, leadership, and all efforts of one's organization is of primary concern to individuals who care about others and target ways to meet their needs. Quality may be described as a level of excellence that meets or exceeds customer expectations (as well as needs). To know our customers' expectations we must understand both the assets and needs of our community. Elements of quality include the following:

To Demonstrate a Professional Commitment

A personal commitment to the profession of parks, recreation, and leisure services demands high ethics and standards from leisure services practitioners. A hallmark of a professional is one who is ethical, well-educated (and seeks ongoing education), exceeds standards as set by the profession, and constantly strives to do the best

possible job. One aspect of that commitment, then, is following through on all tasks that have potential to improve services. Leisure professionals do this by adhering to "best practices," which in programming requires that providers conduct various assessments as part of the cyclical program process. It is through following the steps of excellent practices that professionals most contribute to the field.

To Ensure Accountability

Accountability is a term that refers to being publicly responsible for one's actions and choices. By conducting asset reviews and needs assessments programmers can determine, in advance, what is available and what is needed by the people in the service area. Through determining where assets lie and any gaps exist, programmers can respond to the expressions of need as well as strengths. Thus, when the time comes to indicate how resources have been utilized, leisure services professionals have the necessary information to support programming and development decisions. These preprogram assessments provide a solid basis for the evaluation process (another element of the program planning cycle) and as such aid in addressing accountability.

To Allocate Resources Appropriately

Another reason to conduct needs assessments and asset reviews is that they help to inform about where programmers need to focus their resources. With the information gathered from the community, informal groups, formal institutions, and individual constituents, leisure services professionals can tell if they should increase staffing in one area, or facility maintenance in another. This can help predict where future needs will be, and how one might attend to those needs based on the information gathered from the assessments. Resource allocation includes issues of finances, staffing, equipment, facility use and maintenance, and other elements required to conduct the business of the organization.

To Increase Profits

The amount of revenue raised by various programs is becoming increasingly important in decision-making processes. As it stands now, almost every agency or organization offers some programs that make money, some that break even, and some that lose money. Those that make money are often used to subsidize the programs that lose money. As budgets continue to be cut and resources shrink, generating revenue in programs will become increasingly important. By planning and offering programs in which people have an interest and that will contribute to the community assets, programmers can better ensure revenue generation.

For those parks, recreation, and leisure services businesses that have a for-profit orientation, asset inventories and needs assessments are very important pieces of the decision-making process needed to increase company profits while maintaining customer satisfaction. Further, through use of asset mapping and needs assessments leisure services professionals can maintain customer loyalty while simultaneously working to recruit new customers.

Program Management

Program management is one of the primary reasons to conduct asset inventories and needs assessments. The intent is to understand constituents and the community well enough so that the programs are both appropriate and appealing to a wide constituent base. These tools (asset maps and needs assessments) provide the information used to initiate the program cycle; they can also be used to set goals and objectives around which the remainder of the program cycle is built. To address program quality leisure services professionals consider the following:

To Manage Duplication of Services

Duplicating services within an agency or with another community organization can result in a waste of resources and unhealthy competition. By thoroughly mapping community assets programmers learn what resources (e.g., people, finances, facilities, transportation) are available and where they are located. Programmers then can make educated decisions about providing particular services in specified locations. They may choose to duplicate a program or service if the program is considered a "core" service, or they may choose to use resources in other program areas. In this way programmers manage the agency resources wisely.

To Maintain and Address Safety Issues

Safety is an ongoing concern in all programming efforts. By mapping how facilities, equipment, and programs are distributed and used (as well as maintained), leisure services professionals can better understand where potential hazards might exist. This is particularly important in therapeutic recreation and outdoor recreation settings, including playgrounds and other structures. By understanding peak use times, traffic patterns, use trends, and attitudes toward other participants, professionals can structure programs for maximum

safety and enjoyment. This raises the quality of programming efforts in all areas.

To Help Prioritize Program Plans

By understanding constituents' wants and needs, and knowing the community assets (including their locations and accessibility) programmers can do the most effective job of prioritizing the implementation of program plans. They can learn how many people want and need which type of program and respond in-kind. This might result in increased partnerships and particular programming choices. Bear in mind that there will be times when programs serve only a very small portion of the constituent base. It is imperative not to fall into the trap of only offering programs and services to members of the majority group. Specialized programs and services have a definite place in programming efforts, and all members of the constituency have equal rights to have their leisure needs met.

To Plan a Variety of Enjoyable Programs

People want to enjoy their recreation and leisure experiences, and to be able to access those experiences in a relatively 'hassle-free' manner. Asset maps and needs assessments help programmers to design and implement a wide variety of enjoyable programs because so many individuals, groups, and institutions are involved in the programming process. By mapping community resources and asking lots of questions about various elements of parks, recreation, and leisure services, programmers can augment and make more enjoyable the programs and services that currently exist, as well as those being planned. Participant involvement in

Figure 4.3 Volunteers often serve in after-school activities.

planning contributes to a sense of ownership in the program—this often heightens enjoyment.

To Develop and Meet Individual Goals

Finally, yet another reason for asset mapping and conducting needs assessments is the information gathered can aid in developing and meeting individual goals and contributing to asset development throughout the community. This is especially pertinent in therapeutic recreation, yet is also applicable in other settings. Participant goals might include skill development, broadening of leisure experiences, personal enhancement, health, or simple enjoyment. Contributing to asset development could include utilizing informal neighborhood networks to address transportation or child-care needs, developing partnerships with schools to share facilities, or establishing a volunteer network of talented community members.

◆◆◆

Many excellent reasons for undertaking asset mapping and needs assessments exist in the programming process. If leisure services providers believe in a service orientation (a hallmark of servant leadership) and in participant empowerment, they will want to work with their assets and provide constituent groups opportunities to participate in dialogues related to services. Professionals in parks, recreation, and leisure services are committed to enhancing the viability of the profession—conducting asset inventories and needs assessments are clear ways to augment the professional position. Finally, what is learned from asset mapping and needs assessments aids tremendously in program management—it is an integral and necessary part of the programming cycle.

The Process of Asset Mapping

As mentioned, asset mapping is an information-gathering process related to the resources of an agency, organization, neighborhood, or community. Through systematic methods leisure services professionals can identify, map, and record the following types of assets and capacity in their local area:

- **People:** develop a community profile outlining the knowledge, skills, talents, expertise, and experience of individuals (both personal as well as professional). Consider individual leadership roles, resources, networks, and connections. Find out who has what skills, talents, and resources, and where they live.

- **Places:** natural resources, buildings, and meeting places (such as a coffee house), as well as services and programs offered where people live, work and visit. Consider parks, waterways, transportation corridors, energy resources, and vacant spaces. Also note location, size, features, and amenities of these places.

- **Partnerships and networks:** local partnerships, volunteer groups, connections, and networks that link the community and its members. Consider cultural connections as well as existing and potential relationships between people, agencies, and services.

- **Associations, groups, institutions:** local associations such as the Chamber of Commerce, community groups, church groups, youth groups, schools, local government, health services, youth and adult recreation and sport associations, and civic organizations (e.g., Rotary, Junior League). Consider parks and recreation departments, long-term care facilities, libraries, police and fire departments, and utility providers.

- **Local business information:** economic linkages, local businesses and business leaders, and community development groups. Consider local stores and merchants, banks, job training groups, radio/television stations, nonprofit agencies, small business incubators, and local agriculture and industry (Bonner Foundation, n.d.; Community Strengthening Branch, 2006).

When engaging in asset mapping programmers will want to examine as many different sources of information as possible. Thus, they might examine local printed (or web-based) information such as newspapers, annual reports, community directories, agency brochures, and activity schedules. The U.S. Census Bureau publishes data (including income, education, and business information), and other types of archived materials online.

After examining available materials, programmers will want to collect observable data such as map locations and facility/grounds information. Programmers can use local sources to confirm and verify the information. By contacting local formal institutions, informal associations (such as neighborhood groups), and local individuals, programmers can ensure a complete inventory of the assets and resources at their disposal. See Figure 4.4 below for a graphic that might be used to help sort information.

Accessing Information

We have established a shared meaning for a variety of terms and established the need for conducting pre-program assessments as an integral component to the programming cycle. Now we need to examine whom to ask and what to ask—Just how do programmers go about collecting detailed information and opinions? Who is involved in these processes? What kind of information is solicited?

Constituents

Current users of parks, recreation, and leisure services are easily identified—they are all the individuals who are actively participating in one or more leisure programs. Their frequency, intensity, and duration of participation might vary, but they are currently engaged in some form of recreation and leisure pursuit.

Nonusers, on the other hand, are all those people within the service area who, for some reason, are not currently participating in leisure programs or services. Because users and nonusers are distinctly different from one another, it is important in any asset mapping or assessment of needs that both groups are equitably sampled. These two groups form the constituent group and both are important to the programming process.

Leisure services professionals include users in the assessment processes because it is important to keep community members involved. One tries to determine how to address the loyalty of these individuals so as to retain their business. Programmers include nonusers in needs assessments because they wish to add these people to their user list. Being service-oriented, programmers want everyone to participate and have an opportunity to have their leisure needs met through the efforts of their agency; programmers want the community to benefit from their involvement in recreation programs.

Individual Assets	**Institutional Assets**	**Organizational Assets**

Individuals and their...
   Knowledge
   Skills
   Talents
   Experiences
 	
 Consider:
   Professional
   Personal
   Resources
   Leadership
   Networks
	Faith-based organizations
	 Colleges and universities
	 Long-term care facilities
	 Fire departments
	 Hospitals and clinics
	 Mental health facilities
	 Libraries
	 Police departments
	 Common schools
	 Utilities
	 Transportation services
	 Banks
	 Major employers
	 Sport and recreation services and activities
		Community centers
		 Radio/TV stations
		 Small businesses
		 Large businesses
		 Home-based enterprises
		 Religious organizations
		 Nonprofit organizations
		 Clubs
		 Citizen groups
		 Business associations
		 Chambers of Commerce
		 Cable and phone companies
		 Shopping centers
		 Private foundations

Governmental Assets	**Physical and Land Assets**	**Cultural Assets**
City government State capitol Federal natural resource management agencies Economic development dept. Military facilities School service center Small Business Administration State education agency Telecommunications agency	Agricultural areas Energy resources Forest lands Industrial areas Lakes, ponds, streams Underground and surface mining areas Natural resources/landmarks Parks/recreation areas and facilities Vacant land and lots	Historic/arts groups Ethnic/Racial diversity Heritage and history Crafts, skills Cultural traditions Museums Theater, dance, opera companies Archeological resources and sites Architecture Music

Figure 4.4 General asset categories

External Inventory

An *external inventory* occurs when one looks outside of the organization to determine what resources exist—asset mapping—and what *markers* exist in identifying the needs of constituent groups. The resources in the community might be found at other leisure services agencies, the environment at large, the local tax base, and so on. Markers include those social indicators that illustrate the community might need something. By taking a "read" on the surrounding environment programmers begin to get a picture of who is in the service area, the available assets, the constituents' needs, and their shared interests. This type of inventory is very much like taking inventory at a department store. What is available (i.e., stock) and at what price (i.e., cost)? If "something" is lacking, can relationships with others be built to make "this" available to the constituents?

Social Indicators

Social indicators are pieces of data that are typically gathered and maintained by governmental or nonprofit agencies. They include such statistics as juvenile arrest rates, mortality and birth rates, population and age

Social Indicators	
Childbearing	• Overall fertility rate • Estimated maternal mortality ratio • Contraceptive prevalence among married women of childbearing age
Education	• School life expectancy (expected number of years of formal schooling), total and by sex
Health	• Life expectancy at birth by sex (years) • Infant mortality rate by sex and race/ethnicity • Child mortality rate by sex
Housing	• Average number of persons per room to total; urban and rural areas
Human Settlements	• Population distribution by urban/rural residence • Average annual rate of change in urban and rural populations
Illiteracy	• Illiteracy rate by sex for ages 15–24 and 25+
Income and Economic Activity	• Per capita Gross Domestic Product ($US) • Adult economic activity rate by sex
Population	• Estimated population by sex and race/ethnicity (thousands) • Sex ratio (males per 100 females) • Average annual rate of change of population
Unemployment	• Unemployment rate, total and by sex, age, and race/ethnicity
Water Supply and Sanitation	• Estimated percentage of population with access to improved drinking water sources for total, urban, and rural areas • Estimated percentage of population with access to improved sanitation facilities for total, urban, and rural areas
Youth and Elderly Populations	• Percentage of total population under age 15 • Percentage of male population aged 60+ • Percentage of female population aged 60+ • Sex ratio (men per 100 women) in the population aged 60+

Source: http://unstats.un.org/unsd/demographic/products/socind/socind2.htm

Figure 4.5 Common social indicators collected by the United Nations group information, education levels, rates of disease, vaccination rates, income, and other factors that attest to the general health (or lack of health) of a community. This information is relatively objective and can be helpful in assessment and efforts to program for unstated needs in the community. Typically, these indicators are relatively stable, and we need to remain attentive to when changes occur—change could be indicative of new needs. State and federal governments collect data for these reports periodically and much of this information is available on the Internet. Figure 4.5 presents a list of the social indicators commonly gathered by the United Nations in its efforts to improve quality of life for global citizens.

Measuring developmental assets is another way to understand the health of a community. From over a decade of research we know that the more assets a young person has, the more positive and successful her or his development will be (Search Institute, 2009). Unfortunately, this same research demonstrates that the average young person in the United States experiences only 18 of the 40 assets. Overall, 62% of young people have fewer than 20 of the 40 assets. Thus, by learning about and measuring these assets, leisure services providers can determine programming needs and what community resources are available to help achieve goals.

Comparative Inventories

Comparative inventories are just that—identifying and counting the physical resources and parks, recreation, and leisure programs in a variety of communities. Usually these inventories are compared across cities or towns of similar sizes. This can take both an assets approach and a discrepancy perspective. Leisure professionals might use the information learned to develop supportive programmatic relationships, or if a discrepancy exists in terms of programs and resources, they might say that similar services are needed in the underserved area. Comparative inventories relate well to identifying normative needs. A variety of commercial, nonprofit, and public parks and recreation agencies conduct comparative inventories. These physical inventories are becoming more accessible and commonplace to local parks and recreation entities as technology such as global positioning systems (GPS), digital mapping, and other locator services become easier to use.

Environmental Resources

By taking an inventory of community resources programmers get a feel for the assets—program, open space, facility—and gaps that might exist between what

is and what should be. A needs-based approach to this element of inventory is particularly useful if one is utilizing normative needs in determining program plans. For instance, programmers would want to gather information about available resources in the community (e.g., number and location of playgrounds, pools, parks, campgrounds) as well as about other organizations and their resources (e.g., facilities, equipment, staff) and programs. In this process programmers develop inventory lists of what is available to the constituents in the community.

In addition to counting the physical resources, identifying the resources that are accessible to people with disabilities (and those that need retrofitting to become accessible), those that need repair or replacement, identifying safety concerns, and where resources are located are also important. It could very well be that there are "enough" resources in terms of quantity, but that they are all clustered at one end of town and do not serve all people equally well. Leisure services providers need to strive to gather complete data for the entire service area.

Social Values

Understanding the social mores and values of a community is very important when developing program plans. Some communities have strong religious ties and the influence of the church is quite strong throughout community institutions. Other communities have social mores that attribute a great deal of importance to the extended family; yet other communities manifest strong values toward, and an emphasis on, youth development. Some have an economic or entrepreneurial orientation while others have an underlying worldview that stresses the common good.

Figure 4.6 Staff collect environmental resource information through GPS receivers.

Each of these community types would have different assets and needs, in part driven by the social mores of the surrounding area.

Internal Inventory

An internal inventory is conducted from the vantage point of having a good look at oneself. In this inventory process, an organization conducts a thorough review of itself—its facilities, staff, financial resources, open space, existing programs, equipment, and so on. This is an important element of asset mapping. During this inventory process personnel look for evidence of areas that need attention, new relationships to be built, an infusion of new ideas, and ideas or programs that need to be retired. In this effort, programmers should strive to conduct an unbiased self-audit. This type of audit often occurs as part of an agency accreditation process (e.g., CAPRA—Commission for Accreditation of Park and Recreation Agencies). These efforts are often very revealing and can uncover untapped assets.

Philosophy/Mission/Vision

Continual and periodic checks of the organizational philosophy, mission, and vision are the only way to stay focused and be sure that program efforts are aligned and leading toward the achievement of the mission. Knowing that staff continue to support and buy into the organization's mission is important in ensuring a well-focused and collaborative staff. Professional programmers will frequently examine agency mission and vision statements, and review the agency's philosophy for viability, timeliness, and appropriate focus. This provides the direction for all programming efforts.

Staffing

Staff are some of the most important assets. Thus, knowing who constitutes staff (e.g., office staff, maintenance staff, program staff, administrative staff) is an important component of asset mapping and needs assessments. To program effectively, leisure services providers need to know how many staff they have, as well as the strengths, limitations, interests, skills, and needs of the staff. Availability, where staff are assigned, and other information would also be helpful in determining the best use of these very important resources. In addition, knowing their level of training and certification in various areas is often a necessity (e.g., pool operations [CPO], first responder, therapeutic recreation specialist [CTRS]). This information is often found in employee files and on resumes. In addition, some organizations keep training files in one location for all staff to utilize. With computerization of this type of information, the process is becoming easier and faster for individuals to access. This allows for quick identification of individuals who have training in a specific area so those staff may be appropriately utilized. Of course, understanding the difference between confidential and public information is crucial when accessing information about any staff member.

Recent and Past Programs

Internal reviews are not complete without a review of recent and past programs implemented by one's organization. In this process, leisure professionals can identify a variety of characteristics: traditional programs, those held periodically, those that generate revenue, the types of participants attracted to each program, programs that "flopped" or were successful, goals the programs addressed, and other program traits that help to identify assets and needs of constituents. The success of this effort is incumbent upon detailed programming records and documentation.

Equipment, Facilities, and Supplies

Part of our internal review will include an objective inventory of what is available in terms of supplies (e.g., office as well as program planning supplies), equipment (e.g., quantity, size, condition), and facilities (e.g., amount of space, its strengths, its shortcomings). Each of these elements has an impact on what can be offered, how often, the prioritization of resource allocation, and more. Before beginning, then, leisure professionals must know what is available.

Budgetary Issues

Lastly, in the internal component of an assessment leisure providers must come to know and understand the financial situation of their organization. Whether programmers have an unlimited budget, are required to have programs break even or generate revenue, or are operating on a "shoestring" budget, they must include this component in a complete assessment process. Whether tax-supported, profit-driven, or supported by grant funds is also important to know—each of these has a different impact on programming efforts (see Figure 4.7).

The Process of Gathering Needs Assessment Information

Now that it is quite clear why a leisure services provider undertakes asset mapping and needs assessments, the next step is to consider how to go about this. You already know that one of the characteristics of the cyclical program process is that it begins with assessment and "ends" with assessment ("end" assessment is called *evaluation*). Because program evaluation is so important, a good deal of time is spent in later chapters of this text discussing the various steps of developing a data collection, analysis, and reporting system.

The steps for conducting asset maps and needs assessments are the same as for program evaluation; therefore, the information here is not repeated here. Instead, in this section we will discuss the various avenues through which input from constituents can be gathered, as well as other sources from which we obtain information. The primary questions to bear in mind prior to beginning an assessment are: *Why* are you doing this assessment (i.e., what is the purpose)? *What* information do you want to collect? *How* are you going to obtain these data? *From where* will you get the information we seek? *When* will you gather the information? *From whom* will we collect information? And, *who* will use the information once it is obtained? After answering all of these questions, you begin the data collection process.

People as Resources

Leisure services professionals know that to best serve all constituent groups, it is best they collect information from both users and nonusers of their programs and services. Similar techniques for collecting data from both of these groups can be used. There are advantages and disadvantages for each method, and this should be taken into consideration when deciding upon

a technique to use. No matter the chosen technique(s), programmers typically aim to collect similar types of information.

Types of Data

One of the major categories of information gathered from our constituents is data about themselves. These data help increase understanding of who the constituents are; what interests, desires, and assets they have; and what they are currently doing (if anything) in parks, recreation, and leisure services settings. Programmers collect several different types of data, such as:

Demographic Data. Demographic data include factual information that describes a person and their style of living. Typical demographic items include: age, sex, race/ethnicity, physical and cognitive disabilities, religion, income, level of education, marital status, parental/family status, occupation, military status, and zip code (or some other indication of where they live). This type of information provides a feel for some, but not all, assets and needs. For example, one can be fairly certain that those individuals with children would be interested in and have a need for family

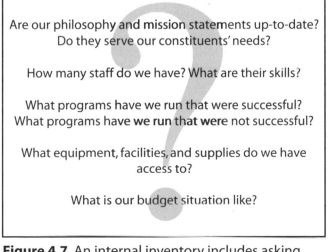

Are our philosophy and mission statements up-to-date? Do they serve our constituents' needs?

How many staff do we have? What are their skills?

What programs have we run that were successful? What programs have we run that were not successful?

What equipment, facilities, and supplies do we have access to?

What is our budget situation like?

Figure 4.7 An internal inventory includes asking tough questions of an organization

Photo courtesy of Austin Parks and Recreation Department

Figure 4.8 People are rich resources of information

(parents and children) recreation, while those who do not have children may not have that need.

In addition, once a programmer gathers some basic information, we can request additional details, if needed. For instance, after learning that an individual has a disability, we can follow up and ask if any special accommodations for full inclusion are required. This information enables programmers to staff appropriately as well as manage the environment for participant success.

Current Activity Involvement. Similar to the demographic data collected, this section of an assessment is factual; programmers want to know in what events or experiences people currently participate. Leisure services providers also might ask how often they participate, with whom, where, what days of the week, for how long, during what time period, and at what cost. This provides a picture of who the users are and can help to clarify relationships people have with one another, the resources, and existing programs. The information gathered also reveals what people are *not* doing and this can be very informative. As information is collected, programmers begin to see patterns and reasons for various levels of participation.

Skills and Needs Information. In addition to asking about physical, emotional, psychological, social, and spiritual needs, it is often helpful to get a picture of the perceptions people have of their own skill levels. This helps in planning appropriate levels of activities and in matching participants based on skills. This is good information to have whether developing athletic leagues, cooking classes, or arts-and-crafts sessions. It is important to note that by asking constituents (called self-reporting) about their skill levels, programmers will not always get accurate results. Some people have a tendency to underestimate their skills, while others overestimate their abilities. In some instances (e.g., water-based programs) skill testing may be necessary prior to assigning individuals to program groups to ensure participant safety.

Attitudes, Beliefs, and Values. Assessments are used to gain information about constituents so as to best meet their needs and wants. Needs and wants are both influenced by attitudes, beliefs, and values (although wants are influenced much more heavily than needs); thus, asking about these characteristics of constituents provides a more complete picture of who they are, what they might want, and some ways to help people to connect to meet those desires. Questions about the importance of various recreation and leisure experiences fall under this category. An example of such an item is "Indicate your level of

agreement with the following statement: It is important that every child be exposed to sports before the age of twelve." Scores from this item could be indicative of respondents' beliefs about the need for youth sports.

Preferences, Opinions, Interests, and Intentions. Other data programmers collect from constituents is about an individual's preferences, opinions, interests, and intentions. This information can provide leisure professionals with background data to help them plan programs more efficiently. Programmers might ask about when constituents would prefer to participate in a certain activity (e.g., season, time of day, day of week), where they would want to participate (e.g., indoors or out-of-doors, what part of town), and with whom (e.g., friends, family, alone). This information is particularly important for a programmer to learn about nonusers. In addition, it would be helpful to know what recreation and leisure opportunities the respondent is interested in and whether or not they have an intention to participate in activities currently offered or that are in the process of being developed.

The most popular approaches to conducting assessments are asking members of advisory boards/ councils, holding town hall meetings, and making comment cards available to constituent groups at a variety of locations. These methods tend to be relatively easy to implement, convenient, low cost, and require little staff expertise.

Advisory Boards

Many parks, recreation, and leisure services organizations have identified advisory boards that consist of people who live in the community. These individuals serve to aid the organization in decision making and are often a wonderful source of information about community assets, needs, wants, and interests. While advisory boards differ in how often they meet and in the functions they provide to a particular organization, they do offer an opportunity for staff to better understand the local community, its assets, and culture. One caveat to bear in mind is that advisory board members may have no expertise or specialized knowledge in parks and recreation programming or operations. Thus, while board members can be invaluable in some respects, there may be limitations to their direct influence over programming.

Town Hall Meetings

In the United States, open meetings are a part of every city, county, and state governmental process. Thus, for public parks and recreation organizations open meetings may be utilized to aid with decisions about budgeting, resource allocation, capital improvements, and so on. Often called *town hall meetings*, these events are typically well-advertised to the general public and provide opportunities for community members to express their opinions about the matter at hand. Organizations that are profit driven and fall into the commercial or entrepreneurial sector also might decide to hold open meetings to solicit input from a variety of constituent groups. In this way agencies are proactive and responsive to the wishes of their clients and potential participants. Open meetings often are the first step in developing networks and relationships across individuals, groups, associations, and businesses. If open meetings are the only method of information gathering and one has to be present to participate, those without transportation to the meeting site could be left out of the process. For those with access, technology can used to gather information either synchronously (at the same time) or asynchronously (at different times).

Comment Cards

In addition to face-to-face meetings, comment cards can be a useful way to gather information when used appropriately. For instance, if comment cards are available only at our facility, only the individuals who enter that facility will have the opportunity to share their thoughts. Thus, to be effective, programmers will want to ensure wide distribution (perhaps as an insert with a utility bill or some other mass mailing). In addition, respondents should have the option of putting their comment cards in the mail (at the organization's expense) or dropping them into a "suggestion box." If the box drop-off method is an option, the receptacle must be in an easily accessible location. It is counterproductive to have a suggestion box kept behind the staff counter where visitors rarely see it. Providing drop boxes at public locations such as banks or grocery stores can increase the card return rate. Many comment cards may be found online, providing another avenue for customers to provide input relative to a service or program.

Focus Groups and Interviews

Another form of gathering data directly from constituent groups involves using focus groups. Focus groups are essentially group interviews where groups of individuals are brought together to respond to a particular question. Thus, if programmers want to know about the assets, interests, wants, and needs of the community, they would bring together a group of constituents and ask them to discuss those topics within the group. By playing off of one another in their discussion of

the question, a great deal of information is brought to light. Much planning and preparation is required prior to conducting focus groups. For instance, the facilitator will need to decide if she or he will gather a homogeneous (people with similar backgrounds) or heterogeneous (people from mixed backgrounds) group. Will the facilitator allow for open topic discussion or utilize a structured interview technique? How long will the session last, and what techniques will be used to ensure that all group members have an opportunity to participate? How will the information be recorded (e.g., voice recording, note taking, video recording), and how will people be notified of this? Figure 4.9 is an example of a note sent to specific constituents, inviting them to a focus group meeting.

Observations

Observing what people do is an excellent method of gathering information about participation rates and behaviors. Through observation leisure services providers can tell quite a bit about current users of a particular area or facility. Some external clues about constituents such as sex, approximate age, apparent race/ethnicity, and physical abilities and qualities can be noted. In addition, information about the activity in which the person is participating, with whom, for how long, at what intensity level, and the time of day may also be noted. This type of information may also

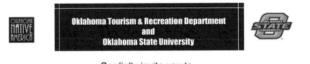

Oklahoma Tourism & Recreation Department
and
Oklahoma State University

Cordially invite you to
participate in the
2010 SCORP Recreation Rally

**Willard Hall Living Room 010,
Oklahoma State University, Stillwater**

March 21, 2010

10:00 a.m. to 3:30 p.m.

As a professional in management of outdoor recreation resources and opportunities for Oklahomans, you are invited to participate in the Statewide Comprehensive Outdoor Recreation Planning Rally.

The rally will include planning and break-out sessions on a variety of topics: Accessibility for people with disabilities; cultural resources and diversity; trails; policy; public domain; air and water quality; environmental issues; and funding/grants. We anticipate that each participant will be able participate in at least three discussions. An appropriate professional will facilitate each roundtable.

Registration is free and light refreshments will be served throughout the day, participants are free to take a lunch break. Parking is free in the Willard Hall parking lot. Additional parking is available at the OSU Student Union.

Please register to help us plan which topics need to be focused on. If you are unavailable to attend, please encourage other appropriate staff members to attend.

Please direct any questions to Lowell Caneday, Ph.D., Oklahoma State University at (555) 515-7777 or email@osu.edu

Figure 4.9 Focus group invitation

be telling in noting who is *not* using the facility or participating in programs. For example, if an agency exists in an ethnically mixed area yet programmers never or rarely observe people of color in the facility, this could be indicative that programs are not meeting the needs of minority group members.

Key Informants

Key informants are specially selected individuals from the community, usually informal community leaders. These individuals might be representatives from key businesses, churches, or civic organizations such as the Elks, Women's Civic Club, or other community groups. In addition, youth representatives from the local high school or people from homeowners' associations might serve as key informants. The selected individuals are those directly impacted by the recreation opportunities under consideration and as such, have a vested interest in the assessment. For instance, if a new skate park was under consideration, key informants might include potential users (of all ages), people living and working near the potential site, and the managing agency. Input from all impacted groups would be important to the success of the venture. One drawback to key informants is that, by their nature, they may be biased (i.e., they are already in favor of or against the new development).

Direct Assessment

The therapeutic side of the profession engages in direct assessment of individual patients and clients. When a new client enters a clinical therapeutic recreation setting an intake assessment is conducted. The recreation therapist must learn as much as she or he can about the client to determine the best course of therapeutic intervention for each particular person. This assessment may be repeated later on during that person's stay to determine if needs are being met or have changed. Programmers who are in community therapeutic recreation settings (often called *inclusion specialists*) also must conduct some level of assessment at intake so as to best serve the individual through recreation and leisure services. By determining assets, strengths, areas of deficits, and level of functioning, the recreation therapist can develop, plan, and implement appropriate leisure activity strategies within the given resources. See Figure 4.10 (pp. 104–105) for a sample assessment.

Surveys: Mail, Telephone, In-Person, and Electronic

Lastly, as with program evaluations, programmers can gather assessment data through the use of paper-and-pencil, oral, or electronic surveys. Whether conducted by mail, telephone, computer, or in person depends upon available resources and the time and talents of our staff. Mail surveys can be costly and response rates may be low, yet are useful in that they have the potential to reach almost all individuals in one's constituent base. Telephone surveys are often perceived as intrusive by those on the receiving end, yet can be done quickly and efficiently. Electronic surveys only reach those who have computers and access to an online service, yet they tend to be quick to complete.

By handing a survey to an individual or group of individuals in person, programmers are readily available should questions arise. In addition, this technique usually results in a high response rate. If this method is chosen, programmers do need to be sure to survey nonusers as well (e.g., distribute the survey to people at a shopping mall rather than our facility to ensure a mix of people). Surveys can be quite useful for collecting information for assessments because constituents have time to look them over, consider the information, and respond with some thought. In addition, programmers can ask a lot of questions at one time and obtain a good deal of information from a wide variety of people. A sample survey appears in Figure 4.11 (pp. 106-107).

Records as Resources

In addition to gathering information directly from people, it is also possible (and oftentimes desirable) to collect information about constituents from existing documents, records, and archives. Programmers can obtain a good deal of background data this way without being an imposition to individuals. See Figures 4.12 (pp. 108-109) and 4.13 (p. 110) for examples.

Registration Information

When people register for programs and services at most leisure services organizations, they must complete some type of paperwork. If a mini-assessment is built into every registration form, ongoing information can be collected from users of those services. Unfortunately, this method of gathering data does not provide any insight into those who have never registered for a program. As with other data collection techniques, depending upon the analysis, the information gleaned from registration records can be useful in what is *not* found as much as what is found. For instance, by asking for information about age of registrants programmers might find that very few of the constituents are people over the age of 45 years old; or by asking where they live, programmers might learn that very few individuals visit the facility from "across the river." This type of information can assist with programming efforts.

Activity Analysis/Program Plans

Every program that is offered should be based on written documentation including goals and objectives, tasks to be completed, staffing and equipment needs, numbers of individuals served, marketing efforts, target populations, and other information. By analyzing these records, and in conjunction with other information, leisure providers can identify patterns in their programming efforts. These might point to a particular type of program and/or service where programmers tend to focus energies, elements of the constituent group they tend to neglect, how they respond to public fads and trends, how they spend their money, and other program-related information.

Census Bureau and Almanacs

The U.S. Census Bureau conducts a nationwide research project every ten years gathering data about individuals. The data are primarily demographic and include such information as race/ethnicity, number in household, ages, income levels, family and marital status, and so on. These data are then utilized in ongoing projections about the population. Programmers can also find information about the year's most watched television shows, films, and sporting events; where and how often people travel; how people spend their money; and the most common recreation activities in which people participate. This information is updated annually, found in almanacs (in paper and on the Internet), and can be extremely useful in planning new programs.

Social Indicators

We mentioned social indicators earlier in this chapter. This type of information is often maintained by governmental or nonprofit agencies. Again, social indicators speak to the general health and wealth status of an area or state. The information can be helpful to parks, recreation, and leisure services programmers in identifying social assets and deficits to which we can then respond.

Both people and records can serve as resources for gathering data in the conduct of an assessment. Each can be a rich source of data and should be well utilized in programming efforts. The information can be gathered formally or informally and from a variety of sources. It should be reemphasized that assessments should be conducted periodically so that new information is constantly coming into the agency providing up-to-date justification for program development.

Summary

The aspects of servant leadership most related to this chapter include listening, foreseeing issues, and healing. Clearly, through conducting asset reviews and needs assessments (with genuine interest and intent) programmers are engaged in the processes of listening and foreseeing issues. The characteristic of listening helps leisure providers to be self- and other-aware; it can help to foster empathy, foresight, and a commitment to others. Similarly, the ability to foresee issues and plot an appropriate course comes from an awareness of others and oneself. If programmers have a good understanding of the assets available and of their constituents, they will be best positioned to make wise choices relative to possible future directions.

The ability to offer healing is another trait of servant leadership. This ability relates to "matters of the heart" and empathy. It is our contention that an attitude and desire for healing can only occur in a setting where we know our community—its assets, strengths, attitudes, and culture. This comes about through the conduct of assessments.

Asset reviews and needs assessments are the first steps to the program planning cycle. Through these assessments leisure services professionals gather information about interests, wants, intentions, needs, and assets from a variety of constituent groups and respond to what they find. In this way programmers remain aware of and responsive to their constituents. In addition, needs assessments and asset reviews provide an avenue for ongoing dialogue between an agency and the people in its service area. This allows programmers to maintain the goal of empowering constituents in influencing the programs and services. There are many reasons for conducting needs assessments and those reasons fall into three broad categories—service orientation/participant empowerment, desire for quality and to exceed expectations, and for program management.

Data collection is an important process and information may be gathered from external as well as internal sources. Leisure services providers might undertake an external inventory of resources, examine social indicators, or reflect on the local social norms. Internally, they could examine values and mission, staff resources, past programs, physical structures, and finances. The actual process of gathering and analyzing data is very similar to that done in program evaluation (discussed in Chapters Eleven and Twelve). The most common sources of needs assessment information are advisory boards, town hall meetings, and comment cards. Other sources (continued on p. 111)

COLUMBIA SPECIALTY HOSPITAL OF TULSA
ADMISSION DATABASE—THERAPEUTIC RECREATION

THERAPEUTIC RECREATION THERAPIST _____ signature/title _____ dates of assessment _____

ASSESSMENT DATA	PROBLEMS IDENTIFIED	SHORT-TERM GOALS	INTERVENTIONS
INDEPENDENCE WITH COMPLETION OF LEISURE TASK ____ verbal cues required and/or ____ physical assistance required	____ No functional deficits ____ Functional deficits related to: ____ verbal cuing required ____ physical assistance required	Within ____ week(s) patient will complete ____ with ____ verbal cue(s) and/or ____ with ____ physical assistance	____ Functional therapy ____ Therapeutic group ____ Community reintegration ____ Patient/Family education ____ Other
ENDURANCE WITH COMPLETION OF TABLE TOP LEISURE TASK WITHOUT SIGN/COMPLAINT OF FATIGUE X ____ seated X ____ standing X ____ in bed X ____ bedside	____ No functional deficits ____ Functional deficits related to endurance: ____ seated ____ standing ____ in bed ____ bedside	Within ____ week(s) patient will complete without sign/complaint of fatigue: X ____ seated X ____ standing X ____ in bed X ____ bedside	____ Functional therapy ____ Therapeutic group ____ Community reintegration ____ Patient/Family education ____ Other
MOBILITY TO TREATMENT SESSIONS ____ distance physically in wc ____ feet ____ independence with wheelchair ____ walking distance ____ feet ____ walking independently	____ No functional deficits ____ Functional deficits related to: ____ wheelchair independence ____ wheelchair distance ____ walking independence ____ walking distance	Within ____ week(s) patient will: ____ propel wc ____ feet ____ with ____ assistance ____ walk ____ feet ____ with ____ assistance	____ Functional therapy ____ Therapeutic group ____ Community reintegration ____ Patient/Family education ____ Other
USE OF THE UPPER EXTREMITIES TO COMPLETE LEISURE TASKS utilized RUE x ____ % utilized LUE x ____ %	____ No functional deficits ____ Functional deficits related to: ____ use of RUE to complete leisure task ____ use of LUE to complete leisure task	Within ____ week(s) patient will utilize: ____ RUE x ____ % ____ LUE x ____ % to complete leisure task.	____ Functional therapy ____ Therapeutic group ____ Community reintegration ____ Patient/Family education ____ Other
L/R NEGLECT WITH LEISURE TASKS ____ cues required to attend midline ____ cues required to attend to right ____ cues required to attend to left	____ No functional deficits ____ Functional deficits related to attention to: ____ midline ____ right ____ left	Within ____ week(s) patient will complete leisure task with: ____ cues to attend to midline ____ cues to attend to right ____ cues to attend to left	____ Functional therapy ____ Therapeutic group ____ Community reintegration ____ Patient/Family education ____ Other
ATTENTION TO LEISURE TASKS ____ cues required to attend to task ____ time patient is able to tend to task	____ No functional deficits ____ Functional deficits related to: ____ cuing required to attend to task ____ time patient attends to task	Within ____ week(s) patient will attend to task with ____ cues x ____ minutes.	____ Functional therapy ____ Therapeutic group ____ Community reintegration ____ Patient/Family education ____ Other

Figure 4.10 An example of a direct assessment

Continued>>

ASSESSMENT DATA	PROBLEMS IDENTIFIED	SHORT-TERM GOALS	INTERVENTIONS
COMMUNITY RESOURCES Patient identifies ____ current resources Patient identifies ____ past resources	____ No functional deficits ____ Functional deficits related to: ____ identification of resources ____ use of resources	Within ____ week(s) patient will identify ____ community resources to assist with maintaining or improving level of functioning present at time of discharge.	____ Functional therapy ____ Therapeutic group ____ Community reintegration ____ Patient/Family education ____ Other ____
IDENTIFICATION OF LEISURE TASKS Patient identifies ____ current tasks Patient identifies ____ past tasks	____ No functional deficits ____ Functional deficits related to: ____ identification of leisure tasks ____ use of leisure tasks	Within ____ week(s) patient will identify ____ current leisure pursuits to assist with maintaining or improving level of functioning present at time of discharge.	____ Functional therapy ____ Therapeutic group ____ Community reintegration ____ Patient/Family education ____ Other ____
ORIENTATION Patient is oriented to: ____ person ____ place ____ time ____ situation	____ No functional deficits ____ Functional deficits related to:	Within ____ week(s) patient will be oriented to: ____ person ____ place ____ time ____ situation	____ Functional therapy ____ Therapeutic group ____ Community reintegration ____ Patient/Family education ____ Other ____
EDUCATION Patient/family knowledge of: adequate inadequate Community transportation ☐ ☐ Sr. Citizen Center ☐ ☐ Sr. Nutrition site ☐ ☐ Adult day health programs ☐ ☐ Purpose of use of leisure activities ☐ ☐ Purpose of use of commun. res. ☐ ☐	____ No functional deficits ____ Requires education in designated areas Barriers to learning: ____ language barrier ____ motivation to learn ____ ability to read ____ emotional state ____ physical limitations ____ financial situation ____ cognitive limitations	Within ____ week(s) patient/family will verbalize knowledge of: ____ Community transportation ____ Sr. Citizen Center ____ Sr. Nutrition site ____ Adult day health programs ____ Purpose of use of leisure activities ____ Purpose of use of community resources ____ Other ____	____ Patient education ____ video instruction ____ 1:1 sessions ____ demonstration ____ Family education ____ video instruction ____ written instruction ____ 1:1 sessions ____ demonstration ____ Home program notebook ____ Community reintegration sessions ____ Other ____

OTHER:

LONG-TERM GOALS: At time of discharge patient will

Figure 4.10 An example of a direct assessment (continued from previous page)

Jones County Parks Community Center Needs Assessment

On Tuesday, September 9th, residents of Jones County went to the polls and approved all parts of Vision 2025. Government officials and area community leaders from Jonesville and surrounding cities spent countless hours gathering information that resulted in a four-part proposition that was designed to attract and retain quality jobs, enhance education and economic development and provide a better quality of life. Each Jones County community had something to gain. A regional recreation/community center for southwest Jones County residents is a component of the Vision 2025 package, which is to be constructed on a 15-acre tract between the two communities.

Throughout the years, citizens of Jones County have identified the need for a community/recreation center, which has resulted in research and studies for this type of facility. To help us complete our research, your input is vital to prioritize program and facility requirements. As you answer these questions, please think of your own needs as well as those of other members of your family.

1. In the following tables (A - F), please rank order the items in order of importance (1 = MOST important, 5= least important) to you and your family members. Be sure to rank each list within each table only with items in that list (rank the fitness items against each other, then rank the group activities, then the education/culture items, etc.).

A

Rank	Fitness
	Jogging track
	Free weights
	Circuit weights
	Aerobics/dance studio
	Other

B

Rank	Group activities
	Volleyball court
	Basketball court
	Tot exercise area
	Gymnastics
	Other

C

Rank	Education/culture
	Computer lab
	Stage for skits and shows
	Audio listening rooms
	Kitchen
	Other

D

Rank	Arts/crafts
	Ceramics studio
	Painting studio
	Weaving/looms
	Photography
	Woodworking

E

Rank	Social
	Billiards
	Card/table games
	Meeting/party rooms
	Teen lounge
	Other

F

Rank	Support needs
	Child care center
	Adult care center
	Teen-only times
	Adults-only times
	Other

2. In your immediate family, which groups have the GREATEST need for a recreation/community center facility? Please check no more than three (3) boxes.

☐ Toddlers/tots (up to 4 years) ☐ Adults ☐ Multiple generations
☐ Children (5 to 12 years) ☐ Seniors (over 60 years) ☐ People with disabilities
☐ Teens (13 to 17 years) ☐ Other _____

3. In addition to serving the basic needs of our constituents, we may be able to phase in additional specialty recreational needs. Please rank order the following list of items you would like to see as a part of this ongoing effort. A rank of 1 is your highest priority, 10 is your lowest priority.

Rank	Rank	Rank	Rank
	Indoor pool with splash pad		Skateboard park
	Hardball/racquetball courts		Indoor rock climbing wall
	Indoor play structure (playground)		Performing arts theater
	Indoor tennis courts		Soccer complex
	Disc golf course		Walking/jogging trail

Figure 4.11 Example of a community needs assessment

Continued>>

4. Please think of your potential use of the new recreation/community center facility. At which times of the day would you or your family use the center MOST OFTEN? Please check no more than three (3) boxes.

☐ Early morning (5:00 - 8:00a)   ☐ Mid day (noon - 2:00p)   ☐ Evening (6:00 - 8:00p)

☐ Mid morning (8:00 - 10:00a)   ☐ Afternoon (2:00 - 4:00p)   ☐ Night (8:00 - 10:00p)

☐ Late morning (10:00a - noon)   ☐ Early evening (4:00 - 6:00p)

To help us plan for all community members, please tell us a little about your family. This information is all confidential and will only be reported in aggregate - we will not be able to tell who answered which items.

5. How many people live in your household? _____

QTY	CATEGORY
	Infants to 5 years
	6 to 10 years
	11 to 15 years

QTY	CATEGORY
	15 to 18 years
	19 to 45 years
	46 to 60 years

QTY	CATEGORY
	61 to 70 years
	70 years and older

QTY	CATEGORY
	People with developmental disabilities
	People with sensory impairments

QTY	CATEGORY
	People with mobility impairments
	People with other special needs

6. Please indicate the number of individuals in your household who fall into the following categories:

Once you have completed the Assessment, you can -
- Fold the survey with the return address visible and drop it in the mail, or
- Take the completed survey to Citizens Bank and Trust (318 E. Main Street) in Jonesville, or
- Take the completed survey to Pat's Grocery Store (141st and Elm) in Jonesville

THANK YOU VERY MUCH FOR YOUR PARTICIPATION!

UNIVERSITY MAILING SERVICES
STILLWATER OK 74075-9988

POSTAGE WILL BE PAID BY ADDRESSEE

BUSINESS REPLY LABEL
FIRST CLASS PERMIT NO. 325 STILLWATER OK

NO POSTAGE NECESSARY IF MAILED IN THE UNITED STATES

Jones County Needs Assessment
003 North Cordell
Account AA-5-78634

Figure 4.11 Example of a community needs assessment (continued from previous page)

A Recreational Needs Assessment
for the
Town of Dryden Recreation Commission

A Study Completed by the *REC 601/602 Recreation Research & Evaluation I & II* Class
Department of Recreation & Leisure Studies
State University of New York at Cortland

Dr. Sharon L. Todd

William Allen	Diane Holtsford	Cynthia Rice
Damara Canery	Benjamin Jones	Sarah Schreiber
Patricia Cole	Rebecca Koenig	Geoffrey Sorenson
Angela Dufield	Matthew Levy	Jennifer Sylstra
Annette Havens	Angela Petrie	Jeffrey Tillapaugh
Jennifer Hayes	Shelena Retamar	Chad Totman

June 2006

Figure 4.12 Needs assessment report Continued>>

Discussion and Recommendations

The response rate on the telephone survey was adequate and representative enough to allow generalizations to the residents of the Town of Dryden. However, it is worth noting that only registered voters were part of the sampling frame, which may have introduced a bias in the sample. These respondents may be more likely to be active in their communities and care about quality of life issues in general. Since 60 percent of the sample was female, there may also have been a gender bias (e.g., females may have tended to answer the telephone more often than males when both were present). The focus groups, though small, gleaned useful feedback and ideas. Based on the results from the survey, the following conclusions and recommendations are provided:

◆ ***Respondents in the sample have lived in the Town of Dryden a moderate length of time.***
Although a majority of the sample had resided 15 years or less in the Town of Dryden, another 35% had lived there 16 to 30 years, making the average length of residence nearly 17 years. As noted in other studies (Smith, 2000; Todd & Anderson, 2006), the longer a person resides in a community, the more he or she tends to develop an "attachment" to that place. On the other hand, Todd & Anderson (2006) also found that long-time residents may take their environment for granted and not notice or value the resources around them.

RECOMMENDATION: Recreation often provides the means through which a place becomes even more meaningful and special, strengthening the bond between residents and the environment in which they live. It is important for the Town of Dryden to remind its inhabitants of the self-directed recreational opportunities available through its parks and open spaces. It should also consider offering organized recreational programs to facilitate not only this sense of place, but also a sense of community, in all residents.

◆ ***Awareness of the Dryden Recreation Department is quite low.***
While only 1 in 2 residents were definitely aware that the Town of Dryden had its own community recreation department, more than a third of the respondents did not know the Dryden Recreation Department existed before receiving their phone interview calls. While awareness seemed to drop with distance from the Village of Dryden, notable exceptions occurred. For instance, a majority of Bethel Grove residents were aware of the department, but within the Village of Dryden, almost a third were unsure of its existence.

RECOMMENDATION: The Recreation Department needs to continue to gain exposure in the community. It can promote itself through many avenues (offer notable programs at reasonable prices, connect its name with parks and places, take advantage of publicity and promotion to gain a positive public image). A newsletter or program brochure targeted to every household could significantly raise awareness and unity, perhaps helping to erase the "west vs. east" division. Having an actual positive hands-on experience in the department's parks and recreation programs would make the most impact. Word of mouth could then have a ripple effect throughout the community to continue to raise awareness, which will help when more resources are needed.

◆ ***Usage of town parks is relatively low.***
While approximately half the respondents had used the Dryden Lake Park and/or Trail in the past for recreational purposes, only 42% reported ever using Montgomery Park and just a third had used other parks or open spaces in the Town of Dryden. Rate of visitation to the three parks was quite low, with most residents visiting the areas just a few times a year. By contrast, two-thirds of the sample had visited other parks and open spaces outside the Town of Dryden.

RECOMMENDATION: Open spaces and trails abound in the Town of Dryden, but citizens need to know where they are and how they can be accessed for recreation. More and better signage would increase the visibility of these opportunities. Parks and open spaces have multiple uses, and if managed creatively and effectively, can attract any types of users. Managing the type, level, location, and time of various uses can lead to complementary relationships instead of competitive ones (e.g., Dryden Lake Trail draws walkers/bicyclers in the spring, summer, and fall, and cross-country skiers in the winter to create year-round opportunities). The Recreation Department should continue to explore alternative programs and special events that will draw people to the parks. For instance, Dairy Days and Music in the Park have revitalized summer use of Montgomery Park; possibilities for ice skating, a skate park, etc. could potentially draw even more residents to that park on a regular basis.

Figure 4.12 Needs assessment report (continued from previous page)

TABLE OF CONTENTS

Figure 4.13 An example of a record (program booklet) that could be used for data collection (continued from p. 103) of information include direct observation, focus groups, surveys, and an examination of old records. The servant leadership orientation dictates that we ask for and utilize needs assessment information from both users and nonusers, and ensure representation from all groups within our community.

Programming from Here to There

The Field Museum's Center for Cultural Understanding and Change website (www.fieldmuseum.org/calumet) offers a wonderful example of asset mapping in action (The Field Museum, 2003). The asset mapping covers the Lake Calumet region, which spans southeast Chicago, Illinois, and northwest Indiana. The Center collected data related to social assets, which they defined as the relationships people create to address the needs of everyday life. They looked at three types of assets: 1) the visible indications of people's capacity to organize, 2) the ways in which people organize (both formally and informally), and 3) the attitudes and values that underlie strategies and guide action. Included in the maps are local resources, networks, places of importance, prevalent issues, connections, and potential connections. To collect the information, the asset mapping team used GIS, focus groups, photo elicitation techniques, interviews, and participant observation.

The use of GIS enabled the mapping team to juxtapose social assets with geographical, historical, demographic, health, crime, land-use data, and aerial maps—providing a comprehensive layering of information. In addition to the maps themselves (which can be viewed on their website), the mapping team learned that when people think of their environment they include physical space, economic security, health, safety, education, and local aesthetics. Not surprisingly, the length of time people lived in the area impacted their involvement in the community. That involvement included formal structures, such as participation on community boards, and informal structures such as neighbors working together. Further, the mapping revealed that people in the region had diverse views about accessing and preserving green space. In terms of recreation resources, the mapping team learned that parks, waterways, wetlands, and forests were "huge assets." In these various settings residents engaged in gardening, water activities, and sports. Cultural events and festivals enabled citizens to feel connected to their own histories as well as the history of the area. Other local resources facilitated the development of social assets; these included informal neighborhood gatherings, local activist organizations, as well as churches, libraries, and other public buildings.

References

Beaulieu, L. (2002). *Mapping the assets of your community: A key for building local capacity.* Southern Rural Development Center. Retrieved August 28, 2008, from http://srdc.msstate.edu/publications/227/227_asset_mapping.pdf

Bonner Foundation. (n.d.). *Community asset mapping: A critical strategy for service.* Retrieved February 22, 2009, from http://www.bonner.org/resources/modules/modules_pdf/BonCurCommAssetMap.pdf

Castleman, C. (n.d.). *Open space guidelines and standards: A guide to understanding the new versus the old.* Reston, VA: National Recreation and Park Association.

Community Strengthening Branch. (2006). *Community building initiative (CBI): Asset mapping guide.* Community Strengthening and Volunteering, Department for Victorian Communities, Melbourne, AU. Retrieved August 28, 2008, from http://www.buloke.vic.gov.au/Buloke/extranet.nsf/0/1F3BCA2F8EC7FA5ECA257221002FFF86/$file/Asset%20Mapping%20Guide%2010March06.pdf

Kretzman, J. & McKnight, J. (1993). *Building communities from the inside out: A path toward finding and mobilizing a community's assets.* Institute for Policy Research, Northwestern University.

Kretzman, J., McKnight, J., Dobrowolski, S. & Puntenney, D. (2005). *Discovering community power: A guide to mobilizing local assets and your organization's capacity.* ABCD Institute. Retrieved August 28, 2008, from http://www.sesp.northwestern.edu/abcd/kellogg/

Rossman, J. R. & Schlatter, B. (2008). *Recreation programming: Designing leisure experiences* (5th ed.). Champaign, IL: Sagamore Publishing.

Search Institute. (2009). Retrieved February 21, 2009, from http://www.search-institute.org

The Field Museum. (2003). *Journey through Calumet: Asset map.* Retrieved January 14, 2009, from http://www.fieldmuseum.org/calumet/

Programmer Profile

Lydia Kuyvenhoven

Photo provided by Lydia Kuyvenhoven

Current Position: Director of Youth Programs, Camp Tall Turf, Grand Rapids, MI
Favorite Book: *Pride & Prejudice* by Jane Austen
Favorite Recreation Activities: Running, biking, cooking

▶ **Describe the path your career has taken.**

- I graduated with a double major in Spanish and Recreation from Calvin College in Michigan. While a student I worked as a camp counselor and program director for Camp Tall Turf.
- After graduating I volunteered with AmeriCorps and conducted after school programs in a middle school. After finishing my year of service, I worked for Camp Fire Boys and Girls and ran their after school programs in Grand Rapids, Michigan.
- Currently, I work with children and teens at Camp Tall Turf. The mission of Camp Tall Turf is reconciling and equipping youth for lives of service in God's world. The vision expands on this mission stating: To pursue and advance God's vision of wholeness, unity, justice, peace, and healing for today's increasing diverse and urban world by rebuilding relationships that make a positive and lasting difference in the lives of youth. In my role as the director of youth programs I develop year-round programs, hire staff, manage our camp programs during the summer and our youth development programs (including our Leaders in Training program) throughout the school year.

▶ **Do you have any advice for new programmers?**

It's very important to keep learning and stay involved. Meet people, make connections and network!! These are skills that are hard to learn in the classroom but are so important for professional development. I am in my current position at Tall Turf because of the connections I made and maintained.

▶ **Describe the joys of working in your current position.**

I think the most rewarding part of working in my current position is seeing change and growth in both campers and staff. Tall Turf's program model "grows up" with kids as it seeks to keep them involved throughout their lives. I started as a counselor at Tall Turf and now am the Director of Youth Programs. Some of my leadership staff were campers who attended camp when I was a counselor. It's very exciting to see them staying involved and invested in their communities!

▶ **What is the most creative program you have developed?**

As part of the Tall Turf program team, I have worked on and developed a Latino Family Camp. The Latino population has been growing tremendously in the Grand Rapids community, but is also very underserved, especially by camps. Culturally, camps are not well-known within the Latino community. Families are generally very hesitant to send their children away overnight anywhere. We felt that by offering a family camp experience, the families would come to know and build a trusting relationship with Camp Tall Turf and its staff such that in the future they would be willing to send their children to youth camp sessions and programs.

▶ **What is an innovative approach to recruiting diverse staff?**

Recruiting a diverse staff takes a lot of time and patience, but the rewards are tremendous. One technique that has been very beneficial for Tall Turf is recruiting from within. We have programs for kids ages 8–17. We stay involved in their lives so that by the time they are 18 they are able to and excited to work at the summer camp. Of course, not everyone wants to work at camp, but this "funnel" has been very successful. We are even seeing it move beyond summer staff to full-time year round staff. Overall, we just make sure we are reaching a diverse audience with our recruitment materials.

Programming for People | 5

In spite of the vast array of settings in which leisure programmers may work, programmers all share in the opportunities and challenges of working with people. In Chapter Four we presented several tools to help assess individual and group needs. In this chapter we want to provide information that will help leisure programmers understand and empathize with the people they serve. This task involves addressing the diversity of people as well as common developmental milestones. It is a cliché (yet true) to say that people come in all sizes, shapes, colors, abilities, and backgrounds. In fact, each person is a unique individual. At the same time, however, individuals share many traits and characteristics with others. People may be like others based on demographic characteristics (e.g., age, sex, race/ethnicity, sexual orientation, physical and mental abilities and qualities) and like others based on interests, needs, and values. These shared traits and characteristics allow leisure programmers to learn about people and use that information to best serve those people in the development, implementation, and evaluation of programs.

It is likely that material about people (e.g., ages, stages, diversity) has been presented in other courses related to parks, recreation, and leisure services. This is because this type of information helps leisure professionals to understand people, and people are the foundation of our profession. Thus, the information presented in this chapter is an overview of material related to understanding people so that leisure professionals might program appropriately. Servant leaders make it a goal to continually develop their knowledge and understanding of various constituent groups so as to further enhance their programming skills. We begin this chapter with an overview of diversity and then provide more specific information related to human development.

Diversity is a concept referring to how individuals differ from one another—remembering that at the same time, people are also similar to one another.

Dimensions of diversity refer to the various dimensions, traits, or characteristics on which individuals differ; these are often referred to as demographic variables. As people, we recognize core and secondary characteristics of individuals; it is these traits upon which others make assumptions about us, and we about them. They include such things as sex, age, socioeconomic status, level of education, and others (Loden, 1995; Loden, 2009; Loden & Rosener, 1991).

The assumptions made based on the dimensions of diversity are known as *stereotypes*. Stereotypes are part of a perceptual and thinking process whereby specific traits are ascribed to people based on their apparent membership in a group—they may be positive or negative. For instance, a negative stereotype might be one where all members of an ethnic group are believed to be lazy. A positive stereotype might be when an individual is perceived to be highly responsible and dependable simply because she or he belongs to a particular age group. *Prejudice* and *discrimination* are often outgrowths of stereotypes and severely limit the people against whom individuals are prejudiced or discriminate. These two terms refer to actions taken based on stereotypes. Commonly, those actions include either including or excluding someone from programs, services, and full acceptance in a group.

The term *racism* is often used to mean an action or attitude that prejudges another person based on her or his perceived race or ethnicity. However, current use of the term more often refers to those forms of prejudice that invoke the privilege of power. These forms of prejudice are often institutionalized (e.g., supported through institutions such as schools, governments, media) and prevent members of a particular race or ethnic group from accessing constitutional and/or human rights. *Social justice* is the term that encompasses the efforts undertaken to address and overcome prejudice and discrimination.

As mentioned earlier, while all are unique individuals, people do share cultural traits with one another. Various groups share assumptions, beliefs, and values (usually unspoken); learned responses; and ways of being, knowing, and doing. People transmit culture from one generation to the next through language, material objects, rituals, institutions, and art. Culture(s) are usually based on the various dimensions of diversity inherent in who each person is.

Dimensions of Diversity

Various dimensions of diversity have a large impact on individual perceptions of the world. Core dimensions of diversity often result in the strongest reaction from others (e.g., they may immediately like us or scorn us). The core (or primary) dimensions include elements of identity we notice upon seeing and meeting people. These dimensions of diversity are extremely difficult, if at all possible, for us to change. The five *primary dimensions* of diversity include sex/gender, race/ethnicity, sexual orientation, physical and cognitive abilities and qualities, and age. *Secondary dimensions* of diversity include such characteristics as educational level attained, family status, socioeconomic status, geographic location (e.g., where a person grew up or currently lives), religion, military status, and work experience (including longevity, type of employment, and role within an organization). Figure 5.1 illustrates the dimensions of diversity model.

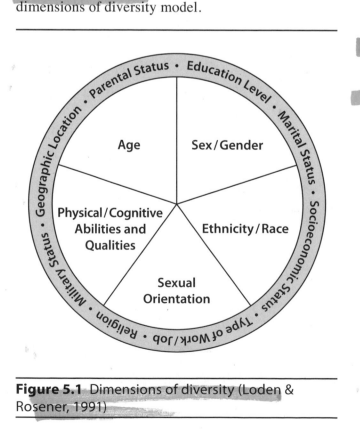

Figure 5.1 Dimensions of diversity (Loden & Rosener, 1991)

These dimensions of diversity are not to be viewed as rigid classifications, but rather as aspects of the human experience that are subject to change within individuals or in society. For example, while religion is considered a secondary characteristic, some religious groups are very identifiable by how they dress and/or speak (e.g., the Amish, Muslims, Othodox Jews, or Sikh), and they often become the victims of strong social sanctions. Likewise, the meaning attached to a particular demographic variable or status may vary considerably based on historical context. One notable example is military status, which may be viewed positively or negatively based on the circumstances of a particular war. For example, the way people treated returning service members has been very different for veterans of the wars in Iraq, Vietnam, and World War II.

Both primary and secondary dimensions of diversity impact leisure in many ways—they are evident in leisure choices, preferences, and participation rates. For instance, males may choose to not take a dance class because they fear the reaction of their friends, family, and others. Further, research tells us that people who have higher levels of education engage in more, and a wider variety of, leisure activities than others. These influences impact the way leisure programmers develop and implement programs. Servant leaders do their best to be aware of how dimensions of diversity influence themselves and others so the programs they develop are as open, inclusive, and welcoming as possible.

Sex and Gender

Sex refers to the biological differences between females and males. These differences include such things such as our reproductive organs and genetic make-up. Gender, on the other hand, is a psychological phenomenon; it is the way we view femaleness (i.e., what is feminine) and maleness (i.e., what is masculine) and is taught to people very subtly throughout life. Evidence exists of a cultural concern for sex and gender roles in various settings. In parks, recreation, and leisure programming the issue of sex and gender arises in the gendered nature of programs offered. By this, we mean people perceive certain programs as "designed" for males and others as "designed" for females. For instance, people who participate in recreation programs (especially children) could probably tell us which activities are "for whom." For example, they might say that gymnastics and aerobics are for girls and women, while football and martial arts are for boys and men. In programming, leisure services professionals often inadvertently (and sometimes purposively) perpetuate these gender stereotypes based on sex and gender.

Society is becoming increasingly accepting of the idea that both sexes benefit from participation in a wide variety of recreation and leisure opportunities. For instance, more and more people recognize the many beneficial outcomes of participating in team sports (which has been predominantly a male domain) and we have seen a tremendous rise in girls' sport involvement because of this. Likewise, it is becoming more acceptable for males to engage in traditional female activities such as cooking and dancing. Leisure programmers influence the way activities and events are gendered through activity selection (e.g., offering only contact sports such as football and karate) and in the time of day offered (i.e., activities held during the day are not available to people who work during the day). Leisure services professionals also contribute to gendering parks, recreation, and leisure through promotional efforts (e.g., when fliers only have pictures or graphics of females on them, thus subtly excluding males), and in customer relations (e.g., a man calls to register for an aerobics class and the staff member informs him "it is an activity for ladies").

Ethnicity and Race

Ethnicity refers to the commonalties passed down through history and tradition from one generation of people to the next. As a term, ethnicity is a more accurate description of the culture with which one identifies than race. In the mid-1990s King, Chipman, and Cruz-Janzen (1994) identified seven components that constitute ethnicity: a historical link, shared geographic beginnings, linguistic commonalties, shared religious beliefs, common social-class status, mutual political interests, and a joint moral (values) base. Individuals who have most or all of these seven aspects of ethnicity in common would be considered to share an ethnic heritage and culture.

Race, on the other hand, refers to a group of people who share a genetic make-up, which results in biological characteristics that can be used to distinguish one group from another (e.g., people of Spanish descent have a darker skin color than people of Scandinavian heritage). Over the generations, the human genetic make-up has mixed and few contemporary researchers acknowledge race as a distinguishing element. Race has relatively little to do with differences in preferences and needs related to parks, recreation, and leisure services programming. It becomes significant primarily as information that may provide insight into a person (e.g., someone who has been systemically marginalized and underserved) within the current and/

or historical social construct. However, because we are all exposed to and affected by institutional racism throughout our lives, this knowledge may be more of a hindrance to us than help. As servant leaders, the most important task before us in this regard is to be open to learning about the experiences of all individuals involved.

A servant leadership approach would indicate that programmers should gain information about the members of ethnic groups with which they might work. Each culture is very complex in its attitudes, beliefs, values structures, and leisure preferences. These preferences might relate to the choice of activity, day of the week on which to participate in an activity, preferences for coed or single-sex recreation, or a desire for intergenerational or segregated program opportunities. Other program attributes such as music, colors, signage, and other elements also matter.

Having said this, it is important to recognize that within each culture individuals are unique; not all women of Asian descent share the same beliefs about gender roles, for instance. Gender, age, physical abilities and qualities, and sexual orientation all interact with one's ethnicity to result in differences within these cultural groups. Learning through observations, interactions, and personal research, then, would be important to gain a solid understanding of people who belong to a variety of ethnic groups. This is commonly referred to as gaining cultural competence.

In programming for people who are of various ethnic backgrounds leisure services professionals should recognize that ethnic groups differ in their perceptions and use of time, beliefs in the importance of the individual over the group, use of language and patterns of communication, leisure preferences, and values. Ethnic groups are *not* different in terms of intellectual, physical, or emotional abilities and needs. Learning about specific ethnic groups will reveal appropriate programming approaches and strategies to best serve them. Certainly, going beyond celebrating ethnic festivals, hanging posters of famous people of color in a facility, and eating ethnic foods is required of leisure services programmers. Programmers can use leisure opportunities as a subtle way to teach and learn about various ethnic groups and develop a greater appreciation of various cultures among all people.

Sexual Orientation

Sexual orientation includes identifying oneself as gay, lesbian, bisexual, transgendered (often referred to as GLBT), and heterosexual. For many, this core dimension of diversity is the most easily hidden of all the core elements (e.g., one cannot tell if someone is straight or gay simply by looking at her or him), yet it still engenders strong social reactions in many communities. People of all sexual orientations engage in a variety of leisure activities and are involved in every type of leisure services organization. Leisure services programmers have long catered to the needs and desires of people who are heterosexual—family programming, husband-wife activities, coeducational dances—yet, the needs of GLBT participants have typically been ignored.

Gay, lesbian, bisexual, and transgendered people differ from heterosexuals in terms of emotional and sociosexual attraction, but are similar in leisure preferences. There certainly are no differences based on sexual orientation in physical, cognitive, or emotional abilities. Specific needs of GLBT participants generally fall in the area of emotional support and social opportunities. Many leisure services providers specifically cater to the needs of gays, lesbians, and bisexuals, particularly in tourism; and increasing numbers of public agencies are responding to the needs of gay or transgendered youth. Generally, programmers can offer a safe environment for people who represent all sexual orientations through their programming efforts.

One of the most needy and underserved minority groups in parks, recreation, and leisure services settings is that of GLBT adolescents and teens. An often confusing time in life for all young people, GLBT adolescents and teens face additional stressors. They may just be realizing they are "different" from their peers and are trying to come to terms with what being GLBT means on an intrapersonal level. Further, people who are gay, lesbian, bisexual, or transgendered may face overt hatred and ostracism from their families, friends, and others at a time when they most need their support. Thus, parks, recreation, and leisure professionals may choose to provide a supportive and safe place for GLBT adolescents to experience leisure, as we commonly do for heterosexual teens.

Physical and Cognitive Abilities and Qualities

In this dimension of diversity, cognitive and physical disabilities are addressed as are other physical qualities that might foster negative reactions—obesity, wearing thick glasses, having severe acne, or being "ugly" in cultural terms. Too often people with disabilities and other "less-than-perfect" physical qualities are discriminated against relative to equal access to parks, recreation,

and leisure services experiences. Assumptions and prejudgments about desires and capabilities are often made upon seeing a person with Down Syndrome, a person with a service animal, a person who is obese, or even a person who has visible birth marks.

Physical and cognitive qualities and ability issues can no longer be ignored. At some point in our lives, everyone will come into contact with people with varying qualities and abilities. People with disabilities live in every community and have a wide range of abilities and limitations, as well as needs and interests. Based on the 2000 census, an estimated 49.7 million people (19.3%) in the United States ages five and older have at least one disability: 35.8% of those individuals have physical disabilities, 19.2% have cognitive or mental impairments, 17.5% have sensory impairments, and 12.2% have conditions that make it difficult to go outside the home (Waldrop & Stern, 2003). As people live longer, we will see increasing numbers of people with age-related disabilities. In addition, the recreation profession is experiencing an increasing need to provide programs and services for wounded service members returning from various conflicts. There is no question that all parks, recreation, and leisure services programmers should be planning and designing activities and events that include people with physical and/or developmental disabilities, and who have varying physical qualities.

In addition to the desire to do the right thing and program for all constituents in a service zone, leisure providers are also required to do so by law. Several laws address the rights of people with disabilities, and the responsibility of agencies and organizations to meet those rights and needs. One of the more prominent pieces of legislation is the Americans with Disabilities Act of 1990 (ADA). The ADA continues to have a profound impact on parks, recreation, and leisure services, as well as on the lives of those with disabilities.

The Americans with Disabilities Act (ADA)

The ADA consists of five subsections, or titles: Title I relates to employment issues, Title II relates to public transportation and accommodations by state and local governments (this is the title that relates to recreation programs and services), Title III addresses public accommodation by private and nonprofit businesses (including restaurants, hotels, movie theaters, and recreation facilities), and the other titles address telecommunications and enforcement issues. The Americans with Disabilities Act of 1990 makes it illegal to discriminate against a person on the basis of her or his disability. Parks, recreation, and leisure services program directors are responsible to ensure both the law and the spirit of the ADA is followed so as to facilitate a full range of leisure experiences for all people. The ADA states that leisure services providers *must*:

- Make reasonable accommodations for people with disabilities to enable full enjoyment of services, programs, and facilities (including policies, communication, and physical access); and

- Provide services, programs, and activities with the most interaction possible.

The ADA states that leisure services providers *shall not*:

- Deny a qualified person with a disability the opportunity to participate or benefit from services available to people without disabilities;

- Offer less effective opportunities for those with disabilities;

- Provide separate aids, benefits, or services for people with disabilities unless those services are necessary to make programs and services available;

- Aid or perpetuate discrimination in any form; or

- Use facilities or sites that result in the exclusion of people with disabilities.

The ADA Amendments Act (ADAAA)

Effective January 1, 2009, this act broadens the definition of *disability* (for example, this amendment adds cancer to the list of recognized disabilities) and clarifies other language subject to legal interpretation (such as *major life activities*). Major life activities now include self-care, working, communicating, concentrating, thinking, reading, and other activities of central importance. The ADAAA also seeks to find a reasonable balance between employer/service provider responsibilities and recipients' needs and rights (Employer Law Report, 2008).

Parks, recreation, and leisure services professionals are required by law to offer programs and services in such a way as to fully include people with disabilities in activities. Servant leaders make every effort to be fully inclusive of all people. *Reasonable accommodation* is a phrase used to refer to some of the

responsibilities related to serving people with disabilities. Programmers must maintain inclusive programs and services by making reasonable accommodations to enable anyone who has a disability to participate fully. Furthermore, full inclusion of people with disabilities in leisure programs is the right thing to do. Necessary program modifications and adaptations will vary for different people who have various disabilities, but most involve minimal changes and/or expense. Learning about inclusion, adaptations, modifications, and assistive technology should be a part of recreation programmers' ongoing professional education.

Assistive Technology (AT)

In efforts to serve all constituents, recreation programmers will want a working knowledge of assistive technology (AT). AT includes equipment, supplies, and devices designed to facilitate full inclusion of people with disabilities in parks, recreation, and leisure programs and services. These items might simply be modifications of existing equipment (such as strapping Velcro to a paint brush so a person with limited

Figure 5.2 An accessible sidewalk includes a curb cut and tactile strip for the visually impaired.

hand and finger mobility can paint) to equipment and devices specifically designed for use by people with physical limitations. Understanding a participant's functional limitations and strengths will aid the programmer in making the best determination of AT needs. This requires open communication with participants.

Age

One core element of diversity that we will all experience if we live long enough involves the stages of human development, or aging. This is the only dimension of diversity we all share, regardless of other personal characteristics. Because of this, parks, recreation, and leisure programmers need to reflect on the changes through which human beings move as we age. While there are many ways to examine human development, and many theories related to lifespan issues, we will present this information from a life-stage development perspective. It is a relatively common way of thinking and is familiar to many.

People who are close in age tend to have similar cognitive, physical, social, and emotional capabilities. As long as programmers remember that exceptions always exist, this knowledge can facilitate programmers to design and implement activities appropriately matched to these capabilities. By using this information, leisure professionals can ensure enjoyable, safe, and successful leisure programs for everyone, whether offering intergenerational or age-segregated programs. In the following sections of this chapter, we will present information about human growth and development to assist the programmer in making appropriate choices for people of various ages.

Developmental Assets

Before we begin to examine the life stages common to childhood, we would like to present a framework for viewing youth development, which we mentioned earlier in this text—developmental assets. A great many parks, recreation, and leisure services organizations use

Table 5.1 Developmental assets: External assets (Search Institute, 2008)

Asset Category	Developmental Asset	Definition
Support	Family support	Family life provides high levels of love and support.
	Positive family communication	Young person and her or his parents communicate positively and young person is willing to seek their counsel.
	Other adult relationships	Young person receives support from three or more nonparent adults.
	Caring neighborhood	Young person experiences caring neighbors.
	Caring school climate	School provides a caring, encouraging environment.
	Parent involvement in schooling	Parents are actively involved in helping a young person succeed in school.
Empowerment	Community values youth	Young person perceives that adults in the community value youth.
	Youth as resources	Young people are given useful roles in the community.
	Service to others	Young person serves the community one hour or more per week.
	Safety	Young person feels safe at home, school, and in the neighborhood.
Boundaries and Expectations	Family boundaries	Family has clear rules and consequences, and monitors the young person's whereabouts.
	School boundaries	School provides clear rules and consequences.
	Neighborhood boundaries	Neighbors take responsibility for monitoring young peoples' behaviors.
	Adult role models	Parents and other adults model positive, responsible behaviors.
	Positive peer influence	Young person's best friends model responsible behaviors.
	High expectations	Both parents and teachers encourage the young person to do well.
Constructive Use of Time	Creative activities	Young person spends three or more hours per week in lessons or practice in music, theater, or other arts.
	Youth programs	Young person spends three or more hours per week in sports, clubs, or organizations at school and/or community organizations.
	Religious community	Young person spends one or more hours per week in activities in a religious institution.
	Time at home	Young person is "out with friends with nothing special to do" two or fewer nights per week.

this information as a foundation for program planning. It is a perspective that forces leisure professionals to examine families, neighborhoods, and institutions for the positive impact they have on "growing" successful young people. For many years, programmers have considered youth from a deficit or need-based perspective. One example of where this is evident is in the language related to "youth at risk." A perspective of young people as "problems to be addressed" has led leisure services professionals to develop programs as a way to fix or prevent problems—for instance, an agency might offer midnight basketball as a way to keep potential troublemakers off of the streets. This perspective can limit one's view of the strengths and benefits youth can offer to the community. Developmental assets help to refocus one's perspective from a negative or limiting position to a positive or strengthening position.

The Search Institute (2008) began surveying youth in 1989 in the United States and Canada to learn about the experiences, attitudes, behaviors, and developmental assets of young people. From this research, the Search Institute identified the positive building blocks commonly found in young people's lives.

These building blocks are known as developmental assets—the "relationships, opportunities, values, and skills, that when present in the lives of youth, make young people less likely to become involved in risk behaviors and more likely to be successful in school, relationships, and life in general" (Benson, Scales, Leffert & Roehlkepartain, 1999, as cited in Scales & Taccogna, 2000, p. 69). The Search Institute has identified 40 developmental assets for adolescents, those in middle childhood, and youngsters in early childhood—20 external assets and 20 internal assets for each age group (see Tables 5.1 and 5.2). When present, these assets contribute to healthy, successful, and thriving youth.

External Assets

External assets are positive experiences young people receive from the people and institutions (such as parks, recreation, and leisure services organizations) in their lives. The external assets include four categories (see Table 5.1 on p. 120).

Table 5.2 Developmental assets: Internal assets (Search Institute, 2008)

Asset Category	Developmental Asset	Definition
Commitment to Learning	Achievement motivation	Young person is motivated to do well in school.
	School engagement	Young person is actively engaged in learning.
	Homework	Young person reports doing at least one hour of homework every school day.
	Bonding to school	Young person cares about her or his school.
	Reading for pleasure	Young person reads for pleasure three or more hours per week.
Positive Values	Caring	Young person places high value on helping other people.
	Equality and social justice	Young person places high value on promoting equality and reducing hunger and poverty.
	Integrity	Young person acts on convictions and stands up for her or his beliefs.
	Honesty	Young person tells the truth, even when it is not easy.
	Responsibility	Young person accepts and takes personal responsibility.
	Restraint	Young person believes it is important not to be sexually active or to use alcohol or other drugs.
Social Competencies	Planning and decision making	Young person knows how to plan ahead and make decisions.
	Interpersonal competence	Young person has empathy, sensitivity, and friendship skills.
	Cultural competence	Young person has knowledge of and comfort with people of different cultural/racial/ethnic backgrounds.
	Resistance skills	Young person can resist negative peer pressure and dangerous situations.
	Peaceful conflict resolution	Young person seeks to resolve conflict nonviolently.
Positive Identity	Personal power	Young person feels she or he has control over "things that happen to me."
	Self-esteem	Young person reports having high self-esteem.
	Sense of purpose	Young person reports "my life has a purpose."
	Positive view of personal future	Young person is optimistic about her or his personal future.

- *Support:* Young people need to experience support, care, and love from their families, neighbors, and other adults. They need organizations that provide positive, supportive environments.

- *Empowerment:* Young people need to be valued by their community and have opportunities to contribute to others. For this to occur, young people must feel safe and secure.

- *Boundaries and expectations:* Young people need to know what is expected of them and whether activities and behaviors are "in or out of bounds."

- *Constructive use of time:* Young people need constructive, enriching opportunities for growth through creative activities, youth programs, congregational involvement, and quality time at home.

Internal Assets

Internal assets involve nurturing the internal qualities that guide choices made by young people and create a sense of purpose and focus in their lives. Through these assets young people learn to internalize wise, responsible, and compassionate behaviors. The internal assets include four categories (see Table 5.2 on p. 121):

- *Commitment to learning:* Young people need to develop a lifelong commitment to learning.

- *Positive values:* Young people need to develop strong values to guide their choices.

- *Social competencies:* Young people need skills and competencies that equip them to make positive choices, build relationships, and succeed in life.

- *Positive identity:* Young people need a strong sense of their own power, purpose, worth, and promise. (Search Institute, 2008)

Research conducted by the Search Institute (2008) and others has shown the most common assets among young people are positive peer influence, family support, positive view of personal future, school engagement, time spent in a religious community, and the value of integrity. The least common developmental assets include youth as resources, a caring school, community that values youth, reading for pleasure, and involvement in creative activities. In addition, the research indicates that the average young person has 18 of the 40 assets;

and, as youth age, they tend to lose assets (Scales, 2000). Girls have more assets than boys. Scales also found that only 8% of youth are "asset-rich" (have 31 to 40 assets), and 42% were "asset-poor" (had 20 or fewer assets); this was true across racial and ethnic groupings. The more assets youth have, the more resilient they are and the more positive behaviors they exhibit. Typically, those who had a minimum of 23 or 24 assets engaged in few high-risk behaviors (Search Institute, 2008).

Thus, it becomes clear that asset building can have a tremendously positive effect on the development of young people, and that parks, recreation, and leisure services professionals are in a unique position to nurture these traits. Asset building is something each person can consciously incorporate into our programming efforts. Some of the strategies one might consider include cooperative programming, involvement of young people in decision making related to special programs, establishment of goals and objectives directed toward skill development in social skills, and the establishment of adult mentors to augment the number of caring adults in young peoples' lives. Leisure professionals might also consider age-appropriate service opportunities in communities, opportunities for leadership development through programming, and establishing ground rules that enhance respect and caring for all.

With this orientation in mind, we would like to now consider the generalities of what we know about human development across the lifespan. As mentioned earlier, this is not an exhaustive presentation of developmental issues, but rather an overview or starting point. Generally speaking, we know that as people develop they grow physically, cognitively, socially, and emotionally. Thus, leisure services professionals should bear this developmental process in mind while programming.

Life Stages and Age Groups

Behavior results from a combination of physical, cognitive, and socioemotional aspects of a person—it is both a holistic process and a product. Generally speaking, *physical development* includes physical energy and growth, the acquisition of fine and gross motor skills, physical coordination, and activity preferences. *Cognitive development* includes the ability to think abstractly, academic achievement, reasoning and logic, and limitations in mental abilities. *Socioemotional development* consists of relationships with others (e.g., peers and adults), fears, worries, self-control, and moods.

Before we delve into the various life stages, we offer a caveat, or caution, about how life stage information is utilized. It is important to remember that individuals may fall within an identified age range, yet be an exception to the traits and characteristics representative of a particular life stage. Therefore, while the following information can be helpful in many ways, predicting *specific individual* behaviors based on age group or life stage is not possible.

Young Childhood (5-7 years)

Physical Development

In terms of physical development, children ages five to seven years have lots of energy; it comes in spurts, and is often difficult to keep under control. As they continue to practice large motor skills, children at this age enjoy a great deal of running, hopping, skipping, climbing, throwing, and catching. In addition, chasing and being chased are favorite activities. Because children at this age struggle with fine motor control they may experience frustration when practicing fine motor skills (e.g., tying shoes). Their high level of physical activity is balanced by a similar need for rest as youngsters in this age group tend to tire quickly and easily.

Cognitive Development

Five- to seven-year olds tend to be concrete thinkers and are very literal in interpreting meanings. Consequently, a Caucasian child might ask, "why is her nose flat?" when meeting a new playmate who is of Asian descent. At this age youngsters have no concept of the social meaning that might be attached to such a question; it is merely an expression based on a concrete observation. Thus, at this age, children operate from perception and intuition rather than logic. It is difficult for young children to focus on more than one thing at a time and they only see things from their own perspective (and they believe everyone else sees things as they do, as well). Young children can accept and work with basic rules, but they will change rules when needed to avoid failure. Due to their heavy reliance on concrete thinking, movement is often necessary for learning and understanding directions. At this age children have wonderful capacities for fantasy, and active imaginations. In addition, in this stage children are curious and ask a lot of questions—they are trying to figure out how the world works.

Socioemotional Development

Young children do not have strong social skills (e.g., communication, conflict resolution, an 'other-orientation'). They tend to be egoistic with everything centering on themselves. In this age group, children engage in some sharing, but do not necessarily seek out ways to share. In addition, a separation of the sexes with boys and girls playing apart from one another is common. Children at this age are generally very honest; this is due in part to a lack of mastery over the nuances of lying. Organizational skills are not a strong suit for young children and items are often lost or left lying about.

Youngsters at this stage of development can be overly sensitive to comments and actions of others (e.g., they may be very hurt if a child sticks out her tongue at them). If there is difficulty in understanding directions, youngsters of this age can be easily frustrated. They need a good deal of encouragement and support from adults and seem to crave adult affection. Children of this age are very impulsive and unable to control their emotions; they tend to use physical aggression to resolve problems, and start and stop crying quickly.

Middle Childhood (8-11 years)

Physical Development

As children move into middle childhood physical coordination improves as do abilities in gross and fine motor skills. High energy levels are still apparent, although since children at this stage do not tire as easily as they did just a few years earlier, they have a reduced need for rest. While children at this age are able to be still for longer periods of time, active participation is still needed for optimum learning to occur. It is not uncommon for early signs of preadolescence to occur in girls at ten or eleven years of age (e.g., onset of menstruation, change in body shape). Youth at this stage are capable of rhythmic movement and begin to show an interest in group activities such as sports.

Cognitive Development

At the middle childhood stage logic, reasoning, and the ability to effectively deal with abstractions develop. One of the characteristics of eight- to eleven-year olds is that they ask a lot of "why" questions as they begin to sort out and understand cause-and-effect relationships. At this age self-concept begins to solidify. Youngsters in this stage of development tend to be easily motivated and are able to work within activity rules. In addition, they have wonderful senses of humor and enjoy challenges (appropriate to their level of development).

Children are now able to consider more than one aspect of a situation at one time, and they understand general concepts better than when younger.

Problem-solving skills are improving and at this age youngsters are able to work independently for short periods of time (particularly when playing video and computer games). Whereas children ages five to seven might give up when faced with frustration, in middle childhood, children tend to persevere longer—they begin to believe that they can make something happen if they try hard and long enough.

Socioemotional Development

As children move out of the egoistic phase (focused on self-interests) they become interested in their peer group. Because children are beginning to form attachments to groups, they become very concerned about fairness and equality. They share better, yet the sexes (for the most part) remain separate (e.g., girls/boys have the "cooties"). Those children in this age group who are maturing more quickly than others may describe girl/boyfriend relationships. As groups develop, so too do relationship skills; youngsters at this age develop some tact, but are not always sensitive to others' needs. At this stage children understand the social meaning attached to the dimensions of diversity presented earlier in this chapter and will share related learned behaviors with others. Adults remain important figures in the lives of these youth, although older children are beginning to test adults in their desire for independence.

It is important to remember that children between the ages of eight and eleven years old do not take criticism from peers or adults very well (they tend to be sensitive and defensive), and are easily embarrassed. An increased awareness of peers and others' expectations impacts the development of self-esteem. This may be seen in an increase of girls "primping" and boys striving to look "cool." Researchers have documented

Figure 5.3 In middle childhood, youth develop relationship skills.

that at about age ten or eleven years self-esteem in girls begins to drop (Clay, Vignoles, & Dittmar, 2005).

Young Adolescence (12–14 years)

Physical Development

In the early teen years, youth experience a balance in their energy output; generally they have calmed down since early and middle childhood. The impulsivity of the previous years has lessened. At twelve to fourteen years of age most girls have experienced the onset of puberty and the development of secondary sex characteristics. There is great variation with boys; some boys have reached puberty, others are just beginning the sexual maturation process. For many young people in this age group, abilities related to coordination and fine and gross motor skills are well-developed. They have a great capacity to try new tasks. Adolescents continue to need opportunities to practice and develop individual skills. Physical activities that appear to be (and sometimes are) reckless are favorites of young people in this life stage. Risk-taking behaviors and challenges are viewed as desirable, in part for the thrills and excitement they provide.

Cognitive Development

Most young teens are gaining experience in logic, reasoning, and problem-solving skills while also improving in their organizational skills and rules management. Twelve- to fourteen-year-old youth have the capability to understand multiple perspectives (i.e., they can see and begin to appreciate others' viewpoints) and to deal with abstractions. Teens begin to develop the ability to formulate and test hypotheses (i.e., "what if…" situations). In this period of early adolescence, youth are beginning to develop a sense of self-identity. These are years of much exploration (e.g., drugs, questioning sexuality, risk-taking behaviors) as the search for self ensues. Young adolescents are capable of understanding and developing strategy in their play and appreciate knowing reasons for why things are the way they are.

Socioemotional Development

In our society, peers are a very important source of support for young teens as they strive to make the transition from family dependence to independence. Their peer group easily influences young people in this age group and the need for belonging seems all-important. Common tools used by young adolescents to stay in touch and develop relationships include online social networking sites, blogs, and cell phone texting. While being connected is important, so too is a need to have time alone. Sociosexual relationships (i.e., attractions to others based on sexuality) begin to develop, as does sexual exploration.

Emotions and moods can range widely as changes in hormones interfere with other cognitive, social, and physical changes. Self-esteem, particularly for girls, fluctuates tremendously in this developmental stage. Research to determine why self-esteem for teenage girls drops so steeply is ongoing. Concerns with body image (as body shape changes with physical maturity) and embarrassment are important issues to this age group of teens. Boys often work through determining a sense of self through being "cool" and engaging in between-boy competitions. That is, teenage boys often engage in showing-off behaviors and spontaneous public competitions (e.g., basketball "jam" contests at the neighborhood court). Teen girls often subscribe to social images of what is beautiful and may experience negative effects on their own psyche (e.g., anorexia, bulimia).

Adolescence (15–17 years)

Physical Development

Well into being teenagers, fifteen- to seventeen-year olds tend to be very concerned about their physical development and body image. Most males reach puberty during this period; most girls have already reached puberty. As physical growth outpaces their ability to adapt, boys' coordination takes a dip (e.g., they may appear gangly—all arms and legs). By this age most girls have accepted their post pubescent bodies. Skills acquisition becomes important and is made possible by physical capabilities—this is the age at which

Figure 5.4 Peers are a very important source of support for young adolescents.

many physical skills are refined. A great deal of sleep is needed during this life stage and many teens are constantly tired; this may be a factor in leisure choices as they begin to seek less structure (new emphasis on just hanging out with friends) and various forms of physical activity (including watching television and playing computer games). Reckless behavior (that suggests a sense of immortality) and exploration (e.g., sex, drugs) continue from early adolescence into this life stage.

Cognitive Development

Many teens hold an idealistic view of the world and believe situations can change if people just try hard enough. At this age the ability to handle abstractions, test hypotheses, and engage in problem solving come together. Cognitive abilities have reached a point of development where further growth results in increasing sophistication rather than the development of new skills. Teens have a wide variety of interests and a strong need to experiment and stretch themselves. They understand the need for rules in games and activities and enjoy sophistication in terms of rules and strategy.

Socioemotional Development

Moving toward young adulthood, older teens strive to achieve self-identity, freedom from adults, and responsibility for themselves. Group affiliation remains important and mixed-sex activities are sought. This stage of development can be difficult for teens as the pull for independence and desire for familial security coexist. Moodiness might reflect the struggle in maintaining changing relationships with parents and other adults. Many teens in this age group often seem like two different people—one mature young adult, and one immature youngster. Music becomes important as an avenue for self-expression. It serves as an outlet for moods as well as a sign of growing independence. In addition, for males, competition becomes increasingly important. Females often drop out of team sports during this stage of development.

Young Adulthood (18–25 years)

Physical Development

Young adults are at their physical peak. Most physical abilities are well-developed by this age, and while nuances may be refined, increased physical prowess is unlikely. The activity level of young adults is relatively high, but it can be slowed somewhat by life changes (e.g., beginning a career, relocation, establishing a family). Most people in this age group desire structured competition and recreation play. Often a concern for fitness drives physical activity, and activity is often secondary to job or career. Interests in physical activity often include both individual and group activities. Young adults welcome outdoor recreation and other forms of physical recreation. High energy, some high in risk-taking behaviors (especially for males), and a need to "do" are traits of this group.

Cognitive Development

Building on the cognitive skills of the late teens, young adults are creative and capable of handling abstractions quite well. Cognitive skills are sharp and are often considered at a peak during these years. Problem solving and hypothesis testing are further refined as young adults build on previous knowledge and experience. Intellectual development tends to increase in sophistication, as does an understanding of strategy and complex rule structures.

Socioemotional Development

It is during the young adult years that most people in our culture search for a life partner and a sense of stability, continuing the process of separating from their family of origin. Enjoyment is often experienced in mixed-sex activities and one's circle of friends expands through college, work, and neighborhood connections. People take risks at this life stage to develop intimate and social connections with others. A concern for work and work efforts begins; competitiveness often reaches a high point in this life stage.

Figure 5.5 Competition can be a valued form of recreation for young adults.

Early Adulthood (26–40 years)

Physical Development

At early adulthood, many people are still at their physical peak. Some slowing down is evident as family and career take priority, and finesse generally becomes more important than strength. Those in early adulthood strive to perfect skills rather than using brawn. Physical activities often take on a family orientation. Personal activity involvement tends to be focused on a few activities in which an individual works to hone her or his skills. Involvement in team sports lessens while individual lifelong sports begin to take on increased importance.

Cognitive Development

Cognitive skills and abilities of human beings are at a peak in early adulthood. One's creativity, use of logic and reasoning, and understanding abstractions reach a high point and many people enjoy stretching their cognitive skills through mental challenges. An awareness of the influences of greater society and global issues on self and family occurs. Perseverance, the ability to work toward one goal for a prolonged period of time, is characteristic of people at this life stage. A solid understanding of self has typically developed for people in this age range, and individuals are engaged in planning for long-term concerns.

Socioemotional Development

Persons in early adulthood generally have decided and are settled in their decisions relative to children and family. Often, the family orientation is one that goes in both directions; that is, there is a concern for both one's children and aging parents. For those without children, in the early years of middle adulthood a "couple" orientation, and a focus toward developing one's work and career are often evident. Work-related stresses may begin to interfere with one's personal and leisure life. Values are firmly established and a commitment to community is often evident.

Middle Adulthood (41–60 years)

Physical Development

As individuals pass early adulthood, changes in physical abilities become evident. Most people experience a general slowing down with changes in eyesight, strength, and flexibility. Metabolism begins to slow and weight gain is common; for women, menopause occurs. Physical activity tends to decline as personal work and family situations change.

Cognitive Development

As with early adulthood, people in this age group experience strong cognitive skills and abilities. Much of one's focus is on career; creativity and the use of cognitive skills are focused in that direction. An understanding of global and social issues is increasingly important to individuals and families. It is during these years that people experience a sense of their own mortality. At this stage some experience a concern with falling into boredom in both work and leisure. In addition, many fear being put into situations when they will fail; thus, some leisure opportunities are missed.

Socioemotional Development

Many people in this age group are focused on current social position and preparing for security in retirement. Family, grandchildren, aging parents, and extended family also become increasingly important. Social relationships tend to be stable and long lasting. Concern about the future and work-related stresses may influence one's emotional and mental stability. This is the life stage when it is common for adults to experience midlife crises—often a radical change in behaviors and attitudes occurs. Midlife crises are experienced by both women and men, and by people from all walks of life. Adults have a desire for respect by others and to experience a variety of life experiences.

Older Adulthood (61+ years)

Physical Development

As medical and lifestyle changes are introduced and accepted, people tend to live longer and healthier lives. Due to longer life spans, adults aged 61 and older exhibit tremendous variation in physical abilities and limitations. While everyone experiences changes in balance, eyesight, hearing, strength and flexibility, how each person is affected by and deals with these changes is based on one's own physical make-up, mental attitude, environment, and opportunities. Some people seem as young and vibrant as those many years their junior, while others are quite frail.

The great disparities between well, active seniors (most aged 61–70) and frail elderly (most aged 71–100+) require that recreation and leisure services leaders take care to avoid categorizing all older adults as having limited physical or cognitive abilities. In fact, many people in their sixties and early seventies are as active and healthy as people in their fifties. Women tend to outlive men in all racial and ethnic groups; therefore, the senior age group includes higher numbers of women than men.

Cognitive Development

As with the changes and differences in physical condition, a similar variation in cognitive and mental processes between individuals is found at this life stage. Eventually mental processes slow, but as a whole, older adults remain sharp and in control of their mental capacities until well into old age. Diseases such as dementia (e.g., Alzheimer's) affect the mental capabilities of some older adults, but these people are exceptions rather than the norm. Leisure programmers who work with older adults who experience major memory loss will need to structure activities and interactions accordingly; programmers will also find the joy of relating to individuals who are living in "the here and now."

Work-related stresses are reduced at this stage as people experience retirement and life changes. However, as retirement arrives older adults may experience stresses related to a change in life (i.e., from worker to retiree). People at this stage of life tend to be more cautious than in younger years and like to think through new ideas prior to engagement. People in this age range are often preoccupied with health concerns.

Socioemotional Development

As people age, social connections become increasingly important. Ironically, this occurs at the same time that people begin to deal with social isolation as life partners and friends die and thoughts of their own mortality increase. Conflict in response to the desire for and lessening of social contacts may occur. Much reflection over one's life is common as people realize their own mortality. Because of this, a renewed interest in religion may occur. Furthermore, retirement may result in great joy and an apparent rejuvenation, or it may cause new stresses as financial stability and quality of life become salient issues.

People in this life stage often experience a "second wind" where they begin or renew leisure activities. Older adults often choose to participate in outdoor recreation such as gardening, walking, and bird watching. Fear often increases and is related to physical safety and well-being, as well as the fast pace of life lived by young people. Some individuals in this life stage may experience boredom; many offset this experience through volunteerism.

Servant Leadership and Programming for People

This chapter easily fits most attributes of a servant leader. After all, parks and recreation professionals are in the business of providing parks, recreation, and leisure services experiences for people from all walks of life. The two traits most emphasized, however, are the ability to offer healing and the ability to empathize with others. The ability to offer healing relates to 'matters of the heart,' which includes the ability to connect with others and facilitate a sense of belonging. By allowing ourselves to develop relationships with people, we embrace this idea. Further, by developing an understanding of human beings and learning about the physical, cognitive, social, and emotional stages of development, as well as various unique cultural perspectives, leisure professionals enhance their ability to be responsive to others.

Empathy requires that individuals develop the capacity to share in others' experiences and ideas. As people, we can only do this through sharing experiences and developing our own sense of cultural competence. As we recognize, accept, and fully integrate the uniquenesses of others into our professional lives, we are engaging in behaviors related to empathy. Thus, using the knowledge and appreciation of others as a perspective from which to program underlies the servant leadership approach to program design and delivery. Understanding the complexities involved when working with people also involves a servant leader commitment to the growth of others as individuals, and in building the community. As we come to know others and to more fully appreciate their

needs, wants, and desires from their perspectives we are able to put into action the ideals of this approach to programming.

Summary

In this chapter we have provided a basis for understanding people—the one common element in all leisure services settings. Elements of diversity and life span issues affect us all. If leisure services professionals are to be true to a servant leadership approach to programming, professionals need to consider cultural influences as well as any adaptations or modifications needed by potential participants within all programming efforts. By being knowledgeable about general traits of people and empathizing with each person's life experience, leisure programmers can plan and implement enjoyable programs that allow for success and address participant needs. In addition, commitment to include and foster the growth of each individual, regardless of background or ability, provides an opportunity for all to build community with others in a safe environment.

We introduced the framework of developmental assets—a way to contribute positively to the growth

Figure 5.7 The Wounded Warriors program is helping injured service members to re-engage in recreation and leisure experiences.

Figure 5.6 Older adults often experience leisure through volunteering.

and development of young people. There are 40 developmental assets; 20 are external assets young people receive from the people and institutions around them, and 20 are internal assets that help young people to develop personal strengths and skills to be successful in the world.

It is important to remember that while people all pass through the various life stages, not everyone does so at the same chronological age. In their development people are affected by social mores and stereotypes, genetic disposition, opportunities, their own abilities and limitations, and others' expectations. By understanding the basic elements of human development—physical, mental/cognitive, and socioemotional—programmers can take appropriate actions with regard to activity selection, timing, equipment use, and other aspects of program planning.

Programming From Here to There

A program example that integrates many attributes of servant leadership with recreation is the Wounded Warrior Program. This program utilizes sports and recreation to enhance the physical and emotional rehabilitation of injured service personnel, and is becoming increasingly common throughout the United States. The programs differ across the country, but most offer recreation activities in conjunction with psychological counseling. The injuries faced by returning service members include such injuries as post-traumatic stress disorder (PTSD), amputations, traumatic brain injuries, spinal cord injuries, and other muscular and skeletal wounds. Thus, many communities and military recreation programs are hiring Certified Therapeutic Recreation Specialists (CTRS) to provide recreation activities and therapy as part of the healing and reintegration processes. Common recreation programs include outdoor activities such as skiing, kayaking, rock climbing, biking and fishing. Sports such as basketball, football, softball, and track and field events are also common aspects of Wounded Warrior programs. In addition, individual fitness activities such as weight lifting and swimming are provided. A core element to the success of such programs is connecting with the real needs of real people, many of whom have special needs. More information about Wounded Warrior programs may be found online by using "wounded warrior" as a key term in any online search engine.

References

Americans with Disabilities Act of 1990 (ADA), 42 U.S.C. § § 12101–12213

Clay, D., Vignoles, V. & Dittmar, H. (2005). Body image and self-esteem among adolescent girls: Testing the influence of sociocultural factors. *Journal of Research on Adolescence, 15*(4), 451–477.

Employer Law Report (2008). *ADA Amendments Act passed by House and Senate; President expected to sign bill.* Retrieved January 30, 2009, from http//www.employerlawreport.comKing, E., Chipman, M. & Cruz-Janzen, M. (1994). *Educating young children in a diverse society.* Needham Heights, MA: Allyn & Bacon.

Loden, M. (2009). Retrieved January 9, 2010, from http://www.loden.com/Site/Welcome.html

Loden, M. (1995). *Implementing diversity.* Chicago, IL: Irwin.

Loden, M. & Rosener, J. (1991). *Work force America: Managing employee diversity as a vital resource.* Homewood, IL: Business One Irwin.

King, E., Chipman, M. & Cruz-Janzen, M. (1994). *Educating young children in a diverse society.* Needham Heights, MA: Allyn & Bacon.

Nondiscrimination on the basis of disability by public accommodations and in commercial facilities, 28 CFR § 36 (1994).

Scales, P. (2000). Building students' developmental assets to promote health and school success. *The Clearing House, 74*(2), 84–88.

Scales, P. & Taccogna, J. (2000). Caring to try: How building students' developmental assets can promote school engagement and success, *National Association of Secondary School Principals. NASSP Bulletin, 84*(619), 69–78.

Search Institute. (2008). *What kids need: Developmental assets.* Retrieved February 12, 2009, from http://www.search-institute.org/assets/

Waldrop, J. & Stern, S. (2003). *Disability status: 2000.* (Census 2000 Brief 2003.C2KBR:17). Washington, DC: U.S. Census Bureau.

Programmer Profile

Barbara Cobas

Photo provided by Barbara Cobas

Current Position: Guest Activities Specialist, Royal Caribbean International
Favorite Book: The Bible
Favorite Recreation Activity: Traveling!

▶ **Describe the path your career has taken.**

- I graduated with a B.S. in Spanish and Minor in Business from Calvin College in Michigan.
- I have worked at Royal Caribbean International Cruise Lines for six years. In those six years I have had a variety of positions including: Cruise staff (shipboard), social hostess (shipboard), training specialist (shoreside), activities manager (shipboard), casting specialist (shoreside), and guest activities specialist (shoreside).
- In my current position, I manage and support the onboard activity program for Royal Caribbean International. I am the operational support for our Activities Managers, Open Deck Managers, Sports Supervisors, and Administrators for 20 ships all over the world. I support all on board programs, from karaoke to bingo, from surf machines to rock climbing walls and everything in between. I manage, promote, and cast appropriate managers based on their skill sets and what our guest demographic requires.

▶ **Describe the joys of working in your current position.**

I am fortunate to work in a very fast paced, fun, and challenging workplace. I have a team that is incredibly hard working and dedicated to delivering guests an amazing vacation experience while also providing our shipboard staff outstanding support to deliver those experiences. On a normal day we are working on budgets, individual performance issues and goals, creative projects, and forward movement planning. I enjoy the variety of my position, and there is never a dull moment.

▶ **Do you have any advice for new programmers?**

Always remember who your guest is. Keep up with the trends, read the newspaper, attend every conference you can get to, listen to people's interests, and keep your eyes open all the time for trends that are up and coming. Your programming must provide guests with a balance of what people expect (unchangeable activities) while also providing them with the stimulation of new and up and coming events. You must be cutting edge, while also being traditional. Understand and study your demographic by tracking your attendance trends and talking to your constituents about what they want to see in your programming.

▶ **Where do you go to get creative ideas for developing programs?**

Every year, I attend the National Recreation and Park Association conference and the International Attractions and Parks Association conference to see what is up and coming in the industry. I also believe it is very important to open your viewfinder even further to find the places where people are having fun and being entertained. We can find a gem in a Cirque du Soleil show as easily as we can find a gem at a Carnival Fairgrounds or by simply watching TV. The important part is opening your perspective wide enough to see them. We very recently just saw a commercial that used a dance element, which was brilliant. We are now trying to determine how we translate that into our programming because it was so relatable. You can never let your mind rest in this fun and hands-on industry…if you do you may miss something!

▶ **How do you ensure that our programs remain contemporary or culturally relevant?**

I believe we stay contemporary by continuously trying new programs. Similar to television, each season starts with a handful of shows and slowly those that don't get the ratings drop off the map. Then there are those shows such as *Friends*, *ER*, or *Lost* that were unexpected and instant successes. It is similar with programming. We must continuously throw new and exciting activities out to our guests. Some will flop and others will be unexpected hits. We must be constantly evolving and changing to meet our guests' expectations. Just keep trying anything that you feel entertains and remember the TV seasons!

Program Design | 6

Unless someone like you cares a whole awful lot, nothing is going to get better, it's not.
—Dr. Seuss (1971)

The program design step in the program planning cycle integrates the philosophy of the organization with needs, assets, and knowledge of human development into programs and services. In the program design process, the programmer's focus turns to the potential beneficial outcomes to be produced through a specific program. This process requires that recreation programmers look at a variety of factors. Constant changes in society, participants, and staff dictate the need for a plan as well as require great flexibility by programmers.

In addition to this need for constant adaptation in response to external changes, programming is a process that includes far more than scheduling specific activities. In reality, a program includes the interaction of the organization's philosophy, the needs of customers, the overall program mix (both activities and services) offered by the organization, specific program goals and objectives, physical environment (e.g., facilities and space), people (e.g., staff and participants), equipment, scheduling, budgets, concern for safety, and other less tangible factors such as policies and procedures, and stage within the product life cycle. The design phase in the programming process works to ensure the most positive interface between these components. While several other subcomponents of the program design stage such as pricing, promotion, and actual implementation of the program are discussed later in the book, in this chapter we focus on understanding the various factors that impact the program design process. It is important that as leisure professionals program they understand the resources available in each of these areas.

The Program Audit

We have already examined the role of an organization's principles, values, and philosophy in the program planning cycle. In addition, we have explored the importance of assessing the needs, wants, and assets of potential participants and communities as we develop a program. In designing programs, these elements serve as the building blocks or the foundation for goals and objectives upon which specific programs are developed. When beginning the program design process, it is important to consider two questions. First, what is the organization already offering in terms of programs and services? Second, how can the specific program being designed fit into these existing program offerings as well as further meet the needs and wants of participants? To answer these questions, programmers must begin and end with an audit of the organization's existing programs and services. A program audit of an organization examines all the individual factors of programs described throughout this chapter, and asks where the new or adapted program will fit within the overall program mix of the organization. We present an example of a program audit at the end of this chapter.

Factors to Consider in Program Design

Within the actual design phase of programming the programmer has to make myriad decisions related to a variety of factors. For example, Table 6.1 presented on pages 134-135 presents an overview of the Symbolic Interaction Theory, which provides one framework through which programmers may view programs. The following sections will examine many of the elements discussed in this theory as well as other factors that programmers will need to consider in the program design process. These factors include program areas and formats, equipment, physical environments,

Table 6.1 Practical theories: Symbolic interaction theory Continued>>

Background

Symbolic Interaction Theory comes from the field of social psychology (Blumer, 1969; Denzin, 1992). It has been used to understand and interpret human behavior in areas such as qualitative research for quite some time, and has recently been proposed as a parks, recreation, and leisure services programming theory (Rossman & Schlatter, 2008). From this theoretical perspective

- People act based on symbolic meanings they find within any given situation. Thus, people interact with and gain meaning from others, equipment, facilities, rules, and so on in any given experience;

- Meaning is created from communication between and among individuals, because through communication people create symbols that have shared meanings; and

- Meaning is established and revised through an interpretive process (Schwandt, 1999). In other words, we first create meaning internally, then check it externally with other people.

In addition, human beings constantly engage in "self-reflexive" behaviors, making choices about how they will act and respond within a situation rather than just passively reacting to it [the situation]. This means that program planners must come to understand participants and their behaviors. To do this the programmer must first actively enter the setting or situation of the people involved ... to see their particular meanings for the situation, what they take into account, and how they interpret this information (Schwandt, 1999). In other words, the program planner must view the situation as potential participants might. Professionals must see programming through the participants' eyes, determine what the participants find important, and how the participants interpret the setting and situation in which they find themselves.

In further examining the Symbolic Interaction Theory within a programming context, Rossman and Schlatter (2008) have noted the following six program elements that interact during the course of a recreation program or leisure experience. As a result, programmers must pay attention to each of these elements individually as well as how they interact together in the program design process:

- **Interacting people:** When a person enters into a leisure experience, it changes. Thus, it is important for programmers to understand the needs and wants of each participant. Effective programming involves matching the right group of individuals with the correct service so that the benefits sought can be obtained.

- **Physical setting:** The physical setting can impact a program in several ways. Programmers must take advantage of the unique aspects of their settings, understand the limitations of specific settings, and how those settings can be altered and adapted to enhance programs.

- **Leisure objects:** Programmers must understand what equipment, props, and other objects are essential to support the interactions intended in a program.

- **Structure:** Rules and formats guide the interactions that take place in programs. Programmers should provide enough structure so the program creates the type of interactions desired. Unclear structure or overly structured events can create unnecessary barriers to achieving desired program outcomes.

- **Relationships:** Programs can either foster or inhibit the relationships of those involved. Understanding the pre-existing relationships of participants, as well as the type of relationships the agency wants to foster through the program, is an important element of program design.

- **Animation:** This last element deals with how a program is set in motion and sustained. It brings all the elements together and looks at the flow of program, as well as how the program will be perceived by participants as they move through the experience.

Table 6.1 Practical theories: Symbolic interaction theory (continued from previous page)

In summary, programmers need to bear in mind that participants play a role in shaping the nature of all recreation and leisure experiences in which they participate. This is done through their interactions with others, the equipment, and facilities as well as the meanings they give to these interactions. No matter the program, each individual will experience the same event differently from others. If programmers understand how people shape meanings, they will better understand how that meaning also shapes actions and can contribute to creating programs that achieve the desired outcomes (goals).

Practical Applications of the Theory

To illustrate this theory consider the following: If we were planning a theme park ride we would want to keep in mind that different people give different meanings to the structure of the ride (some might ascribe excitement and thrills to a ride while others see it as having meanings of personal lack of control and fear). These views are affected by interactions with others, the structure of the ride, signage, and other sensory input. For example, while waiting in line for a theme park ride we can influence a person's view of the upcoming experience by what we say and how we say it. In addition, certain colors (of the equipment and structures), and smells in the air, can increase or decrease the excitement or anxiety levels of those waiting. These different perceptions affect the way people view the ride, their desire to participate, and the nature of the leisure experience they derive from it. By understanding, planning for, and being responsive to these meanings, programmers can best meet a variety of participant needs.

Disney does this extremely well. For instance, while standing in line for a virtual reality movie ride about the human body at Disney World, customers are moved through an environment that gives the impression of moving through a biological sanitation and cleansing zone. There are white, sanitized walls; moving sidewalks with scientific-looking grids; voices on loudspeakers that remind "biologists" (guests) to be sure and go into the "cleansing hydrospray;" and the Disney cast members (employees) attending this ride are dressed like physicians and biologists. All of this preparation and lead-in sets the tone to make even waiting in line part of the ride. It also is a wonderful example of how leisure professionals can influence the way people interact with the environment.

Your turn

If you were to offer a Family Play Day at your local YMCA, what are several key elements that you could address from a symbolic interaction perspective? How would you become acquainted with the meanings that participants might hold for such an event? What would be your goals? What type of shared meaning would you want to create? How would you go about doing this (think of the various methods of communication available to you; consider the use of symbols, color, sound, and smells)? Identify at least three examples of ways that you could shape how participants would experience the overall event.

Photo courtesy of Austin Parks and Recreation Department

policies and procedures, risk management, staff, staff-customer interactions, flow or animation of the program, scheduling, and the program life cycle (see Figure 6.1). We will address each one of these factors individually and collectively using a program audit as a way to understand the overall scope of programs and services.

Program Areas

In Chapter One, we acknowledged that no universal definition for leisure exists that explains what leisure is in every society and every situation. We also indicated that a great variety of activities and endeavors are often referred to as recreation. As a result of these differing perspectives, parks, recreation, and leisure services organizations have traditionally found it necessary and desirable to catalog recreation behavior into program areas. We present an abbreviated list of possible activities organized by program area in Table 6.2.

Classifying the activities that offer satisfying leisure and recreation experiences can be a difficult task. The possible categories are limitless and the means of classification are often arbitrary. Leisure activities may be classified based on the type of activities, participant involvement (e.g., passive or active), indoor/outdoor, skill level, cost, season of the year, outcomes, age, sex, level of risk, facility or setting, goal structure, and so forth. Furthermore, any one activity could be classified in a number of different ways. For example, in Table 6.2 scuba diving is commonly classified under aquatics although it could also fit under adventure

recreation, outdoor activities, or even environmental activities. Despite the problem of overlap, these classification systems are designed to facilitate generalizations about leisure activities and programs, and to contribute to the development of theory in program development.

Within each of the noted program areas, unique program design features may come into play. Due to the sheer number of possible program areas we do not try to present the design features of all activity types that could be offered to participants, but we do encourage programmers to offer a wide range of activities in many different program areas. In this chapter, we present some overall design considerations that are common for the activities presented in Table 6.2.

Program Formats

Within each program area a variety of different formats may be used to conduct each activity. Program formats may be viewed as the way in which an activity is organized and structured for delivery to the customer. More specifically, program formats may be viewed as the configuration or "way in which experiences are sequenced and linked to one another to increase the likelihood that customers will achieve desired benefits" (Edginton, Hudson, Dieser & Edginton, 2004, p. 275). Different beneficial outcomes are emphasized in different program formats for the same event. As a result, it is important to match the appropriate program format with the needs and wants of constituents.

For the purpose of this book, we will explore the following formats: competitive, drop-in (including opportunities to promote self-directed experiences), special events (including performances and exhibits), clubs (including special interest groups), instructional experiences (including classes, workshops, and seminars), trips, outreach, and service opportunities. As with program areas, some overlap exists between format types. For example, a special event may include a competitive tournament, opportunities for service, resource information (e.g., drop-in format), and the chance for a specific club to display some of its products (e.g., art display). Despite this overlap, we feel there is enough difference to warrant individual consideration of the program formats (see Table 6.3, p. 138).

Competition

Within a competitive format, performance of an individual or a team of individuals is compared to the performance of another individual or team, or an established criteria or standard. Thus, individuals or teams

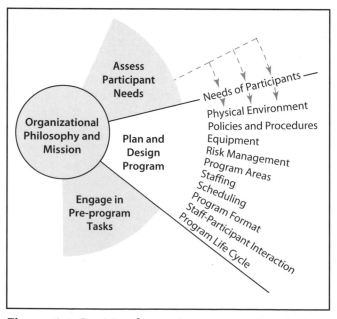

Figure 6.1 Decision factors in programming design

may compete against themselves, the environment, or other individuals or teams. Within leisure services organizations, competition may take many different forms such as:

- A one-day tournament or meet where teams or individuals play one another (e.g., wheelchair basketball tournament, track meet, chess tournament, cricket match)

- A contest where individuals compare abilities through parallel performances with a set standard determining the winner (e.g., gymnastics or ice skating competition, cook off, fishing tournament, voice competition, spelling bee)

- League play where teams or individuals play one another over an extended period of time (e.g., bowling league, fantasy football, bridge club)

Although the competition format has traditionally been dominated by sports, a variety of other program areas lend themselves to competition including board games, music, cooking, and drama. Several tournament designs such as single elimination, double elimination, ladder, and round robin tournaments are presented in the Appendix of this text.

Competition is a popular and important format for many leisure services organizations. Programmers should, however, be very aware of its limitations and try to avoid the "win at all costs" mentality. This mindset causes many people to avoid or drop out of participation because they feel they are not skilled enough to compete. Participants, particularly in youth leagues, need to feel that coaches or leaders, as well as parents and spectators, respect their efforts. Skill development and dignity in play should serve as a foundation to competitive activities. To this end, we suggest that programmers strive to remember the two principles listed on the following page.

Table 6.2 Program areas and sample programs

Adventure Education
Backcountry travel
Initiative activities
Rock climbing
Ropes courses
Whitewater kayaking

Aquatics
Aquacize
Swimming lessons
Pool parties
Scuba diving
Spray park activities
Water polo

Arts and Crafts
Ceramics
Jewelry making
Leathercraft
Paper making
Painting
Photography
Weaving
Woodcraft

Cognitive and Literary
Book clubs
Creative writing
Debates
Visiting museums

Dance
Ballet
Folk
Hip-hop
Modern
Social/ballroom
Square
Stepping
Tap

Drama
Films/movies
Plays
Puppetry
Reenactments
Storytelling/dramatic readings

Environmental Activities
Birdwatching
Camping
Environmental education
Nature crafts
Outdoor living skills

Extreme Sports
Bungee jumping
Inline skate competitions
Motocross
Snowboarding

Fitness/Wellness Activities
Aerobic activities
Fitness activities
Nutrition education
Weightlifting

Hobbies
Collecting
Creative work
Education and learning
Gardening

Music
Children's rhythms
Composition
Instruction
Instrumental (individual or group)
Listening
Performance
Study/practice
Vocal (individual or group)

Self-Improvement/Education
Advocacy groups
Conferences
Genealogy research
Leisure education
Retreats
Stress management activities

Service/Volunteer Opportunities
Coaching
Direct service
Fundraising
Interpretive guide or docent
Service learning
Service on advisory boards

Social Recreation
Board games
Mixers
Parties
Picnics
Social integration games

Sports and Games
Competitive athletics
Dual sports and games
Individual sports and games
Team sports and games

Travel and Tourism
Ecotourism
Field trips
Travelogues
Trips and tours

(1) Provide participants with opportunities to compete with others of similar skills and abilities, or utilize mechanisms to equalize the competition between individuals. For instance, in golf and bowling, less skilled participants are often given a handicap in an effort to create opportunities for players of all abilities to compete evenly with each other. In other circumstances, programmers can be creative in adapting activities or equipment so individuals of varying abilities can play together. For example, in an intergenerational game of softball the size of the ball and bat could be changed to accommodate differing skill levels and developmental stages. Less skilled, younger players could use a bigger bat and try to hit a bigger ball while players with more advanced skills would use a regulation size ball and bat. In addition to physical skills, programmers will want to consider social, emotional, and cognitive readiness for particular programs.

(2) Participants should always feel that they are competing in a safe and fair environment. Safety (both physical and emotional) is always a high

priority in programming efforts, and these efforts should be easily discernible by those involved. Furthermore, participants feel more in control of their own circumstances if they can be a part of the development of rules and guidelines to keep things fair and equitable.

Additionally, organizations should continually examine their philosophical position concerning competition so they can be intentional about the outcomes they want to provide through the competitive programs. The level and intensity of competition provided in a league or tournament can be encouraged or discouraged depending upon the policies and procedures put into place by the organization.

Drop-In

Programmers use casual or drop-in programs to encourage spontaneous participant involvement. This format usually involves setting aside a specific period of time for unstructured play. For example, a recreation center may schedule open gymnasium time when individuals can drop-in and play pick-up basketball, volleyball, or badminton. Other program facilities that may lend themselves to drop-in time include ice rinks, swimming pools, tennis courts, driving ranges, bowling centers, craft facilities, music rooms, and computer labs.

Generally, drop-in activities do not require any advance commitment from the participant (i.e., they do not need to register for a class). For example, the city of Cedar Falls, Iowa offers an indoor park experience for young children from October to April each year. Parents and their preschool children can drop into the gym on Tuesday or Thursday morning from 9:00 a.m. to 11:00 a.m. During this time a variety of equipment, mats, and toys are provided for children to play with in an indoor setting. Parents may choose to pay each time they visit or buy a pass for a particular weeklong session.

Another form of drop-in programming is that of a resource center that empowers individuals to be self-directed in planning their own leisure experiences. Creating resources such as providing information, creating connections between people, and offering equipment rental may be all that some people need to be self-directed in terms of their leisure needs. For example, many college or university-based outdoor recreation centers provide students with an area to study books, maps, and other resources to plan outdoor trips in the surrounding area. Many also offer students a shared adventure board so they can connect with other students with similar interests. Other common services include environmental information,

Table 6.3 Summary of program formats

Competition—Performance of an individual or team is compared to the performance of another individual or team, or established criteria or standard.

Drop-In—Setting aside time and space for unscheduled activities to occur spontaneously.

Special Events—Planned occurrences designed to entertain, inform, or provide enjoyment to participants; tend to be periodic.

Clubs—Groups of individuals organized around the enjoyment or practice of a specific activity or purpose.

Instructional—Experiences designed to teach and further develop skill levels of participants.

Trips—Excursions that entail travel to and from a specific area or event.

Outreach—Programs that reach out to participants where they reside, play, or hang out.

Service Opportunities—Opportunities for participants to volunteer and give back to something or someone in a specific way.

video/DVD rentals, a bulletin board to sell used equipment, and an equipment rental program (see Table 6.4). An arts center might provide a kiln, woodworking shop, or photo or glass blowing lab to constituents.

Very little is needed from an organization in preparing for drop-in activities. Equipment may or may not be provided. Staffing is usually minimal and limited to general supervision of the area or facility. For safety purposes, programmers should be aware of several issues. For example, programmers need to be alert to the situation where parents drop off young children and then leave. In essence, drop-in programs may end up being used as childcare centers. Some drop-in programs are purposefully designed this way, while leaders of other programs may be faced with unique problems because of absent parents. Programmers should be prepared to deal with between-participant altercations, troublesome participants, and gang infiltration. In addition, in urban areas the numbers of homeless individuals who enter drop-in programs for protection from the elements are increasing. Organizational policies related to addressing these types of situations are necessary to ensure access and actions consistent with the organiza-

tional mission and concerns for risk management.

A programmatic concern related to providing drop-in opportunities is scheduling, as the drop-in approach is often overlooked or underplanned (Russell & Jamieson, 2007). Further, time is usually limited to what is left over before or after structured and scheduled programs are held. Programmers are thus encouraged to remember this program format in developing the overall program plan for a facility. Careful attention must be paid to understanding when people want to be able to drop-in and at which facility, and then program accordingly.

Special Events

Special events describe programs that deviate from the norm and are offered in compressed time periods (e.g., one to three days in length) such as festivals, play days, carnivals, banquets, celebrations, shows, pageants, exhibitions, fairs, and other activities or combination of activities. Jackson (1997) has noted that special events are "extraordinary, nonspontaneous, planned occurrences designed to entertain, inform, or provide enjoyment and/or inspiration to audiences and/or spectators" (p. xii). Two unique characteristics of special events require specific attention—volunteers, and the use of sponsors to provide financial support of some kind.

The use of special events as a means to deliver services continues to grow. In the early 1990s, over 20,000 recurring community festivals were held in the United States each year (Janiskee, 1996); this figure has continued to grow as a variety of organizers and sponsors see this format as a way to meet goals. Corporations and businesses have embraced this format as a key element in their marketing strategies and image promotion. In difficult economic times, however, a decrease in such events is not uncommon.

The enthusiasm of community groups, nonprofits, and individuals for special events has also grown as programmers in these types of agencies see these events as a way to draw specific attention to and/or advocate for a specific product, program, service, philosophy, message, or group (Allen, O'Toole, & Harris, 2008). The importance of festivals and special events can be seen in many ways. For example, the Travel Industry Association of America reported that one-fifth of adults visited a special event (fair, festival, or other event) while on vacation (Goldblatt, 2004). Figure 6.2 on page 140 presents a few possible goals of special events for various types of organizations.

Like program and format types, we can categorize special events by noting similar features. Table 6.5

Table 6.4 University of Oregon Outdoor Program

Wouldn't it be great if there was...

...a place where anyone can launch a wilderness trip of their dreams...

...a place where there is a free and open room with wilderness maps, guide books, magazines and other outdoor information...

...a place where transportation and quality equipment and experienced advice are readily available for any outdoor trip...

...a place that offers a wide variety of events, clinics and natural history classes....

...a place that nurtures a sense of community among outdoor folks such as yourself...

Wouldn't it be great if there was a place where people were encouraged to grow and develop leadership skills in an cooperative and experiential environment...

Welcome to the UO Outdoor Program!

Adapted from http://outdoorprogram.uoregon.edu/

illustrates one grouping model. In terms of special events, many programmers feel that the larger the event, the better. However, this is not always the case. As with most programs the most important consideration is whether or not the event meets the goals and objectives of the program. Thus, small special events can be very successful if they are well-planned and designed. For example, some nursing homes sponsor an "over 80" party each year to commemorate Older Americans Month. The goal of this event is to celebrate the lives of residents who have lived 80+ years with their family and friends in the community. A variety of special events are often included such as living histories, photo displays, biographical information, and intergenerational activities. The success of these types of events is founded in the collaboration of local social services and families to celebrate the gift of life.

As special events grow in scale the tasks unique to planning and implementing them become more complex. Crowd control, parking, trash pick-up, portable toilets and hand-washing stations, accessibility issues, installation of temporary utilities, concessions (and sales tax issues), public safety (e.g., police, fire protection), and juggling a wide variety of tasks are all examples of the extra details that may accompany a large special event. As a result, special events are often the result of a variety of partnerships with a wide range of community organizations. This allows for one agency or organization to take the lead while delegating tasks to others. Thus, programmers should allow plenty of lead time for planning and organizing.

Consider a 2008 special event in Uruguay, South America, which set a Guinness world record for the largest barbeque. In this event, close to 1250 chefs grilled 26,400 pounds of beef on a grill running almost a mile long. The event was sponsored by Chabad-Lubavitch, a nonprofit organization that promotes Judaism throughout the world. The purpose of the event was to educate Uruguayans about Jewish dietary rules and promote kosher consumption among Uruguay's Jewish population (Chabad-Lubavitch, 2008). Many such examples of large special events throughout the world happen on a regular basis. The impact of large national and international special events is tremendous both for participants and the communities where the events take place. Consider the economic impact of the 2008 Beijing Olympics; some economists estimated that the Games brought a profit of over 30 million dollars to the city. Additional revenues were raised from merchandising, tourism, and sponsors. Tourism alone increased in Beijing by 7% each year between 2001 (the year Beijing was announced as the host for the Olympics) and 2008, when the Games were held. Moreover, 9 out of 10 tourists who attended the Games also visited other cities in China, leading to even greater economic opportunities (Yang, 2008).

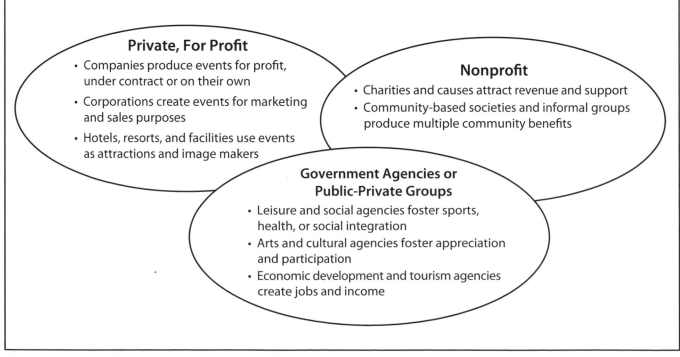

Figure 6.2 Possible goals for special events (Getz, 1997)

Clubs

Clubs, or special interest groups, are groups of individuals organized around the enjoyment or practice of a particular activity or purpose, usually for an extended period of time. Clubs in leisure services settings are normally organized around an activity interest, but can also be organized around some unifying factor such as age group, the exchange of information or ideas, or a specific issue. The club format offers both socialization and continuous opportunity and support for participation in a specific activity or event.

Clubs typically sustain themselves through dues they collect from members, and sometimes, through the sale of club goods (e.g., crafts, food). In addition, most clubs have officers and some type of bylaws to govern the group. This helps the club to respond to member needs and desires. Furthermore, clubs often program their own events for both club and nonclub members. Club members may receive discounts on goods and services from within a community. The possibilities for clubs are endless. Examples of the interests of clubs include gourmet cooking, model airplanes, civil war reenactments, ham radio operations, running, rugby, bird watching, book-of-the-month, current events, ultimate Frisbee, hiking, and computer games.

The club format requires little involvement of the leisure services organization once the club has been established. Clubs exist for their members and, as a result, it is the members of the club who take on the leadership role of directing the club activities. This involvement can be very empowering for members as they work together to develop their own internal organization, which may be formal or informal. Formal clubs typically develop a constitution and a set of bylaws. A constitution states the intended purpose of the club and the fundamental principles by which the club operates. The bylaws establish the rules by which the club is to function.

Beyond sometimes providing club leadership, parks, recreation, and leisure services organizations may offer assistance in helping interested parties connect (especially initially). They also can provide meeting space and help to ensure that club membership is accessible to all interested parties. In addition to encouraging full access to membership, leisure services organizations ensure that all aspects of the

Table 6.5 Special event groupings (Adapted from Jackson, 1997)

Neighborhood Events
A gathering or program put on by homeowners' associations, local merchant groups, perhaps a church or school.

Community Events
These events expand to several neighborhoods, up to and including suburban satellite cities or quasicities. These may include festivals named after food and flowers (e.g., the Strawberry Festival of Poteet, TX; the Lilac Festival of Rochester, NY), commemoration of historic events (e.g., Tom Mix Film Festival in Guthrie, OK), amateur athletic competitions, and other similar festivals.

Metro Area Events
Those whose operations and appeal encompasses several contiguous cities, communities, and neighborhoods. Most often, these events include large family-oriented festivals, musical offerings, major athletic competitions, historically or geographically themed happenings, and so on.

Statewide Events
Obviously those aimed at involving the entire state. A primary example is the celebration of a state's 100th anniversary of statehood, but there are others which are primarily political, social, educational, and professional in nature.

Regional Events
Ordinarily, statewide events broadened and clustered by contiguous states; often the link between state and national events. Often these are seasonal and relate to natural events (e.g., Buzzard Weekend in Hinkley, OH—one weekend each spring when the buzzards return from their migration to roost in the rocky cliffs of the area).

National Events
Large scale events that include such things as political party conventions and other conventions that are national in scope (e.g., NRPA, AAHPERD). The Race for the Cure, benefitting the American Cancer Society, is another example of this event level.

International Events
Events that draw an international audience including sporting competitions (e.g., the Olympics). Other important events focus on issues dealing with global health, social, political, religious, and economic issues. The International Women's Conference in Beijing in 1996 was an example of this.

Promotional Events
Events that can be any of the above-mentioned events that include a promotion of a product or service. An example of this is the annual MacWorld Expo, promoting new products.

club are conducted within the spirit and philosophy of the sponsoring organization. A golf or country club is one example of a club format. It is primarily focused on providing grounds and facilities for potential participants, yet it also offers other amenities (e.g., a pro shop, sandwich shop, rental equipment). On occasion, a country club will sponsor either educational or competitive events for its members and/or the general public.

Another interesting type of club is a "Friends" organization. This might be a "Friends of City Park" club, for instance. The Friends group exists to assist with various tasks at the park. Members might get together once a month to pick up litter, paint buildings, mow grass, weed a flower box, or provide some other type of volunteer work to the park. Club members might pay dues, which are often used to purchase food, supplies, and equipment during club activities. Figure 6.3 illustrates an example of the club format.

Instructional

Instructional formats are very common within a variety of program areas. Instructional formats include classes, seminars, workshops, clinics, and specialized camps. The goal of each of these formats is to teach and further develop skill levels of participants. The difference between each of these formats lies in the length of time devoted to instruction. Classes are usually offered over an extended period of time (e.g., several weeks or months) while seminars, workshops, and clinics are conducted over a short period of time (e.g., several hours or a day). Instructional camps are typically one week long and may be day or overnight programs.

The instructional format is usually highly structured, has a high degree of leader control, and a limited number of participants. Techniques for presenting information in an instructional setting include lecture, video and other visual aids, interactive technology, computer assisted instruction, demonstration, guest speakers, class member experimentation, and practice. It is the leader's responsibility to choose the most appropriate means of instruction considering the program purpose, activities, participants, group size, location, and equipment available.

One consideration for developing instructional formats includes maintaining an appropriate instructor to participant ratio. These ratios are typically based on best practices and safety issues and include consideration of facility size and layout, as well as participant skills, age, needs, and developmental stages. Although it may vary according to the technique and information

being presented, a reasonable class size is between 10 to 20 participants per leader. Scheduling of classes should allow for enough time for participants to practice each skill presented. Skills should also build on each other as participants move through the class, workshop,

---

The Bike Club is Back!

Last summer The Bicycle Shop of Chaska initiated the first Bike Club for the community of Chaska. We met each Wednesday and Friday evening at the Bicycle Shop and explored the various trails in and around Chaska.

Starting May 3rd

This year we are setting things up a little different and offering some educational maintenance classes as well. Wednesday nights will still be devoted to the recreational rider, but in addition we will spend approximately 30 minutes after the ride going over various routine maintenance schedules on your bike. These will include changing a tire, adjusting derailleurs, truing wheels, etc. There is a group of riders that ride Tuesday and Thursday evenings off road. We will be coordinating with them for the rider who is looking for more bumps and stumps. The group we have not yet been able to satisfy is the roadies. We would like to support their sport and would be more than interested in cooperating with any individual or group that would like to start a road club.

The Benefits of the Club

To encourage people to participate in the Club and learn more about the area trails, new and changing bikes and equipment, not to mention the opportunity to meet new and exciting people (as if this were not enough!) we are offering 10% off any accessories purchased on that day.

Family First

Again, our emphasis is on the family and to encourage community involvement; so don't be afraid to bring your family down for a ride and encourage your friends and neighbors to come too. We will be setting up a Family Bike Ride this summer with the City of Chaska as a part of River City Days. Look for more information to come. In addition to the Family Bike Ride we will be conducting another Bicycle Rodeo with the Chaska Police Department to encourage and teach proper bike safety and maintenance to children.

Figure 6.3 An example of a club program format (compliments of Chaska, MN)

Winter Mass Registration

A registration flyer with specific skills for each level and class times is available at the front desk of the CCC. Registration will continue to be taken after mass registration at the front desk of the CCC. Please be prepared to show proper ID. For more information, call Lori at 555–5633 ext.106.

Date   Saturday, December 20, 1997
Time   9–11 a.m. Residents and Members
           11 a.m.–12 noon Non-Residents
Place Community Room in the CCC

Learn to Swim Program

Winter Swimming Lessons

Swimming lessons are offered on Tuesday and Thursday evenings and Saturday mornings. All classes are taught by American Red Cross trained instructors and lifeguards. Each session is eight weeks and meets one day a week. Various levels of swimming are offered for each hour listed below. For specific skills and levels offerings, please pick up a flyer at the CCC Front Desk.

Tuesday Evening

Dates   Session I   January 13–March 3
            Session II March 17–May 5
Times   4:45–5:25 p.m., Levels 1 – 3
            5:30–6:10 p.m., Levels 2a – 4
            6:15–6:55 p.m., Levels 1 – 3

Thursday Evening

Dates   Session I   January 15–March 5
            Session II March 19–May 7
Times   4:45–5:25 p.m., Levels 2a – 5
            5:30–6:10 p.m., Levels 1 – 4
            6:15–6:55 p.m., Levels 1 – 2b, 6, 7

Saturday Morning

Dates   Session I   January 10–Feb. 28
            Session II March 21–May 10
Times   9:00–9:40 a.m., Levels 1 – 4
            9:45–10:25 a.m., Levels 1 – 4
            10:30 11:10 a.m., Levels 1 – 3, 6, 7
            11:15–11:55 a.m., Levels 2a – 5

Leisure Pool Schedule

January 5 – May 31, 2005

Schedule is subject to change depending on swimming lessons.

	Sun.	Mon.	Tues.	Wed.	Thurs.	Fri.	Sat.
9 a.m.							Swim Lessons 9 am – 12:50 pm
10 a.m.		Tot Time 10:15 am–12:15 pm				Tot Time 10:15 am–12:15 pm	
11 a.m.							
12 p.m.							
1 p.m.	Open Swim 1 – 5 pm	Leisure Swim 1 – 3 pm	Leisure Swim 1 – 3 pm	Leisure Swim 1 – 3 pm	Leisure Swim 1 – 3 pm	Leisure Swim 1 – 3 pm	Open Swim 1 – 5 pm
2 p.m.							
3 p.m.		Waterslide Open Swim 3–4:55 pm	Waterslide Open Swim 3–4:30 pm	Waterslide Open Swim 3–4:55 pm	Waterslide Open Swim 3–4:30 pm	Waterslide Open Swim 3–4:55 pm	
4 p.m.							
5 p.m.			Swim Lessons 4:45–6:55 pm		Swim Lessons 4:45–6:55 pm		
6 p.m.	Open Swim 6–8:30 pm					Open Swim 6–9 pm	Open Swim 6–9 pm
7 p.m.		Open Swim 7–8:30 pm	Open Swim 7–8:30 pm	Open Swim 7–8:30 pm	Open Swim 7–8:30 pm		
8 p.m.							
9 p.m.							

Introducing a New Water Tot Program

To better meet the needs of parents and children of the preschool age, a new format for preschool age swim lesson is being introduced. Each class is 30 minutes.

Monday Evening

Dates   March 17–May 4
Times   6 to 18 months
            5:00–5:30 p.m.

            18 to 36 months
            5:35–6:05 p.m.

            3 to 4 years
            6:15–6:45 p.m.

Adaptive Swim Lessons

Preregistratioin is required so that ample instructors are available to provide quality lessons. Contact Lori at 555–5633 ext. 106 for more information.

Dates   Session I   January 10–Feb. 28
            Session II March 21–May 10
Times   Saturdays 12:00–12:45 p.m.

Semi-Private and Private Lessons

Available for ages 6 and older, and all skill levels. Lessons will be structured and based on needs of each student, and time available in the pool area. The intent for these lessons is to progress children through a level they may have difficulties with. Contact Lori at 555–5633 ext. 106 for more information.

Figure 6.4 An example of instructional program format (compliments of Chaska, MN) seminar, or clinic. Furthermore, sessions need to be scheduled at times when the potential participants are available (see Figure 6.4 on p. 143).

Outreach

In many situations, constituents cannot travel to the parks, recreation, and leisure services agency for services and programs due to a variety of factors. Poor health, lack of resources (e.g., money, transportation), lack of time, and psychological reasons (e.g., people think they don't know how to do an activity) are a few examples of possible barriers preventing constituents from going to parks, recreation, and leisure services sites. To overcome these barriers many leisure services organizations reach out to people where they reside through outreach programs. In this format we can reach out to individuals who are alienated or excluded from services, or who are simply not aware of available services.

Outreach does not simply involve the provision of a set of activities. Rather, outreach involves myriad programs, services, and personal interactions, which respond to situation-specific, site-specific, and individual-specific needs. An outreach approach may be used to provide needed programs such as mobile libraries or art-in-the park activities. Outreach programs can also be used as intervention mechanisms that address specific social problems. An example of this is using family recreation activities to teach parenting skills at a local school.

Further, outreach activities serve as a mechanism to maintain a leadership presence with a specific group or neighborhood. With this orientation the leader does not directly suggest options to participants, but rather serves as a role model who "is around" to serve as a resource to the community, neighborhood, or individual. The ability of staff to assimilate to the environment and relate to participants impacts the success of the outreach program. In rural areas where parks, recreation, and leisure services facilities are often in short supply, a recreation provider may move from community park to community park to deliver mobile recreation programs to area residents (most often, the young people). The recreation provider may have limited equipment and supplies in her or his vehicle to use during the recreation event.

Examples of outreach programs are extensive. Public recreation departments have mobile recreation programs that travel to different locations throughout the summer. Nonprofit organizations reach out to their constituents through a variety of programs, such as book and zoo mobiles. Both Girl Scouts and Boy Scouts offer scouting programs at schools during lunch hours in an attempt to meet students at times and places that are convenient to members. Therapeutic recreation specialists who work for non-profit and commercial healthcare providers reach out to individuals who are homebound through recreation programs. The benefits of implementing in-home therapeutic recreation programs for seniors include providing engaging experiences that meet physical, social, and cognitive needs in a familiar environment. These types of activities provide opportunities for the recreation therapist to gather important observations about the senior's home environment and any lifestyle difficulties (Chow, 2002).

A specific example of an organization conducting recreation activities as part of home health care is Alternative Solutions in Sparta, New Jersey. As can

---

Table 6.6 Alternative Solutions, Home Healthcare Recreation Program

If you are responsible for the care of a senior citizen, young adult or child, and feel that more can be done for that person, contact us. **We provide In-home Recreation Therapy.** One of our trained recreation therapists will visit the client, complete an intake summary, and develop a program of activities specifically designed for that person. The therapist will visit the home of the client for a minimum of two hours per visit to conduct the activities. Recreation Therapy will provide a tailored leisure program to fit individual needs.

For Well Seniors, Young Adults, and Children we provide: Stimulating Activities, Strengthening Activities, Fun Activities, Crafts and Art Projects, Cooking Programs, Educational Programs, and Sing-A-Longs

For Hospice Clients we provide: End of Life Review

For Dementia/Alzheimer's Clients we provide: Reminiscence Programs, Walking Programs, Simple Arts and Crafts, Easy-to-Do Cooking Programs, Story Telling, Poetry, Creative Writing, and Pet Therapy

Source: http://www.activitytherapy.com/inhomerecreation.htm

be seen in Table 6.6, Alternative Solutions offer a wide range of activities for a variety of clientele. Another opportunity for in-home care involves respite programs for parents and families of children with disabilities. Respite programs offer to care for, and provide recreation programs for children with special needs while parents or caregivers take a needed break. Respite programs range from in-home experiences where volunteers visit a person's home and provide recreation programs for a few hours, to situations where children, youth, or adults attend a weekend-long camp program giving daily caretakers time off.

Trips

Trips are closely identified with the program area of travel and tourism, yet they may be viewed as a specific format for delivering desired outcomes in a wide range of program areas. For example, a Little League baseball team might take a trip to see a professional baseball team play; a painting class might hold a session in a nearby wooded area rather than a typical classroom; or a group of seniors might go on an overnight trip to see a Broadway play. Because most people respond positively to going someplace new and different, trips can add value to traditional recreational services.

Taking trips adds responsibilities for programmers—making necessary arrangements to ensure the trip runs smoothly is a must. Issues of inclusion and accessibility, securing safe and reliable transportation, scheduling breaks while en route, taking into consideration any medical needs (i.e., current and potential), and so on are some of the special logistics that must be considered when programming a trip. Figure 6.5 on page 146 presents a trip control plan, which is completed prior to taking a trip from a college campus. Trip leaders also have additional responsibilities to make sure the group stays together and varying needs are met. Oftentimes additional supervision is needed for trips, especially with children. Volunteers are often enlisted to provide this additional supervision, but it is still up to the programmer to organize and provide the needed information for success. It is the programmer's responsibility to see that volunteers are screened. In fact, many organizations can only "hire" volunteers who have passed a federal and state background check—especially if they are to work with or around children.

Service Opportunities

Although authors differ in classifying whether service opportunities are a program area or a program format, the importance of this topic cannot be overlooked. We have chosen to discuss it as a program format because programmers can develop formats in which to use volunteers in a variety of program areas.

Volunteers perform a wide range of services within programs without financial reward. Thus, volunteers provide valuable services to organizations. Successful volunteer programs commonly provide a great deal of satisfaction to the volunteer. Volunteering skills and energy to coach youth sports, serve as a Big Sister/Brother, referee youth basketball games, play a game with a hospital patient, take a Girl Scout troop camping, or establish fishing habitat often provides the same satisfaction that others receive from being participants in these activities. It also provides the additional satisfaction of contributing to the development and enjoyment of others.

Most parks, recreation, and leisure services organizations have volunteer programs—especially those within the public and nonprofit settings. An example of a comprehensive volunteer program is Special Olympics. Special Olympics is the largest sports organization in the world for people with intellectual disabilities. Almost 3 million athletes from more than 180 countries play 30 Olympic-type sports; they compete in nearly 30,000 competitions per year. Over 750,000 volunteers support the events at the local, state, regional, national, and international levels. The goal is the same at each level: to improve opportunities for people with intellectual disabilities and, in the process, to make the world a more accepting place for everyone (Special Olympics, 2008).

By varying the time commitment and skill level needed to be a volunteer, Special Olympics reaches out and provides a wide range of volunteer opportunities (see Figure 6.6, p. 147). Individuals can make a one-day commitment to serve as a volunteer buddy, driver, or game official, or make a longer-term commitment to serve as a coach or board member on the local, state, or national level. Special Olympics also engages volunteers in office related tasks such as website management, publicity, answering telephones, and clerical work (http://www.specialolympics.org/volunteers.aspx).

◆◆◆

Creativity is needed in all aspects of programming and decisions regarding program areas and program formats. In addition to considerations in those areas, programmers also need to plan for equipment and supplies, the physical environment, budgeting, and risk management. These areas will be addressed in this next section of this chapter.

Equipment and Supplies

Equipment and supplies are critical components of implementing programs and can influence when and where programs can be offered, as well as the costs associated with specific programs. As a result, it is important for programmers to consider the need for equipment and supplies in the design of programs. For our discussion we will refer to equipment as permanent and reusable items (e.g., balls) while supplies are materials that are consumed during an activity and not reusable (e.g., clay, paint).

In designing programs, programmers must know what type of equipment is needed for the activity as

---

Outdoor Trip Control Plan

Trip Leader: _____ **Assistant Trip Leaders:** _____

Expedition Goals and Objectives:
1. _____
2. _____

Travel Plans/Directions to Location:
Description of Arrival Route/Total Miles/Time: _____
Miles: _____
Travel Time: _____
Descriptions of Return Route/Total Miles/Time: _____
Shuttle Description: _____
Parking Area(s): _____

Wilderness Area/Park:
• Emergency Phone Numbers: _____
• Permits Required as well as Permit/Camping Fees: _____
• Maximum Backcountry Group Size/Watercraft Limit: _____
• Planning resources: _____

Itinerary:
Day 1: _____
Day 2: _____

Emergency Action Plan 1:
Emergency Contact Numbers:
• On-Site as well as Home Contact Numbers _____
• Health issues or concerns within the group _____

Emergency First Aid Procedures – Include evacuation procedures
1. _____
2. _____

Documents/Essentials:
Includes such things as: drivers' licenses, medical waivers, insurance documents, travel documents, permits, maps, budget sheet, money, etc.

Group and Individual Equipment Lists:
Includes such things as first aid kit, group gear, repair kit, shelters, cooking gear, etc.

Rations and Daily Menu: _____
_____

Figure 6.5 Example of an outdoor trip control plan

well as the participants (including assistive technology such as listening systems or beep balls), what equipment is available through the organization, and where needed equipment can be obtained. In many situations, equipment is shared between different programs and organizations, or must be rented. To ensure equipment availability, then, programmers need to pay specific attention to scheduling programs and events across programs (within one organization) and organizations (between two or more organizations). For instance, a kiln and pottery wheels may be shared between two organizations, and each might provide its own supplies (e.g., clay, glaze). Each will have to work with the other when scheduling so as to avoid double-booking the equipment and facility.

Equipment may also be manipulated through the program design process to achieve desired outcomes. For example, programmers can purposely use objects that are unfamiliar to participants (e.g., paint with sponges, play tag with teddy bears). Changing the equipment used in a game can alter the activity level, the degree of challenge, and potentially alter the experience of the whole game.

Cheers for Volunteers!

Special Olympics volunteers are vital to the success of all of our programs! Coaches and workers at athletic events, lunch makers, fund raising committee members, special event "worker bees," volunteer coordinators, games committee members, gift wrappers, envelope stuffers and more. . . . Special Olympics wouldn't happen without you!

In future issues, we will endeavor to list all of the volunteers who make Special Olympics happen. For now, we would like to thank all of you, over the past many years, who have contributed so much time and energy.

Figure 6.6 Example of a volunteer acknowledgement

For many people, equipment is an invitation to play. Something novel and unusual arouses our curiosity as well as desire to participate. Likewise, the "same old" equipment can be a demotivator for people. For example, if someone brings out a basketball for a basketball game there are a number of assumptions and expectations that go along with this piece of equipment and game (e.g., this activity is only for tall, skilled, and coordinated people). When programmers use equipment that is unfamiliar, participants have fewer expectations and as a result may be more open to trying new activities (e.g., using a soft foam ball to play basketball). Developing new equipment or simply modifying existing equipment can also be very cost-effective for organizations and will be discussed in Chapter Seven.

Physical Environments

Identifying where a program or service will be offered is an important element of program design, and it encompasses the variables of location and atmosphere. Location refers to such issues as accessibility, usability, and safety of the location. Accessibility may refer to a number of components such as ease of access as it relates to travel time or actual distance, parking, and accessibility of the facility for people with disabilities.

The types of areas and facilities used to deliver recreation programs are almost endless. Grassy fields, lakes and their waterfront, urban open spaces, virtual reality machines, and multipurpose rooms are all different types of environments in which programming occurs. When designing programs, leisure professionals must bear in mind that the suitability for the activity and customer perceptions of an area or facility are important. Professionals must determine if the area or facility offers all the necessary amenities to deliver the program (e.g., adequate space, lighting, privacy, toilets). The actual atmosphere portrayed by the area or facility is also important: Is it warm and inviting to a wide variety of constituents? Other issues for consideration include participant comfort and safety.

Once the physical environment of a program has been identified, a programmer can often enhance the environment to improve the overall program. Ideas for actually creating or enhancing the environment are presented in Chapter Ten, where we discuss how to facilitate the program experience for participants.

Budget

Budget concerns include all aspects of potential income and expenditures for programs, both individually and collectively. Both the income and expenditures for programs are influenced by many of the factors listed in Figure 6.1 (p. 136), which ultimately dictate the price charged for programs and services. Budgeting and considerations in setting fees and charges are examined in greater detail in Chapter Nine. It is mentioned here to encourage programmers to begin to be aware of costs throughout the program design phase of the programming cycle.

Policies, Procedures, and Rules

Policies, procedures, and rules are the boundaries within which programs are developed and implemented. Policies should flow from the mission, philosophy, goals, and objectives of an organization and give direction to the operation of an agency. They direct the behavior and actions of employees so actions are consistent with the philosophy, values, goals, and objectives of an organization.

Policies tend to be broad in their scope and application, whereas procedures are the specific actions or approved steps required to carry them out. Unlike policies, which many times involve the entire organization, procedures tend to be applied to departmental or interdepartmental activities. Examples include how customer registrations are to be handled, how staff are hired, how fees and charges are calculated, and how environmentally friendly purchasing can be achieved.

Rules are the narrowest boundaries, in that they deal with specific activities or behaviors. In general, rules guide the behaviors of individual staff and participants during specific programs or events. Although rules are necessary for the managed presentation of recreation activities, rules do not have to be overtly constraining or ruin the fun. General guidelines for rules are presented in Figure 6.7.

In designing programs, programmers must understand and follow the policies and procedures of the organization. For example, if the organization believes it must serve as a model of environmental responsibility and promote an outdoor ethic in participants, then the programmer would be well advised to design a program that is environmentally friendly. Likewise, as programs are designed programmers should give some thought to how rules and guidelines will be developed and implemented, and how they augment the organizational mission, and set the tone for servant leadership.

Risk Management

Risk is an important aspect of many recreation programs. For many people, especially young people, risk is a powerful motivator for participating in many leisure activities. The rush of adrenalin that results from participation in a challenging tennis match, skiing a black diamond slope, rafting a wild river, or racing in an elite bicycle competition creates a desire for a specific type of recreational experience. Yet, this often creates a paradox for the programmer that can be seen in the words of Willi Unsoeld, an experiential educator from Germany, when he told the following story, "We used to tell them in Outward Bound, when a parent would come and ask us "Can you guarantee the safety of our son Johnny?" And we finally decided to meet it head on. We would say, "No. We certainly can't Ma'am. We guarantee you the genuine chance of his death. And if we could guarantee his safety, the program would not be worth running. We do make one guarantee, as one parent to another. If you succeed in protecting your boy, as you are doing now...we guarantee you the death of his soul!" (Miles & Priest, 1990). Yet, program administrators are responsible to participants as well as insurance agents and supervisors who are concerned with injuries that may occur when people are exposed to risk. At the same time, risk presents so much opportunity for growth. So what is a programmer to do?

The answer to this question can be found in understanding the importance of risk management, embracing the full duality of risk, both its potential for loss and for adventure (Cline, 2003). Risk management

> **Rules should:**
> * Have reasons
> * Be equitable
> * Define responsible behaviors
> * Be appropriate for participants
>
> **Rules must be:**
> * Enforceable
> * Clear and succinct
>
> **When using rules, you should:**
> * Design rules in conjunction with participants whenever possible
> * State rules in positive terms
> * Clarify, practice, and monitor rules continuously
> * Follow through with enforcement
> * Give a warning when rules are broken
> * Have only a few rules

Figure 6.7 General guidelines for rules (Jordan, 2007)

becomes an extension of the vision and values of an organization as well as its policies and procedures. We believe in managing risks to maintain high quality programs, rather than from a perspective of minimizing lawsuits. Presenting high quality programs is a very proactive position, while operating from a mindset to minimize lawsuits is a defensive (and often ineffective) approach. Leisure services professionals are still accountable to attorneys and insurance agents who view only one side of risk, the potential for loss; yet, we must not take all risk out of our programs for then we destroy the character of the experiences we provide. As Cline (2003) states "this is not to say, we should not continue to engage in meaningful dialogue with all of the stakeholders involved in our program, but rather that we should start to consider defining risk for ourselves, in a manner that supports both our ideals and our goals" (p. 26).

Within this context, programmers use risk management to articulate the steps to minimize the undesirable risks found in the administration of parks, recreation, and leisure services. At the same time, it is important to create opportunities for exploration to help participants grow, develop, and live life to the fullest. Other aspects of managing risks include informing participants of the potential risk and level of challenge involved so that they can make informed decisions about their participation. Accepting inherent risks, understanding the safety precautions being taken, and understanding one's role in self protection are all important parts of managing risks (White, 2008).

Risk management helps programmers recognize the risks that are inherent in everything we do—we might slip in the bathtub, burn ourselves while cooking dinner, or trip over our own feet as we walk down our front walk. These types of risks we accept as integral to living, and if they occur we consider them to be accidents. We do not accept (or expect) some risks, however, which might include the following: slipping in the shower at the recreation center because the cleaning crew did not rinse the slippery soap film off the floor; burning ourselves while at a park-sponsored cookout because gasoline was used to light the charcoal; and tripping on the sidewalk at a golf course where the concrete had buckled and not been repaired or cordoned off. In one set of instances, the injury was due to expected and accepted hazards of daily living. In the second set of examples, the injuries were due to hazards that could have (and should have) been addressed.

How are unexpected and unacceptable risks addressed in parks, recreation, and leisure services? Risks are typically managed in four ways—eliminating the risk, accepting the risk, transferring the risk to another (through insurance), and reducing the risk (see Figure 6.8). Parks, recreation, and leisure services programmers must utilize all four strategies. Professionals eliminate risks by choosing *not* to offer something (e.g., in many states gymnastics programs were eliminated because of the concern for participant injury). Professionals accept the risks inherent in many programs—there is a risk, for instance, of spraining an ankle in many sports; yet we still offer and engage in these activities. Risks are transferred through insurance policies, which are commonly selected and purchased by agency administrators. For instance, many agencies carry multi-million dollar policies to cover personnel in the event of a negligence lawsuit. Risk reduction describes those actions that limit the negative risks inherent in an activity. For example, we know that in bicycle riding there is a risk of falling off the bike and sustaining head injuries. Thus, in parks, recreation, or leisure services sponsored bicycle events, we require the wearing of helmets to reduce this risk.

Skilled programmers are able to identify potential risks and manage those risks through planning, implementation, evaluation, and follow-up of an event.

Figure 6.8 Water-based activities are high risk.

Such a process should involve staff and participants in relationship to a number of factors such as areas and facilities, and/or policies and procedures related to the programming process. Risks usually are addressed through the development and utilization of a risk management plan, through proper activity selection, appropriate staff and supervision, periodic facility checks, and a thorough pre-program safety check. Before we get into some of the details of risk management, we should discuss the meanings of several related terms.

Negligence

Negligence is a term that describes an act that results in personal injury to another person or their property. As a legal term it refers to a situation where an individual was careless in the course of her or his duties resulting in injury to another party. For negligence to exist, four elements must be present: *duty, an act or standard of care, proximate cause,* and *injury/damage*. If any one of these four elements is not present, there is no negligence (and no standing for a lawsuit).

Duty. The term *duty* refers to an obligation one person owes to another individual based on a legal relationship between that individual and the other. Typically, in parks, recreation, and leisure services settings a programmer and participants are engaged in the conduct of a leisure or recreational pursuit. In this case a legal relationship (duty) exists between the leisure services professional and the participant. The programmer has a duty, or obligation, to provide reasonably hazard-free activities and facilities to all participants and staff.

In leisure services programming, the duty owed to participants includes a responsibility to plan and implement programs in a safe and prudent manner, to warn of hidden (e.g., slick floor) and visible hazards (e.g., tripping hazard), to provide staff who are skilled and competent in their job duties, and maintain a safe environment through appropriate policies and proce-dures—this duty is owed when participants are using leisure facilities, in the conduct of activities, and in the general provision of leisure services.

Act/Standard of Care. The second element of negligence is the *act*. This refers to the actions (or omissions) of a person (e.g., leisure services programmer) in light of the duty owed to participants. A certain *standard of care* is required to minimize hazards for participants. When a person claims negligence, a programmer will be held to a standard of care which

> would be measured by the moral qualities, judgment, knowledge, experience, perception of risk and skill that a person in the capacity of a professional would have. (van der Smissen, 1990, p. 43)

In other words, a leisure services programmer must act in the same way that another person competent for a similar position and in a similar situation would act. The term, *standard* also refers to a generally accepted practice in the field (sometimes referred to as an *industry standard*). These types of standards may be established by legal precedent or through professional associations. For example, the American Camp Association (ACA) offers standards for camps and conference centers, while the Association for Challenge Course Trainers (ACCT) has established standards for practices related to the operation of challenge courses. Comparisons can also be made to the operating procedures and policies of similar recreation organizations or agencies (White, 2008). Programmers and leaders can breach the standard of care in three ways: *malfeasance, nonfeasance,* and *misfeasance*.

Malfeasance. Doing something that one ought not to have done (which may also be illegal) is considered malfeasance. For instance, malfeasance would have occurred if a programmer scheduled a soccer team for five-year olds to play against a team of thirteen-year

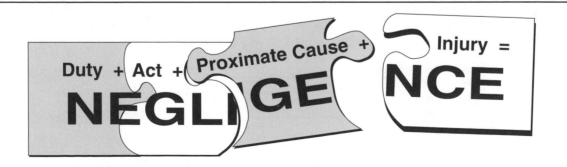

Figure 6.9 For negligence to exist, all four elements must be found.

olds. The potential for injuries due to physical mismatches is extremely high and this scheduling match should not have been made.

Nonfeasance. Nonfeasance is the neglect of duty; it is often thought of as passive negligence because it results out of uninvolvement. An example of nonfeasance would be failing to maintain a facility by passively allowing it to age without regular maintenance or upkeep. If, due to this neglect of duty, an individual were to become injured (by a swing set chain breaking, for example), nonfeasance might be the claim and negligence the result.

Misfeasance. Those acts whereby a programmer did not exercise the appropriate level of care for the rights of the participants are termed misfeasance. This type of breach of duty includes both a failure to act as well as the improper conduct of an act. An example of misfeasance in an act of omission, for instance, might include the following: a festival was held in a recently mowed field where poison ivy was known to grow. No attempt was made to check for poison ivy, nor was the area sprayed to kill the plant. Festival goers were exposed to the plant, and came down with severe cases of poison ivy, which caused health complications for some.

As an example of improper conduct consider the following hypothetical situation: an amusement ride attendant was strapping in a rider on a Ferris wheel ride. The attendant wasn't paying attention and incorrectly connected the straps. During the course of the ride the rider fell out and was injured. The act (strapping in) was appropriate, but it was done incorrectly. This is an example of misfeasance during an act of commission.

Proximate Cause. In addition to duty and a breach of that duty, the third element that must exist for negligence to be proven is *proximate cause*. For negligence to be attributed to an action, it must be shown that the injury was the direct result of the action—this is proximate cause. For example, if the festival goers who were exposed to poison ivy were exposed not at the festival location, but earlier in the day while they were fishing in the local river, the earlier exposure would be the proximate cause, not the festival incident.

Injury/Damage. The fourth element that must exist for negligence to be found is actual injury (to a person) or damage (to physical property). The injuries might be physical (e.g., fracture, sprain, head injury), emotional or mental (e.g., anguish, humiliation and embarrassment, emotional trauma, psychogenic shock), or economic (e.g., replacement cost for equipment, loss of one's job, future medical bills).

◆◆◆

Understanding the four elements of negligence is critical to beginning the process of identifying and then reducing and minimizing risks and hazards. To provide high-quality programs and minimize risks, the area in which parks, recreation, and leisure professionals might choose to focus throughout the programming process is on the act/standard of care. This is a part of program planning.

Program Planning

Planning is a necessity in risk management; plans must be reasonable, well thought out, and based on professional knowledge of the activities, participants, and the environment. Plans should be continuously updated and documented (i.e., written down) so that programmers have a record of the plans and a solid knowledge base. It becomes important, then, to attend to and follow the program plan, and to document changes as they occur. In this way, leisure services professionals can protect themselves from some assertions of negligence related to planning, particularly if the plan was well-done and approved by supervisors.

The planning process should include a thorough consideration of the risks involved in the program and how they will be addressed. Furthermore, the program plan is the document where programmers indicate an understanding of the agency risk management plan, potential participants; the activity; and the areas, structures, and facilities. For example, Figure 6.5 (p. 146) presents an outline for an Outdoor Trip Control Plan (TCP). This outline is used to plan for all outdoor trips sponsored by the Calvin College Outdoor Program. It serves as the program plan for each trip that leaves campus. The form helps leaders think through a variety of logistics including identifying specific risks associated with each trip, as well as how the leader will deal with the risks throughout the trip. The TCP helps programmers think of a variety of issues related to risk management including: activity selection, equipment needed, travel plans, as well as forms and documentation needed for a specific program.

Activity Selection. In the process of program planning, an activity of some sort is selected and offered—even if an agency only provides facilities for others' use. It might be a special event, something focused on skill development, a sport league, an activity related to the arts, or one of many other recreation or leisure activities. In selecting an activity or event, programmers must try to foresee every possible negative risk and address that risk. Obviously, there are times when programmers will not be able to foresee everything, but by asking several people to participate in this process, a number of the potential undesirable risks can be addressed. Certainly, the activity must be a fit for the anticipated participants as well as the available areas and facilities.

In addition, some activities have more inherent dangers or risks attached to them than others. For instance, all water-based activities have high levels of inherent risks; board games have very low inherent risks. Highly active activities have the potential for more injuries than do less active events. We do not advocate removing all risks from every event, but the risks must be known to and accepted by participants. In addition, the risks must be manageable and should enhance or be integral to the nature of the leisure pursuit. For instance, risks abound in snowboarding—indeed, that is the draw and thrill of the activity for many participants. The risks are known to and accepted by participants (in fact, lift tickets are contracts that stipulate this), are managed (by clearly identifying slope difficulty, providing monitoring by ski patrol members), and without which, snowboarding would not be snowboarding.

To wisely choose appropriate activities in our programming efforts, we must have a solid knowledge and understanding of the activity itself; how it impacts participants (and how participants impact it); how it interacts with the environment; and how, in the course of the activity, participants interact with one another as well as staff. In addition, programmers must continually learn about changes in activities and events as technology and the collective professional understanding increases. Technological advances may necessitate changes in approaches to programming and activity selection, and as professionals we are expected to be aware of these changes.

As programmers, we should also be concerned with the sequencing and progression of activities we offer. It is important to offer activities in such a way that the skill development of participants matches the skills required by the activities. We might sequence events from easiest to most difficult (in terms of physical skills), from low activity to high and back again, or from simplest to most complex (in terms of rules and intellectual involvement). Choices related to sequencing and progression are impacted by the goals of the program, needs of the participants, staffing and equipment issues, and external factors such as time of day and weather conditions.

Being Facility and Equipment Aware. Another aspect of risk management that is extremely helpful in the programming process is being aware of the areas and facilities to be used for the planned events. Legal concerns about leisure services facilities and environment fall into two general categories—agency liability for maintenance of facilities, and leader liability for conducting an activity on unsafe premises. Programmers should be concerned about both of these issues.

Equipment can cause risk management problems in several ways—through improper use of equipment, inadequate maintenance of equipment, and improper substitution of equipment. Programmers need to be well-aware of equipment limitations, maintenance, and availability in planning parks, recreation, and leisure programs. Improper use of equipment includes such things as attempting to stand on a six-foot-diameter earth ball, using a badminton racket for tennis, and using a water ski for snowboarding. Examples of inadequate maintenance include failure to maintain bases on softball and baseball fields and failing to keep a pool filtration system in working order. Improper substitution of equipment might include using a carpet cutter (which utilizes an unprotected razor blade) instead of scissors in a crafts project and substituting folded blankets for mats under gymnastics equipment.

Forms, Forms, Forms. Program planning involves many steps including an attempt to anticipate all types of risks associated with a program. Unfortunately, no one can anticipate all risks. One way to address these unknown and unanticipated risks is to encourage the use of risk management forms as part of the program process. You probably recognize the names of various risk management forms—waivers, assumption of risk forms, releases, incident/accident report forms, and medical information forms (see Figure 6.10). Each of these forms has a particular

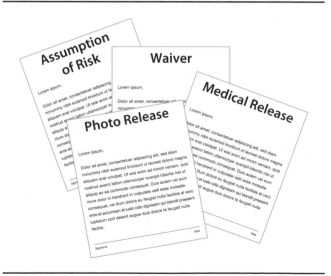

Figure 6.10 Program planning includes the use of waivers and releases.

purpose in an overall risk management plan.

The purpose of using forms in risk management is to limit the liability of individual employees and that of a particular agency. Many people have raised questions about the effectiveness of waivers and release forms; the courts have found them to be useful in determining participant understanding of the risks involved in an activity. In other words, risk management forms *are* useful and *do* serve a purpose. As a program is developed planners should consider the potential risks involved and decide which forms, if any, would be appropriate to aid in minimizing liability risks to the agency and personnel. Understanding what forms are necessary and the process of using these forms are discussed in Chapter Ten, which looks at facilitating the overall customer experience in recreation programs.

◆◆◆

In addition to the concerns related to equipment and supplies, the physical environment, and risk management, other components of program design must be considered. The following sections will address the issues of staffing, program goals and objectives, scheduling, and program life cycle.

Staffing

Staffing leisure programs is a comprehensive task and includes the recruiting, selecting, training, supervising, evaluating, and compensating of individuals. While management of staff is beyond the scope of this chapter, we will mention a few issues directly related to staff and program design. As might be imagined, when designing programs, supervisors need to be aware of interests and skills of their staff, as well as understanding what they are passionate about. One author noted that the world has plenty of talent (i.e., creativity), but lacks passion: "the best creative work represents passion fulfilled, whereas a neurosis may be thought of as passion thwarted. Enthusiasm is the elixir that pervades creativity, inspires it, frees it so that anything seems possible, and enlists others in the cause" (Wilson, 1981, p. 19).

Staffing is important to designing and delivering programs because passionate leaders tend to be willing to put extra time into an activity or event to make it special. They love what they do, and they believe in what they are doing. They are growing, learning, and improving themselves throughout their professional efforts. They are also able to incorporate the ideas, hobbies, and interests about which they are passionate into programs.

Understanding the passions of staff enables supervisors to develop creative programs built on these passions.

In addition to passion, part of the program planning process includes matching staff with activity leadership and with participant needs. Some activities are highly staff intensive (e.g., aquatic activities, activities with participants who have severely disabling conditions) while others require very little staff supervision (e.g., drop-in activities, board games). Matching appropriate staff and the appropriate numbers of staff with an event is important to managing risks. Staff should be knowledgeable about the activity, participants, facility, and policies and procedures related to the program and the agency. Just as leisure services professionals would never think to place a noncertified person in a lifeguard stand, so too should they avoid placing staff who have few skills or knowledge about a particular program in a similar position of responsibility.

Not every staff member is equally suited to all activities in terms of temperament, knowledge, and experience. For instance, if hiring an inclusion specialist leisure professionals would want to be sure the individual has the background, skills, certifications, and knowledge base necessary to fulfill the job duties. A job description is a first step to matching staff to programs and program participants. It also is important to learn about each staff member in terms of their interpersonal skills, preferences, and previous experience. In this way, the best staff and combination of staff can be selected and assigned to particular programs.

Program Goals and Objectives

It is difficult to design programs without appropriate goals and objectives. Clearly, in the design and planning process, a programmer has something in mind she or he would like to have happen. It will happen as envisioned when the programmer has carefully written and followed the goals and objectives. We mentioned earlier, in Chapter Three, that goals are broad statements of intent and objectives are the steps to reach those goals. As programmers, we will want to bear in mind that there are four general levels of goals: *societal, agency, leader*, and *participant* (Russell & Jamieson, 2007).

Societal goals are the aims or ideals of a community. These goals tend to be culturally relevant (meaning they change with the times), and may or may not be in the best interest of all community members (i.e., citizens; Jordan, 2007). Examples of societal goals include the goals of healthy living for all, equal opportunity and access, and maintaining a litter-free neighborhood.

These goals may directly or indirectly impact the provision of leisure services. Typically, societal goals exist at the agency level.

Agency or organizational goals are those espoused by the parks, recreation, and leisure services organization. Often, these goals are identified in the mission statement or a statement of purpose. Agency/organization goals might include things such as to exhibit a servant leadership approach to service delivery, to increase the social capital of the community, and to develop community leaders among staff. As an example, one goal of the Wellness Center at Oklahoma State University is for Oklahoma State University to become "the healthiest university in the county." This goal drives the development of specific program goals and objectives. To this end, the Center offers nutritionally sound cooking classes, fitness programs, stress reduction lessons, physical rehabilitation, cardio kickboxing, and a "wellness-walk-about" walking program.

Leader goals might mirror those of the agency, but usually other elements exist as well. A leader might have a personal goal to be promoted, to develop new skills, to make a lot of money, or to make a real difference in the lives of others. When goals of the leader are synchronous with those of the agency, the greatest compatibility and leader satisfaction occurs.

Participant goals are quite diverse. People may desire to participate in leisure experiences to exercise, to learn a new skill, to be with others, to do something different, to experience excitement, to respond to peer or parental pressure, and for many other reasons. The specific goals or needs of participants are often identified during the needs assessment phase of program development (as discussed in Chapter Four). As the programmer, it usually is best to focus on one or two participant goals in the planning of programs—it would be impossible to meet them all.

As indicated, goals and objectives are developed for each program in its design phase. These provide structure and give direction to the event. Jordan (2007) has indicated that goals are broad statements that describe the intent of a particular program, and that program goals include the following:

- *Skill development* (e.g., throwing, drawing, jumping, singing) and *knowledge development* (e.g., history of the area, rules of the game, factual information about natural phenomena such as stargazing or plant growth).

- *Interpersonal skills* (e.g., decision making, problem solving, communication) and *social goals* (e.g., being with others, sharing, helping) are common reasons people participate in a wide variety of leisure experiences.

- *Democratic living skills* (e.g., cooperation, ideals of fair play, equality) often are the focus of leisure activities, particularly for young people and those who volunteer.

- *To have fun* and serve as diversionary (i.e., non-utilitarian) activity is a perfectly legitimate goal of recreation and leisure activities. In fact, many participate in leisure experiences with having fun as the primary goal.

- *Health benefits*. Many people engage in leisure for the physical exercise and mental health benefits derived from it. Physical exercise makes participants feel better physically, emotionally, and mentally.

Writing Objectives

Developing specific and measurable objectives in the program planning phase will give a programmer and staff focus for the actions needed to achieve the desired outcomes—objectives provide direction to program offerings. Bloom (1956) conceptualized three different realms of objectives as including *cognitive*, *behavioral*, and *affective* objectives. *Cognitive* objectives are those that deal with thinking, *behavioral* objectives deal with physical actions and skills, and *affective* objectives deal with feelings and emotions.

In parks, recreation, and leisure services, all three objectives are addressed through programming, although one may be emphasized more than another. For instance, in working with the frail elderly a programmer might focus on designing cognitive objectives dealing with mental stimulation and memory retention; for participants in rehabilitation a programmer might focus on objectives such as coordination and strength; and when working with young children a programmer might focus on affective objectives such as sharing and cooperation.

Objectives are defined as specific, measurable statements needed to reach a goal. In that light, objectives must be related to goals. Writing down objectives as they are developed aids in focusing the program and provides a framework and reasoning for the entire event. The aim of writing objectives, whether they be cognitive, behavioral, or affective, is to design them in such a way that if they were turned into a question, an individual could answer without hesitation, "yes" or "no." If the best answer is "sort of" or "maybe" the objective is not written as specifically as needed. A number of program planners use the acronym, SMART, to help write objectives. With this pneumonic, programmers can remember that objectives are Specific, Measureable, Achievable, Realistic, and Trackable.

ABCDs of Writing Behavioral Objectives

To aid in the development and writing of objectives for program design some people find it helpful to follow the ABCD method. Remember, objectives go hand-in-hand with goals. Thus, prior to writing objectives, one must know the goal for which one is striving. For example, if one of the goals of a tiny tot soccer league is to help participants develop specific gross motor skills objectives should relate to this goal—objectives are the steps to achieving goals.

Writing an objective is much like writing a sentence—each objective has a *subject*, *verb*, *object*, and *modifier*. In this case, the subject is *who* will do the behavior, the *what* is the verb (or behavior the subject will be doing), the *how* is the phrase that explains the behavior to be done, and *how well* addresses the modifier. These elements are the ABCDs of writing objectives related to our stated goal and these elements are further defined as follows:

A = Audience. The audience identifies *who* is doing the action (i.e., behavior) described in the objective. The audience should be identified as specifically as possible. Audiences commonly found in program design objectives include staff, the programmer, participant, camper, client, etc., and names of specific individuals or groups of individuals (participants) who are to do the task. For example,

Figure 6.11 Objectives serve as a map to reaching goals.

Participants will…

B = Behavior. The behavior is the *action* the audience must do (i.e., verb in the sentence), and it is required in a behavioral objective. *Each objective should have only one verb or behavior in the sentence*; otherwise, the objective is extremely difficult to measure. Common behaviors in youth sports programs (specifically soccer) include dribbling, passing, punting, stopping, running, and throwing. For example,

Participants will *dribble the ball…*

C = Condition. A condition helps to *describe* the behavior in specific terms. Anything that serves to further identify the behavior in the objective is considered a condition. Often, a condition can be recognized by the way it describes how or when an action is to be accomplished. For instance, if an objective specified that the audience was to dribble the ball, by when should they accomplish this task? For example,

Participants will dribble the ball *one-half the length of the field by the end of the second practice…*

D = Degree. The degree in an objective describes *how well* the behavior will be accomplished. To what degree of competence will the audience be held? Various ways of stating degrees include such things as 90% of the time, with fewer than four errors, without any supervisor prompts, and so on. In some situations the degree is implied in the condition and action of the objective. It is important to note that the degree must match the behavior—it should answer the question, how well must the audience do the behavior? Therefore, if the action is implementation, how well must the person implement that task (e.g., on time, fully including *all* participants)? As an example,

Participants will dribble the ball one-half the length of the field by the end of the second practice *without losing control of the ball.*

Thinking through the program in advance and working with colleagues are ways to ensure solid goals and objectives that will lead to positive programming. In addition, being as specific and measurable as possible in writing objectives will make program design and development a smooth process.

Scheduling

The issue of scheduling is twofold. First, scheduling is concerned with offering programs that fit with the timing needs of customers. Timing may refer to a multitude of variables including: time of day, day of the week, season of the year, length of time, and frequency of offerings. With increased demands being placed on people's time, it is critical for programmers to identify the best time of day, week, month, or year, as well as the amount of time that people are either willing or able to spend on a specific program or activity. For example, some people might be able to commit to a weekend volleyball tournament, but not a league that stretches over a long period of time.

The issue of timing also includes identifying which types of programs should be offered at the same time. This is often referred to as packaging or bundling services. The concept suggests that as time constraints continue to grow there will be a need to cluster services that allow individuals and families to have a quality leisure experience under the same roof at the same time. For example, a fitness center might offer childcare, instructional leagues for children, aerobic classes, and open weight room hours in an attempt to meet the needs of the whole family at the same time. This concept has been applied successfully at many large commercial malls in which group childcare, food concessions, shopping, and entertainment opportunities are offered at one convenient location during the same hours.

The second issue of scheduling is making the best use of the areas, facilities, and equipment that an organization controls. The scheduling of parks, recreation, and leisure programs should complement the selected program areas and formats discussed earlier in this chapter. This often involves creative thinking as recreation facilities and programs usually experience peak times when space is hard to find, as well as downtime when demand is relatively low.

With these two issues in mind, scheduling may be thought of in at least three different patterns (Russell & Jamieson, 2007). The first involves the seasons or natural block periods in the year (e.g., holidays). This approach may be most convenient for organizations located in regions of the country that experience seasonal change (i.e., winter, spring, summer, fall). Promotional efforts can be easily coordinated within this scheduling pattern. Pamphlets, fliers, and brochures can be coordinated to focus on each program that is being offered during a specific season (see Figure 6.12).

The second scheduling pattern is based on a shorter duration such as a monthly or weekly focus. This pattern is most appropriate for facility-centered programs (e.g., swimming pools, ice rinks) where the traffic flow of participants is constant and where program activities occur the same day each week, indefinitely. Communicating the program schedule by the week or month helps to keep regular users informed and reminded of upcoming programs.

The third, and perhaps most critical pattern for consideration in scheduling, is the daily time frame for activities. This approach requires programmers to understand the lifestyle patterns of constituents. Traditionally this approach has focused on morning sessions, early afternoon sessions, late afternoon sessions, early evening sessions, and late evening sessions (Russell & Jamieson, 2007). However, with the increased complexity of individual schedules and the changing lifestyle patterns of participants, programmers need to focus on all possible time periods (e.g., midnight basketball, teen lock-in overnights) for providing programs that meet the needs of all target markets.

Figure 6.12 Many recreation agencies publish program brochures for specific seasons of the year.

Program Life Cycle

The program life cycle concept is drawn from the discipline of marketing. The concept is derived from an analogy of human biological development and suggests that parks, recreation, and leisure programs have a definable life span. Following the human development model, the program life cycle has been adopted as a way to trace the evolution of programs and services. The life cycle presented in Figure 6.13 includes the following stages: introduction, take-off, maturation, saturation, and decline or extension.

During the introduction stage, potential customers are slow to accept the program. This reluctance is overcome during the take-off stage as participation in the program grows rapidly. The take-off stage continues until the rate of participation begins to slow down; this is when the program reaches maturity and moves into the saturation stage. During the saturation stage, the program relies on repeat involvement for its survival. Very few new participants seek out the service. Typically, the saturation stage is longer than previous stages as program involvement peaks and begins to decline slightly. At that time, existing participants drop out, and there are few new participants to take their place.

In the last stage the program begins to decline. At this time, programmers can consider various strategies for extending or stretching the program life cycle, if desirable. At this point in the program life cycle, programmers will want to examine a number of critical questions. Could the program be revitalized by assigning new staff, adopting a fresh approach, using a different facility, or developing an alternative structure or format? Can new customers be developed? Can the program be adapted to meet the particular benefits sought by different target audiences? It is also important to remember that not all programs can be revitalized; in this case we need to acknowledge this, reduce the time and money invested in the program, and let it cease.

The program life cycle is important to program design in a number of ways. First, the cycle facilitates preplanning; the programmer can be proactive in program implementation instead of reacting to what has already happened. By utilizing the life cycle concept, program design, implementation, and evaluation can be planned systematically. Understanding the program life cycle also assists the programmer in making decisions about promotion, program duration, resource allocation, and cessation of programs. Perhaps the greatest benefit of understanding the program life cycle is that it reminds the programmer of the importance of constantly developing and designing new programs and services to replace those on the decline. Alternatively, planners may choose to reinvent programs to reinvigorate them before they become a major drain on the resources of an organization (Bowling, 2001).

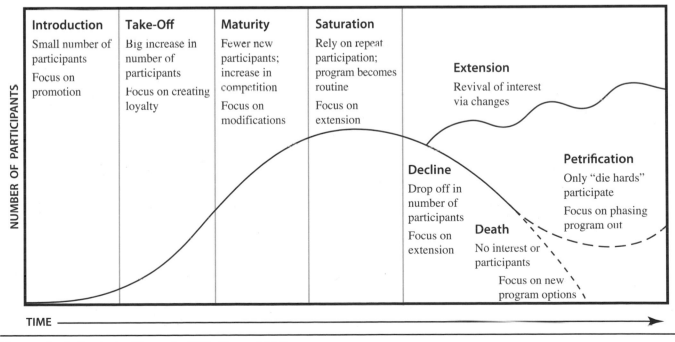

Figure 6.13 Program life cycle (O'Sullivan, 1991)

The Role of the Program Audit

In the opening section of this chapter we raised the importance of beginning and ending with an agency program audit. Traditionally, audits are associated with financial procedures and expenditures. For our purposes, we want to think about an audit as an overall evaluation of all the program offerings, sometimes referred to as the overall program mix of an organization. Such an audit allows the programmer to develop a snapshot of all the current programs and services offered by the agency within a specific time period and determines where additional programs may be needed (see Figure 6.15 p. 160).

Now that we have reviewed many of the factors that would be examined through an organizational program audit we can return to discussing the program audit itself. Foundational questions for a program audit include:

- Who are various target markets the organization is trying to serve through its programs?

- What are the needs and assets of each target market?

- What beneficial outcomes does the organization want to offer this target market?

Once a programmer has answered these questions, she or he can utilize a program grid (see Figure 6.14) for each target market and look for gaps in the overall program mix in serving this market. For example, consider a youth serving organization with a target market of young children, which offers all the programs listed in Table 6.7 (on p. 160). Programmers could place these programs into the overall program grid and see where gaps and opportunities might exist. In the example in Figure 6.15 (on p. 160), a programmer might see that many fitness, sports, and adventure activities are offered, but few options in the following program areas exist: cognitive and literary, dance and drama, hobbies, and music. Knowing this, programmers can ask additional questions related to staff capabilities, vision and mission of the organization, facilities and equipment, finances, scheduling, and other pertinent information. The answers to these questions influence programmers' decisions to add or delete programs to/from the current program grid for the potential participants. Specific questions may include:

- Do the organizational vision and mission statements direct staff to offer a well-rounded program or specialize in one specific area such as sports or fine arts?

- Is the programming emphasis on cooperation, competition, or individually focused activities?

- Does the agency have the staff, equipment, facilities, finances, and other necessary resources to offer a particular type of program?

- Are potential constituents or target groups demanding a particular type of program?

- Does the agency offer similar activities at other times of the year?

- How do the programs fit with the schedule of programs and services offered for a particular target market?

- How well do the programs address the needs of the underserved and marginalized populations?

Using program audits in this manner can help program planners suggest programs that fill a specific need rather than over-program in one specific program area.

A Servant Leadership Approach: Empowering Participants

In previous chapters we have indicated that parks, recreation, and leisure professionals need to be servant leaders and work to empower participants to meet their own leisure needs whenever possible. Within the program design phase, this means assisting participants in designing some aspects of their own programs. However, it should be noted that some participants simply do not have the inclination, time, or skills to take control of their own leisure experiences. As a result, programmers often take the responsibility for designing programs and events that meet the needs of specific target audiences. In this process, programmers can still work to empower participants and foster creativity through program design. Listening to participants through assessments and evaluations may foster both empowerment and creativity providing choices in programs, and letting participants make their own decisions within the program once it has begun.

By truly understanding and utilizing servant leadership as an approach to programming people can integrate the notion of service to others through-out the programming process. Individuals act out of a servant leadership orientation when they maintain connections to the community they are serving and by continually reminding themselves to be inclusive of all people. This means that leisure services professionals must become familiar with the people who are their potential customers—professionals need to get out into the neighborhoods within their community. Program design should be culturally relevant to the people an agency intends to serve. If an agency is a public parks, recreation, and leisure services organization, staff will need to work hard to understand all the people within the service zone. If programming for a nonprofit organization that addresses people who are economically disadvantaged, then staff will need to be sure to program based on the constituents' needs and desires, and not their own. Lastly, if programmers work for a commercial, for-profit entity, it would be in their interest to be sure that they understand the potential market to ensure financial viability. For all providers, programming with a servant leadership approach can lead to long-term organizational success.

	Monday	**Tuesday**	**Wednesday**	**Thursday**	**Friday**
9:00	**Daily Welcome** • Songs • Drama • Announcements	**Daily Welcome** • Songs • Drama • Announcements	**Daily Welcome** • Songs • Drama • Announcements	**Daily Welcome** • Songs • Drama • Announcements	**Daily Welcome** • Songs • Drama • Announcements
10:00	**Small Group Time** • *Name Games* Make sure everyone knows one another • *Initiatives* Help the group work together	**Clubs** • Drama • Arts & Crafts • Nature Activities • Sports & Games	**Field Trip** Make sure field trips are checked out in advance. Create a number of bus activities for campers to do en route. Count number of campers both on and off the bus to ensure everyone gets back to camp safely.	**Clubs** Encourage a good selection of clubs each week to give campers a variety of choices.	**Small Group Time** • Special Event Preparation
11:00	**All Camp Activities** • Active Games	**Small Group Time** • Low Organized Games		**All Camp Activities** • Sports	**All Camp Activities** • *Special Event* (e.g., carnivals, parades, treasure hunts, parties)
12:00	**Lunch and Quiet Time** • Low Organized Games	**Lunch and Quiet Time** • *Story Time* Read stories to campers. Use the library.		**Lunch and Quiet Time** • Board Games	**Lunch and Quiet Time** Make a special meal to go with the special event.
1:30	**Clubs** Have counselors do commercials to promote clubs	**Rotating Activities** • Swimming • Arts & Crafts • Sports & Games		**Rotating Activities** Use resources in the community • Bowling • Rollerskating • Swimming	**All Camp Swimming**
2:30	**All Camp Swimming**		**All Camp Swimming**		
3:30	**Camper's Choice**	**Camper's Choice**	**Camper's Choice**	**Camper's Choice**	**The Big Show** Have clubs or small groups present skits, songs or other presentations
4:00	**Closing Activities** • Songs	**Closing Activities** • Announcements	**Closing Activities** • Drama	**Closing Activities** • Stories	**Closing Activities** • Spirit Stick

Figure 6.14 An example of a generic weekly/daily program grid

Program Areas/Formats	Competition	Drop-in	Special Event	Clubs	Instructional	Trips	Outreach	Service
Sports & Games								
Music								
Aquatics								
Arts & Crafts								
Fitness								
Social Recreation								
Hobbies								
Cognitive & Literary								
Self-Improvement & Education								
Dance & Drama								
Environmental Activities								
Adventure Education								
Other								
Other								

Figure 6.15 Program audit form

Table 6.7 Possible programs for a youth-serving organization

Soccer League	Fall Campout
Soccer Clinics	Sports Outing (traveling to watch a local college)
Swim Lessons	Sports Tournaments
Basketball Clinics	Dive-In Movies at the Pool
Parent/Child Canoe Trip	Drama and Plays
Video Arcade Competition	Pool Parties
Challenge Course Team Building	Board Game Bash
Poster Contest	Baby-Sitter Certification Program
Rap and Hip-Hop Artist Lessons	Language Lessons
Wii or Guitar Hero Competitions	Financial Fair with Carnival-Type Games
First Aid and CPR Training	Kayak or Canoeing Trip
Bike Trip	
Break Dancing Events	
Cooking Contests or Festivals	
Power Hour (fitness and supervised play in an after-school program)	
Drop-In Activities (e.g., basketball volleyball, dodgeball, kickball, swimming)	
Parent/Child Fitness Hour	
Punt, Pass, and Kick Competition	
Enchanted Forest (Halloween Event)	

Summary

Parks, recreation, and leisure programs should flow from the needs of customers as well as the values and philosophy of the organization. Once needs have been identified and the goals and objectives of the program to be established are in line with the philosophical foundation of the organization, it is time to design the actual program.

The factors impacting program design addressed in this chapter include program areas, program formats, equipment, physical environments, policies and procedures, risk management, staff, writing goals and objectives, scheduling, the program life cycle, and other considerations. Once staff understand these factors, they can conduct a program audit to identify programs that may be needed to strengthen the overall program offerings of an organization. The next chapter will examine how to integrate these factors in program design decisions with innovation to ensure that programs (both individual and collective) serve the customers of parks, recreation, and leisure organizations.

In terms of connecting program design with the characteristics of servant leadership, programmers are encouraged to build consensus throughout the process. This entails making sure that programs meet the needs of participants and that participants have input into the process whenever possible. This can be accomplished in a variety of ways including providing choices in programs, and involving participants in program decisions once the program begins. For example, within a summer camp program, campers can be involved in developing cabin rules and expectations for the duration of the program. A second important servant leader characteristic to be incorporated into the planning process is stewardship. This involves a number of elements including: making wise decisions related to the resources used in planning and implementing programs, as well as helping participants take responsibility for their own experience and realizing how they impact the experiences of others.

Programming from Here to There

In Chapter Two we discussed how in today's changing environment we have seen a blurring of the traditional lines between public nonprofit and commercial organizations. Public and nonprofit organizations are being asked to be increasingly innovative and entrepreneurial while commercial (for-profit) organizations are being asked to be more socially responsible.

This is evident in the following profile of the Tampa Bay Club Sport organization, the largest provider of social sports leagues for adults in the Bay area. Tampa Bay Club Sport is a commercial (for-profit) organization that offers a yearly membership and works with a variety of area municipalities to offer its programs. The organization was established in the late 1980s and has been in continuous operation since 1995. Currently it serves over 14,000 league participants annually.

The organization offers a variety of program areas including sports and games, social recreation, fitness/wellness activities, service opportunities, and aquatics; its main emphasis is on sports in a variety of program formats (e.g., leagues, tournaments, special events, trips, and outreach). Examples of specific programs include: entering a team in Tampa's Dragon Boat Annual, Club Sport and Creative Loafing Field Day competition, poker tournaments, happy hours, dodgeball tournaments, kickball league, and sports leagues (e.g., football, soccer, basketball, golf, tennis). Tampa Bay Club Sport also organizes corporate events from outings to picnics to teambuilding activities.

A number of elements add to the uniqueness of this organization, these elements include:

- Programs and formats: The organization specializes in sports and games and uses a variety of different formats to offer these programs.

- Collaboration: The organization owns no facilities and instead works with a variety of public, nonprofit, and commercial organizations to offer programs. Facilities include municipal fields, recreation centers, public beaches, restaurants, churches, bowling centers, golf courses, fitness centers, and tennis complexes.

- Target market: Although programs are open to everyone over the age of 18, the majority of participants are young active professionals in their mid 20s to early 30s. Priority is placed on creating a social environment to meet new people while enjoying sports and staying active. Individuals can join with others or they can join alone and be placed on teams.

- Marketing strategies: Memberships are encouraged, but not required. Memberships offer individuals discounts on program registrations and serve as a marketing tool.

For additional information on Tampa Bay Club Sport visit their website at www.tampabayclubsport.com/

References

Adler, R. & Elmhorst, J. (1999). *Communications at work* (6th ed.). New York, NY: McGraw Hill.

Allen, J., O'Toole, W., & Harris, R. (2008). *Festival and special event management*. NY: Wiley.

Bloom, B. (1956). *Taxonomy of educational objectives*. New York, NY: Longman.

Blumer, H. (1969). *Symbolic interactionism: Perspective and method*. Englewood Cliffs, NJ: Prentice Hall.

Bowling, C. (2001, June). Using the program life cycle can increase your return on time invested. *Journal of Extension, 39* (3).

Chabad-Lubavitch (2008, April 13). *Uruguay: Biggest BBQ event begins with Kosher Beef* from: http://lubavitch.com/news/article/2022594/Uruguay-Biggest-BBQ-in-the-World-Begins-With-Kosher-Beef.html

Chow, Y. (2002, Second Quarter). The case of an in-home therapeutic recreation program on an older adult in a naturally occurring retirement community. *Therapeutic Recreation Journal, 34*(2), 203–212.

Cline, P. (2003). Re-examining the risk paradox. *Wilderness Risk Management Proceedings*. 23–28.

Denzin, N. K. (1992). *Symbolic interactionism and cultural studies*. Cambridge, MA: Blackwell.

Edginton, C., Hudson, S., Dieser, R., & Edginton, S. (2004). *Leisure programming: A service centered and benefits approach* (4th ed.). Boston, MA: WCB, McGraw-Hill.

Getz, D. (1997). *Event management and event tourism*. Elmsford, NY: Cognizant Communication.

Goldblatt, J. (2004). *Special events: Event leadership for a new world*. The Wiley Group.

Jackson, R. (1997). *Making special events fit in the 21ˢᵗ century*. Champaign, IL: Sagamore Publishing.

Janiskee, R. (1996). The temporal distribution of America's community festivals. *Festival Management and Event Tourism, 2*(1), 10–14.

Jordan, D. (2007). *Leadership in leisure services: Making a difference* (3rd ed.). State College, PA: Venture Publishing, Inc.

Miles, J. C. and S. Priest (1990). *Adventure education*. State College, PA: Venture Publishing, Inc.

O'Sullivan, E. (1991). *Marketing for parks, recreation and leisure*. State College, PA: Venture Publishing, Inc.

Rossman, R. & Schlatter, B. (2008). *Recreation programming: Designing leisure experiences*. Fifth edition. Champaign, IL: Sagamore Publishing.

Russell, R. & Jamieson, L. (2007). *Leisure program planning and delivery*. Champaign, IL: Human Kinetics.

Schwandt, T. A. (1999). On understanding understanding. *Qualitative Inquiry, 5*(4), 451-464.

Seuss, D. (1971). *The lorax*. New York, NY: Random House.

Special Olympics (2008). *Special Olympics celebrates 40 years*. Retrieved February 22, 2009, from http://www.specialolympics.org/40th_anniversary.aspx

van der Smissen, B. (1990). *Legal liability and risk management for public and private entities*. Cincinnati, OH: Anderson.

White, N. (2008). *Managing risk in recreation programs, facilities and services*. Article found at www.play-safe.com

Wilson, M. (1981). *Survival skills for managers*. Boulder, CO: Volunteer Management Associates.

Yang, S. (2008, April 2). Beijing 2008: The economic impact of the Olympics. *Business Today*. Retrieved January 9, 2010 from http://www.businesstoday.org/index.php?option=com_content&task=view&id=478&Itemid=47

Programmer Profile

Photo provided by of Dana M. Bates

Dana M. Bates

Current Position: Executive Director (and Founder) New Horizons Foundation, Romania
Favorite Book: *Trust: The Social Virtues and the Creation of Prosperity* by Francis Fukuyama (1996)
Favorite Recreation Activities: Hiking and reading

▶ **Describe the path your career has taken.**

- Graduated with a B.S. in Philosophy from Gordon College.
- I have worked at Gordon College as Teaching Assistant and Wilderness Trip Leader as well as an adjunct professor at Northwestern College, serving as the Director of the Romania Semester Abroad Program.
- I am currently the executive director of New Horizons. The mission of New Horizons is "to develop caring citizens who feel empowered to act." The overall foundation offers a wide range of adventure and service learning activities to achieve this mission. Programs include a summer camp as well as service learning clubs (IMPACT clubs) throughout Romania and now in Honduras. In my current role, I supervise staff, help develop programs, and work to obtain the resources needed to sustain the overall organization. I am also working on my Ph.D. at the University of Wales and studying an Eastern Orthodox theology of human flourishing.

▶ **Describe the joys of working in your current position.**

Having staff who are doing a great job which is allowing me to pursue some of my academic desires, which is where I flourish; this allows me to give back to the Foundation/New Horizons in ways that are personally sustainable.

▶ **Do you have any advice for new programmers?**

Find quality staff. Poor staff will be a thorn in the organization's side and threaten to scuttle the entire mission.

▶ **What is the most creative program you have developed?**

Our IMPACT clubs have offered a creative way to engage Romanian youth to get involved in their communities. IMPACT clubs utilize adventure education activities, service learning opportunities, and moral education to build social capital in a post communist context. Our IMPACT clubs have been selected by Heart of a Child Foundation as an international best practice (see www.new-horizons.ro) and won a competition for best foundation model by NOKIA phones; from this we have received needed finances to open 150 more clubs.

▶ **Describe a program example that demonstrates a servant leadership philosophy.**

The IMPACT clubs described above strive to encourage servant leadership in young people by getting them involved in their communities through a wide variety of service learning opportunities which are identified and organized by the young people themselves. One concrete example would be that youth built the very first viable outhouse in the local national park, and they also built the second, and third one as well!

▶ **What is the biggest challenge you face as a programmer?**

Funding. There is not a culture of corporate or even private giving in Romania, and the government, while improving is still somewhat corrupt and has shown little interest in funding programs of public interest. That may change as things do seem to be improving.

Creativity and Innovation 7

As we think about the actual design of programs, the breadth and complexity of the possibilities can appear overwhelming. To begin to overcome this obstacle, we believe that it is helpful to remember that programming is not an act—it is a process. The task of programming becomes manageable when we realize that we simply need to start the process and then continue on the journey, working on one aspect at a time toward constant improvement. In Chapter Six we examined the key elements of designing programs; in this chapter we pay particular attention to helping programmers gain the tools necessary to develop creative programs.

The acronym CPR—Creativity, Passion, and Research—developed by Clark (1995) is helpful as it suggests that these three concepts are intertwined and are responsible for breathing life into programs. We believe that if all programmers practice CPR in their programming efforts, programs will remain vital, contemporary, and desirable. In addition, the process and product of programming will benefit both the programmer and constituents.

Creativity

Creativity is important in all aspects of the program planning cycle from interacting with customers, to facilitating the actual leisure experience, to dealing with staff challenges, to developing new programs and services. Creativity also assists programmers in dealing with the ambiguity brought on by continual change. All leisure providers in parks, recreation, and leisure services face a work environment that is constantly changing. On one hand we are being asked to document outcomes, respond to the needs of customers, and provide quality services, while on the other hand we are asked to deal with budget cuts and staff reductions. Programmers everywhere must meet the challenge of doing more, doing it faster, doing it better, and with fewer resources. This is particularly relevant to the idea of creativity as recent research contradicts the premise that

people produce the best results under time pressures (Silverthorne, 2002).

Creativity implies making something from nothing or using something in an innovative or new way. Being creative means seeing opportunities in problems as well as other unique situations. Many of us know someone whom we would label as being creative. In fact, many believe that only some individuals are blessed with this talent. However, we believe that everyone has the potential to be creative. The idea that creativity is some rare, magical trait or process associated with the arts is an outdated perspective. Some of us may still conjure the image of a secluded genius working on some problem or invention tirelessly until she or he has a "eureka" moment. Researchers agree that creativity is an interaction between an individual and the environment (including other people) (Amabile, 1998). Individual characteristics found to be common to creative people include expertise, good thinking skills, and high intrinsic motivation. Of these three, some of the most recognized creative people in our world credit their intrinsic motivation as the key to their accomplishments rather than a specific skill or innate intelligence. Another characteristic of creative people is that they are flexible and are not tied to the way things have always been (Csikszentmihalyi, 1996). While creative problem-solving skills are viewed as one of the top characteristics of creative people, Figure 7.1 (on p. 166) illustrates how the *approach* to problem solving is more critical to creativity than the *knowledge* of problem solving.

For leisure programmers to reach their creative potential, we must understand the nature of creativity and ways to enhance our own creative thinking. First, we must understand that creativity is a learned skill that can be fostered and developed in both staff and participants. Over ten years ago, Csikszentmihalyi (1996) presented five steps to creativity—they still hold true today. The steps include:

- **Preparation**—becoming immersed (whether aware of it or not) in interesting problematic issues that arouse curiosity

- **Incubation**—ideas churn around below the threshold of consciousness

- **Insight**—the "Aha!" moment when the puzzle starts to fall together

- **Evaluation**—deciding if the insight is valuable and worth pursuing

- **Elaboration**—translating the insight into its final work and working out the details

Imagine a…problem as a maze.

One person might be motivated to make it through the maze as quickly and safely as possible to get a tangible reward, such as money—the same way a mouse would rush through for a piece of cheese. This person would look for the simplest, most straightforward path and then take it. In fact, if he [*sic*] is in a real rush to get that reward, he might just take the most beaten path and solve the problem exactly as it has been solved before.

That approach, based on extrinsic motivation, will indeed get him out of the maze. But the solution that arises from the process is likely to be unimaginative. It won't provide new insights about the nature of the problem or reveal new ways of looking at it. The rote solution probably won't move the… (organization or program) forward.

Another person might have a different approach to the maze. He might actually find the process of wandering around the different paths—the challenge and exploration itself-fun and intriguing. No doubt, this journey will take longer and include mistakes, because any maze—any truly complex problem—has many more dead ends than exits. But when the intrinsically motivated person finally does find a way out of the maze—a solution—it very likely will be more interesting than the rote algorithm. It will be more creative. (Amabile, 1999)

Figure 7.1 Problem-solving as a maze

These steps are not necessarily linear, and are revisited often throughout the creative process. In addition, creativity in any field comes from being well-grounded in that discipline; thus, understanding the programming process, our constituents, local environment, and other factors that go into successful programming are precursors to creativity.

Second, several researchers have noted that a person's work situation is an important variable in enhancing creative thinking (Hanna, 2008). Managers can help staff by creating an environment that focuses on small increments of progress rather than just the big results, set clear and meaningful goals while offering adequate resources and time, and view successes and failures as learning opportunities. With this thought in mind, programmers must look for ways to harness their creativity and passion, and apply these resources to designing programs.

Developing creative skills and learning to be creative involves recognizing one's blind spots and trying to overcome them. Blind spots are sensory "lock outs" of our environment caused by conditioning or prior expectations. For example, read the quote presented in Figure 7.2. How many letter *Fs* do you see? Research has shown that approximately 50% of the population will see only three *Fs*, approximately 10% of the population will see all six *Fs*, while the remaining portion of the population will see either four or five *Fs*. The reason for this disparity is that we are conditioned to speed read over the small words in sentences and as a result many of us miss or discount the *Fs* in the word "of." Research supports the notion that we are conditioned to repress our creativity; thus, without a conscious effort, many of us lose our ability to use our innate creativity as we grow older. As a result, we need to consciously work to redevelop our creative selves. A good place for us to

FEATURE FILMS ARE THE RESULT OF YEARS OF SCIENTIFIC STUDY COMBINED WITH THE EXPERIENCE OF YEARS

Figure 7.2 How many Fs do you see?

start is to be aware of the mental blocks to creativity presented in Figure 7.3.

There are infinite ways to be creative in program design. As individuals remove the mental blocks to creativity, they are often empowered to try new and innovative program ideas and approaches. Specific techniques for encouraging creative thought include brainstorming/brainwriting, discontinuity, forced analogy, mental imagery or visualization, mind mapping, and unconscious problem solving. We discuss these in detail throughout this chapter. Figure 7.4 presents specific actions each of us can take in efforts to increase our creativity.

THE RIGHT ANSWER—By the time the average person finishes college, they have taken over 2,600 quizzes, tests, and exams, most of them seeking the one right answer to solve the question. Thus, the "right answer" approach becomes deeply ingrained in our thinking. We need to relearn that life is ambiguous and there are many right answers, all depending on what we are looking for.

BE PRACTICAL—Break this constraint by being a magician… ask "what if" questions and use the provocative answers as stepping stones to new ideas. Cultivate your imagination and encourage "what iffing" in others.

AVOID AMBIGUITY—Look at something and think what else it might be. Pose a problem in an ambiguous fashion so as not to restrict the imagination of the problem solvers. Try using humor to put you and your group in a creative state of mind.

TO ERR IS WRONG—If you make an error, use it as a stepping stone to a new idea you might not have otherwise discovered. Differentiate between errors of "commission" and "omission." Strengthen your "risk muscle" by taking at least one risk every twenty-four hours. Remember the two benefits of failure: first, if you do fail, you learn what doesn't work; and second, the failure gives you an opportunity to try a new approach.

PLAY IS FRIVOLOUS—It is not so important to be serious as it is to be serious about important things. The next time you have a problem, play with it. If you don't have a problem, take the time to play anyway. You may find some new ideas. Make your workplace a fun place to be!

THAT'S NOT MY AREA—Develop the outlook that wherever you go, there are ideas to be discovered. Schedule idea-hunting time into your day and week. Develop different kinds of hunting grounds. The wider and more diversified your knowledge, the more places you have to draw from.

DON'T BE FOOLISH—In a time when things are changing very quickly, who is to say what's right and what's foolish? Occasionally let your "stupid monitor" down, play the fool, and see what crazy ideas you can come up with.

I'M NOT CREATIVE—Creative people think they are creative. Less creative people don't think they are creative. This is an example of a self-fulfilling prophecy. If you want to be more creative, believe in the worth of your ideas and have the persistence to continue building on them. With this attitude you'll take a few more risks and break the rules occasionally.

Figure 7.3 Mental blocks that prevent creativity (Adapted from von Oech, 1983)

PLAY MORE—Get involved with children's activities; you may find that toys aid the creative thinking process. Jigsaw puzzles (for spatial thinking), building blocks, drawing, role-playing/acting, just talking and asking questions, all contribute to creative thought and practice. Gaming, as a hobby, can improve problem-solving and creative skills. There are many types of games that involve intellectual thought and creative solution; investigate miniatures, board games, card games, computer games and simulations, and so forth. Positive creative exercise can be found in such activities.

CREATE YOUR OWN CREATIVE SPACE—Having your own special place for creative outlet has many benefits. A very famous creative space is Henry Thoreau's cabin described in *Walden.* Vance and Deacon (1995) in their book, *Think Out of the Box,* describe a concept called the "Kitchen for the Mind" which is a room filled with creativity-stimulating objects and decor—a resource-rich environment. Vance and Deacon recommend that you take a space in your home or organization and make it a place that stimulates you to think and be creative. Make a conscious effort to surround yourself with the tools and resources you need to be creative. Think about your ideal creative space. What do you need (e.g., computers, art supplies, musical instruments) and where will you locate your space?

KEEP RECORDS—Keep a daily journal and record your thoughts, ideas, sketches, and so on as soon as you have them. Review your journal regularly and see what ideas can be developed.

DEVELOP OUTSIDE INTERESTS—Develop an interest in a variety of different things, preferably well away from your normal sphere of work. For example, read comic books or magazines you wouldn't normally read. This keeps the brain busy with new things. It is a common trait of creative people that they are interested in a wide variety of subjects.

DON'T WORK TOO HARD—You need time away from a problem to be creative after periods of intense focus. Indulge in relaxation activities and sports to give the mind a rest and time for the subconscious to digest information. Relaxation and good health are important to mental and physical health—essential prerequisites to creative thinking. For example, while jogging some individuals are able to clear their minds and think through problems. Some have been able to visualize computer programs, develop ideas, and process solutions to different problems when engaged in various forms of exercise.

Figure 7.4 Steps to improve creativity (Adapted from von Oech, 1983)

Brainstorming/Brainwriting

Creative thought may be divided into divergent and convergent reasoning. Both abilities are required for creative output. Divergent thinking is essential to the novelty of creative products whereas convergent thinking is fundamental to determining appropriateness. *Divergent thinking* is the intellectual ability to think of many original, diverse, and elaborate ideas. In other words, thoughts diverge or separate from the norm. *Convergent thinking* is the intellectual ability to logically evaluate, critique, and choose the best idea from a selection of ideas. This type of thinking requires that a judgment be made about an idea.

The basis of brainstorming is divergent thinking; people in groups generate ideas while withholding judgment. It is generally accepted that brainstorming is highly productive in generating a large quantity of ideas, which ultimately yield higher quality ideas. The greater the number of ideas generated, the greater the likelihood of coming up with new and potentially effective program alternatives and program delivery methods. Thus, the *number* of ideas generated is the goal of brainstorming. Brainstorming is a process that works best with a group of people when the six rules presented in Figure 7.5 are followed. Figure 7.6 provides a number of idea-generating questions for brainstorming related to parks, recreation, and leisure programming.

Many different forms of brainstorming have emerged since the original concept advocated by Osborn in 1957. Nominal groups involve individuals working independently to generate ideas, which are later combined. Mongeau and Morr (1999) believe that nominal groups produce more quantity and quality ideas than face-to-face groups. Another type of brainstorming utilized by organizations is electronic brainstorming. Individuals can complete this technique independently with no knowledge of others' ideas, or they can interact with one another through a live chat service. Electronic brainstorming may enable exposure to other ideas without the risk of feeling judged by other group members.

Brainwriting is another technique to generate creative ideas (Heslin, 2009). With this technique each member of a small group (4 or 5 people) writes down ideas on a slip of paper independently from the others. It is helpful if each person uses a different colored writing implement. Then, the slip of paper is passed to another group member, who then inserts her or his own ideas. When each group member has provided at least one idea, the slip of paper is placed in the center of the table—this is repeated up to 25 times. In the second stage, group members separate from one another and through recall, write down as many of the generated ideas as possible. This encourages attention to the ideas. In the final stage, the group members develop ideas on their own; these ideas are then combined for consideration.

It is our belief that in the spirit of creativity and recognition of different cognitive styles, leisure programmers should utilize a variety of techniques, as well as create new methods. One consistent belief among researchers is that fostering a judgment-free environment and postponing the evaluative phase of decision-making to a later time will generate the most ideas.

Discontinuity

The more familiar we are with something, the less stimulating it is for our thinking. When we disrupt our typical thought patterns, those ideas that create the greatest stimulus to our thinking do so because they force us to make new connections in order to understand the situation. Thus, to enhance our creativity we will want to insert interruptions into our day. We could change our working hours, travel to work a different way, listen to an unfamiliar radio station, read a magazine we wouldn't normally read, try a new recipe, or watch a

---

1 Identify a well-defined and clearly stated problem.

2 Arrange the group so each member can see the others (a circle often works well).

3 Trade off the job of writing down all the ideas as they occur. Write on newsprint, overhead transparencies, or some other medium which can be seen by all.

4 Have an appropriate group size. Most sources advocate groups between five and twelve people. With skilled leadership, however, effective sessions can be conducted with larger or smaller groups.

5 Use a location that is different from the normal working environment. Such a setting can be more conducive to creativity. Aim for comfortable seating, room, lighting, and temperature. Be sure there is room for the people who like to pace while they think.

6 Share responsibility to help enforce the following guidelines: suspend judgment, accept and record every idea presented, and encourage people to build on the ideas of others (i.e., piggy-back on others' ideas).

Figure 7.5 Guidelines for brainstorming

television program or film we wouldn't normally watch. Provocative ideas are often stepping stones that get us thinking about other ideas. Butting ideas against each other can cause friction that creates new thought-paths.

Forced Analogy

Forced analogy is a very useful and fun-filled method of generating ideas. The idea is to compare the problem with something else that has little or nothing in common and gain new insights as a result. People can force a relationship between almost anything, and arrive at new insights. Think about

similarities between companies and whales, management systems and telephone networks, or the relationship between a supervisor and a pencil. Forcing relationships is one of the most powerful (and fun) ways to develop new insights and new solutions. A useful way of developing the relationships is to have a selection of objects or cards with pictures to help generate ideas. Choose an object or card at random and see what relationships you can force with the topic at hand. For example, imagine a leisure services organization as a matchbox (see Table 7.1). What comparisons could you make? Analogies can also be made by imagining a particular object to use as a tool or a particular person as a resource. This type of exercise can be insightful in realizing the importance of flexibility or the adaptability of organizational structure. For leisure programmers, a possible analogy might be to compare leisure programming to a three-ring circus—lots of things go on at once.

Mental Imagery/Visualization

Mental imagery has been used in sports psychology for a long time. Athletes are asked to visualize themselves winning or performing their technical best. This type of mental imagery can also be used to design programs. Mental imagery provides a unique access to the unfolding of a program or event and can be used to experience the program from a participant's point of view, to anticipate and/or solve problems, to identify critical moments of interaction with participants, and to experience the entire operation of a program. For example, mental imagery might involve visualizing the event or program as one would expect it to unfold and then

---

1 Try to define what something is not.

2 What is everybody else NOT doing?

3 What if we _____ ?

4 What could we adopt and/or adapt from other places? What else is like this?

5 Plug in a variety of opposites. For example what if we…

Magnify/Minify:
What to add? Greater frequency? Stronger? Larger? What to subtract? Eliminate? Split up? Less frequent?

Substitute/Combine:
Who else instead? What else instead? Other place or time? How about a blend, an assortment? Combined purposes or ideas?

6 How can we modify programs? How can we change meaning, participants, motion, degree of difficulty, equipment, sound, odor, taste, form, and/or shape.

7 How can we put the program to other uses? New ways to use it? Other uses if modified?

8 How can we rearrange: the layout? the sequence? the pace?

9 How can we reverse? Opposites? Turn it backward? Turn it upside down? Turn it inside out?

10 What are the assumptions of the problem? What happens as we drop some of these assumptions either individually or in combination?

Figure 7.6 Idea-generating questions for brainstorming (Adapted from Russell, 1982)

Table 7.1 Forced analogy: Comparing a leisure services organization to a matchbox

Matchbox Attributes	Organization Attributes
Striking surface on two sides	Organizations need protection from unexpected risks.
Sliding center section	The organization should be flexible/moveable in order to respond to changing situations. The core of the organization is protected by its cover.
Made of cardboard	Inexpensive mode of structure. The structure is not important; it is built to protect what is inside.

identifying the necessary steps to making all those elements happen.

Mental imagery and visualization can also be used to improve the quality of programs and events by visualizing all the thousands of specific moments that combine to create the total customer experience. These moments may be thought of as "moments of truth" in which staff have opportunities to impact the quality of the experience for participants. These "moments of truth" may be visualized in terms of a cycle of service. According to Albrecht and Zemke (1985), a cycle of service is *a repeatable sequence of events in which various people try to meet the customer's needs and expectations at each point.* The cycle begins at the very first point of contact between a constituent and an organization. It ends, only temporarily, when the constituent considers the service complete, and it begins anew when that person decides to come back for more.

By visualizing a cycle of service chart, staff can identify potential moments of truth for the customer (see Chapter Six). In many ways the chart forces staff to see things as the constituent sees them, without contaminating personal perceptions with knowledge of what is *supposed* to happen behind the scenes. It is important to engage in this visualization process, then, from several different constituent perceptions. What would the program look and feel like from the perspective of a child, teenager, adult, or senior? What would this experience be like for an individual who uses a wheelchair, walker, or crutches? How would a customer with a visual impairment experience this cycle? How about the experiences of someone who represents an ethnic or religious minority group—How would the cycle of service appear to them? By doing this from several different perspectives, we avoid the trap of only seeing the world through eyes of "people like us."

According to Albrecht (1992) this tool works best when it is important to focus staff attention on the participant's chain of experience and how the succession of "truth moments" builds to a complete perception of quality by the completion of the cycle. Thus, this cycle allows staff to realize that the participant experience is cumulative and should be managed as such.

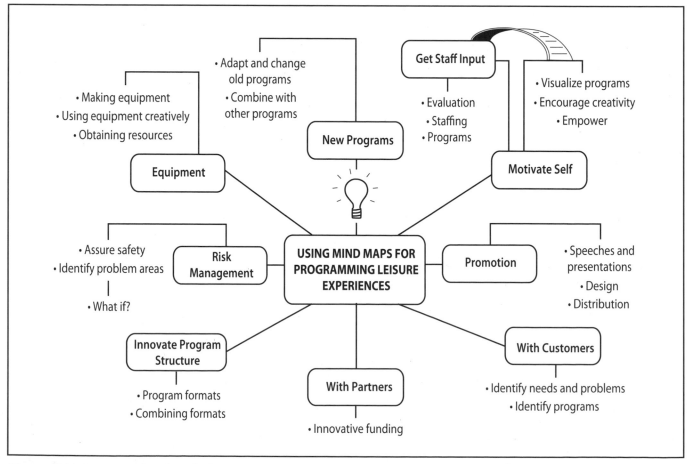

Figure 7.7 An example of a mind map

Mind Mapping

In addition to visually anticipating all aspects of a program individuals can also use their cognitive abilities to map out the program in their minds. In some ways people's brains are very much like computers; in other ways they are quite different from a computer. Whereas a computer works in a linear fashion, the brain works linearly and associatively—comparing, integrating, and synthesizing as it goes. Mental association plays a dominant role in nearly every cognitive function, and words are no exception. Every single word and idea has numerous links attaching it to other ideas and concepts in our minds. Mind maps are an effective method of taking notes and useful for generating ideas by association. To make a mind map, individuals begin by writing a word representing the main idea in the center of the page and work outward in all directions with additional words, producing a growing and organized structure composed of key words and images. Using images of objects (e.g., a bridge, light bulb) and pathways to depict ideas and using different colors in the process aid in cognitive stimulation. Key features of mind maps include clustering of ideas through association and the visual memory it creates for individuals (see Figure 7.7).

Mind maps help organize information. Because of the large amount of association involved, they can be very creative, generating new ideas and associations that have not been thought of before. Every item in a map is, in effect, the center of another map. The creative potential of a mind map is useful in brainstorming sessions. A person only needs to start with the basic problem at the center, and generate associations and ideas from it to arrive at a number of different possible approaches. By presenting perceptions in a spatial manner and using color and pictures, a better overview is gained and new connections can be made visible.

Mind maps are very individualized and original. For example, if one were to compare the mind maps of two different individuals around a central theme they would be different. Research has shown that even simplified mind maps (with as few as seven related words) of any two individuals would average only one word in common, and anything above two is very unusual (Buzan & Buzan, 1996). The guidelines for developing mind maps are presented in Figure 7.8.

Unconscious Problem Solving

This method relies on the unconscious mind to continually process the various sensory inputs stored in short-term and long-term memory. It entails using the

---

Step One: Lighten Up
Let go of finding the perfect program, solving all the problems of the organization, or writing the perfect program evaluation. Mind mapping is simply a brain-dumping process that helps stimulate new ideas and connections. Start with a playful attitude—you can always evaluate later.

Step Two: Think Fast
Our brains work best in 5 to 7 minute bursts so capture that explosion of ideas as rapidly as possible. Key words, symbols, and images provide a mental shorthand to help us record ideas as quickly as possible.

Step Three: Judge Not
Similar to brainstorming, this phase of mind mapping asks us not to evaluate, but rather to record everything that comes to mind even if it seems to be totally unrelated.

Step Four: Break Boundaries
Break through the idea that we have to write on white, letter-size paper with black or blue ink. Use ledger paper or easel paper or cover an entire wall with butcher paper… the bigger the paper, the more ideas we will have. Use wild colors; fat, colored markers; crayons; skinny felt-tip pens; or anything else you can find.

Step Five: Center First
Our linear, left-brain education system has taught us to start in the upper left hand corner of a page. However, our mind focuses on the center…so mind mapping begins with a word or image placed in the middle of the page that symbolizes what we want to think about.

Step Six: Free Associate
As ideas emerge, print one- or two-word descriptions of the ideas and connect them to the thought that generated the idea. Allow the ideas to expand outward from thoughts as they emerge.

Step Seven: Keep Moving
Keep moving. Avoid getting stuck on one idea. The more ideas generated, the better.

Step Eight: Allow Time for Organization
Compare your individual mind map to the maps of other people who are working on the same problem. Begin to look for linkages, that is, pieces of information that can be linked together in some way. Sometimes we will see relationships and connections right away, while other times it may take some time. Just remember the main purpose of mind mapping is to get ideas out and on paper.

Figure 7.8 Mind mapping—The basic rules (Adapted from Wycoff, 1991)

unconscious mind to solve problems. It is a process of listening and a readiness to record ideas as they percolate into the conscious mind. Some of the greatest thinkers were great relaxers. Albert Einstein was a daydreamer and spent much of his relaxation time sailing on a lake. Ralph Waldo Emerson enjoyed fishing. Thus, a person learns that while it is important to work diligently on a problem under the stressful pressure of deadlines; the opposite condition of relaxing and dispensing with a problem is also very valuable.

A practical application of this technique is to saturate oneself in a problem and then take a break. For instance, some people write down the problem on a writing pad and leave it by their bedside. When they wake up, they lie in bed, think some more about the problem, and write down their thoughts—even in the dark. This process is particularly helpful when planning special events. Often, thoughts wake people from sleep—particularly related to things they need to attend to the next day (e.g., security, ticketing, trash recycling) and can be difficult to remember them in the morning. By writing them down during the night, a person can be sure to tend to the needed tasks and still get a good night's sleep.

Passion

Creativity is an important starting point; passion will carry us through the additional planning phases. Passion carries with it a connotation of being dramatic, powerful, and emotional. While these characteristics may indicate how people express passion, passion itself is more accurately characterized as an unfailing dedication to an ideal. Thus, the idea that passion is something rare and not sustainable is more myth than reality. In today's world of strategic planning, mission, vision statements, and values clarification (see Chapter Three) rather than answering the what or how, passion answers the question, "why?" According to Cassidy (2006), passion tends to be personal and unique to individuals, usually internalized, even hidden from others. On the other hand, when expressed with others, passion tends to be contagious and attracts both people and opportunities.

Passion is often demonstrated by intensity and duration. For instance, when programmers make a long-term commitment to gradual and continuous improvement of programs and the organization, they demonstrate a strong sense of passion. One way in which this passion can be demonstrated is a commitment to research. This includes a new look at resources that are a part of the programmer's "bag of tricks," as well as searching for new ideas.

The pursuit of research is one step in the professional development of a leisure programmer. In conjunction with practical, hands-on experience, it provides us the building blocks to create innovative and unique programs, as well as respond spontaneously to people and situations. Leisure programmers who become too comfortable with their current level of programming knowledge tend to do a disservice to participants, the organization, the program, and themselves.

Creativity and passion are integral to the conduct of research. This might seem contradictory because for many, the idea of research is limited to traditional views of white lab coats, endless forms and reports, and overwhelming statistics. Therefore, the idea that research can be vital and creative rather than dry and boring can be a stretch of the imagination. For this reason, we often find that leisure programmers are less committed to this aspect of service delivery than it merits. As we mentioned previously, creativity is the ability to make something out of nothing, or to use something in a new or innovative way. The leisure programmer who approaches research with passion and thinks creatively is likely to find the process both productive *and* enjoyable.

Research and Resources

No one questions the need for healthcare professionals to continually educate themselves about current and changing medical techniques and practices. While the consequences of being comfortable with the status quo in leisure services is not generally a matter of life or death (as it can be with health issues), the vitality and life of a program may be put in serious jeopardy if research is neglected. Furthermore, the programmer who is not actively involved in expanding her or his programming repertoire may very well experience a resulting decrease in enthusiasm and passion for the program. In addition, as activities become stale and tedious through repetition and a lack of energy, staff and participants also lose passion. Consequently, even programs that have a high turnover in participants need to reflect a commitment to expanding ideas and implementing change.

Research goes far beyond conducting a survey or an experiment of some sort. Most agree that research is a diligent, careful, and exhaustive inquiry into a subject to discover or interpret facts, theories, or applications. This means that *all* avenues of gaining knowledge and gathering resources should be utilized. This includes looking to disciplines beyond parks, recreation, and leisure services for information and ideas. Related disciplines that may prove valuable in this search include education, psychology, social work, health services, parenting/childcare, and business. As servant leaders concerned with maximizing abilities to meet constituents' varied needs, it is important to undertake a thorough search for new viewpoints and material. This requires expanding one's thinking as well as looking to other people, organizations, media, documents, and other potential sources for assistance and guidance throughout the programming cycle.

Adapting Resources

A logical starting point when approaching research creatively is to challenge oneself to look in new ways at the resources that already exist. For example:

1. Find unique and different uses for equipment the department possesses;

2. Expand the target group, change locations or rules, and/or alter timing for particular programs; and

3. Adapt activities to meet different objectives.

Sometimes a very minor adjustment or change precipitates the most dramatic results. Using resources in new ways enables programmers to spark interest and enthusiasm in participants and staff.

Equipment

Introducing familiar equipment in a new way addresses the issue of blind spots that occur when we associate objects and meanings with previous experiences. Consequently, if we present participants with a basketball, paint brush, or hula hoop and give no instructions, we can predict with a fair amount of certainty how participants will use these pieces of equipment. Those with the basketball will dribble and pretend to shoot a basket; those with the paint brush will look for something to paint; and those given the hula hoop will put it around their waist and try to keep it up as long as possible. If we give participants rules that are incompatible with the conventional uses of the equipment, however, we suddenly create a new game. For instance, we could give participants access to art supplies and tell them they need to use the basketball to create an art project. We could tell those with paint brushes to use them when playing air hockey, and we could suggest to those with hula hoops that they create a dance using the hoops as props. Although the equipment remains the same, by changing other variables, the possibilities suddenly seem limitless.

Another strategy is to introduce new or unique equipment to a familiar activity. For example, to provide a variety of tactile experiences to young children we could fill a wading pool with rice instead of sand or water. This not only provides easy cleanup, but it also stimulates the children with a distinctive medium to explore. Leaders can also vary activities by altering the number of pieces of equipment typically used—imagine what might happen when a doubles tennis game is suddenly played using two balls.

Equipment may also be adapted to create a homemade version that is often simpler and more cost-effective than the commercial alternative. For example, before taking her sixth grade class to a winter camp, a teacher at New Branches School in Grand Rapids, Michigan downloaded instructions off the web and provided class time for students to make their own snowshoes out of simple supplies found at the local hardware store. Not only did this save money while providing students with their own snowshoes, the process of making them increased student knowledge and emotional investment in the camp experience.

Another way to adapt equipment is to look at new products and determine if they can be effectively (and safely) duplicated with existing resources. For example, Trak Paks are an innovative product in terms of how they are packaged. They are small fanny packs that contain objects representing abstract characteristics and concepts to be used when working with groups. For instance, among the 24 "starter" items, each pack contains a key (e.g., What was the key to our success?), a bragging stone (e.g., talk about what you did that contributed positively to the group), and a battery (e.g., What about this activity gave us a charge?). The idea of using small objects as symbols and metaphors in group processing is the real innovation, and the idea can be borrowed and expanded upon by creating a customized pack for your own use. All of these strategies improve programs by increasing variety and innovation. A guideline for making equipment and resources for attaining inexpensive equipment is presented in Figure 7.9 (see p. 174).

As mentioned throughout this text, good programmers consider the needs of all constituent groups. One outcome of this integrated thought process is that we become more aware of adaptive or assistive devices commonly used when programming for people who have disabilities. By using these pieces of equipment for all users, we can change the nature of an activity. An example would be playing beep baseball, rather than sighted baseball. By blindfolding players and using adaptive equipment, programmers can encourage everyone to use more of their senses and make an old game new.

People, Places, Timing

As leisure services programmers, we can also be creative by rethinking what we offer, where we offer it, to whom, and when. While it is a valuable skill to think in terms of developmentally appropriate activities, it is also true that programmers often think too narrowly in terms of individual skills and interests. By expanding their thinking, staff may begin to realize that they may want to offer an activity that has traditionally been targeted at one particular age group to others. For example, people typically think about playgrounds being a resource for young children. However, a playground may also be incorporated into an obstacle course for teens or adults. Programmers wanting to involve

Design Considerations

1. Concerns in deciding between "homemade" versus manufactured: quality, safety, and versatility.
2. Are materials easily obtained and available in sufficient quantities?
3. Is it safe for the age level and maturity level of those using it?
4. How durable is it? Is maintenance required?
5. Will it be interesting and challenging as well as aid in meeting the goals of the program?

Helpful Hints

1. Make one sample model before you mass-produce; you may decide on alterations.
2. Whenever feasible make enough for each participant to have one (e.g., small apparatus) or at least one piece for every group of 3–5 participants.
3. Any wood apparatus should be sanded and finished to avoid splinters; corners should be rounded off when feasible.
4. Use resources in the community to help you construct the equipment.
5. Use bolts in place of nails whenever possible, especially if equipment is to be dismantled or stored after use.
6. When soliciting for "new materials" take a sample model with you and explain how your participants will benefit by using the donor's gracious gift.
7. Allow yourself ample time to construct the equipment to ensure a quality product.
8. Trips to toy or sporting goods stores (or magazine, catalog, or Internet browsing) may prove useful in obtaining ideas concerning a variety of equipment available for creative modification or utilization.

Safety and Legal Liability

The importance of maintaining a safe and healthful environment cannot be overemphasized both from a humanistic and from a legal point of view. The use of homemade equipment places an additional responsibility on the individual who utilizes such equipment. Each piece of homemade equipment should be built at least to required specifications with effort being made to improve upon its design in terms of safety. The equipment should be regularly inspected and defects immediately corrected. A program of preventative maintenance that anticipates and removes potential hazards before they arise is the best way to avoid the hazards of legal liability.

Resource Banks for Inexpensive Equipment and Supplies

- Sporting goods businesses (old bike tires, old bowling pins, damaged products)
- Electrical companies (colored wires, large/small wire spools)
- Stores (feed sacks, plastic flags, barrels, fruit crates, large baskets, old displays)
- Tennis or golf clubs (old tennis balls, old golf balls, old nets)
- Card stores (mailing envelopes, old wrapping paper, ribbon)
- Auctions, garage/rummage sales, and pawn shops (any number of miscellaneous items)
- Furniture/Appliance stores (large cardboard boxes, packing material, old mattresses)
- Travel agents (old travel posters)
- Art stores (leftover or damaged paper, other merchandise)
- Churches (old candles)
- Garment factories (old buttons, ribbon, yarn, fabric scraps)
- Building supply companies (wood and lumber, tiles, wallpaper books, color samples)
- Hardware/Paint stores (linoleum, rope, chain, wood, leftover paint, end rolls of wallpaper)
- Carpet companies (remnants, scraps)

Figure 7.9 Considerations when creating homemade equipment (Adapted from Marston, 1997) senior citizens in a fitness activity by utilizing a playground as part of an obstacle course could tap into the popularity of Bingo with this population. Bingo cards could be placed at strategic places on the obstacle course to be subsequently used in the game of Bingo; or BINGO could be used as an acronym during promotion for a different program (e.g., Be Involved Now—GO Fitness!). Programmers do need to take care that when trying to increase the appeal of a program the program is not misrepresented to the target audience.

Changing settings can also add interest to an otherwise familiar activity. Moving a football game to a mud hole or swimming pool adds a whole new and exciting dimension to the game. Changing the time for an activity is also a factor—both daily and seasonally. A barbecue on the beach may appeal to teens; schedule it for midnight under the stars and participation may soar (however, excellent crowd control and chaperones are a necessity). The Winter Carnival in Saranac Lake, New York (Saranac Lake Winter Carnival, 2009), is a good example of integrating traditional winter activities such as skiing, skating, curling, pond hockey and broomball with activities typically played indoors or during the summer. Their 2008 event featured such innovations as inner-tube races, a treasure hunt, snowflake volleyball, an arctic barbecue, and an ice palace fun run.

Rules and Procedures

Changing objectives or rules of familiar games can also create excitement and enthusiasm among participants. Using the example of *baseball*, imagine if making a rule that players could run the bases in any order they desired; or if a larger, smaller, or a different type of ball was used for the game. Think about the changing dynamics of playing Capture the Flag if the rules included any of the following:

- If half of any team is captured, play is discontinued while negotiations for release are held.

- Persons who are jailed may get "early release" by performing a talent for the "parole board" made up of impartial judges.

- Players must hold hands with at least one other player on their team at all times; any time players fail to do this, they must join the other team.

Introducing such elements to an activity teaches flexibility and openness and is often used to foster cooperation rather than competition. It can also be used as the means to include players of varying abilities as seen in the case example presented in Table 7.2. The importance in this situation was not whether adjustments were made for Lenny or whether all players changed how they were going to play, but the fact that these children helped Lenny redefine how he saw himself. We can certainly hope that it is only a matter of time before Lenny becomes active in determining his own game adaptations.

PACE (Patience, Alternatives, Creativity, Enthusiasm)

The acronym, PACE, developed by York and Jordan (1992), incorporates all of these areas when looking specifically at programming for persons with disabilities. The underlying idea is that to be successful,

---

Table 7.2 A case example of adapting games (Adapted from Morris & Stiehl, 1989)

The fifth-grade students at Adamsville Elementary had been modifying games for quite a while when Lenny first arrived. That day they happened to be playing a variation of kickball. Lenny had never played kickball. In fact, he had not played many games because most people agreed that a boy who used a wheelchair could not participate in vigorous activities.

The children immediately began to introduce themselves to Lenny and invited him to participate in the game. Lenny was frightened—he had been alone before, but never in this sense. This time he was alone in his belief that he could not participate in such a game. The other children were already embracing a "can do" spirit and were determined to include this newcomer.

Lenny was assigned to the team at bat, some members of which had been deciding on a strategy of including him in a manner equal with his abilities. Instead of kicking the ball and running bases, Lenny had to maneuver his wheelchair through some obstacles and then squirt a water pistol at a paper cup, knock it over, and return home without colliding with any of the obstacles. If he did so, he was pronounced "safe."

Sometimes Lenny succeeded, and sometimes he did not. His classmates and he determined what he could do, verified their strategy with teachers, and then agreed that this was an acceptable option. Lenny was no longer merely a spectator. His was not a case of token involvement, but of genuine participation—of inclusion.

a programmer must consider and meet the individual needs of participants. The key to this effort is

P. Have the *Patience* to accept progress at any rate

A. Seek *Alternatives* by modifying activities, skills, equipment, rules, and presentation

C. Act *Creatively* through improvisation, modification, and adjustment

E. Be *Enthusiastic*

Figure 7.9 (see p. 174) suggests several specific ways programmers can modify programs and may prove helpful to those delivering recreation and leisure programs.

People

It is not uncommon to hear managers talk about people being their most important resource. While actions speak louder than words as to whether this belief is put into practice, it is an ideal that servant leaders should be passionate about making a reality. One benefit of this approach is that people feel valued, but the real purpose of utilizing people as resources is because they can truly help us. Trying to provide quality leisure services in a vacuum is like trying to make a pizza with only flour, water, and oregano. It is unnecessarily limiting, nearly impossible, and certainly frustrating. There is nothing so gratifying as realizing that "we are all in this together." If we are thinking and acting creatively, we will effectively utilize people within our organization as well as in the community at large.

In addition, being aware of others and trying to see the world from their perspectives and through their lenses, helps us to avoid assuming that everyone is like us—that their interests and needs are the same as ours. It helps us to avoid the trap of believing that we know all our constituents. Further, by always paying attention and desiring to know more about others, people can increase their cultural competence, and thus, their cultural responsiveness.

Within Our Own Organizations

With the onset of technology came a broadening of our world—we live in an era in which even young children are aware of events that occur across the globe. While it is a good thing to broaden our horizons, particularly from the perspective of becoming more culturally sensitive, it can be a mistake to overlook the resources available in "our own backyard." Even

before our first day on a job, the networking process within the organization has begun; initial contacts with staff and constituents become the foundation for future relationships.

Management. If our organization is structured in such a way as to support the needs of constituents, then it is also likely that it is responsive to personnel who are functioning in direct service and middle management roles since they are the key to success. However, even in organizations that are not effectively supporting programmers and activity leaders, upper management can be a valuable resource. Therefore, even if it is difficult to get past obstacles such as political posturing or inaccessibility, leisure programmers need to be proactive about tapping the knowledge and experience of management personnel. These are often people who have walked in your shoes and are willing to tell about it. Find out the strengths of different managers in your organization and start to build your own expertise by learning from theirs.

Constituents. Throughout this text we have talked about the servant leader's desire to empower constituents and how this commitment usually proves to be mutually beneficial. Not only do participants gain a sense of program ownership, but programs and programmers also benefit in a variety of ways. First of all, participants are a source of ideas. Put simply, they expand the volume of input when given the opportunity. They also improve the quality of ideas since they are in touch with the needs and desires of the population to be served (i.e., themselves), are often highly invested in the program, and committed to the organization. Third, they serve as a link for programmers trying to network in the community. Lastly, constituents can help us to avoid making culture-blind mistakes. By involving our constituents, our awareness will be raised and we might offer programs we would not otherwise offer. For example, offering single-sex swimming opportunities might open up a world of swimming to people of various religious groups who otherwise would not use a public pool because females and males are discouraged or not allowed to see one another in swimming attire.

Colleagues. One of the real joys of working in the parks, recreation, and leisure services profession is that it is very people-oriented. So much job satisfaction comes from the people we serve and also from the people with whom we work. The experiential nature of our programs and the practical side of our field enable us to collaborate with coworkers. At the minimum, we should make the time to share ideas with other staff on a regular basis. This process inevitably leads to new ideas that no one would have conceptualized independently, which result from the building of one idea upon another—creativity at its best. It is also helpful (indeed, often necessary) to work with colleagues throughout the programming cycle on specific projects or areas of development.

Community: Partnerships and Networking

One of the most important tools of resource attainment is the ability to network and establish partnerships with other entities. Minimally, this requires strong and effective social skills to meet new people and build relationships; ideally, this requires the ability to envision how two individuals can share resources for their mutual benefit.

Businesses (Partnerships, Mentors, Donors). Forming a partnership can take many forms. One example is mentoring programs that exist in urban areas between youth-serving organizations and businesses. These programs often require members of the business community to donate time on a weekly basis to a youth who is identified "at risk" and in need of positive adult role models. In Oklahoma, the Association for Electric Cooperatives supplies hundreds of volunteers each year to assist with the Oklahoma Special Olympics Track and Field games. Another example of a partnership is soliciting sponsorship in the form of cash or product donations from businesses for a program or organization. In exchange, the leisure organization typically offers free publicity or advertisement of the products, test marketing, or service recognition in the community.

An example of an enterprise that involved several partnerships is the 10-mile sustainable mountain biking trail in Murphy-Hanrehan Park Reserve near Minneapolis-St. Paul. Requiring complex planning, funding, building, and maintenance, this endeavor spans several years and organizations. The result is a trail that challenges the most avid of mountain bikers while protecting the park's natural resources. The flow chart in Figure 7.10 (see p. 178) highlights both the tasks and organizations involved in this venture.

Leisure Services Organizations. Just as we want to broaden our knowledge base into other disciplines, we also want to expand our resources by networking with professionals in other parks, recreation, and leisure services organizations. Possible strategies to facilitate this information exchange include

1. Contact directors of similar programs and inquire about their most successful programs and traditions.

2. Mix business with pleasure by visiting museums, amusements parks, outdoor recreation areas, and parks, recreation, and leisure settings, and take notes about innovative programs or ideas.

3. Participate in a staff exchange for whatever time or distance is feasible—this could be as little as one day at a local organization or as much as one year in another country.

While it is important to talk with professionals who work in similar settings or with similar populations, we unnecessarily limit our programs and creativity by maintaining these contacts exclusively. We can learn a great deal by collaborating across the lines that have historically served as barriers. These include parameters such as whether the organizations are

• Private, commercial, or public nonprofit

• Youth-serving or adult-focused

• Therapeutic or nontherapeutic

• Urban or rural

• Outdoor or indoor; and so on

The complexity of our world often requires us to compartmentalize; we could use this to aid us in delivering quality services, rather than limit our potential. We need to find out what others are doing (and not doing) in our local communities as well as nationally and internationally. Think about the possibilities if staff at museums, amusement parks, libraries, youth organizations, fitness clubs, special recreation districts, daycare centers, golf courses, travel agencies, and nature centers networked successfully.

Professional Associations

Professional associations serve as a means to advance the interests of their membership. This overall mission involves benefits to both professionals and the association. Membership in the association entitles members to benefits such as subscriptions to journals, trade magazines, and newsletters; reduced costs for conferences and workshops; special notifications (e.g., mail, email, Twitter) of information; and access to listserves and discipline-related chat rooms, among other perks. By sharing their time, talents, and ideas, members, sustain associations. Thus, professional associations may be viewed from the dual perspective that they are a resource as well as an opportunity to serve.

Professional associations vary a great deal in their scope, geographic parameters, and size. Some associations such as the Association for Challenge Course Technology (ACCT) are narrowly specific while others like the American Association for Health, Physical Education, Recreation, and Dance (AAHPERD) have a much broader appeal. Within a particular association, such as the National Recreation and Park Association (NRPA), different levels of the association serve specific geographic regions. NRPA serves the entire country, for example, while separate, related groups serve geographic regions or states. Both the scope and level of the association affect the size that it attains which also affects the benefits that can be provided to members (due to resource limitations). Parks, recreation, and leisure services professionals often begin their involvement at the local level and build on this as they become involved in and serve the parent organization.

Examining professional associations more closely, we find that they serve eight basic functions, including

- **Advocacy**—promoting the profession to the public at large, including legislative interests;

- **Promotion of standards**—promoting high quality of service and ethics by establishing and publicizing industry standards;

- **Research**—the study and dissemination of trends and issues related to the profession;

- **Education**—providing opportunities for ongoing education and training, usually through the form of conferences, workshops, seminars, or institutes;

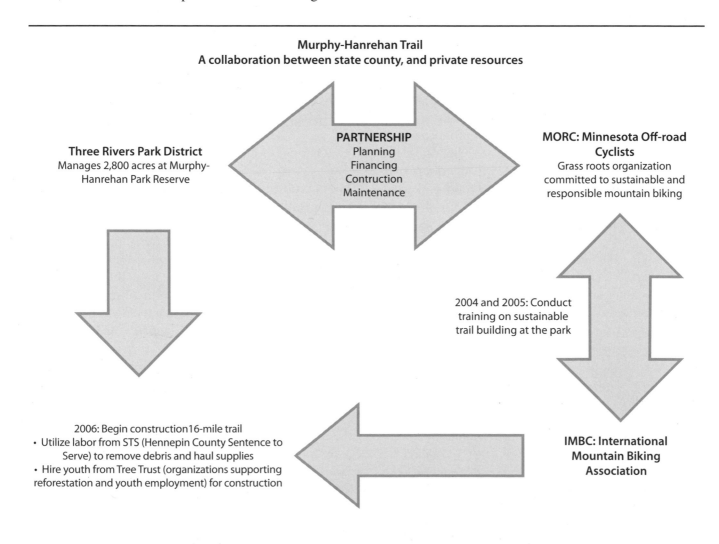

Figure 7.10 Flow chart of mountain bike trail development through partnerships

- **Communication**—disseminating information regarding association activities, as well as current research and job opportunities via magazines, journals, newsletters, and computer technology;

- **Networking**—by providing opportunities for people with similar interests to meet, those individuals can jointly problem solve, share resources, and reaffirm their commitment to the profession;

- **Recognition**—acknowledging the contributions and efforts of individual members, influential people outside of the membership and students via certificates, plaques, scholarships, and prizes; and

- **Insurance and retirement benefits**—tangible benefits such as health insurance, liability insurance, and retirement are often provided to members and organizations at reduced rates. (Edginton, DeGraaf, Dieser & Edginton, 2006)

The first three of these functions involve the profession as a whole while the remaining five focus on individuals. These benefits of participation in leisure services professional associations are often applicable to professional organizations in other fields. Whether it is personal contacts, conference or workshop attendance, or written resources, many valuable ideas can be borrowed from professional associations like those listed in Figure 7.11 (see p. 180).

Because of the large membership and the structure of large associations, many opportunities to network with people who come from different backgrounds and settings are available. These cross-specialty relationships can be quite fruitful. For instance, within NRPA conferences and workshops are beginning to appear that are a result of cross-discipline collaboration. The National Therapeutic Recreation Society and the American Parks and Recreation Society (two branches of NPRA) have joined forces to offer an annual conference related to the inclusion of people with disabilities in community recreation settings—the National Institute on Recreation Inclusion. Also at NRPA annual congresses, a session titled "Call of the Wild" has become extremely popular. Every year, over 600 people sit in on these sessions to listen to five-minute presentations about creative programming ideas. Program information is shared via handouts and participants have opportunities to ask questions.

Written Materials

The wealth of written information available to parks, recreation, and leisure services professionals should be a source of great comfort in research efforts. Because of the many resources, programmers do not have to work in isolation or without easily available resources. Written materials are often fairly compact and can be easily transported from place to place. We also realize, however, that the breadth of written materials (even before the technology explosion) have become overwhelming to programmers. For most organizations, limitations of time and money require that research be focused and efficient. From the thousands of materials available, decisions need to be made about which to access, read, purchase, and use in programming efforts. In addition, one of the disadvantages of written materials is that they become outdated in a fairly short period of time; therefore, programmers need to remember to update their most helpful books, and supplement information from other resources.

Textbooks

As parks, recreation, and leisure services students, you are required to purchase and read many textbooks to prepare for your future profession. While some students sell back their textbooks, many recognize the value of retaining their textbooks to serve as a resource in the workforce. In particular, those texts that address leadership, programming, evaluation, and ethics may be good sources of information and guidance in your professional life. These types of books often address the overall questions of "How?" and "Why?" which can be helpful in job-related situations. For instance, we might learn or be reminded about how we can determine what our constituents need and want; and why we should make our building accessible even if it means we don't have funds to provide childcare. Utilizing texts and class notes as resources provides many entry-level practitioners with an edge over those who do not have access to these types of materials.

Activity and Programming Books

Activity and programming books are often helpful in answering the question "What?" as in "What are we going to do?" "What are we going to need?" and "What are we going to accomplish?" While we all, as programmers, have our favorite activities and programs that we can offer without relying on books or additional resources, we also need to develop systems to help us access specific information about activities we don't know as well. In this way, research helps expand one's programming repertoire and incorporate new ideas into existing programs. This may be something as simple as designating a bookshelf in the office for the latest programming books, which can be purchased in bookstores, on the Internet, or ordered through a variety of catalogs.

Other ways to address programming resources include creating a personal file that contains details for conducting activities that have been successful in the past, or attending sessions and exhibitions at professional conferences to find out what current resources and products are available. Other materials can found by searching the Internet using keywords such as recreation programming, arts and crafts, group games, cooperative games, outdoor activities, fitness, games, children, parenting, seniors, rainy day, education, leisure time, park activities, and so on.

Children's Literature

Children's literature can provide a wealth of ideas and information to assist with programming efforts. Books that may prove helpful for particular programs fall into a variety of categories. Classics from the 20th century include individual books such as *Charlotte's Web*, as well as series such as *The Boxcar Children Mysteries*. Many times it is the author, such as Dr. Seuss, who makes a work of literature stand out as a potential resource. In a similar vein, a popular character such as Curious George or Dora the Explorer, may offer ideas for programs. Many children's books

---

4-H of the USA
www.4husa.org

American Alliance for Health, Physical Education, Recreation, and Dance
www.aahperd.org

American Camp Association
www.ACAcamps.org

American Therapeutic Recreation Association
www.atra-online.com

Association for Challenge Course Technology
www.acctinfo.org

Association of College Unions International
www.acui.org

Association of Experiential Education
www.aee.org

Association of Outdoor Recreation and Education
www.aore.org

Boy Scouts of America
www.scouting.org

Boys and Girls Clubs of America
www.bgca.org

Canadian Parks/Recreation Association
www.cpra.ca

Christian Camp and Conference Association
www.ccca.org

Easter Seals
Easterseals.com

Employee Services Management Association
www.esmassn.org

Girl Scouts of America
www.girlscouts.org

International Festivals and Events Association
www.ifea.com

International Special Events Society
www.ises.com

JCC Association [Jewish Community Centers]
www.jcca.org

National AfterSchool Association
www.naaweb.org

National Association for Interpretation
www.interpnet.com

National Association of Recreation Resource Planners
www.narrp.org

National Intramural Recreational Sports Association
www.nirsa.org

National Recreation and Park Association
www.nrpa.org

North American Association for Environmental Education
www.naaee.org

Paralyzed Veterans of America
www.pva.org

Resort and Commercial Recreation Association
www.rcra.org

Travel and Tourism Research Association (TTRA)
www.ttra.com

World Leisure
www.worldleisure.org

YMCA of the USA [Young Men's Christian Association]
www.ymca.net

YWCA of the USA [Young Women's Christian Association]
www.ywca.net

Figure 7.11 A selection of professional associations of interest to those in leisure services can be utilized in programs that serve all ages. For example, Dr. Seuss's 1990 book, *Oh, the Places You'll Go…* makes a wonderful banquet theme for a variety of occasions. To think creatively about how to use children's literature programmers need to break away from the idea that its value is restricted to children. Staff also need to think beyond the typical "story time" approach, although this certainly is a valuable activity. By using one's imagination and including participants in program design a wide variety of possibilities are opened up.

Trade Books

Much of the information available on parenting and childcare, for example, is not in the form of textbooks or program resources, but are found in trade books. These are books published by companies or individuals who sell to the general public. While some trade books are available in public and university libraries, many of the current and most helpful sources of information for programs that serve children, youth, and families, and are about leadership, sports and games, educational activities, and nature are found in bookstores. While browsing through an actual bookstore is almost a lost art, it can often yield great finds. Resources focused on families or youth will commonly provide guidance and ideas in the form of activities, behavior management strategies, and developmental milestones. Other types of trade books that often prove helpful are health and medical guides, cookbooks, and travel books.

Journals

Professional journals may be categorized into two groups based on the audience targeted. One type of journal includes those that target practitioners and promote best professional practices in a specific area. These types of periodicals are often connected with a specific professional association and are provided to members as one of the benefits of their membership. For example, *Camping Magazine*, produced by the American Camp Association, offers camp professionals a variety of current information on such topics as programming, managing areas and facilities, supervising staff, meeting professional standards, dealing with risk management, and working with children.

A second type of journal is research-based and tends to be targeted at university professors and researchers within the parks, recreation, and leisure field as well as practitioners who are interested in practical applications of completed research. Research journals provide readers with current information about issues related to parks, recreation, and leisure services.

Figure 7.12 (pp. 182-183) provides a list of selected research and professional journals related to the profession. Many professional journals and periodicals are available on the web, or through a university or public library.

Periodicals

We define periodicals as magazines and newspapers that are circulated to businesses, public agencies, and residential households either through hard copy and/or electronically (e-zines). They may be published as infrequently as quarterly or as frequently as weekly. Periodicals that programmers may wish to consult include national newspapers (e.g., *USA Today, The New York Times*), local newspapers, news magazines (e.g., *Time, Newsweek, U.S. News and World Report*), hobby magazines (e.g., *Better Homes and Gardens, Backpacker*), magazines of general scope with wide circulation (e.g., *Reader's Digest, Latina Magazine, Vibe*), society and culture periodicals (*Exceptional Parent, Teen Vogue, Vista*), and specialty magazines (e.g., *Computer Digest, Games, Ranger Rick*).

Articles. Articles in periodicals often prove to be good indicators of trends and issues; thus, they provide a window into the topics that are important to constituents now and in the near future. For example, in a 2009 e-zine article (March 14, 2009) in *Medical News Today* Brunner reported that children at risk of being overweight who live in proximity to parks, green spaces, or recreational areas are more physically active that than those who live at a distance. For each park located within one half mile of their home, girls were twice as likely to walk for leisure, while boys increased their leisure walking by 60%. This information can be valuable in helping programmers to effectively use open spaces in local neighborhoods, and to develop programs that take advantage of the nearby parks and green spaces.

In researching for this text, we found a wide range of other articles about leisure-related trends. They included information about how Baby Boomers will reinvent retirement, the decrease in young people playing outdoors, increase in budget travel, a decrease in hunting and fishing, improvements in consumer technology such as cameras and computer games, an increase in bicycle riding, and a decrease in visitation to national parks.

In addition to articles that inform programmers about national, state, and local trends, the articles also serve as a good source of evaluative information about products and programs. For instance, each year *Good Housekeeping* and *Consumer Reports* magazines

Professional Journals

Camping Magazine. Bimonthly. Trends and issues in the organized camp industry; includes research in youth development, management tools, and programming ideas. *http://www.acacamps.org/campmag/*

Journal of Experiential Education. Three issues/year. Scholarly journal with range of articles in outdoor adventure programming, service learning, environmental education, therapeutic applications, and more. *http://www.aee.org/publications/jee*

Journal of ICHPER-SD. Quarterly. International Council for Health, Physical Education, Recreation, Sport and Dance. Covers topics related to health, physical education, recreation, sport, dance, and the Olympic movement. *http://www.ichpersd.org/i/journal.html*

Journal of the Philosophy of Sport. Semiannual. Covers issues related to contemporary philosophy of sport. *http://www.humankinetics.com/Jps/journalAbout.cfm*

The Journal of Physical Education, Recreation & Dance. Nine issues/year. Provides information on teaching strategies, legal issues, assessment, adapted physical education, leisure for older adults, and equity issues. *http://www.aahperd.org/aahperd/template.cfm?template= johperd_main.html*

NCPAD Newsletter. Monthly. Publication of the National Center on Physical Activity and Disability. Includes articles related to health, disability, programs, and activities. *http://www.ncpad.org/newsletter/newsletter.php?letter= current&PHPSESSID=0*

Paleastra. Quarterly. Resource that features articles and stories related to physical activity for the disabled. *http://www.palaestra.com/*

Recreational Sports Journal. Two issues/year. Publication of the National Intramural-Recreational Sports Association. Provides empirical, theoretical, and applied research in recreational sports. Topics include leadership, student development, programming, facility management, assessment, marketing, and organizational development. *http://www.humankinetics.com/RSJ/journalAbout.cfm*

Parks & Recreation Magazine. Monthly. Includes columns, articles, and product reviews related to the parks and recreation profession. Programming ideas, risk management, facilities, recreation across the ages, therapeutic recreation, and other aspects of the field are topics. *http://www.nrpa.org/content/default.aspx?documentId=507*

Sports and Spokes. Six issues a year. International publication dedicated to wheelchair sports and recreation activities. *http://www.pvamagazines.com/sns/*

Strategies. Six issues a year. Focus is on research and practice related to physical education teaching strategies. *http://www.aahperd.org/naspe/template.cfm?template=str ategies_main.html*

Research Journals

Adapted Physical Activity Quarterly. Quarterly. International multidisciplinary journal focused on issues related to physical activity for those with special needs. Includes case studies, techniques for adapting equipment, facilities, methodology, and book reviews. *http://www.humankinetics.com/apaq/journalAbout.cfm*

American Journal of Recreation Therapy. Quarterly. Goal is to provide CTRSs with the latest research, techniques, and advances in the use of recreational intervention to improve client health and well-being. *http://www.pnpco.com/pn10000.html*

ATRA Annual in Therapeutic Recreation. Quarterly. Features a mix of research-based and program-oriented articles. *http://www.atra-tr.org/annual/index.htm*

Journal of Leisure Research. Quarterly. Devoted to original investigations that contribute to knowledge and understanding of the leisure studies field. *http://www.rpts.tamu.edu/journals/JLR/*

Journal of Park and Recreation Administration. Quarterly. Established to bridge the gap between research and practice for administrators; provides a forum for the analysis of management and organization for the delivery of parks, recreation, and leisure services. *http://hotel.unlv.edu/recreation/journal/*

Journal of Teaching in Physical Education. Quarterly. Features research articles based on classroom and laboratory studies, summary and review articles, and current topics. *http://www.humankinetics.com/JTPE/journalAbout.cfm*

LARNet: The Cyber Journal of Applied Leisure and Recreation Research. Encompasses a wide range of recreation and leisure topics including leisure behavior, recreation and play, travel and tourism, campus recreation, community recreation, employee recreation, military recreation, and other aspects of the profession. *http://larnet.org/*

Figure 7.12 Research and professional journals and magazines related to recreation

Continued>>

Research Journals (continued)

Loisir et Societe/Leisure and Society. Semiannual. Multidisciplinary journal specializing in the study of leisure; serves as a forum for critical debate on the relationship between free time and the evolution of societies.
http://www.erudit.org/revue/ls/apropos.html

Leisure Sciences. Five issues/year. Focus is on the theoretical and empirical investigation and analysis of leisure and leisure behavior.
http://www.tandf.co.uk/journals/authors/ulscauth.asp

Leisure Studies. Quarterly. Focuses on all aspects of leisure studies from a variety of disciplines; focus is on the whole range of leisure behavior in the arts, sports, cultural and informal activities, tourism, and urban and rural recreation.
http://www.tandf.co.uk/journals/titles/02614367.asp

Therapeutic Recreation Journal. Quarterly. Devoted to publishing scholarly and substantive manuscripts in therapeutic recreation; includes needs of persons with disabilities, challenges facing the profession, and the provision of therapeutic recreation services.
http://www.nrpa.org/content/default.aspx?documentId=511

Related Journals of Interest

AARP The Magazine. Bimonthly. Serves the needs of those 50 and older. Includes information on games, activities, finances, travel, food, and health.
www.aarpmagazine.org

Child Education. Monthly. Includes issues affecting children, activities, growth and development, and reviews of other publications.
http://www.udel.edu/bateman/acei/cehp.htm

Childhood Education. Six times a year. Includes issues affecting children, activities, growth and development, and reviews of other publications.
http://www.udel.edu/bateman/acei/cehp.htm

Creative Kids. Monthly. Includes games, stories, and opinions by and for kids ages 8–14 years.
http://www.prufrock.com/client/client_pages/prufrock_jm_createkids.cfm

The Gerontologist. Bimonthly. Provides a multidisciplinary perspective on human aging including social policy, program development, and service delivery.
http://gerontologist.oxfordjournals.org/

Gifted Child Today. Monthly. Includes articles about working with gifted children, children with disabilities, and is full of practical ideas.
http://journals.prufrock.com/IJP/b/gifted-child-today

Intellectual and Developmental Disabilities. Quarterly. Features policy, practices, and perspectives for professionals and families interested in mental retardation and developmental disabilities.
http://aaidd.allenpress.com/aamronline/?request=get-static&name=mr-info#1

JADARA: The Journal for Professionals Networking for Excellence in Service Delivery with Individuals who are Deaf and Hard of Hearing. Quarterly. Deals with practical applications of research findings, program descriptions, social services, mental health, and other issues relatead to deafness.
http://www.adara.org/pages/publications.shtml

Journal of Creative Behavior. Quarterly. Academic journal that focuses on current research in creative thinking.
http://www.creativeeducationfoundation.org/jcb.shtml

Journal for the Education of the Gifted. Quarterly. Offers research related to gifted and talented children, including programming ideas.
http://journals.prufrock.com/IJP/b/gifted-child-today

Journal of Environmental Education. Quarterly. Environment issues and educational practices related to the natural environment.
http://www.heldref.org/jenve.php

International Journal of Multicultural Education. Open-access e-journal reports empirical research, theoretical, and practical articles related to multicultural education.
http://ijme-journal.org/index.php/ijme

Science Activities. Quarterly. For K-12 teachers to provide hands-on activities in the biological, physical, environmental, chemical, earth, and behavioral sciences.
http://www.heldref.org/sa.php

Skipping Stones: An Award Winning Multicultural Magazine. Five issues a year. Magazine for youth that encourages communication, cooperation, creativity, and the celebration of cultural richness.
http://www.skippingstones.org/

Figure 7.12 Research and professional journals and magazines related to recreation (continued from previous page) rate the safety and educational level of children's toys, while trade periodicals like *Skiing* or *Outside Magazine* often include information and reviews on new equipment. Programmers can use these sources to prioritize equipment expenditures and as a basis for making decisions. Furthermore, programs of excellence are sometimes featured in periodicals such as *World Traveler*, city magazines such as *Seattle,* or entertainment sections of newspapers. Other magazines such as *Family Fun* contain activity ideas appropriate for a variety of ages.

Comic Strips. While reproducing comic strips for publication can prove prohibitive due to copyrights, comic strips can be used in a variety of ways at very little expense. One example is to use them as a springboard to a comic strip drawing/writing activity as part of an arts program or a session related to self-expression. This might take the form of a book of original comic strips that participants compile for their own enjoyment or to sell to raise financial support for a program, agency, event, or particular purchase. Another idea might be to hold a comic strip contest between participants—perhaps entries could be printed in newsletters and/or displayed for public enjoyment, while the winning cartoon could be incorporated into a program brochure or T-shirt design.

A creative use of comic strips developed into an activity that became a tradition at the Recreation Center at Camp Walker, an army base located in Taegu, South Korea. During the 1980s when *Garfield* was popular, programmers held Garfield birthday parties, which incorporated the character as well as characteristics he possessed. The menu always included lasagna and activities such as Garfield trivia and "Pin the Nose on Odie." One of the advantages of using comic strip characters is that many have longevity that contrasts with the television industry. Children today still enjoy some of the same characters as their parents such as Marmaduke, Calvin and Hobbes (reproduced in book collections and shelved in children's sections at libraries), and Charlie Brown. This can be particularly helpful when planning intergenerational programs.

Pamphlets and Newsletters

Pamphlets and newsletters are not as accessible to programmers as other written materials from the standpoint that they are not indexed or catalogued in the same way as books, journals, and periodicals. However, they are easy to access from the standpoint that they are often free or available at a minimal cost, and may be obtained through the mail or online. We recommend that programmers ask for such things from staff at various organizations when meeting in person, talking on the phone, or corresponding via the Internet or e-mail. A valuable resource addressing a wide range of topics are the Federal Trade Commission pamphlets published by the government and available through the Consumer Information Center in Pueblo, Colorado.

Calendars

Calendars come in all shapes, sizes, and levels of detail. In programming efforts we might use the pictures and graphics calendars include or the information they contain. Many businesses make calendars available free of charge to those who ask, and they often contain wonderful pictures of wildlife and scenery that can be used for collages, making puzzles, decorating, and other art projects. Furthermore, calendars contain information about specific dates of interest or recognition for a variety of cultural groups.

For many years, recreation programmers have been incorporating this information by celebrating the changes in seasons and specific holidays such as Thanksgiving, Chanukah, Valentine's Day, and Martin Luther King, Jr. Day. These widely known holidays only scratch the surface of potential ideas. Many calendars include information about less publicized anniversaries, birthdays, and other significant events that can provide new ideas for creative programming. websites publish information about odd, strange, or bizarre holidays throughout the year.

On the humorous side, Tom and Ruth Roy have developed over 60 wacky holidays published in newspapers as well as the Wellcat Holidays website (e.g., Cook Something Bold and Pungent Day). This endeavor began on the radio when Roy encouraged his listeners to celebrate Northern Hemisphere Hoodie-Hoo Day by going outside and yelling "Hoodie-Hoo" in an effort to chase winter away (Houck, 2002). Over a decade later, individuals and organizations can be seen and heard celebrating each February 20th.

Perhaps the most comprehensive source of serious, whimsical and multicultural calendar information is *Chase's Calendar of Events* sold through bookstores and the Internet. According to the publisher's website,

> Since 1957, *Chase's Calendar of Events* has been the ultimate reference calendar: the standard day-by-day directory to special days, weeks and months as well as holidays, historical anniversaries and fairs and festivals. Each edition of *Chase's Calendar of Events* has more than 12,000 listings. It's a "must have" for broadcasters, journalists, advertising and

PR agencies, event planners, activity directors, speakers, librarians or anyone looking for something to celebrate each and every day! The book is revised annually and the new edition always publishes in the fall for the following year. (McGraw Hill, 2008)

As can be seen, calendar information varies considerably and may be viewed as humorous and frivolous or important and meaningful. Programmers may also want to research significant dates relating to their particular field or potential participant groups.

Movies, Television, and Radio

A fruitful source of ideas for themes and activities may be found in movies, television, and radio. Often referred to as a "drug" due to its powerful appeal, one of four Americans indicate they would not trade their televisions for a million dollars, and the average child watches almost four hours daily (McDonough, 2009). Radio is also widely utilized and has the added attraction of being mobile and offering a wide variety of stations in most locations without additional costs to the listener. Both of these mediums offer programming ideas that could be easily implemented or adapted for individual needs.

A good starting point when examining modern television and radio media is PBS (Public Broadcasting System) and NPR (National Public Radio) stations. Focusing on educational topics, the quality of content in programming is generally high and varied. These programs can serve as a source of positive fads in the listening and viewing realm of the public. On the radio, interesting current trends and issues are often reported as well as presentations that capture aspects of daily living, such as Garrison Keillor's *A Prairie Home Companion*.

On television, the ongoing popularity of shows like *Barney and Friends*, *The Wiggles*, *Curious George*, and *Clifford* may be capitalized on by incorporating it into existing or new programs. Through these shows children can learn about science, planets, conflict resolution, diversity, making friends, the environment, and other important social and cultural issues.

Adults are also avid television viewers in our society and may enjoy special events designed around popular television shows. Examples include a costume party around the characters in *Heroes*, or contests that highlight local talent à la *American Idol* or *Dancing with the Stars*. Game shows such as *Jeopardy, Survivor,* and *Deal or No Deal* have

spawned a variety of special events and recreation programs in communities across the U.S.

Cable television has also opened up a vast array of possibilities for programming ideas. Nickelodeon and Disney channels broadcast shows appropriate for children and general family viewing. In addition, science and nature specials are frequent fare on the Discovery Channel and Animal Planet and, used judiciously, may be a wonderful supplement for programs that utilize particular themes.

Television and radio can also be sources of songs to augment programs for children and adults of all ages and cultures. PBS shows like *Maya and Miguel* and *Sesame Street* present songs that preschool and school-age children can easily learn. Theme songs for shows such as *The Backyardigans* and *The Magic School Bus* will have appeal to older children. Theme songs (both past and present) can also provide content for talent shows and trivia contests for participants of all ages. Videos of shows can often be purchased from the network, retail stores, or catalogs.

When utilizing movies, television, and radio shows for ideas, programmers need to be careful that content will appeal to participants and will not conflict with constituent or organizational values. For example, *The Mighty Morphin Power Rangers* has enough appeal for children that it continues to air, but recreation programmers should be aware that some parents are concerned about the violent content in the show. Programmer concerns might include how the violence might affect participants, be received by parents, or conflict with their organization's values, mission, and vision. Even animated movies rated G may be objectionable for images that may be too frightening for children of certain ages. Using the theme or characters from popular books and movies such as *Twilight* and *Harry Potter* may be objectionable to some of the people served (some criticism revolves around the vampirism and sorcery depicted). In these situations, communication with constituents through town hall meetings, focus groups, and needs assessment becomes even more crucial (see Chapter Four). Furthermore, since television viewing is widely overused in American households, we would caution against utilizing this resource too frequently. A creative programmer can develop a memorable experience by involving participants in creating a theater or environment complete with refreshments, ushers carrying flashlights, tickets, "live" previews or commercials presented by staff or participants, and other elements of this medium.

Electronic Media

The category of electronic media includes avenues that communicate information via digital and computer technology. These resources have several advantages, one of which is that they tend to be more current than written materials. They are also readily accessible to most (but, not all) constituents; computers are found in many homes and most businesses. Those who do not have home access to services such as e-mail and the web can often access online resources at nearby public libraries, county court houses, Internet cafés, and recreation centers. Electronic media can minimize paper waste and the need for physical storage space for resources such as bookshelves or filing cabinets. Electronic media is critical to the recreation programmer who wishes to keep informed of fast-paced trends and changes as well maximize resources available via electronic communication.

Recordings: Audiotapes, Videotapes, CDs, DVDs and Internet Downloads

Audiotapes, videotapes, digital recordings, CDs, DVDs, and Internet downloads provide recreation programmers with a good deal of flexibility to utilize electronic media at a time that best fits a program. One service that is commonly provided to constituents is making sports, fitness, and instructional recordings available for individual viewing. This enables participants to do several things, such as:

- Continue their fitness and conditioning at home;

- Learn new skills and techniques for a particular activity at an appropriate pace;

- Learn safety techniques;

- View and evaluate videotapes for personal purchase; and

- Become interested in new activities.

Many organizations (especially those that are non-profit in orientation) provide educational recordings for youngsters (e.g., conflict resolution skills, anti-drug messages) and adults (e.g., parenting skills, behavior management). In this fashion, constituents are provided an important service related to continuing education. Oftentimes, successful television programs, such as *Bill Nye the Science Guy* that are no longer airing, are available via DVD or download.

Furthermore, libraries and recreation centers commonly offer recorded audio books to constituents. These materials can also be great sources of programming ideas.

Recordings may also be utilized by an organization as a promotional tool or to enhance a particular program. For instance, recordings of sound effects are often used to set the mood for a party (e.g., spooky noises at Halloween, nature sounds during a yoga class). In addition, recorded music can be a catalyst for programs such as dances and lip sync contests; stories from audio-recorded books can be used to set the stage for skits and plays. The ability to quickly download a vast array of music and videos electronically also provides an efficient way to incorporate these materials into programs. Having said this, programmers are cautioned that with the use of any commercial product, we will need to understand and adhere to any related copyright issues with use of the materials.

As is always the case with technology, we inherit some challenges in addition to the benefits with such progress. While the advances can serve as invaluable tools to creatively deliver programs, the very same aids can prove to be an impediment to the goals we are trying to accomplish. Programmers have seen cell phones and MP3 players dominate participants' time in the midst of a leisure experience, cutting the users off from interactions with their co-participants. While this most commonly occurs in what might be considered down time (for example when transitioning from one activity or location to another), programmers have also observed players balance the responsibility of being goalie in a noncompetitive game of soccer while taking cell phone calls. This type of use, of course, involves safety concerns as well as social and activity related issues. Thus, programmers will want to clearly share the agency's electronic use policy with participants. One innovative use of technology on a trip that involved a long van ride required each participant to submit a favorite song(s) to the leader, who created a montage of music to be listened to by the entire group en route. This enabled the use of something participants valued within a structure that promoted interpersonal interactions. Such policies and practices are important for all ages, as many young participants have open access, and adults often feel so dependent on their technological gadgets that they do not consider the effects on other group members or their own leisure experience.

Internet (World Wide Web)

The Internet is so accessible that it is no longer considered a new technology. Resources that can be accessed are seemingly limitless. People can find information about trends, product information, activity ideas, and social networking. In addition, programmers use the web for promotion, to share information, and to connect with constituents in a variety of ways. One common use of the web for recreation programmers is to search for information related to program ideas. A pragmatic approach to search for information is to use keywords. Such a search opens up many different links of information from which to choose. In Table 7.3, we provide a list related to recreational programs. The list is certainly not exhaustive and we hope that this list helps to challenge you to think of additional related keywords. Clearly, by using more than one keyword at a time the search can be expanded or narrowed.

Summary

In this chapter we focused on suggesting ways that recreation programmers can apply their creativity and passion to the process of research. By thinking and acting innovatively, we can find a vast number of resources not available through traditional methods. This requires that we utilize people, organizations, written materials and electronic technology across disciplines. By persevering in our quest for constant improvement, we take the most important step in delivering quality services to our constituents. As servant leaders we must remember that equipping ourselves with the best resources available, within the financial constraints of our organization, is imperative to provide quality programs.

The greatest resource inherent to all organizations to make this happen is the creativity and passion of its staff. While creativity and passion take many different forms and vary from individual to individual, key elements include open-mindedness, perseverance, collaboration, resourcefulness, and commitment. Violin virtuoso Anne Akiko Meyers captures the essence of this as she reflects on her own passion for music:

> I have to practice for a couple of hours every day, or my fingers will get stiff. But I don't overdo it. It's like that in life, too… If you concentrate too hard on school, work or whatever, you run the risk of extinguishing what you love about it. But if you take a step back every now and then, it can grow beyond your dreams. (Akers, 1998, p. 65)

In terms of servant leadership and creativity, several attributes come to mind—self-awareness, listening, and conceptualization. One of the most important questions a servant leader can ask her or himself is, "What don't I know?" When we ask this question we are exhibiting a willingness to engage in self-reflection. This typically leads to increased self-awareness, which is an attribute of a servant leader. The key, of

---

Table 7.3 Keywords to explore the Internet for programming ideas

Recreation, leisure, play, activities, education, curriculum, board games, yard games, social activities, party, fun programs, club sports	**Therapeutic recreation**, disability, disabled sports, Special Olympics, special education, mental retardation, wheelchair, blind, adapted sports, Para Olympics, recreation and disabled
Outdoor recreation, outdoor education, nature activities, parks, science experiments, water, boating, adventure, camp	**Arts and crafts**, pottery, ceramics, wood working, hobbies, cooking, culture, drama, theater, skits, music, singing, home and family
Culture(al), cross cultural, multicultural, diversity, personal differences	**Fitness**, exercise, aerobics, weight lifting, cardio workout, physical education
Youth, children, seniors, teens, retired; African Americans, Native Americans, Hispanic; girls, boys [and another keyword]	**Sports**, relay races, athletics; small group, large group, team, individual; competitive, cooperative, tournament
Parks and recreation department, Girl/Boy scouts, Campfire, boys and girls clubs, church, YMCA, YWCA, JCC, CYO, recreation club	**Military recreation**; armed services recreation; morale, welfare, and recreation; campus recreation; intramurals

course, is to answer the question and then engage in behaviors to learn about those areas in which we lack. The acts of lifelong learning are vital to maintaining and enhancing our creativity.

By consulting constituents, scouring the recreation literature and Internet, and staying abreast of current movies and books, programmers demonstrate the servant leadership trait of listening. This listening is part of our continuing education and it enhances our abilities to conceptualize what may be—it helps us to be creative and responsive to our constituent groups.

Programming from Here to There

In Clearfield City, Utah the Community Services program implemented a Farewell 2 Fat program (their version of *The Biggest Loser* TV show), where over the course of 8 weeks, teams exercised and ate a balanced diet to lose weight. Each team worked with a nutritionist, kept food journals, and worked with a personal trainer. A bulletin board in the community recreation center was created to highlight the progress made by each team and staff found that posting the information became a source of motivation for participants. The department partnered with exercise equipment companies and presented the winners with exercise gear/equipment to assist them in continuing the healthy habits they developed. In a three-year period, the program grew from 23 registrants to more than 50 participants, several of whom have participated each year the program has been offered. The true success of the program can be seen in one participant who experienced so much success that she implemented the program in her neighborhood—after one year her husband had lost over 100 pounds.

Several other recreation departments have offered similar programs—conduct an Internet search of "recreation programs biggest loser" to find other community and campus recreation agencies that have developed successful programs around the theme of this particular television show. Similar searches using the titles of popular television shows, movies, and books reveal other creative program ideas.

References

Akers, P. (1998). Note of distinction. *World Traveler*, April, 44–48, 64–65.

Albrecht, K. (1992). *The only thing that matters*. New York, NY: Harper Business.

Albrecht, K. & Zemke, R. (1985). *Service America*. Homewood, IL: Dow Jones-Irwin.

Amabile, T. (1999). *The creativity maze*. Harvard Business School Working Knowledge. Retrieved March 26, 2009 from http://hbswk.hbs.edu/item/0543.html

Amabile, T. (1998, September-October). How to kill creativity. *Harvard Business Review*.

Buzan, T. & Buzan, B. (1996). *The mind map book: How to use radiant thinking to maximize your brain's untapped potential*. New York, NY: Plume.

Brunner, S. (2009). *Kids who live near parks are physically more active*. Retrieved March 25, 2009, from http://www.medicalnewstoday.com/printerfriendlynews.php?newsid=142287

Cassidy, L. (2006). *Beyond motivation—passion*. Retrieved February 26, 2009, from EzineArticles.com at http://ezinearticles.com/?Beyond-Motivation---Passion&id=228801

Chase's Calendar of Events 2009. Editors of Chase's Calendar of Events. (2008). Chicago: IL: McGraw-Hill.

Clark, S. (1995) *Innovative programming: How to survive the jungle*. Speech given at Academy for Youth Leaders, October 10, 1994, University of Northern Iowa, Cedar Falls, IA.

Csikszentmihalyi, M. (1996). *Creativity: Flow and the psychology of discovery and invention*. New York, NY: HarperCollins.

Edginton, C., DeGraaf, D., Dieser, R. & Edginton, S. (2006). *Leisure and life satisfaction*. Dubuque, IA: McGraw-Hill.

Hanna, J. (2008). *Getting down to the business of creativity*. (Online). Retrieved February 26, 2009, from http://hbswk.hbs.edu/item/5902.html

Heslin, P. A. (2009). Better than brainstorming? Potential contextual boundary conditions to brainwriting for idea generation in organizations. *Journal of Occupational and Organizational Psychology, 82*(1), 129–145.

Houck, J. (2002, April 7). Couple turn oddball holidays into hobby. *Tampa Tribune*.

Marston, R. (1997). Personal interview. University of Northern Iowa.

McDonough, P. (2009). *TV viewing among kids at an eight-year high*. Retrieved January 9, 2010, from http://blog.nielsen.com/nielsenwire/media_entertainment/tv-viewing-among-kids-at-an-eight-year-high/

Mongeau, P. & Morr, M. (1999). Reconsidering brainstorming. *Group Facilitation*. (Online). Retrieved March 7, 2009, from www.findarticles.com

Morris, G. S. & Stiehl, J. (1989). *Changing kids' games*. Champaign, IL: Human Kinetics.

Rossman, R. & Schlatter, B. (2003). *Recreation programming* (5th ed.). Champaign, IL: Sagamore Publishing.

Russell, R. (1982). *Planning programs in recreation*. St. Louis, MO: C.V. Mosby Company.

Saranac Lake Winter Carnival. Retrieved February 26, 2009, from http://www.saranaclakewintercarnival.com

Seuss, D. (1990). *Oh, the places you'll go!*. New York, NY: Random House.

Silverthorne, S. (2002, July 29). *Time pressure and creativity: Why time pressure is not on your side*. (Online). Retrieved February 26, 2009 from http:/hbswk.hbs.edu/item/3030.html

von Oech, R. (1983). *A whack on the side of the head*. New York, NY: Warner Books.

Waltz, M. (September, 2007). Hold onto your handle-bars. *Park and Recreation, 81–85*.

Wellcat Holidays. Retrieved December 20, 2004, from http://www.wellcat.com/holiday.html

Wycoff, J. (1991). *Mindmapping: Your personal guide to exploring creativity and problem-solving*. New York, NY: Berkely Trade Publisher.

York, S. and Jordan, D. (1992, May 23). *Programming with PACE*. Presented at the Central District AAHPERD Conference, Des Moines, IA.

Photo provided by Jermel Stevenscn

Programmer Profile

Jermel Stevenson

Current Position: Parks and Recreation Director, Rowlett, Texas
Favorite Books: *Leading with Soul* by Lee Bolman & Terrence Deal (2001)
　　　　　　Jesus, CEO: Using Ancient Wisdom for Visionary Leadership by Laura Beth Jones (1996)
Favorite Recreation Activity: Fishing
Certifications: Certified Parks and Recreation Professional (CPRP)

▶ **Describe the path your career has taken.**

- Graduated with a Bachelor of Applied Arts in Community Parks and Recreation Management, and a Master's in Public Administration from Central Michigan University.
- Since completing my undergraduate degree, I have worked in a variety of positions in a number of different places:
    - City of Phoenix, Arizona Parks and Recreation, Parks and Recreation Supervisor
    - City of Detroit, Michigan Parks and Recreation, Acting District Manager/District Supervisor
    - City of Kentwood, Michigan Parks and Recreation, Adult Sports Coordinator
    - City of Kalamazoo, Michigan Parks and Recreation, Youth Programs Assistant
    - City of Warren, Michigan Parks and Recreation, Recreation Instructor
- I am transitioning to the first Directorship position of my career. As of January, 2010, I will be the Parks and Recreation Director for the City of Rowlett, Texas (suburban city of Dallas)
- During my tenure with the City of Phoenix I had the most exciting experiences! The City of Phoenix serves a population of about 1.5 million residents living within an area of 517 square miles. In my role as a Park and Recreation Supervisor, I am charged with:
    - Managing the programs and maintenance within 54 parks and 5 recreation centers, and assisting in the administration of a $17 million operating budget and an $8 million capital improvement budget in the Northwest District of the city;
    - Supervising five recreation coordinators and over 120 other staff who provide a wide range of recreation services; and
    - Working with a variety of special interest groups and grass roots organizations like neighborhood associations and faith-based organizations. Most recently, I had the pleasure of working with a table tennis club in developing a program to increase awareness of table tennis in the Northwest District.

▶ **Describe the joys of working in your current position.**

The diversity of the Northwest District is amazing and I love the various challenges that this diversity brings. The northern portion of the district is described as affluent with residents able to pay for programs and services. With this affluence comes the challenge of maintaining the market share for what we do well. This includes providing a well-rounded program (e.g., sports leagues and youth programs) and clean, well maintained fitness centers and parks. I enjoy keeping my programs and services competitive with our suburban counterparts.

In the more western portion of the district I have the joy of working with strong and thriving neighborhood associations and engaged community leaders. This area of the district has a large Spanish speaking population with its own unique interests and needs. Recently we worked with a variety of partners (including the National Basketball Association) to build a new playground in an area park. I also enjoy finding grants and sponsors to help offset the cost of services and programs based on our residents' income levels.

▶ **Do you have any advice for new programmers?**

New programmers need to keep current with new trends. One of the best ways to do this is to get involved and stay active in your state parks and recreation association, as well the National Park and Recreation Association. Make it a habit of reading the local newspaper of your city or town. Know what is going on in your community! In addition, I love reading *Governing Magazine*, which offers resources to keep up with trends in the public sector.

▶ **Describe the most creative program you have developed.**

The most recent creative program I have been involved with would be the "After Dark in the Park" and "Light Up the Sky" event held on July 4, 2009. Historically these two celebrations and festivals were financed and organized by the city of Phoenix Parks and Recreation Department. In 2009, the program was at risk of being cancelled due to budget reductions. I was tasked with the responsibility of organizing and delivering these two major festivals.

The first step was finding ways to finance both events. As a result, the department approached corporations, media, and a variety of grass roots organizations. We were able to raise a total of $90,000 to finance both events. In addition, all full-time staff worked the two events. What makes this event significant is while many of our suburban communities near our District cancelled their shows/festivals, we were able to organize and deliver not one, but two festivals for our community!

▶ **Share your ideas for developing creative programs.**

I love to visit other park systems and businesses as a way to find new ways to market our programs. In addition, I enjoy going to conferences within the parks profession as well as outside of the field; these events keep me fresh and my creative juices flowing.

▶ **How do you keep programs contemporary or culturally relevant?**

I listen to the community and then work with community members to make their ideas happen. In addition, I try to stay up to date with the services and programs that are being offered by commercial recreation organizations in the Phoenix area as well as our suburban counterparts. For example, I am in the process of working with community groups to convert tennis courts to small soccer fields with turf on them. This is culturally relevant because we have seen a decline in some segments of our community relative to tennis and an increase in space needed for soccer.

Program Promotion | 8

In the circular diagram, reading around from top: Conduct Summative Evaluation, Assess Participant Needs, Plan and Design Program, Engage in Pre-program Tasks, Implement Program, Conduct Formative Evaluations, Make Adjustments and Continue Implementation, with Identify Organizational Philosophy and Mission at the center.

*In this and like communities, public sentiment is
everything. With public sentiment nothing can fail,
without it nothing can succeed.*
— Abraham Lincoln

Effective communication with customers is a vital ingredient of success for all organizations. Without the ability to "get the word out" about organizations and programs agencies would have no staff, volunteers, or customers to serve. This has been substantiated by over a dozen studies that have examined constraints to recreation participation in public parks and recreation. Respondents in these studies have identified lack of knowledge as one of the leading barriers to their participating in recreation programs (Jackson, 2005).

Every parks, recreation, and leisure services organization faces the task of finding ways to effectively communicate with its various publics and constituents. As a result, effective use of program promotion is an important tool for leisure services managers. In this chapter, we present material about the promotion process, tools, and techniques used in promoting organizations and programs, and information about how to develop an effective promotional mix.

In examining the topic of promotion, many express confusion surrounding definitions of related terms such as marketing, advertising, publicity, and selling. It can make discussions about program promotion confusing. As a result, we begin by defining many of these terms and demonstrating how they relate to one another within the context of an organization's promotional mix.

Marketing

Although marketing often is confused with terms like promotion, advertising, and publicity, it is a much broader concept. As presented earlier, marketing is the umbrella for all management functions that foster desired exchanges. It is a customer-oriented approach to delivering services and requires extensive knowledge of who is served in recreation programs. The real contribution of marketing is that it leads institutions to search for meaningful positions in the larger market. Instead of all parks, recreation, and leisure services organizations offering the same services, marketing leads each organization to shape distinct service mixes to serve specific market segments. Programmers do this by managing such variables as price, place (i.e., location of service), and promotion. Thus, marketing at its best creates a pattern of varied institutions, each clear in its mission, market coverage, specialization area, and services and programs provided.

Public Relations

Public relations is similar to marketing in that it is a broad management function that is concerned with all aspects of relating with the public. Specifically, public relations is telling the story of a program or organization in effective ways (Ries & Ries, 2004) and establishing beneficial relationships between the organization and its various publics. This process emphasizes two-way communication whereby organizations share information and, at the same time, evaluate the public's attitudes about the organization and its programs. As Berkman and Gilson (1987) noted many years ago, public relations is "any process that evaluates public attitudes, identifies the policies and procedures of an organization with the public interest, and plans and executes a program of action to earn public understanding and acceptance" (p. 501). As information is gained and shared, organizations can develop and sharpen strategies to disseminate information that casts the organization in a positive light.

Promotion

Promotion is often viewed as a part of both the marketing process and the process to develop a public relations strategy. Generally speaking, promotion is any form of communication used to inform, persuade, remind, and/or educate people regarding the benefits offered through an organization's programs and services. Effective communication communicates *with* the potential customer rather than *to* the potential customer. The communication process is not complete until the potential participant acts upon the message she or he has received. In their communication programs, organizations may be involved with one or more of the four basic types of promotion: advertising, publicity, personal selling, and sales promotion.

Advertising

Advertising is paid, nonpersonal communication regarding programs, events, goods, services, organizations, and ideas. This communication is transmitted through various media by business firms, nonprofit organizations, and/or government agencies, which are in some way identified in the advertising message as the sponsor. Advertising includes such varied media as magazines, newspapers, radio, television,

websites (e.g., pop up ads), cell phones, outdoor media (e.g., billboards, signs, skywriting), novelties, cards, catalogs, directories, and direct mail by post and electronic media. Advertising is a huge business. Total advertising expenditures in the United States were close to $280 billion in 2007 (AdAge.com, 2008), up from $240 billion in 2002, when American companies spent about $2.37 per American per day for the entire year on some form of advertising (Ries & Ries, 2004).

Publicity

Publicity is nonpersonal communication regarding programs, events, goods, services, organizations, and ideas transmitted through various media, but not paid for by an identified sponsor. As a result, the media generally controls the message rather than an organization or agency. Publicity may be found in a wide variety of media. For example, a newspaper may offer to run a feature article on a program, public service announcements may appear on television and radio, or a staff member may participate on a radio or television talk show. Other types of less formal publicity include

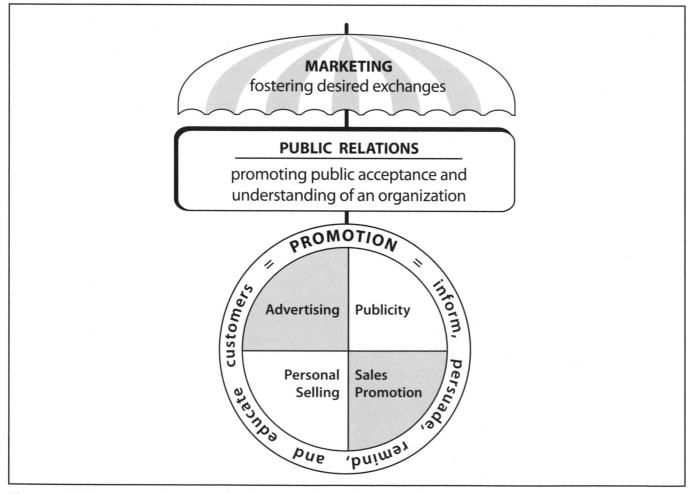

Figure 8.1 The relationship among marketing, public relations, and promotion

links on web pages, blogs, and information shared on social networking sites such as YouTube, Facebook, and MySpace. The relationship between advertising, publicity, personal selling, and sales promotion is presented in Table 8.1.

Personal Selling

We agree with Kotler and Andreasen (1996) that personal selling refers to "attempts by an organization, staff member, or volunteer by using personal influence to affect target audience behavior" (p. 573). This means personal selling promotes one-on-one contact; it tends to be used most often in the commercial sector. Public and nonprofit organizations are sometimes reluctant to employ this method of promotion for two reasons. First, public and nonprofit organizations typically perceive their programs or services as inherently good and as a result the general public should automatically accept them. Second, organizations often view personal selling as synonymous with manipulation and believe it is unethical (Ries & Ries, 2004). It is interesting to note, however, that word-of-mouth (i.e., personal selling) is often cited by participants as one of the best ways to communicate opportunities

---

Table 8.1 Examples of advertising, publicity, personal selling, and sales promotion

Advertising
- An ad for XYZ Cruise Line (paid, demand directed)
- An ad showing XYZ Cruise Line as an environmentally friendly vacation choice (paid, image driven)

Publicity
- A report on the local/national news about the success of XYZ Cruise Line's partnership with a local craft cooperative to sell souvenirs on their cruises (nonpaid, image driven)
- A newspaper article showing the economic value of an XYZ Cruise (nonpaid, demand directed)

Personal Selling
- A presentation by a representative of XYZ Cruise Line at a senior center travelogue program that promotes the advantages of a group cruise on XYZ Cruise Line (nonpaid, personal contact)
- A speech at a local college or university by a representative of XYZ Cruise Line about the benefits of working in the cruise industry (personal contact, image driven)

Sales Promotion
- Ad in a travel magazine that includes a coupon for a cruise on XYZ Cruise Line (paid, demand directed)
- A packaged deal offered with the airlines through travel agents (nonpaid, demand directed)

---

for participation in programs (Rosen, 2002). In this day and age, this word-of-mouth communication can be direct (e.g., face-to-face, on the telephone) or indirect (e.g., online social networking sites, blogs). Researchers have found that recommendations from friends and relatives rank right after convenience and customer service as reasons customers choose travel services related to places to visit, where to stay, what to eat, and which airlines to fly (Pethokoukis, 2005). It is important to remember that every time a member of an organization and a member of the public interact there is an opportunity to inform, persuade, remind, and/or educate about the organization and its programs. Personal selling can occur at all these contact points.

Sales Promotion

Sales promotion involves paid communication activities (other than advertising) that stimulate consumer behavior. Sales promotion for parks, recreation, and leisure programs includes incentives (e.g., coupons), giveaways, 2-for-1 registration or membership deals, demonstrations, and various other limited-time efforts not in the ordinary promotion routine. These might be made available through all of the same media used for advertising.

As presented in Chapter Two, organizations can adopt a wide variety of philosophical orientations to serve as a foundation. Whatever an organization's philosophical framework, it still must promote its programs in some way. As a result, the focus of the remainder of this chapter will be on identifying promotional strategies (i.e., using a mix of advertising, publicity, personal selling, and sales promotion) to promote a parks, recreation, and leisure organization, as well as promoting specific events and programs.

Promotional Tools and Techniques

Promotional tools and techniques are like ambassadors for an organization and the programs it offers. Through various promotional tools and techniques organizations are able to compete for the attention of customers. This is important because in today's fast-paced world, people are bombarded daily by promotional messages. Although estimates vary, experts suggest that the average American sees thousands of marketing messages a day (including logos). In 2004, Ries and Ries estimated that Americans saw the equivalent of 237 television ads each day. With such tremendous competition for attention and so little time to make an impact, a promotion "has to say something, say it well and say it fast. It has to connect with individuals and get them to think, 'This is good. This could be for me.'"

To be effective, a good fit must exist between the program, the promotional tool and/or technique, and the target group programmers are trying to reach. Thus, understanding the audience and their needs is one crucial element to successful promotion. Servant leaders desire to be fully inclusive and to reach all potential constituent groups. Thus, programmers must be aware of their potential audiences and audience abilities to read and understand written and verbal language. For instance, leisure services professionals may have potential constituents for whom English is a second language. Thus, providing promotional information in alternative languages might be important. Using accessible language is another basic principle for promotional materials. By using common words and writing/speaking at a level at which most people can understand (i.e., 8th grade reading level), leisure professionals can reach most groups. Furthermore, staff must consider the needs of those with disabilities and other conditions that serve to marginalize particular groups of constituents. If staff only provide promotional information in a written format, those who cannot read or those who have visual impairments may not be able to access that information without assistance.

To explore how to fit these factors together programmers must understand the wide variety of tools and techniques available, as well as the strengths and weaknesses of each approach. What follows is a discussion of a variety of promotional tools and techniques used in promoting parks, recreation, and leisure programs.

Broadcast Media

Most consider radio and television to be broadcast media. Networks operate both radio and television at the national, state, and local levels. Distinguishing characteristics of broadcast media include passive audience involvement, immediacy, and public control (Berkman & Gilson, 1987). This means that while it requires some active involvement to read a newspaper or magazine, radio and television can "just be there." In addition, television and radio are on the air 24 hours a day. As a result they tend to be regarded as having the most up-to-date stories with the greatest potential to offer late-breaking news and events.

The airwaves are commonly viewed as public resources monitored or managed by the government through the Federal Communications Commission

(FCC). Station managers must apply for licenses to operate, and must prove to the FCC that they are serving the public through such things as public service broadcasting and public service advertising. Cable, digital, and pay-per-view television are somewhat different in that viewers pay for these services directly. To operate, however, these stations still need FCC approval.

Schroeder (2002) noted that broadcast media (especially visual media) have a far more pervasive influence on most Americans' lives than newspapers and magazines due to the sheer volume of exposure most Americans have with radio and television. Consider the average American who wakes to the sound of a radio alarm, eats breakfast watching a morning news show, and rides to work listening to the radio. While on the job a radio may be playing in the background; then it is back home in the car listening to the radio. Following dinner, the television is often turned on for the remainder of the evening. While this scenario may not represent all Americans, Elliott (2008) reported that 99% of U.S. homes have at least one television. The typical American home includes 2.5 people and 2.8 televisions; 82% of U.S. homes have more than one television. We also know that Americans continue to listen to radio. Over one fifth of Americans say they listen to more radio than they did five years ago even with the increased availability of podcasts and MP3 players (Sass, 2006).

Beyond advertising, radio and television also offer other potential opportunities for parks, recreation, and leisure services programmers to promote their programs. For example, talk shows are becoming an increasingly popular format for both radio and television and offer an opportunity for more lengthy promotion of an idea or service than a traditional 15 to 60 second commercial would allow. The format for talk shows is usually question and answer, giving the programmer an opportunity to make specific points concerning her or his organization, program, or event. Opportunities for being invited on talk shows may be enhanced by developing a long-term relationship with broadcast media staff—both television and radio—in one's local area.

Radio

Radio is enjoying a healthy revival after its popularity dipped during the 1950s, 1960s, and 1970s when television became ubiquitous. The reasons for the rebirth of radio are multifaceted. First, is the fact that television has become too expensive for many advertisers. Because of the great competition among radio stations for advertiser dollars, advertising time slots are rarely sold out. Thus, costs are negotiable. Second, radio allows organizations to target specific groups as radio stations keep extensive data on their listeners. A third advantage of radio advertising is the portability of the medium. Radios and radio stations are everywhere—in cars, on the beach, on the Internet, and on bike paths. Anywhere potential customers go, radios can be taken along. Fourth, the advancement of satellite and online radio is increasing to expand listenership. According to a recent study, the weekly Internet radio audience increased 50 percent between 2005 and 2006; more than one in five Americans reported listening to Internet radio each month (Rose & Rosin, 2006).

Disadvantages of radio include the need to help listeners visualize programs and services as well as the fact that people often listen to the radio in conjunction with other activities. This tendency to become involved in a variety of activities while listening to the radio is referred to as "clutter" by advertisers. The more clutter that exists, the more difficult it is to focus listeners on specific advertisements. As a result, organizations that use radio often run ads frequently to increase exposure. It helps that radio offers high-frequency (i.e., multiple runs) ads at a low cost. The continued growth of satellite radio and MP3 players may negatively impact the influence of radio promotional efforts as listeners can skip over the advertisements.

Radio offers an additional opportunity to organizations planning programs and events in the community. Oftentimes radio stations broadcast live from community events. These appearances can either be paid or public service opportunities, and they provide invaluable exposure for organizations and their specific events and programs. By developing relationships with radio personalities, parks and leisure services professionals can facilitate this type of opportunity.

Television

The figures related to television usage are staggering as television viewing surpasses all other uses of free time, accounting for over 30 hours a week of Americans' free time (Elliot, 2008). As a result, the major advantage of using television to promote parks, recreation, and leisure programs and services is that it reaches a large number of potential customers (offering almost universal access). Other advantages of television include frequency and visual representation. Television offers great frequency potential as one commercial can be run over and over again for a long period of time. Television also offers the ability to offer a visual representation of the benefits of participating in a specific program or service from the comfort of one's own living room.

A last advantage of both radio and television is the ability to segment the market as specialized programs make it easier to deliver highly targeted commercials. For example, advertising an upcoming cooking class during a cooking show on television would appropriately target people with interests in such an activity.

Disadvantages of using television include cost as well as clutter. Producing and airing television commercials is expensive. Simply producing television commercials can run anywhere from $1,000 to several hundred thousand dollars. A similar range exists in buying air time; a 30-second spot during the Super Bowl can run into millions of dollars while the same length spot on a local cable or news show can cost under $1,000.

Advertising on television suffers from a lot of noise and clutter in that commercials offer individuals the opportunity to channel surf, to get a snack, or take a break before returning to continue watching their program. Likewise, television viewing is often a secondary activity, meaning that people are doing other things while watching a show.

Television can be an effective marketing tool, when it is used wisely. Many large commercial organizations (e.g., Disney, Carnival Cruise Lines) can make the commitment to national television campaigns while smaller regional or local organizations might choose to use television sparingly and only during specific time slots (see http://www.wdwpublicaffairs.com/AssetDetail.aspx?AssetId=c3446026-e1ac-4dc3-8a02-a87cc695b8b3). For many public and nonprofit organizations television is out of reach except through the use of public service announcements. However, one emerging trend in the television industry may make television exposure more affordable and available—especially to public and nonprofit organizations. This trend is the expansion of cable, digital, and direct television giving consumers increased options. Many communities now have channels for local access programs, some of which are set aside for local government use. These channels can offer an excellent opportunity for promotion of city parks, recreation, and leisure services programs and events. Listing upcoming activities, showing slides/photographs of recent activities, and uploading short video segments are all possible through this type of media.

Technology

It is hard to predict what the future holds concerning technology, but it is important to stay current and understand the potential of existing and emerging technology in delivering and promoting programs and services. A majority of the new technology is interactive in nature, making it possible for viewers to interact with and through the media. Leading the way in a new wave of emerging technology is the computer, which has taken U.S. homes by storm. In 1990, fewer than 10 percent of all U.S. homes included a computer; by the end of 2001 this had risen to over 51 percent (U.S. Census Bureau, 2001). In a recent study, researchers found that almost 90 percent of respondents owned a personal computer and over 80 percent had Internet access (Carrol, Rivara, Ebel, Zimmerman, & Christakis, 2005). Ninety percent of school age children (ages 6 to 17) in the U.S. had access to a computer in 2000, with 80 percent using a computer at school and over 65 percent with a computer at home (U.S. Census Bureau, 2006; Lukovitz, 2008).

One of the major factors behind this surge is the diffusion of online services (e.g., SBCGlobal, Suddenlink, Earthlink), which have grown tremendously in the last five years. Online advertising offers a tremendous opportunity to businesses—large and small. In addition, computers have also made such promotional opportunities as CD-ROMs, DVDs, webcasts, and information kiosks available to the general public.

Managers of leisure services organizations must look to maximize the opportunities offered by computer-related technologies. At the same time, they must also remember the limitations of emerging technologies, especially in terms of physical access. The issue of access has been called the *digital divide* and most researchers attribute the differences in computer ownership and Internet access to differences in income and education. While the digital divide seems to narrowing (Carroll et al., 2005), we still need to be aware that older individuals, those with lower incomes, those with disabilities, and other marginalized groups may not have access to needed computer technology. To access information online, for instance, individuals with disabilities may need specialized software. To help constituents use web-based information, website designers will need to use universal design principles. These principles will enable programmers to reach everyone who has physical access to a computer. In particular, by doing so, leisure professionals will better serve those who:

- may not be able to see, hear, move, or are unable to process some types of information easily or at all;

- may have difficulty reading or comprehending text;

- may not have or be able to use a keyboard or mouse;

- may have a text-only screen, a small screen, or a slow Internet connection;

- may not speak or understand fluently the language in which the document is written;

- may be in a situation where their eyes, ears, or hands are busy or interfered with (e.g., driving to work, working in a noisy environment); and

- may have an early version of a browser, a different browser entirely, a voice browser, or a different operating system (World Wide Web Consortium [W3C], 2008).

Universally designed websites overcome these difficulties and allow access for all. People who have disabilities, for instance, might use software that reads text (e.g., screen readers), or allows for navigation via a keyboard, switch, mouse, or voice command. These devices are known as assistive technology and open the world to many people who would not otherwise have such access (W3C, 2008).

CDs and DVDs

Most new computers come equipped with drives that both read and burn CDs and DVDs; thus, organizations have the opportunity to produce CDs and DVDs very economically to promote their image, services, and programs. For example, the CD displayed in Figure 8.2 relates the story of Outward Bound, specifically Outward Bound West. The CD includes pictures, video clips, slide shows, interactive quizzes and games, and information about the overall organization as well as specific courses. With an Internet connection, individuals looking at the CD may also access the web directly from the CD to gain additional up-to-date information. The CD may be used for a variety of purposes including appealing to and persuading potential participants, appealing to and educating parents of younger potential participants, attracting future staff members, and introducing the organization to potential funders.

Electronic Kiosks

Interactive computers operating from small kiosks are being placed in a wide range of locations. Many municipal governments have begun to use kiosks to increase access to information and services. Customers can now pay bills, renew licenses, and obtain information about a variety of services at these kiosks. Several states now use electronic kiosks to promote tourism and quickly disseminate information. Interactive multimedia kiosks have been placed in locations ranging from park headquarters and trailheads to remote interstate highway visitor centers. The kiosks offer a wide variety of information that individuals can use to plan their recreation experiences.

Many visitor centers, colleges/universities, hotels, and tourist attractions also make use of electronic kiosks (see Figure 8.3). Sometimes used as electronic bulletin boards, these kiosks provide individuals with 24-hour-a-day access to information about many services and programs offered by local, state, and federal government, nonprofit agencies, and commercial organizations in the local area. Advantages of kiosks include interactivity, the ability to search for specific, up-to-date information, and the ability to provide information in text, visual, and audio formats. In addition, kiosks may offer the same information in several languages for access by diverse users. Disadvantages of electronic kiosks include machines falling into disrepair, the need to maintain and update technology and information, and issues related to accessibility for those with disabilities.

Mobile Phones

Text messaging on mobile phones has exploded over the last few years as friends and family find new ways to communicate with one another. Recognizing the power of this medium, new services have begun to utilize text messaging to promote products and pro-

grams. Customers can receive text message coupons by signing up for them or by texting a particular service, which then sends a text coupon. In some cases, services track the location of an individual through a GPS feature on the phone and send geographically appropriate coupons for services in that area. Customers redeem a text coupon by showing the merchant the coupon/message on the cell phone display screen. Coupons may contain numerical or bar codes for the seller to track how the individual accessed the coupon, thereby improving future ads.

Alexander (2007) noted that this type of advertising is a spur of the moment opportunity and offers the potential to change a coupon quickly to take advantage of changing conditions. Consider a bowling center that is experiencing a slow night; the manager could choose at a particular moment to text a "buy one game, get a second game free" coupon to a large segment of people in the community in hopes of encouraging immediate business. Disadvantages of cell phone coupons as a promotional tool include irritating recipients who may perceive unsolicited text messages as spam. Further, text messages typically cost the receiver a fee (whether by individual message or as part of a bundled phone package) and this may be considered to be intrusive and unethical.

http://www.outwardbound.org/docs/info/ob-west.htm

Figure 8.2 Outward Bound West promotional CD

Figure 8.3 Example of a screen on an electronic kiosk

Internet

The Internet is a collection of millions of interconnected computers located in countries throughout the world—all linked by phone lines, high-speed cables, or wireless connections to form a gigantic computer network system. The Internet is becoming the preferred means of communication and information retrieval by millions of people worldwide—especially by organizations interested in a fast, global, inexpensive means of reaching customers. To "travel" on the Internet, people use a variety of communication options. A few options are discussed in this section, including e-mail and the World Wide Web.

E-mail. E-mail, an abbreviation for electronic mail, enables individuals to send text and graphic messages back and forth to each other quickly. E-mail has rapidly become one of the preferred methods of communication between individuals, whether they are in close proximity (e.g., the same building), across town, or on opposite sides of the world. Using e-mail, organizations can set up distribution lists of specific target groups or ask users to sign up for lists. Such lists (commonly called listserves) provide an easy way to communicate with groups of people about specific programs or upcoming events. E-mail lists are also a means by which individuals can keep up-to-date with a specific topic, or a way to notify a large group of people about cancellations or changes in programs. An agency will want to be careful about using electronic mailing lists for the sole purpose of advertising; such a practice can quickly degenerate into electronic junk mail (i.e., spam).

World Wide Web (WWW). If any function of the Internet is exciting, intoxicating, and habit forming it is the World Wide Web, commonly referred to as the web. The web may be thought of as a superhighway on which a computer user who is "online" can travel throughout the world to specific websites of individuals, organizations, and agencies, which constantly add to and update their sites. Websites may include photographs, text, audio, and video, all packaged in such a way as to provide organizations with a visually attractive means to provide accurate, up-to-date information. The Internet, including the web, gives customers an opportunity to send and receive information, and purchase programs and services without ever leaving their homes.

The web offers parks, recreation, and leisure services programmers a variety of options for promoting programs and services. Websites, or home pages, can be used by organizations to inform and educate about their overall program or specific special events. For example,

the homepage of the Grand Rapids Children's Museum (http://www.grcm.org/) is simple, yet eye-catching, and provides people who visit this site access to a wide range of information with an additional click of the mouse. Organizations can use their websites in a variety of ways—participants might sign up for specific listserves, register for a program, check the events calendar, report scores, and purchase products via a secure server. Some organizations have separate websites for staff. On these sites they might accept online applications for employment, and provide links for information related to benefits, staff schedules, and internal policies and procedures. Commercial organizations commonly include advertising in online magazines and newspapers that are updated on a continuous basis.

Advertising on the web is not simply an electronic version of a print, radio, or television advertisement. The web offers the opportunity to actually interact with potential customers. Thus, the use of the web for marketing and promoting organizations, products, and services will continue to increase and evolve. E-commerce sales, where individuals can make a purchase through a computer, have risen dramatically over the last five years; parks, recreation, and leisure services agencies have seen a similar increase in demand for online access to services.

The web offers leisure services organizations a number of opportunities to advertise and promote programs including: advertising on the agency home page, linking to and being linked on related sites, developing pop-up advertisements for use on other sites, and producing and distributing webcasts or short video programs. Advertising on an agency or organization's home page may include selling advertising space to related entities. Hostelling International-USA, discussed in detail later in this chapter, posts the following invitation on their home page (http://www.hiusa.org/about/advertising.shtml):

> If your organization is looking for increased visibility, consider advertising on Hostelling International-USA's website. HI-USA is an active travel community of young adventurous travelers traveling across America and around the world. We have nearly 100,000 U.S. members and over 3 million Hostelling International members worldwide. We average over 5.5 million hits per month with over 55,700 unique visitors. Consider advertising opportunities (web and/or print) with HI-USA. Please contact...

Pop-up advertisements are another form of advertising on the web. Pop-up ads and banner ads are small windows that suddenly appear while an individual is surfing the web. They offer an interactive and difficult-to-ignore vehicle for advertisers. However, many consider pop-up advertisements as controversial and bothersome. Some companies have even gone so far as to sue advertising companies for attaching pop-up ads on websites without the authorization of the original website manager and for not sharing the profits of related sales. Like so many areas of Internet law, the issue of pop-up ads has not yet been totally resolved. Thus, parks, recreation, and leisure services organizations may wish to be cautious about using this medium to promote programs.

The Internet offers a number of other opportunities to promote an organization or program. These opportunities will continue to grow and evolve as new technology becomes available. Consider the video sharing websites such as YouTube where users can upload, view, and share video clips. Created in 2005 and purchased by Google in 2006, YouTube offers a staggering number of videos with more being added each day. Likewise, viewers continue to grow; in January 2008 alone nearly 79 million users viewed approximately *3 billion* video clips (Yen, 2008).

Although the uploading of videos containing commercial advertisements is prohibited, organizations can post short videos about their programs. Consider the UCLA adaptive recreation program which has produced a YouTube video introducing people to one of its programs. The video discusses the importance of inclusion and shows a number of program components (see http://www.youtube.com/watch?v=KiBzq1uq6Cc). As part of a promotional plan, staff can create videos to upload to the Internet and place a link to that video on their website. This helps to educate and introduce people to their programs and services in a very dynamic way. Another example of effective use of the Internet for marketing is Paradox Sports. This is an organization that provides opportunities for individuals with physical disabilities to experience human powered outdoor sports such as climbing, kayaking, and skiing. In their YouTube video, Paradox Sports use high energy background music to engage those watching the video (see http://www.youtube.com/watch?v=CkOYQZiesfI). They also offer a running slide show on their home page (paradoxsports.org) illustrating people actively engaged in outdoor activities.

In addition to providing access to videos on the web, computers provide a means for individuals to download audio and visual media for their personal use. Streaming and podcasts allow individuals and organizations to distribute audio and video files quickly and inexpensively. Podcasting became popular in the early 2000s, fueled by the explosion of iPods and MP3 players. While not specifically used in promoting programs, such technology can be used in a variety of ways to share information with potential participants. This technology can also be used in programming such as audio programs (interpretive narratives) in museums and zoos. In the future, new technologies will create opportunities for organizations to promote and educate constituents about their programs and services.

A potential challenge with increased access to technology is the ability for any individual to upload videos, photos, and text (such as with blogs), some of which may not depict an agency or organization in a positive light. The concept of "freedom of speech" in the U.S. gives individuals the right to post or publish most material without legal repercussions. Thus, a person attending a festival for instance, could take personal video or photos and upload them without the express permission of the sponsoring agency. If the material depicts a negative situation, an organization might find itself having to defend what has been posted.

Display Media

Display media is a broad category of tools, which includes billboards, bulletin boards, exhibits, point-of-purchase advertising, posters, and signs. As is evident from this list, display media may be found in both indoor and outdoor environments and includes both two- and three-dimensional objects. Parks, recreation and leisure services organizations may use such display media to highlight program services and organizational efforts, or for purposes of interpretation. Displays may be used as part of an actual program (e.g., a display in a museum) or as a vehicle to facilitate promotional efforts aimed at public involvement or support of a program (e.g., to promote a special event).

Billboards

Billboards, often referred to as part of the outdoor advertising industry, offer an excellent and affordable way to catch the customer on the move, whether traveling by foot, in a car, or via public transportation. Billboards may be found on the side of a building, within stadiums or arenas, on the sides of buses and taxis, and along roadways. The key to using billboards is "location, location, location." Altstiel and Grow (2006) identified the following characteristics of effective outdoor advertising. Outdoor advertising is...

• best used as a secondary medium (reinforcing a message a customer has received via another medium)—outdoor advertising serves as a great reminder of an organization or an upcoming program/event;

• easy to see and read at a high speed—keep it simple; and

• visually striking and grabbing; think big—billboards should make use of a unique size or shape whenever possible and use bold colors and visuals.

The price for billboard advertising varies considerably depending upon location, but overall it is an effective and relatively inexpensive means of promotion. For public and nonprofit organizations, billboard space may be even more affordable through public service programs. An example of a series of educational billboards by the city of Wyoming, Michigan is presented in Figure 8.4; the billboards are posted along a bike trail and play off an old technique named for a Burma Shave advertising campaign.

Burma Shave was a brand of shaving cream that developed an advertising gimmick of posting humorous rhyming poems on small, consecutive highway billboard signs. Over 7,000 signs were developed and posted throughout the United States from 1925 to 1963. Creative use of such signs might include creating innovative signs to advertise programs or selling

space on a biking or hiking trail to promote related products. For example, a commercial go-cart track operator could advertise a brand of ice cream being sold at a concession stand as customers race around the go-cart track.

A traditional use of billboards includes promoting special events (see Figure 8.5) such as the "Would you go over the edge?" event. This event is a fundraiser for two specific programs of the West Michigan Community Blood Centers. Note that the billboard is easy to read, simple, and points individuals to a website for more information. The event provides an opportunity for participants to rappel from the highest building in Grand Rapids—a distance of over 400 feet. A minimum donation of $1,000 is required to reserve a place on the rope.

Bulletin Boards

A bulletin board is generally a two-dimensional display prepared on a flat surface that can be used to present information about a specific organization, program, staff member, or service or as a means to promote an upcoming event. A bulletin board may be fixed or portable, and it may be static or dynamic (e.g., mechanical panels or digital messaging). Location of the bulletin board is a very important determinant of the effectiveness of the display. Using attention getting devices like an unusual design, striking color combinations, or leading statements to catch people's attention is a good idea. Whenever possible try to involve participants in the creation of bulletin boards. For instance, using children's arts and crafts projects can be a creative way to encourage parents to read about upcoming classes and events. Themes can be used to highlight upcoming programs during a specific time of year. Bulletin boards are intended to be temporary and should be changed periodically to remain current and stimulating.

Figure 8.4 A Burma Shave style billboard along a bike path

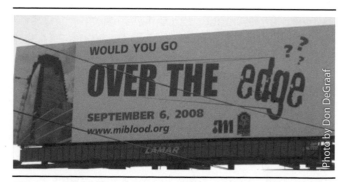

Figure 8.5 Billboard promoting a special event as a fundraiser for a local nonprofit

Exhibits

An exhibit is typically three-dimensional and may be used as an interpretation tool to educate the public about an issue or event. For example, the Cook County Forest Preserve outside Chicago uses exhibits to educate the general public about the use of prescribed burning in specific areas of the preserve. Other types of exhibits include display boards that promote the overall organization and/or specific programs and events (see Figure 8.6). Such displays are often portable, allowing them to be set up in a variety of different locations. In addition, they frequently include props such as items to give away, a running slide show on a laptop computer, and items that reflect the agency or programs being highlighted. Programmers will want to consider public places where people congregate and attempt to create displays that educate and remind people about their programs. One public recreation director asked a local bank for a permanent display table. Every month, staff set up a new display promoting upcoming events. As with websites, it is important that exhibits offer information through a variety of media (e.g., audio, visual, text) to ensure access to all.

Point-of-Purchase Advertising

Point of Purchase advertising is often considered an organization's last chance to promote its programs and services to potential customers. Typically, P-O-P is employed when a person registers for or arrives at a program. Thus, P-O-P can make use of a variety of formats including posters, banners, floor stands, signs, display racks, web ads, telephone messages, and other channels. Point-of-purchase advertising serves either as a reminder to buyers, when a program or service is advertised in another medium, or as a stimulus to impulse buying (Altstiel & Grow, 2006). The P-O-P ads may be temporary or permanent and be located inside or outside of an organization. For example, many youth centers on military bases use banners at the center to remind parents and youth when it is time to register for sports leagues or specific special events.

Posters

Posters offer an alternative to large stationary billboards. They can be professionally produced (and mass produced) or created by staff or customers on-site. They may be available in print or electronic forms. As a result, posters are a very versatile form of promotion. Posters may also be given (or even sold) to the general public. Many of them are created by artists and trea-

Figure 8.6 An example of an exhibit: Becoming an Outdoors Woman (Oklahoma State University)

Join The Right To Time Movement!

www.timeday.org

It's true: Overworked Americans are neglecting and abandoning their pets in record numbers

Home Alone
Again.....

Hi, my name is Rover. I never see my human companion anymore. He leaves for work before I wake up and by the time he gets home he's always dog tired. Sure, he walks me around the neighborhood every now and then, but it's just not the same.

Even a dog's life isn't what it used to be.

Give Rover (and yourself) a break.
Participate in TAKE BACK YOUR TIME DAY,   Oct. 24th.

Figure 8.7 Take Back Your Time poster (Courtesy of timeday.org)

sured by collectors. This desirability is considered a secondary benefit of posters—their staying power. When suitable for framing, posters have the potential to be around for years. For example, Figure 8.7 features an educational poster that promotes a specific event, Take Back Your Time Day. This poster is a part of a series (found at www.timeday.org/) that is a part of the Take Back Your Time initiative. The goal of this effort is to challenge the epidemic of over-work, over-scheduling, and time famine that threat-ens health, families and relationships, communities, and the environment.

In developing posters, it is important to pay close attention to design, layout, and general aesthetics. The message must be eye-catching, worthwhile, attractive, and understandable to all constituent groups. For example, an eye-catching poster or brochure advertising the world's largest banana split might be created in the shape of a banana split, use realistic photographs, and show pictures of excited or playful people at the location. In addition to getting peoples' attention, consider other elements of attractiveness—it is more than just aesthetic appeal. Attractiveness also addresses a sense of inclusion where potential constituents can envision themselves involved in the depicted pro-grams and activities. Leisure services professionals accomplish this when using photos, graphics, and text that are welcoming and appropriate to a broad audience. As staff design (or ask others to do so) promotional posters, they might ask the following types of questions:

- Do graphics, pictures, and text send a message of being inclusive?

- Do the graphics represent people from all age groups? Are people of a wide range of racial and ethnic groups visible? Are both sexes depicted?

- Are people who have disabilities among those pic-tured, and/or do we include symbols that illustrate our willingness to meet people's needs?

- Is the text gender neutral and welcoming to all?

- Are the graphics and text culturally appropriate and meet local customs and mores?

- Do we offer posters in different languages and place them in relevant locations?

As with other display media, success with the use of posters is based on location. For example, it would be ineffective to hang a poster promoting a youth program sponsored by a nonprofit organization in a bar. Posters can, however, be placed in a variety of locations such as buses, bus shelters, airports, city benches, and so on. Ultimately, the flexibility in displaying posters makes them an effective and inexpensive means of promotion.

Presentations

Presentations include any opportunity to present information concerning an organization, program, or service to a group of people. Examples of presenta-tions are public speaking at local civic clubs, schools, religious institutions, and conferences. Such public speaking opportunities may include slide shows and vid-eos. Slide shows and videos may also be used as stand-alone presentations. Computer software (e.g., Microsoft PowerPoint, Keynote) enables individuals to create slide shows that can be informative, entertaining, and aesthetically appealing.

When well done and geared to a specific audience, presentations on videos or DVDs can be excellent promotional tools. DVDs last a long time, are nearly indestructible, and relatively easy and inexpensive to mail. Many private independent camps produce promotional videos, which are sent to potential customers as DVDs or downloaded from websites. A single DVD might include one video for parents and another for the potential camper. Each video is geared toward its intended audience so that parents might receive informa-tion about nutrition, safety, and staff, for instance. Campers, on the other hand, might view a video that highlights friendships, activities, and the camp environment. Organizations typically follow up with the recipients using other promotional methods such as a phone call, letter, and a brochure.

Commercial entities such as fitness clubs and re-sorts also use DVDs as promotional tools. For example, Walt Disney World sends a free DVD (which includes interactive elements) to potential guests so that they can "tour" the park, decide what they would like to do when visiting, and know where to make reservations that best suit their needs. Agencies and organizations that specialize in working with people with disabilities in clinical settings might produce electronic presentations with family members in mind. Highlighting the benefits of recreation therapy and introducing departmental staff are common elements in such productions.

If programmers choose electronic presentations as an element of promotion, they should remember to depict contemporary scenes (including hair styles and the way people are dressed), and offer closed-captioning for all visual elements. In addition, if used as a part of a presentation, videos should be kept short and complement other elements of the presentation. When conducting in-person presentations it is important that the speaker know the topic well, be enthusiastic, be an effective communicator, and know how to appropriately use any audiovisual tools.

Print Media

Print media offers a wide range of options in terms of promoting and advertising an organization's programs and services. Despite the emerging potential of television and computer technologies, print is still one of the most important worldwide advertising mediums. Generally, print media includes newspapers and magazines; we also include several other mediums in this category (e.g., annual reports, brochures, fliers, newsletters, the yellow pages).

A major consideration concerning print media (beyond newspapers, magazines, and the yellow pages) is how the brochure, flier, or other printed material is distributed. Before the time and expense of developing printed material is committed, organizations need to identify strategies to reach their intended audiences. Creativity is an important element of this decision. Consider the city of Des Moines, Iowa, where the Convention and Visitor's Bureau identified taxi drivers as city ambassadors and created a brochure rack for the backside of the driver's seat. This rack contains brochures on a wide range of recreation opportunities offered by commercial, nonprofit, and public parks, recreation, and leisure services organizations throughout the area.

Annual Reports

Annual reports are comprehensive summaries detailing the financial status, program services, physical descriptions, and prospective changes in a parks, recreation, or leisure services entity. Considered a "must" by many government and nonprofit organizations, an annual report is often submitted to a governing body or board of directors (of the organization) and is available to

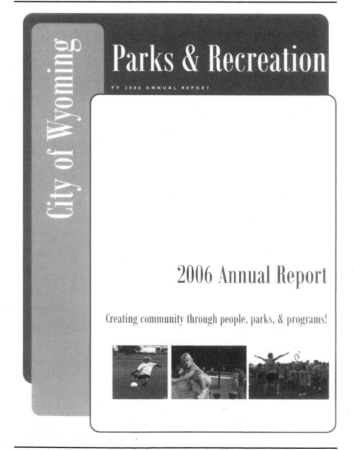

Figure 8.8 City of Wyoming (MI) Parks and Recreation Annual Report cover page

Figure 8.9 Camp Tall Turf Annual Report

the general public. In some organizations, the annual report may replace a brochure—especially in organizations that change a good deal from year to year. Annual reports may also be used to explain how an entity has changed or how it is responding to a changing world. Figures 8.8 and 8.9 present the cover of two different Annual Reports, one from a municipal organization (City of Wyoming) and one from a nonprofit organization (Camp Tall Turf). Each of these organizations uses their annual report in different ways. In its document, the City of Wyoming includes information about a wide range of programs as well as financial performance. The theme of the report focuses on the benefits provided to citizens through the recreation department. The Camp Tall Turf annual report is mission focused and gives an overview of its programs; it also recognizes donors, documents financial performance, and updates readers on ongoing capital campaigns. Both of these organizations use their annual report to tell a story about how their

programs contribute to the public good. Important points to remember with annual reports are to pay close attention to the overall image of the report, write at a level at which potential readers are comfortable, avoid jargon, and think through and select appropriate distribution channels. In this way, the potential of the annual report to promote the overall organization is maximized.

Brochures

A brochure may be viewed as an organization's business card. As a result, brochures are often created for the organization as a whole, or for major components of an overall program as well as for specific one-time events. Brochures come in a variety of sizes and shapes and may include different types of information (see Figure 8.10 below, plus 8.11 and 8.12 on p. 208). In Figure 8.10, a traditional one-page trifold brochure is presented which informs the public of the services of Wilderness Inquiry, a

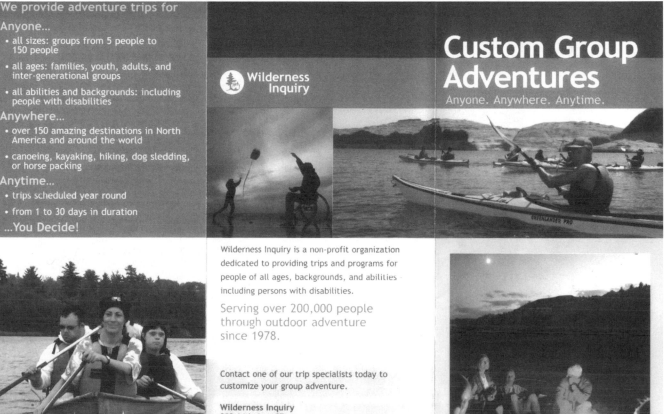

Figure 8.10 Trifold brochure promoting wilderness programs (Wilderness Inquiry)

nonprofit organization in Minneapolis, Minnesota. The brochure does not advertise a specific program or event, but rather presents an overview of the services the organization can provide. The tagline *Anyone, Anywhere, Anytime* connects to the values of inclusion and emphasizes a willingness to work with customers to co-create a program.

Figure 8.11 presents the cover of an extensive 104-page book that features a schedule of over 150 special events in Chicago in the summer of 2007; the cover was also developed as a flier. The theme of the summer was the *Art of Play,* and the brochure includes a calendar and description of events and festivals, descriptions of where to play in Chicago, an introduction to the Chicago International Toy and Game Fair, and resources for planning a trip to Chicago (e.g., travel packages, hotels, transportation choices). Many of these events took place in a variety of Chicago's parks; the brochure is a good example of how a number of different city departments joined together to provide and advertise a wide range of recreational opportunities.

Last but not least, Figure 8.12 presents two mini-brochures used by commercial organizations to inform and persuade people to use their services by including discount coupons for their programs. In examining the differences between these brochures, the reader can see that a brochure promoting a specific event may include a description of the event, when and where the event will be held, a registration form, and/or contact information where a person can get additional information. A brochure promoting a specific organization might include a brief history of the organization, its mission, and an overview of its programs. A brochure promoting a facility or location might include pictures and descriptions of the equipment and facility features.

When developing a brochure, it is important to remember the ultimate use of the brochure. Will customers put it in their pocket and use it as a guide? Will office staff be mailing the brochure (i.e., will it fit in an envelope)? Understanding the intended use of the brochure, the audience, and the image to portray are important early steps to creating effective brochures. Additional factors impacting the development of brochures include content (see Table 8.2), layout and design (see Table 8.3), accessibility (e.g., offering large-print versions), timing to ensure maximum visibility and impact, means of distribution, and costs (e.g., type of paper, printing, number of photographs, color or black-and-white, staff time, and distribution method). Paying attention to the issues of inclusion addressed in the section on posters is important as well.

Figure 8.11 Example of a flier (City of Chicago)

Figure 8.12 Examples of mini brochures

Fliers

One of the most widely used forms of promotion in parks, recreation, and leisure services organizations is the flier. A flier is a short, written message that is usually printed on one side of an 8.5 by 11-inch sheet of paper and handed out, posted on a bulletin board or in a hallway, or folded and sent through the mail. As a result, fliers must be able to catch the attention of people quickly and deliver a short, understandable message upon which an individual can then act. Fliers can be used to promote upcoming special events (see Figure 8.13 on p. 210) or longer-lasting programs (see Figure 8.14 on p. 211). In addition, fliers may be used as fact sheets or as educational tools to provide vital details about upcoming programs and events.

Costs for producing fliers vary. Fliers created in-house can be inexpensive and easy to produce, while elaborate glossy fliers produced by professional printers can be quite expensive. Regardless of cost, effective fliers are kept simple and constructed around a central theme or idea. For instance, fliers promoting specific programs or events should include the name of the program/event; the target audience; location,

Table 8.2 How to write effective copy for brochures (Sources: Altstiel and Grow, 2006; Kerstetter, 1991; Learning Resources Network, 1997; Stern, 1992)

- Find examples of promotional materials that you admire and analyze what could work for your organization.
- Write in language that sells. The first goal is to get people to stop and read the text. The copy on brochures should be benefit-oriented and motivating. Remember, customers buy benefits rather than programs. Use the brochure to create a relationship with the prospective customer.
- Use headlines to convey the essentials and make sure your headlines stick out. Headlines should be simple and catch the reader's attention. Four out of five people will never read beyond the headline; thus, you must write a headline that appeals to reader's self-interests. Use benefit words that have impact. Recent research has reported that headlines with a benefit are read by an average of four times more people than headlines that don't list benefits.
- Under each headline you must elaborate on the benefits you have promised in the headline. Be specific and offer proof of the headline's claims. Vary sentence length and structure in your writing. Limit sentence length to 17 words or less. Readership studies show comprehension decreases at word 18. Strive to achieve a rhythm and variety in your writing.
- Include testimonials when possible. Coupling the testimonial with a photo of the participant creates a highly motivational piece.
- Give your copy closure by asking for an action. Call readers to action by asking them to register, make a phone call, a visit, or request they get more information. Give readers time constraints or limits within which they must act. Include a registration form or questionnaire with the brochure.
- Include a graphic or photo on the cover that will draw the reader in. Continue to use visuals throughout the brochure whenever possible. Captions should be included with all photos and other visuals.
- Let prospects know how to reach you. Registration information, pages, and forms should be geared for convenience, speed, and even fun. While registration information is often moved to the back of the brochure, the reader should be able to find the registration phone number in ten seconds. Other important information includes location (a map), hours of operation, address, phone numbers, and website address.
- Show what you write to a number of people and ask them to give you feedback.

Table 8.3 Design tips for brochures and fliers (Learning Resources Network, 1997; Stern, 1992)

- Find examples and be aware of current design trends.
- Use the front and back covers of brochures. Front and back covers are being recognized as prime space to promote classes, special activities, or the program in general. The use of photos, clip art, color, and humor draw in the audience.
- Increase the amount of white space, especially at the top and sides of the margin. More white space makes the brochure more readable and helps call the reader's attention to what is most important. Throughout the brochure avoid a cluttered look.
- Use clip art, photos, and graphics wisely. A wide array of line drawings are available. Use visuals that relate to the copy; avoid arbitrary art as a filler.
- Use typefaces carefully—and creatively. Use specific styles and sizes to help direct the reader's eye. Use fonts that complement each other. For example, use serif fonts (i.e., letters with hooks and extensions like this font) for body copy and sans serif (i.e., letters without hooks and extensions like the font for this Table title) for headlines.
- Pay attention to the leading (i.e., space between lines) of text copy. Keep columns ragged right (rather than justified) and less than 50 characters wide.
- Use accents with care. Accents are italics, bolds, boxes, rules, screens, and colors. These are used to highlight certain works or passages. Used sparingly they help with highlighting. Overused, they lose their punch.
- When the brochure is in final draft form, step back and pretend you are looking at it for the very first time. See how all the elements work together.
- Get additional training. Work with printers, go to workshops, and look into design courses.

date and time; the sponsoring agency; and a point of contact if additional information is needed. Figure 8.13 (below) is a good example of a special event flier; the original uses vibrant colors and photographs to attract readers and a number of co-sponsors of the event are listed at the bottom. As with all types of promotional strategies, issues of inclusion and accessibility should be addressed. One way to do this is to include the universal symbols of accessibility (see Figure 8.15 on p. 212) on the brochure, indicating available accommodations. Another type of inclusion is addressed in the flier presented in Figure 8.16 (see p. 212), which is offered in both English and Spanish to reach a wider audience.

international children's festival

Experience the SIGHTS, SOUNDS & TASTES of over 25 countries!

Saturday, April 19, 2008 ▪ 10am-5pm
Mill Point Park ▪ Downtown Hampton

Don't miss this unique opportunity to expose your children to the world around them. FREE. *For all ages.*

Festival offers the opportunity for Girl Scouts to complete badge requirements!

PRESENTING SPONSOR: *Busch* GARDENS. EUROPE

ADDITIONAL SPONSORS: at&t Unity WHRO Coalition for Youth

FOR MORE INFORMATION: www.hampton.gov/parks • (555) 555-5555

Figure 8.13 International Children's Festival flier

Magazines

The major advantage of using magazine advertising is the ability to target a specific group of potential customers (see Figure 8.17 on p. 213). This is because magazines offer organizations an opportunity to access individuals who share common lifestyles or special interests. Other advantages include a good deal of flexibility in reproduction quality (i.e., magazines offer

much greater quality than newspapers while still offering a wide range of options in terms of costs, size, and quality of the ad), and long life, which means the magazine will reach and be retained by an audience over a long period of time (Altstiel & Grow, 2006).

Disadvantages of magazines include early closing dates, a slow pace of reading, and clutter. Magazine production takes time, so ads must be

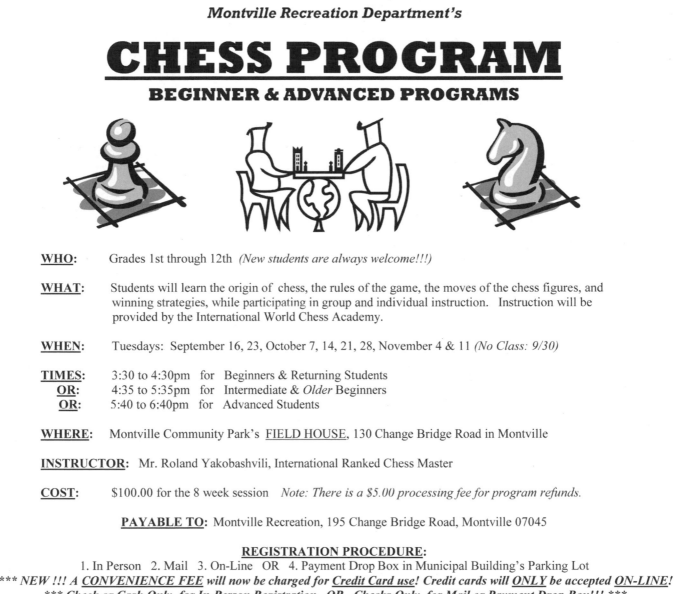

Montville Recreation Department's

CHESS PROGRAM
BEGINNER & ADVANCED PROGRAMS

WHO: Grades 1st through 12th *(New students are always welcome!!!)*

WHAT: Students will learn the origin of chess, the rules of the game, the moves of the chess figures, and winning strategies, while participating in group and individual instruction. Instruction will be provided by the International World Chess Academy.

WHEN: Tuesdays: September 16, 23, October 7, 14, 21, 28, November 4 & 11 *(No Class: 9/30)*

TIMES: 3:30 to 4:30pm for Beginners & Returning Students
OR: 4:35 to 5:35pm for Intermediate & *Older* Beginners
OR: 5:40 to 6:40pm for Advanced Students

WHERE: Montville Community Park's FIELD HOUSE, 130 Change Bridge Road in Montville

INSTRUCTOR: Mr. Roland Yakobashvili, International Ranked Chess Master

COST: $100.00 for the 8 week session *Note: There is a $5.00 processing fee for program refunds.*

PAYABLE TO: Montville Recreation, 195 Change Bridge Road, Montville 07045

REGISTRATION PROCEDURE:
1. In Person 2. Mail 3. On-Line OR 4. Payment Drop Box in Municipal Building's Parking Lot
*** NEW !!! A *CONVENIENCE FEE* will now be charged for *Credit Card use!* Credit cards will *ONLY* be accepted *ON-LINE!*
*** *Check or Cash Only* for *In-Person Registration* OR *Checks Only* for *Mail or Payment Drop Box!!!* ***
***For On-Line Registration !!!* Go to the town's website at: www.montvillenj.org**
Click on Municipal Services & then click on Parks & Recreation & then click on On-Line Registration

CLASS SIZE IS LIMITED!!! FIRST COME, FIRST SERVE!!! DON'T GET CLOSED OUT!!!

QUESTIONS ??? Call Recreation at: 973-331-3305 or visit our website at: www.montvillenj.org

Figure 8.14 Learning to play chess program flier

submitted well in advance of publication. In addition, because some magazines are read slowly, it may take a long time for a reader to actually act on an advertisement. In a magazine, clutter refers to the number of advertisements included in any one issue of the magazine. Some magazines include over 50 pages of ads; in some cases 50% of the magazine content consists of advertisements. Another concern is that more people are turning to online magazines (e-zines) to obtain information, leaving the future of printed magazines in doubt (Altstiel & Grow, 2006).

An additional promotion opportunity offered by magazines is feature articles. These articles may be written about an organization as a whole, promote an upcoming event, or describe a past program. Articles may also be developed along specific themes (e.g., developing one's leisure repertoire; how to solve the summertime blues; fun family travel tips). Although such an article may not be directly related to a specific organization it can offer an indirect promotional boost. Magazine staff, a free-lance writer, or a parks, recreation, and leisure services professional may write and submit an article for publication.

Newsletters

A newsletter is a means of communicating with an organization's membership and/or constituents. Newsletters let people know an organization is alive and well, and when well-written, can produce loyal readers and a good response. Many years ago, Beach (1993) identified three main newsletter categories: *promotional newsletters* for marketing programs and services (readers receive the newsletter at no cost); *informational newsletters* for employees or members which are about people, places, and ideas (readers receive the newsletter as part of membership in an

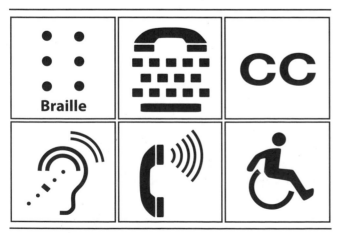

Figure 8.15 Common symbols used to denote inclusion and accessibility

Take a break from holiday shopping and weekend work. Bring your son, daughter, nephew, niece, or neighbor to the Phoenix Bikes Family Mechanics Winter Workshop! It's free!!

Family Mechanics Bike Workshop

Phoenix Bikes Mechanics will help you fix up your bike and learn basic bike maintenance that will keep everyone riding throughout the year.

Workshop will be conducted in English with Spanish translation. Participants should bring a bike to fix up or can practice on one at the shop. Space is limited to 14 participants. To register for you and a child, call 703-575-7763 or email phoenixbikes@gmail.com. Priority will be given to registered participants, though drop-ins are welcome, if there is space. Children under 18 must be accompanied by an adult.

Descansa de las compras navideñas y los quehaceres del fin de semana. Trae a tu hijo/a, sobrino/a o vecinos al Taller de Bicicletas para la Familia de Phoenix Bikes! Gratis!!

Taller de Bicicletas para la Familia!

Los mecánicos de Phoenix Bikes te enseñaran como arreglar tu bicicleta, también el mantenimiento rutinario para poder montarla durante todo el año.

El taller se presentara en inglés con traducción en español. Los participantes tendrán que traer una bicicleta para arreglar o practicar con uno en el almacén. Tenemos cupo para 14 participantes para este evento. Para registrarte junto con tu hijo/a u otro participante, llama al 703-575-7763 o envíanos un mensaje a phoenixbikes@gmail.com. Los que se registren, tendrán prioridad en el taller el sábado pero todos están bienvenidos a llegar y participar si hay espacio. Niños/as menores de 18 años tendrán que ser acompañados por un adulto.

Figure 8.16 Promotional flier in both English and Spanish

HIKEBIKECLIMB GALLUP

RED ROCK STATE PARK & PYRAMID ROCK TRAIL

With elevation from 6,660' to 7,487', Pyramid Rock Trail is the highest point in the Red Rocks vicinity. This 3 mile round trip trail takes you past amazing rock formations and the summit is surprisingly large and roomy providing a breathtaking panoramic view of the beautiful surrounding landscape.

Directions from Gallup: Travel 6 miles east on Route 66 (Hwy 118), turn left (north) onto Hwy 566, after .5 mile turn left again into Park Entrance & follow signs to Pyramid Trail.

HIGH DESERT TRAIL SYSTEM

A narrow, single track mountain biking and hiking trail, High Desert Trail System provides a wide variety of terrain with the least technical beginning at the East Trail. Three loops off of the trail - First Mesa, Second Mesa, and Third Mesa - increase in technical difficulty of terrain.

Directions to East (Gamerco) Trail Head: Travel north from Gallup about 3 miles on Hwy 491, turn left onto Chino Road (9th or the Gamerco Road), travel about 300 yards and turn left at the first road. Trail Head and Parking Area are at the corner.

MENTMORE ROCK CLIMBING AREA

Mentmore Rock Climbing area features more than 50 bolted top rope climbs and 31 sport climbs ranging in height from 25 to 45 feet with difficulty levels of 5.0 through 5.13.

Directions: Travel west on Route 66 (Hwy 118) .5 mile from Interstate 40 exit 16 in Gallup. Turn right (north) onto County Road 1 for about one mile, the road makes a sharp turn to the left (west) and becomes Mentmore Road. Take Mentmore Road about 1.5 miles up and over the hill. At the bottom of the hill the road turns sharply to the right. At this turn go straight through the open gate to the Mentmore Rock Climbing Area Parking Lot.

For further information regarding all areas contact
Charlie Koehler 505-726-2048

Figure 8.17 An example of magazine advertising: Hike Bike Climb Gallup Ad (Designed by OnLine Design, Albuquerque, NM)

Official newsletter for the
Boys & Girls Clubs
of Hall County

Spring 2008

CLUBHOUSE

770 532-8102 • One Positive Place, Gainesville, GA 30501

BOYS & GIRLS CLUBS
OF HALL COUNTY

10th Annual Rubber Duck Derby

Ducks are available for adoption.

As part of their rigorous daily workout, 15,000 bright yellow ducks sporting fashionable black sunglasses, are swimming laps and lifting weights in preparation for the 10th Annual Rubber Duck

Derby. This year's event will be held Saturday, May 17, at Clarks Bridge Park, 11 am - 2 pm. "Adoptee" parents will wait anxiously in hopes of winning one of many great prizes including the Grand Prize - a new 2008 Camry LE donated by Milton Martin Toyota.

"This is always such a fun event," said Larry Baldwin, chairman. "We would like to ask everyone to help by adopting ducks for $5 each and then come out on race day for a fun filled day for the entire family." "We would like to thank Edmondson-Telford Center and INK - Interactive Neighborhood for Kids for hosting Family Fun Day."

Scenes from last year's Rubber Duck Derby and Family Fun Day.

Thanks to our presenting sponsors:

WATERFRONT • TOYOTA scion • HOME PLACE • fieldale farms corporation • Gainesville JEWELRY • News CHANNEL WNEG TV • Magic 102.9

ADOPT A DUCK
WIN A CAR

770-656-DUCK
rubberduckderby.com
May 17, 2008

2008 Camry LE
TOYOTA

A. G. Edwards is a division of Wachovia Securities, LLC. A.G. EDWARDS FULLY INVESTED IN OUR CLIENTS. *A. G. Edwards & Sons, Inc.* Member SIPC

Billboard showing this year's grand prize - a 2008 Camery LE.

Ed Hollis Named 2008 Youth of the Year

Youth of the Year finalists (left to right) Stacy Young, Jasmine Covarrubias, Ed Hollis, Eboni Norman and Teryan Rucker.

Today, more than ever young people are discovering the value of giving back to the community, club service, and volunteerism.

This is the work of Ed Hollis. Not only does he help build and strengthen our communities but also our youth through his leadership abilities. Ed believes in making a difference in

the club that he has attended since he was 6 years old. He has inspired many by contributing his time, talent and enthusiasm to make a difference in the lives of others. He is committed to improving the quality of life in the youth that we serve.

Ed Hollis is a true exam-
Youth continued on page 2

Figure 8.18 Newsletter from a Boy's and Girl's Club (Hall County, GA) organization); and *subscription newsletters* that try to make readers richer, smarter, or healthier (readers pay for the newsletter). The majority of newsletters in the parks, recreation, and leisure field are either promotional or informational in nature.

In developing newsletters, it is important to remember the purpose of the newsletter—this will guide design decisions. Consistency is also important. A well-designed newsletter has its own look or brand—see Figure 8.18. Rather than appearing like a collection of different sections and articles, everything in the newsletter should flow together. The style and appearance should assist readers in recognizing the newsletter immediately when it arrives. Setting up a consistent style enables an agency to establish a visual language to which people respond, often without knowing it. For example, by placing a list of articles in a specific shaded box in the same location every issue, readers quickly learn just where to look and what to look for, so it is easy to find what interests them. It is also important to remember that many people only scan newsletters, so pictures, headlines, subheadings, highlighted quotes, and empty space are important to use. Such design features allow readers to get a quick handle on what is being presented.

Some newsletters are provided in hard copy, others in electronic format; some organizations use both forms of delivery. Electronic newsletters can be emailed to listserve subscribers as an attachment in Portable Document Format (pdf) so that all computer users can access them, or a link can be provided in an e-mail and the newsletter made available on the web. When available on the web, newsletters are typically provided in both pdf and html format. This facilitates access for many different types of computer users. Benefits of online newsletters include the low cost, and the ability to use color photos and text. Hard copy newsletters need to be mailed out or made available at a variety of locations. This form of newsletter tends to have longer "staying power" where people hold on to the newsletter and peruse it multiple times before discarding it.

Newspapers

With a few exceptions (e.g., *USA Today*, the *Wall Street Journal*, the *New York Times, Chicago Tribune*), newspapers are usually locally produced. Most newspapers are printed daily, although some small town papers or neighborhood papers are available less frequently (e.g., semiweekly, weekly, biweekly). In the late 2000s, the United States began to see a drop in newspaper readership and some papers ceased operating.

The advantages of using newspaper for promotion are its geographic sensitivity, the fact that it fosters immediate customer response, and offers a fast production turnaround. In addition, 60 percent of readers actually say they look forward to newspaper ads as compared to only 7 percent of television viewers. On television and radio, commercials are often perceived as an intrusion into entertainment time, whereas in newspapers they seem to be regarded as part of the overall entertainment value. This often prompts readers to act on information provided in a newspaper ad in a timely manner (Alstiel & Grow, 2006). Disadvantages of using newspapers are poor demographic selectivity (i.e., we have no idea who the readers are; there is no way to target consumers), poor production quality, a short life span, and clutter. In addition, it should be remembered that while newspapers are good at reaching some groups, like senior citizens, they are less successful at reaching young people. Many in younger generations prefer to obtain their news electronically or through television. In their report, Altstiel and Grow reported that the average age of a newspaper reader was 53. To reach younger audiences, many newspapers offer an electronic version of their paper. Despite concern over declining readership trends, newspapers and their online equivalency offer a wide variety of opportunities for promotion including ads, classified ads, editorials and letters to the editor, feature articles, and sports news.

Newspaper Advertising and Classifieds. Both advertising and classified ads are initiated by the organization and are forms of paid promotion. Advertising space may be found throughout the paper (whether hard copy or online), while classifieds are organized under predetermined categories in a specific section. Rates for both advertising space and classifieds are quoted either by the line or by the column inch. Although there is usually a flat rate per line, newspapers will often offer discounts for local advertisers as well as for increased volume (i.e., the more space you buy during the year, the lower the line or column inch rate will be).

Newspaper advertising is a mainstay for many commercial recreation and leisure services organizations (especially small, local operators—see Figure 8.19 on p. 216). Organizations such as bowling centers, roller skating rinks, movie theaters, and community theaters often use newspaper advertising. Public and nonprofit leisure services organizations tend to rely on newspaper advertising more for special events rather than the day-to-day operation of the organization.

Editorials and Letters to the Editor. Newspaper editors are often accessible to the general public and will consider and encourage thoughtful, well-documented points of views on issues that concern their readership. Editorials offer recreation programmers the opportunity to comment on issues by offering individual viewpoints or an organization's view on the subject. Quick response time is important as one becomes aware of local issues that involve the organization. Editorials offer high visibility for the organization and make a contribution to public debate on important issues.

Letters to the editor also offer individuals an opportunity to contribute to the public debate. Such letters, when timely, well-thought-out, and well-written, are often published. If an individual or organization has a strong position on an issue within the community, letters to the editor may be used to educate others about their position. Other uses for letters to the editor include thanking volunteers and sponsors in the community for their support, or responding to earlier positive or negative letters to the editor written by citizens. To maintain good will, organizations will want to be on the lookout for such letters and respond to the individual with a personal contact, as well as through the paper. It is also important to follow up with the newspaper editor (often in the form of a letter) either

acknowledging positive publicity or responding to negative publicity in a constructive manner.

Features. Reporters are always looking for news in their communities. If an organization has an event or program that is timely, unique, interesting, or new, staff should contact the newspaper for possible coverage. A news release or a personal call could be used to inform the paper of noteworthy items. When dealing with newspaper reporters, staff should be careful to avoid saying anything they would not want to read in print—everything should be considered "on the record." Feature stories offer high volume, but short-lived coverage for the organization. Encourage the use of photographs with articles to help bring the written word to life. Some newspapers will print photos with captions without an accompanying article. This visual presentation of an event or program can be just as intriguing to readers as a full-length article.

Sports News. Sports editors are often open to including a wide variety of information about community sports leagues (including hunting and fishing contests). Feature articles prior to the start up of a league or following league play are possibilities, while ongoing opportunities to inform the public may be found in game announcements, game summaries, and box scores. Some newspapers expect such information to be submitted in writing (typically by e-mail or directly to the news agency website), while others allow scores and other pertinent information to be phoned into the paper. Whatever the method, it is important for the programmer to build a relationship with her or his contact at the newspaper.

Yellow Pages

The yellow pages are considered by some to be a lifeline that ties a company to its customers and potential customers—especially for commercial organizations. Traditional yellow page services are changing in response to the online opportunities that computers and

Figure 8.19 An example of a newspaper advertisement: Mary Free Bed Hospital & Rehabilitation Center from the Grand Rapids (MI) Press. (Courtesy of Mary Free Bed Hospital)

Figure 8.20 Saskatoon Golf Club-AT&T Yellow Pages Grand Rapids Area (AT&T Michigan)

mobile phones offer. Yet, traditional hard copy telephone books still exist and offer opportunities to place ads, like the one presented in Figure 8.20. The advantage of this medium is they provide 24-hour access for people and are still available in most homes and businesses. Telephone books also lend themselves to cooperative advertising whereby national companies offer advertising for local branches in the yellow pages of large urban areas. For example, Schwinn or Mongoose might financially assist a local bicycle shop that sells its products to be listed in a larger company ad (Janes, 2006).

A challenge for leisure services organizations is to identify the yellow page categories where they should be listed. For example, a YMCA could be listed under fitness centers, childcare, youth sports, or swimming pools. Another challenge of traditional yellow pages is competing with the new online yellow pages which offer search capabilities, links to creating online maps and directions, coupons, consumer reviews, and a host of other possibilities.

Other Promotional Tools

The techniques and tools used to promote organizations, programs, and events are endless. With a little creativity and hard work, individuals can continually create new and innovative promotion techniques. For instance, in the early 1990s, one leisure services organization printed pertinent information concerning an activity on narrow slips of paper and inserted them into a batch of homemade fortune cookies (Clark, 1993). While the following is not an exhaustive list, we provide it here so it might generate additional creative ideas about potential promotional tools.

Awards and Citations

Agencies frequently look for ways to recognize staff, volunteers, customers, community organizations, and groups for their contributions to the success of the agency. Awards are thought of as publicity and can serve as a public relations tool. Awards can be meaningless if given too freely, but are effective when presented when deserved. Examples of awards include certifications for the completion of classes, volunteer appreciation certificates, outstanding service awards for staff, and recognizing the efforts of community groups that have assisted in programs or done other noteworthy service (see Figure 8.21, p. 218). The process of giving awards can itself become a promotional tool. When giving awards, if it is appropriate to inform local newspapers, radio, and television through a press release about it, do so. A picture and a short article in a community paper can promote a positive image for an organization and spark additional interest in its programs and services.

Celebrities/Spokespeople

Using celebrities to promote an organization and/or a specific program or event can be fun and worthwhile. Celebrities serve as attention-getters, but seldom in and of themselves make the sale. Organizations look to both local and national celebrities to promote their programs. National organizations are often more suited to attracting big-time stars, but local affiliates and organizations can look for local radio and television personalities to promote events. We offer one note of caution in selecting a spokesperson—make sure the person embodies the values of your organization. Altstiel and Grow (2006) identified the following internally directed questions in using celebrities: Can we afford this person? Does she or he have any "skeletons in the closet" that may lead to embarrassment for the organization? Will the celebrity connect with customers and enhance the organization's overall image? How will people of various backgrounds, cultures, and demographics respond to this spokesperson? One example of use of a celebrity spokesperson is the use of professional wrestlers at grand openings of stores and malls. The characters draw huge crowds for pictures and autographs, and visitors often buy goods while waiting for autographs. Some would find the use of professional wrestlers to be exciting and appealing, while others might find this choice of celebrity endorsement to be undignified and offensive.

Contests

Contests can bring attention to an organization or to a specific event or program. Contests often serve as a lead in to a specific event, priming individuals or groups for the main event. Contests can range from coloring contests for children, to poster design competitions for adults, to fundraising drives. They can be embedded in larger events (e.g., hospital bed races as part of a community health fair) or may be the main event (e.g., dragon boat races, pet shows). Prizes are often given to winners; examples of prizes include cash awards, trips, donated merchandise, or a variety of novelty items with an organization or agency logo on them.

The Oklahoma State Parks Division conducted a successful (in terms of its promotional value) contest in 2007. Staff invited people from across the state to submit an original drawing or essay responding to the theme, "What Parks Mean To Me."

Certificate of

Appreciation

Presented to:

<Name of Recipient>

In recognition of your service to the sport and recreation industry

Presented on:

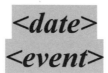

<date>
<event>

Hon Judy Spence MP

Minister for Police,
Corrective Services and Sport

Local Member

<Electorate>

Figure 8.21 Queensland Government Certificate of Appreciation

Close to 500 people of all ages and backgrounds participated, and five grand prize winners were selected to spend a weekend in a state park lodge. The pictures and essays were used to create 2008 calendars, which were distributed across the state, promoting state parks. In addition, CDs of the essays and drawings were prepared and provided to state legislators. Because legislators could see the personal influence of parks on citizens, funding for state parks was positively influenced. In addition, the winning essays and drawings were framed and hung in Oklahoma highway welcome centers. This provided a very personal view of the value of state parks and increased park visitation.

Coupons

Coupons such as "Buy One Registration, Get a Second Registration for Half Price" are effective means to encourage individuals to try new programs or services, thereby creating a returning customer base. Coupons may be incorporated into various types of promotion such as fliers and brochures. It seems coupons are everywhere: in the mail, on receipts, on the Internet (print them yourself), on brochures, as text messages on cell phones, and so on. One reason for this increased use of coupons for retail products is that coupons are an effective approach to persuade customers to save money and try new programs and services. Coupons have been used very effectively in leisure services for senior citizen participation. By showing a special senior's discount card, seniors can receive reduced rates for programs and services (often during a specific/nonpeak time of day or day of the week). At the beginning of each new year coupons are commonly used to encourage new and loyal customers to continue involvement in activities and services.

Direct Mail

Direct mail is carried out by an organization that wants to share a complex message with a large constituency at a reasonable cost (see Figure 8.22, a postcard sent by the YMCA to generate new family memberships). This form of communication involves mailing a brochure, letter, or other piece of promotion directly to an individual whom the organization has targeted as a potential customer, donor, or stakeholder in the organization. Mailing lists may be generated from past participants, new residents, people in a specific geographic area, or individuals who have expressed an interest in a particular program area. Unfortunately, many people feel bombarded by "junk mail" which has lessened the effectiveness of direct-mail techniques. Another

consideration that might lessen the enthusiasm for direct mailing is the environmental cost. Direct mailing can consume a great deal of resources (mainly paper), which may give the organization an unfavorable image. Despite these concerns, with careful targeting and message development, direct mail can be an effective means of promotion.

Involvement in Special Events

Neighborhood festivals, art fairs, and other special events take place throughout the year. Having a presence at these types of community events is important to promote an organization's involvement in the community and/or increase name recognition for an organization with the general public. Involvement can take on a variety of forms such as hosting a game booth, providing entertainment, facilitating hands-on projects for children, or simply staffing an information booth where staff disseminate brochures, fliers, and other promotional materials about programs and services. Organizations can also sponsor specific special events of their own as a way to promote a cause,

Figure 8.22 Direct mail flier: YMCA of Greater Grand Rapids

celebrate a holiday, and/or promote a specific service or program. Such special events are hard work, but are a good way to renew or maintain personal contact with other organizations and individuals in the community on a large scale.

Logos, Emblems, and Trademarks

Logos, emblems, and trademarks are visual symbols that represent an organization. Logos and emblems have an important advantage over other forms of communication—the advantage of speed. If a logo is well-designed, it will catch the eye, generate interest, and be recognized instantaneously. Logos, emblems, and trademarks can be used in a variety of ways. Good trademarks and logos can stand alone as well as be used on stationary, envelopes, decals, T-shirts, and vehicles—almost anything an organization utilizes as a sign (on the door of the city car, for instance) can include their logo or signature trademark.

From a design standpoint, logos and trademarks may take the form of a symbol, type (or lettering) or a combination of the two. The logo of the American Camp Association (see Figure 8.23) relates the idea of providing opportunities for adults and children to connect in ways that enrich lives and build tomorrows. The most successful logos and trademarks are original, simple in nature, appropriate to the product and organization, and easy to remember (Janes, 2006).

Photographs

"A picture is worth a thousand words" is an adage that runs true for promoting the benefits of recreation programs. Thus, photographs should not be overlooked in the overall promotional mix. Although photographs are usually used in conjunction with other promotional tools (e.g., newspaper articles, brochures, newsletters, websites) there are several specific considerations to keep in mind. First and foremost, organizations should build a photo file so they have quality pictures available

when they are needed. Such a file should be continually updated and expanded, and captions (including the date and name of the event) should be kept with all pictures. A wide range of pictures should be kept, including pictures of staff members, facilities, group shots, and perhaps most important—pictures of participants in action.

Although photographs may be rented or purchased from advertising agencies, it is best for pictures to be taken from actual programs and events sponsored by the parks, recreation, or leisure services organization. Oftentimes organizations hire photographers or designate in-house staff to take photos. Digital cameras have become less expensive and easier to use over time; thus, they provide a viable option for organizations to take and use pictures in a variety of publications. In addition, digital photos allow for easy storage of pictures on CDs, DVDs, USB flash drives, and hard drives. A third option may be to involve local newspapers and let them know of opportunities for a good photo shoot. If a photographer does take pictures, she or he is often willing to share them with the agency for promotional purposes.

As with print media used for promotional purposes, it is important to be as inclusive as possible with photographs without staging situations that do not represent the community. In recent years, one university received a good deal of bad press for digitally inserting the faces of two Black students into a picture of all-white fans at a sporting event. This staged photograph was discovered by one of the students in the photo and the university received negative publicity on a national level.

An important consideration when shooting pictures during a program is to ask participants to sign a media release. Permission should be gained prior to publishing any customer photographs where individuals might be identifiable, especially if a monetary gain is experienced, if the subjects are minors, or have special needs. Failure to do so could result in a lawsuit based on invasion of privacy.

Press and/or Information Kits

To take advantage of unexpected opportunities to promote an organization staff may wish to develop a press kit. Such a tool can be distributed on a moment's notice to program visitors, dignitaries, potential customers, and/or media representatives. A press or information kit might include items such as a brief history of the organization, a current Fact Sheet about the organization, frequently asked questions, and an organizational chart. Additional details

Figure 8.23 American Camp Association logo

about staff (professional biographical information), brochures, the annual report, and a list of major accomplishments or programs offering unique products from past programs (e.g., a child's arts and crafts project) might also be included. Other common press kit materials include a list of major supporters or customers of the agency or organization, as well as reprints of articles about the organization, letters of support from customers and community figures, and a CD with approved logos and photographs (Janes, 2006). By keeping these types of materials on file within the organization, the needed information can be quickly accessed to create a customized press or information packet. A press kit may be assembled in a binder or folder for easy access, or provided electronically to recipients. It is important to keep information used for such press or information packets current.

Press Releases

A press release serves to make a specific statement that the organization hopes will be picked up to receive free publicity in the media. Press releases may publicize an event, provide information about the organization, or announce the opening of a new facility or program. A well-written press release will stress the benefits of the event and emphasize its community appeal. In many cases, organizations develop relationships with the media that will facilitate the publication of press releases. One type of press release is a news release.

Historically, a news release was the way for an organization to communicate with the media (e.g., radio, newspapers). This is no longer the case and in many instances (up to 80% of the time) unsolicited press releases are not even read by news staff (Janes, 2006) as media outlets receive a large number of press releases daily. Starting in the mid 2000s, many agencies began to make use of social messaging utilities such as Twitter to share news release information directly with constituents as well as media representatives. By developing a relationship with local media staff (e.g., news writers, radio personalities), a programmer can greatly improve the possibility of getting the word out through press releases. Part of the relationship development process is to learn how each media member prefers to receive information (e.g., phone, fax, e-mail, direct mail), what they believe is newsworthy, and the type of information that fits their needs. Figure 8.24 (see p. 222) presents an example of a press release that includes succinct information about the five *Ws* in the first paragraph (e.g., who, what, why, when, and where). Editors often call for

additional information, so be sure to include a contact person and her or his contact information.

In addition to newspapers, programmers can send news releases to a variety of sources. For example, local churches may accept news releases for inclusion in their church bulletin. A local sporting goods store may be willing to place short announcements in store newsletters and on their website. The community human services department may be willing to include information about programs for people with disabilities as part of a local radio talk show. When sending out news releases, address them to specific individuals whenever possible and give two to three weeks advance notice of an event.

Promotional Merchandise (Novelty Items) and Prizes

Organizations can use a variety of promotional merchandise to promote their organization, specific program, or event. Novelty items (imprinted in some way with the logo and/or contact information of the organization or program) include bumper stickers, lapel pins, pens, pencils, mugs, clothing (e.g., T-shirts, sweatshirts), calendars, banners, flags, small toys, matchbooks, postcards, patches, magnets, and other merchandise. For example, T-shirts can be printed and handed out to volunteers during a special event. In such a capacity, the T-shirt may be viewed as a sign of appreciation to the volunteer as well as a way to designate who is available to help participants during the event. T-shirts may also be sold to the general public during an event as a means to generate funds and promote the organization or event for the future (see Figure 8.25 on p. 223)

Promotional items are often used as prizes leading up to specific events or during the actual program or event. For example, tickets for special events may be given to radio stations or other commercial organizations for giveaways prior to the event. Prizes and giveaways of novelty items can create a sense of goodwill between organizations and customers when used wisely.

Public Service Announcements

Public service announcements (PSAs) are short messages aired on the radio, television, or Internet intended to inform or educate viewers and listeners about the work of nonprofit organization and others that serve a public interest (Janes, 2006). There was a time when radio and television stations were required (by law) by the Federal Communications Commission (FCC) to run public service announcements. And, with the increase in computer use for viewing and listening to a wide variety of media, agencies have turned to the Internet as a site for PSAs.

Although the FCC law is no longer in effect, most radio and television stations still include PSAs as part of their programming. This is in part because they need to fill otherwise empty airtime with interesting material, but more so because the stations want to be good citizens (especially when license renewal time comes around; Janes, 2006). Public and nonprofit leisure services organizations can take advantage of this opportunity by creating their own PSAs. The organization can advance an idea (e.g., *It Starts in Parks* campaign) or provide information about its programs or services (e.g., promote a specific upcoming event). A survey of public service directors indicated television stations were most apt to use PSAs under the following conditions (Wright, 2000):

- The PSA contains information relevant to their audience.

- Television executives are familiar with the non-profit sponsor or the cause it represents.

- A local connection or link can be made (with an individual, agency, or effort occurring in the community).

- The PSA is sent in a timely manner and includes information about the sponsoring organization.

(continued on p. 224)

PRESS RELEASE
FOR IMMEDIATE RELEASE
Thursday, April 24, 2008

CONTACT: Media and Marketing
Sterling Clifford (555) 555-5555
Kia McLeod (555) 555-5555 or c (555) 555-5555

Rec and Parks rolls out the green carpet for EcoFest
FREE trees for city residents

BALTIMORE (April 24, 2008)---It will be so easy to 'go green' in Baltimore this weekend. On Saturday, April 26th, Mayor Sheila Dixon will join Baltimore Green Week to kickoff the 5th Annual EcoFestival and the 2008 Arbor Day FREE Tree Giveaway in Druid Hill Park. The goal is to raise awareness about how local residents can make the Baltimore region cleaner and more environmentally safer. City residents will also have an opportunity to save a little green and slash energy bills with FREE trees.

Planting trees has both environmental and economical benefits, including reducing utility bills by up to 30 percent, increasing property values, improving air quality, and fighting water pollution. Last year, Baltimore City Department of Recreation and Parks planted and distributed 5, 683 trees.

FREE Trees will be distributed in the morning *(at Mansion House Drive)* from 9 to 11 a.m. and during EcoFestival *(at the TreeBaltimore display)* from 11 a.m. to 5 p.m. in historic Druid Hill Park. The first 50 participants at the Department of Public Works' Household Hazardous Waste Drop-off Days *(at Patterson High School)* will also get FREE trees.

Celebrate EcoFest and Arbor Day with live entertainment, workshops, vendors with sustainable products, healthy food, Tree awards, demonstrations, and more! Pick up a FREE tree to plant in your front or backyard; two per household. This event is FREE and open to the public. FREE trees will be available on a *first-come, first-served basis, while supplies last*.

For more information on the 2008 Arbor Day FREE Tree Giveaway or the 5th Annual EcoFestival, please call (555) 555-5555 or visit us on the Web at www.baltimorecity.gov/recnparks.

###

Figure 8.24 Press release for the City of Baltimore Plant a Tree

Figure 8.25 Examples of promotional items

Parks, recreation, and leisure services organizations meet many of these conditions and would be well-suited to make use of PSAs through a wide variety of media. The Ad Council sometimes provides assistance for public and nonprofit organizations to develop a PSA. The public or nonprofit organization pays for material costs, and receives creative and media support free of charge (Ad Council, 2009). Over the years The Ad Council has been deeply involved in American life, creating over 1,000 campaigns to communicate positive messages about healthy lifestyles. Their focus areas include improving children's quality of life, preventative health, education, strengthening families, and environmental preservation. Through their efforts, the Ad Council has created many memorable characters (e.g., Smokey Bear, McGruff the Crime Dog, Vince and Larry—The Crash Dummies). It has produced the following familiar slogans:

- Only you can prevent forest fires (U.S. Forest Service).

- A mind is a terrible thing to waste (United Negro College Fund).

- Help take a bite out of crime (National Crime Prevention Council).

- This is your brain. This is your brain on drugs (Partnership for a Drug Free America).

- The toughest job you'll ever love (United States Peace Corps).

Word of Mouth and Testimonials

Last, but certainly not least, the essence and image of an organization is communicated daily through word-of-mouth by customers, staff, and a variety of other people both within and outside the organization. Such word-of-mouth publicity contributes to the overall image of the organization. In his book, *The Anatomy of Buzz*, Rosen (2002) equates word-of-mouth exchanges to creating a "buzz" over an organization or program. Understanding the importance of creating a favorable buzz as well as understanding the networks people use to spread the buzz is imperative if organizations want to capture the power of word-of-mouth testimonials. Networks that support word of mouth information-sharing include informal neighborhood groups (e.g., garden clubs, book clubs), informal sharing by happenstance (i.e., someone runs into an acquaintance at the grocery store), and through electronic social networking and messaging sites (e.g., MySpace, Facebook, Twitter). Many organizations use testimonials to record positive impressions that people have with their programs and services. Testimonials can then be used in a variety of promotional formats.

Factors to Consider When Promoting Programs

Given tight budgets and time constraints, practitioners will probably not be able to do everything they want to promote their program, service, or idea. As a result, organizations must give concerted thought to making decisions that will maximize the effectiveness of a promotional campaign as well as make the best use of time and money. These decisions are dependent on many factors. The following questions serve as a guide to assist programmers in making these decisions.

What Are the Promotion Objectives?

The overall goal of promotion efforts is to encourage the public to derive full benefit from the program and services that an organization provides. Within this broad goal, however, the objectives of specific promotional efforts should be clearly established as to whether the promotional effort is intended to inform, educate, persuade, or remind.

For example, if an organization's objective is to inform, then it may attempt to create mass awareness of a new program or service by emphasizing advertising and publicity. Consider a nonprofit organization that is partnering with a public parks and recreation department to run a new summer adventure program for teens. Both organizations would want to generate as much awareness of the new program as possible. Promotional techniques might include publicity in daily and community newspapers; PSAs on local radio stations; displays and exhibits; wide distribution of brochures through city centers, public agencies, and tourist accommodations; and the hanging of posters in libraries, restaurants, community centers, and other public locations.

Who Is the Target Audience?

It is important for an organization to understand the *entire* target audience (e.g., consider age, sex, race/ethnicity, educational level, those with disabilities, those with and without families) for the overall organization as well as for specific programs and services. To be most effective, staff will gear the promotional tool to the intended audience—programmers need to think about how the audience lives, where they go, and what they are most likely to look at, listen to, or read. Thus, one challenge programmers face is to determine the tool that fits into that picture.

For example, a staff member could develop the best newspaper ad in the world, but it probably would not reach teenagers because most teenagers do not read newspapers. The staff would be better off developing a public service announcement for MTV, developing online pop-up ads, or posting information on a social networking site. Likewise, a great web page will not be effective if we are trying to reach customers who do not have access to a computer.

Once staff have identified the target market, they must still understand the similarities and differences among groups within the market area. For example, in examining differences among various ethnic groups, Guion and Kent (2005, p. 2) noted that successful ethnic marketing:

- Values the cultural uniqueness of the target group.

- Values cooperation and bridge building with community leaders and other organizations working within the community.

- Values the cultural beliefs, symbols, and practices of the target group.

- Values differences in languages, accents, practices, and social conduct.

- Values word of mouth and interpersonal communication to spread the message.

What Is the Budget?

Clearly, the amount of money an organization has available for promotional activities has a substantial influence on the types and numbers of promotional tools and techniques used, as well as the frequency with which they can be used. As a result, programmers should be sure to utilize as many free and low-cost techniques as possible, but should not overlook the hidden costs in terms of staff time needed for creating effective promotional techniques. Many publicity tools are dollar free, but staff intensive. Consider the amount of time it may take to develop relationships with a magazine editor in getting a feature article published or in creating in-house promotional items. Programmers need this information before making

decisions concerning the most appropriate promotional tools and techniques.

What Is the Program?

The actual program may dictate the most appropriate promotional technique. Different events have different potential for using various promotional techniques. For example, television is a much better medium to promote active events; each media type has different potential for demonstration, visualization, explanation, believability, and color.

At What Stage Is the Program within the Product Life Cycle?

In Chapter Six, we noted that programs go through a life cycle beginning with introduction and ending with decline. In the introduction stage, the promotional objective typically is to inform and educate prospective customers and stimulate trial and use. In the middle stages of the program life cycle, advertising is often used to persuade and remind clients of the availability of the program or service. During the final stage of the program life cycle, promotional activities are commonly reduced and phased out as fewer and fewer people are interested in the program (Janes, 2006).

What Is the Time Frame?

The issue of time is relevant on many different levels. First and foremost, is the timing of the promotional technique in conjunction with what is being promoted? For example, if there is a short time span until an actual event or program is to take place radio, newspaper advertisements, or fliers may be the best choice as such mediums can be created quickly and can prompt potential customers to move quickly. A second related issue of time revolves around the amount of lead time needed to create the promotional piece. For example, brochures and magazines take a long time to produce, but they have a longer life than fliers and newspaper advertisements.

Coordinating the Promotion Mix

In answering the questions presented in Figure 8.26 (see p. 226), programmers should be able to identify the promotional tools and techniques that are most appropriate for specific programs or events. At the same time, it is important to remember the overall promotional mix of the organization. Thus, programmers should examine the overall promotion strategy of the organization using the same questions listed in the preceding section. Ideally, the promotion mix for the organization as a whole will include some combination of all four components of promotion (i.e., advertising, publicity, personal selling, and sales promotions) discussed earlier in this chapter.

The key to a successful promotion mix is integrating a wide variety of techniques. Each element must dovetail with others. Using a variety of approaches generally ensures reaching a wider audience. It is important, however, that all efforts be coordinated to ensure that each impression the customer or potential customer receives will fit with what she or he knows or believes about the program and the organization behind it.

Developing a Promotion and Overall Marketing Strategy

In examining the importance of promotion to an organization, consider the communication challenges facing the following three organizations (one public, one nonprofit, and one commercial):

- South Carolina Department of Parks, Recreation, and Tourism (public organization). Created in 1967 by the state of South Carolina with the following mandate: to help foster and promote the state's emerging tourism industry; to protect and promote South Carolina's state parks; and to help communities plan and develop recreational opportunities for local residents. The vision of the organization is *"Shaping and sharing a better South Carolina through stewardship, service, economic development and marketing"* (http://www.discoversouth-carolina.com/).

- Hostelling International-USA (HI-USA; nonprofit organization). HI-USA is a nonprofit membership organization founded in 1934. The mission of HI-USA is *"to help all, especially the young, gain a greater understanding of the world and its people through hostelling."* The organization operates a network of inexpensive, safe, and clean hostel accommodations throughout the United States. HI-USA, in cooperation with other worldwide national associations, belongs to the International Youth Hostel Federation (IYHF). Although services are primarily offered to young people, HI-USA focuses its promotion efforts on teachers, school administrators, potential partners, and potential funders for the program as well as young people (http://www.hihostels.com/).

- West Michigan Whitecaps (commercial organization). The Whitecaps is a professional minor league baseball team, a Class A affiliate of the Detroit Tigers, based in Grand Rapids, Michigan. The Whitecaps play a 140-game schedule and their home park is Fifth Third Ballpark, a privately owned stadium built in 1994. The mission of the Whitecaps is to *"provide affordable family entertainment to the entire West Michigan community by providing friendly faces, open minds, our time and energy, and a welcoming atmosphere"* (http://www.whitecaps-baseball.com).

For each of these organizations it is important to develop an integrated marketing strategy in terms of informing, educating, persuading, and reminding the community and target audiences of its programs and services. We encourage you to have a look at the associated websites of these three entities and evaluate the promotional tools you see. In Figure 8.27, you can see a visual of how HI-USA describes their relationship with individuals by using a continuum. Table 8.4 (see p. 228) presents some of the various objectives of an overall marketing strategy for each organization and Table 8.5 (see p. 229) presents various techniques used in each of these areas to

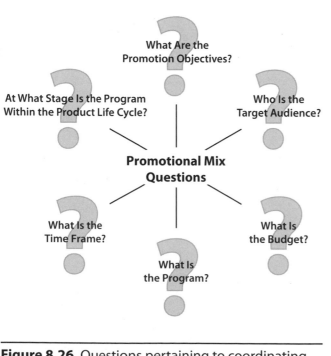

Figure 8.26 Questions pertaining to coordinating the promotional mix

accomplish these objectives. The programs and promotional efforts of the organization offer a mechanism to move potential travelers looking for a "cheap sleep" to travelers who believe in the mission of HI-USA; these individuals include short-time volunteers within the organization as well as lifelong supporters.

Promoting Programs: A Servant Leadership Approach

Some people believe promotion is wasteful, an opinion that is reflected in the following quote attributed to Ralph Waldo Emerson:

> If a man [*sic*] can write a better book, preach a better sermon, or make a better mousetrap than his neighbors, though he builds his house in the woods, the world will make a beaten path to his door. (cited in Fern, 1985, p. 69)

This suggests that promotional efforts are not needed if the product, program, or service is of high quality. This view would seem to fit with servant leadership, which we have proposed as a framework for delivering recreation programs and services. As servant leaders, programmers follow the needs of their constituencies rather than creating interest in programs through promotion. This orientation still requires outreach to constituents, however.

In dealing with this criticism, let's go back to the quote from Emerson. In many instances better books, sermons, and mousetraps have been produced. Yet...

> many have remained unread, unheard, and unused. Unless the world knows that organizations, programs and services exist, as well as believing that they offer "want satisfying" benefits, these offerings will remain unsuccessful. (Crompton & Lamb, 1986, pp. 379–380)

Thus, without promotion an organization and its programs and services literally do not exist in the public consciousness.

Effective promotion increases the net benefits provided by an organization in many ways. First, it increases the number of people who are aware of an organization's services, thereby overcoming an identified barrier to recreation participation. Second, it can decrease the cost of services by increasing the number of people participating in (and thus paying) for services. When promotion decreases net costs to participants and increases individual and community benefits, it is often viewed as a positive investment.

As a result, we believe servant leaders should invest in promoting their organizations, programs, and services within the following ethical principles. First and foremost, promotion should not be misleading and should be about developing trust between constituent and organization. This is a difficult task, as indicated by a 1999 poll which found that 74 percent of respondents strongly or somewhat believed that most advertisers deliberately stretch the truth about the products and programs they advertise (Ware, 2002). An organization seeking to overcome this perception and build the lasting patronage of its customers will succeed only if it provides accurate and honest information about its programs and services. Thus, servant leaders should resist the tendency to overpromise. If an organization promises more from a program than it is able to deliver, its credibility can be damaged and it will not be truly serving the customer.

A related issue to overpromising is not giving customers enough information to make good decisions. Servant leaders provide customers with the information they need to make informed (continued on p. 231)

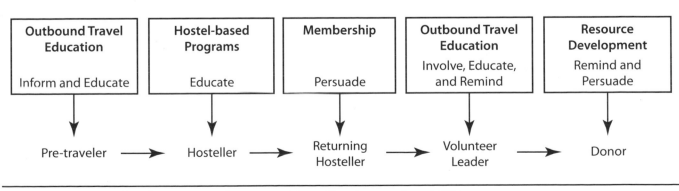

Figure 8.27 Example of promotional strategy: Hostelling International-USA

Table 8.4 Objectives in a marketing strategy for various types of organizations

	West Michigan Whitecaps — Commercial Organization	Hostelling International-USA (HI-USA) — Nonprofit Organization	South Carolina Department of Parks, Recreation, and Tourism (SCPRT) — Public Organization
Informing — How can the organization introduce itself to potential customers?	The Whitecaps compete with a variety of local entertainment options. The first step in attracting potential fans is to inform people of the opportunity to watch professional baseball in West Michigan. In addition, the Whitecaps work with local businesses to inform them of the potential advertising opportunities that exist with the team.	HI-USA is a unique experience combining education, cross-cultural exchange, and affordable travel. Need to inform teachers, school administrators, group leaders, and individual travelers about the opportunities HI-USA provides as well as hostel locations, costs, and how to find more information.	Tourists have many different options when planning their trips. The first task of SCPRT is to inform potential visitors of the possibilities, to get them to think that South Carolina is a possible destination for them. SCPRT also informs potential businesses about how they can benefit if they become involved with SCPRT.
Educating — How can the organization educate potential customers about the benefits of the experience?	Once people become aware of watching baseball as a recreation option, the Whitecaps try to encourage people to think about the experience as more than a baseball game. It is an affordable family experience that includes baseball, as well as other promotions and events. Potential sponsors and advertisers need specific information related to costs, potential return on investment, access to spectator time and attention, and the target audience. The Whitecaps also educate the community about the public service they provide through their Caps in the Community Program.	For most people travel is a life-changing experience. A tremendous number of organizations exist to assist people with travel yet few exist that specialize in the educational aspects of travel. HI-USA programs focus on the benefits of travel and help HI-USA educate the public about the benefits it provides. This enables the organization to expand its target audiences (e.g., participants, funders, volunteers), develop an understanding about the benefits of travel, and arouse a desire to get involved with HI-USA.	Once potential visitors are aware that South Carolina is a viable vacation spot, they need more information about the various opportunities that South Carolina provides. Visitors must move beyond knowing South Carolina has beaches and mountains to knowing what specific opportunities exist for education (historical sites), food and lodging, and entertainment (beaches, parks, golf courses).
Persuading — How can the organization get customers involved with the organization?	For the Whitecaps, persuading means getting people in the seats, motivating them to purchase food and other concessions, and ensuring a positive experience so visitors will return for future games. The Whitecaps also work to persuade area companies to advertise in the park and sponsor promotions for individual games.	In addition to being given information, participants, funders, and volunteers may need to be persuaded to become involved in a HI-USA program or to stay at a hostel. The quality of the experience, unique nature of the program, opportunity for personal enrichment, location of the program or hostel, social interaction that takes place in hostels, frequent guest program, and group rates are all considered to be 'persuaders.'	Success is gauged not by individual involvement with SCPRT, but rather by the relationships with a variety of tourism-related entities across the state (e.g., lodging, food, entertainment providers). Thus, SCPRT creates opportunities for these types of organizations to tell their story. In addition, SCPRT offers planning resources to visitors as they plan their overall trip.
Reminding — Keeping the organization on people's minds. How can the organization encourage loyal customers?	For the Whitecaps reminding entails repeating the message that the Whitecaps are a viable option for constituent entertainment dollars. In addition, the Whitecaps focus on techniques and approaches to help one-time visitors to become fans and return again and again.	Individuals and organizations have many alternatives on which to expend their time and money while traveling. Therefore, it is necessary to remind travelers about the personal and community benefits that accrue from their support of HI-USA. At the same time, HI-USA strives to demonstrate appreciation for their patronage. This approach is crucial for confirming and reinforcing future support of the organization.	SCPRT reminds target groups about recreation and tourism opportunities by engaging in a variety of promotional efforts to keep South Carolina on people's minds and encouraging them to return again and again.

Table 8.5 Marketing tools and techniques for various types of organizations

	West Michigan Whitecaps Commercial Organization	Hostelling International–USA (HI-USA) Nonprofit Organization	South Carolina Department of Parks, Recreation, and Tourism (SCPRT) Public Organization
Informing How can the organization introduce itself to potential customers?	• Season schedule • Website (www.whitecaps-baseball.com) • Advertising spots on TV and Radio • Newsletter (*The Breaker*) • Baseball clinics • Press releases • *Caps in the Community* – giving back to the community through volunteerism • Billboards	• Local council newsletters • Annual guidebook • Website (www.hiusa.org) • Hostel programs generate positive publicity in newspapers, magazines, and other media outlets • Brochures for individual hostels • National partnerships with organizations like the Girl Scouts, Greyhound, local parks and recreation departments	• Magazine ads (target travel magazines) • Exhibits at trade shows (NY Times travel show) • Travel brochure to be mailed by visitor and convention bureaus • SCPRT website (www.scprt.com) • Discover South Carolina website (www.discoversouthcarolina.com) • Posters
Educating How can the organization educate potential customers about the benefits of the experience?	• Clinics • Intercity youth baseball/softball programs • Agency website • Ballpark tours	• Programs like Travel 101, Cultural Kitchen, etc. • Agency website • Annual reports • Memberships • Partnerships • Press kits	• Links on the SCPRT website to partnering organizations (and vice versa) • Agency website • Visitor centers • Electronic kiosks • CD/DVD
Persuading How can the organization get customers involved with the organization?	• Clinics • Intercity youth baseball/softball programs • Promotions and special events—free giveaways and coupons, fireworks, camping on the outfield (complete with movie) after the game • Special group nights (group pricing) • Radio broadcasts of games	• Agency website • Partnership opportunities • Presentations to groups • Yellow Pages	• Promotions (coupons, incentives) • Agency website • Direct mail and emails
Reminding Keeping the organization on people's minds. How can the organization encourage loyal customers?	• Merchandise—T-shirts, caps, mugs • Intercity youth baseball/softball programs • Logo and mascot • Word of mouth (online, face-to-face) • Newsletters • Radio broadcasts of games	• Annual report • Merchandise • Fundraising events • Agency website • Direct mail and email • Word of mouth (online, face-to-face) • Membership renewals • Volunteer opportunities	• Links on the SCPRT website to partnering organizations • Word of mouth (online, face-to-face) • Awards and citations to partners

Table 8.6 Practical theories: Motivation-based theories

In developing recreation programs and then promoting them, it is important to know what motivates individuals to want to participate. Inherent to understanding motivation is being aware of the needs or desires of constituents, and how these needs or desires are satisfied. Maslow's (1943) hierarchical needs theory is probably the best known general theory of motivation. Maslow presented this view of motivation in a pyramid shaped model that depicts various levels of needs. According to Maslow, higher order needs are ignored until lower order needs are met.

Maslow's hierarchy

Although many have questioned this theory, it has stood the test of time and offers a framework to guide programming efforts to meet specific needs of individuals. An example of addressing lower level needs prior to higher order needs is the breakfast program offered in public schools. It is well known that in order for children to learn (a higher order function) their lower order needs must be met first. Otherwise hunger and discomfort will drive children's behaviors (which will likely be in conflict with their learning related goals).

Another approach to understanding an individual's motivation to participate in a particular program can be viewed through Deci and Ryan's (1985, 2000) self determination theory. They suggest that people are intrinsically motivated out of a desire to explore and understand their environments, and this desire forms the basis for most actions. Deci and Ryan further explain that motivation is based on the innate need for experience. It includes three components:

- Competence: when people experience the desire to interact proficiently or effectively with their environment;

- Autonomy/Self-determination: when people feel that they are the origins of their actions (this includes the idea of choice); and

- Relatedness: when people feel loved and connected to others, feel that others understand them, and feel meaningfully involved with the broader social world.

Thus, according to these two authors, people would be motivated to participate in parks, recreation, and leisure service programs out of a need to experience their skills and talents (competence), to make choices about participation (self-determination), and to feel connected to others (relatedness). As programmers, then, we would want to ensure opportunities for people to experience success and competence by offering activities in a wide range of skill levels. We could provide opportunities for choice by offering a variety of activities, activity times or locations, and fellow participants. Lastly, by paying attention to how, when, where, and with whom we design programs, we can provide opportunities to facilitate social interaction among participants.

If we follow motivation theories as the driving force behind recreation programming, we need to remember that as leisure service providers we do not motivate people. Rather, we create and manipulate environments to facilitate people to motivate themselves. True motivation is intrinsic—it comes from within an individual. Thus, our goal is to develop social, psychological, and physical settings that support individual motivators. For instance, we know that lighting (e.g., subdued, bright) and colors (e.g., pastels, neon) affect people's moods, and thus, "motivate" people to behave in certain ways.

Staff often develop adolescent and teen programs from their understanding of human development and motivation theory. From human development we know that adolescents are strongly motivated to experience a sense of belonging with their peer group, and with risk taking. In response to this knowledge, many urban area programmers provide special outdoor adventure programs for teenage youth where group bonding can occur in an atmosphere of excitement and risk. When structured activities and spaces in which to meet these needs are not provided, we may see an increase in gang membership or other undesirable groupings.

Your Turn:
How might you develop a promotion strategy for a summer camp or other program using these two theories as a foundation? How would each theory influence the messages you might want to send? How does the theory you choose impact the choice of promotional tools or strategies to best assist in delivering these messages? Do the theories imply an influence by the culture or demographics of constituents (e.g., age, sex, religion, family status, education level, income)?

(continued from p. 227) decisions. Thus, the educational aspect of promotion is especially important to servant leaders. Promotion is an opportunity to serve through education.

When looking at all aspects of marketing, public relations, and promotion, servant leaders will realize the importance of building relationships. An organization's ability to develop relationships with consumers, community organizations, sponsors, and other partners is a powerful tool to reach and help motivate potential customers in today's marketing environment (see Table 8.6). "It is no longer simply good enough to provide a good quality experience for consumers… organizations must be skilled at forming relationships with all stakeholders and partnering organizations to provide meaning to their experience and approach marketing (and public relations and promotion) holistically (Shepler, 2006, p. 304). Inherent in relationship building is the ability to develop consensus with various constituent groups about specific programs to accomplish desired outcomes. This relates to not overpromising as well as giving everyone (potential customers, customers, partners, community) the information needed to make good decisions related to being involved with a specific program or organization. This demands that programmers see the promotion process as a two-way street whereby organizations offer information and listen to feedback from everyone involved. Building this kind of information-sharing requires the intentional integration of a number of characteristics of servant leaders presented in Chapter One, including the ability to empathize with others, listen to others, and the ability to be aware of the potential of our programs. Emphasizing these characteristics in the promotion process demonstrates a commitment to serve the needs of others; it also emphasizes the attributes of openness and persuasion, rather than control.

Summary

Promotion is primarily communication that seeks to inform, educate, persuade, or remind various target groups about an organization's programs and services. Organizations that have a successful promotion strategy utilize a well thought out promotion mix. The promotion mix is a set of four communication tools available for an organization's use. These tools are advertising, publicity, personal selling, and sales promotions. Within these components are a wide variety of techniques and tools programmers can use in promoting their programs and services. To identify the most appropriate techniques for specific programs

and events, a programmer must consider a variety of factors. These factors are discussed in question format and include the following:

- What are the promotion objectives?

- Who is the target audience?

- What is the budget?

- What is the program?

- At what stage is the program within the product life cycle?

- What is the time frame?

- Where do the promotional efforts for this specific program fit within the overall promotion mix of the organization?

It is also important to remember to coordinate the individual activities with the overall promotion mix of the organization. This is accomplished by using the same questions listed above. Ultimately, it is important to pick the right mix of techniques within one's budget that promote individual programs and the organization as a whole. Ideally, the promotion mix for the organization will include some combination of all four components of promotion.

A servant leadership approach to promotion means seeing promotion as an investment rather than a wasteful activity. Servant leaders resist the tendency to overpromise in their promotional efforts. Other considerations for servant leaders include giving customers enough information to make informed decisions and using promotion as a tool for education.

Programming from Here to There

Block (2002) offers a radical example of putting servant leadership principles into practice in developing a marketing plan. His example cites a plan developed around a nonprofit community center that offers health and recreational services including a fitness facility, daycare center, and youth activities. Block challenges the underlying values and the core 'reason for being.' He asks,

> Is it in competition with other community centers in nearby towns? Is it in competition with private fitness centers and private daycare

centers? Most of its employees believe they are in competition and act accordingly. They think that their objective is to be the Number One community center in the region. Instead, why not decide that its mission is to support community everywhere, to support fitness wherever people choose to work out, to support daycare for all families who need it.

This would indicate that the center's real purpose is to act on a set of values about interdependence, civic engagement, family, health, and caring for the next generation. If we would take these values seriously, we would believe that we have a stake in the success of all community centers, fitness facilities, and daycare operations. We would create an alliance of those other organizations and work to improve them all. We would look at the strengths of each operation and have the best teach the rest. We would share operating information and perhaps have overlapping board memberships to support young or struggling centers.

The marketing strategy would be to get more people exercising, more kids cared for, more community involvement in the area. The community center I have in mind has 2,000 members. All the community centers, fitness centers and daycare facilities in the region have about 8,000 members. There are 75,000 people living in the region. Why not say that the marketing goal is to get another 10,000 people actively participating, regardless of where they go?

Now you might say that most organizations already belong to an association that promotes their interests. But most associations protect the boundaries of their individual members rather than overlap and expand their boundaries. Few competitors are committed to each other's success....The climate for this kind of thinking is increasingly receptive with the increase of alliances and partnerships, but the mindset of "This is my unit, my division, my organization" is still strong. (pp. 131–132)

Taking a servant leadership approach to all aspects of the organization demands having a broad view of what is good for our communities and working with other organizations to serve the common good. Staff of the community center presented above recognized the broader vision of encouraging people to be active and worked to best meet the needs of the entire community. Thus, for servant leaders, understanding the *why* of the organization must precede questions of *how*.

References

AdAge.com (2008). *Coen's spending totals for 2007.* Retrieved August 21, 2008, from http://www.adage.com/.

Ad Council. (2009). *About Ad Council.* Retrieved on February 22, 2009, from www.adcouncil.org/default.asp?id=68

Alexander, S. (2007, August 29). Text-message coupons may be a new line to discounts. *Star Tribune.* Retrieved January 9, 2010, from http://www.startribune.com/science/11619671.html

Altstiel, T. & Grow, J. (2006). *Advertising strategy: Creative tactics from the outside/in.* Thousand Oaks, CA: Sage Publications.

Beach, M. (1993). *Newsletter sourcebook.* Cincinnati, OH: North Lights Books.

Berkman, H. & Gilson, C. (1987). *Advertising concepts and strategies* (2nd ed.). New York, NY: Random House.

Block, P. (2002). *The answer to how is yes: Acting on what matters.* San Francisco, CA: Berrett-Koehler Publishers.

Carroll, A., Rivara, F., Ebel, B., Zimmerman, F., & Christakis, D. (2005). Household computer and internet access: The digital divide in a pediatric clinic population. *AMIA Annu Symp Proc.* 111–115.

Clark, S. (1993). *Taming the recreation jungle: 100 ways to improve the quality of recreation programs.* Seattle, WA: Book Partners.

Crompton, J. & Lamb, C. (1986). *Marketing government and social services.* New York, NY: John Wiley & Sons.

Deci, E. & Ryan, R. (2000). The "What" and "Why" of goal pursuits: Human needs and the self determination of behavior. *Psychological Inquiry, 11*(4), 227–268.

Deci, E. & Ryan, R. (1985). *Intrinsic motivation and self determination in human behavior.* New York, NY: HarperCollins.

Elliot, A. (2008). *Average U.S. home now receives a record 118.6 TV channels.* Nielsen Media Research.

Fern, D. (1985). A better mousetrap. *Inc., 7*(3).

Guion, L. & Kent, H. (2005). *Ethnic marketing: A strategy for marketing programs to diverse audience.* Florida Cooperative Extension Service, Institute of Food and Agricultural Sciences: University of Florida.

Jackson, E. (2005). *Constraints to leisure*. State College, PA: Venture Publishing, Inc.

Janes, P. (2006). *Marketing in leisure and tourism: Reaching new heights*. State College, PA: Venture Publishing, Inc.

Kerstetter, D. (1991, July). How to write effective copy for brochures and fliers. *Resort and Commercial Recreation Association*, 5.

Kotler, P. & Andreasen, A. (1996). *Strategic marketing for nonprofit organizations* (5th ed.). Englewood Cliffs, NJ: Prentice Hall.

Learning Resources Network. (1997, September). *The fundamentals: The ten best brochure/catalog ideas*. Manhattan, KS: Learning Resource Network.

Lukovitz, K. (2008). *Up to age 11, most kids aren't heavy Internet users*. New York: MediaPost Communications.

Pethokoukis, J. (2005, December 2). Small biz watch: Studies show effectiveness of word of mouth. *U.S. News and World Report*. Retrieved August 23, 2008, from http://www.usnews.com/usnews/biztech/articles/051202/2sbw.htm

Ries, A. & Ries, L. (2004). *The fall of advertising and the rise of PR*. New York, NY: Harper Business.

Rose, B. & Rosin, L. (2006). *The infinite dial 2006: Radio's digital platforms*. New York, NY: Arbitron.

Rosen, E. (2002). *The anatomy of buzz: How to create word-of-mouth marketing*. New York, NY: Doubleday.

Sass, E. (September 18, 2006). *Americans say they are listening to more radio, not less*. American Media Services.

Shepler, B. (2006). Relationships: Community, sponsorships, and stewardship. In Janes, P. *Marketing in Leisure and Tourism: Reaching New Heights* (pp. 303–324). State College, PA: Venture Publishing, Inc.

Schroeder, J. (2002). *Visual consumption*. London, UK: Routledge.

Stern, G. (1992). *Marketing workbook for nonprofit organizations*. St. Paul, MN: Amherst H. Wilder Foundation.

U.S. Census Bureau. (2006). *U.S. Census Bureau reports on ecommerce sales*. Washington DC: U.S. Census Bureau.

U.S. Census Bureau. (2001). *U.S. Census Bureau reports on computer, Internet access*. Washington DC: U.S. Census Bureau.

Yen, Y. (2008, March 25). YouTube looks for the money clip. Available from *CNNMoney.com*— http://techland.blogs.fortune.cnn.com/2008/03/25/youtube-looks-for-the-money-clip/

Ware, L. (2002). *Selling it: The incredible shrinking package and other marvels of modern marketing*. New York, NY: W.W. Norton & Company.

World Wide Web Consortium (W3C). (2003). *World Wide Web Consortium Web guidelines*. Retrieved December 27, 2003, from http://www.w3c.org/

Wright, K. (2000). *2000 survey of PSA Director results*. New York, NY: West Glen.

Programmer Profile

Photo provided by Mark Freidline

Mark Freidline

Current Position: Director of the Outdoor Pursuit Center at Miami University, Ohio
Favorite Book: *The Power of One* by Bryce Courtenay (1996)
Favorite Recreation Activities: Mountaineering and whitewater boating
Certifications: Wilderness First Responder (WMI), Top Rope Instructor (AMGA), Kayak Instructor (ACA), Swift Water Rescue (ACA), Lifeguard (ARC), Certified Outdoor Leader (WEA), Mountain-eering Skills Course (RMI), Level I Avalanche Course (AAI), Instructor Judgment Training Workshop (Outward Bound), Advanced Open Water Diver (PADI), Ropes Course Instructor (OWLS), and High Course Technical Training (CDI)

▶ **Describe the path your career has taken.**

- Graduated with a B.A. in Biology from the University of Northern Iowa and an M.S. in Recreation Administration from Aurora University.
- Since completing my undergraduate degree, I have held the following outdoor recreation positions:
    - Challenge Course Facilitator for Aurora University's Outdoor Wisconsin Leadership School (OWLS)
    - Outdoor Intern for Augustana College Campus Recreation
    - Adjunct Instructor for the University of Iowa Touch the Earth program
- I currently work as the Director of Miami University's (Ohio) Outdoor Pursuit Center. Miami University is a public institution with an enrollment of 16,300 students. The Outdoor Pursuit Center is committed to providing enjoyable, challenging, and affordable experiences that allow individuals and groups to learn the skills necessary to safely enjoy the outdoors. We hope that through these experiences, participants will develop an appreciation and a connection to the natural environment. Specifically my duties include:
    - Supervising the domestic and international trip program
    - Instructing academic backpacking, rock climbing, fly fishing, and outdoor leadership courses
    - Supervising the 2,600 sq. ft. indoor climbing wall
    - Supervising and facilitating low and high challenge course programs
    - Supervising rental equipment and retail operations

▶ **Describe the joys of working in my current position.**

Working with student employees, developing and leading international experiences, and helping students develop a passion for the outdoors.

▶ **Do you have any advice for new programmers?**

Programmers need to make it a priority to learn the financial policies and procedures used in their organization. Early on in my career, I organized a program that overlapped the organization's fiscal year. While the revenue for the program (approximately $70,000) came in before the end of the fiscal year, the majority of the expenses came in the beginning of the next fiscal year. This led to one extremely positive year and a negative net revenue the following year.

▶ **How do you enchance the anticipation phase of recreation programs?**

One of the primary goals of our international programs is to foster the development of intellectual curiosity. Assignments are designed to encourage students to question, challenge, and explore concepts and topics of interest. Students are asked to research topics and become "experts" on a particular area of the culture or environment where they will be traveling. The students are then asked to present their findings and thoughts to the other members of the group prior to the trip.

▶ **Describe a program example that demonstrates a servant leadership philosophy.**

Our outdoor program is a part of an overall collegiate curriculum; as a result for the last eight years, we have offered a 30-day study abroad course in outdoor leadership. During this course, students compare and contrast a variety of different leadership models and theories which include servant leadership. Later in the course, students have the opportunity to take over the leadership of the course for 3 to 5 day segments. Students are encouraged to incorporate leadership styles and decision-making processes that focus on building community and the growth of individuals, rather than personal recognition.

▶ **How are you able to balance social responsibility and social justice with customer-expressed desires?**

The Outdoor Pursuit Center uses international programming to introduce students to the concepts of social responsibility and social justice. In our study abroad program to Kenya, students spend several days living in a Maasai village and stay with families in manyattas (low, rounded houses built by spreading cow dung over a wood framework). Students have the opportunity to discuss social issues and concerns such as health care, education, poverty, nutrition, body modification, etc. Students then are challenged to educate others and/or address some of the challenges that Maasai living in that environment face.

Pricing Program Services | 9

For many of us, dealing with finances is considered a chore, something that we don't like to do but something that we know is necessary. Several years ago Block, (1996) noted

> money is vital to how we govern because it is the universal measuring device. It does not measure everything we care about, but it is the common language we use to measure the health of our institution, as well as our promises to each other and how well we have delivered on those promises. We have created the financial function to help become fully informed and communicate about performance. Financial functions also help people, through budgets, to document and keep track of their promises. These intentions are service-oriented and a critical means for people at all levels to fulfill their stewardship responsibility. (p. 135)

When people think about finances and funding in terms of stewardship they fulfill a major characteristic of servant leaders. The concept of stewardship helps programmers to see the bigger picture. Making sound financial decisions in terms of budgeting, funding, and pricing become key elements in fulfilling the mission of the organization. In particular, setting a price for a service has received considerable attention by all types of leisure services organizations. This attention includes involvement by public and nonprofit organizations that are being asked to do more with less, as well as commercial organizations that struggle with increased competition for the customer dollar. Two related challenges (especially for public and nonprofit administrators) are maintaining the balance between customer demand for programs and the organization's ability to deliver the programs while ensuring access to people of all income levels. One central element to meeting these challenges is understanding how to price programs and services in a fair and competitive manner. In this chapter we will

examine various pricing strategies and will help you understand the elements of program costs and other factors as they apply to developing pricing strategies for parks, recreation, and leisure services organizations. Figure 9.1 (p. 238) presents a nine-step process to help programmers set a price for programs and services. Inherent in this process is understanding how a servant leadership approach to programming will impact the process of establishing price points for programs and services.

Step One: Understand Trends

We live in a complex world that is constantly changing. In fact, change has become the one "constant" of our lives. This is especially true in the area of financing and pricing leisure services. The increased complexity of environments where leisure services are provided has placed greater demands on programmers to be responsive to fiscal operational concerns. In the following sections we discuss some trends that impact program-related fiscal and pricing decisions.

Decrease in Tax Support: Doing More with Less

Parks, recreation, and leisure services directors within public agencies commonly cite a lack of resources as one of the largest constraints at the local level, affecting everything from the provision of quality programs and services to the acquisition and development of land and facilities. Decreases in funding from tax revenues begun in the late 1970s, combined with cutbacks in federal grant-in-aid programs such as the Land and Water Conservation Fund, have created an environment where public parks, recreation and leisure services departments have been forced to do more with less. Crompton and Kaczynski (2003) noted that in the 1990s support for public parks, recreation and leisure programs rebounded with strong investment in capital

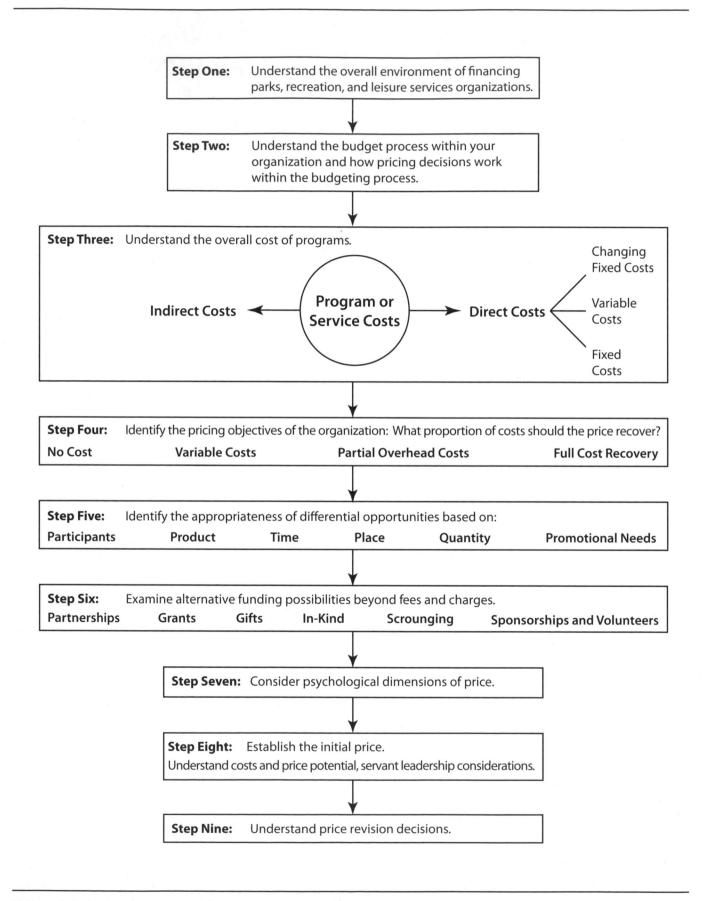

Figure 9.1 A nine-step process for setting a price (adapted from Crompton & Lamb, 1986)

projects and programs. Their analysis indicated the recession in the late 1970s and early 1980s had a devastating impact on overall budgets, but that as the economy improved in the late 1990s, so did tax supported budgets. Through the early 2000s, funding was relatively strong, however, when the recession hit in 2008, funding sources again became very difficult to access.

Today, public parks and recreation departments generate approximately 33% of their budgets through fees and charges. As we move forward in the 21st century, there is evidence that tax dollars will remain a large part of budgets and the state of the economy will continue to play a role in funding public parks and recreation (Kaczynski & Crompton, 2006). Like the government sector, nonprofit organizations are dealing with a tight funding environment. Less support from federal and state governments, as well as increased competition for limited grant funds and donors have all contributed to a difficult funding environment for nonprofits, including those providing recreation services (Hailman, 2003).

Although commercial organizations typically do not receive tax dollars, more and more of them are applying for government and private grants; thus, they must be concerned with the state of the economy and being efficient in their operations. It is clear that all types of organizations and agencies need to continue to seek out innovative funding sources to fulfill their missions. We discuss many of these additional funding sources later in this chapter.

Contracting Services

Over the last 25 years, contracting services with outside entities has become an important alternative for delivering recreation services within the public sector. For example, the U.S. Forest Service uses the private sector to manage a number of campsites throughout the system as well as to operate their online campground reservation system. In 2008, this contract with *Reserve America* was worth $97 million dollars (Mosquera, 2005). This type of arrangement continues a trend over the last fifteen years, during which time over 94,000 full- and part-time positions have been contracted out to the private sector (Crompton & Kaczynski, 2003).

Initially, contracting was seen as a way for public organizations to cut costs, but over the last few years all types of organizations have increasingly viewed contracting as a viable means of providing services. Consider the following examples of contract services: public parks and recreation departments contract out park maintenance to private landscape firms, the U.S. military contracts with nonprofit organizations to offer

summer camps for dependents of American military personnel, and corporations contract out special event planning (e.g., group picnics, golf outings, theme parties) to public parks, recreation, and leisure services departments. In each of these examples, decision makers viewed contracting to outside entities as a way to provide services effectively and efficiently. As leisure services agencies continue to operate in the 21st century, contracting services will continue to be a viable option in many situations (e.g., concessions and specialty services such as janitorial, maintenance, or security services).

It is important to note that some drawbacks to contracting out services do exist; these include a decrease in local control, loss of jobs, decreased accountability, and potential of increased fees. Thus, weighing the advantages and disadvantages of contracting out services in each specific case is important. A critical question related to the use of contracting in today's competitive environment asks what tasks should be contracted out, and what should be done "in house." Leisure services professionals also need to know how to make arrangements to ensure that contracting benefits all parties involved.

Expanded Definition of "Cost"

In 2007, former vice president Al Gore and the United Nations' Intergovernmental Panel on Climate Change won the Nobel Peace Prize. Gore received this award in part for his involvement with the film, "An Inconvenient Truth," which won two Oscars. In accepting the award, Gore said "it [climate change] is the most dangerous challenge we've ever faced, but it is also the greatest opportunity we have had to make changes" (MSNBC, 2007). This effort and thousands like it around the world have brought a new wave of awareness and public support for addressing the environmental issues of the day. This support for the environment continues as individuals use the "power of the pocketbook" to direct companies to develop products and services that are "green." One outgrowth of this commitment has been an expanded definition of *cost*. Environmental costs, as well as other social costs, are now being viewed as part of the overall costs of providing programs.

In the future, stronger considerations will be given to understanding the economic, environmental, and social costs connected to the program process. For example, an organization may identify a demand for a mountain biking program in a nearby natural area. The program may be economically feasible, yet the organization may decide against providing the program due to the environmental costs connected with the program. An additional example may find the economic costs of offering a program (e.g., an educational program for teen parents) to be so high that the program is not feasible. The lack of this program, however, may produce a higher social cost than is acceptable (e.g., increased child neglect, community crimes); therefore, the organization may decide to offer the program in spite of the costs.

Yet another social cost of offering programs is ensuring that programs and services are fully accessible, particularly to those with disabilities. For instance, a deaf person may require an interpreter to fully access a program; a person with cerebral palsy might require an aide who accompanies her or him to a program. The Americans with Disabilities Act makes it clear that we cannot add these costs to the price of receiving programs or services to the individual who needs that service—the cost must be considered part of the cost of doing business, and must be shared among all participants (Skulski, 2009). This type of cost sharing also holds true with efforts to address the access needs for those with mobility and other types of impairments (e.g., door threshold ramps).

A challenge programmers and program supervisors face is articulating to others the true cost of implementing a program. This is in part because whereas economic costs are often relatively easy to calculate, calculating the social or environmental costs of a specific program can be difficult. Despite this difficulty, parks, recreation, and leisure services professionals will be increasingly called upon to make complex decisions regarding what programs to offer in what locations. At the same time, with society recognizing the true environmental costs of our current lifestyles, many opportunities exist for expanding recreation programs and services as well as partnerships with other public services. For example, recognizing the health costs of our sedentary lifestyles as well as the rising costs of gasoline provides opportunities to expand bicycle programs and related infrastructure (e.g., bike lanes, bike trails) to reduce the environmental impact of our actions while also promoting more active, healthy lifestyles.

Risk Management

In addition to environmental and social costs, programmers should always be prepared for the cost of a potential lawsuit. Highway billboards, yellow pages, and newspaper ads encourage and entice people to file lawsuits to recover costs from injury or property loss. The fear of being sued is an ever-present part of doing business in the United States. Costs associated with a litigious society are passed on to the customer in a variety of ways; these costs are sometimes referred to as a "lawsuit tax" and are built into the price people pay for goods and services. These costs are established to cover the expenses that manufacturers and retailers incur when they pay liability insurance. In 2006, it was estimated that each U.S. citizen paid $886 per year to cover her or his share of lawsuit costs, totaling $3,544 for a family of four (Kotner, 2006). Parks, recreation, and leisure services agencies are not exempt from these costs. Thus, an increasing cost of providing recreation programs is protecting the organization from lawsuits. Finding creative ways to offer safe programs while maintaining some elements of risk, an important aspect of leisure experiences for many people, will continue to be important.

Projecting Economic Impact

Due to increased competition over financial resources for public and nonprofit organizations, leisure professionals have seen a move to using economic impact studies to obtain and maintain additional financial support. Public and nonprofit organizations are collecting data on the positive economic impacts of events and facilities. Economic impacts include: direct impacts (i.e., the amount of money participants or visitors spend on local goods and services); indirect impacts (i.e., ripple effects of re-circulating participant/visitor spending throughout the community); and induced impact (i.e., the proportion of household income that is spent locally on goods and services). An example of how recreation programs and facilities can contribute to a community's economic well-being is by attracting new residents to a community, such as retirees. According to Crompton

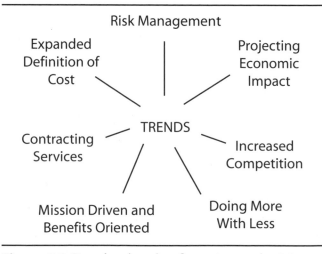

Figure 9.2 Trends related to financing and pricing

(2008), a growth industry in the U.S. is the increasing number of relatively affluent, active retirees. "Their decisions as to where to locate with their substantial retirement incomes is primarily governed by two factors: climate and recreational activities" (p. 195).

Increased Competition

In a market economy such as in the United States, theoretically, competition is good for the consumer. This is because increased competition can keep prices low and quality high. In addition, increased competition can be good for an agency or organization. Competition among parks, recreation, and leisure services organizations can increase the overall size of the market as well as keep staff focused on meeting the needs of the customer. As competition between parks, recreation, and leisure services organizations increases, programmers need to examine the implications on pricing leisure experiences. This might entail looking for ways to cooperate with competitors (Godbey, 1997). As Godbey noted

> …There are more win-win situations than win-lose situations in the provision of leisure services…. The numbers of consortiums [and partnerships] which can be developed in leisure services is almost infinite. What is important is imagination, communication, and the will to do it. (p. 218)

Mission Driven and Benefits Oriented

Previously in this text, we articulated the importance of vision and mission for all organizations. This importance can be seen in motivating employees, designing programs, and evaluating the effectiveness of the overall services of an organization. This mission driven approach has led many organizations to focus on the benefits they provide through programming. For public organizations this means the development of a new paradigm where government is perceived as flexible and adaptable, responsive to customers, offers choices of services, and empowers citizens. This approach will be reflected throughout an organization, including its budget. The budget will be used to align resources with the mission of the organization over time. In so doing, the budget process will become focused on the benefits and values programs offer to customers. Thus, the organizational budget will tell the story of the organization and what it is trying to accomplish.

Step Two: Understand Budgets

Budgets are found in all types of organizations and at every level of the organization. Budgets may be viewed as "a financial plan that translates the operational and strategic plan of the organization into achievable activities over a specific period—usually a year" (Brayley & McLean, 1999, p. 135). Budgets serve several functions, some of which include:

1. a means of planning and forecasting;

2. a mechanism to establish and communicate program priorities;

3. a method to allocate resources;

4. an opportunity to build organizational consensus;

5. a historical record of past priorities;

6. a means to commit the organization to a course of action;

7. a reference point to monitor and control expenditures of fiscal resources, including program control as well as audit control (by outside agencies);

8. a monitoring system; and/or

9. a process to translate the programs to reality. (Zietlow, Hankin, & Seidner, 2007)

As may be seen from this list, budgets are used in different ways. Further, a great deal of variety exists in how budgets are developed and in the types of budgets used. Figure 9.3 (see p. 242) presents descriptions of a few budget types used in parks, recreation, and leisure services organizations. In this text we do not attempt to provide an exhaustive presentation of budgeting processes. At this point, we believe that it is enough to recognize the importance of budgeting and to encourage programmers to understand how pricing programs impacts the overall budget process of an organization.

Lump Sum Budgeting

Lump sum budgeting was used primarily before 1900, and was practiced in most cities and states. For each of the departments in a city or state, a lump sum of money was appropriated and no attempt was made to analyze how the money was to be spent. This gave departments freedom to use the money in any way they deemed necessary (Deppe, 1983).

Line-Item Budget

The line-item budget is a common form of budgeting in government bodies. The line-item budget appropriates specific dollar amounts to each item of expenditure listed in the budget. It lists these expenses line-by-line as they are paid out. The agency is limited to spending only the dollar amount printed on the line across from each item. Rather than listing the items of expenditure at random, the line-item budget organizes expenditures into specific categories or accounts. Line-item budgets allow for adjustments with minimal difficulty but require detailed planning and preparation; some accuracy is lost as expenditures are collapsed into lines (Brayley & McLean, 1999).

Program Budget

Program budgets present expenditures in the form of specific programs; essentially think of having sub-unit budgets, one for each program. This helps to direct one's attention to individual programs instead of the overall organization. From a control and coordination perspective, program budgeting links spending directly to planned activity levels of the services and products. Program budgets focus on values of programs rather than just costs, and offer limited budget cost detail as expenditures are collapsed together (Brayley & McLean, 1999; Zietlow, Hankin, & Seidner, 2007).

Performance Budget

Performance budgets link the amount of resources that are consumed in producing a program or service with its outputs. Actual outputs can be measured by a variety of performance indicators including workload measures, efficiency measures, and effectiveness measures. Workload measures refer to the volume of work being completed. Efficiency measures refer to how well resources of an organization are used. Effectiveness measures refer to the extent to which a program achieves its stated goals (Edginton, Hanson, Edginton & Hudson, 2004).

Planning, Programming, Budgeting System (PPBS)

This approach is similar to management by objectives used by many organizations. The PPBS budget process is a performance-based budget that focuses on the establishment of goals and objectives, long-range planning, and evaluation. Within this budget system programmers are required to identify system-wide goals and objectives and relate programs and services to these goals. PPBS also requires programmers to think about costs and the scope of programs over a five-year period, as well as examine alternative options to determine which programs and services best meet the goals and objectives of the organization (Deppe, 1983). PPBS provides a method to focus on service goals and offers a means for comparative analysis of programs and services; yet, it is often difficult to determine the importance of needs and value of each program and thus difficult to make comparisons across the entire organization (Brayley & McLean, 1999; Zietlow, Hankin, & Seidner, 2007).

Zero-Based Budget

Budgets, whether line item or program or performance, are usually arrived at by changing the past year's budget slightly, perhaps based on new economic assumptions or noted actual versus budget variances from the prior year. Under a zero-based budget system a comprehensive evaluation and justification of all programs is carried out each year. Each department is asked to build its budget from zero each year, justifying every dollar expenditure to guide current appropriations. Key components include: identifying objectives, determining the value of accomplishing each activity or program, evaluating different funding levels; establishing priorities, and evaluating workload and performance measures. Although this approach is hard work, Zietlow, Hankin and Seidner (2007) recommend it every 5 to 10 years because of how it forces a disciplined look at the expenses of an organization.

Rolling Budget

Rolling budgets involve recreating the budget within a budget year and projecting out at least the following 12 months. This keeps the organization's focus on a full year ahead. Rolling budgets take advantage of advances in information technology that allow for ongoing monitoring of expenses and outputs. Implementing rolling budgets does not necessarily require any fundamental change in the way an agency engages in the budgeting process (Zietlow, Hankin, & Seidner, 2007).

Figure 9.3 Types of budgets

Indirect Costs	+	Direct Fixed Costs	+	Direct Variable Costs	=	TOTAL COST
Administrative salaries		Instructor salaries		Supplies		
Office equipment		Facility rent		Equipment rental		
Organization promotion		Program promotion				

Figure 9.4 Total cost of a program

Step Three: Calculate the Overall Costs/Understand the Price Potential

Prior to making any pricing decisions, it is important to gather effective program cost information. A cost may be seen as a monetary measurement of the amount of resources needed to create, implement, and evaluate programs (see Figure 9.4). Knowing and understanding all aspects of these costs enables programmers to make informed decisions about the overall mix of programs offered by a specific organization. It also serves as a starting point for making pricing decisions. Before establishing the overall costs of a specific program, an organization must determine which costs are to be included. To accomplish this task, programmers must first understand two types of costs—indirect and direct. This will help to accurately classify and allocate specific costs to the overall cost of an individual program.

Indirect Costs

Indirect costs are those costs that an organization incurs regardless of whether or not it operates a specific program. For example, computers and other office equipment, administrative salaries, organization-wide promotion, and custodial services are indirect costs for all programs and services. The organization will have these expenses whether or not it operates any one specific program or service. Nevertheless, these costs are typically attributed to specific programs. The difficulty arises in determining how to allocate these types of costs to specific programs.

Figure 9.5 presents several types of cost allocation methods available to programmers. In this process, programmers are faced with a number of decisions about how costs can or should be allocated. Rossman and Schlatter (2008) offer three principles to guide these decisions.

1. Implementing cost allocation should be an attempt to assign indirect costs to specific programs in a fair and equitable manner. The goal of cost allocation is to reflect the full cost of creating, implementing, and evaluating a program.

2. The chosen method of cost allocation should accurately reflect how much of an indirect cost a specific program actually uses or consumes. Obviously, this is a difficult task and is sometimes based on an educated guess. In this instance, organizations have some discretion in allocating indirect costs. It should be remembered, however, that all indirect costs must be accounted for at some point. It pays for the organization to be as accurate as possible in this process.

3. In any cost allocation method there is a trade-off between accuracy and cost. Programmers need to try to achieve as much accuracy as possible within the limits of reasonable effort.

Direct Costs

Direct costs are those that may be traced directly to a specific program. Whereas indirect costs are incurred regardless of whether or not a program is offered, direct costs are incurred only when a program is implemented. For example, hiring an aerobics instructor to

---

Equal Share of Indirect Expenses
In this method, each functional line or program unit is charged with an equal share of indirect expenses. With this method, no effort is made to base the indirect costs to be assumed by a unit on actual costs used by the unit.

Percentage of Budget
In this method, each line unit is assigned a percentage of indirect expenses that equals its percentage of the overall budget of the organization.

Time Budget Study
With this method, the time a service unit (i.e., general administration) spends on each line item or program is studied. The percentage of time is then used to allocate indirect expenses of the service unit to line or program units. The actual allocation of expenses is similar to the percentage of budget method, except that more accurate data are being used to develop the percentage figures for allocating indirect expenses.

Space or Measurement Studies
This method of cost allocation is used in instances where one can determine the appropriate proportion of expenses to allocate to a specific line item or program by measuring the relative proportion of overall costs that are being used by each line item or program. This method is useful in situations where one can accurately determine the proportion of costs to be allocated. Allocating expenses connected to a fertilizing program in parks, or maintenance expenses for a building are examples where this method works well.

Figure 9.5 Cost allocation methods (Rossman & Schlatter, 2008)

teach a class may be seen as a direct cost of offering an aerobics program. Therefore, this cost may be allocated directly to this program. Direct costs include both fixed and variable costs of a program.

Fixed Costs

For our purposes, a fixed-cost item is assumed to remain constant during a specified time period (in a program), regardless of the number of participants. An example of a fixed cost would be rental of a facility for the aerobics class mentioned previously. This cost would be directly related to the program. It would also remain constant regardless of the number of participants in the program. Whether 1 or 25 people participate, the rental fee would be the same. It is thus considered a fixed cost. Programmers should bear in mind that fixed costs do have their limits. Consider the room where the aerobics class is being offered; it is small and thereby limits the number of participants to 25. Rossman and Schlatter (2008) describe these types of limitations as setting the relevant range for the program (i.e., for the aerobics class the relevant range would be 1 to 25 participants). All fixed costs, then, are fixed within this specified relevant range.

Connected to the idea of fixed costs in specified relevant ranges is the idea of *changing fixed costs*. Rossman and Schlatter (2008) identify changing fixed costs as those costs that "change in the same direction, but not proportionately with change in volume or number of participants" (p. 347). These costs change within the relevant range of the program. In other words, they are costs that change after certain numbers of participants are added within the relevant range. For example, within the aerobics class an instructor would be hired to teach the class. This cost would be a direct fixed cost allocated to the program. However, let's say that the instructor would require one assistant to help with the program if the program enrollment exceeded fifteen participants. Therefore, within the relevant range of the program, the instructional cost would change after the fifteenth participant as it would be necessary to add an assistant when the sixteenth person was added to the class. From the 16th to the 25th participant, the agency would have the additional cost of an assistant aerobic instructor. In this case, the cost of the assistant's salary would be a changing fixed cost.

Another example of a changing fixed cost is the additional costs of making programs and services fully accessible—particularly to those with disabilities. For instance, a deaf person may require an interpreter to fully access a program or a person with cerebral palsy might require an aide who accompanies her or him to a program. The Americans with Disabilities Act makes it clear that we cannot add these costs to the price of receiving programs or services to the individual who needs that service—the cost must be considered part of the costs of doing business, and must be shared among all participants. This holds true for programmatic as well as physical accessibility related costs (e.g., hearing amplifier systems, door threshold ramps).

Variable Costs

Variable costs are those costs that may be directly attributed to a program and vary proportionately with changes in volume (i.e., number of participants). They include such costs as supplies, equipment, and food. For example, within the aerobics class each participant who enrolls in the class is given a fitness manual. If the manual costs $4, then for each participant who enrolls in the program, an additional cost of $4 is added to the program. Some programs have a number of variable costs. For instance, each additional camper

---

Efficient Use of Financial Resources
Pricing allows organizations to make efficient use of financial resources by assisting organizations in recovering costs and making a profit. Depending on the pricing philosophy of the organization, prices can be set to maximize profits or recover all or part of the costs connected with a program.

Fairness or Equitableness
Pricing can be used by public and nonprofit organizations to promote equity. For example, municipal governments can charge higher prices for private goods in order to subsidize both merit and public goods. Likewise, state parks can charge nonresidents more than residents to acknowledge the support provided by residents through tax dollars.

Usage Maximization
Prices can be set low to encourage participation. This approach can be used to promote new programs or to expose participants to alternative programs and services provided by the organization.

Commercial Sector Encouragement
For public organizations, pricing can be used to encourage or discourage the commercial sector. By identifying prices based on the competition, public organizations can encourage potential customers to examine all options for programs and services.

Market Disincentivism
Prices can be used to reduce demand for specific programs and services by increasing program cost. This approach to pricing can be used to reduce overcrowding or to protect a fragile resource (e.g., environmentally sensitive area).

Figure 9.6 Pricing objectives

who enrolls in a day-camp program may add the following variable costs: a T-shirt, camp bag, lunches and snacks, arts-and-craft supplies, and field trip admissions. Other programs such as our aerobics class have few variable costs.

Step Four: Determine the Cost Recovery

Once programmers know the cost of delivering a service they can begin to decide what proportion of the cost a price should recover. It is a fairly common situation where all program costs are *not* covered in an established price. For instance, the $2 fee commonly charged for swimming pool entry does not cover the real per-person costs of operating the pool. The program is said to be subsidized when some or all of its costs are covered by other means.

Establishing a price is an opportunity for an organization to meet its pricing objectives. Pricing objectives may differ by program or by organization and should be reflected in the organizational philosophy. Further, pricing is a means of accruing revenue, and leads to a number of other outcomes. For example, public and nonprofit organizations may charge particular prices that may lead to:

- income redistribution (to other programs or services);

- the promotion of efficient use of resources within the organization;

- the promotion of equity (ensuring that those who benefit from a service bear the cost of that service);

- maximal opportunities for participation by a wide variety of constituents;

- the development of positive constituent attitudes; and

- the production of revenue. (Howard & Crompton, 1980; see Figure 9.6)

In the mid 1980s, Crompton and Lamb (1986) identified three categories of services provided by public and nonprofit organizations—private, merit, and public. *Private services* primarily benefit those who use the service. *Merit services* are those that have tremendous societal good (i.e., the benefits are meritorious in and of themselves). Lastly, *public services* are those that benefit the local community where the services are offered. Based on which category of service we promote, different decisions about pricing are made (see Figure 9.7). Figure 9.8 (pp. 246-247) presents one example of how Portland Parks and Recreation Programs uses these categories of service to make cost recovery decisions. An explanation of the continuum of possible positions for cost recovery connected to these categories follows.

No Cost Recovery

All programs and services have costs associated with them. Thus, when programs and services are provided free of charge to participants, alternative sources of funding (e.g., grants, sponsorships) are required to offer the program.

Characteristic:	PUBLIC SERVICE	MERIT SERVICE	PRIVATE SERVICE
Who benefits?	Everyone in the community	Individuals who participate and all others in the community	Individuals who participate
Economic desirability or technical feasibility of pricing	*Not Feasible* Services cannot be priced and/or it is undesirable that they should be priced	*Feasible and Desirable* Services can be priced	*Feasible and Desirable* Services can be priced
Who pays?	*The Community* through the tax system— no user charges	*Individual Users* pay partial costs	*Individual Users* pay full costs
Example	Municipal parks	Youth sports programs	Renting a facility for a private party

Figure 9.7 Differences between services according to type of service (adapted from Crompton & Lamb, 1987)

COST RECOVERY POLICY FOR CITY PARKS AND RECREATION PROGRAMS
Non-Binding City Policy, NCP-PRK-3.06

PURPOSE

WHEREAS, a healthy parks and recreation system makes Portland a better place to live, work, and play; and

WHEREAS, the mission of Portland Parks & Recreation is to ensure access to leisure opportunities and enhance Portland's natural beauty; and

WHEREAS, an objective of Vision 2020 is to provide a wide variety of high quality park and recreation services and opportunities for all residents; and

WHEREAS, when organizing recreational opportunities for the public, Portland Parks & Recreation offers activities that promote positive community values such as:

Lifelong learning;
Health and a sense of well being;
A sense of community;
Respect for the natural environment; and

WHEREAS, Portland's citizens have made a significant investment in parks and recreation facilities so that all citizens can have access to a broad range of positive leisure activities, and all Portland citizens benefit when the community has recreation sites that are clean, safe, and accessible to all; and

WHEREAS, Portland Parks & Recreation is obliged to protect these investments through sustainable operations and maintenance practices; and

WHEREAS, participation in positive recreation activities brings personal benefits to the individual participants such as an increased a sense of well being, life long learning, and enjoyment; and

WHEREAS, public recreation programs also bring benefits to the entire community such as increased community involvement and cooperation, a more attractive location for businesses and employees, better educated and more responsible youth, improved public safety and health, stronger and more cohesive neighborhoods, and greater respect for the environment; and

WHEREAS, broad participation in public recreation programs by a diversity of citizens from all segments of Portland increases both personal and public benefits; and

WHEREAS, the public interest is furthered in ensuring access to public recreation for groups experiencing barriers to participation; and

WHEREAS, with multiple benefits accruing to both personal and public interests, it is appropriate for public recreation programs to be supported by a blend of participant fees and taxpayer funding; and

WHEREAS, the annual City budget determines the amount of taxpayer support that is available for organized public recreation opportunities; and

WHEREAS, charging fees for participation is a way to increase the availability of those programs by supplementing taxpayer resources; and

WHEREAS, charging fees creates the responsibility to balance the availability of recreation programs with their affordability; and

WHEREAS, recreation programs exist in a voluntary market place where customers have complete choice about whether to participate, and where consumer choices are sensitive to the prices charged and the selection of offerings; and

WHEREAS, Portland Parks & Recreation has prepared a cost of service study that identifies current cost recovery levels for the various types of recreation programs;

POLICY

NOW, THEREFORE, BE IT RESOLVED by the City Council of the City of Portland that the cost of service study presented by Portland Parks & Recreation be accepted; and

BE IT FURTHER RESOLVED that the following cost recovery policy guide Portland Parks & Recreation's efforts to organize and set prices for recreation programs;

1) Public Interest – The public has an interest in the availability of a broad range of organized recreation opportunities that encourage good health, lifelong learning, respect for the environment, and a sense of community.

2) Balance of benefits – Benefits of participation in public recreation accrue to both the participant and to the public and, therefore, it is appropriate that recreation be funded by a balance of participant fees and public resources.

3) Focus of cost recovery goals – The mission and goals for public recreation activities and programs apply to all citizens of Portland and interests in particular activities are determined by individual participants. The public interest lies in encouraging participation and reducing barriers to access of public recreation. Hence cost of service analysis and cost recovery goals are expressed in broad demographic groups for which there is particular public interest or for whom there exist significant barriers to participation. These groups are identified as follows:

a) Youth: in order to invest in the future of our community.

b) Adults: in order to increase the diversity of community participation in public recreation.

c) Low income citizens: in order to ensure access and mitigate financial barriers to participation.

d) Disabled citizens and seniors: in order to improve opportunities for inclusion and participation.

e) New immigrants: in order to increase awareness of, and improve access to, recreation programs.

Figure 9.8 Portland Cost Recovery Plan

Continued>>

4) Cost recovery goals – Cost recovery goals express a balance of public and personal benefits defined in terms of the broad demographic groups identified as follows:

    a) Youth: Pricing for youth programs offered outside of low income neighborhoods should be set to recover 42% of total costs.

    b) Adults: Pricing for adult programs offered outside of low income neighborhoods should be set to recover 63% of total costs.

    c) Low income citizens:

        i) Youth: Pricing of youth programs in low income neighborhoods should be set to recover 23% of total costs.

        ii) Adults: Pricing of adult programs in low income neighborhoods should be set to recovery 26% of total costs.

5) Targeted recreation programs – Portland Parks & Recreation will provide recreation programs targeted to the special needs of disabled citizens, seniors, and new immigrant populations. The disabled citizens recreation, senior recreation, and outreach programs for new immigrant populations will have lower cost recovery rates than general recreation programs because of the fixed costs of organizing these programs. However, to the degree that disabled citizens, seniors, and new immigrants participate in general recreation programs, they are subject to the same prices as the general population, including pricing as appropriate for youth or low income citizens. Exceptions are for multiuse passes, golf, Pittock Mansion, and Crystal Springs Rhododendron Garden, where the bureau may continue the existing tradition of offering separate senior rates.

6) Pricing – Prices are to be set by recreation staff under the authority of the Director of Portland Parks & Recreation. In setting prices, the bureau will balance the goals of program availability and affordability within the constraints of budget allocations, market economics, and cost recovery goals approved herein.

7) Financial assistance – In addition to pricing which reflects cost recovery goals for low income neighborhoods and youth programs, Portland Parks & Recreation will seek to ensure affordability of recreation activities through scholarships, certain free youth activities, time-limited price promotions, and by cultivating volunteers and partnerships. Certain youth activities should be free and regularly available at community centers and SUN Community Schools as appropriate to ensure accessibility and participation as determined by Portland Parks & Recreation.

8) Cross-subsidization – Cost recovery goals, as determined by this policy, are intended to be averages across the recreation programs. Over- or under-realization of these cost recovery goals by any particular site or activity is acceptable in order that programming and pricing fit the realities of the marketplace and particular neighborhoods while maximizing participation, making efficient use of facility capacity, and maintaining a broad array of recreation offerings.

9) Activities requiring permits – A permit is required for certain activities in Portland parks. When permits for picnics or weddings result in exclusive use of an area, pricing should be set to achieve 100% recovery of total costs. When the purpose of a permit is to reserve a limited area for a limited time, such as a small group picnic, then prices should be set to recovery 100% of the direct costs incurred by the bureau.

10) Rental of facilities – Various facilities are available for use by groups and private parties. Pricing should be set to recover 100% of direct costs for rentals during normally open hours. For events during normally closed hours, prices should be set to recover all incremental costs incurred by the bureau, including staff, maintenance, and utilities. However, recognized friends of parks groups and City of Portland neighborhood associations may have reasonable use of facilities free of charge during normally open hours.

11) Waivers of Fees and Charges – Waiving or reducing certain fees and charges for recreation activities, permits, and rentals is within the public interest in order reduce barriers to participation, or optimize utilization and revenue generation of existing facilities.

The bureau shall establish an appropriation during the annual budget process to offset revenues lost by waiving fees and charges. Total fees and charges waived annually shall be constrained within this appropriation. The bureau may request budget adjustments during the fiscal year.

12) Updating of goals – Information about cost recovery levels should be updated annually, and cost recovery goals should be reviewed and updated at least once every two years.

Whenever the Council approves a cost recovery goal that is higher than the current level of recovery prices should be raised incrementally over time in the affected program categories in accord with market acceptance in order to optimize revenue generation in balance with program availability and participation. Whenever the Council approves a cost recovery goal that is less than the current level of recovery the bureau shall present a budget decision package during the subsequent annual budget process identifying the additional amount of General Fund discretionary resources necessary to achieve the goal and provide options for program changes or reductions in lieu of additional resources.

13) Compliance with budget – Notwithstanding the policy goals for cost recovery described above, the bureau's first responsibility in organizing and pricing recreation programs is to operate within the budget set by City Council. Cost recovery goals are guidelines for program design and pricing, subsidiary to budgetary allocations and economic realities. Furthermore, cost recovery goals are subsidiary to the bureau's responsibilities for parks system development and maintenance requirements.

14) Recreation enterprises – Golf and the Portland International Raceway continue as enterprise operations and should continue to recover 100% of their full costs.

15) Interagency services – Services provided to other bureaus or governmental agencies should recover 100% of their full costs, consistent with the City's Comprehensive Financial Management Policy.

BE IT FURTHER RESOLVED this resolution is non-binding city policy.

HISTORY
Resolution No. 36257 adopted by Council September 29, 2004.

Figure 9.8 Portland Cost Recovery Plan (continued from previous page)

Variable Cost Recovery

Programs and services are priced to cover the variable costs associated with the program. In this context, variable costs are direct operating and maintenance expenses, which can be easily documented and allocated to specific programs. Within this option indirect costs and direct fixed costs are covered by other funding options. Many programmers take this position for programs, services, and facilities where both participants and nonusers benefit from a program. For example, facilities and amenities offered by public and nonprofit agencies add to the quality of life of a community. As a result, nonusers receive benefits from the existence of facilities, and nonusers should therefore pay the indirect fixed costs required to make these programs, services, and facilities available.

Partial Cost Recovery

Programs and services are priced to cover variable costs plus some proportion of fixed costs. The remaining portion of the fixed costs represents the subsidy given to the particular program by other funding sources. The amount of subsidy is dependent upon the extent to which nonusers benefit from a participant's involvement in a specific program or service. As the benefits to nonusers increase, the proportion of fixed costs met by the subsidy should increase. Benefits to nonusers could include such things as increased property values and decreased crime.

Full Cost Recovery

In this case, programs and services are priced to produce sufficient revenue to cover all the fixed and variable costs associated with the service or program, as well as help the organization meet all of its indirect costs. Full cost recovery is an appropriate strategy for those programs and services that benefit only participants and offer few external benefits to the general community. Some difficulties are connected with full cost recovery. As previously noted, it can be difficult to allocate all the indirect costs of an organization. In addition, it is sometimes difficult to identify the number of participants who will be involved in a program; this has implications for the total possible revenue generated by a program.

◆◆◆

Revenue production is the primary objective of pricing for many recreation providers, yet pricing strategies may also be used in other ways. For example, some programs might be underpriced in an attempt to familiarize customers with a new program or facility. In addition, some prices might be subsidized (e.g., childcare) to encourage participation in other programs the organization offers. Further, recreation providers have some flexibility in determining pricing as different strategies generally are applied to specific programs to meet the desired objectives of the organization.

Step Five: Consider Differential Pricing

When leisure professionals look at the appropriateness of differential pricing they are essentially considering charging different prices to different groups for the same service, even though there is no real difference in the costs of providing the service to each of the groups. There are many potential reasons for considering differential pricing, such as reaching underserved participants or to stimulate demand for service during specific times. We offer six potential criteria to be considered when implementing differential pricing: participants, product, place, time, quantity of use, and incentives.

Price Differentials Based on Participants

Participant price differentials are based on the perception that some groups may find it difficult to pay a recommended price while others can pay more. Four groups are frequently identified as less able to pay than most: children, those with severe disabilities, senior citizens, and the economically disadvantaged. Despite the designation of these groups, Havitz, Morden, and Samdahl (2004) have noted a disparity in how these groups are served by public parks, recreation, and leisure services. For example, fewer than 20 percent of agencies charging fees commonly offer discounts for unemployed participants as compared with more than 75% that offer discounts for children and senior citizens. Commercial recreation organizations often offer differential pricing based on age (e.g., child or senior discount) or the size of the group, rather than financial ability. Discounts based on age this can be contradictory because many seniors have more discretionary income than other social groups.

Havitz, Morden, and Samdahl (2004) highlighted this issue in a recent study noting the difficulties in providing price differentials for the economically disadvantaged. Consider the difference between an unemployed 40-year-old and a retired 62-year-old seeking fee assistance at a public recreation facility. "The unemployed adult must complete an entire set of paperwork to document financial need. In contrast, the retiree need only produce a valid photo ID to gain a significant price discount…these subsidies are available regardless of whether the participant is a fixed income pensioner, a financially secure full professor, or a wealthy corporate CEO" (p. 181). To be fair to various constituent groups, organizations will want to look for creative and equitable ways to use price differentials.

While not always based on economic realities, participant price differentials are one way to address the concern about equal access to programs and services. Organizations can charge fees based on costs while considering special needs, rather than charge artificially low fees overall. One technique is to offer discount tickets that may be provided to any disadvantaged group. Vouchers are often given to low-income families for program access, and many organizations offer a sliding fee scale, which is applied based on income levels.

Price Differentials Based on Product

Product price differentials are based on offering extra levels of service for additional charges. For example, many fitness organizations have a basic membership fee and, for an additional charge, members may join an executive club. The basic service provided is the same for all—the use of fitness facilities. However, executive club members receive extra benefits such as a complementary laundering of workout clothes, as well as access to a whirlpool, sauna, and a more plush locker room. The prices of these additional services are sometimes set to cover the incremental cost of providing them, and other times prices are set to cover the incremental costs and help subsidize other aspects of the program.

Price Differentials Based on Place

Price differentials based on place are often found at spectator events (e.g., concert, theater, sports event) where a higher price is charged for better seats (e.g., closer to the performance). Another example of price differentials may be seen in public organizations charging higher prices for nonresidents and nonprofit organizations charging higher prices for nonmembers. In both of these examples, if a service or program is being used to capacity, a price differential based on place may serve as an effective method to discourage use by nonresidents or nonmembers.

Within nonprofit organizations, if the service or program has spare capacity, price differentials may be used to encourage individuals to become members. In commercial ventures, individuals who live at a distance may be offered a price break to lure them to the organization. Many destination resort entities use this tactic—particularly during the slow season.

Price Differentials Based on Time

With differential prices set on a time basis, identical programs are offered at different times and priced differently. Typically, programs and services offered during periods of lower demand are priced lower than programs offered during peak hours. For example, bowling centers commonly offer reduced prices on bowling during weekday afternoons, usually nonpeak time. Likewise, movie theaters offer matinee prices to encourage participation during "slow" times. Thus, differential prices set on a time basis encourage fuller and more balanced utilization of the program capacity.

Price Differentials Based on Quantity

Price differential based on quantity reflects the lower costs of buying in bulk. The season or multiuse discount pass for such programs and facilities as swimming pools, fitness centers, golf courses, zoos, amusement parks, and museums are all examples of price differentials based on quantity. The purpose of price differentials based on quantity is twofold. First, it tends to stimulate additional demand for a program or service. Second, quantity price differentials reduce the costs of meeting levels of demand by helping organizations forecast the number of participants for specific programs and services.

Price Differentials as Incentives

Price discounts may be used as incentives to persuade people to try a new service or program. Incentives such as coupons (see Figure 9.9 on p. 250) and discounts are effective in encouraging participation (especially for new users/constituents). It is important, however, that programmers emphasize to customers that such discounts are for a limited duration or restricted to a particular set of circumstances, and that after a given time or change in circumstances, the regular price will be charged. Without this caveat, new participants may feel cheated when the price increases.

Step Six: Examine Alternative Funding

As discussed in step one, leisure services professionals have seen a decrease in tax support across the United States, and public and nonprofit programmers are being asked to do more with less through self-generated revenue. Crompton and McGregor (1994) substantiated

Figure 9.9 An example of a discount coupon

this trend reporting that self-generated revenue increased from 14 percent of the total local public expenditures on parks and recreation in 1964 to 21.4 percent in 1990–1991. This trend continues as evidenced by a 1999 study by the Municipal and County Parks and Recreation Services conducted in North Carolina which found that local government parks and recreation agencies continue to rely heavily on user fees for revenues for program delivery. Likewise, McCarville, Sears, and Furness (1999) reported that government agencies continue to show increasing interest in applying fees for services and that pricing recreation services represents one of the greatest ongoing challenges confronting public administrators. The challenge of a decrease in tax support is pushing public and nonprofit organizations to continue to look for alternative funding to offer programs.

Commercial leisure organizations are also searching for alternative funding sources. Innovative funding sources enable commercial organizations to stay competitive by keeping immediate fees and charges low. Although it is impossible to identify all categories of alternative funding sources, the following funding strategies are discussed: gifts and donations, grant writing, in-kind contributions, partnerships, scrounging, sponsorship, and volunteers.

Gifts and Donations

For many public and nonprofit organizations, gifts and other outright donations are definite possibilities for raising funds. Gifts and donations may be made for specific programs or to the overall organization. Americans have always been generous people. As early as 1832, Alex de Tocqueville, in his book *Democracy in America* (2003), highlighted efforts in the U.S. for individuals to form clubs and associations to address difficulties, rather than looking to government to solve problems. Fast forward to the early years of the 21st century and this generosity continues to be evident. In 2006, American giving reached a record high, with donations totaling $295 billion (Giving USA, 2007).

Beyond outright gifts and cash donations, one strategy being used by an increasing number of public and nonprofit agencies is the development of a gift catalog. A gift catalog is an attractive brochure that outlines a wide variety of needed equipment, as well as facilities and programs that might be sponsored by individuals or organizations in the community. For each project or item, a price tag is attached so a potential donor can choose their gift to the organization from an extensive "wish list."

Another option for stimulating gifts and donations is creating a support group for the organization. The Friends of Hartman is an example of an organization that encourages gifts and donations to Hartman Reserve, a public outdoor education center in Cedar Falls, Iowa. This Friend's group encourages donations and gifts of all types including cash, fundraising activities, memorial donations, an endowment, and volunteer efforts. Friends groups are common in parks, libraries, zoos, and museums and provide opportunities for individuals to become involved in fundraising and to advocate for the goals of the organization.

It is important to note that not all gifts or donations are viewed as assets (nor are they always accepted). For instance, if an organization is given a large tract of land located in another county or a building that requires major renovation, the gift could prove detrimental rather than beneficial. Likewise, it is important to consider the message being sent by the benefactor as well as the gift. Many parks, recreation, and leisure services organizations would think twice about accepting large gifts from major tobacco companies, for instance, because of the perception of incongruent health messages.

Grant Writing

Private foundations and other philanthropic organizations are potential sources of funding for parks, recreation, and leisure services organizations. In addition to federal, state, and local government grant-in-aid programs, corporations and over 62,000 private foundations provide funds for a variety of programs and services (Loe, 2002). In the late 1980s federal grant-in-aid programs distributed billions of dollars for a wide range of issues; private foundations distributed additional money to all types of programs. Private foundations include family foundations, corporate foundations, and community foundations. The top 10 family foundations in the United States commonly contribute upwards of $300 million annually (Thompson, 2007). Although it is difficult to identify the specific dollar amounts awarded to parks, recreation, and leisure services, grants within the related fields of health, human services, cultural activities, and the environment, have all fared well with grant-in-aid programs. The largest share of grant money in 2002 was given to children and youth organizations—this accounted for over 15 percent of total grant dollars and over 20 percent of the total number of grants awarded that year (Lawrence, 2002).

Grants should not be viewed as easy money, however, as there is strong competition among an increasing number of applicants for both public and private grants. Furthermore, grant writing is a skill that requires a good deal of time and commitment to do well. For organizations that invest the energy in doing their "homework" and presenting their ideas to the right funders, however, grants can greatly increase an organization's ability to offer quality programs.

In-Kind Contributions

In addition to money, all organizations can benefit from in-kind contributions. These refer to resources made available to a program by individuals or organizations that require no financial transaction. Although in-kind contributions may include materials and supplies, they more than likely involve the sharing of labor, facilities, and/or equipment.

Consider the following example of an in-kind contribution to the Make-a-Wish Foundation. This agency arranges to bring to life the wishes of children under the age of 18 who are terminally ill. Since 1980, when Disney helped the newly formed charity grant its first wish, a visit to one of Disney's theme parks remains the Foundation's most requested wish for children. In 2005, Disney granted 5,000 wishes for the Make-a-Wish Foundation; this included providing tickets, lodging, and special behind-the-scene tours to the awardees (Disney, 2005). As another example, a small charter fishing boat in Hawaii donated a day of marlin fishing to a fourteen-year old boy. The result: a record setting 547-pound blue marlin, the largest catch ever by a child (Make-a-Wish Foundation, 2006). These contributions did not involve an exchange of cash, rather they offered in-kind assistance from a profit-oriented organization to a nonprofit organization.

Partnerships

Whereas in-kind contributions are noncash donations, partnerships are a means for two or more organizations to join to further the goals and objectives of all parties. Partnerships are established because each organization recognizes that it cannot achieve its vision solely with existing resources. By identifying a purpose for a partnership, all parties acknowledge the collaborative benefits, thus allowing partners to focus their efforts on making the partnership a success. To be successful organizations must clearly define goals, understand their partners' strengths and weaknesses, and know the real cost of their involvement and anticipated cost of future involvements. Each partner must realize that they each give up some level of control to reap the benefits of the partnership. Furthermore, they should focus on outcomes, recognize that partnerships usually require a long-term commitment, and arrange management to facilitate the process.

The National Recreation and Park Association (NRPA) has initiated a number of successful partnerships with both nonprofit and commercial organizations. Several of these partnerships include:

• *Sajai Wise Kids*. The Sajai Foundation partners with NRPA to develop a science-based curriculum that teaches children about activity levels and nutrition, and how to balance these two concepts in their lives. This exciting youth program offers a quality program to a variety of parks and recreation agencies to deliver wellness messages and practical, hands-on activities. The partnership advances the missions of the Sajai Foundation (which is to inspire healthy, wise youth) and the mission of NRPA (to create healthy lifestyles and livable communities).

• *Tennis in the Parks, 2008*. Tennis in the Parks brings together NRPA and the United States Tennis Association. Together, they provide resources and support to communities committed to growing and improving tennis programs, infrastructure, and advocacy efforts in their local communities.

• *Partnership for Play Every Day*. A collaborative initiative bringing together the YMCA of the USA, NRPA, and the National Association for Sport and Physical Education, is increasing the spaces and quality of play for our country's children and youth. The partnership's focus is to bring together the public, private, and non-profit sectors to advance polices, programs, and practices that ensure all children and youth engage in at least 60 minutes of physical activity every day. As part of a specific outcome of this partnership, Visa recently awarded a jump off grant to the San Francisco Recreation and Parks Department to enhance youth volleyball programs. The grant helps SFPARD to enhance facilities, purchase equipment, and provide scholarships to area children to attend volleyball camps and clinics.

These partnerships (as well as others) address a number of contemporary issues such as youth development, health and wellness, environmental stewardship, facility development, advanced technology, and community development. Because of their concern for improving quality of life, leisure services organizations are well situated to partner with a variety of organizations to expand services and meet their goals and objectives. The YMCA of Silicon Valley offers additional examples of successful partnerships (see Figure 9.10).

Scrounging

Scrounging involves locating and soliciting miscellaneous items and recycling them for short-term or long-term use. It requires creativity and inventiveness to see the potential use for discarded materials in programs. With enough space dedicated for storage, a wide range of items can be scrounged and stored for later use. As many practitioners in the field can attest, leisure services programmers are legendary scroungers. Staff can turn an old appliance box into a puppet theater, discarded tires become swings, old military parachutes are used for playground games, and so on. One example of a formalized scrounging program is often seen in children's museums. The museums collect a variety of junk items from area businesses to place in large bins. Items might include buttons, pipe cleaners, wire, old posters, and paper, among other things. Children are encouraged to use the materials for creative art projects on-site. In addition, parents can pay a fee and fill a small, medium, or large bag with items for children to use for creative projects at home.

Sponsorships

Sponsorships can include in-kind contributions as well as cash and products. The purpose of sponsorships is to provide the parks, recreation, or leisure services organization with additional revenue while providing the sponsor with market recognition and promotional opportunities. The key to successful sponsorships is that both parties benefit from the relationship. In return for their financial contributions, the corporations receive several benefits including name recognition on promotional materials. In developing sponsors, programmers must be aware of organizational philosophies and community values. For instance, beer companies would not be appropriate sponsors for a teenage softball league, and a local casino may not be appropriate to serve as a sponsor for family night at a YMCA.

Volunteers

Volunteers enable many parks, recreation, and leisure services organizations to stretch their finances and

Y We build strong kids,
strong families,
strong communities.

YMCA of Silicon Valley

Y Partners

The YMCA works collaboratively with many organizations to fulfill our mission of building strong kids, strong families and strong communities. Here are just a few of our partnerships.

Project Cornerstone

Project Cornerstone is working to mobilize our entire community to shift from reacting to children and youth as problems to connecting with them so they thrive. As a catalyst for change, Project Cornerstone aims to ensure that every aspect of our diverse community—individuals, businesses, community organizations, schools and government—understand and embrace the fact that interacting with young people is important... and that every interaction makes a difference.

Healthy Silicon Valley

Healthy Silicon Valley partners with more than 100 organizations and individuals to promote healthy nutrition and physical activity in Silicon Valley. The YMCA serves as fiscal agent for Healthy Silicon Valley.

City of Morgan Hill

Morgan Hill's Centennial Recreation Center is a unique partnership between the City of Morgan Hill and the YMCA of Silicon Valley. The YMCA provides health and fitness services to center members.

United Way of Silicon Valley

The United Way brings diverse people and resources together to address the most urgent issues their communities face. Through unique partnerships and approaches, the United Way mobilizes resources beyond the dollars that are pledged through their fund-raising efforts.

YMCA Activate America®

YMCA Activate America® is the YMCA's approach to directly address our growing health crisis in communities across the nation. Locally, Activate America works both internally with YMCA members and externally with community partners to promote healthier eating habits, more physical activity, and improved well-being in spirit, mind and body. Key partnerships include Cambie Su Vida with Dr. Dan Delgado, director of the Pediatric Weight Lifestyle Clinic, the Santa Clara County Public Health Department's Black Infant Health program, the Santa Clara County Public Health Department's STEPS Collaborative, the Gilroy REACH Proyecto Movimiento, the Redwood City School District's Active Kids Collaborative, East Palo Alto's Get Fit Collaborative, the Santa Clara County Office of Education's Fit for Learning initiative, El Camino Hospital's South Asian Heart Center, the Health Improvement Program of the Stanford Prevention Research Center's Living Strong, Living Well program, and the Lucile Packard Children's Hospital Pediatric Weight Control program. Local funders include the David and Lucile Packard Foundation, the Santa Clara County Public Health Department, and Kaiser Permanante. Federal funders include the Center for Disease Control, the Department of Education, JC Penney Afterschool, and the YMCA of the USA.

Figure 9.10 YMCA partners (adapted from http://www.ymcasv.org/association/html/about_partners.html, information retrieved February 26, 2010) provide programs and services beyond their staffing capability; the impact is large. In 2007, 60.8 million Americans (26.2% of the U.S. population) volunteered on a regular basis (Bureau of Labor Statistics, 2007). The economic impact of volunteers is immense, helping organizations expand the impact of their programs. As organizations consider utilizing volunteers, it is important to remember volunteers are not "free." They need to be supported in a variety of ways, including training, supervision, evaluation, and recognition. Volunteers do, however, significantly expand the reach of public and nonprofit organizations, leverage scarce financial resources, and actively engage citizens in the work of a democracy. Their involvement helps generate networks of trust and reciprocity, and build caring communities.

Step Seven: Consider the Psychological Dimensions of Price

In addition to considering the social and environmental issues surrounding pricing, leisure services professionals also need to consider the human elements in pricing. Programmers might set logical prices for programs, yet potential customers may not respond positively to these decisions. Customer reactions to prices are often irrational. They might stem from historical perspectives, previous experiences, self-interest, and emotion—human elements. Hence, in addition to economic principles, establishing a price that will be acceptable to customers requires consideration of the following psychological dimensions of pricing: à la carte pricing, protection of self-esteem, price-quality relationship, establishing a reference point, consistency of image, and odd pricing.

Total Cost Versus à la carte Pricing

In recent years, leisure services professionals have seen a move to an à la carte model of pricing for services. Such an approach offers the customer multiple options as well as the opportunity to pay for only the services rendered. As an example, in recent years airlines have eliminated meals for most passengers and replaced that service with food that can be purchased on board. Similarly, many airlines now charge for checked bags and on-board Wi-Fi. In the past, all passengers paid for checking bags even when they did not take luggage because a charge for transporting bags was built into the ticket price. The airlines see this as a way to generate additional, much-needed revenue.

Although this approach may raise income, the strategy can also backfire. If customers (and competitors) balk and see the service as no longer worth what they are being asked to pay, they may turn elsewhere for service. Likewise, à la carte pricing can raise questions about costs that organizations must include as a part of all programs; costs include those associated with such needs as risk management and accessibility.

Protection of Self-Esteem

Protection of self-esteem is a psychological dimension of pricing that applies specifically to public and nonprofit organizations—those that deal with customer groups in need of subsidized services. It is important for customers to pay some portion of the costs of a program or service. Through such payments (no matter how small) customers make a commitment to the program and the stigma of receiving a handout is minimized or eliminated. For instance, many Boys and Girls Club of America programs charge an annual membership fee of $5.00; in many instances the youth are allowed to pay the fee over the course of a year.

Price-Quality Relationship

As most of us know from personal experience, the price of a program or service is often perceived as a reflection of the quality of that program or service. Marketing studies have shown that consumers' perceptions of product quality vary directly with price. This means that to some degree, if program fees are high, the program is perceived to be high quality; likewise, if the program fees are low, the program may be perceived as being low quality. As a result, a high-quality program may not be well-attended if potential customers perceive the price of the program as too low.

Price also serves as a cue to targeted client groups that a service or program is designated for them. If a service targeted to a middle-income group is priced too low, it is possible the group may not recognize it as being intended for them. Greater involvement in some programs may follow from increasing the price rather than from reducing it. Calculating this balance point can sometimes be a bit of trial and error.

More recent analysis indicates the perception of the relationship between price and quality has decreased over the last 15 years, especially in terms of higher priced products and services, as well as for customers who are familiar with the product (Volckner & Hoffmann, 2007). Despite this trend, the relationship between price and quality still needs to be considered in the price setting process.

Establish a Reference Point

Establishing a reference point refers to setting an initial price for a program or service. This first price establishes in a person's mind the "fair" price for the service based on the consumer's experience with similar services and/or from introductory information provided by the recreation provider. In this way it becomes the reference point against which future price changes are compared. Pricing experts believe such reference points act as internal standards against which program characteristics and price information are compared (McCarville, 1996). In the mind of the consumer, this impacts on the price-quality relationship. For instance, if the initial price for a program or service is $50.00, that becomes *the* price for that type of program. If the price is later cut (in a promotional effort), people feel like they are getting a good deal. If the price goes up, people may feel "ripped off." Thus, programmers have much more flexibility in pricing an initial service or program that has no reference point. Once the reference point has been set, programmers must remain aware of its pricing history as well as the "going rate" of providing the service (i.e., consistency of image).

Consistency of Image

Similar to the price-quality connection, organizations create an image in the eyes of consumers and use pricing to reflect this image. For example, state park campgrounds offer low-priced family vacation opportunities, whereas Hilton Family Resorts offer high-priced luxury family vacations. If state parks offered a product at a

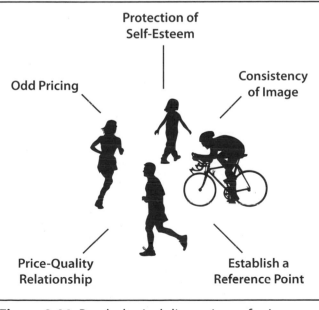

Protection of
Self-Esteem

Odd Pricing

Consistency
of Image

Price-Quality
Relationship

Establish a
Reference Point

Figure 9.11 Psychological dimensions of price

high price, it would be inconsistent with what customers expect. Price must be consistent with customers' perceptions of an organization and its offerings. Similarly, a very low price for a resort vacation would probably leave consumers wondering what types of problems exist, or what the hidden costs might be.

Odd Pricing

This psychological pricing strategy has long been used in the commercial sector. A program or service may be said to carry an odd price if it costs 49¢ rather than 50¢, $9.95 instead of $10.00, or $19.96 rather than $20.00. Odd prices are thought to create the illusion of lower prices. While there is little concrete evidence to support this contention, this pricing strategy is used frequently.

Step Eight: Establish the Initial Price

The eighth step of the pricing process is to determine an actual price for the program or service. In the steps prior to this one, programmers were asked to understand and gather a wide range of information relevant to pricing. Thus, the first phase of the initial price setting step is to revisit step three of the pricing process to understand the overall cost of the program. In addition, this phase examines the price potential of programs based on the going rate charged by competitors or current demand. The second phase of setting the initial price involves considering how the cost could change as a result of the information presented in steps five, six, and seven. The last phase of determining the price is understanding how a servant leadership approach to programming might impact pricing decisions.

Understanding Costs and the Price Potential of Programs

Establishing the initial price is based on cost-based pricing (discussed in step three) which identifies all costs of a program and then sets a price based on these costs. Cost-based pricing for individual programs is often presented using break-even analysis. This means that prices are determined by matching all costs with potential revenues. In this system, a program neither makes nor loses money. Alternatives to cost-based pricing include competition-based pricing and demand-based pricing.

Table 9.1 Cost of an aerobics program

Cost Items Description	Total Costs
Indirect Costs	
Allocated %: Administrative Overhead	$200.00
Direct Fixed Costs	
Facility rent: 3 x a week for 12 weeks (36 rentals)	
Room rental: $30/hour at local fitness club ($30 x 36)	$1,080.00
Instructor salary: $25/class ($25 x 36)	$900.00
Changing Fixed Costs	
Class aide for $7/class	
From the 16th to 25th participant ($7 x 36)	$252.00
TOTAL FIXED COSTS	**$2,732.00**
Variable Costs	
Fitness manual	$4.00
T-shirt	$5.00
TOTAL VARIABLE COST/PERSON	**$9.00**

Cost-Based Pricing: Using Break-Even Analysis

Cost-based pricing is based on all costs associated with offering a program. As discussed in step three of the pricing process, this includes allocation of indirect costs, fixed costs, changing fixed costs, and variable costs. Cost-based analysis will provide valuable information to help establish prices. This information is often presented in two ways: organizing the data on a table or spreadsheet, or by placing the cost data on a graph. This enables programmers to visually understand the break-even point of their programs. To illustrate these techniques, the aerobics program cited in step three will be developed further. Table 9.1 presents the beginning set of facts regarding this program.

The information in Table 9.1 (costs of program) may be placed in a cost volume profit table. Table 9.2 illustrates the amount of cost in relation to the number of people in the program. Thus, various costs based on different participation levels for an aerobics class are presented. You'll remember that various participation levels reflected in the table represent the relevant range of the program. At the bottom end of the spectrum are eight participants since this organization has a policy not to operate a program with fewer than eight participants. The top end of the range is 25 participants, which is the highest number of people the room will accommodate. The cost per participant, which is the final row in Table 9.2, is known as the break-even point. As each volume is specified, the cost per participant represents the price that needs to be charged for the organization to break-even and cover all costs involved in the program.

The information presented in Table 9.2 can also be presented in a graph. This format allows programmers to include a revenue line, which represents various levels of revenue as compared to the costs presented in the cost volume profit table. Plotting the revenue line also illustrates the potential loss or profit of a program at a specific price level. In Figure 9.12, using a price of $175 yields a break-even point between 13 and 14 participants.

Cost-based pricing allows programmers to isolate specific activities and to match their costs with the revenues they generate. As stated in step three of the pricing process, understanding all aspects of costs is an important starting point for identifying the actual price of a program or service.

Competition-Based Pricing

Unlike cost-based pricing, competition-based pricing has no relation to the actual cost of a program or service. Rather, it is based on the prices charged by competitors for similar programs and services. To establish competition-based pricing, programmers need to identify competitors, check their prices, and compare this information to their own program or services. Taking this information into consideration, the price established for a program may be raised or lowered from

Table 9.2 Cost volume profit table for an aerobics program

Cost Items	Number of Participants						
	8	10	12	15	16	20	25
Indirect Costs	$200	200	200	200	200	200	200
Direct Fixed Costs	$1,980	1,980	1,980	1,980	1,980	1,980	1,980
Changing Fixed Costs	0	0	0	0	$252	252	252
Variable Costs ($9/person)	$72	90	108	135	144	180	225
TOTAL COSTS	**$2,252.00**	**2,270.00**	**2,288.00**	**2,315.00**	**2,576.00**	**2,612.00**	**2,657.00**
Cost per participant (break-even)	*$281.50*	*$227.00*	*$190.66*	*$154.33*	*$161.00*	*$121.65*	*$106.28*

the "prevailing market price" (i.e., what competitors are charging) based on a number of different variables. These variables include the unique characteristics of one's own program, the relative strengths or weaknesses of competitors, location, and the possible reaction of competitors to the price set by the programmer. This approach is popular with many organizations because prices for programs can be determined relatively easily and quickly. As you can see, whereas cost-based pricing works by identifying costs and then setting a price, competition-based pricing is a reverse approach where the price is set and the organization works backward to see if it can cover costs.

Demand-Based Pricing

A third method used to establish an initial price for a program or service is demand-based pricing. This method is based on setting a price with respect to buyers' expectations and needs. Under this approach the programmer looks beyond the costs connected to produce a program and instead considers the intensity of demand for the program or service. Thus, to make pricing decisions the programmer needs to have some idea of the possible demand for a particular program at various prices. This demand schedule then becomes the basis for determining which level of pricing would be most profitable for the organization.

◆◆◆

Moving beyond simple cost-based pricing is important for parks, recreation, and leisure services organizations.

By understanding what other organizations are charging for similar programs and services, programmers can develop a range of prices that are likely to be acceptable to users for a particular program or service. Determining this range requires that an organization addresses what potential customer groups are willing, or able, to pay for a particular service.

In addition to understanding the going rate of a program, programmers should also examine the expectations and needs of customers in terms of price. In some instances a price based on costs will be out of the price range of most constituents. For parks, recreation, and leisure services organizations this might mean not offering the program or looking for alternative funding sources to subsidize it. The point to be made here is that at times the going rate may not cover costs; especially for public and nonprofit organizations. As a result, step four of the pricing process (i.e., determining the proportion of cost that the price should recover) becomes extremely important for programmers in that it gives them a strategy on which to build a price for their programs and services. Comparing this strategy to the actual cost of the program or service gives the programmer direction as to how to proceed in steps five, six, and seven of the pricing process.

For example, if the price of a six-week aerobics program is set at $120, the break-even point of providing the program is between 20 and 21 participants. However, an analysis of prices charged by competitors reveals an average cost of $80 for a similar series of classes. Further analysis of the demand for the program

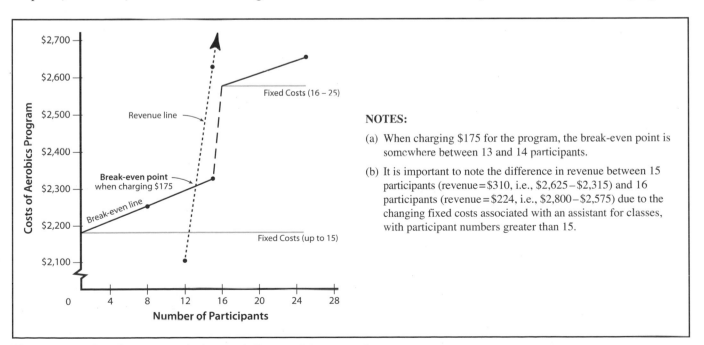

NOTES:

(a) When charging $175 for the program, the break-even point is somewhere between 13 and 14 participants.

(b) It is important to note the difference in revenue between 15 participants (revenue = $310, i.e., $2,625 − $2,315) and 16 participants (revenue = $224, i.e., $2,800 − $2,575) due to the changing fixed costs associated with an assistant for classes, with participant numbers greater than 15.

Figure 9.12 Break-even analysis graph for aerobic example (perhaps through a needs assessment) indicates that potential customers are not willing to pay more than $80 to participate in this program. With this information programmers can begin to make decisions related to pricing, decide not to offer the program, or look for alternative funding sources to cover the costs.

These decisions may be influenced by the service orientation of the organization (e.g., public, nonprofit, commercial). A commercial organization may decide not to offer the program at all, or to offer it at a loss because it serves as a way to introduce new customers to their organization where they will spend money on other programs, services, and goods. Public or nonprofit organizations may examine the program and feel it is a merit good (i.e., has value both to an individual and to society) and, as a result, decide to offer the program and set a price based on partial overhead recovery while looking for additional funding sources. Public or nonprofit organizations may also decide to differentiate the price, set the price for the program at $80 (the going rate), offer discounts for certain groups, and identify other funding sources.

Understanding how costs contribute to the break-even point of a program or service can also provide focus in lowering costs, thereby lowering prices. For instance, the bulk of the cost to offer this program lies in facility rental. As a result, we might search for a less expensive alternative location in which to hold the classes. Another venue might offer a better price or more space so we can add more participants. Furthermore, there might be a potential to share facilities with another organization, or the program might be offered at a different time when the price for renting the facility is reduced.

Step Nine: Understand Price Revision Decisions

Once a price has been established there is still a need to periodically review the price and examine the need for revisions. In most cases, "revised" is synonymous with "increased," thus, it is important to develop a systematic process for making price revisions. Figure 9.13 provides an example of such a process used by a city parks and recreation department. The one additional consideration that an organization might consider in the price-revision process would be to solicit participant input about potential price changes. This input helps to prepare constituents for a price change and can give programmers insights into various psychological considerations in price revision decisions. In the mid-1980s, Crompton and Lamb (1986) identified four psychological elements

programmers should consider: tolerance zone, customer adjustment period, changing the perceived value of a service, and anchor pricing.

Tolerance Zone

The tolerance zone refers to the degree to which small price increases will not encounter client resistance and adversely impact involvement with the program or service. This concept suggests that a series of small incremental increases in price over a period of time are less likely to meet customer resistance than a one-time major increase.

Customer Adjustment Period

When it is necessary to raise prices beyond the tolerance zone, organizations may encounter customer resistance. This often manifests itself in a decreased demand for the program. After an initial period, however, constituent groups will usually adjust, accept the new price, and return to the program or service.

Changing the Perceived Value of the Service

One means to reduce customer resistance when prices are raised beyond the tolerance zone is to raise (at the same time) customer's perceived quality of the program or service. If customers think that the quality of the program is commensurate with the new price being charged, they are less likely to react adversely to the price increase.

Anchor Pricing

Anchor pricing refers to identifying a price that exists between two already established prices—a high and low price (the anchors). Any time an agency charges a new price for a service or program we should assess the new price to see if it falls between the lowest and highest prices charged for other programs. Research has indicated that the lowest and highest prices charged for other programs are likely to be the most noticeable to constituents. Thus, these prices serve to *anchor* potential customers' judgments about the quality of services offered by the organization. Keeping prices within these two anchor points is less likely to arouse customer resistance than if prices are outside of these anchors.

A Servant Leadership Approach to Pricing

A servant leadership approach to pricing is crucial if we are committed to empowering staff and customers in the creation, implementation, and evaluation of programs and services. It is easy to give lip service to a philosophy, but through the pricing process programmers have an opportunity to "put our money where our mouth is"—this can be a difficult task. One metaphor, mentioned in the opening of this chapter, that can help programmers understand a servant leadership approach to pricing is the image of a steward—someone who practices stewardship and cares for others, the environment, and other resources.

In the opening chapter of this book programmers identified stewardship as holding something in trust for another. Historically, the concept of stewardship has often been thought about in terms of financial manage-ment; yet today we see the concept of stewardship being applied on a much larger scale. This larger vision of stewardship means that we consider all stakeholders, including future generations, and promote ways for participants to govern themselves, creating a strong sense of ownership and responsibility for outcomes.

In terms of pricing, this means that programmers must hold themselves responsible for understanding a broad definition of costs, making sure they think through the impact of programs not only on the agency's finances, but also on the environment and society as a whole. In addition, programmers should involve constituents as much as possible in pricing decisions through research, advisory boards, and advocacy groups. Pricing does not have to be an adversarial process. Educating constituents (especially in public and nonprofit organizations) about the costs, philosophy, and strategies in the pricing process can help them become partners in very meaningful ways.

Fee Review—Recreation Programs

Program: _____

Date: _____

1. Is this a public, merit service, or private service? _____
2. What are the total costs of the program? _____
3. What is the anticipated revenue at current prices? _____
4. Does the fee cover direct operating costs? ❏ Yes ❏ No
5. How much, if any, of the direct support costs are covered? _____
6. To what extent is the program tax supported? _____
7. Are fees, in general, comparable to those of other similar service providers in the area? ❏ Yes ❏ No

   Exceptions:

   _____ _____   _____

   _____   _____

   Comments:

   _____   _____

   _____   _____

8. Can we, or should we, charge "what the market will bear?" ❏ Can ❏ Should ❏ Are Now

   Why? _____   _____

9. How does the fee of one program compare to the fee of like programs (i.e., adult ballet vs. adult tap)?

   _____   _____

   _____   _____

Figure 9.13 Price revision analysis form

Emmett, Havitz, and McCarville (1996) described an excellent example of an organization taking a servant leadership approach to pricing. Although somewhat dated, this example shows us the possibilities of using the pricing process to creatively engage customers and address issues of equity in programs. Emmett, Havitz, and McCarville documented the pricing policies of a nonprofit recreation center operating in a large Canadian city. After a major capital campaign to renovate their facility, programmers realized that they would have to charge fees to offer and maintain their programs. They also wanted to ensure that the new fees and charges would not preclude anyone from using the facility. With this in mind, programmers developed a unique approach to customer subsidies for those who could not afford to pay membership fees. This approach enabled potential participants to personally negotiate with staff and develop a mutually acceptable price level for the basic membership. Consequently, no one is excluded from programs and services for financial reasons and everyone received identical services.

What is unique about this process is how staff empowered constituents to make decisions related to the price they are able to pay. When staff met with potential customers they could negotiate in terms of any number of relevant issues (e.g., family income, housing costs, living costs) that might influence their ability to pay. No proof of need was required, and honest disclosure was assumed by all applicants. The process was focused on specific needs rather than unbending policies, criteria, and standards.

Over the first six years of operation, the assisted-member policy had no negative effect on the Center's total revenues. In fact, revenues rose consistently from 1989 to 1995. Most importantly, the policy was effective, as reflected in the following quote:

> The Center generously grants me membership assistance. You can't understand how important this is to me. I feel as though I can contribute to my community in a positive way even though I lie well below the poverty level and cannot always contribute financially. The Center confirms my importance as a member of this community... by supporting me. I feel confident that one day I will be helping others in my position today. I intend on being a member for the rest of my life. Thank you. (Emmett, Havitz & McCarville, 1996, p. 74)

Block (2002) offers one last caution when dealing with budgeting and pricing decisions from a servant leadership perspective. For Block, financial decisions are "how questions" dealing with how to do something. When programmers focus only on the how questions, they often avoid questions of mission and purpose. If staff become too focused on what is financially feasible, they operate in a world where efficiency, methodology, and instrumentality become the primary goals. When this happens programmers often pursue these goals at the expense of depth and intimacy. Thus, according to Block, the work of servant leaders is to keep in perspective

> the benefits of instrumental values, for commerce and barter are essential elements of a viable economic system....While at the same time, seek to sustain enough idealism, intimacy and depth so that we can act on our vision of what the world might become. (p. 147)

Balancing the financial requirements to stay in business with the mission and vision of the organization is the task of the servant leader.

Summary

Pricing has emerged as a important administrative tool for programmers in parks, recreation, and leisure services. As may be seen from this chapter, the process of setting a price is complex and encompasses a variety of factors. To assist programmers in this process we have provided a nine-step process to determining a price for a program or service. This process includes understanding the overall environment of financing parks, recreation, and leisure services organizations; understanding the budget process; understanding the overall cost of programs; identifying the pricing objectives of the organization; examining the appropriateness of differential opportunities; exploring alternative funding; considering the psychological dimensions of price; setting the initial price; and understanding price revision decisions.

Following this process does not give programmers a simple formula by which a price can be established. This process does, however, encourage programmers to consider myriad complex variables that must be addressed in establishing specific prices for programs and services. Lastly, we offered the symbol of *steward* as a metaphor for incorporating a servant leadership perspective into the pricing process. As a steward of program resources, we not only focus on financial decisions, but we also place these financial decisions within the larger context of the organizational mission.

Save Money Now!

Charges

Leisure Card charges are reviewed annually. Card holders and their stated dependants or carers pay £1.20 per person per session at the Leisure Centres. One adult and two children would normally pay £5.20 for a swim at Macclesfield Leisure Centre. Leisure Card holders pay only £3.60. All prices correct until 31st March 2004.

Charges for the cinema, sports development and bowling club will vary.

Before Travelling

Please check details with the Leisure Centres and clubs before travelling. The centres operate different opening times and have different programmes throughout the day. These can also vary during and outside school term times.

Car Parking

At Wilmslow Leisure Centre those paying for a Leisure Card activity can claim back their car park fee by producing the relevant portion of the ticket at reception. Normal car parking restrictions apply.

For Further Information

Please contact the Leisure C
or Michael Harding, Busines
Manager at:

Macclesfield Leisure Centr
Tel: 01625 669607
Email: m.harding@maccle

Designed and
Council, Res

www.

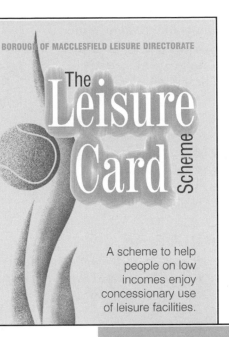

BOROUGH OF MACCLESFIELD LEISURE DIRECTORATE

The Leisure Card Scheme

A scheme to help people on low incomes enjoy concessionary use of leisure facilities.

Staff Use Only

For those currently unemployed

I certify that the person named is unemployed and registered at this office.

Official Signature _____

Date _____

Qualifying Stamp

Fee Paid   £ _____

Proof Of Residence Seen   ☐

Proof Of Concession Seen   ☐

Concession Type (In Words) _____

Centre Of Issue _____

Card Number _____

Expiry Date _____

Receptionist's Initials _____

Receipt Number _____

Did You Know? continued

Tennis courts and bowling greens within the parks throughout the Borough, are available free of charge except during school holidays, weekday evenings and weekends. *Equipment not provided.*

Leisure Card holders can save money at Knutsford Studio Cinema, where an adult will be admitted at the concessionary price. Contact the cinema on 01565 633005 for further details.

Leisure Card holders can apply for allotments at a reduced rate. Contact Leisure on 01625 504511.

Prestbury Bowling Club offers use of its facilities to Leisure Card holders for a nominal fee. Contact Derek Gower on 01625 573397 for further details. The club will offer training and advice to new players.

We are currently seeking more clubs to join the scheme.

Where Do I Apply?

Application in person can be made to any of the following:

Macclesfield Leisure Centre
Priory Lane, Macclesfield SK10 4AF
Tel: 01625 615602

Wilmslow Leisure Centre
Rectory Fields, Wilmslow SK9 1RU
Tel: 01625 533789

Poynton Leisure Centre
Yew Tree Lane, Poynton SK12 1PU
Tel: 01625 876442

Knutsford Leisure Centre
Westfield Drive, Knutsford WA16 0BL
Tel: 01565 653321

Figure 9.14 Leisure card program to assist low-income constituents

Programming from Here to There

The Leisure Card is an innovative approach to implementing a price differential for use in recreation programs and facilities (see Figure 9.14 on p. 261). It was developed by the Borough of Macclesfield, England. The Leisure Card program is designed to simplify the process through which people with low incomes access a variety of leisure facilities and programs. Residents show qualifying documents once when the card is issued, and no personal documents are kept. The Leisure Card is valid for six-months and a card-holder may access facilities and programs simply by showing the card at registration.

References

Block, P. (2002). *The answer to how is yes: Acting on what matters*. San Francisco, CA: Berrett-Koehler Publishers.

Block, P. (1996). *Stewardship: Choosing service over self-interest*. San Francisco, CA: Berrett-Koehler Publishers.

Bureau of Labor Statistics. (2007). *Volunteering in the United States, 2007*. Washington D.C.: U.S. Department of Labor.

Brayley, R. & McLean, D. (1999). *Managing financial resources in sport and leisure service organizations*. Champaign, IL: Sagamore Publishing.

Crompton, J. (2008). Evolution and implications of a paradigm shift in the marketing of leisure services in the USA. *Leisure Studies, 27*(2), 181–206.

Crompton, J. & Kaczynski, A. (2003, Winter). Trends in local park and recreation department finances and staffing from 1964–65 to 1999–2000, *Journal of Park and Recreation Administration, 21*(4) 122–144.

Crompton, J. & Lamb, C. (1987). Establishing a price for government services. In P. Kotler, O. Ferell, & C. Lamb (Eds.), *Strategic Marketing for Nonprofit Organizations: Cases and readings*. Englewood Cliffs, NJ: Prentice Hall.

Crompton, J. & Lamb, C. (1986). *Marketing government and social services*. New York, NY: John Wiley & Sons.

Crompton, J. & McGregor, B. (1994). Trends in the financing and staffing of local government park and recreation services 1964/65–1990/91. *Journal of Park and Recreation Administration, 12*(3), 19–37.

de Tocqueville, A. (2003). *Democracy in America*. New York: Penguin Classics

Delaney, P. (1991, July). Give a little… Receive a lot! *Resort and Commercial Recreation Association, 6*.

Deppe, T. (1983). *Management strategies in financing parks and recreation*. New York, NY: John Wiley & Sons.

Disney. (2005). *Disney worldwide outreach*. Retrieved September 06, 2009, from http://www.disney.com

Edginton, C., Hanson, C., Edginton, S. & Hudson, S. (2004). *Leisure programming: A service-centered and benefits approach*. Dubuque, IA: McGraw-Hill.

Emmett, J., Havitz, M., & McCarville, R. (1996). A price subsidy policy for socioeconomically disadvantaged recreation participants. *Journal of Park and Recreation Administration, 14*(1), 63–80.

Giving USA. (2007). Charitable Giving. As cited by the *National Philanthropic Trust* (www.nptrust.org/philanthropy/philanthrophy_stats.asp)

Godbey, G. (1997). *Leisure and leisure services in the 21st century*. State College, PA: Venture Publishing, Inc.

Hailman, S. (2003). *Understanding trends impacting nonprofit organizations' budgets*. Excerpted from materials developed by Campaign Consultation, Inc., for the ASK to Sustain Institute held in San Diego, CA, October, 2003. Retrieved January 9, 2010, from http://eclkc.ohs.acf.hhs.gov/hslc/Program%20Design%20and%20Management/Fiscal/Financial%20Management/Budgets/UnderstandingTre.htm

Havitz, M., Morden, P. & Samdahl, D. (2004). *The diverse world of unemployed adults*. Waterloo, Ontario Canada: Wilfrid Laurier University Press.

Howard, D. & Crompton, J. (1980). *Financing, managing, and marketing recreation and park resources*. Dubuque, IA: Wm. C. Brown.

Kaczynski, A. & Crompton, J. (2006). Financing priorities in local governments: Where do parks and recreation services rank? *Journal of Park and Recreation Administration, 24*(1), 84–103

Kotner, A. (2006, April 10). Frivolous lawsuits are a heavy price to pay. *San Diego Business Journal*. Available through Goliath: Business Knowledge on Demand. www.goliath.ecnext.com

Lawrence, S. (2002). *Foundation giving trends*. New York, NY: Foundation Center.

Loe, C. (2002). *Foundation center releases estimates of 2002 foundation giving and assesses prospects for 2003*. Press Release from the Foundation Center. New York, NY.

Make-a-Wish Foundation. (2006). *Adventure wishes granted: Deep sea fishing*. Retrieved September 06, 2009, from http://www.wish.org

McCarville, R. (1996). The importance of price last paid in developing price expectations for a public leisure service. *Journal of Park and Recreation Administration, 14*(4), 52–64.

McCarville, R., Sears, D., & Furness, S. (1999). User and community preferences for pricing park services: A case study. *Journal of Park and Recreation Administration, 17*(1), 91–105.

Mosquera, M. (2005). *GAO again sides with rec-site losing bidder*. Retrieved January 9, 2010 from http://gcn.com/Articles/2005/11/04/GAO-again-sides-with-recsite-losing-bidder.aspx.

MSNBC staff (2007, October 12). *Gore, U.N. climate panel win Nobel Peace Prize: Warming is greatest challenge ever.* www.msnbc.msn.com/id/21262661/.

Rossman, R. & Schlatter, B. (2008). *Recreation programming: Designing leisure experiences* (5th ed.). Champaign, IL: Sagamore Publishing.

Skulski, J. (2009). *Planning for inclusion: Implementing an accessibility management program in a parks and recreation business model*. Retrieved January 9, 2010 from http://www.ncaonline.org/index.php?q=node/728

Thompson, W. (2007). *The complete idiot's guide to grant writing* (2nd Edition). Exton, PA: Alpha Publishing.

Volckner, F. & Hofmann, J. (2007, March). The price-perceived quality relationship: A meta analysis assessment of its determinants. *Marketing Letters. 18(3)*, 181–196.

Zietlow, J., Hankin J., & Seidner, A. (2007). *Financial management for nonprofit organizations*. Hoboken, NJ: John Wiley & Sons.

Programmer Profile

Ron Coplin

Photo provided by Ron Coplin

Current Position: Coordinator of Saint Mary's Adult Partial Hospitalization Program; Chair of Activity Therapy, Pine Rest Christian Mental Health Services.
Favorite Book: *Lonesome Dove* by Larry McMurtry (1989)
Favorite Recreation Activities: Hunting, fishing, and gardening
Certifications: Certified Therapeutic Recreation Specialist (CTRS), Crisis Prevention Intervention (CPI), and CPR

▶ **Describe the path your career has taken.**

- B.S. in Education, History, and Recreation and Parks Administration (with an emphasis in Therapeutic Recreation) from Central Michigan University.
- Master of Arts in Recreation and Parks Administration, with an emphasis in Therapeutic Recreation from Central Michigan University.
- I have worked as a recreation therapist in a number of different organizations including the State of Michigan Psychiatric Hospital, Pine Rest Christian Mental Health Services, and Bulthuis and Coplin Consulting. My current employer is Saint Mary's Adult Partial Hospitalization Program. The Adult Partial Hospitalization Program is provided through a joint operating agreement between Pine Rest Christian Hospital Mental Health Services, Saint Mary's Health Care, and Metro Health. The program is a short-term, intensive treatment program offered to individuals experiencing significant mental and/or emotional problems. Our goal is to provide intensive treatment to assist individuals in managing these problems. The target population includes adults, ages 18 and older, who meet the criteria for admission and cannot be adequately treated through traditional outpatient services.
- As coordinator of this program my job is to make sure our interdisciplinary team, which is made up of chaplains, activity therapists, social workers, pharmacists, nurses, and psychiatrists, works together to enhance the therapeutic value and treatment of each patient. As coordinator I am in contact with the Program Manager, and lead the Team Meetings as well as staff meetings. I am responsible for staffing issues as well as the content of Psycho-Education Groups. I have to make sure that the program is meeting the State of Michigan and regulatory governing boards' regulations and guidelines.

- As a Clinical Recreational Specialist, I plan, lead, and process psycho-educational groups. I conduct initial patient assessment determining patient needs and, based on those needs, schedule the patient for programming. I supervise student interns and complete daily progress notes on each patient.
- As Chair of the Activity Therapy Department it is my job to make sure all Activity Therapists are up to date on certifications and licensing. I am the department spokesperson in Hospital Management Meetings. I am involved in hiring and firing of Activity Therapy Staff and act as a negotiator in staffing issues. I am involved in many of the Activity Therapy Staff's yearly evaluations.

▶ Describe the joys of working in your current position.

I think the joy of my current position is the variety it offers each and every day. I am involved with direct patient care and I delight in seeing patients use the skills taught to make progress in their treatment. At the same time I am involved a lot in the day-to-day operation of the program, and get to work with experienced professionals from many disciplines working together for a common goal. I love being able to program, lead clinical groups, and still be involved with administrative duties of the day-to-day operations of the program.

▶ Do you have any advice for new programmers?

You do not know it all, as much as you would like to, you cannot control if a person will use the skills you have taught them. Only they control that. You will fail some of the time. Just because you have a degree doesn't mean you've earn professional respect. Respect comes with experience, acting professionally, listening and learning. Don't be late, people do notice, and it will end up hurting you.

▶ How have you incorporated needs assessments into therapeutic recreation?

In our clinical settings, needs assessments are very important. Our activity therapy department uses a variety of standardized as well as customized assessments created by our staff. These customized assessments have been developed based on the nature of the patients admitted to each particular unit. The majority of these assessments include a leisure component, which is used in developing a treatment plan for each individual. In addition, we assess relationship issues, addictions, trauma, work stress, physical and emotional health issues, etc. All these findings are incorporated into the individual's treatment plan, which is managed by a team of therapists. Individuals are then assigned various group sessions and programs, based on their therapeutic needs.

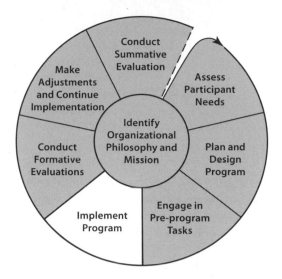

Facilitating the Program Experience | 10

In the early 1990s, Albrecht (1992) identified three components to providing quality services: a service strategy, customer-oriented front-line staff, and customer-friendly systems (see Figure 10.1). The service strategy refers to understanding the vision and mission of an organization, which we discussed in Chapter Three. Front-line staff refers to the importance of the customer-leader interaction, which we have discussed throughout this book (particularly as it relates to servant leadership). In this chapter, we examine the area of user-friendly systems (including making the system convenient, accessible, and pleasant for the user) and the participant-leader interaction that takes place during the experience itself.

For most program participants (customers), involvement with an organization begins long before they participate in an actual program. In fact, the total customer experience may be thought of in terms of several distinct phases. Clawson and Knetsch (1966) developed one of the most widely used models explaining the recreation experience. They labeled the phases or stages of recreation experiences as anticipation, travel to the site, participation in on-site experiences, travel back home, and recollection. Likewise, O'Sullivan and Spangler (1998) identified three phases of an experience as pre-experience (including need recognition, alternative selection, preparation, and anticipation); participation (including everything connected to experiencing the

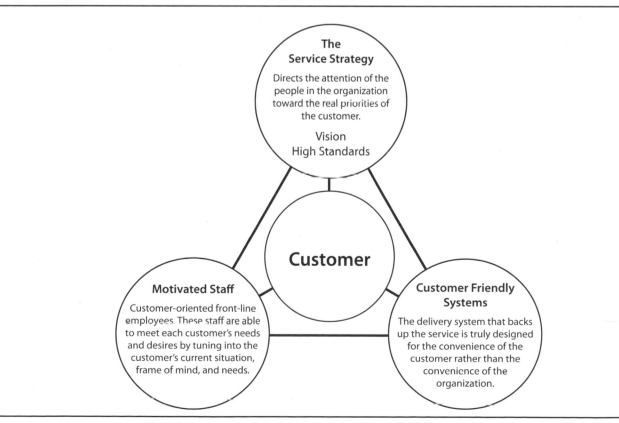

Figure 10.1 The service triangle (Albrecht, 1992)

actual event or program); and post-experience (including remembering and beginning the planning process once again). Figure 10.2 offers a graphic of the stages. Within each of these phases identified by O'Sullivan and Spangler, programmers and their organizations have an opportunity to enhance the customer experience. In this chapter we will emphasize ways to assist programmers and organizations to reach the goal of providing meaningful leisure experiences to their customers at every stage.

Facilitating the Pre-Experience

The pre-experience stage refers to anything and everything involved prior to engagement in the actual experience. Initially during this stage, potential customers must make decisions concerning their involvement in various recreation opportunities; this decision is often based on what needs/wants they are trying to meet. These questions usually start on a macro level asking many broad-based questions and gradually become more focused (see Figure 10.3).

O'Sullivan and Spangler (1998) explain the process of making decisions as moving from need recognition to searching for activities that would fulfill the need, to choosing a specific provider of one of these activities, and going to the activity. For example, "Pat" realizes a desire or need to escape and relax, and realizes she has a variety of generic

alternatives that would meet this need (e.g., physical activity, entertainment, socialization). Having decided on a physical activity, Pat would then construct a list of possible activities (e.g., walking, yoga, swimming, biking) that would meet her need. From this list of possible activities, Pat makes a decision to swim. Next, Pat must identify all the potential locations/service providers where she could swim on the chosen day and time; she then selects the local YWCA as her service provider.

Typically, a consumer's excitement in making these decisions is high during the planning stage. Thus, to facilitate the decision-making process, organizations should provide potential customers with needed information to make informed decisions. As mentioned in the previous chapter, the process of educating potential customers through the most appropriate medium is one of the goals of promotion and marketing. Additional considerations in facilitating the planning process for customers include serving as a general resource and creating customer-friendly registration procedures. Once the individual makes a decision (and registers or commits to a program), the emphasis of the organization then shifts to facilitating the person's anticipation of the upcoming event.

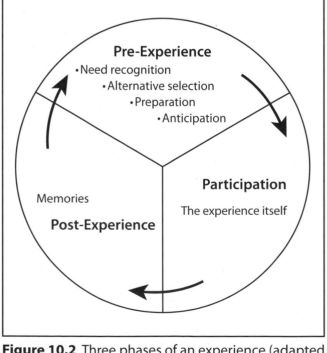

Figure 10.2 Three phases of an experience (adapted from O'Sullivan & Spangler, 1998)

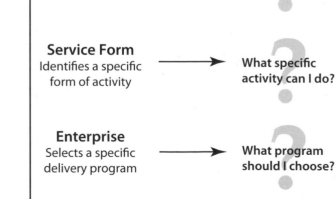

Figure 10.3 Consumer decision-making questions

Assisting Potential Participants to Make Wise Decisions

In managing an individual's pre-program experience, programmers must identify how promotional materials can best be used, as well as how they will be distributed. Within a servant leadership perspective, we believe promotional materials should provide potential participants the information they need to make informed decisions. In this regard it is important for promotional materials to *accurately* describe programs, services, and potential benefits. A critical element of facilitating a customer's pre-program experience is managing expectations. Promotional materials are often the first step in this process and must set the stage for open and honest exchange between potential participants and program staff.

In addition, a servant leadership approach to programming suggests that we should go beyond promoting an individual organization. Being responsive to customer demands means that we empower them to meet their own needs. This may mean recommending that a customer try an alternative program that might better meet their needs even if the program is offered by a different organization. In the short run, this customer resource approach may result in an occasional loss of a customer; however, in the long run the organization will develop a reputation based on integrity and customer responsiveness that will benefit both the participant and the organization.

Customer Friendly Registration Procedures

Organizations exist to meet the needs of participants, and to be successful at this, organizations must become customer-oriented. Nowhere is the need to become customer-oriented more evident than in the registration process. Historically, registration procedures have been created to help organizations manage programs and services by developing a record of people who want to, and are qualified to, participate in a specific program or service. The need for registration procedures is well-documented (see Figure 10.4). Customers generally recognize these requirements and are willing to go through the registration process. Yet, in many cases, registration procedures have been created for the convenience of the organization rather than the customer. In today's competitive environment where the emphasis is on providing quality services, organizations may wish to rethink the registration process with the needs and interests of the potential

participants in mind. Today, constituents want a registration process that is accurate, convenient, accessible, easy to understand, and that works for them.

Registration Information

Keeping accurate and well-organized records is an important part of the registration process. Organizations will want to collect a wide range of information during this process. The more complete the information collected, the less chance that programmers will need to contact participants to request additional information at a later date. Information collected from customers during the registration process typically includes:

- date of registration

- contact information: registrant's name; address; day, evening, and cell phone numbers; e-mail address

- registrant information: age, sex, T-shirt size, special requests (e.g., to be registered with a friend)

- name of the program the customer is registering to attend

- amount and method of payment

- fee waiver and/or scholarship request

- proof of age (if required to verify ages for restricted sport leagues)

- liability waivers

Registration is necessary under the following conditions:

- when a fee needs to be collected;

- when the number of spaces in a program is limited;

- when the program has high variable costs and it is important for programmers to make informed decisions about supplies and equipment; and/or

- when the program has qualifying criteria for admission. In outdoor programs, for example, certain qualifications may need to be demonstrated before an individual can participate in a program.

Figure 10.4 Common needs for registration procedures

- medical information, medical release form, and insurance information

- media (e.g., photo, video) release

- indication of any special accommodations needed (information needed to address inclusion needs)

- code of conduct agreement (behavioral expectations of participants, parents, guests, etc.)

- emergency contact: name, relationship, contact information

It is not uncommon for registration forms to be used as a means of gathering demographic and personal interest data from participants. This information could be gathered from responses to the bulleted items above, but may also entail including additional questions for this purpose. For example, organizations might include a question about future programs registrants would like to see offered in the community, how they heard about the program, or what other community resources they utilize.

In addition to the information collected from customers, organizations must also share information during the registration process including:

- a short program description with start and end dates and times

- the fee for each program participant

- acceptable methods of payment (e.g., credit card, check, money order, cash)

- instructions regarding where and how to submit the registration form and any fees

- a list of any program-specific requirements (e.g., special equipment, clothing, footwear, previous skill level required, age and/or size prerequisites)

- staff member contact information to request accommodations for a person with a disability

- who to contact with additional questions

- what to expect once the registration is received (timetable for acknowledgement, processing)

- the location where the program will meet

- policies related to cancellations, delays, refunds, other programmatic issues

For example, Figure 10.5 presents a web page from the City of Boynton Beach that provides policies and procedures related to the registration process. This web page informs customers about how to register, and links provide information about refunds, cancellation, insurance, and fees.

Registration Methods

Parks, recreation, and leisure services professionals use several basic registration methods. These include registering over the Internet, at a central location, at a program location (i.e., the site where the program is being held), by mail, by telephone, via fax, or through a combination of methods. Each of these methods has advantages and disadvantages; it is up to the programmer to develop the method(s) that best serve the customer for various types of programs.

Internet Method. A high-quality website is imperative for all parks, recreation, and leisure services organizations. These sites usually include registration information and the forms needed to register for various programs. Many sites offer interactive registration forms where once a person has completed a registration, she or he simply hits the "submit" button and the registration is processed. Other sites offer downloadable or printable (usually pdf format) forms that must be downloaded to one's home computer, then completed with a pen or pencil, and faxed or mailed in to be processed.

The major advantage of interactive web-based registration is flexibility for both the customer and the organization. People can peruse programs and register for them from the comfort of their home at a time convenient for them, it is inexpensive for both constituents and leisure services organizations, and materials can be updated quickly and easily. In addition, confirmation emails can be sent immediately (and automatically) for received registrations, thereby confirming the process for customers.

Many of the disadvantages of the Internet method resemble those of registering by fax (e.g., no face-to-face interaction with staff, inability to see the program site, need for additional payment procedures). Additional disadvantages of the Internet are the potential lack of security involved in sending personal information over the Internet (e.g., credit card information, medical information), and the lack of computer access for many constituents. Furthermore, if not properly designed, registration forms may not be accessible to people with disabilities.

Central Location Method. In the central location method, participants registering for a program or service offered by an organization must go to one central location such as the organization's headquarters, a central office, or a municipal hall. All the materials and information needed to register are found at this location. Oftentimes with this approach, registration activities are available only on specific dates and times. The advantages of this approach include a quick registration process, easy supervision of registration, the centralization of fee collections, and increased customer service due to a centralized flow of information.

Disadvantages of the central location method are that programmers lose the opportunity to excite potential participants, participants are unable to become familiar with the setting by seeing the program location, and due to conflicts or transportation difficulties, some constituents may be unable to travel to the registration site. In addition, the volume of customers may be high; this can cause long lines and increase the chance of error in the registration process. To alleviate any negative feelings that might arise during the centralized registration process, many parks, recreation, and leisure services organizations take the opportunity to add value during the registration process. Value-added elements include offering such perks as refreshments,

---

Business   Community   Government   Online Services   Departments   City Contacts

Home > Government > Departments > Recreation and Parks > Recreation Program Registration

WELCOME

Advisory Boards

After School Care

Beach and Boat Decals

Department Staff Directory

Funfare Magazine

Golf

Parks

Programs and Activities

Recreation Centers

Rentals

Special Event Permits

Special Events

Summer Camp

Transportation

Volunteers

Recreation Program Registration

New Hours of Operation

The Clubhouse is opening an hour earlier, Tuesday through Friday to enable staff to assist customers for their convenience. The new registration hours are:
Tuesday - Thursday – 10 a.m. – 6 p.m.
Friday – 10 a.m. – 5 p.m.
Saturday – 10 a.m. – 2 p.m.

Recreation Program Registration

Intracoastal Park Clubhouse is the central registration area for all recreation programs. The friendly staff at the Clubhouse will help you register for any of the recreation classes, activities and programs listed in each issue of the *Funfare! Magazine* at the various recreation centers in Boynton Beach.

Registration Dates

Registration for programs beginning in January is December 2 for Residents and December 9 for Non-residents.

Payment

Checks or money orders should be made payable to The City of Boynton Beach. Visa & MasterCard are also accepted at the Clubhouse.

Returned Checks

The City of Boynton Beach charges a service fee of $20 for all returned checks.

Mail-in Registration

Mail completed registration form (please find the attachment below) and check or money order to:

City of Boynton Beach Recreation & Parks Department
Program Registration
PO Box 310
Boynton Beach, FL 33425-0310

Figure 10.5 City of Boynton Beach web page identifying registration alternatives free child care, tours of facilities, opportunities to meet staff face-to-face, program-related videos/DVDs, and information about upcoming programs.

Program Location Method. In the program location method, registration takes place at the program site, such as a recreation center, swimming pool, golf course, or camp. This approach helps familiarize participants with the program site, and participants have a greater probability of interacting with program staff. These advantages are important features, particularly when registering young children. During the registration process youngsters can meet staff and become familiar with the location before returning to the site without their parents. Disadvantages of this method include extra time and effort, and the feeling of being given the "runaround" if a customer is registering for several programs at different locations. In addition, this method makes supervision and cash control more difficult than the central location method. In offering value-added services in this approach, organizations can provide many of the same perks as in the central location method.

Mail-In Method. As we might imagine, the mail-in method requires constituents to complete a registration form and mail it to a centralized processing location. This is a common registration process and is typical of public, private nonprofit, and commercial leisure services providers. Advantages of this method include that it is easy and time efficient for participants, it allows for flexibility of staff in processing the applications, and it centralizes the cash control element of registration. The major disadvantage of this method is that it does not allow for any direct interaction between participants and staff, and as a result some may experience a delay in knowing if they are registered for a specific program. In addition, there is always the chance that registration forms will be delayed or lost in the mail. Participants also lose the opportunity to see facilities prior to the start of the program. Fewer opportunities to offer value-added services exist using the mail-in method, although discounts and coupons can be offered for "early bird registrations."

Telephone Method. Telephone calls for registration purposes are usually directed to a central location that offers the advantages of centralized cash control (payment is typically by credit or debit card), ease of supervision, and efficiency for customers. Disadvantages include lack of face-to-face interaction between staff and participants and the need for additional procedures to pay for programs and services, especially when payment needs to be received before registration can be confirmed. In addition, participants

do not have an opportunity to see the program location. Further, registering by phone can be frustrating unless organizations have a method of managing a high volume of calls as they are received. A computerized telephone service can help to implement a queuing process whereby people "will be helped in the order in which their phone call was received," but this is extremely impersonal and some constituents will hang up before being helped. In addition, not all constituents have telephones, and for some, such a call may be long distance.

Scan and Email, or Fax-In Method. This approach enables constituents to register via email or facsimile and offers many of the same advantages and disadvantages of telephone registration. With this method, a potential participant completes the registration form by hand, and then either faxes it directly or scans it into a computer to be emailed. Disadvantages of this method are the lack of interaction between constituents and staff, and the limited availability of computer or fax machines. An advantage of this method, however, is that potential participants can submit a registration form for programs 24 hours a day.

Combination of Methods. The majority of parks, recreation, and leisure services organizations offer a variety of registration methods to improve convenience and accessibility for constituents. This fits well with a servant leadership approach to delivering programs as programmers strive to be open to the needs of customers and seek a variety of ways to meet these needs. Example registration forms may be found in Figures 10.6 and 10.7 (see pp. 273 and 274)—note that one is presented in Spanish to accommodate the needs of the local population.

Providing a variety of registration methods can be challenging for organizations and requires a good deal of thought, planning, and organization. The increasing use of computer software in the registration process is assisting organizations in coordinating various registration methods and information collection. Computers with appropriate software enable programmers in multiple locations to link to a centralized database, thus increasing the ability to manage the overall registration process. A wide variety of software packages are available to assist with data management on several levels. Software specifically developed for the parks, recreation, and leisure services field can assist professionals to: access facility and program usage reports, maintain up-to-date program lists, provide programmers with demographic profiles of participants, manage photo ID/entry processes, and provide maps and directions to program sites. Complex software packages can also help to manage financial processes and information, facility scheduling, locker management, equipment rental, and work orders to repair or replace structures and goods. Further, to engage participants some software provides activity statistics (e.g., for sports leagues), a site to upload participant photos and comments, and interactive program and activity evaluations. In addition, many software programs can send automated emails to program registrants in the event of a cancellation or other program-specific news. Examples of such commercial software include RecWare, Schedule Star, The Sports Manager, Class, RecTrac, and Park Works.

Issues Related to Registration

Regardless of the registration method(s) chosen by an organization, programmers will want to ensure the overall quality of programs and services. Parasuraman,

Zeithaml, and Berry (1985) developed a model identifying five dimensions of quality for a number of different services, which remains useful today. Listed in order of importance the five dimensions are reliability, responsiveness, assurance, empathy, and tangibles. Researchers in parks and recreation have examined dimensions of quality in recreation facilities and programs and found a similar set of dimensions.

Reliability refers to the ability to perform the promised service consistently and accurately. *Responsiveness* is the willingness to help customers and provide prompt attention; another word for this is timeliness. *Assurance* indicates courteous and knowledgeable staff conveying trust and confidence. The *empathy* dimension includes offering caring and individualized attention to all constituents. Lastly, the *tangible* dimension represents the physical facilities, equipment, and appearance of personnel—do they demonstrate excellence? Many of these dimensions are relevant for programmers to

---

City of Bloomington Parks & Recreation

Program Registration Form

Hours: 8 a.m. - 5 p.m.
Phone: 555-555-5555
Fax: 555-555-5555

Name _____
(parent/guardian if participant is under 18 or under legal guardianship)

Home Phone _____

Work Phone _____

Street Address _____

Emergency Contact _____

City _____ State _____ Zip _____

E-mail Address _____

City of Bloomington Resident?   Yes   No
   If you are unsure of your residency status, please call 349-3700.

How did you hear of this program?   Program Guide   Newspaper   Flyer   Friend   E-Mail   Website   Previous Participant   Other _____

Participant Name	M/F	Birthdate	Program Name	T-shirt Size/Short Size	Class Code #	Fee

Inclusive Service Request:

Reasonable accommodations are needed to participate in above program(s) related to specific needs associated with a disability. (circle one) **YES**   **NO** If **YES**, please complete an Inclusion Assessment and the Inclusive Recreation Coordinator will contact you. We request at least two weeks notification for reasonable accommodations requests. *In some cases reasonable accommodations may take longer.*

Include Your Voluntary Donation

☐ Youth Scholarship Fund
☐ Bloomington Tree Fund
☐ Bloomington Parks and Recreation Foundation

$1
$3
$5
Other $_____

Total $ _____

The undersigned is the adult Program Participant, or is the parent or legal guardian of the Program Participant. The undersigned hereby states that s/he understands the activities that will take place in this program, and that the Program Participant is physically and mentally able to participate in this program. The undersigned recognizes, as with any activity, there is risk of injury. In the event that the Program Participant sustains an injury in the course of the program, and the City of Bloomington Parks and Recreation Department is unable to contact the appropriate person(s) to obtain consent for treatment, the City of Bloomington Parks and Recreation Department and/or its employees or volunteers are authorized to take reasonable steps to obtain appropriate medical treatment. The Program Participant and/or his/her parent or legal guardian shall be responsible for the cost of such treatment. The Undersigned now releases the City of Bloomington, the Bloomington Parks and Recreation Department, its employees, agents, and assigns, from any claims including, but not limited to, personal injuries or damage to property caused by or having any relation to this activity. It is understood that this release applies to any present or future injuries and that it binds the Undersigned, Undersigned's spouse, heirs, executors and administrators. The Program Participant may be photographed and videotaped while participating in Parks and Recreation activities, and consent is given for the reproduction of such photos or videos for advertising and publicity.

I have read this release and understand all of its terms. I agree with its terms and sign it voluntarily.

_____   _____
Signature (parent/guardian if participant is under 18 or under legal guardianship)   Date

Method of Payment:
   Cash (do not mail cash) _____
   Check or Money Order _____
   Visa/Mastercard # _____
   Expiration Date _____
   Signature _____

Make check or money order payable to:
Bloomington Parks and Recreation Department

Mail registrations to:
Bloomington Parks and Recreation
P.O. Box 848
Bloomington, IN 47402

Figure 10.6 An example of registration form (Bloomington, IN)

FORMA DE INSCRIPCION PARA LA CLASE DE RECREO: haga el favor de llenar completamente

Una forma para cada familia

Informacion de pades or beneficirio   Direccion de e-mail:_____

Nombre	Apeilldo		
Direccion		Cuidad	Codigo Postal
Numero de casa #	Numero de trabajo #	Numero de Telefon y contacto de emergencia	

☐ Marca aqui si la direccion es nueva

Nombre de Particitante	Nombre de clase y Actividad	Curso	Codigo de clase	Honorarios de clase
NOMBRE APELLIDO				
EDAD FECHA DE NACIMIENTO / /				
SEXO (Haga un circulo al rededor de la repuesta correcta) MUJER HOMBRE				
NOMBRE APELLIDO				
EDAD FECHA DE NACIMIENTO / /				
SEXO (Haga un circulo al rededor de la repuesta correcta) MUJER HOMBRE				
NOMBRE APELLIDO				
EDAD FECHA DE NACIMIENTO / /				
SEXO (Haga un circulo al rededor de la repuesta correcta) MUJER HOMBRE				
NOMBRE APELLIDO				
EDAD FECHA DE NACIMIENTO / /				
SEXO (Haga un circulo al rededor de la repuesta correcta) MUJER HOMBRE				

ACCEPTAMOS EFECTIVO/CHECQUE O GIRO POSTAL

USO OFICIAL UNICAMENTE Fecha recibido		USO OFICIAL UNICAMENTE Recibo#
Numero de Cheque#	Cantidad de Cheque:	Cantidad de efectivo $

La Cuidad de Coolidge propone obedecer la acta de incapacidad de los americanos. (ADA) Si usted tiene cualquier necesidad especial favor de llamar (520) 723-4551. Necesitas formas adicionales?

Yo entiendo que la Cuidad de Coolidge no llueva seguro de accidents para estas programas y yo por este medio renuncio y pongo de acuerdo de no tener el patrocindor inoco de cualquier demanda de dano personal o danos y perjuicio ocurrido por la participacion de la programa del la Cuidad de Coolidge. Yo tambien doy permiso por fotos y videos tomado de participantes para el uso de la Cuidad de Coolidge.

Firma de padre o beneficiaro:_____   Fecha:_____

Enviar por correro: Cuidad de Coolidge * Inscripcion para la clase de recreo * 660 S. Main St. * Coolidge, AZ 85228

Figure 10.7 An example of registration form (Coolidge, AZ)

address in the registration process and in preparing constituents to participate in programs and services. Consider how staff treat potential participants in the registration process. By performing their duties accurately, being knowledgeable about programs and services, listening to customers, and making appropriate suggestions for improving programs, staff exude an attitude of quality assurance.

By understanding what constituents value in terms of service delivery, programmers are in a better position to identify specific situations where problems may occur. This may require the use of what is called *outside-in thinking,* where a person looks at tasks from the constituents' perspectives rather than her or his own. To do this a programmer might ask a staff member to pretend to be a potential participant and, using each registration medium offered (e.g., online, walk-in, phone, fax, mail), register for a program. In this way, the staff member experiences the process just as an actual registrant would. Another way to identify specific issues relative to service quality is to create a cycle of service (discussed in Chapter Two) specifically for the registration process. Once identified, staff can address the issues and ensure that the process flows properly. Some critical points within the cycle of registration include well-prepared staff, ease and accessibility of the registration process, additional paperwork, and payment methods.

Prepared Staff

The most important relationship in the process of creating, implementing, and evaluating leisure programs is that of the potential participant and front-line staff member. The initial formation of this relationship occurs prior to the actual start of the program or service. Thus, the first impression created for participants as they interact with staff for the first time is critical to developing a positive relationship. As noted in the previous section, staff must be competent as they interact with all constituents. In addition, they must be knowledgeable about the organization and its programs. To be most successful, administrators will want to examine how they can train staff to best prepare them to react to customers in a way that fosters a sense of reliability, responsiveness, assurance, and empathy.

In many parks, recreation, and leisure services organizations, seasonal, part-time, or volunteer staff deliver programs and services. Preparing these staff to meet the demands of interacting with various constituents can be a challenge. Despite the importance of front-line staff and the fact that they constitute the majority of person-

nel recruited by parks, recreation, and leisure services organizations, they are often the lowest paid and receive the least amount of training and development of all organizational staff. More needs to be done to enhance their preparation, training, and status within organizations.

Many organizations fail to produce benefits to the participant because they fail to realize the importance of developing and supporting their front-line staff. It may be helpful to redraw the organizational chart with a fresh look to include customer benefits as a fundamental part of what goes on in successful organizations. Such a chart might also reflect the benefits staff will receive from working within an organization (see Figure 10.8). In this approach values or benefits flow outward—internal service departments deliver value to the front-line staff, who then deliver value to the constituent.

In working through such a structure, programmers can begin to work with front-line staff to identify ways the interactions between constituents and staff can be improved. It becomes important to regularly provide staff development opportunities to learn more about the organization, potential participants, and how to effectively communicate with the public. During training, organizations might acknowledge the joys and challenges of interacting with constituents, answering the same questions a hundred times each day (seemingly), and dealing with the problems of others. By acknowledging these difficulties and working through them *with* staff, the organization fosters a servant leadership perspective for delivering programs

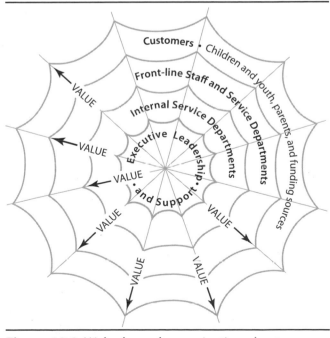

Figure 10.8 Web-shaped organization chart (adapted from Albrecht, 1992)

and services, and meets the participant's needs relative to the five dimensions of quality.

Ease and Accessibility of the Registration Process

In addition to preparing, training, and maintaining quality front-line staff, leisure services professionals also impact participants' pre-program experiences through the actual registration process. When adopting a method or methods of registration, ease and accessibility for customers are important dimensions to keep in mind. Customers are, after all, the reason leisure programs and services are offered. Their perceptions are paramount to an organization's success. Suggestions for making the registration process user-friendly include:

- Provide enough knowledgeable staff to handle the registration process.

- Schedule registration times and choose locations/methods that are convenient for all potential customers—particularly those who have not previously participated in programs and services.

- Make all forms and other information readily available for all potential constituents (in multiple languages and accessible to those with disabilities).

- Establish well-organized queuing systems to make sure customers are served in the order they arrive (or call). Queuing refers to standing in line or being on hold on the telephone while waiting to be served.

- Provide clear and easy-to-follow registration forms. Arrange the form in such a way that customers can complete as much of the registration form as possible before needing assistance. Consider aesthetics, language, reading comprehension level, length of form, use of words, and any other factors of communication that may arise.

- Process registrations in an efficient and timely fashion.

Common Forms Used in the Registration Process

At the time of registration for a specific program or service, a number of other tasks are commonly completed. These tasks often involve providing detailed information such as department policies and procedures related to cancellations, refunds, and rain-outs; and filling out additional forms such as a code of conduct agreement, fee waiver or scholarship request, agreement to participate, parental permission, inclusion questionnaire, medical history and treatment release, liability waiver, and media release.

Code of Conduct Agreement

Many agencies and organizations ask participants and guardians to read, accept, and sign a code of conduct agreement prior to participation and involvement in a recreation or sporting activity. Some state laws (such as Title 5 of the New Jersey Athletic Code of Conduct, PL 2002-74) and local ordinances (such as the Kennebunkport, ME Recreation Code of Conduct; see Figure 10.9) mandate the implementation of such codes for all youth sports. A code of conduct serves as a guide to, and acknowledgement of, expected behaviors related to involvement in recreation and athletic programs. The code may apply to students, parents, participants, coaches, officials, spectators, and/or others who are involved in a recreation or sporting activity.

Fee Waiver or Scholarship Request

All types of parks, recreation, and leisure services agencies and organizations are faced with situations whereby an individual wants to participate in a program or service, but her or his financial situation will not allow participation. Thus, it is relatively common for public and nonprofit entities to offer an opportunity for potential participants to request a reduced program fee, or to have the fee waived altogether. Public, nonprofit, and commercial organizations may also provide fee assistance in the way of scholarships. Funding for scholarships might come from outside entities (e.g., Lions Club, Junior League) or from a budgeted line. Whether requesting a fee reduction, waiver, or scholarship, such requests will require information gathering. Some forms used for this purpose are quite simple whereby an individual is asked to write a 500-word essay indicating her or his need for the financial support and how the program will benefit her or him. Other forms might require detailed financial information and a copy of one's most recent tax statement or pay stub. Figure 10.10 (see pp. 278-279) is an example of a scholarship program and the required form.

Agreement to Participate Form

Vital to a strong risk management program, this form is used to help constituents understand the risks and responsibilities associated with participating in particular activities. Agreement to (continued on p. 280)

Town of KENNEBUNKPORT, ME

P.O. Box 566, Kennebunkport, ME 04046
ph: 207.967.4243

Recreation Code of Conduct

Kennebunkport Parks & Recreation CODE OF CONDUCT

This CODE OF CONDUCT has been written for all persons involved in a youth sports program of Kennebunkport. It cannot cover every possible circumstance, but it will serve as a guide of expected behavior and consequences. Safety is our primary concern, violence will not be tolerated. Extreme misconduct may result in exclusion from participation or in police action. Alcohol and other substances are never permitted. Complaints may be channeled through the recreation department at 967-4304.

I For Players...
- Players must show respect for parents, teammates, opponents, game officials, staff, and the facility itself.
- Players shall refrain from swearing or using obscene or vulgar language at any time, even if it is not directed at a particular person.
- Fighting is prohibited.
- Arguing with an officials decision is not allowed.
- CONSEQUENCES: If a player breaks any of these rules, coaches shall (in addition to any penalty assessed by officials), (a) first time: sit out for a quarter, a half, or a game as circumstances may reasonably require; (b) second time: in addition to the above, report incidences to the Recreation Director for further action.

II For Coaches...
- Respect all players, opponents, parents, game officials, and recreation personnel.
- Play by the letter and spirit of the rules of the game.
- Fair/equal play: all players must play as close as reasonably possible to one half of the game, and every player must sit on the bench for at least one quarter.
- Never openly dispute or argue an officials decision.
- Never use obscene or vulgar language to anyone, at anytime, anyplace.
- CONSEQUENCES: Coaches will have to meet with the Recreation Director and/or Committee in the event of complaints. Extreme misconduct may require exclusion from participation.

For Parents and Spectators...
- Encourage your child to play by the rules and as a team player.
- Applaud good effort, whether in victory or defeat.
- Never create a disturbance or interfere with the progress of the game.
- Never swear or use obscene or vulgar language, even if not directed at a particular person.
- Avoid all verbal abuse of players, coaches, and officials. Fighting is prohibited.
- If you have a concern to discuss with the coach, contact the coach by telephone or set up an appointment to meet. If you cannot reach the coach, call the Recreation Director. Do not attempt to confront the coach before, during, or after a game or practice. These are emotional times for both parent and coach; this period does not promote objective analysis of the situation.
- CONSEQUENCES: Should any spectator create a disturbance or interfere with the progress of the game, officials are required to stop the game. A warning may be issued, depending upon the seriousness of the disturbance. It is up to the coach of the team responsible for the person creating the disturbance to leave the bench and instruct the person to leave the building. If the person refuses to leave, the game will end, and the team responsible for the problem will forfeit the game. In any event, the game will continue only after the person leaves.

For Officials...
- Act in a professional manner at all times.
- Strive to provide a safe and sportsmanlike environment in which players can properly display their sports skills. The game is under your control.
- Adopt a zero tolerance attitude toward verbal or physical abuse, and never use foul language when speaking with a coach, player, spectator, or other official.
- Be fair and impartial at all times.
- Violence must never be tolerated.
- Never openly criticize a coach, player, spectator, or other official.
- CONSEQUENCES: Complaints about officials behavior (not judgment) must be made in writing to the Recreation Director.

All signatures indicate an understanding of and adherence to the above CODE OF CONDUCT.
Player: _____ Parent: _____ Coach: _____

Figure 10.9 Code of conduct form

Bloomington Community Parks and Recreation Foundation

Recreation Scholarship Program

General Information

Bloomington Community Parks and Recreation Foundation seeks and receives contributions from individuals, social groups, clubs, businesses, and service organizations to assist in providing scholarships for youth enabling them opportunities to participate in recreation programs.

1. Need is the primary criterion upon which scholarships are considered. Accepted participants are expected to pay at least 25% of the registration fee. No full scholarships will be awarded.

2. Scholarships are not guaranteed and are available on an as-needed basis.

3. Bloomington Community Parks and Recreation Foundation cannot provide scholarships for programs when primary costs are contractual (such as trips or performances, tickets or admissions) or for programs conducted by non-parks and recreation employees (i.e., Bloomington Blades, little league).

4. Scholarships are not available for special registration fees (i.e., Kid City) or late fees.

5. Bloomington Community Parks and Recreation Foundation reserves the right to limit the amount of scholarships awarded to an individual during the program session, particularly if the demand for scholarships by the community is high. No family will be awarded more than $500 per calendar year.

6. Approval of any scholarship application does not automatically register that person into the program of choice. Registration for any program is the responsibility of the family requesting assistance. **All payments must be received prior to registration deadlines and participation.**

7. Scholarship applications will be accepted up until **two weeks prior to the program start date**.

8. Confidentiality: All information provided will only be used to determine the level of scholarship awarded.

ELIGIBILITY

- **City of Bloomington residency required with proof of residency (current utility bill, housing lease, etc.) -** must be primary residence of participant.
- IU students/families are eligible with residency requirement.
- Only those under 18 years of age are eligible for scholarship assistance.
- **Proof of Income** – All applicants must show proof of income, such as most recent income tax return, last four (4) payroll stubs, or a letter from the appropriate social service agency (Bloomington Housing Authority, Welfare Department, Head Start, etc.).

APPLICATION PROCESS

- Complete the Scholarship Application Form (one form per family please). All information requested must be supplied. Incomplete forms will not be considered.

Applications and attachments should be submitted to:

Bloomington Parks and Recreation Department
BCPRF Scholarship Committee
401 N. Morton Street, Suite 250
P.O. Box 848
Bloomington, IN 47402

Phone: 555-555-5555
Fax: 555-555-5555
Email: parks@bloomington.in.gov

All information submitted will remain confidential.

Updated 04/2005

Figure 10.10 Scholarship application information and form

Continued>>

Bloomington Community Parks and Recreation Foundation

Recreation Scholarship Program

A separate scholarship application form must be submitted for each child, and individual applications should be submitted a minimum of **two weeks prior to the requested program's start date**.

<table>
<tr><td>OFFICE USE ONLY</td></tr>
<tr><td>Date Received: _____</td></tr>
<tr><td>Date Reviewed: _____</td></tr>
<tr><td>Approved/Denied: _____</td></tr>
<tr><td>Amount Awarded: _____</td></tr>
<tr><td>Committee Rep: _____</td></tr>
</table>

Child's Name: _____ Age: _____

Address: _____
  (Street)   (City)   (Zip)

Program Requested: _____

Parent/Guardian's Name: _____

Address (if different from above): _____

Phone (daytime): _____ Phone (evening): _____

Number of household members UNDER 18 years of age: _____ Number of household members OVER 18 years of age: ____

INCOME
Please check:

☐ Proof of household income
☐ Proof of in-city residency
☐ Monetary child support/alimony (if applicable) $_____
☐ Employer: _____
☐ Other local, state or federal assistance (i.e. child care assistance, food stamps, etc):_____
_____

☐ Rent/Mortgage payment: $_____

Please give a brief statement of reasons for applying for assistance: _____
_____
_____
_____

Have you received a Bloomington Parks and Recreation Scholarship in the past? _____ If so, when? _____

I/We, the undersigned, understand that the information given will be kept confidential. The information provided is true and complete to the best of my knowledge and belief. I consent to the disclosure of such information for purposes of income and verification related to my/our application for financial assistance. I understand that any willful misstatement of material fact will be grounds for disqualification. *I agree to pay any outstanding balance I have on my household account after all scholarship money has been applied.*

_____   _____
Applicant's Signature   Date

All information submitted will remain confidential.

Updated 04/2005

Figure 10.10 Scholarship application information and form (continued from previous page) participate forms explain that accidents may occur and the organization cannot guarantee the safety of participants. In addition, participants are reminded that they must assume elements of responsibility for their own safety. An agreement to participate form formalizes the fact that customers agree to participate and assume the inherent risks associated with the activity. When using agreement to participate forms with children, programmers should properly inform both children and parents or guardians about the activity, its risks, and expectations of participants. Both the child and the parent or guardian should sign this type of form.

Parental Permission Slip

A permission slip is a signed statement indicating that parents/guardians will allow their minor children (under age 18) to participate in a specific program or service. Commonly used before taking young people on a trip (e.g., to a nearby waterpark or theater) or engaging in a high risk activity (e.g., downhill skiing, gymnastics), permission slips serve as a way to inform parents or guardians about program plans. These simple forms provide written (or electronic) documentation indicating that parents or guardians are aware and approve of their child's participation in a particular event or program. Staff may also use a variation of the permission slip to gather information identifying the people who are allowed to pick up a minor from an event.

Inclusion Questionnaire

Figure 10.11 presents an inclusion questionnaire in use by the City of Bloomington (IN) Parks and Recreation Department. When an individual (or her or his parent or guardian) indicates that she or he will need accommodations to participate in a program or service, it becomes important for staff to understand the nature of that need. Thus, an inclusion questionnaire is used to gather information to assist staff in understanding and planning for any needed accommodation. The form might include personal information such as type of disability or impairment, activity interests and preferences, communication and social skills, mobility challenges, medications, personal toileting needs, food and eating limitations, activity restrictions, assistive technology needs, and other information that might help staff provide the needed assistance.

Medical History and Treatment Release

Some programs may require participants to complete a medical history form prior to participation. For instance, many fitness programs (e.g., high-impact aerobics classes, aquatic programs, weight training classes,

highly active programs for seniors) or programs for those recovering from medical procedures typically require that participants provide a brief medical history. Staff keep this information in a confidential and locked location and the forms are only accessed if the participant requires medical attention while engaged in a sponsored program. Medical history forms may be simple health disclosure forms used to collect basic information such as name, address, emergency contact phone numbers, sex, birth date, height, weight, age, blood type, medical insurance policy type and number, and physician information (e.g., phone, address). The form may also include questions about one's health history and prior injuries, fears, medications, allergies, and so on. More complex medical forms may include a form signed by a doctor that documents the health of a participant and indicates her or his fitness to participate in certain programs or activities. The type of information collected depends on the nature of the activity or program. For instance, if a program is going to be held outside at a park, it would be wise to know (and be prepared for) someone who is allergic to bee or insect stings. Treatment release forms tend to be attached to another form (e.g., registration form, inclusion questionnaire, medical history form). Participants (or parents/guardians) sign these statements indicating their willingness to accept medical treatment should they be unable to give such permission at the time of an injury.

Liability Waiver

Liability waivers are agreements between the organization and the participant that state that participants will not hold the organization liable for any damages if ordinary negligence is the reason for the injuries or damages. Waivers commonly include information about the program or activity, its inherent risks (physical, emotional, psychological), behavioral expectations, a statement that all risks cannot be negated and that injuries can occur, a list of potential injuries, and a statement that the individual signing the form understands and accepts the risks of participation. Legal concepts such as *exculpatory* and *indemnity* clauses are typically included on these forms. As with all issues related to risk management, agencies will want to involve attorneys in the creation and implementation of such forms.

Media Release Forms

Organizations are frequently on the search for photo, video, and audio opportunities to promote their programs and services. Photographs, movies, and audio recordings might be used (continued on p. 284)

Inclusion Questionnaire

This form is intended to assist in identifying reasonable accommodations which may be beneficial for successful participation. **To assist us in meeting your needs, we require that registration for each program and reasonable accommodation requests be made at least two weeks prior to the program registration deadline. In some cases reasonable accommodations may take longer.**

Please complete as thoroughly as possible. *Thank-you!*

PARTICIPANT INFORMATION (to be completed by parent/guardian if participant is under 18)

Name _____ Date of Birth _____

Address _____ City _____ Zip _____ Phone _____

Parent/Guardian (if applicable) _____ Home Phone_____

Work Phone _____ Email _____

Recreation Interests

Please identify any interests the participant has:

Community Examples: traveling	Outdoors hiking, fishing	Physical ice skating, golf, tennis	Wellness tai chi, yoga, relaxation	Educational language, outdoors, financial	Hobbies cooking, music, dance, reading	Creative sewing, painting, stained glass

Are there any recreation activities the participant is interested in learning? _____
_____

Which Bloomington Parks Recreation activities has the participant registered for in the past? _____
_____

Social (please check all that apply)

____ Shows interest in others
____ Will play/interact cooperatively with others
____ Is tolerant of others, not easily agitated or annoyed
____ Can listen and follow direction
____ Is aware of safety concerns (traffic, staying with group, using sharp objects, hot stoves, etc)

____ Will sit quietly to watch a program, movie, etc
____ Can identify and take responsibility for personal belongings

Comments/Areas of difficulty: _____
_____

1

Figure 10.11 Inclusion questionnaire

Continued>>

Other Information

Circle each diagnosis that applies to the participant and/or identify any condition not listed.

Amputation	Down Syndrome	Muscular Dystrophy
Arthritis	Epilepsy	Psychiatric Disability
Attention Deficit Disorder	Hard of Hearing	Spina Bifida
Autism Spectrum Disorder	Learning Disability:	Spinal Cord Injury Level:
_____	_____	_____
Behavioral Disorder	Mental Retardation, mild, moderate,	Traumatic Brain Injury
Cerebral Palsy	severe	Vision Impairment
Deaf	Multiple Sclerosis	Other_____

Does participant have seizures?   YES   NO   If yes, please indicate type and describe: _____

_____

Date of most recent seizure _____

Does anything trigger the seizures? _____

Medications

Medication	Time	Dosage	Purpose	Side Effects/Contraindications

Allergies (include food/medication/other) activity restrictions, special diets or other medical concerns:_____

_____

_____

Communication Skills

How does the participant communicate? (Circle the ones that apply)

Speech   Read Lips   Communication Board   Sign Language   Computerized Device

Any communication devices that are used at home or work are also needed in recreation settings, please provide any resources available, including, but not limited to communication board/books, computer devices etc..

How can staff assist the participant in communicating needs? _____

_____

_____

Feeding Skills

Does the participant eat and drink independently? YES   NO   If no, what type of assistance or adaptive equipment is needed? _____

_____

_____

Figure 10.11 Inclusion questionnaire (continued from previous page)

Mobility Skills

Does participant walk independently?   YES   NO   If no, please identify any mobility devices used or assistance needed: _____

Describe transfer techniques used: _____

_____

If the participant uses a wheelchair, is a wheelchair lift required? YES   NO Explain: _____

_____

Transportation Skills

Does participant drive or use public transportation independently YES NO
If no, how will participant get to and from the programs? _____

_____

Restroom Skills

____ Wears Attends/Depend   ____ Uses toilet independently
____ Indicates need to use toilet   ____ Washes hands independently
____ Uses toilet with physical assistance

Concerns/Restrictions

Activity concerns or restrictions related to health/social issues: _____

_____

_____

Do you feel the participant requires one to one supervision?   YES   NO
(*Level of supervision will ultimately be determined by the Inclusive Recreation Coordinator.*)

Additional Comments: (Please attach additional pages if needed)

_____
_____
_____
_____
_____
_____
_____
_____

This assessment expires one year from date of the assessment or in the event of significant change.

Termination of inclusive recreation services must be completed through the Inclusive Recreation Coordinator. At no time may a participant or parent/guardian terminate inclusive recreation services without consulting the Inclusive Recreation Coordinator.

_____   _____
Signature (parent/guardian if participant is under 18 or under legal guardianship)   Date

Please return to Bloomington Parks and Recreation:
401 N. Morton, Ste 250
P.O. Box 848
Bloomington, IN 47402
Phone: 812-349-3700 Fax: 812-349-3705

3

Figure 10.11 Inclusion questionnaire (continued from previous page) in brochures, calendars, television commercials, and various web-based settings such as social networking sites, photo sharing sites, blogs, and other promotional opportunities. Sometimes issues of privacy arise when using such media for promotional purposes (especially when working with protected classes such as children, those with developmental and cognitive disabilities, and prisoners); thus, to simplify the process of using photos, videos, and audio recordings many organizations ask registrants to sign a media release prior to participating in programs and services. Failure to sign a media release would not preclude individuals from participating, but administrators would need to determine any legal repercussions before media depicting those persons were used for promotional purposes.

In addition to the forms and registration information, administrators will want to examine their programs and decide if any other paperwork is needed. Many organizations combine several forms into one. This can create problems, however, because participants may be willing to sign one aspect of the form, but not another. For example, an individual may agree to sign a liability waiver, but not consent to a media release. If these two components are wrapped into one form this could create undue problems for both the agency and the individual.

◆◆◆

We have talked about the registration process and the many forms that might be completed as a part of that process. To foster and maintain a servant leadership approach to all aspects of programming it is important to try to build an orientation to customers into all program cycle elements. Cost and payment for programs and services is an integral part of this process. No matter an organization's orientation (i.e., commercial, nonprofit, public) payment of some sort usually accompanies the delivery of a program or service. Costs across and within programs can be flexible. For example, one program might cost more than another, and two different constituents might pay different amounts to participate in the same program. Some of these individuals might be on a flexible pay scale, while others might barter for an exchange of services.

Payment Methods

Ease of registration includes resolving several questions concerning payment methods. In their efforts to best serve constituents, programmers and administrators must answer several questions about payments:

Who Should Collect Payments?

To facilitate positive interactions between an agency and potential participants, programmers will want to make it as easy as possible for constituents to obtain information, make reservations, and offer payment for programs and services. In most cases parks, recreation, and leisure services organizations handle these arrangements themselves, yet some organizations delegate some of these tasks to intermediaries, thus freeing the organization to focus on program or service delivery. Examples of intermediaries include travel agents who make hotel and transportation arrangements, ticket agents who sell seats for a sporting event, businesses that sell trail passes for bicycles or cross-country skiing, and the use of a commercial entity such as PayPal for online payments. Although the organization may have to pay a commission for this service, intermediaries are able to offer customers greater convenience in terms of where, when, and how the program cost can be paid. Even after commissions, the use of intermediaries often offers a net savings in administrative costs to the organization.

When Should Payments Be Made?

Customers face four basic options related to when payments for services or programs can be made. They include:

1. in advance of the program;

2. at the onset of the program;

3. after the program is completed; and

4. with some combination of methods (e.g., a deposit may be required prior to the program starting with the balance due at the start or completion of the program).

Asking customers to pay prior to a program beginning can help build customer commitment and provides the organization with needed capital to finance program planning. Other approaches may be initiated to assist customers in the payment process. One approach that offers customers flexibility and encourages early payment is when an organization offers discounts for early payments, for payment in full, or cash payments.

How Should Payments Be Made?

Participants can pay for programs and services using cash, checks, money orders, direct bank transfers, credit cards, debit cards, prepayment cards/gift cards, and vouchers. Organizations that engage in a barter system may also allow participants to build up internal payment accounts where after volunteering for ten hours at the agency, for instance, an individual earns $10.00 in program points. These points may then be used to pay for a program or service. Cash may appear to be the simplest form of payment, but handling money can raise questions about security and may be inconvenient when exact change is required. Accepting payment by check is commonly practiced, but concerns exist related to accepting checks from individuals who do not have sufficient funds (which you will not know in advance) or who live out of town. Credit cards are also widely accepted although they can create additional paperwork for the leisure services organization and add to operating expenses.

Debit cards have become a popular means for paying for services. Debit cards look like credit cards, but act more like plastic checks because the money comes directly from the customer's checking account upon use. Related to both debit cards and credit cards are prepayment cards. These are based on cards that store a dollar value on a magnetic strip or in a microchip embedded in the card (e.g., a prepaid calling card for telephone use). As services are purchased, a staff member scans the card and a specific amount is deducted from the total value of the card. These cards may be most helpful when offered as an opportunity for customers to provide a leisure experience to someone else as a gift or for parents/guardians to give to children in place of money. In some agencies these cards can be used at the snack bar, concession stands, for equipment rental, or in other service areas. Another form of payment, vouchers, can also be used effectively, especially when organizations wish to subsidize the cost of a specific program. Whatever the method of payment, programmers must remember that for many transactions, the simplicity and speed with which payment is made may influence the customer's perception of overall service quality.

Facilitating the Anticipation Experience

Once an individual makes a decision and commits to a specific program or service she or he begins to prepare for and anticipate the upcoming experience. Some experiences require extensive preparation, while others are nearly instantaneous. For example, compare someone who chooses to go for a hike in a local park (very little advance planning or preparation) to someone planning a two-week backpacking experience with an ecotour operator (extensive planning and preparation). For more involved experiences, the planning and anticipation can be as exciting as the actual experience. Consider the planning one might engage in when preparing for the backpacking trip; it could include reading about the destination or route of the trip, researching and buying the gear and food needed for the trip, or exploring the history of the people and places to be visited along the way. This preparation becomes a vital part of the person's overall experience and offers the programmer a unique opportunity (with a little planning and foresight) to enhance the experience before it even begins.

Organizations and programmers can accomplish this enhancement in a variety of ways. For example, the agency can send program packets to participants and include such things as packing lists, an explanation of policies and procedures, a welcome letter from program staff, and material that explains the logistics of programs so customers begin to anticipate what to expect. Other possibilities for program packets include reading lists of relevant books, website addresses, videos and CDs/DVDs, and other resources. Staff might send periodic pre-experience emails or make phone calls to registrants to check in with them, answer questions, and generate excitement. For example, youth coaches often contact their players prior to beginning practice and tell them what to expect, when and where practices will begin, how to dress, and respond to any expressed concerns.

Building the anticipation for a program or event is a great way to add value to services. In Grand Rapids, Michigan, the local parks and recreation department offers a skills clinic for youngsters about to participate

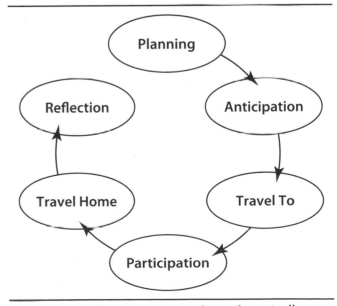

Figure 10.12 A program experience is typically considered to have six stages.

in a youth sports program. The morning workshop not only helps prepare the children for the upcoming program, but it also provides one of the meeting times for a mandatory parents' orientation to the program. Each parent orientation lasts approximately 30 minutes and requires that parents sit through a short video explaining the philosophy of the program (i.e., skill development and fun) as well as outlining the behavior expectations for parents during games and practices.

One area that programmers have to guard against in building anticipation for programs is making false promises or facilitating too much pre-program "hype." Thus, a critical component of the anticipation process is managing the expectations of customers, as expectations play a crucial role in the evaluation of the overall quality of a program or service. As we discussed in Chapter Two, quality—a perception of excellence—is the extent to which the services received by a customer equal or exceed expectations. Customer expectations for programs and services are developed in many ways. Factors that influence customer expectations include agency image (as seen through the web, logos, public persona, etc.), staff professionalism, word-of-mouth communications from staff and other customers, personal needs, past experiences, external communication (such as promotional materials), and the concept of equity (primarily applicable in the public and nonprofit sectors).

Within this list of factors, organizations can have the most direct impact on customer expectations through external communication. As noted in Chapter Eight on program promotion, external communications may be used to inform, persuade, educate, and remind customers about various elements of a program. To be most successful within the anticipation phase of an experience, organizations should attempt to inform and educate customers about the upcoming experience. A good rule of thumb in this process is to be realistic in program information and description, and then over-deliver during the actual program. By being realistic and over-delivering, organizations exceed the expectations of customers. This ultimately aids in enhancing participant perceptions of quality.

Facilitating the Travel To Experiences

Another often overlooked component of a parks, recreation, or leisure experience is the experience of travel to a program. Travel time to programs may be viewed as part of anticipating the experience and can be used by programmers as a transition zone into the experience itself. For example, when individual con-

stituents transport themselves to a recreation experience or event (e.g., by foot, bicycle, motor vehicle), rather than seeing this as outside the immediate realm of the parks, recreation, and leisure experience, programmers can influence that experience by providing suggestions for scenic routes and/or the quickest routes with the approximate travel time for each. Programmers might provide ideas for short activities or audio stimulation (e.g., songs or stories on audiotapes or CDs, or downloaded to one's MP3 player) to be played en route.

In other instances, when recreation programmers provide transportation to a special event (e.g., a bus is utilized to transport seniors to a festival) beyond the most immediate concerns of safety and convenience, the transportation itself can be a stand-alone programming opportunity. The tone is set and the entire experience impacted by the music played, songs led, drinks and food provided, decorations used, and games and activities engaged in (or not) while in transport. Regardless of the means used to get to a program, the travel-to experience does have an impact on the upcoming on-site experience for most constituents; thus, the travel-to time presents another opportunity to enhance the overall experience.

Facilitating the Participation Experience

From an early age, we are taught to deal with complexity by breaking things down into their separate parts. In this text, we have broken the programming

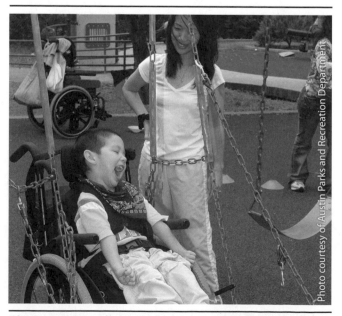

Figure 10.13 All people can experience joy when participating in a planned recreation activity.

process into specific tasks to accomplish. Yet at some points all these tasks must come together in order to see the whole picture and experience the moment. We are reminded that participants want and expect to be positively, emotionally, and memorably impacted by their experiences. This ability to "see things whole" takes place during the participation phase of the experience. It is where all the hard work comes together and the program takes on a life of its own. Thus, the role of the programmer changes from that of an organizer and planner to a facilitator—someone who helps facilitate the experience for participants in such ways as to deliver the positive benefits they seek. In addition to physical preparation, program facilitators must also consider preparing the human resources.

Staff Preparation

Just as participants prepare for upcoming programs, so too, do recreation programmers. This preparation can be quite simple, such as gathering equipment and supplies. However, it can also be quite extensive, such as creating a unique physical environment, completing pre-program checklists to ensure safety, understanding the process of activity analysis, preparing staff and/or volunteers, and making sure necessary supplies and equipment are available. By addressing these elements of planning, programmers can use the time prior to the program to enhance the experience of constituents in a number of ways.

Creating the Physical Environment

As noted earlier in this chapter, the physical environment or "tangibles" of an organization is one of the major dimensions that impacts the provision of quality services. As a result, prior to the beginning of a program, programmers can address a number of areas related to the physical environment that will facilitate the overall experience of participants.

The overall aesthetics of a facility or area provides subtle messages to customers about the organization. The appearance of the reception or registration area, the cleanliness of the bathrooms, and the condition and level of repair of exercise equipment all present the organization in a positive or negative light. As one airline executive lamented, "If our bathrooms are dirty, people think our planes will not fly." This is also the case for parks, recreation, and leisure services programs. When the environment is not clean and well maintained, constituents may have questions about the quality of programs and services.

It is important to note that the facility and equipment do not necessarily have to be new; a clean, orderly, and well-maintained area can present a positive image for an organization. This is especially relevant from a servant leadership approach to programming, which encourages programmers to be good stewards of resources and equipment. This attitude often spills onto participants, and when we take care of the environment, participants tend to take good care of the resources as well.

In addition to assuring the basic cleanliness in the program area, programmers can also use decorations and sound (e.g., music, sound effects) to set the stage for the upcoming program. Being aware of the physical environment of a proposed program or service can be a crucial component to the overall customer experience. For example, using decorations can enhance the overall program experience by creating ambiance and drawing participants into the emotion of experience.

Different lighting, colors, decorations, sounds, and spatial arrangements create unique moods within programs and programmers can manipulate these attributes to accomplish specific objectives. For example, rock-and-roll music, informal dress, bright lights, and brightly colored malt shop decorations might be used to create one type of mood, whereas classical music, formal dress, intimate lighting, and European café decorations will create a different type of mood. In setting the mood for programs and services, programmers must work hard to create the appropriate atmosphere. This includes having all props and equipment ready prior to participants arriving for a specific program or event.

Some recreation departments have developed "decoration tool kits" that include a variety of tools and resources to help in the decorating process. This tool kit might include such things as duct tape, staple gun, fishing line, zip ties, string, glue, rubber bands, scissors, pliers, hammer, screwdrivers, utility knife, paper punch, bungee cords, tacks, paper clips, staple remover, paper, pencils, markers, and a balloon pump. The decoration tool kit helps to ensure that everything needed to put up decorations is present and available when needed. It is particularly helpful when volunteers are setting up for events without the involvement of staff. In addition, this type of tool kit provides everyone the tools to be creative "in the moment" of setting up decorations. Finding decorations for programs can be an art in and of itself. As discussed in Chapter Eight, scrounging can be one effective method to create innovative decorations on a shoestring budget.

Risk Management

Many organizations utilize checklists immediately prior to beginning programs, which may focus on a variety of areas. For example, adventure education programs that utilize ropes courses have facilitators/leaders conduct a walk-through of the course and complete a checklist to ensure that the structures and equipment are safe and ready to use. This type of checklist is related to good risk management. Other checklists may be used to ensure that the programmer or leader did not leave any task undone prior to the start of a program, thus serving as a reminder about maintaining the quality of the overall program. Still other checklists fill a combination of these functions and direct programmers through the program design and implementation process. Figure 10.14 presents a list of questions for staff developing an outdoor trip program to help focus risk management efforts.

Rationale

Is there a rationale/reason for going on the trip? What are the goals and objectives for the trip? Do these goals and objectives fit into the overall philosophy of the organization?

Participants

Who are the participants? What are needs of the participants? Does meeting these needs fit into the rationale and philosophy of the organization? Do the participants match the needs as established by the trip rationale? Are they compatible with routing, scheduling, activities, and location?

Activities

Does the chosen activity or activities match the needs of participants as established by the trip rationale?

Location

Does the chosen location match the needs of participants as established by the trip rationale? Is the location compatible with the types of activities we want to do while on the trip?

Route

Does the chosen route and schedule match the needs of participants as established by the trip rationale? Are the route and schedule compatible with the activities and the location on the trip?

Group

Do the groups formed match the needs of participants as established by the trip rationale? Are the groups compatible with the routing, scheduling, activities, and location of the trip?

Staff

Do the staff match the needs of participants as established by the trip rationale? Are they compatible with the routing, scheduling, activities, and location of the trip? Are staff compatible with each other?

Equipment

Do the equipment lists match the needs of participants as established by the trip rationale? Are they compatible with the staff, routing, scheduling, activities, and location of the trip?

Food and Water

Does the food and water provision match the needs of the participants as established by the trip rationale? Are the provisions compatible with the equipment, staff, routing, scheduling, activities, and location of the trip? Are meals balanced? What kind of water purification system will be used?

Accommodations

Do the accommodations match the needs of the participants as established by the trip rationale? Are the accommodations compatible with the provisions, equipment, staff, routing, scheduling, activities, and location of the trip? Have advanced reservations been made where necessary? Have payments been made in advance?

Transportation

Does the chosen means of transportation match the needs of the participants as established by the trip rationale? Are the methods of transportation compatible with the accommodations, provisions, equipment, staff, routing, scheduling, activities, and location of the trip?

Communication

Does the chosen means of communication match the needs of the participants as established by the trip rationale? Is the method of communication compatible with the transportation, accommodations, provisions, equipment, staff, routing, scheduling, activities, and location of the trip?

Budgeting

Do the financial arrangements meet the needs of the participants as established by the trip rationale? Is the method of budgeting compatible with the communication, transportation, accommodations, provisions, equipment, staff, routing, scheduling, activities, and location of the trip?

Risk Management

Is the method of risk management compatible with all the above elements of the trip? Has a risk management plan been developed? Are staff familiar with the risk management plan? Do staff have all necessary certifications and skills to lead the trip?

Figure 10.14 Pre-programming checklist for an outdoor program (adapted from Priest & Gass, 1997)

Activity Analysis

Activity analysis is an important task for programmers to undertake prior to the beginning of most programs. Analyzing activities helps programmers make quick adjustments as needed during an actual event so that everyone can participate fully and safely. *Activity analysis is a systematic process through which we learn the nuances of activities so that we can design, implement, adapt, and evaluate appropriate programs for various constituent groups.* We use it in conjunction with needs assessments and other forms of information gathering, and it is used during many phases of the programming cycle. Because of the impact the utilization of this information can have on the design and implementation of programs and services, the function of analyzing an activity is significant in programming efforts. This process is particularly important when working with those who have developmental, cognitive, and/or physical disabilities. Understanding the demands of a particular activity helps programmers to most appropriately match participant abilities with activity requirements.

Activity Analysis by Domain

Activity analysis has been approached from several different perspectives. One way to analyze activities (i.e., to break them down into understandable parts) is to examine the requirements of different domains for participant success. These domains include examining the *psychomotor (physical), cognitive (intellectual), affective (emotional),* and *social interaction* demands of an activity. Stumbo and Peterson (2004) offer descriptions of what might fall within each of the domains.

Within the *psychomotor domain* we might look at what body parts are involved (e.g., feet, hands, legs, eyes), the types of movements required by those body parts (e.g., kicking, throwing, twisting, bending, standing), the types of locomotion required (e.g., scooting, walking, crawling, skipping), level of exertion, necessary degree of fitness, skill level, endurance, rhythm, and sensory demands.

The *cognitive* domain requirements might include the complexity of instructions and rules, required academic skills (e.g., reading, writing, math), level of concentration and ability to focus, level of factual knowledge/understanding/evaluation/analysis/synthesis required, ability to think quickly, abstract thinking, and use of verbal and other communication skills.

Affective requirements of an activity include opportunities to communicate feelings, level of potential enjoyment, opportunities to display creativity, control over one's environment, self-discipline, impulse control, self-esteem, interacting with others, and teamwork.

Finally, many activities require some degree of *social interaction.* In this domain, we examine the levels of competition/cooperation, the ability to work within rules, individual or small group involvement, level of structure in the activity, the mix of participants (in terms of age, sex, ethnicity, abilities, and so forth), interaction levels, proximity, and touching.

Activity Analysis by Social Interactions

Another way of conducting an activity analysis is to focus solely on *examining the social interactions* required in the activity. This was first developed and presented in 1974 by Avedon and later adapted by Smith, Austin, and Kennedy (2001). The different interaction possibilities, with examples of each, follow:

- Intraindividual—within one person; the activity involves no outside person or object (e.g., running or jogging)

- Extraindividual—directed to an outside object; no interaction with another person is involved (e.g., art project or reading)

- Aggregate—a number of people all concentrate on an object with no interaction between them (e.g., group bicycle ride, riding on a roller coaster)

- Interindividual—dyad (two people interacting) in a competition format (e.g., board games, tennis)

- Unilateral—three or more people in a competition where one of them is 'it' (e.g., tag, keep away)

- Multilateral—three or more people in a competition where there is no 'it' (e.g., golf match, swim meet)

- Intragroup—two or more people cooperating toward the same goal (e.g., barbershop quartet, relay teams)

- Intergroup—two or more intragroups engaged in competition (e.g., team sports)

Activity Analysis by Activity Dimensions

A third way of conducting an activity analysis is to *look at the various dimensions of different leisure activities and search for commonalties*. These dimensions can include body contact, element of chance, kind and intensity of competition, space required, time required, kinds and use of props, role-taking functions, rules and their complexity, levels of participation, leeway for emergent leadership, respite opportunities, suspense, role switching, pleasure/pain (win/lose), use of rewards and punishments, obstacles, trust, real-life themes, amount of ritual, genderizing games, humor, challenge, locomotion, movement of body parts, competency required, and interactiveness (Farrell & Lundegren, 1991).

Whichever method (or combination) of activity analysis is utilized, the key point is to examine the different attributes or characteristics of the activity so that they can be easily understood and matched to constituent needs, desires, and capabilities. When one considers program elements in this way one can best determine if and what types of modifications are necessary for optimum participant and programmatic success.

Modifications as a Result of Activity Analysis

One important reason for conducting activity analyses is to most appropriately match activities with potential participants As a result of conducting an activity analysis we can see how to best modify or adapt an activity for maximum participation, enjoyment, and success—especially for people with special needs or who have a disability. General guidelines for use in adapting or modifying programs and activities for people with special needs have been developed over the years. First, programmers will want to review the results of the activity analysis to identify the particular demands of the activity or event. Through this process we also identify environmental and equipment requirements so that we can determine how much and what type(s) of modification is needed for anticipated participants.

Overall guidelines for adapting activities for full inclusion of all participants include:

1. Programs should include enjoyable activities that are suitable for the chronological age of participants.

2. Activities should be selected to include a wide variety of leisure pursuits.

3. Activities should resemble those found in community-based settings as much as possible to permit learning that can be used in other settings.

4. Programs should include opportunities in all program formats with emphasis on pursuits that stimulate motivation and provide enjoyment.

5. Difficulty levels should be such that self-confidence is instilled through repeated success in different environments.

More specifically, programmers should examine activities and events (in a task analysis process) and modify only the components necessary to ensure inclusion. In addition, as we modify particular activities we will want to consider the following guidelines:

1. Change as little as necessary.

2. Avoid making assumptions about a person's abilities based on an apparent, perceived, or actual disability.

3. Where possible, involve the person in the modification process.

4. Consider all levels of competition (e.g., a person with a special need might be able to compete at one level, but not another).

5. Offer activities that are characteristic of what is offered to the general population.

6. Develop common denominators for activities that encourage everyone playing by the same rules. For example, in wheelchair basketball, everyone plays in a wheelchair (whether needed for ambulation or not) and follows the same rules. The common denominators for equality in participation are the common rules and the wheelchairs.

7. Develop ways for people to participate rather than watch or help the leader.

8. Start at the level where participants are currently functioning.

9. Provide everyone with opportunities to exercise free choice.

Five general categories of modification for specific activities have been identified over the years: (1) procedural and operational adaptations (e.g., modify the rules, walk rather than run, shorten the time for the game, use buddies); (2) environmental adaptations (e.g., adjust boundaries, change playing surfaces, use bright lighting); (3) equipment adaptations (e.g., add aids to existing equipment, use special equipment), (4) change equipment (e.g., use a beachball in place of a volleyball); and (5) human intervention (e.g., a person might physically assist individuals by pushing their wheelchairs or by verbally guiding a person through a task). By considering all of these modification opportunities and then following the general guidelines as suggested previously, we can provide recreation and leisure programs with dignity for all.

Staff and/or Volunteer Roles

In Chapter Seven we encouraged programmers to visualize their program come to life. Later in this chapter we discuss how this can help with sequencing and pacing activities throughout the event; visualizing can also help with thinking through a staff plan for programs and events. As experienced programmers visualize their program, they pay special attention to the role of staff and volunteers in implementing that program. A question programmers commonly ask is, "How can staff and volunteers enhance and facilitate the program or event for participants?" In developing and implementing a staffing plan for a program or event, programmers will want to begin by thinking about the following questions:

1. **Prior to the event:** What type of (and how many) staff and volunteers are needed (consider staff skills, participant needs)? How will they best be utilized? How will the organization attract, train, and retain the staff and volunteers needed? Will staff need to conduct background checks on staff and volunteers?

2. **During the event:** How will we supervise and offer support to staff and volunteers?

3. **After the event:** How will we evaluate and thank staff and volunteers?

Prior to the actual event, programmers will want to identify the number of staff needed and any specialized skills or certifications needed by staff or volunteers to implement the program. This can be done in a variety of ways. In many situations, standards that dictate a staff-to-participant ratio needed for specific programs may already be in place. For example, the American Camp Association recommends the following staff-child ratio for camps:

- One staff member for every five campers ages 4 and 5 (every six campers in this age range at day camp).

- One staff member for every six campers ages 6 to 8 (every eight campers in this age range at day camp).

- One staff member for every eight campers ages 9 to 14 (every 10 campers in this age range at day camp).

- One staff member for every 10 campers ages 15 to 17 (every 12 campers in this age range at day camp).

Beyond knowing the specific number of staff needed, programmers must also understand what specific skills or certifications are needed by each staff person to implement the program or event. These are often identified in formal job descriptions (see Figure 10.15 on p. 292), which include both the overall responsibilities and duties of a position as well as the qualifications needed (i.e., knowledge, skills, and abilities). In many situations, organizations may have developed job descriptions already in place; in other cases the programmer may need to develop job descriptions, especially in the case of a one-time program or special event. Many parks, recreation, and leisure services agencies require that all staff and volunteers working with minor children undergo state and/or national background checks. Generally, the costs of the background checks are covered by the hiring agency. See Figure 10.16 (pp. 293-294) for an example of a background check policy and permission form.

When utilizing a range of staff and volunteers to conduct short-term events, many programmers will create a briefing card. A briefing card provides needed information for individuals in specific positions (see Figure 10.17 on p. 295), and serves as a way to ensure that staff have information they need to do their jobs.

In addition to knowing what type of (and how many) staff or volunteers are needed, parks, recreation, and leisure services organizations will also want to know how those people can be best utilized. Volunteers like to feel useful and to have an identified purpose with what they do. A well-defined job description will aid this process as it will facilitate the (continued on p. 295)

CALVIN COLLEGE INTRAMURALS
POSITION ANNOUNCEMENT—Intramurals Coordinator

Supervision
- Reports to the Intramural Director
- Assists in the supervision of Intramural Assistants

Overall Responsibilities
- Responsible for planning, organizing, and supervising the Calvin College Intramural program

Duties Include:
- Organizing tournament schedules
- Coordinating gym time in the Physical Education Building to avoid potential conflicts with athletics and open gym time
- Assisting in the scheduling of sports assistants to assure building and activity coverage at all intramural events
- Assisting in the registration process for intramural events
- Assisting in promoting the intramural program
- Maintaining and updating the College's intramural Web page
- Attending and assisting with all intramural staff meetings
- Assisting with other duties as assigned.

Qualifications
- Basic computer skills (e.g., word processing, spreadsheets) required. Experience with Web page design and management preferred
- Ability to relate to people and communicate effectively
- Able to take direction as well as being responsible and self-directed
- Prior experience programming sports and recreation events

Job Clarification
Level C—Pay scale $5.45 to $7.20 an hour

Hiring Process
- Turn in application by Thursday, September 10. Applications are available in front of the Director's office (PE 262B). Questions can be directed to the Director (555-5555, office & 555-5555, home).
- Interviews will be held Friday, September 11 and Monday, September 14
- First staff meeting, Wednesday, September 16 at 3:30 p.m.

CALVIN COLLEGE INTRAMURALS
JOB DESCRIPTION—Intramurals Assistantship

Purpose of the Position
Offer students an opportunity to gain experience by providing coordination and direction to the Calvin Intramural Program. Responsible for planning, organizing, and supervising the intramural program.

Supervision
- Reports to the Intramural Director
- Assists in the supervision of all intramural personnel

Duties Include:
- Organizing tournament schedules
- Coordinating gym time in the Physical Education Building to avoid potential conflicts with athletics and open gym time
- Assisting in the scheduling of sports assistants to assure building and activity coverage at all intramural events
- Serving as the office manager of the program including managing the registration process
- Promoting the intramural program
- Maintaining and updating the intramural Web page
- Leading intramural staff meetings
- Recruiting and hiring intramural staff
- Assisting with other duties as assigned

Qualifications
- Basic computer skills (e.g., word processing, spreadsheets) required. Experience with Web page design and management preferred
- Ability to relate to people and communicate effectively
- Able to take direction as well as being responsible and self-directed
- Prior experience programming sports and recreation events
- Experience with the Calvin intramural program preferred

Job Clarification
Semester stipend of between $1,000 and $1,200 depending on experience

Hiring Process
- Turn in application by the middle of April. Applications are available in front of the Director's office (PE 262B). Questions can be directed to the Director (555-5555, director@calvin.edu).
- Interviews will be held in late April/early May with the position starting the following fall.

Figure 10.15 Sample job descriptions

**nne **rundel
R E C R E A T I O N A N D P A R K S
1 Harry S Truman Parkway
Annapolis, Maryland 21401
Attention: Mark Oliver
(410) 222-7311 ext. 3404 * FAX (410) 222-4509
www.aacounty.org/recparks

BACKGROUND CHECK PROGRAM
GENERAL INFORMATION

COUNTY POLICY

"Any person convicted of illegal use of drugs, drug distribution, child abuse or violent crimes shall be prohibited from participation in leagues or programs sponsored by the Department of Recreation and Parks."

As written, the policy does not allow for organizational discretion in granting exceptions to individuals with criminal convictions as referenced above. For the purpose of this policy, violent crimes are defined as homicide, rape, sexual assault, robbery, assault, and battery.

Anne Arundel County Department of Recreation & Parks does not hire or fire volunteers; the Athletic Associations are responsible for those actions.

WHO MUST HAVE A BACKGROUND CHECK

1. Anyone who has care, custody and/or control of youth participants in any program or activity. This condition applies to programs or activities sponsored by the Department of Recreation & Parks, or any group or organization permitted the use of a County park or Board of Education field or facility. The background check must be completed prior to any personal involvement with the children.

2. All Coaches who participate in the Department's Coaches Certification Program must have a background check prior to receiving their Certification Card.

3. All Officers, Board Members and Sports Commissioners with Youth Organizations that participate in County-sponsored leagues.

4. All Board of Director's of Coaches Associations affiliated with County-sponsored youth sports.

5. All Coaches, Officers, Board Members and Sports Commissioners with Level 1 Accredited Youth Organizations regardless of their affiliation with a County-sponsored league.

6. All Coaches and Officers in Organizations that have opted to apply the Background Investigation Policy to their assistant coaches and/or officers.

HOW BACKGROUNDS WILL BE PROCESSED

1. Individual will complete and sign the Authorization and Release for the Procurement of an Investigative Report form. Additionally, the President of the organization will sign the form.

2. The signed Authorization and Release for the Procurement of an Investigative Report form must be delivered to Recreation & Parks at the address identified above, Attention: Mark Oliver, or given to a departmental representative.

3. The Investigative Report will be completed within one week upon receipt. If a negative report is received by Recreation & Parks, a departmental representative will call and discuss the information with the individual.

   If deemed necessary, a meeting will be held between the individual, the President of the Organization and representatives of Recreation & Parks.

Figure 10.16 Background check policy

Continued>>

AUTHORIZATION AND RELEASE
FOR THE PROCUREMENT
OF AN INVESTIGATIVE REPORT
(Revised July 2007)

Anne Arundel
RECREATION AND PARKS
1 Harry S Truman Parkway
Annapolis, Maryland 21401
Attention: Mark Oliver
(410) 222-7311 Ext. 3539 FAX (410) 222-4439

I, the undersigned, do hereby authorize Anne Arundel County Department of Recreation & Parks, by and through its independent contractor, Kroll Background America, Inc., to procure an investigative report on me that includes social security verification and criminal history records.

I understand that I am entitled to a complete and accurate disclosure of the nature and scope of any investigative report of which I am the subject upon my written request to Kroll Background America, if such is made within a reasonable time after the date hereof. I also understand that I may receive a written summary of my rights under 15 U.S.C. Section 1681 et. seq.

I further authorize any person, business entity or governmental agency who may have information relevant to the above to disclose the same to Anne Arundel County Department of Recreation & Parks, by and through Kroll Background America, including by not limited to, any and all courts, public agencies, and law enforcement agencies regardless of whether such person, business entity or governmental agency compiled information itself or received it from other sources.

I hereby release Anne Arundel County Department of Recreation & Parks, by and through Kroll Background America and any and all persons, business entities and governmental agencies, whether public or private, from any and all liability, claims and/or demands, by me, my heirs or others making such claim or demand on my behalf, for providing an investigative report hereby authorized. I understand that this Authorization/Release form shall remain in effect for the duration of my association with Anne Arundel County.

INDIVIDUAL'S NAME IS POSTED ON R&P'S WEBSITE WHEN BACKGROUND IS COMPLETE
BACKGROUND CHECKS ARE GOOD FOR THREE YEARS
PRINT CLEARLY AND COMPLETE ALL REQUIRED INFORMATION

FULL FIRST NAME	FULL MIDDLE NAME	FULL LAST NAME

OTHER NAMES / DATES	SOCIAL SECURITY NUMBER

DATE OF BIRTH (MM-DD-YY)	DAYTIME TELEPHONE	NIGHT-TIME TELEPHONE

CURRENT STREET ADDRESS	CITY	STATE	ZIP CODE

LIST ALL PREVIOUS ADDRESSES (COUNTY & STATE) FROM AGE 18 TO PRESENT

1. _____ COUNTY   STATE   DATES   3. _____ COUNTY   STATE   DATES

2. _____ COUNTY   STATE   DATES   4. _____ COUNTY   STATE   DATES

Have you ever been convicted of a crime or convicted in a military court martial?   ☐ YES   ☐ NO

Are you currently under any investigation or have a pending charge?   ☐ YES   ☐ NO

I certify that the information contained on this Authorization/Release form is true and correct, and acknowledge that I may be precluded from coaching due to false, omitted or fraudulent information.

SIGNATURE	DATE	ORGANIZATION / TROOP NUMBER

Background Policy and Database can be accessed on the Department's Website at www.aacounty.org/recparks

Figure 10.16 Background check form (continued from previous page)

(continued from p. 291) matching of workers to needs. Program coordinators will want to consider availability, strengths, limitations, previous experience, interests, and other volunteer attributes to assist with this effort.

Once a programmer knows how many staff or volunteers are needed the next step is to recruit, attract, and hire the necessary individuals and train them to implement the program. This process will vary depending on who is attracted and for what position. Some positions may have a very formal interview process while others will not. For example, a programmer might pull staff from throughout the organization to run a one-time special event, hire part-time staff for general help, contract with someone who has special skills (e.g., karate instructor), or recruit volunteers from the community. Figure 10.18 (on p. 296) presents one means of recruiting volunteers through the Internet; volunteer recruitment also occurs at recruitment fairs, through mass media (e.g., newspapers, radio), and through targeting mailings.

The next step in preparing staff to implement a program is orienting/training staff and/or volunteers to implement the program. Again, this process can be very detailed, such as conducting a staff training week for staff working at a resident camp in the summer or could be as simple as meeting with volunteers an hour prior to a day long carnival to kick off an organization's summer program. When using volunteers or staff in a one-time event the briefing cards mentioned earlier and seen in Figure 10.17 offer a useful means of communication. Typically, briefing cards include such information as times for arrival and departure, responsibilities, any needed clothing or equipment, reporting structure, and so on.

Throughout an actual program or special event, programmers will need to put into place a supervisory plan to support staff and/or volunteers. Such a plan typically includes identifying who will be the "on-call" individual who is available to staff during the event if problems arise. In addition, name the contact who will serve as the on-site planner to ensure that staff and volunteers understand what needs to be done. Of course, in addition to knowing who these people are, it is important to note how they can be contacted during the event (e.g., cell phone, walkie-talkie).

The staffing element of programming would not be complete without thinking about evaluation and appreciation. In terms of evaluation, how will programmers obtain feedback for staff involved in the activity? Will a wrap-up meeting, a series of one-on-one meetings, or a short feedback/evaluation form work best? Whatever methods used, they must allow the programmer to obtain the needed feedback to improve future programs. In addition to evaluation, programmers will want to think about how to express their appreciation to staff and (especially) volunteers who helped make the program a success. Methods of appreciation vary and often include certificates, T-shirts, letters, cards, banquets, and letters to the editor in the local paper.

Event: *4th of July Carnival*

Volunteer: *Isaac Hovda*

Contact Number: *555-9876*

Time In: *8:30 a.m.*   **Time Out:** *11:30 a.m.*

Position: *Card Booth*

Duties:

1. *Assist Rochelle D. at Card Booth*
   - *8:30–9:00 set up; 9:00–11:00 Booth Open; 11:00–11:30 clean up*
   - *Supplies and set-up materials are at your booth. For additional material see Sandy at the Main tent.*
2. *Help participants create a thank-you card for someone serving in the military.*
3. *Please wear your volunteer T-shirt.*
4. *Have Fun!*

Before You Leave:

1. *Return all supplies to the volunteer tent using the boxes provided.*
2. *Please complete an event evaluation.*

Thanks for helping create a successful event!

Briefing Card

Figure 10.17 Volunteer briefing card

Preparing Supplies and Equipment

In preparing for programs, it is important for programmers to know what supplies and equipment will be needed and where they can be obtained. In this context, we will refer to equipment as durable and reusable items (e.g., canoe paddles, floor mats) while supplies are materials that are consumed during an activity and not reusable (e.g., paper, paint). In many situations, equipment is shared between different programs and organizations. To ensure equipment availability, then, programmers need to pay specific attention to scheduling programs and events across programs (within one organization) and organizations (between two or more organizations). For instance, a kiln and several pottery wheels may be shared between two organizations. Each organization will have to work with the other when scheduling so as to avoid double-booking the equipment. Likewise, supplies must be budgeted for and purchased prior to the start of a program.

Being a good facilitator of an experience demands that programmers have done their homework in setting up the experience and are flexible enough to respond *in the moment* to enhance the overall experience. When done correctly, the result is magical, creating an experience that exceeds expectations. It is important to recognize that participants play an important role as programs unfold; part of the challenge for the programmer is to respond to participants as they respond to each other and the program. Review the story presented in Figure 10.19; the action required forethought and planning and it all came together in the moment to create a lasting memory for the young boy described.

In facilitating the actual program experience programmers/leaders must think about several things. First and foremost, programmers must understand how the activity or program will flow—this includes thinking about how the sequencing and pacing of the program will be managed. Second, programmers will need to examine how staff will interface with customers

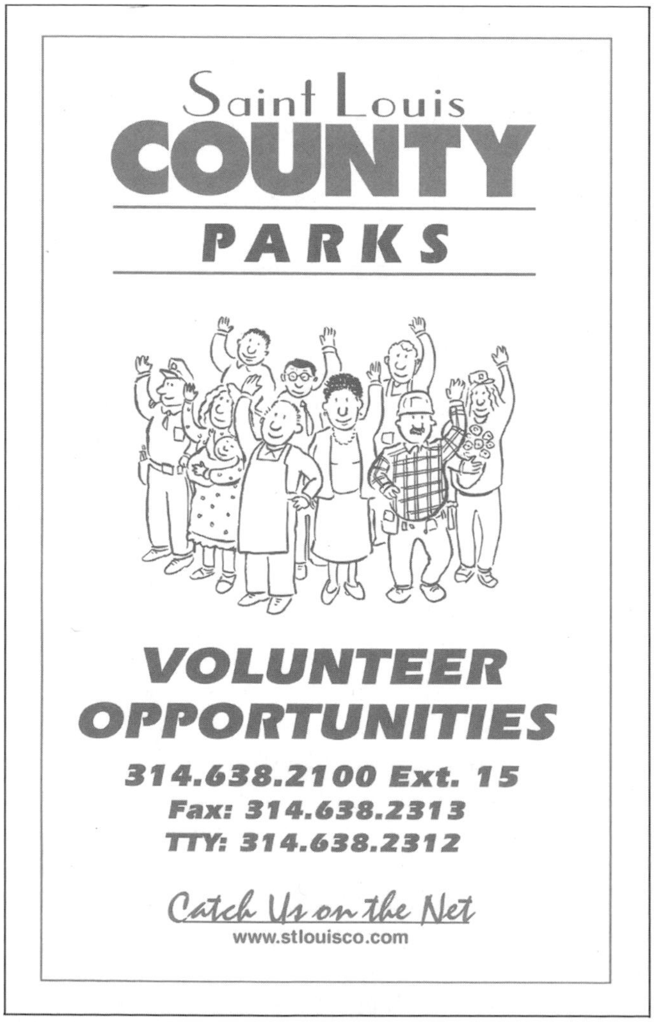

Saint Louis COUNTY PARKS — VOLUNTEER APPLICATION

9801 Mackenzie Road • St. Louis, MO 63123

Name: ______

Address: ______ Zip: ______

Phone: ______ Work: ______

Fax #: ______ E-Mail: ______

Birthdate: ______ Location Preferred: ______

Type of Volunteer Service Preferred: ______

How referred to us: ______

Are you now a student? ❑ Yes ❑ No

If so, where? ______

Are you presently ❑ Employed ❑ Retired

Check one: Most recent ❑ or current ❑ employer's name/address:

______

Employer's Phone: ______

Previous work experience: ______

Times you are available? ❑ Morning ❑ Afternoon ❑ Evening

Days available (circle): M T W T F S S

Have you been a volunteer elsewhere? ______

If so, with whom, responsibilities & dates: ______

Special skills: ______

Figure 10.18 St. Louis Park System volunteer application form throughout the experience (this includes how customer problems and complaints are handled). Thinking these situations through before and while the program is being delivered can serve to create a program environment that enhances a participant's overall experience.

Sequencing/Pacing

In several places in this text, we have discussed how mental imagery can help programmers think about how a program or an event will unfold, thereby helping them sequence programs and events. Once the event has begun, we can often change the sequence of events as the situation and participants demand. Thus, sequencing and pacing are two concepts that we need to understand as we facilitate and lead leisure programs. When sequencing we accept the responsibility for ordering activities in ways to enhance participant success and enjoyment. In this way we continue our commitment to servant leadership by putting the needs of participants first, and doing what is best for them.

Creating Magic

It happened one evening at the end of the Christmas parade. Folks, if you have not seen the Christmas Parade at Disney World, then someday you simply must. It is not just two people and an old horn, it's a parade's parade… Standing right on the corner of the main street where it meets the square, I watched the parade and saw something happening that I'll never forget…The parade was coming to an end as the Santa Claus float was rapidly approaching. Across the street a father stood on the edge of the sidewalk while his son was off the curb in the street itself where he could get a good close-up view. As he stood there this father reached into his coat pocket and took out a long, white card about four-inches high and twelve-inches wide and held it up behind his son's head. On the card in large block letters was printed the name "Richard." And when Santa rounded the corner, he called out, "Merry Christmas, everyone," and then added, "Oh, hello there Richard!" Well Richard's mouth dropped open, his eyes almost burst from his head, he doubled up, and just shook all over in ecstasy.

That was a magical movement. One of those superb moments of pure delight that remain with you forever. I am sure all his days Richard will remember the night Santa called out to him at Disney World. And the whole setup was so simple. His father simply wrote "Richard" on a card, put it in his pocket, and got ready. He cared enough about magic that he wanted to add it to his son's life. And believe me, he did.

Figure 10.19 Creating Magic (Van Matre, 1990, p. 78)

This role requires that we consider what we know about the potential participants (e.g., age, abilities, skills), resources (e.g., available equipment and facilities), activity (e.g., complexity of rules, physical and other domain requirements), and our own skills to conduct activities in a progression that enhances program goals.

We can sequence *within* an activity (e.g., begin a painting workshop by mixing paints before moving on to putting paint on a canvas) and within a program (e.g., early in a tai chi class we teach simple, easy-on-the-body exercises before moving on to more complex, physically demanding elements). It is usually appropriate to utilize both forms of sequencing in programming. In some cases, sequencing is critically important for safety reasons. For instance, in swimming, gymnastics, skiing, scuba diving, and in facilitating ropes courses, sequencing is very important to the safety and well-being of participants. If we move to advanced skills before participants have a clear understanding of foundational skills, people could get hurt (i.e., physically, emotionally, and/or psychologically).

Closely related to sequencing is pacing. Programmers and activity leaders pace activities by manipulating the tempo (e.g., some activities are full of quick movements while others are much slower in their movements and pace); and by sequencing or scheduling activities in a certain order (e.g., by alternating fast-paced and slow-paced activities). Pacing is important to managing fatigue levels of participants and to respond to learner readiness (particularly in skill-based activities such as learning to play soccer). This is important because different individuals may need different pacing in order to learn certain skills. If people are overstimulated and/or fatigued, learning and attending to task drop off. Thus, pacing and sequencing are designed to match the readiness of participants with activities.

Interfacing with Constituents within a Servant Leadership Context

This function of a parks, recreation, and leisure services programmer is perhaps the most critical to organizational success. Being available and responsive to customers are tasks involved in the customer interface role. As mentioned in an earlier chapter, interfacing with constituents begins the first time the programmer and customer come into contact with one another. This may be in passing as the programmer initially greets participants, at registration, on the telephone, through promotional materials, or any other time the "long arm" of the programmer reaches out and touches a potential participant. Thus, we must always be aware of how others might perceive us at all times.

Different aspects of interfacing with participants involve different skills. All interfacing, however, involves treating people with respect, exhibiting an attitude of service to others, and doing what is necessary to maintain human dignity. When we interface with constituents we display our leadership capabilities. In this role we may need to remind ourselves that rather than being an end in itself, leadership is a vehicle or a means to an end—it helps us to help others.

Good leaders have a whole host of skills. We would like to suggest that leaders in programming focus on the skills listed below. Many of these skills are rooted in the ten characteristics of servant leadership presented in Chapter One; other skills relate to being creative and taking risks (discussed in Chapter Seven); and still others relate to having integrity and realizing that delivering recreation programs takes place within a values framework. This framework exists for both the organization and the individual programmer. Thus, programmer/leader skills include, but are not limited to:

1. listening effectively and communicating clearly.

2. seeking out and enabling great ideas in others—empowering them to be the best people possible.

3. engaging in creative thinking and other risk-taking behaviors.

4. having courage to stand in the face of conflict and confusion.

5. sharing and drawing others into the organizational vision and mission.

6. practicing an orientation toward others—putting others' needs ahead of one's own.

7. selling the benefits of involvement in parks, recreation, and leisure services.

8. being willing to support and defend a moral position.

9. knowing and understanding the role of our profession in overall quality of life.

10. being a servant to others.

Interfacing with customers also includes dealing with customer dissatisfaction. Pre-program checklists serve programmers in minimizing customer complaints, yet no matter how well-planned leisure programs may be, at one time or another, a participant will not be satisfied with the service provided. One early study into customer complaint behavior found that the average business never hears from 96 percent of its unhappy customers; and, for every complaint received the average company had twenty-six customers with problems, six of which were serious (Albrecht & Zemke, 1985). However, Wuest (2001) cited several studies that suggest customers with concerns that are addressed and resolved in a timely manner are often more loyal than customers who never had complaints in the first place. Therefore, it is important for organizations to take a two-prong approach to dealing with customer complaints. First, organizations must examine how they can encourage constituents to share their dissatisfaction with program staff. Second, an organization needs to provide staff with direction and the authority to handle participant dissatisfaction as it arises or is brought to the staff's attention.

Parks, recreation, and leisure services organizations can encourage comments and possible complaints from participants in a variety of ways. Many of these are discussed in Chapters Eleven and Twelve on program evaluation. In addition, many organizations utilize customer complaint/suggestion forms available in hard copy, electronically, or both (see Figures 10.20 and 10.21 on pp. 299-300). A written approach to complaints is favored by many organizations for several reasons. First, it allows information to be organized in a way that allows for an orderly, well-thought-out response. Second, it provides a safety valve or buffer for customer complaints, enabling the organization to handle concerns at the earliest possible time. This minimizes the concern that complaints won't be addressed until much later, when the situation may become more volatile. Third, a written complaint system provides document-based evidence, which facilitates long-term tracking.

One difficulty with written complaint forms is that they can be long and time-consuming, which may discourage participants from giving feedback. A second problem with complaint forms is that organizational response is not immediate and participants can become frustrated. As a result, all staff must be prepared prior to the implementation of programs and services to deal with customer dissatisfaction in later aspects of the program.

CARROLLTON TOWNSHIP
RECREATION

COMPLAINT FORM

DATE: _____

COMPLAINANT: _____ _____
(Please Print)

Phone Number: _____

Complaint: _____

_____

_____

_____

_____

_____

_____

_____

_____

(If more space is needed write on the back)

Signed: _____

• •

Follow Through _____

_____

_____

_____

_____

_____

_____

Signed _____ Date_____

Figure 10.20 Simple complaint form

NYC Parks & Recreation Patron and Visitor ADA Complaint Form

Date of Visit: _____

Person completing form (***check one***): ☐ Complainant ☐ Authorized Representative

Name: _____

Telephone #: (____) - _____

E-Mail: _____

Mailing Address: _____

_____

_____

ALLEGED VIOLATIONS

Describe the circumstances and the <u>specific location</u> that prompted your specific ADA complaint. Please be specific and provide details (attach additional pages if necessary).

_____

_____

_____

_____

_____

REQUESTED ACTION

Please describe the accommodation or request that would help to provide you with greater access to our facilities, programs, or services.

_____

_____

_____

_____

_____

_____   _____

Signature   Date

Figure 10.21 ADA complaint form

If we are serious about developing programs and services to be customer-centered, staff must avoid simply responding to constituent complaints—we must actively seek them out. Each complaint offers an opportunity for organizations to recover from the problem or concern and improve. Staff should also understand what they are authorized and not authorized to do to resolve a complaint. In some organizations staff have the authority to offer refunds for programs or vouchers for another program without seeking approval from administration. This helps to address the need for immediacy when working directly with constituents. In other situations staff are authorized to offer discounts on merchandise to apologize for a mistake. From a servant leadership perspective program leaders want to avoid having to pacify or make irate participants wait until a supervisor can review the situation.

When examining these types of questions it is helpful for staff to consider the priorities to be managed in each situation. Albrecht (1992) identified five critical priorities that organizations should discuss with staff as a means of helping them decide how to focus their energies in situations related to customer complaints. These priorities, which create the acronym SPACE, include

- *Speed.* How time-critical is the response to the customer? To the organization?

- *Personal Touch.* How important is it to manage the constituent's state of mind?

- *Accuracy.* How important is precision, conformance to specifications, safety, security, information clarity, and error prevention?

- *Cooperation.* How important is it to dovetail with another person's task or with what the customer is doing?

- *Economy.* How important is it to minimize the resource cost involved to the organization?

For example, if a disgruntled constituent complains to a staff member about an unexpected change in the program schedule, the staff member and her or his program supervisor might have already agreed that the sequence of priorities in addressing this complaint will be using a personal touch first, then economy, followed by cooperation with the constituent, speed (to avoid wasting the customer's time),

and accuracy. It's not that accuracy is not important, but it holds less importance on the priority list, which is keyed to keeping the customer's good will within the resources of the organization.

In addition to deciding on a sequence for addressing complaints, the programmer will need to identify what steps exist within the staff member's authority for solving the problem. Barneto (2006) offers the BLAST approach to addressing customer dissatisfaction:

- Believe the customer—in her or his mind, a wrong has been committed.

- Listen to the customer and hear what is said and not said (is she or he really upset about the schedule change or is something else going on?).

- Apologize for the change in the schedule while explaining why the change took place.

- Satisfy the customer's needs; perhaps looking for other alternatives with the customer while offering a $10 discount on a new registration fee might satisfy this person's concern.

- Thank the customer for bringing her or his dissatisfaction to your attention.

In this case, all five of the SPACE considerations are important and the BLAST approach gives the staff member a framework for dealing with the complaint. If these priorities are discussed between program

SPEED	**B**ELIEVE
PERSONAL TOUCH	**L**ISTEN
ACCURACY	**A**POLOGIZE
COOPERATION	**S**ATISFY
ECONOMY	**T**HANKS

Figure 10.22 SPACE and BLAST considerations to help staff to focus on customer complaints

supervisors and staff, employees can provide input into what is important on the frontlines. This framework can also help supervisors organize and share their expectations with staff in various situations.

Facilitating the Travel Home Experience

The travel home phase is similar to the travel to phase in that it may or may not be within the purview of the parks, recreation, and leisure services programmer. As with travel to the site of the experience, travel home is an opportunity for additional programming. Typically, we want this programming to assist in the reflection process of the experience. It tends to be less active than the travel to phase (in part because participants may be tired) and can aid in the transition from an enjoyable activity to warm and positive remembrances of that event. If we have direct impact on this phase we might ask participants to respond to questions about the activity verbally or in writing (e.g., trip journals are used by many groups). In this way, we can help constituents capture their thoughts, feelings, and memories in such a way as to prolong the leisure experience.

Facilitating the Reflection Experience

The reflection, recollection, or reminiscence stage may be viewed as the aftermath of an experience. As we

move to an experience economy (discussed in Chapter Two) customers are looking to create lasting memories. In fact, this is often a goal of trips with family or participating in programs with friends. It is important to remember that an experience can last forever, and its impact on the individual can remain for life. As a result, we want to encourage programmers to think about how they can create mechanisms that foster positive reflections about the experience offered by a parks, recreation, and leisure services organization. This not only enhances the overall experience for participants, but also makes it more likely that the individual will become a repeat customer. Past experiences can be an important driver for future purchases; they can also facilitate excellent word-of-mouth promotion for the organization.

Parks, recreation, and leisure services organizations often engage the memories of previous participants in attracting them to future programs and events. Consider when Disney celebrated the 25th anniversary of Disney World in Orlando with an advertising campaign entitled "Remember the Magic." The advertisements resembled vintage home movies and featured scenes of people swimming, meeting Mickey Mouse, and enjoying themselves in the park over the past 25 years. The campaign's aim was to encourage viewers to remember their first encounter with Mickey Mouse and invited viewers to return with their own families.

These types of advertisements can be so powerful that Braun, Ellis, and Loftus (2002) remind organizations to act ethically in this process. They found in

---

Use Photographs
Take pictures and send them to participants following the program.

Help Participants Create Remembrances
Children's art projects are often kept by parents and children to provide a visual symbol by which to remember programs.

Provide Promotional Items such as T-shirts, Stickers, or Pins
Hurricane Outward Bound ends their courses with participants pinning fellow classmates while telling the person what they enjoyed about her or him during the course.

Journals
Encourage participants to keep a journal during their program experience.

Sponsor Program Reunions
This can be done at locations and times convenient to different groups of participants.

Send Out Newsletters
Ask participants to contribute poems, stories, and photos of the event, and create a newsletter to send out.

Letters
Have participants write themselves a letter during the program experience and then mail it to them three to six months after the program ends.

Figure 10.23 Techniques to enhance the reflection stage of the customer experience

their research that memory ads can make events (even impossible ones) seem likely to have happened to consumers as children. "Recreating" peoples' memories and leading them to believe something occurred that did not, is of course, a form of lying. Thus, programmers are cautioned about going too far with this approach.

As we can see, programmers can no longer neglect the reflection stage of an experience as this stage influences one's view of long-lasting satisfaction of participating in a program or event. One person's experience can be lived again and again (often with friends or family), and through such memories, participants keep the experience alive. Figure 10.23 presents several techniques to enhance the reflection aspect of a participant's experience.

Summary

Facilitating the program experience clearly relates to the servant leadership principles of "conceptualizing what may be" and "foreseeing issues." When we imagine (and plan for) the potential impact of the various phases of a recreation program, from pre-experience to post-experience, we are conceptualizing what may be. In particular we think about, plan, and prepare for the influences of our efforts on our potential and existing customers when we engage in the preparation and reflection phases of programming. By foreseeing registration issues and potential challenges for constituents for whom English is a second language, those who lack private transportation, those without access to the Internet, and those who have traditionally been excluded from our services, for example, we can enhance the opportunities for engagement in programs.

In the process of creating, implementing, and evaluating recreation programs, programmers must pay attention to creating customer friendly systems that enhance all phases of a customer's experience — planning, anticipation, travel to, participation, travel home, and reflection. In facilitating the pre-program experience, organizations will want to pay attention to a variety of factors, recognizing that everything the organization does communicates some message (intended or otherwise) to customers. The look of promotional material, the accessibility of the registration process, the paperwork that is required before participating in a program, the set-up of the environment when participants arrive for the start of a program, the staffing of the program, and the interactions with staff all contribute to the expectations and perceptions of customers before and during the actual program. As a result, effective programmers are not only concerned with developing a program, but also thoroughly plan the events leading up to the program as well as how the program will "play out" in the actual delivery of the program or special event. This chapter has presented a number of key areas for programmers to address in an effort to improve the quality of the overall experience for the customer.

Programming from Here to There

Many agencies and organizations offer information related to planning recreation events. One example is offered by the U.S. Department of Justice. In a July 1999 newsletter titled, *Youth In Action*, the steps to planning a specific type of recreation activity — special event — are identified in an easy-to-access format. The information includes background material, a timeline that indicates the planning steps that occur 16 to 20 weeks before the activity, entertainment, prizes, decorations, and evaluation. Another example of an entity that provides unique planning information is that provided by the University of California at the website: http://www.specialevents.ucla.edu/index.html. This site provides specific information needed for anyone or any group that wishes to plan a special event on the UCLA campus. Protocol guidelines, event policies, and planning resources such as budget checklists, logistics information, timeline templates, invitation style guide, and strategic questions are found on the site. Florida State University offers similar information at http://union.fsu.edu/eventplanning/SEPforms.html. Policies, required forms, event planning templates, marketing information, and FAQs are available and accessible to all. In looking at these sources, it is easy to see that facilitating the recreation experience takes thoughtful preparation.

References

Albrecht, K. (1992). *The only thing that matters*. New York, NY: Harper Business.

Albrecht, K. & Zemke, R. (1985). *Service America: Doing business in the new economy*. Homewood, IL: Dow Jones-Irwin.

Avedon, E. (1974). *Therapeutic recreation service: An applied behavioral science approach*. Englewood Cliffs, NJ: Prentice Hall.

Barneto, A. (2006, August 7). *Dealing with customer complaints — B.L.A.S.T*. Retrieved January 17, 2009, from http://ezinearticles.com/?Dealing-With-Customer-Complaints---B.L.A.S.T&id=263054

Braun, K., Ellis, R., & Loftus, E. (2002). Make my memory: How advertising can change our memories of the past. *Psychology & Marketing, 19*(1), 1–23.

Clawson, M. & Knetsch, J. (1966). *Economics of outdoor recreation*. Baltimore, MD: Johns Hopkins Press.

Farrell, P. & Lundegren, H. (1991). *The process of recreation programming: Theory and techniques* (3rd ed.). State College, PA: Venture Publishing, Inc.

O'Sullivan, E. & Spangler, K. (1998). *Experience marketing: Strategies for the new millennium*. State College, PA: Venture Publishing, Inc.

Parasuraman, A., Zeithaml, V., & Berry, L. (1985). A conceptual model of service quality and its implementation for future research. *Journal of Marketing, 49,* 41–50.

Priest, S. & Gass, M. (1997). *Effective leadership in adventure programming*. Champaign, IL: Human Kinetics.

Smith, R., Austin, D., & Kennedy, D. (2001). *Inclusive and special recreation: Opportunities for persons with disabilities* (4th ed.). Boston, MA: McGraw-Hill.

Stumbo, N. & Peterson, C. (2004). *Therapeutic recreation program design: Principles and procedures* (4th ed.). San Francisco, CA: Benjamin Cummings.

Van Matre, S. (1990). *Earth education*. Warrenville, IL: The Institute of Earth Education.

Wuest, B. S. (2001). Service quality concepts and dimensions pertinent to tourism, hospitality, and leisure services. In J. Kandampully, C. Mok, & B. Sparks (Eds.), *Service Quality Management in Hospitality, Tourism, and Leisure* (pp. 51–66). New York, NY: Haworth Press.

Programmer Profile

Photo provided by Vicki Proctor

Vicki Proctor

Current Position: Camp Services Director, Campfire, Tulsa, OK
Favorite Book: *The Man Who Walked Through Time* Colin Fletcher (1989)
Favorite Recreation Activities: Kayaking and backpacking

▶ **Describe the path your career has taken.**

- Graduated with a B.S. in Education from Ashland College in Ohio and an M.A. in Education from Ohio State University
- Places I have worked: Yucca Girl Scout Council, Bluestem Girl Scout Council, Camp Fire USA Green Country Council
- I currently work with young people through Camp Fire USA Green Country Council in Tulsa, Oklahoma. Camp Fire is a youth serving nonprofit found throughout the United States that strives to build caring, confident youth and future leaders. The Green Country Council currently serves 2,500 boys and girls, ages 3 to 18, and their families. Members learn how to play together, work together, and appreciate their similarities and differences in a constructive and positive manner. Specifically, my duties include: Providing resident and day camp programs in the summer months; conducting campouts, field days, and trips focusing on outdoor related topics and skills; overseeing risk management in the camps and Council; and running the Oklahoma *Becoming an Outdoors-Woman* program, but mainly delivering outdoor programs to the youth and families we serve.

▶ **Describe the joys of working in your current position.**

Working with kids outdoors. I see their eyes light up when they have woods in front of them and know that they're getting ready to explore and have great adventures. The satisfaction of taking a group of kids on a caving or backpacking trip and watching them go through the process of discovery, gaining confidence, and becoming in tune with the natural world. Watching elementary age kids conquer their fears and learn to appreciate nature.

▶ **Do you have any advice for new programmers?**

Delegate, delegate, delegate. You need to get people involved by empowering them to do even the smallest of tasks. The more you can have people do and help with, the more time you have for other logistics of the program or event. In addition, constantly be aware of your surroundings and the people for whom you're programming. Be flexible and willing to change something at the last minute. Constantly watch the flow of the program and how the participants are feeling and responding. Awareness of everything is the key.

▶ **What is the most creative program you have developed (or been involved with)?**

Becoming an Outdoors-Woman workshop (search for it on the web): Pulling together a weekend workshop for women to become more comfortable in the outdoors. The thrill of coming up with new and creative classes, finding instructors to teach the classes, then organizing all the details to pull off a good workshop.

▶ **How do you communicate your values and traditions to staff and constituents?**

Be a role model first. Believe in what you're doing and embrace the values and traditions as your own. That will come across to staff and participants.

▶ **Describe the importance of integrating evaluation in the program design process.**

We have broad goals for Camp Fire USA and we have specific outcomes for each of our programs. Staff are trained to what the outcomes are and how to work with participants—then the participants are surveyed at the end to see how we did. Then we have outcome measurement results for funders—and information on where we need to improve our training of staff for the next time.

The Essence of Program Evaluation

11

Many people cringe when they hear the word *evaluation*. For those who have not participated in the process of evaluation, it often conjures up images of tedious statistics that no one understands (or cares about). Evaluation, however, is fairly straightforward and an integral component of the program cycle; it is *not* a distinct and separate concern that someone else must deal with. Leisure services professionals must constantly remind themselves that programming does not stop with implementation of a program. Indeed, it is through evaluation that parks, recreation, and leisure services professionals engage in a continuous learning process about the delivery of leisure services. Among other things, programmers learn how to better prepare, implement, and provide programs and services to constituents—these are all elements of strategic planning, discussed in Chapter Three. As such, evaluation is a very important component of the servant leadership approach to programming.

Program evaluation is considered to be a critically important element of program delivery and agency success. As an integral element of planning and programming, evaluation should be considered in the program planning cycle well *before* a program is implemented. This enables leisure professionals to seek out continuous feedback about programs, facilities, staff, organization, and participants and make adjustments as needed throughout the programming process. Thus, evaluation becomes a process within a larger process.

The evaluation process is systematic. This means that evaluators follow defined steps and tasks to accomplish evaluation goals. Obviously, leisure programmers want the evaluation to result in useful and usable information. To make sure this happens, we must first learn about what evaluation is, how to do it, and how to use it. Therefore, in this chapter we will present information about terms, the components of evaluation, evaluation models, and selected evaluation techniques.

Definitions and Terms

As we've mentioned in earlier chapters, when learning new material, it is wise to begin with a presentation of terms and their definitions. This enables everyone to understand the use of the terms and concepts as they come up later in the chapter—it also helps in making sense of the material. Multiple definitions exist for many terms related to evaluation and in this section we present the most inclusive and commonly used definitions. These will help provide a common frame of reference to discuss evaluation in more depth.

Evaluation

Every author cited in this chapter agrees that evaluation is about *judging the value or worth of something*—in this case—leisure services and programs. The other common element to the many definitions of evaluation is that evaluation is a *way to determine if program goals and objectives have been met*. In addition to these two elements, *evaluation is a systematic process* (meaning that it can be followed and understood, is purposeful, and has identifiable steps) *of collecting information* about activities, characteristics, and outcomes of programs to make judgments about the program, improve the program effectiveness, and/or inform decision making.

Patton (2002, 2008) and Bamberger, Rugh, and Mabry (2006) suggest an approach to evaluation called *utilization-focused* evaluation. This type of evaluation emphasizes development and implementation of evaluations with a focus on *the intended use by intended users*. We, too, believe that evaluation should be done for specific people (e.g., users) and for specific reasons. Knowing one's purpose and audiences ahead of time helps to define the evaluation process, focus the evaluation questions, and provide direction to the evaluation report. It gives the evaluation process real-life meaning and ensures its usefulness to the agency. Further, it lends support to our emphasis on servant leadership.

Assessment

Commonly related to identifying needs, this is a *process of gathering information and data about the impacts of people, places, and things on individual participants and communities* so that appropriate parks, recreation, and leisure services might be provided to aid in meeting individual and group needs. Assessment is the act of collecting information about what is or what exists—and then using this information in program, staff, and facility planning. Space, facility, and equipment inventories are common examples of assessments. Needs assessments were discussed in depth in Chapter Four; programmers use similar techniques for needs assessments and evaluations.

Measurement

A loosely used term, measurement typically refers to assigning a number to an attribute or characteristic that provides a way of quantifying that element. When conducting both assessments and evaluations, measurement is used to help evaluators understand what they are examining. For example, when measuring levels of satisfaction among participants, evaluators often assign a range of arbitrary numbers to levels of satisfaction (e.g., 1= not at all satisfied to 5 = extremely satisfied). In this way, one can measure levels of satisfaction.

Formative Evaluation

Programmers can view evaluation from two different perspectives—by the timing of it (i.e., when in the program life cycle it occurs) and by what is evaluated (i.e., the content of the evaluation). Formative evaluation is conducted during the implementation process or delivery of an event or service (see Figure 11.1). It may be thought of as evaluation that helps to *form* an event as it occurs. It is continuous and ongoing.

When using formative evaluation, professionals can make adjustments in programs and services along the way. This is a very responsive type of evaluation that helps the programmer to refocus things as she or he sees the need. For example, imagine an arts-and-crafts session for five- to seven-year olds in which the children are working on a nature-based art project. You observe that some of the children are idle and seem to be disassociated from the project; some of them

are beginning to engage in undesirable behaviors. A formative evaluation, using direct observations as a technique, would direct that you first determine what the problem is: Do I have insufficient or inappropriate supplies for the size and needs of the group? Is available space lacking at the worktable? Do the children lack the skills needed to do this activity? Do the youth need staff attention? Once the issues are determined (and this is done quickly), you can then act to rectify the situation. This "on the fly" type of evaluation is considered formative because it occurs during the program event. Be aware that formative evaluation does not always occur on-site during a program or event. It may also occur at staff meetings and at informal times while the program is being conducted elsewhere.

Summative Evaluation

Since formative evaluation is conducted throughout the implementation of the program, it makes sense that summative evaluation occurs once the program is over. It is like a *summary* evaluation—conducted when the program or service delivery has been implemented and is completed (see Figure 11.1). As a part of this process, staff might sit down and discuss how the event went and take notes about adjustments they want to make the next time the program occurs (whether it be tomorrow, next week, or next year).

Figure 11.1 Formative and summative evaluation within the program cycle

In the previous example of the arts-and-crafts program, if only summative evaluation were used very little would be done to help the children at the time of the difficulty. Instead, staff would make observations and take notes for the next day, week, or year to suggest adjustments in how the nature-based art program could be presented in the future. Thus, with summative evaluation, issues related to customer satisfaction are not fully addressed until after the program ends.

Process Evaluation

It is easy to confuse the terms used to describe timing and content issues of evaluation. In fact, process evaluation is sometimes confused with formative evaluation, but it is not an issue of timing; rather process evaluation addresses what is to be evaluated. As the name suggests, process evaluation is about evaluating the process—the *how was it done*—of a program. So, in order to conduct a process evaluation of a wheelchair basketball league a programmer might evaluate how efficiently it was organized and implemented. In this type of evaluation evaluators would look at how the facilities were arranged, how teams were formed, how coaches and officials were recruited and trained, how registration was handled, how the game scheduling occurred, and so on. In process evaluation evaluators are concerned with the efficiency and effectiveness of how programmers did things to get the league underway. The PERT model of assessment introduced in Chapter Three fits well within this type of evaluation.

Product Evaluation

The other half of the content component to be evaluated is product evaluation (see Figure 11.2). Product evaluation is sometimes confused with summative evaluation because it typically occurs at the end of a program or service. Product evaluation, however, is about evaluating the *outcome or product* of an event, program, or service rather than the timing of the evaluation. In the wheelchair basketball league example, to conduct a product evaluation at the end of the season we might look at the league itself—the number of active teams, whether or not player needs were met, how the league was perceived by those not directly involved with it, the pricing and promotion plans, and so on. As a part of product evaluation, professional programmers would summarize these ideas and be better prepared for next season.

Outcomes-Based Evaluation

Another approach to evaluation is called outcomes-based evaluation (Driver, 2008). The focus of this evaluation method is on the impacts, benefits, and/or changes to participants after involvement in a particular program. Commonly used in educational systems and nonprofit organizations and agencies, outcome-based evaluation may look at short-term or long-term impacts. When conducting this type of evaluation, the primary questions will be, "How have participants (or the community) changed as a result of their involvement in this program?" "What have participants learned (about themselves, others, the activity, etc.) from involvement in this program?" A key to responding to outcomes-based questions is being able to demonstrate or document the outcome. Thus, using this type of evaluation programmers look for *indicators* that provide evidence that participants improved in X, Y, and Z as a result of being in the program. Outcomes-based evaluation requires planning ahead and articulating expected achievements. Then, at the conclusion of the program, evaluators look for evidence or proof (indicators) that people met those achievements.

The Need to Conduct Evaluations

As mentioned at the outset of this chapter, practitioners often prefer to avoid evaluation. Sometimes it appears as though a form of "evaluation phobia" exists where people will do just about anything to avoid becoming

Figure 11.2 The content of evaluation consists of both the process and the product.

involved with the process. It is important to reiterate, however, that evaluation is not a stand-alone process—it is integral to the entire programming cycle. As such, it can be helpful to look at the reasons people use to avoid conducting evaluations so that professionals can address and overcome these concerns.

The reasons for avoiding and dismissing program evaluation as unimportant are many, yet none of them outweigh the benefits. Evaluation is crucial to well-run programs because it is through evaluation that we improve both services and service delivery. It is also important to a servant leadership approach to programming since we empower constituents to participate in the program process through evaluations. We have all heard (and sometimes perpetuated) the reasons some programmers use to avoid program evaluation. Some believe that evaluation is not vital to an event or service—after all, "No one uses evaluation results anyway." Others firmly believe that the intuitive approach commonly used to evaluate programs is perfectly adequate to meet organizational needs. In this approach programmers have a gut feeling (intuition) for what worked and what didn't, and they respond to their perceptions accordingly. After all, "We have been doing leisure services programming for a long time and know a good program when we see one, right?"

Evaluation phobia also manifests itself in the following reasons: We have no time for a long drawn-out evaluation process (evaluation *can* occur in a short time period); we cannot spare any staff to conduct the evaluation; or we have no money, copying equipment, or other resources to undertake a thorough evaluation. Others acknowledge that deep down inside they are fearful because they lack the confidence and knowledge about how to conduct evaluations; still others are less than enthusiastic about what to do with "all those statistics." Some practitioners say they prefer to avoid systematic evaluations because "The programs seem to work, so why rock the boat?" Still others believe that evaluation can stifle creativity, and some fear potential change.

In response to these reasons (and others you might have thought of while reading this) for not doing evaluation, we say again—*evaluation is a critical element of the programming cycle*. A program is not complete until programmers have conducted an evaluation and used what they learned to modify existing (or plan for new) programs and services. At that point the programming cycle begins anew. Thus, at this point one might conduct or update needs assessments and asset inventories to support future programming efforts.

Benefits of Evaluation

The ostrich syndrome of putting our heads in the sand when it comes to evaluation of programs and services is counterproductive. It doesn't help the situation, we don't learn from it, and it can hurt us when something we should have noticed (e.g., a safety hazard) ends up hurting someone. Consequences of avoiding evaluation range from losing participants/customers and the revenue they would have generated, to causing serious injury and/or cessation of services. If designed and conducted properly, leisure services professionals have nothing to lose from undertaking evaluations and quite a bit to gain. Programmers have many reasons for conducting evaluations and some of those are presented in the following section (see Figure 11.3).

To Improve Programs, Events, and Services

If one were to ask people why program evaluations are conducted, many would say, "to improve programs and services." People generally understand the relationship between an evaluation and intent to improve programs and services. From evaluations people learn if something needs to be stopped, changed, or augmented to positively impact the perceived quality of services. By conducting an evaluation, professional programmers can assess quality and then make changes to better a program. People are being shortsighted, however, if this is the only reason they think evaluations have any merit. In fact, evaluation helps parks, recreation, and leisure programs and services in many ways.

To Seek Out and Eliminate Detrimental Elements

Similar to improving programs, seeking out and eliminating detrimental elements to services and programs is another reason for conducting evaluations. Improving programs often entails discovering and eliminating elements that detract from full participant satisfaction and program quality. These detrimental elements may include staffing (e.g., lack of interpersonal skills), facilities and grounds (e.g., poor maintenance and cleanliness), participants (e.g., with conflicting goals), agency organization (e.g., tedious and unwieldy registration processes), and program delivery (e.g., insufficient equipment). To minimize factors that detract from quality experiences, we need to ask questions related to omission (e.g., what was not included) as well as commission (e.g., what was included that needs to be changed or dropped).

To Manage Risks and Enhance Safety

Evaluating areas, facilities, staff, participants, policies, and programs on a continuous basis is part of a strong risk management plan. For instance, if there is a deficiency in a piece of equipment or structure (e.g., broken swing), an evaluation will help us find, tend to, and repair or replace the equipment within a reasonable time period. If staff are conducting themselves in a manner that may prove hazardous to participant safety, that too can be addressed in a timely fashion. Evaluation can also help in recognizing if any agency policies are contradictory to local, state, or federal laws and regulations (e.g., if registration procedures inadvertently discriminate against people with disabilities this would violate the Americans with Disabilities Act). Being "in the know" with regard to one's agency will help keep programs operational, effective, and efficient.

To See If the Program Meets Predetermined Goals and Objectives

For most of us, our common world experience tells us that evaluation is somehow related to the goals and objectives of an organization. That is, one has a need to know if an organization and its programs and services are doing what they set out to do. Indeed, in some fashion, parks, recreation, and leisure services professionals attempt to answer questions related to how well programs and services meet the stated goals and objectives for those programs. This requires a solid understanding of the organization values, philosophy, mission, vision, and goals and objectives. It also requires an understanding of potential constituents. In addition, goals and objectives provide the foundation for an outcomes approach to assessment; thus, these tools are necessary if programmers undertake this type of evaluation.

To Improve Decision Making

No agency can offer programs and services to meet the needs and desires of all constituents. Decisions have to be made about what to offer where, to whom, when, how much of it, and at what cost. Leisure services professionals can design and conduct evaluations to help in this very complex decision-making process. Evaluations can provide information that will help set priorities so that programmers can make wise choices relative to program ideas, staffing, budgeting, facility use, and equipment purchases.

To Justify Expenditures, Accountability, and Documentation

Determining benefits and costs of programs and services is one way to accommodate needs of policymakers and those who hold the budgetary purse strings. While this is not easily done, it is required of organizations in commercial, nonprofit, and public sectors. Measuring the benefits of parks, recreation, and leisure services has long been an enigma for those in the profession. How do professionals know if their programs and services are helping to reduce the local crime rate? How do they know that participation in parks, recreation, and leisure services contributes to the physical, mental, socioemotional, and spiritual health of participants? Assessments and evaluations can help professional programmers to determine answers to these questions.

Accountability and documentation are two related concepts that have existed in the leisure services profession for quite some time and recently have been taking on new and stronger meanings. All those impacted by expenditures in our field (e.g., the public, politicians, investors, healthcare professionals) are asking questions about where money is spent, for whom, and the impact those expenditures are having on individuals and the community. In fact, on the clinical side of therapeutic recreation third-party payments to insurance companies demand accountability and documentation of recreation services and their impacts provided to patients. Completing intake assessments, progress notes, and weekly charting are all forms of evaluation that address documentation and accountability.

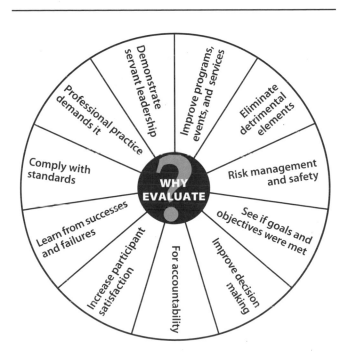

Figure 11.3 There are a multitude of benefits and reasons for conducting evaluations.

Non-therapeutic recreation agencies are also being mandated to provide documentation and accountability as monies become tighter and resources fewer.

To Increase Participant Satisfaction

Presumably, a reason many of us have for going into parks, recreation, and leisure services is to positively impact the lives of others. Through leisure and recreation professional programmers have an opportunity to influence the quality of peoples' lives. Thus, it becomes very important to know if our programs and services are having a positive impact on participants. To maintain high levels of participant satisfaction, programmers must learn about the impact of their programs on quality of life and make necessary adjustments—they do this through assessment and evaluation throughout the programming cycle. Another way participant satisfaction is increased through evaluation is through the very process of asking for input—participants like to be involved in meaningful decision-making processes. This opportunity for input is necessary to maintain a servant leadership foundation to programming.

To Explain Key Successes and Failures—and Learn from Them

Leisure services and programs are as diverse as the individuals served by them. The impacts of those programs and services on various constituents also differ tremendously. Some programs succeed beyond our wildest expectations while others fail miserably and we are stumped as to why. Evaluations can be designed to help leisure providers understand why certain programs succeeded while others failed so that they can incorporate the desirable elements into future efforts. Programs and services often fail, not because the entire event was flawed, but because one or two key elements were lacking. Evaluation helps programmers to identify those key elements to adjust for continued and future success in their programming efforts.

To Comply with Internal or External Standards

In parks, recreation, and leisure services academic programs, we utilize external standards (e.g., NRPA Council on Accreditation) to help monitor and document that curricula are complying with nationally established standards of minimum competency. These standards indicate that each accredited university program meets or exceeds standards set by the profession for professional competence. Similar forms of external standards exist in several program areas of our field—clinical therapeutic recreation sites are often accredited by the

Joint Commission for the Accreditation of Health Care Organizations (JCAHO), city and county parks and recreation programs may be accredited by the Commission for Accreditation of Park and Recreation Agencies (CAPRA), and organized camping organizations adhere to standards established by the American Camp Association. These accreditations speak to our concern for quality; they also serve as a mechanism for recruiting staff and marketing to potential constituents.

To Meet the Obligations for Professional Practice

One of the hallmarks of a professional is the concern for and involvement in ongoing evaluation—of self as well as those program and agency elements with which one is affiliated. Every professional in parks, recreation, and leisure should be intensely interested in her or his skills, competencies, and abilities to impact others' lives through program and service delivery in parks, recreation, and leisure services. Good professional practice means following through the entire program cycle by conducting evaluations and using that information in program development.

To Enact Servant Leadership Principles

We have suggested throughout this text that servant leadership is a strong and desirable foundation for professional practice in parks, recreation, and leisure services. And, a quick review of servant leadership principles informs us that evaluation is a necessary part of the passion and desire to constantly improve our communities and agencies. In 1995, Spears identified the ten hallmarks of a servant leader. The first among them is listening. Listening is what evaluators do when they engage in evaluation of programs and services. Professionals listen to constituent voices on surveys, in focus groups, and through interviews. The second characteristic of a servant leader is empathy. DeGraaf, Tilley, and Neal (2004) state, "Empathy is the capacity for participation in another's feelings or ideas; it is important in dealing with both staff and customers. Servant leaders strive to understand and empathize with others" (p. 5). To get to the point of empathy, programmers must first ask questions, then listen to the answers, and put that into cultural and organizational context. That comes from evaluation.

Another trait of a servant leader is one who continually develops her or his awareness—of others and selves. Again, what better way to do this than through moments of evaluation? Indeed, the notion of collective reflection (i.e., done by an entire agency or organization) is extremely valuable in improving ourselves and our services. Finally, the notion of stewardship serves as a hallmark of a servant leader. Block (1996, p. 6) characterizes stewardship as "the willingness to be accountable for the well-being of the larger organization by operating in service, rather than in control, of those around us. Stated simply, it is accountability without control or compliance." Thorough evaluation processes enable professionals to live this notion of accountability and stewardship.

◆❖◆

It is clear that many excellent reasons exist to support conducting program evaluations. A few reasons also explain why some people avoid them. It is now time to examine some of the issues that can influence the evaluation process and its outcomes. These influences affect all of us as leisure services professionals, and should be acknowledged so that we can all minimize the negative effect they have on the evaluation process and findings.

Influences on the Evaluation Process and Outcomes

As in all spheres of life, evaluation does not occur in a vacuum. It is influenced by the many internal and external events that affect all leisure services organizations. Local politics, ethical issues, and cultural biases are a few of the concerns that need to be addressed early in the program planning evaluation cycle (see Figure 11.4). These elements can affect both the evaluation process as well as outcomes. For instance, in the evaluation process ethical issues arise whenever other people are involved—How much should we push and insist that participants complete evaluation forms? When does encouragement become harassment or coercion? In another vein, outcomes often are affected by local politics—for instance, an evaluation report might be softened so as not to offend the mayor who has strongly advocated for the implementation of this program. Additionally, cultural biases affect all of us at our core, influencing the way we all view the world, how we as professionals ask evaluation questions, and the assumptions we as programmers make about what people do and do not like.

Ethics and Professionalism in Evaluation

The essence of ethics is knowing right from wrong; this strikes at the center of who we each are as a person. Ethics are not something that occur once, nor are they something that a person does. A person either behaves and lives in an ethical fashion, or she or he is willing to be compromised. Ethics are ongoing behaviors and attitudes that protect the rights of others while upholding standards. An ethical person is reliable and has a sense of professionalism and integrity. This means that an ethical individual consistently acts in a particular way when faced with difficult decisions, and others can count on this type of behavior in all situations.

In evaluation (as well as other elements of programming), an ethical person works in such a way as to promote the ideals of the profession while ensuring participant safety and positive experiences. When doing evaluations, ethical issues might arise relative to how the people who are selected to participate in the evaluation process (i.e., the sample) are treated. Some participants avoid completing evaluations because in the past they were harassed, ignored, their opinions were belittled, or they were otherwise treated poorly. Some have even reported feeling manipulated or pressured into answering questions in a certain way. This, of course, is unethical behavior by the individual conducting the evaluation. Programmers must have the utmost respect and care for constituents in all respects, and particularly when in the midst of an evaluation.

Another example of unethical behavior related to program evaluation may occur when evaluating by standards. If an organization typically operates below standards, yet during the two weeks prior to an evaluation visit, organizational staff frantically scurry about to appear as though they do meet standards only to fall back into substandard behaviors once the evaluation is completed, this is unethical.

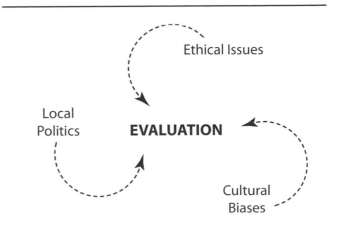

Figure 11.4 Evaluation is impacted by a variety of internal and external influences.

A third example is changing the results or writing a report that misrepresents the findings of an evaluation. This sometimes occurs when an individual is fearful of an unflattering evaluation or if there is pressure to use the evaluation for promotional or political purposes—we are all hesitant to let the public know that we have weaknesses.

Politics in Evaluation

Those who are involved in evaluation often strive to be free of political influences so they can state that the evaluation was unbiased and free from external pressures. However, every evaluation is influenced by internal and/or external politics. Politics are inevitable and should be acknowledged and addressed as forthrightly as possible. Political maneuvering might come in the form of executives from the head office demanding that only certain types of questions be asked to ensure a positive evaluation. Or, it might be evident in pressure to present a report in a less-than-truthful fashion to ensure third-party payment in a clinical therapeutic setting. Professional programmers should all address the political issues and stay true to reliable, valid, and usable evaluations—in this way, evaluation will be an effective component of the programming process in spite of political influences.

Cultural Biases in Evaluation

Cultural biases are inherent in every society. In the United States, the dominant cultural group is representative of people who are white, middle-class, and educated. Therefore, the way most people in the United States view the world is influenced by attitudes, beliefs, and values held by this group of people. Partly due to this, most people in our society know very little about the way program participants who represent minority groups look at the world, the appropriateness of various program interventions in meeting their needs, or the personal consequences of program participation for minority group members. Programmers who have little contact with people who represent the many dimensions of diversity, therefore, may not be the best people to determine the appropriateness of program and evaluation strategies for these groups.

Many evaluators have a tendency to homogenize groups of participants—they either evaluate only people who are similar to one another, or they report findings as though all the respondents were very much alike. This is often done with the underlying assumption that evaluation respondents are reflective

of the dominant cultural group in the United States. This presumed homogenization might result in poor program conceptualization, insensitive measures and evaluation, and inappropriate generalizations of findings. It is important that the entire program process, including evaluations, be contextually relevant to the geographic area and culture of the constituents. In other words, evaluations should involve a diverse group of constituents and be representative of many cultural norms.

Davis (1992) suggested five steps programmers can take to be more culturally sensitive in evaluating programs; these ideas are still valid today:

1. Conduct within-group and between-group comparisons—observe and note that all people of one minority group are not necessarily alike in their thoughts, values, and opinions.

2. Use culturally sensitive evaluators who understand themselves, their personal biases, and other cultural viewpoints.

3. Solicit feedback about interpretations of evaluations before reporting them. One way to do this is to ask those who participated in the evaluation process if your interpretation accurately portrays what they meant by their responses.

4. Analyze the program in context—look at the whole picture—to serve as a basis for different results. Identifying the context or situation helps because context is likely to have more impact on differences in responses than a person's cultural background or skin color.

5. Use multiple variables to determine any differences in evaluation results based on various demographic characteristics (e.g., socioeconomic status, age, religious affiliation, marital status, geographic area of residence).

Effective evaluators will want to consider culture and cultural biases in conceptualizing the evaluation process, collecting data, and interpreting findings. If a target population's cooperation is expected, then its values, beliefs, and traditions need to be taken into consideration during the evaluation design process, implementation, and the dissemination of evaluation findings and recommendations.

Having addressed some of the concerns and external influences related to evaluation, it is now time to examine evaluation on a conceptual level. This entails considering two views of evaluation: the generic evaluation process and several specific evaluation models. Understanding the "big picture" as well as the relationships between the many elements is helpful in understanding how to go about actually conducting an evaluation (see Figure 11.5).

Defining One's Worldview

Before deciding on a particular evaluation model or technique, leisure services professionals should identify and articulate our preferences relative to how we look at the world. A worldview is also known as a paradigm. In evaluation, two primary paradigms are utilized—qualitative and quantitative. Most of us grew up learning and practicing tasks that reflect a quantitative worldview; and for many of us, this has been quite comfortable. In evaluation, the quantitative paradigm means that we try to quantify, or assign numerical values, to different attributes in life. Generally speaking, we are trying to "crunch" numbers in such a way as to reduce multiple responses to a few that are easily understandable. For instance, we might ask seniors to rank order their favorite activities. We then use the numbers to make programmatic decisions for the future; for example, we might offer more of the highest ranked activities.

From a qualitative paradigm, we look at targets of evaluation in a holistic framework and use words as data sources, rather than numbers. This makes a great deal of sense in many respects and enables us to present multiple perspectives in context. We can find a deep, rich "truth" to the ways respondents perceive a program through a qualitative paradigm. Thus, in the previous example, we might ask seniors to tell us their preferred rankings and then ask them *why* they rank ordered items this way. It could be that the number one item is ranked such because it provides the most social interaction, and not because the participants liked that particular activity better than another. This information could result in different program choices than simply responding to the numerical rankings.

Quantitative Paradigm

Those who prefer a quantitative worldview generally perceive evaluation as a time to collect information that can be reduced to numbers for analysis. The quantitative paradigm examines one or more program attributes

or characteristics in isolation from the entirety of the program. For example, a supervisor might evaluate individual staff members and *not* consider their experience, hours, pay scale, training, or access to resources. Depending on the intended use of the evaluation and the disparity among staff based on these traits, this could result in a biased evaluation. Quantitative evaluations typically occur with paper and pencil and everyone is measured in the same way on the same attributes. When programmers ask participants about levels of satisfaction relative to a program, for example, everyone answers the same question on the same scale with the same response choices. This allows programmers to examine responses in a uniform fashion, and collapse the data into readily analyzed numbers. Quantitative methods can be relatively quick to administer and to analyze, and most of us have done this type of analysis throughout our lives.

Qualitative Paradigm

The qualitative paradigm is one where the evaluator examines the program to describe what was (or is being) done and to determine overall program quality. People who prefer this paradigm recognize the existence of multiple truths and that people have different perspectives of the same experience. Determining overall program quality is accomplished through

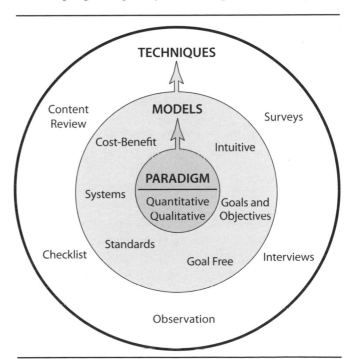

Figure 11.5 When deciding on an evaluation approach, programmers must first decide on a worldview, then a model, and then the techniques to collect the data.

gathering information—which are words (e.g., from interviews, written responses to open-ended questions, observations). The strength of this worldview is that it allows professional programmers to evaluate the interrelationships found throughout the programming cycle. It can be used as exploratory evaluation whereby the programmer looks at the big picture, and after noting areas of interest conducts a more narrowly focused quantitative evaluation. On the other hand, qualitative evaluation can be used to add details, depth, and meaning to what was found in an earlier quantitative analysis.

The qualitative paradigm is particularly useful in evaluation when examining program effectiveness. Using a qualitative perspective, for instance, programmers learn why participation (or nonparticipation) in a program was meaningful to people. If programmers were to ask individuals about levels of satisfaction with a program, they would do so in such a way that would allow the individuals to answer in their own words. In this way, one person's answer may or may not look like anyone else's answer. Leisure services professionals gain a tremendous amount of information from this process.

Patton (2002, 2008) provided a sampling of examples describing when a qualitative paradigm is the most appropriate choice for program evaluation. Adapted, those examples include the following:

- to look at the internal dynamics of a program—how something was accomplished;

- to evaluate individual outcomes—as in therapeutic recreation and in skill development programs;

- to document unusual cases—such as successes/failures/oddities;

- to describe diversity across program sites;

- to conduct a formative evaluation—to provide a holistic picture of existing interrelationships;

- to emphasize detected problems within a complex structure;

- to add depth to quantitative analyses and to increase quantitative understanding;

- to generate new insights and creativity in program and service delivery ideas;

- to evaluate a setting where it is extremely difficult to develop a quantitative instrument; and

- to measure the attributes with which the programmer is concerned.

While most people favor either the quantitative or qualitative paradigm in terms of conducting evaluations, the two can be integrated. For instance, programmers might conduct an evaluation that includes two data collection techniques—interviews and paper-and-pencil surveys. Another approach would be to use a paper survey that includes both closed-ended and open-ended questions. The open-ended items, if worded well, can result in rich word data that are then treated as qualitative data. Once they have decided upon an evaluation paradigm, programmers can then move forward in the evaluation process. An integrated approach to evaluation often provides the strongest form of measurement for a program or service (see Figure 11.6).

The Evaluation Process

Before we get into the specifics of different evaluation models, it is appropriate to consider a generic evaluation process. The generic process, or framework, remains the same no matter which model is used to formulate the evaluation plan. It serves to remind professionals about the needed steps to complete evaluation within the programming cycle. Just like the larger process of programming, the process of evaluation is cyclical. And, as mentioned several times, evaluation is an integral part of the complete program process. Therefore, evaluation is a cycle within the cycle of programming (see Figure 11.7 on p. 318).

The evaluation cycle begins early on in program design. The users and uses, paradigm, model, and techniques of evaluation are clearly spelled out *while the program is being designed and planned*. In other words, the evaluation for a particular program is designed at the same time that the program itself is designed. This enhances our ability to develop program strategies (for implementation) and clearly explain and illustrate program concepts (Kellogg, 2004).

Evaluation involves first understanding the agency/organization and the people who will be using the evaluation results. This information helps to form a value orientation (i.e., how to know something is considered good or bad) relative to program characteristics. A decision then has to be made about worldview (i.e., qualitative or quantitative), the evaluation goals, and the most appropriate evaluation model (based on several factors, such as personal preference, programmer skills, desired information, resources available). Next, an evaluation tool or technique must be selected. Lastly, the program is implemented. Because formative evaluation allows programmers to make corrections in midcourse, some level of evaluation is conducted shortly after the program is introduced and periodically throughout the implementation process. Adjustments are made, and the program is continued (Figure 11.7, p. 318). Upon program completion a summative evaluation is conducted, the data are collapsed and analyzed, a report is written, and the information is disseminated to those who will use it in future programming efforts.

As a reminder, we are advocating a utilization-focused evaluation process, no matter the paradigm or model utilized. According to Patton (2002, 2008) the essence of this orientation is twofold: first, those people who will use the evaluation results must be identified as real people, preferably by name; and second, evaluators must work with those individuals to make decisions about the evaluation process. The utilization focus is based on ten basic premises:

1. Concern for use should be the driving force in the evaluation.

2. Concern for use is ongoing and continuous from the very beginning.

3. Evaluations should be user-oriented.

4. Once identified, the users of the evaluation results should be active in the entire evaluation process.

5. Different groups and individuals have multiple and diverse interests surrounding the evaluation.

6. Careful selection of those who will use the results will allow for high-quality participation.

7. Evaluators have a responsibility to train users in evaluation processes and the use of information.

8. Different groups and individuals will use evaluation processes and findings in different ways.

9. A variety of situational factors affect evaluation.

10. Serious attention to utilization involves financial and staff time costs.

By adhering to these ten premises and bearing in mind the use of the evaluation, a programmer will collect useful data, which have real meaning in terms of program and participant satisfaction. Remember, no matter which of the following models or techniques is used to conduct program evaluation, it is the orientation toward users that sets utilization-focused evaluation apart from other types of evaluation.

Guiding Questions

To begin any evaluation process, an evaluator first needs to know the answers to basic questions that will serve to guide the choice of data collection techniques and tools, the type of analyses undertaken, and the method of interpreting and reporting the findings (see Figure 11.8 on p. 318). Many evaluators find it helpful to prepare a planning worksheet that includes these questions—and the answers—to share with the entire program team. This way, all members of the team understand the foundation and intent of the evaluation.

Why?

First, programmers must decide the reasons for doing this evaluation. *What are the primary and secondary purposes of this evaluation?* Bearing in mind that the ultimate purpose includes the goal of using the evaluation findings (e.g., utilization-focused evaluation),

QUANTITATIVE PARADIGM	QUALITATIVE PARADIGM
• Data consist of numbers	• Data consist of words
• Examines one component of a program	• Looks at a program from a holistic perspective
• Uniform in appearance and in data collection	• Appearance can change based on sample
• Typically use paper and pencil as instrument	• The evaluator is the instrument
• Effective to examine program product	• Effective to examine program effectiveness

Figure 11.6 Characteristics of qualitative and quantitative paradigms

programmers still need to articulate other aims of every evaluation. Is it for program improvement? To satisfy external standards? To calm fears about money being wasted? To compare to other similar programs? Or to document the impacts of programs on participants? Many reasons can exist for conducting evaluations and programmers need to be clear about the reasons for conducting each one.

Who?

The *who* question consists of several subquestions: *Who* is to conduct the evaluation? *Who* will be impacted by the evaluation? *For whom* is the evaluation designed? *Who* (e.g., constituents, administration, local politicians, the board) will have an impact on the evaluation? *Who* will participate in the evaluation process (as part of the sample)? *Who* will receive the evaluation report? Answers to these questions help in terms of choosing an evaluation model, and provide guidance in terms of how to implement the evaluation and treat the results.

What?

What answers the question of what will be evaluated. Programmers need to identify the attributes or characteristics that reflect the stated purposes of the evaluation. Typically, programmers choose among five elements of a program to evaluate: *areas and facilities, personnel, participants, policies and procedures,* and the *program or activity* itself (Henderson & Bialeschki, 2002). Leisure professionals might decide to conduct a comprehensive evaluation or only examine one component—this

is dependent upon time, staffing, money, and other organizational factors.

When?

When will the evaluation be conducted? During what season, which week, and at what time of day? *Timing* is very important to several types of evaluation and should be considered in every evaluation design. In addition to asking about when the evaluation will be conducted, it is equally important to have a sense of the programming and evaluation cycle timelines. This includes when the report will be written and disseminated.

Where?

At which *physical location* will the evaluation be conducted? The area should be conducive to the type of evaluation being administered and should help to reflect the primary and secondary aims of the evaluation. Consideration should be given to addressing location concerns such as accessibility, weather, traffic flow, and so on. For instance, if a programmer wanted to evaluate a swimming or boating program she or he would want to make sure respondents had a dry, warm place in which to respond to the questions. Sometimes agencies mail evaluations to constituent's homes or send them by email, in which case the location is somewhat out of their control.

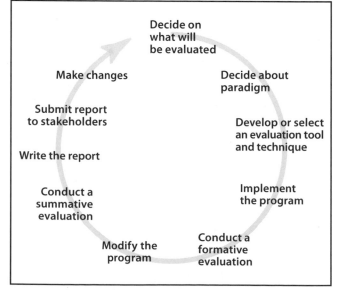

Figure 11.7 The evaluation process is cyclical.

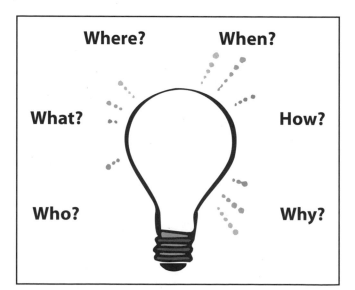

Figure 11.8 Answering six key questions helps to guide a programmer in the evaluation process.

How?

How will the evaluation be conducted? Which *paradigm* (i.e., qualitative or quantitative) will be utilized? Which *model* of evaluation is best suited to get at the types of data desired? Which *techniques* are most appropriate considering all of the pertinent issues (e.g., time, money, programmer experience)? How will the survey be distributed—in person, as a group, by mail, electronically, etc.?

Evaluation Models

Once leisure services professionals have articulated the responses to the guiding questions, they then are faced with choices of models and approaches to evaluation, which will describe how to measure the quality of their efforts. While most programmers tend to have a favorite model or two, having a look at several of them helps put perspective on things and may help in better understanding this element of the programming cycle. Work to fully understand each model, and begin to examine different situations when it might be most useful to apply each model. Each approach has strengths and weaknesses that make it more or less suitable in certain conditions.

As leisure services professionals, at the very beginning of the evaluation process, when we are thinking about needing to conduct an evaluation, it is important to be extremely clear about our intentions. If we are unclear or ambivalent about what we want to find out, we could very well conduct an evaluation that is of little value. Programmers can evaluate a whole host of program elements. They might include resources, activities, facilities, equipment, staffing, policies, participation, outcomes (including knowledge, skills, and attitudes), and impact (e.g., on the community).

Intuitive Model

Intuitive evaluation is used by everyone at one time or another. In fact, it is a method of discrimination (i.e., sorting through) and evaluation used by each of us in various aspects of our lives. The intuitive model is what we use when we have "a feeling" or gut reaction to something. For instance, we "know" a program is going well or not based on our feelings, which are based on receiving a variety of sensory input.

Intuition has been described as being the culmination of various stimuli, both conscious and subconscious, that form an impression on our subconscious. For instance, when we informally observe a program we notice participant reactions, the setting, numbers of participants, types and location of equipment used, placement and reactions of staff, and so on. This information enters our subconscious and is compared with our expectations of what the program "should" be like. The judgment we make based on this comparison is intuitive evaluation. While we are involved with judging value or worth of something, often we are unable to articulate on what we based our judgments. While this model is not based on scientific methods, it is easy-to-use, is used on a day-to-day basis, and is low-cost in terms of time and money. Unfortunately, it is also low in reliability (i.e., consistency) and the evaluator might not address the issues of real concern.

Application. Intuitive evaluation is most appropriate when a quick overview of a program or situation is needed; or, if funding, staffing, or the time to do a more in-depth evaluation is limited. In addition, intuitive evaluation is often used between the planned periodic formative evaluation efforts. This type of evaluation provides a general sense of things, which may then lead to a more structured form of evaluation. To maximize the usefulness of this model, several people might be invited to share their intuition about the success or failure of a program. This allows for triangulation (i.e., using several data sources to verify information) and strengthens the reliability of the overall evaluation.

When to avoid. The intuitive model of evaluation should not be utilized when it is the only evaluation method intended—the lack of systematic process and reliability cause it to be too weak to be used alone. Intuition is not a strong alternative for a comprehensive summative evaluation nor does it work particularly well in process evaluation. In addition, if formal documentation of evaluation is required, this model would not be sufficient—too much is done in a "casual" fashion.

Evaluation by Goals and Objectives

Evaluating by goals and objectives is a clear-cut method to determine if a program or service has accomplished what it said it would (see Figure 11.9 on p. 320). It is also the most commonly used method of evaluation in parks, recreation, and leisure services (Henderson & Bialeschki, 2002). This is one aspect of almost all evaluation efforts—someone in the organization or evaluation hierarchy wants to know if an agency or program has met its goals and objectives. This model is sometimes referred to as the goal attainment model.

It begins with an articulation of the organization philosophy, mission, and vision. Next, program specific goals and objectives are developed, the program is implemented, and those goals and objectives are measured. When used well, goals and objectives serve as the foundation for determining outcomes.

To many in the profession of parks, recreation, and leisure services, writing program goals and objectives is as unappetizing as conducting evaluations. This is because writing meaningful goals and objectives can be difficult; with practice, however, professional programmers can all become skilled in this area. As mentioned earlier in this text, because programs and services should reflect the mission and underlying values of the organization, programmers should have a solid understanding of these elements upon which to base the goals and objectives.

Goals

A goal may be short-term or long-term. It is a course of action that one intends to follow—an aim. It is broad-based and rather global in nature. Objectives are the steps to reaching the goal. They are very specific and measurable. Poorly written or a total lack of goals and objectives may result in activities and programs without focus, unsatisfied participants, ineffective leadership, and evaluation limited in usefulness (Jordan, 2007). Examples of program goals include

• to aid in participant skill development;

• to increase the health and well-being of community members;

• to provide healthy and wholesome recreation opportunities for adolescents;

• to encourage social interaction among participants; and

• to maximize participant fun and enjoyment while also maximizing profit.

To be useful, a program planner will develop objectives to help reach each of those goals (see Figure 11.10). A programmer identifies the goals and objectives for each program to provide structure and focus to leisure experiences—this is done during the planning stages and is related to the anticipated evaluation process. Goals are broad statements that describe the intent of a particular program or event.

Objectives

Objectives are the steps to reaching goals (see Figure 11.10). If one were to picture a staircase, objectives would be the individual steps and the goal would be at the top of the stairs. Each step can have three different types of objectives: *cognitive*, *behavioral*, and *affective*. *Cognitive* objectives are those that deal with thinking, *behavioral* objectives deal with physical actions and skills, and *affective* objectives deal with feelings and emotions. In parks, recreation, and leisure services all three objectives are addressed through programs and services, although one may be more emphasized than another. To utilize evaluation by goals and objectives one would ask questions designed to determine if the stated goals and objectives had been met.

Application. Evaluation by goals and objectives can be very useful in a variety of situations. When a formal, relatively objective evaluation is desired, this is a useful model to follow. In addition, when goals and objectives are well-written and related to the agency mission, this model can be particularly enlightening. As far as program settings go, evaluation by goals and objectives fits in well with therapeutic recreation since, typically, each client is evaluated on her or his progress toward specific goals and objectives. It also works well in military recreation settings and with commercial recreation ventures where goals and objectives are often clearly spelled out.

When to avoid. This form of evaluation is not the best choice when poorly written goals and objectives exist (or there are none). In addition, because the

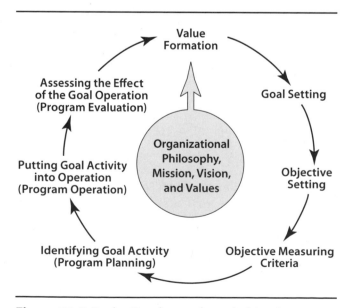

Figure 11.9 Evaluation by goals and objectives (Adapted from Theobald, 1979)

evaluation closely follows the establishment of goals and objectives, someone will need to develop an instrument to measure the specific goals and objectives for each program. This can be time-consuming. Therefore, if staffing concerns exist, another model might be a wiser choice.

Goal-Free Model

The goal-free (or black box) model of evaluation (Henderson & Bialeschki, 2002) is one where the evaluator is unaware of the program goals and objectives before undertaking the evaluation. This often requires the use of an evaluator from outside of the organization. The idea is that the evaluator will examine the program in its totality and evaluate all that is observed. This allows for a very holistic approach to the evaluation process. In fact, because of the holistic approach, this model relies heavily on qualitative methods to gather information. It can provide a wealth of information about the interrelationships of the various factors affecting a program or service.

Application. The goal-free model of evaluation is rich in data and provides an excellent overview of the entire organization or program in process. If program providers want to see how various elements of a program interact, the goal-free model provides this type of information. In addition, it elicits a fresh look at efforts of the organization, in part because a person external to the organization usually conducts the evaluation. Because of its richness and open view, the goal-free

model is a very solid choice to use when one is interested in process evaluation and formative evaluation. It can also be used to provide general information and clues as to what aspects of the program or service need closer inspection.

When to avoid. A goal-free model of evaluation can be time-consuming and costly, especially if an outside evaluator is utilized. In addition, it is not the best method to use when providers want to examine one small element of the organization. Furthermore, the data that result from this model are words—qualitative data. If staff are unskilled in qualitative methods and techniques, or the users (audience) of the evaluation report want numbers (i.e., quantitative data), then another model would be a better choice.

Evaluation by Standards

Evaluation by standards was mentioned earlier in this chapter. It refers to the use of external standards against which a program or agency is measured to determine quality. If standards are met, the program is said to be a quality program. This model provides an objective approach to evaluation—the standards are usually developed and the program monitored by an outside agency or group of professionals. This model is often used in conjunction with the "expert judgment approach" to evaluation. Criteria are established as standards, agency personnel engage in a verification process (indicating which standards are met and which are not), and outside experts come in to review the efforts of the agency in this regard.

Application. This model of evaluation is appropriate when it is mandated by law to meet external standards (e.g., the ADA). It is also a good model when it is desirable to comply with industry standards (i.e., common practice in the field) as this is an indicator of quality. In addition, meeting standards is often good documentation for a risk management plan and can aid in professional networking. Accrediting bodies epitomize this type of evaluation.

When to avoid. Standards should not be used as a basis for evaluation when the standards do not reflect agency practice, mission, or philosophy. Misapplying standards to a program or agency can be detrimental in the long run. In addition, it can be expensive, so if expenses are a concern, this might not be the best evaluation model to follow. Furthermore, standards are a minimum, and if programmers do not intend to exceed most standards they may be doing the agency and constituents a disservice by solely relying on this technique.

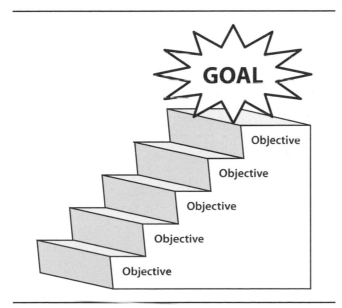

Figure 11.10 Objectives are the steps to reaching a goal.

Systems Models

Systems models to evaluation are commonly used for special events and other programs or services that tend to follow a well-defined path or timeline. These tools often help in decision-making processes and provide a graphic representation of the programming process. They can also serve as evaluation models or techniques. Because these models are visual and detailed relative to what needs to be done and in what period of time, many in our field favor them. Several models fall within the general systems category—we presented information about the two most commonly used: Gantt Charts (see Figure 11.11) and the Performance Evaluation Review Technique (PERT) (see Figure 11.12).

Application. Systems models of evaluation are appropriate for use when we either need or desire a business-like orientation. Because they are systematic and include three broad steps—input, process, output—they are relatively easy to follow. They provide a clear path of checkpoints and time lines for programmers. Another strong suit of these models is that they are process-oriented. At a glance, we can see where the program is in the cycle of development, and make changes as program implementation is anticipated.

When to avoid. Systems models of evaluation are best avoided when the desire is to learn about issues of quality such as participant satisfaction or facility appropriateness for the event. The very nature of systems models of evaluation (i.e., quantitative) limits the type of information gained through their use. In addition, a special event or program may be too large or convoluted to maximize the use of these models in evaluating an event. Systems models are quite broad and may not allow for in-depth measurements of quality.

Importance–Performance Analysis

The Importance-Performance model of evaluation offers information in two areas—the importance of a particular program element or service to constituents, and an evaluation of agency performance related to that particular program element or service. It results in data that can be plotted on a grid, showing where items fall in one of four quadrants (see Figure 11.13 on p. 324). Programmers might find that a program element (e.g., online registration) might be very important to constituents and participants are satisfied with their efforts—they should keep up the good work in this area. If evaluators found that online registration fell into the quadrant where it is very important to constituents, and participants are dissatisfied, then programmers should work to improve performance in this area. If the item being evaluated is not important to constituents (such as a paper brochure describing programs) and constituents are highly satisfied, perhaps programmers would be better served to shift their efforts to a different area. Lastly, if an item is considered to be not important and receives low satisfaction scores, programmers may wish to drop it altogether.

Application. The Importance-Performance evaluation model is a good choice when programmers want to discern the effect of their efforts in specific areas and the related perceptions of constituents. The results can provide information that can aid in decisions related to staffing assignments and efforts, programs to discontinue or improve, and areas where programmers can give themselves a pat on the back for a job well-done.

When to avoid. If well-designed, Importance-Performance analysis provides very clear direction about very specific programming efforts. Thus, if programmers do not intend to use the results to make

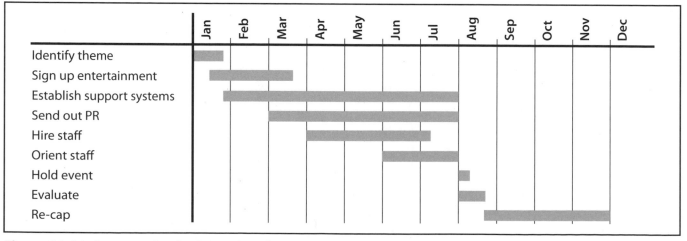

Figure 11.11 An example of a Gantt chart for a special event

indicated changes, this type of evaluation would best be avoided. Further, a well-designed instrument is necessary to elicit useful data; thus, previous experience with the process of developing instruments (whether online or paper/pencil) is highly desirable.

Cost-Benefit Analysis

As an evaluation model cost-benefit analysis is often used in commercial recreation settings and other instances when budgeting is a bottom-line concern (see Figure 11.14 on p. 324). This model helps staff to examine the relative effectiveness of alternative programs and strategies in terms of costs. Further, it determines the relationship of costs to benefits derived from the program. The types of costs that are examined include direct costs (e.g., staff salary, promotion, equipment) as well as indirect costs (e.g., insurance, utilities, maintenance). These are weighed against direct benefits (e.g., revenue generated, customer loyalty) and indirect benefits (e.g., decrease in social problems, a concomitant decrease in property taxes). This type of analysis directly relates to pricing decisions, which we discussed in Chapter Nine.

Application. The cost-benefit model of evaluation is beneficial if we need to adhere to a business approach where money and profit are of primary concern. Also, in a situation where budgetary constraints and the need for cost or benefit documentation exist, this is an appropriate model of evaluation. This model is particularly useful when trying to decide between program priorities as it helps to clearly identify financial advantages and disadvantages of various issues.

When to avoid. Because cost-benefit analysis is concerned with the financial bottom line, it measures monetary efficiency more so than program effectiveness or quality. This model is often most useful when used in conjunction with other types of evaluation that do a better job of measuring actual program quality. Programmers should avoid using cost-benefit analysis as an only method of evaluation when they want to know about participant satisfaction, program leader effectiveness, or overall program quality.

◆◆◆

As you can see, a variety of models can be used in planning the program evaluation process. Some of them fit better with the quantitative paradigm, others fit best with the qualitative paradigm, and others fit either view equally well. It is up to each program evaluator to decide among the models based on several factors. In utilization-focused evaluation, two primary considerations are the user and uses of the evaluation findings. The most appropriate model, then, will be partly determined by these two factors. In addition, the primary and secondary purposes of evaluation have a great deal of influence on the evaluation model selected, as do the skills and preferences of the individual(s) conducting the evaluation.

We have discussed evaluation paradigms, evaluation models, and evaluation techniques. To move further along the evaluation process and begin to design the actual evaluation we look to guiding questions to help focus the evaluation. If, in the evaluation process, a programmer answers the six guiding questions presented

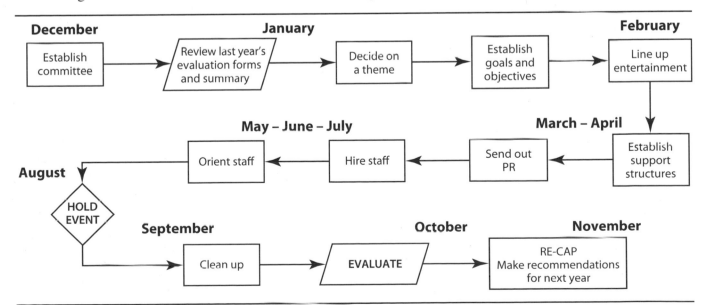

Figure 11.12 A program evaluation review technique (PERT) chart identifies tasks and a timeline in a flow chart format.

in this chapter, she or he will have put together a very viable evaluation system to aid in program development.

Summary

Throughout this text we have been highlighting various key elements of servant leadership as they relate to the topic under discussion. The content in this chapter relates to the servant leadership elements of "conceptualizing what may be," "a commitment to the growth of others," and "listening." When we plan for evaluation before implementing a program, we are contributing to a servant leadership approach to programming. We do so because the process of planning, implementing, and utilizing evaluation information enables us to "conceptualize what may be"—it facilitates our ability to see how we might change programs.

In addition, evaluations of programs, staff, participants, and other aspects of programming demonstrate a "commitment to the growth of others." This growth might be personal and professional growth of staff, or social and emotional growth of program participants. Thus, if we as leisure services professionals *are* committed to the growth of others, evaluation is an absolutely necessary element of programming. Further, conducting evaluations, no matter the methods used to collect information, lets

constituents know that we are actively engaged in listening. Through appropriate use of evaluations we are saying that "your opinion and thoughts are important to us."

It is clear—program evaluation is a very important element within the larger programming cycle. It is integral to program development and aids the programmer in many ways. Evaluation can be used to improve programs and services, to enhance risk management and safety, and to ascertain whether or not predetermined goals and objectives have been met. In addition, program evaluation is used to aid in decision making, justify expenditures, and increase participant satisfaction. Furthermore, program evaluation can be used to explain keys to success, comply with standards, and serve as evidence of a commitment to the profession.

Ethical and political issues can influence program evaluation as can cultural biases held by the evaluator. These need to be addressed in the planning of the program evaluation process. Some people involved in evaluation prefer to adhere to a quantitative worldview, while others utilize a qualitative worldview. No matter one's perspective, several different evaluation models may be utilized in the evaluation process. These models include the intuitive model, evaluation by goals and objectives, evaluation by standards, the goal-free model, systems model, importance-performance model,

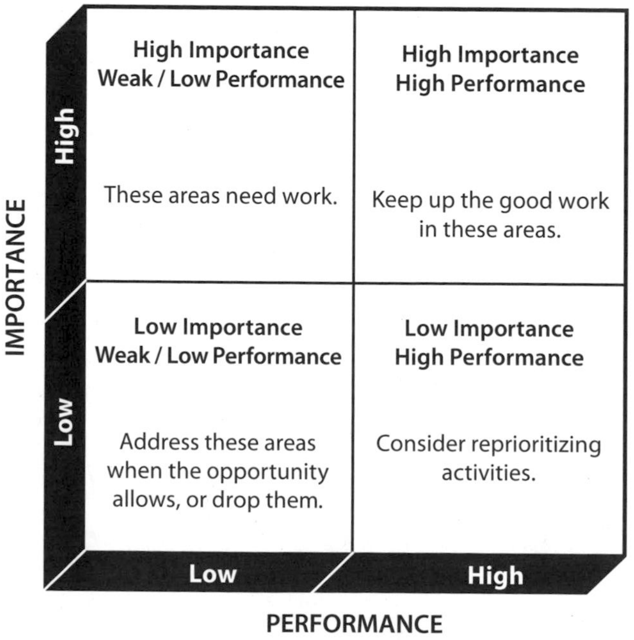

Figure 11.13 Importance-performance grid

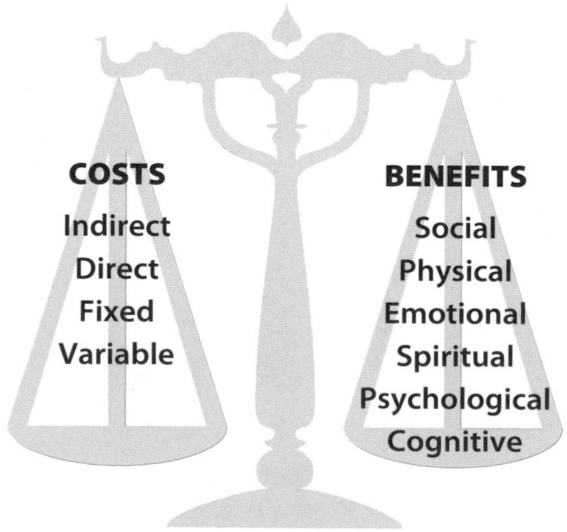

Figure 11.14 Cost-benefit analysis involves weighing the identifiable costs with benefits of a program.

and cost-benefit analysis. Further, when planning the evaluation process, answering the questions of why, who, what, where, when, and how before choosing a model and process can help clarify the evaluation cycle. Deciding which paradigm and model to follow is based on many factors inherent in the planning process.

Programming from Here to There

Evaluation has made a difference in many communities and many organizations. One example of the impact of evaluation can be seen in the decisions and actions of Tulsa Parks staff. In response to a needs assessment and a vocal interest group, in 2001 Tulsa Parks opened a skateboard park that was built on an old tennis court. The park was situated in the midst of a residential area, close to potential users. Because the skateboard structure is made of steel, however, the noise made by users was problematic. Using a public forum (open interview) approach, the City of Tulsa held several meetings in the neighborhood to try to resolve the concerns. What came out of those meetings was a decision to move the skateboard facility to a non-residential area across town. The facility still gets tremendous use and no longer presents noise problems to community members. YouTube videos of skaters at the Tulsa River Skate Park may be found at the following two websites: http://video.aol.com/video-detail/river-skatepark/2044680925/?icid=VIDURVSPR03 and http://video.aol.com/video-detail/grind-this-tulsa-skatepark/2054735921.

References

Bamberger, M., Rugh, J. & Mabry, L. (2006). *RealWorld evaluation*. Thousand Oaks, CA: Sage Publications.

Block, P. (1996). *Stewardship: Choosing service over self-interest*. San Francisco, CA: Berrett-Koehler Publishers.

Davis, J. (1992). Reconsidering the use of race as an explanatory variable in program evaluation. In A. Madison (Ed.), *New Directions in Program Evaluation*, *53*, 55–67, San Francisco, CA: Jossey-Bass.

DeGraaf, D., Tilley, C., & Neal, L. (2004). *Servant-leadership characteristics in organizational life*. Indianapolis, IN: The Greenleaf Center for Servant Leadership.

Driver, B. (Ed.). (2008). *Managing to optimize the beneficial outcomes of recreation*. State College, PA: Venture Publishing, Inc.

Henderson, K. & Bialeschki, M. D. (2002). *Evaluating leisure services: Making enlightened decisions* (2nd ed.). State College, PA: Venture Publishing, Inc.

Jordan, D. (2007). *Leadership in leisure services: Making a difference* (3rd ed.). State College, PA: Venture Publishing, Inc.

Kellogg Foundation, W.K. (2004). *Logic model development guide*. Battle Creek, MI: W.K. Kellogg Foundation.

Patton, M. (2002). *Utilization-focused evaluation (U-FE) checklist*. Retrieved January 14, 2009, from http://www.wmich.edu/evalctr/checklists/ufe.pdf

Patton, M. (2008). *Utilization-focused evaluation* (4th ed.). Newbury Park, CA: Sage Publications.

Spears, L. (1995). *Reflections on leadership*. New York, NY: John Wiley & Sons.

Photo courtesy of Tulsa Parks

Figure 11.15 The Tulsa River Skate Park

Programmer Profile

You

▶ **What will your future Programmer Profile look like?**

It is never too early to start to think about where you want to be as a professional in five to ten years, and how you might get there. The profiles presented in this book offer some general insights for you as you ponder your own professional path. Consider the following:

- *Hobbies*: The programmers profiled in this book have a wide variety of hobbies and interests reminding us not to forget to PLAY. As programmers we must practice what we preach, and continue to look for ways to balance our lives, for it is through our play that we solve problems and create new programs.
- *Education*: All of the programmers profiled noted the importance of education, yet many took different paths and majors to their present position. We strongly advocate the importance of a professional preparation in parks, recreation, and leisure services through higher education and work experience. At the same time we recognize that related disciplines such as education, sociology, and business can also provide excellent backgrounds when partnered with intentional work experiences and educational opportunities related to parks, recreation, and leisure services.
- *Diversity*: As is evident from the programmer profiles presented in this book, our profession needs to do a better job of encouraging diversity as we strive to better reflect the populations we serve. As you move forward in your career, be open to understanding the unique joys and challenges of working with a diverse staff and constituents, and continuously consider ways to encourage greater diversity throughout the profession.

▶ **What will your career path look like?**

Given the importance of being intentional in gaining the experiences and knowledge needed to be successful as a recreation programmer, we encourage you to take some time and ponder the following questions as you develop your own programmer profile now and in the future.

- What are you passionate about? Where do you want to be a year after you graduate? Three years? Five years? Identify three personal and professional goals you would like to accomplish in the next three years.
- What type of volunteer or paid experiences will you need to help you reach your goals? How can you fit those experiences in with your education experiences? Identify several potential organizations or agencies where you might complete a practicum or internship.

- What type of professional associations (e.g., ACA, AEE, ATRA, NRPA, RCRA) might help you reach your goals? Gather information about several of these associations, join those that are appropriate to your goals, and become actively involved.

► **Life experience for programmers from Maya Angelou.**

In concluding our programmer profiles, we would like to pass along some advice from Maya Angelou. Although she is not a recreation programmer, she is a wise woman with a lot of life experiences. She has been called "America's most visible black female autobiographer" by scholar Joanne Braxton and is best known for poetry and her series of six autobiographies. In April, 2006, she was interviewed by Oprah on her 78th Birthday and shared the following insights:

- I've learned that you can tell a lot about a person by the way she or he handles these three things: a rainy day, lost luggage, and tangled Christmas tree lights.
- I've learned that "making a living" is not the same thing as "making a life."
- I've learned that you shouldn't go through life with a catcher's mitt on both hands; you need to be able to throw some things back.
- I've learned that whenever I decide something with an open heart, I usually make the right decision.
- I've learned that even when I have pains, I don't have to be one.
- I've learned that every day you should reach out and touch someone.
- People love a warm hug, or just a friendly pat on the back.
- I've learned that I still have a lot to learn.
- I've learned that people will forget what you said, people will forget what you did, but people will never forget how you made them feel.

Evaluation Tools, Techniques, and Data Analysis

12

Learning about models, tools, and techniques to collect information for needs assessments and program evaluation is essential. The same is true for data analysis. While we as programmers might prefer the quantitative paradigm over the qualitative or vice versa, and we might have a particular model in mind that will answer the questions we have, we still need to know how to go about gathering and analyzing that information. Different techniques are for each evaluation model. Each programmer must decide which is most appropriate for the existing circumstances and then put that technique into action. In this chapter we will provide an overview of selected sampling techniques, several data collection techniques, and data analysis procedures, all of which are necessary elements of needs assessments, asset inventories, and evaluations.

Sampling

Sampling, or choosing which people will participate in a needs assessment or evaluation, is a concern any time evaluators want to systematically collect data from a group of people. Part of the expectation of a systematic process is that with enough information, another person can replicate (i.e., copy) what an evaluator did and come up with information against which he or she can compare his or her results. While we will not offer a comprehensive look at sampling procedures here, we will offer enough background for you to have a general understanding of how to go about choosing individuals to participate in a needs assessment or program evaluation process.

In evaluation terms, a *population* consists of all constituents in one's service zone—they are all people who potentially could be a part of the evaluation process, and they might be users or nonusers. For example, if you were evaluating a specific program, you would only consider asking those who were participants to evaluate it (i.e., staff and

participants). If you wanted to evaluate your entire agency or organization, however, the opinions and attitudes of the entire community might be desirable. Very few agencies, however, have the time, money, or staff to include every possible constituent in an evaluation. In addition, statistically, after a certain number of people, it becomes redundant to include everyone.

A *sample* is a subset of a larger population that could participate in the evaluation process. Evaluators usually try to identify a sample that is representative of the larger population, but there are times when this is not possible or desirable. By selecting a representative sample evaluators can generalize their findings to the larger population and make broad statements about overall program quality. For instance, if you asked people who were members of a representative sample to rank their three favorite activities, after analyzing the data you could say that X, Y, and Z were likely the three favorite activities of the entire population. If the sample was not representative of the population, you could not make such a global statement. Sometimes the sample will consist of the entire population. For instance, if a programmer wanted to evaluate a program in which 50 or fewer people participated she or he would likely survey everyone.

Bearing in mind that leisure services professionals need to be systematic in their sampling methods, programmers need to clearly state the procedures used to select the people who participate in the evaluation process. Depending upon what an agency wants to know, it might involve participants, nonparticipants, key informants, experts, community leaders, staff, administrators, volunteers, partners, funders, policymakers, and others who are appropriate to the project goals.

If generalization to a larger population is desirable, programming professionals will want to use some form of random selection to choose the sample (see Figure 12.1 on p. 330). *Random sampling* is a method that is based on the premise that *every person in the population has the same chance as every other person to be selected for the sample*. For example, if the population is the entire community, evaluators need to find a way to identify *every* community member (e.g., including those with and without permanent addresses, those with and without telephones or Internet access, those who have and have not registered for our programs).

Once the entire population has been identified, evaluators then choose a method to select individuals from among that group so that every person has the same chance of being selected as every other person. This is commonly done by computer or by hand using a random numbers table; it may also be done with a technique called "fishbowl with replacement." In this technique, every name is placed in a fishbowl and drawn one at a time. In order to ensure the equal chance rule, once drawn and the name recorded, the name is replaced in the fishbowl and another name drawn. This continues until we have the desired number of names.

Systematic random sampling is a method that first generates a list of all members of the population, then systematically chooses every *n*th name from that list. Knowing the size of the population and the desired size of the sample will determine what figure is used for *n*. For instance, if your population is 10,000 and you want 100 people in your sample, you would select every 100th name from the list. An example of this technique is to use a membership or mailing list, randomly point to a name on that list, then identify every *n*th name after that to be in the sample.

A couple of nonrepresentative sampling techniques include *convenience sampling* and *purposive sampling*. These techniques do not allow evaluators to make generalized statements to the larger population about the evaluation findings. As one might suspect, convenience sampling is based on the ready availability of people to participate in the evaluation process. For instance, at a festival the sample might be chosen based on individuals who were approached and agreed to participate. This convenience sample offers no representation to the larger population of people who attended the festival. For example, interviewers might find themselves approaching only adults at the festival who were dressed well and looked friendly. Thus, those who were perceived as less friendly were eliminated from the evaluation before they had a chance of being chosen simply because they did not look open to being approached to participate in the evaluation. When reporting evaluation findings interviewers will only be able to say that the *people who were approached* thought such and so. They can not say that *all* festival attendees felt that way.

Purposive sampling is a technique that results in individuals being chosen from the larger population based on predetermined criteria. Criteria might include participation in a particular program, people who have a specific expertise, or that individuals represent a particular group (e.g., female, over 65 years old, ethnic minority). If used, the criteria chosen for sample selection must be made explicit in the final evaluation report so that others have a clear understanding of how evaluation participants were selected. In both convenience and purposive selection, the ability to generalize findings to the larger population is limited. For instance, if either of these two sampling techniques were used one could not say that "from this evaluation it is apparent that the community felt the program was a success." One could only say that the individuals who responded to the evaluation felt the program was a success.

Data Collection Tools

Once evaluators know the population and have decided on a sampling technique they are ready to select a tool or technique for collecting program evaluation data. Evaluation tools and techniques are varied and offer different strengths and limitations for their use. *Instrumentation* refers to the actual tool or instrument used to gather information for an evaluation. Most commonly used are computer-based and paper-and-pencil evaluations, but people can also be instruments when they are interviewers. In any case, evaluators need to be concerned with three elements related to the instrument: reliability, validity, and usability (see Figure 12.2).

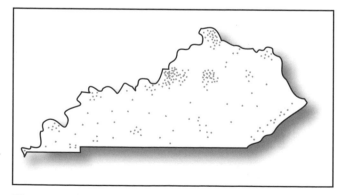

Figure 12.1 Theoretically a random sample would select people who represent the entire population.

Reliability

Reliability refers to just what it sounds like—How reliable is the instrument? Can it be counted on to elicit similar information when used again? Another word for reliability is consistency. Does the instrument measure a phenomenon consistently over time? If programmers cannot count on the instrument to be stable and reliable, then it is of limited use in evaluation. To determine reliability, evaluators often administer the instrument to two different groups or to the same group at two different times, and compare answers. If the responses are similar, one can say the instrument is reliable.

Programming professionals can do several things to increase reliability in quantitative evaluation techniques. First, they need to write clear, unambiguous items. Further, a longer instrument tends to be more reliable than a short instrument because the content is better covered; thus, programmers want to ensure appropriate questionnaire length. In addition, by conducting a pilot test of the instrument before actual use programmers will be able to ensure that the directions are understandable, and that the instrument is appropriate for the individuals completing it (e.g., wording is appropriate for the age group and anticipated literacy levels of the intended participants). If programmers are using a qualitative paradigm, they would want to be sure to use an audit trail. Programmers do this by documenting everything they did so that others might follow their steps without difficulty. The audit trail becomes a record of the entire data collection process. It should be extremely detailed and follow accepted practice relative to the chosen data collection technique.

Validity

Not only are leisure services professionals concerned with consistency of responses, but they are also concerned with whether or not the instrument measures what they intended it to measure. This is validity; it provides credibility to our work. There are several forms of validity, three of which directly relate to evaluation techniques: construct validity, content validity, and face validity. *Construct validity* refers to the overall question of whether or not an instrument measures what it set out to measure—Is it evaluating the appropriate construct or attribute of the program? For instance, if you set out to evaluate the safety of a facility, questions about aesthetics would not be valid items. However, valid items might include those that address facility lighting, maintenance, and cleanliness. *Content validity* refers to the actual content of the instrument—Does the content found on the instrument cover all the areas to be evaluated? Are the items inclusive—is the instrument thorough? Lastly, *face validity* refers to whether or not "on-the-face-of-it," it looks like the instrument measures what it says it measures (Bamberger, Rugh, & Mabry, 2006; Patton, 2008). Having several different people make this assessment is important to ensure accuracy.

To improve instrument validity professional programmers should address the three types of validity mentioned previously, choose an appropriate sample size and technique, and select an appropriate evaluation instrument to match a particular model. Clear instructions, avoiding jargon, using triangulation (e.g., collecting data from multiple sources, using multiple data collection techniques), and conducting a pilot test prior to use will also facilitate instrument validity. If a programmer has utilized a qualitative paradigm where the evaluator is the instrument she or he can increase validity through prolonged engagement (i.e., observing the program over an extended period of time), use of examples and negative cases (i.e., to add to and confirm our written descriptions), and provide thick (i.e., rich or detailed) descriptions of our observations and experiences—the more detailed and thorough, the better.

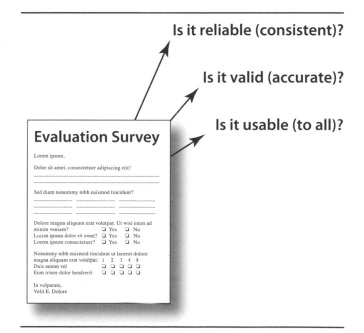

Figure 12.2 Three concerns with evaluation instruments

Usability

In program evaluation, usability (and utility) is an important concern for an instrument. This refers to how easy and convenient respondents find the evaluation process, and to the usefulness of the evaluation report upon completion. It directly relates to utilization-focused evaluation. If an instrument is not usable, it is of limited value.

Usability of a quantitative instrument can be enhanced by ensuring ease of administration (e.g., giving a paper-and-pencil evaluation outdoors in a rainstorm is not reflective of usability), designing the instrument to take a reasonable amount of time for completion (i.e., most evaluations should be able to be completed in 15 minutes or less), making the instrument easy to score and interpret, and keeping the evaluation process to a reasonable cost (Henderson & Bialeschki, 2002; Patton, 1990). In the case of qualitative evaluation methods, to increase usability programmers should make sure they have trained and competent evaluators, be sure they have the time commitment to complete the process, use triangulation (i.e., use multiple evaluators, include both staff and participants, and/or use more than one data collection tool), and explain all variances in the findings. In all cases the final report should be well-written and the information in it easy to use.

What Do You Want to Know?

In the upcoming sections we will share information about how to collect, analyze, and interpret the information obtained from conducting needs assessments and evaluations. Before getting into the tools and techniques of data collection, it is important to have a plan (formulated prior to beginning a program) to guide the evaluation process.

Evaluation planning, which we discussed in detail in the previous chapter, includes having a clear understanding of your evaluation goals—do you want to know about participant knowledge, attitudes, skills, or aspirations? Are you most interested in learning about the effectiveness of your program leaders? Do outcomes drive the program and evaluation process? Or, are you in need of information related to program costs and benefits? The answer to these (and similar) questions will provide guidance in your choices of data collection tools and analysis techniques.

Quantitative Data Collection

As a reminder, the quantitative paradigm presents respondent thoughts, attitudes, and opinions in numerical form. This is also true of quantitative data collection techniques. By assigning number values to standard items on a survey, comparisons within and between groups can be made and numerical norms can be established. For instance, with appropriate questions one could say that levels of participant satisfaction with a particular program are above average. In fact, with quantitative data, if an evaluator uses the right statistical techniques she or he can even say how much above average a certain program is rated. Several quantitative techniques and tools to collect evaluation information exist, a few of which are mentioned here.

Head Counts

Head counting is a method used quite frequently in parks, recreation, and leisure services (in fact, it is often overused, see Figure 12.3). It includes counting participants in attendance at an event, tallying the number of registrants for a recreational sports league, or measuring participant or visitor hours (commonly used in park settings). Head counts are fast, easy to do, and easy to understand. At the same time, however, head counts fall short in terms of measuring program quality, effectiveness, and efficiency. For example, consider a person who asks how successful a program was and the answer was, "Very successful! We had over 100 people show up!" The number of people in attendance is designated as the evaluation criteria, however, those 100 people may have been extremely dissatisfied with the program quality.

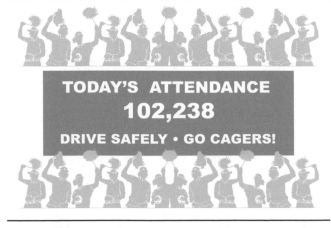

Figure 12.3 Head counts are weak measures of evaluation.

In addition, if only ten people were in attendance (and 100 were expected) that information is not enough to judge the program as a failure. Those ten people might have had a very positive experience and achieved long-term benefits. From the evaluation one might find that the need for such a program was limited, there was a date conflict with another large event, publicity was poor, or some other reason negatively affected participation.

Questionnaires

Questionnaires (also called surveys) are another common method of data collection for program evaluation. They consist of written (i.e., paper or electronic form) standardized items (i.e., everyone is asked the same things in the same format) and can be relatively quick to administer and analyze. Surveys can be administered by:

1. handing them to participants and asking them to drop them in a box when completed;

2. distributing them to a group of people all at once (either orally or on paper/computer) and collecting them when participants are done;

3. mailing them and providing a self-addressed, stamped-envelope (SASE), or business reply envelope (BRE) for return;

4. making them available through e-mail, a website, or another electronic medium;

5. asking the evaluation questions verbally over the telephone or in person;

6. text messaging to a cell phone or other electronic device; or

7. utilizing some combination of media.

When designing questionnaires, one should bear in mind several considerations to enhance reliability, validity, and usability. The following information comes from much practice and working with evaluation questionnaires over a long period of time. You are encouraged to add to the list as you learn more about constructing surveys over the course of your academic and professional careers.

Design and Layout Concerns

Design and layout concerns have to do with the aesthetics or visual appeal of a questionnaire, and they relate to both computer-based and paper-based questionnaires. A well-designed questionnaire or survey can aid in completion and return rates, and enhances the perception of professionalism. Programmers will want to bear in mind several issues (see Figures 12.4 [sides A and B] on pp. 334-335, for examples as marked in brackets):

1. Minimize the use of 'white space' (i.e., empty space) on a survey. Be sure the questionnaire looks aesthetically balanced on the page. If the survey is Internet-based, be aware of various monitor sizes, Internet-access software (browser), and the need to scroll to see content. [A].

2. As much as possible, put questions that address the same general topic together on the survey. As with the previous item, it will be important to indicate if a user should scroll down the page (on a computer) or if internal hot links will be used. [B].

3. Put items that are of the same format (e.g., Likert scale items, semantic differentials) together. This helps minimize confusion with multiple and repeated instructions. [C].

4. Use a common typeface that is easy to read. Consider type, size, color, and style of font. If Internet-based, be aware that potential respondents may not have access to unique fonts that might exist on the computer on which you are working. [D].

5. Use a background (both on paper and computer) that is uncluttered, visually appealing, and in appropriate contrast to the font color. Consider the needs of those with visual impairments who may have difficulty with discerning details (e.g., some of those who are color blind have difficulty discerning greens and reds from other colors).

6. If using both sides of the paper, be sure to give directions on the bottom of the page to turn the page over and respond to all items. If Internet-based, give respondents some idea of how far along they are in completing the survey and whether or not they have to scroll or click a button to continue [E]. (continued on p. 336)

Date: _____   Course Title: _____

D

Course Evaluation

The purpose of this course evaluation is to aid the instructor in making decisions related to the course. Your input will be utilized to determine course content, use of the textbook, how the course is taught in the future, assignments and other methods of student evaluation (e.g., exams), and other elements of this course. Your feedback is greatly appreciated!

Section I: Semantic Differential

Please make an X in the space which best describes how you feel about this course.

A

THE COURSE MATERIAL IS/WAS:	**B**	
highly interesting	____|____|____|____|____	quite boring
very valuable	____|____|____|____|____	worthless
too difficult	____|____|____|____|____	too easy
too slow paced	____|____|____|____|____	too fast paced
very relevant	____|____|____|____|____	irrelevant
confusing, hard to follow	____|____|____|____|____	clear, easy to follow
very practical	____|____|____|____|____	very philosophical
current, up-to-date	____|____|____|____|____	old, out-of-date

C

THE INSTRUCTOR:	**B**	
cared about students	____|____|____|____|____	didn't care about students
was fair to all students	____|____|____|____|____	appeared to have favorites
was difficult to understand	____|____|____|____|____	was easy to understand
had high expectations	____|____|____|____|____	had low expectations
was closed to new ideas	____|____|____|____|____	was open to new ideas
was very knowledgeable	____|____|____|____|____	didn't appear to know the subject
helped me to understand	____|____|____|____|____	did not care if I understood
was boring, lost my interest	____|____|____|____|____	was able to keep my interest

Section II: Open Feedback

Please be as specific as possible and make suggestions for change as you think of them.

1. What aspects of this course have been most beneficial to you (such as topics, techniques, assignments, interaction with classmates)?

PLEASE COMPLETE OTHER SIDE   **E**

Figure 12.4 Sample survey—Side A

Continued>>

2. What do you suggest to change this course (such as length of class, prerequisites, textbook, teaching techniques)?

G

3. Comment on the grading system (such as number of assignments, consistency in grading, assignments matched course goals).

4. In what areas should the instructor improve (such as dealing with students one-on-one, communication, enthusiasm)?

5. What characteristics of the instructor were most helpful (such as explanations, gestures, progression)?

6. Overall, how would you grade this course? (circle one grade)

       A   B   C   D   F

Please explain why you assigned this grade:

7. Any other comments?

8. How many years of college have you attended? (circle one)   1   2   3   4   5   6+

9. What is your sex?   Female   Male

F

10. What is your major? _____

Figure 12.4 Sample survey—Side B (continued from previous page)

7. Typographical errors, blotches, light ink, or other unsightly printing errors are *not* acceptable on paper surveys—the questionnaire should look clean, sharp, and inviting. Internet-based surveys should be free of extraneous graphics, images, animations, or sounds that detract from the intent of the survey.

8. If the survey includes a long list of items, visually separate them with extra white space by groups of five (i.e., insert an extra wide line between items 5 and 6), or use alternate line shading.

9. If same-format items carry over to another page, repeat the instructions and any acronyms (e.g., SA=strongly agree, A=agree, D=disagree, SD=strongly disagree, and NA=not applicable) to remind respondents about the abbreviations used.

10. Ask the most nonthreatening questions first; save demographic questions (e.g., income, race/ethnicity, zip code) for the end of the questionnaire [F].

11. If the survey includes open-ended items, leave enough room for the type and length of response you would like or can anticipate. If Internet-based, be sure the text box provided is set to accept enough characters that a respondent can fully answer the question [G].

12. Consider providing the survey in multiple languages; ensure that translations accurately reflect the intent of the question.

13. If provided electronically, ensure that the entire survey is compliant with Section 508 of the amended Rehabilitation Act of 1973 (discussed later in this chapter).

Wording Issues

How evaluation items are worded directly impacts not only the cooperation of respondents, but also the types of responses received. Poorly worded items may result in an item being skipped over (i.e., not answered), or the answer may not match the intended outcome. Remember, the goal is to develop a questionnaire that is easy to prepare, administer, complete, and score. Helpful hints with wording include:

1. Use wording appropriate to the intended respondents (e.g., items written for children should differ from those written for adults).

2. Avoid technical jargon and unfamiliar language. If intended respondents are representative of the general population, write at a sixth grade level—this is the average reading level of people in the United States.

3. Avoid clichés and local terminology—respondents for whom English is a second language or those with low literacy levels may have difficulty understanding nonstandard English.

4. Provide directions that are clear, concise, and repeated if the questionnaire is lengthy.

5. Use only one idea per item so that the entire question is answerable with a single response.

6. Be as clear, brief, and simple as possible with each item.

7. Avoid leading questions (i.e., ones that suggest a certain response).

8. If using closed-ended items, be sure all possible responses are provided. By using the category "other" with a following open space, an individual can fill in the blank if her or his response is different than those provided.

9. Avoid questions that are worded negatively (e.g., Do you not agree that we need a new swimming pool?).

10. Be sure all questions are relevant to the intent of the questionnaire.

Using Existing Instruments

Previously developed needs assessment and evaluation instruments (data collection tools) may be found in books, professional journals, on the web, and from colleagues. Clearly, if an appropriate questionnaire already exists, it makes sense to use it rather than develop a new survey from scratch. Advantages of using existing resources include saving time, being able to take advantage of others' expertise, and the instrument may have already been tested for reliability, validity, and usability.

Disadvantages also exist, however. It may be difficult to find a survey that can be easily modified or appropriately adapted for a particular use. Well-tested surveys may require a fee for use—this is particularly true in the field of therapeutic recreation where many intake and leisure activity assessment instruments are copyright protected. Further, there is no real 'check-and-balance' process required before publishing instruments to the web or sharing them with colleagues. Thus, it can be easy to pass on a poorly developed instrument for use by others; this only exacerbates problems with the questionnaire and the data collected. Therefore, understanding how to develop instruments as well as best practices in assessment and evaluation are necessary to make good judgments about the use of existing tools.

Web-based Data Collection Tools

Advantages to designing and creating web-based surveys is that the survey is available at all times of the day and night, the data are collected and stored at the same time, the data are easily transferred into a database (e.g. Excel, Access) for easy analysis, and the analysis is relatively quick and easy. Agency staff can create surveys in-house, contract out the work, or use one of many existing online tools. With the increasing popularity of web-based surveys, several software companies offer ready-made templates for the easy creation of online surveys. In many cases, the company will send out emails (invitations and reminders to participate) on your behalf, collect and analyze the data, make graphs and charts, and even put the results into slide format (for use in programs such as Microsoft PowerPoint) for use in presentations. Typically, the more services one uses, the more expensive the process.

Most of the online software programs (e.g., SurveyMonkey, Zoomerang, SurveyGizmo) allow users to create both closed-ended and open-ended questions, record the date and time the survey was submitted, and add images (such as an agency logo) to the survey. The software programs provide overall descriptive statistics, a review of individual responses, and the ability to filter results by variables. Through the filters, for example, evaluators can view the analysis of results by age, income, education level, or other demographic variable. Further, most of the online products allow the user to download results onto a local hard drive facilitating access and long term data storage. Commercial web-based survey programs may offer a free version of their software for public use. It is impor-

tant to understand that the free version typically is extremely limited. Often, the number of returned surveys allowed is 100 or fewer (any additional completed surveys are not collected), only one survey may be conducted per year, or the data analysis is limited to simple descriptive statistics.

Accessibility and Universal Design

As part of the amended Rehabilitation Act of 1973, Section 508 requires that electronic and information technology be accessible to people with disabilities (Section 508, n.d.). While not every parks, recreation, and leisure services entity is mandated to follow this law (it applies to agencies impacted by federal funding), they all should be concerned with the full inclusion and accessibility of everyone in all aspects of our programs—including needs assessments and evaluations.

Any time agencies make public input tools available on the Internet or through some other electronic medium, it is important to ensure accessibility for all. Thus, whether agencies create their own online surveys, contract out (outsource) the work, or use one of the online survey creation tools, they will want to be sure that the survey is compliant with Section 508 rules and guidelines. Several websites exist that provide excellent information related to web accessibility and other accessibility resources. Some web accessibility tips include:

1. Always give users more than one way to accomplish a task. For instance, users might use only voice commands, the keyboard, a mouse, or stylus to navigate an electronic form.

2. If images and photographs are included on a web page, offer a text-only site as well.

3. If a website uses multiple colors or colored backgrounds, be sure to include a version with white background and black print that a user can easily find.

4. Maintain a simple, consistent page layout throughout the site.

5. Keep backgrounds simple; make sure to use an appropriate level of contrast between the color of the background and the color of the text.

6. Use standard HTML throughout the site to avoid inserting features that are only accessible through

use of additional software (e.g., Flash plug-ins).

7. Design large buttons, checkboxes, and readable text; provide an option for a user to increase the font and screen image sizes on their own monitor.

8. Be sure that all graphics include a text description for those who use screen readers. If video clips are used, include closed-captioning of any audio.

9. Test the website with a variety of browsers and accessibility software; several free accessibility-testing programs are available online [http://www.w3.org/WAI/; http://www.webaim.org/; http://www.mardiros.net/bobby-accessibility-tool.html; http://www.tawdis.net/taw3/cms/en; http://www.virtualhosting.com/blog/2008/test-me-25-freebie-website-accessibility-checkers/].

10. Test the website with multiple platforms, operating systems, monitor sizes, and screen resolutions.

Question Formats

Three basic types of formats are used in writing survey questions: closed-ended items, forced-choice items, and open-ended items. The type of format used depends, in part, upon the type of desired responses (see Figure 12.5). *Closed-ended* items are those that have a limited number of choices, but may offer a middle-ground response, such as a Likert scale item or a semantic differential item.

Forced-choice items are a special type of closed-ended question that have limited response choices and respondents are forced to select one of the alternatives. These might be yes/no or true/false questions, checklist, or rank order items. They tend to be either/or types of questions with no middle ground. Closed-ended and forced-choice items can

---

Likert Scale Item

For each of the following items, please rate your level of satisfaction (1 is low and 5 is high).

	not at all satisfied				extremely satisfied
Registration process	1	2	3	4	5
Staff courtesy on the telephone	1	2	3	4	5
Appearance of the reception area	1	2	3	4	5

Semantic Differential Item

Please think about your experience with our agency staff. On the scales below, please place an X indicating where your opinion falls.

Agency Staff are...

warm	_____	cold
happy	_____	grumpy
can't be bothered	_____	helpful
positive attitudes	_____	negative attitudes

Checklist Item

Please circle all of the sports you would participate in, if they were available.

basketball	volleyball	scoop ball
wallyball	soccer	disc golf
double dutch	rugby	softball

Ranking Item

Please rank the following issues by level of importance to you. A number 1 ranking means that item is of the most importance; a 5 is the lowest importance.

___ constructing a new community swimming pool

___ maintenance at our county parks

___ safety for evening and night programs

___ childcare for center activities

___ purchasing new resources for the community library

Open Ended—Single Stage

In the space below, please describe one new activity, service, or program you would like to see us provide.

Open Ended—Multiple Stage

Please describe your concerns about accessibility of this facility.

What suggestions do you have for improvement?

Figure 12.5 Question formats

be difficult to write, but tend to be easy to score, analyze, and interpret.

Open-ended questions are written in such a way as to encourage wordy responses. They are least restrictive in terms of possible responses and can yield a wide variety of answers. Questions that can be answered with a yes or no should be designed as closed-ended items rather than open-ended. Open-ended questions require some thought and time to answer, and some respondents skip over them without answering.

In addition to being concerned with questionnaire layout and question format, a program evaluator must also decide what *type* of questions to ask. For instance, closed-ended items might include Likert scale items, semantic differential items where opposite words are placed on a continuum and respondents are asked to mark on the continuum where their opinions lie, checklists, and ranking items. Open-ended items might be simple (i.e., single stage) or compound (i.e., multiple stage). Each item elicits slightly different types of information. When deciding on question type, keep in mind the users and uses of the evaluation.

Qualitative Data Collection

Following the qualitative paradigm, qualitative techniques are those efforts that elicit rich descriptions and use words to explain the data. They collect information from several different sources to learn about multiple perspectives. The data are not as easily reduced as numerical data, but they do provide a holistic and rich explanation of what has occurred. A whole host of data collection tools exist that are used to collect qualitative data, and a few of the more common techniques are described here.

Review Documents and Records

In program evaluation, reviewing documents and records is done fairly regularly on an informal basis. Document review refers to the *systematic* review and examination of records and documents related to a program. In program evaluation, leisure professionals might study past program plans, reports, and other documents related to an event or service. They might look at registration forms, attendance records, trip permission slips, agency files, sign-in sheets, client treatment plans, and so on. By studying records evaluators can gather information without putting undue demands on participant time and energies.

Observation

Observation is a tool for gathering data about a program or activity that utilizes the program evaluator as the data collection instrument. The program evaluator might be an *open observer* where it is obvious to everyone that she or he is observing the event, or she or he might act as a *covert participant observer* where she or he would engage in the program or activity just like a participant and no one would know an evaluation was being conducted. From either position, the observer makes in-depth observations about her or his experiences and documents what was noted. The aim of observation as an evaluation tool is to see the program through the eyes of participants and make detailed notes about behaviors, the setting, comments people make, and so on. Observation provides detailed descriptions about peoples' activities, behaviors, actions, and interpersonal relationships that are a part of all human relationships (Patton, 2002). It can yield fascinating information.

Observation may be a structured form of evaluation meaning that in advance, the program evaluator knows the answers to the six guiding questions (i.e., why, what, who, when, where, how) of evaluation or it may be more flexible. This technique fits well within the goal-free model of evaluation. It can also be used with a more restrictive checklist of criteria for quality.

A *case study* is a study of observations related to a specific case—a case might be a person or an activity/ program or agency. This type of evaluation enables evaluators to make comparisons between cases. One might note the diversity of participants and programs involved at a particular organization, or the extreme or unusual cases seen. Case studies are used quite frequently in therapeutic recreation and inclusion settings with individual clients, as well as in commercial and tourism-focused recreation settings to identify and highlight examples of excellent business practices.

Sociometry

Sociometry is a technique that examines relationships among and between people—participants, leaders, and spectators. It results in a graphic representation of how people interact with one another, and sometimes, how they interact with equipment or structures (Henderson & Bialeschki, 2002; Russell & Jamieson, 2007). This is done by drawing lines between interacting elements as seen in Figure 12.6 on p. 340. From this information evaluators can examine how the program facilitates relationship building, social skills, and leadership development.

Focus Groups

Focus groups are a special form of group interviewing. When using this technique, programmers assemble a group of people based on preselected criteria. The group of people might be representative of larger constituent groups or they might have certain background knowledge that makes them particularly useful for responding to pointed evaluation questions. A focus group usually consists of eight to twelve people and examines all aspects of one broad question. In groups, the program evaluator can get multiple perspectives, and respondents tend to "play off of each other" resulting in diverse and rich responses. Focus groups can be helpful in needs assessments as well as program or organizational evaluation.

Interviews

Interviews can be time-consuming tools for data collection, but they result in a richness of data and understanding not found with many other techniques (see Figure 12.7 on p. 341). Four primary methods of

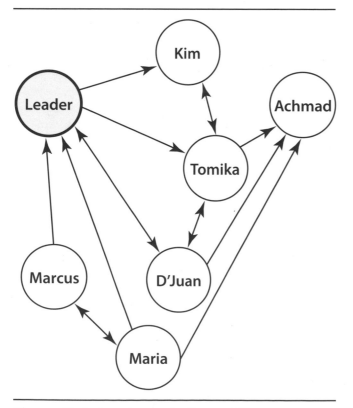

Figure 12.6 A sociometric diagram illustrates interactions between participants.

interviewing, which differ based on amount of structure, are common to needs assessment and evaluation. The *informal conversational interview* is one that occurs when individuals are readily accessible to be engaged in conversation. The interviews might occur in the hallway, between programs, at a park, or any time and place participants and programmers meet. Interview questions are developed as the conversation flows and in-depth information can be elicited from each participant. Of course, with this technique, different people might be asked different questions, so it could be difficult to compare responses. In addition, because it is done on an informal basis, interviewer biases may creep into the questions and the interpretation of the responses. Furthermore, if this is the desired technique, strong efforts must be made to speak with a representative sample of the population.

The second least structured interview format is the *interview guide approach*. With this technique topics and issues to be covered are predetermined, but the sequence differs based on the flow of the interview. This allows for a bit more consistency in terms of response categories than the informal approach, but still allows the free-flowing nature of a conversation. Again, a lot of information can be gathered from respondents using this form of interviewing. Furthermore, multiple interviewers can use the same interview guide to ask large numbers of individuals similar questions.

More structured forms of interviewing include standardized open-ended interviews and the closed quantitative interviews. In the *standardized open-ended interview*, the interviewer uses the exact same wording and sequence for questions with each interviewee. This enhances the ability to compare answers between respondents, but may result in a "stiffness" in the interview process. The *closed quantitative interview* is similar to an oral survey where individuals are asked questions and select answers from among choices. The analysis of data is much simpler for closed quantitative interviews than in other forms of interviewing, but this type of interviewing is very constraining to respondents. It can result in distorted meanings because it doesn't allow for probing or expanding on answers.

Triangulation

Triangulation means to use more than one source of information (i.e., ask questions of participants, staff, and observers), multiple evaluators, or several types of evaluation models or tools in the search of "the truth" relative to what is being evaluated (see Figure 12.8 on p. 342). It makes sense that if participants, leaders, and spectators were asked to evaluate the same program we would receive more detailed and complete information than if just one of those groups were asked the questions. Similarly, if two or three program leaders or supervisors were asked to conduct an evaluation of the same program, we would get a more complete picture of that event than if only one person conducted the evaluation. Lastly, if we utilized multiple tools to collect data, we would also enrich our findings. Often, triangulation is constrained by a shortage of resources (e.g., staff, time, money). As much as possible, however, programmers should try to utilize triangulation in evaluation to ensure reliable, valid, and usable information.

◆◆◆

A wide variety of qualitative and quantitative evaluation techniques and tools are available for use. Each has its own advantages and disadvantages, and each can result in data about programs and services. Data are the information collected from constituents. Once programmers have collected data, they must do what they can to collapse the data into something meaningful. That is the role of data analysis.

Data Analysis

Imagine that we've recently conducted a program evaluation and a sample of 75 people responded to 25 different items on an evaluation form. This results in a potential of 1,875 different pieces of information gathered for one small evaluation! The human brain is not designed to make sense of close

to 2,000 pieces of individual information at once. Therefore, we must collapse the data into smaller, more manageable sizes (see Figure 12.9 on p. 342). This is the purpose of data analysis—to reduce the many individual responses we've gathered so the evaluation will make sense and be relatively easy to utilize. When we collapse the individual pieces of data in the analysis process, this is referred to as *data reduction*. We simply reduce large volumes of information into a smaller, more understandable set of data. This process differs depending on whether one used quantitative or qualitative techniques to collect data.

In quantitative techniques of data collection there are two primary analysis techniques used to reduce data. These provide two different types of general information. *Inferential statistics* are mathematical techniques that allow us to make generalizable statements about the population's (i.e., all constituents') thoughts, feelings, and attitudes. *Descriptive statistics* are mathematical techniques that give enough broad information to provide a general overview or description of the sample's (i.e., respondents') thoughts, feelings, and attitudes.

Inferential Analysis

As mentioned, inferential data analysis allows us to study the evaluation results and make general statements that relate to the entire population, rather than just the sample. Thus, these techniques are more sophisticated than descriptive techniques, and require additional understanding of statistical processes. Because most

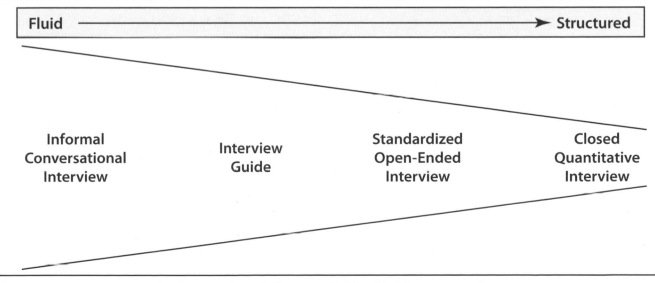

Figure 12.7 Interview methods move from being very fluid to highly structured.

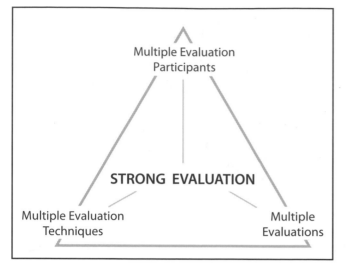

Figure 12.8 Triangulation results in strong evaluations.

evaluations tend to be descriptive in nature, we will cover only descriptive data analysis techniques here. Inferential statistical analysis techniques are usually covered in other academic courses concerned with evaluation and research.

Descriptive Analysis

Descriptive analysis is what most program evaluators attempt to do—provide a description of the feelings, thoughts, and attitudes of respondents relative to a program or service. This can be accomplished through following qualitative or quantitative paradigms and/

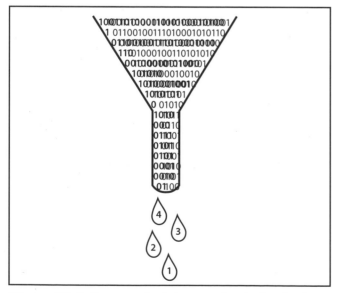

Figure 12.9 Data analysis is a method of reducing large amounts of individual data into a few meaningful pieces of data.

or data collection techniques—both can provide a description of respondents' feelings, thoughts, and attitudes. Before we can provide a general description about how respondents felt about the program, however, we must do something to reduce the large set of data. Techniques for analyzing data for descriptive analysis follow.

Techniques for Quantitative Data Analysis

A quantitative paradigm and quantitative data collection techniques result in numbers. These might be on a Likert scale, in rank order items, or arbitrarily assigned numbers, as in the case of some demographic variables (e.g., female = 1, male = 2). Numbers are relatively easy to reduce to more manageable and understandable terms and we do it all the time in our daily lives. We calculate batting averages, bowling scores, median home costs, and other numbers when we work and play.

Table 12.1 Calculating frequencies

Frequencies are calculated by simply counting the number of one score. On the following item, people identified their level of satisfaction with the registration process.

> On the following scale, please indicate your level of satisfaction with the registration process (1 = extremely low, 5 = extremely high).

Twenty-one people responded to this item and their scores were:

2	3	4
3	2	3
1	4	4
2	1	2
3	2	3
2	1	1
1	1	2

A frequency table for these scores would look like this:

score	frequency
1	6
2	7
3	5
4	3
5	0

Frequencies

Calculating frequencies is the simplest of descriptive data analysis techniques. Evaluators simply count the number of "whatever" they have. For instance, if you indicate that you have four apples, three oranges, and three bananas, you are reporting the frequency of each occurrence of apples, oranges, and bananas. In evaluation, one might indicate that 12 people answered "yes," 47 answered "no," and 7 did not respond to a particular item. These are frequencies. See Table 12.1 for a sample of how frequencies are typically represented in a written report (frequency table).

Percentages

One can see the usefulness of calculating frequencies in the example above—one can take 66 individual responses and reduce them to three easy-to-understand categories. By themselves, however, frequencies are not always useful. For instance, if one had 356 total responses and 297 people answered "yes" while 59 said "no," this does not translate into very meaningful information—the numbers are too large for human brains to really make sense of things. Therefore, one might calculate percentages of each possible response. Percentages are calculated by dividing the frequency of a response category by the total number possible. Thus, continuing the example of 356 respondents, one finds that 83% of respondents (297/356) answered this item "yes" while the other 17% (59/356) responded "no." This presents the responses in a slightly different light and allows one to make statements about the "majority" and "minority" of respondents. Percentages are often reported in conjunction with frequencies to provide an additional dimension of understanding (see Table 12.2).

Measures of Central Tendency

Getting a bit more sophisticated in terms of reducing or analyzing quantitative data, one can also calculate measures of central tendency. This information informs us about how and where scores fall relative to the "middle" of the data set. By examining "middle" scores one gets a

Table 12.2 Calculating percentages

Percentages are calculated by dividing the frequency of one score by the total number of responses—in this case, 21. Using the example of satisfaction with the registration process as in Table 12.1, the percentages are calculated.

> On the following scale, please indicate your level of satisfaction with the registration process (1 = extremely low, 5 = extremely high).

Twenty-one people responded to this item and their scores were:

2	3	4
3	2	3
1	4	4
2	1	2
3	2	3
2	1	1
1	1	2

A frequency and percentages table for these scores would look like this:

score	frequency	%
1	6	28.6
2	7	33.3
3	5	23.8
4	3	14.3
5	0	0.0

Table 12.3 Calculating the mean

The mean is calculated by dividing the total of all the scores by the total number of responses. Continuing with our example with satisfaction of the registration process we calculate the mean below.

> On the following scale, please indicate your level of satisfaction with the registration process (1 = extremely low, 5 = extremely high).

Twenty-one people responded to this item and their scores were:

2	3	4
3	2	3
1	4	4
2	1	2
3	2	3
2	1	1
1	1	2

First, we add all the scores above (sum = 47). Next, we divide that by the number of respondents (21) resulting in a mean of 2.24.

little more information about relative positioning of data. The three measures of central tendency describe the "middle" score include the mean, median, and mode. They may or may not be the same number for any one data set, although the numbers are typically close to one another.

Mean

The mean is another term for mathematical average. Remembering from early years of school math, the mean is calculated by adding all the scores and then dividing by the total number of responses. Therefore, with a Likert scale item where respondents could

---

Table 12.4 Calculating the median and mode

The median is calculated by finding the halfway mark between the scores. Continuing with the example with satisfaction of the registration process we identify the median below.

> On the following scale, please indicate your level of satisfaction with the registration process (1 = extremely low, 5 = extremely high).

First, arrange the scores in descending order:

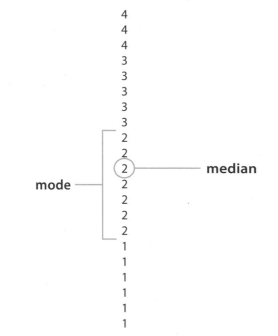

There are 21 scores, so divide 21 by 2 to find the halfway mark. This number is 10.5. Then, starting at the top, count down 10.5 scores. In this case, that places us in the midst of the 2 scores; thus, 2 is the median.

The mode is the most frequently occurring score. We can see from the frequencies table and by looking at the table above that the most frequently occurring score is 2. Thus, 2 is the mode.

---

answer on a scale from one to five, we could calculate the average score (see Table 12.3 on p. 343). When presented along with frequencies, percentages, and standard deviation this information provides a deeper understanding of how individuals responded to a particular item. Be careful to avoid calculating an average of arbitrarily assigned numbers (e.g., female = 1, male = 2) as numerical means of categorical items (words) do not make sense.

Median

The median is another measure of central tendency that provides a slightly different perspective in understanding data. The median is calculated by finding the middle of a series of scores by counting up or down a column. First, we list all the scores individually in descending order (this makes it easier to do additional calculations). If there are 15 total scores, the eighth score in the column is at the middle—that is, it is in the middle of the column whether we count from the top or the bottom. See Table 12.4 for an example of this. Median scores are reported, usually in conjunction with the mean, to help better understand how people answered a particular item. When interpreting the median we report that half of the respondents scored higher than n and half of the respondents scored lower than n. Similar to calculating a mean score, we do not calculate median scores for categorical data.

Mode

Calculating the mode is the simplest of the three measures of central tendency and is also the roughest estimate of where the middle score is found. The mode is the most frequently occurring score or response. There can be multiple modes—if there are two, the data are considered to be bimodal; if there are three modes, the data are trimodal, and so on. While it is mathematically possible to calculate a mode for all types of data, it will be important to be sure the score is meaningful before reporting a mode in a report.

Measures of Dispersion

Measures of dispersion describe how spread out the data are. This is helpful to know because even though measures of central tendency might be similar (or even the same), the scores might look different. For instance, if we were evaluating the safety and risk management aspects of a program facility using a standard evaluation tool with Likert scale items, we might find that two different areas in the building had a mean score of 3.5 on a 5.0 scale. In looking at the individual items that were used in the calculation of these means, however, we might find that one facility received mixed scores of ones and fives, while the other facility received a score of three or four on every item. Obviously, one facility is "okay" on all areas, while the other is excellent in some areas and severely deficient in others. This information would lead us to take different forms of action in these two facilities.

Range

The *range* is the easiest type of dispersion to calculate. It is determined by calculating the difference between the highest and lowest scores and adding one. For example, in the facility safety check above, the range of the first program area with scores of ones and fives would be five ($5 - 1 + 1 = 5$); the range of the second program area where scores were all threes or fours would be two ($4 - 3 + 1 = 2$). Each quantitative item on an evaluation instrument has a range. It gives us an idea about how close together the scores are. See Table 12.5 for an example.

Standard Deviation

Standard deviation is the most commonly used measure of dispersion of data and it should be reported whenever the mean is reported. It is the average of how much

---

Table 12.5 Calculating the range

The range is calculated by subtracting the lowest score from the highest score and adding one. Continuing with our example with satisfaction of the registration process we calculate the range below.

On the following scale, please indicate your level of satisfaction with the registration process (1 = extremely low, 5 = extremely high).

Twenty-one people responded to this item and their scores were:

2	3	4
3	2	3
1	4	4
2	1	2
3	2	3
2	1	1
1	1	2

The highest score (4) minus the lowest score (1) equals 3; then add 1. The range for the above scores is 4.

---

the scores differ from the mean. The smaller the standard deviation, the more closely the scores are clustered around the mean and the more alike are peoples' responses. The higher the standard deviation, the more spread out the scores are from the mean, and the more dissimilar peoples' responses. See Table 12.6 (p. 346).

Techniques for Qualitative Data Analysis

We've already mentioned that using a qualitative paradigm and qualitative data collection techniques result in words rather than numbers (for example, words on open-ended items on a questionnaire or in an interview are considered data). These words provide a rich data set that enables us to gain understanding of what people thought in relation to the items asked. As noted, in analyzing *quantitative* data, evaluators try to reduce the data into smaller, more manageable categories or, even, single numerical descriptors (e.g., the mean).

In analyzing *qualitative* data, rather than reducing the data to one word, evaluators attempt to understand and report the various perspectives that people shared (Bamberger et al., 2006; Patton, 2002). Evaluators work to bring order to the data and organize "words into patterns, categories, and basic descriptive units. Interpretation involves attaching meaning and significance to the analysis, explaining descriptive patterns, and looking for relationships and linkages within the data" (Henderson & Bialeschki, 2002, p. 303). Thus, analyzing data of any type involves both analysis and interpretation.

Open Coding

Open coding is a process used to organize qualitative data so that emerging patterns and themes become evident. This is the process of reducing data into smaller, more manageable pieces and coding it so we can easily find it again later. To begin, evaluators must read and reread the data several times. As they go through this process they can place a code word next to the data to aid them in focusing on their findings. These initial codings are not firm; they will change based on one's growing understanding as one reads through the responses several times (Patton, 2002). Some people put the data (i.e., words) on index cards and sort them into like categories and patterns. Others use the cut-and-paste function of word processing or qualitative analysis programs and computers to move the data around as codes are being developed (see Table 12.7 on p. 347).

Enumeration

Enumeration is a relatively straightforward technique of bringing some sense to qualitative data. It is the coding and counting of words, themes, or patterns based on the code we have assigned. The use of numbers in this analysis technique helps in understanding the strength and frequency of feelings. For instance, if a question asked individuals to identify the strengths of a program, we might get the following responses: great staff!; stale food; staff were warm and inviting; facilities were clean; staff were enthusiastic; I liked the way the staff treated me and my family—we felt very welcomed to this event; good facilities; and facilities were easy to get to. Enumeration might lead us to

say that there were three positive responses about staff, three positive comments about the facilities, and one negative response related to the food (see Table 12.7).

In qualitative analysis we would not want to solely rely on the use of enumeration as this greatly reduces the richness of the responses. To counter the potential for an over-reliance on the use of enumeration, in evaluation reports we often provide direct quotes from the responses to help address the depth of feeling and the various aspects of what it was people expressed. In this way, various perspectives are shared in the words of the respondents, and most accurately understood by those using the evaluation report.

Table 12.6 Calculating the standard deviation

The standard deviation is calculated by following several steps. Continuing with the example of satisfaction with the registration process, we can identify the standard deviation for the item below.

On the following scale, please indicate your level of satisfaction with the registration process (1 = extremely low, 5 = extremely high).

(1) First, arrange the scores in descending order:

score	deviation (s)	squared differences (s^2)
4	1.76	3.10
4	1.76	3.10
4	1.76	3.10
3	0.76	0.58
3	0.76	0.58
3	0.76	0.58
3	0.76	0.58
3	0.76	0.58
2	−0.24	0.06
2	−0.24	0.06
2	−0.24	0.06
2	−0.24	0.06
2	−0.24	0.06
2	−0.24	0.06
2	−0.24	0.06
1	−1.24	1.54
1	−1.24	1.54
1	−1.24	1.54
1	−1.24	1.54
1	−1.24	1.54
1	−1.24	1.54

(2) Second, determine the mean—in this case, the mean is 2.24 (see Table 12.3, p. 343).

(3) Third, determine the difference between each of the individual scores and the mean—those calculations are the "deviation" column (for example, 4 minus 2.24 = 1.76).

(4) Once the deviation is determined, square each of the deviation scores and place that value in the squared differences column.

(5) Then, sum the column of squared differences.

$$\Sigma s^2 = 21.86$$

(6) Next, we divide the sum of the squared differences by the total number of respondents, less one.

$$21.81 \div 20 = 1.093$$

(7) Finally, we take the square root of that figure—this is the standard deviation.

$$\sqrt{1.09} = 1.05$$

Standard deviation (steps 5 through 7) can also be represented by the statistical formula:

$$\sqrt{\frac{\Sigma (s)^2}{(n-1)}}$$

where Σ = "sum of"
s = deviation from mean
n = number of responses, measurements (data)

Constant Comparison

As a data analysis technique, constant comparison offers a systematic way of seeking out the meanings in peoples' responses (Bamberger et al., 2006). It is particularly useful in dealing with interview or focus group data because there is so much of it. In this technique the data are recorded (all verbal interview or focus group data must be transcribed as quickly as possible after the initial interview), read, coded, reread, themes are developed, the data are reread and recoded, and themes are checked for fit. In fact, in this effort, one may ask colleagues to read, code, and identify themes to determine consistency among interpretation. This is important to ensure accurate interpretation of raw data.

According to Henderson (2006), three stages are involved in the constant comparison process (see Figure 12.10). Stage one involves the initial coding, reducing, and organizing of the data into categories. Stage two includes comparing the various categories with one another and with the original data set to ensure appropriate interpretation. The third stage involves reworking the categories (if necessary) to talk about the data and how they fit or don't fit with the evaluation criteria. At this stage it is important to ensure that no categories or important data are missed. If new themes are discovered at this stage, the process begins again.

Table 12.7 Coding and enumeration

In the example below respondents were instructed

"Please comment on the environmental policies of this recreation center."

This was an open-ended item and resulted in diverse responses. Responses are identified below, as is the initial *coding*.

Code	Response
negative—no know	I didn't know there were any!
negative/good	It seems a little carried away at times. I mean, having to reuse paper plates is ridiculous!
positive	I like the concern for the environment.
negative—no know	I never really noticed.
positive	It seems to make sense to me!
positive	In this day and age it is critical to have pro-environment policies everywhere—thank goodness, someone is doing it!
neutral	It's messy to use a compost pile (it smells too).
positive	I like recycling whatever we could.
positive	It's good to get up awareness.
negative/neutral	The area around the can collection place is always sticky.
positive	I'm glad it's happening!
negative—no know	Don't know what they are.
neutral	Okay.

Enumeration involves calculating a frequency for the codes. In this case, it would look like this:

3	Negative—no know(ledge)
1	Negative/Neutral
1	Negative/Good
2	Neutral
6	Positive

1 Initial coding into categories → 2 Compare categories with each other and other data → 3 Rework and redefine

Figure 12.10 The constant comparison process involves three stages.

Content Analysis

Content analysis is used when examining old records, documents, photographs, electronic media, and anything else in "printed" form. In program evaluation we might utilize this technique to examine reports from previous years, to better understand the community, and/or to enable accurate portrayals of things such as historic themes. In this form of analysis we use a systematic process to examine documents in a fashion similar to constant comparison. We look for similarities, differences, and outstanding elements (whether they be positive or negative).

Interpreting the Analysis

Once data is analyzed, evaluators need to interpret it for the users of the evaluation—those to whom they will submit the final report. This involves a cyclical process where evaluators look at their initial assessment or evaluation goals along with the results of their analysis. This helps evaluators to focus their interpretation of the results and final recommendations. In light of the initial goals, one will want to look for results that both support and contradict the broader question, as well as what one found and what one did not find. For example, let's say that one found that 86% of those responding rated interactions with staff as "good or excellent" —one should be pleased with this result. However, one may have reason to be concerned if one discovers that a particular group of people (e.g., teenagers, women, Hispanics, people with disabilities) were not involved in the evaluation process or were the 14% who rated interaction with staff as "poor or fair."

To ensure accurate interpretations evaluators must take their time with the data reduction, analysis, and interpretation processes. To ensure a thorough needs assessment or evaluation, evaluators will want to remain open to making modifications in the midst of the analysis and interpretation processes.

As evaluators become more familiar and comfortable with examining, analyzing, and interpreting data they will come to understand it as it was intended by the respondents. To help users of the evaluation to understand interpretations and recommendations without going through the entire data analysis process, evaluators need to present the findings and interpretation in a relatively straightforward fashion. In part, this is done by making statements about the data and supporting comments with quotes and anecdotes directly from the data set. Evaluators try to present a balance of descrip-

tion with the words of the respondents to provide the depth and richness the data have to offer.

Report Writing

After completing the analysis and interpretation of the data one must present the information in a meaningful fashion to potential users. Bearing in mind that we are proponents of utilization-focused evaluation, we want programmers to present a written report in such a way as to maximize its usefulness. To begin, programmers must remind themselves of the audience—both in terms of their experience with evaluation as well as with the role or position they hold in relation to the program under review. For instance, a report to staff might look slightly different than a report to the Board of Trustees or City Council. A programmer might present the results to one group via a formal written report, another group might receive an executive summary with highlights, and yet another audience might learn of our findings through an oral report with a computer-aided presentation. Agencies may wish to publish highlights or the entire report to the web for public access, or it may be important to keep the final report in-house.

The intended audience(s) is an important element that influences the choice of content, writing style, and format. In some cases an executive summary might be sufficient (i.e., a two to three page summary of the process and major findings with recommendations); in other situations, a full-blown report might be required complete with graphics, figures, and appendices.

Generally, in a written report of an evaluation, we will present background information about the evaluation explaining the why, who, what, when, where, and how questions; findings (i.e., factual information learned from the data analysis); interpretations (i.e., our understanding of the reduced data based on background and other information); judgments (i.e., values and criteria used with the data); and recommendations (i.e., suggested courses of action based on the findings, interpretation, and judgments; Henderson & Bialeschki, 2002; Rossman & Schlatter, 2008). A typical format for a written, formal report follows.

Front Cover

The front cover or first slide (see Figure 12.11) of any evaluation report should include the following:

- Title of program and its location

- Time period covered by the report or date of event

- Name of evaluator(s), with agency affiliation and contact information

- Information about to whom the report is submitted

- Date report is submitted

Table of Contents

Depending upon the length of the report, a table of contents may or may not be necessary. For any report over eight pages in length, a table of contents is helpful for those searching for particular pieces of information. Simple reports that are presented as charts or tables typically will not warrant this element.

Front Matter: Summary

Front matter includes material that is important, yet not integral to the outcome of the assessment. It often includes a section describing the authorizing agency, external funding source, or others who contributed to the initiation of the project. This early part of the report also includes the names and affiliations of those who

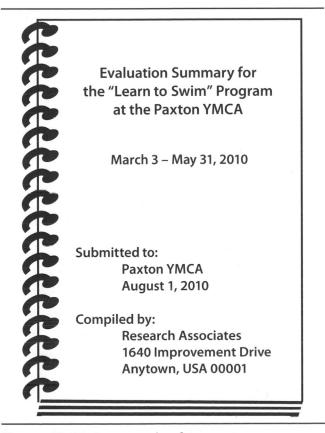

Evaluation Summary for the "Learn to Swim" Program at the Paxton YMCA

March 3 – May 31, 2010

Submitted to:
    Paxton YMCA
    August 1, 2010

Compiled by:
    Research Associates
    1640 Improvement Drive
    Anytown, USA 00001

Figure 12.11 An example of a report cover

assisted with the process and/or report. If, for instance, a colleague conducted the data analysis, this is the appropriate place to note her or his involvement and express appreciation.

A brief summary of the evaluation is also often found in this early section of the report. The summary is usually one page or shorter, explains why the evaluation was undertaken, and reports the major findings and recommendations. This is sometimes referred to as an *executive summary*.

Section 1: Introduction

The Introduction sets the stage and provides a context for the evaluation—this is particularly important when an entire agency or organization is being evaluated. Included in this section is a purpose statement and the goals of the assessment, definitions that will assist the reader in understanding the report, and a short description of the overall process undertaken for the project.

Section 2: Background Information

This is the section of the evaluation report that provides the context to help readers understand all that is to follow. The amount of information and detail will depend upon the targeted audience of the report. Some will require a great deal of information, while others may already have a thorough understanding of the program being evaluated. This section serves to keep things in context as the report is being written and helps the program evaluator to stay focused (see Figure 12.12 on p. 350).

Typical information found in this section (although in varying amounts of depth) includes general information about the organization, its values, philosophy, goals, mission, and vision. Also, material about the origin of the program (e.g., What was the impetus and process for program development? Who are the constituents?), philosophy and goals of the program, participant demographics, characteristics of the program (e.g., facilities, location, equipment, activities, program format and structure), and staffing information are included.

Program-specific information might also be included in this section. This material might include a short program description, the intended target population, numbers and types of staff and volunteers, a program timeline, costs, needed equipment and facilities, registration processes, marketing efforts, partners, sponsors, and other related data. Depending upon the desired material, this section of a formal report could be from one to five pages in length.

Section 3: Methods and Procedures

This section of the report focuses on explaining the evaluation process to the reader. The language should be such that the intended reader understands what is explained. In this section, the report writer describes the paradigm followed (i.e., quantitative or qualitative); how the sample was chosen; and the evaluation model

---

General Organizational Information

History
Philosophy
Mission
Vision
Goals

General Program Information

Philosophy
Purpose
Goals
Target Population
Location and Facilities

Participant Information

Demographics
Historical Involvement
Other Community Information

Program Description

Event
Staffing
Process
Budget

Figure 12.12 Background information in an evaluation report helps provide context for increased understanding.

and data collection techniques used. In addition, information about how the instrument was developed or selected as well as information about its validity, reliability, and usability is found in this section. Other information to include relates to data collection procedures and an explanation of how the data were analyzed. A reader should have enough information from reading this section, that if she or he so desired, she or he could conduct a similar evaluation by following the information given.

Section 4: Analysis and Results

Because of the nature of the material, this section of the evaluation report tends to be the most straightforward. It presents an explanation of the data analysis and the results of those analyses. It is important to include both narrative and graphical information to help explain the findings. Common graphics included in this section are charts (e.g., bar, pie, line), tables (such as frequency and percentage tables), photographs, and other pertinent figures. All graphics require titles or captions, and narrative descriptions to facilitate reader comprehension.

As mentioned earlier, the intended audience and the presentation format will help determine the amount and use of text and graphics in a formal report. A computer-aided presentation will typically use more graphics than text. When reporting percentages (whether in text or in a table) writers commonly use rounded numbers (e.g., 14.7% would be written as 15% to make the data more readable). If this is done, it is often important to indicate that numbers may not equal 100% due to rounding.

Section 5: Interpretations, Conclusions, and Recommendations

The interpretations, conclusions, and recommendations section is where the program evaluator has an opportunity to explain why she or he thinks the findings came out as they did. Taking time to explain program results, utilizing the information found in Section 2: Background Information, is helpful in putting things in context. Providing alternative reasoning is helpful. For instance, one may have found that participants were concerned about a lack of pre-event information, but one is unclear as to why. By looking at all the information one has, one might speculate that the problem was due to poor event planning, a snafu with the mailing process, a poor printing job, poor selection of evaluation techniques, or some other reason. In the recommendations subsection, the program evaluator makes suggestions relative to changes in the program based on the interpretation of the results. This should be worded clearly and in action statements. See Figure 12.13 for an example of this.

Appendices

Appendices provide a place to include additional explanatory information, which serves to enhance the material found in the report. Often included in this section is a copy of the evaluation instrument (sometimes with descriptive statistics included—if appropriate), a copy of the cover letter if a mail survey was used or the introduction page of an online survey, summaries of needs assessments or evaluations from past years, promotional material for the program, cost information, and a list of references from which community information was gathered.

Summary

There is much to be learned about program evaluation. We as leisure services professionals can utilize a qualitative or quantitative paradigm and associated tools for gathering data. Prior to beginning the evaluation, however, we must select a sampling technique appropriate to the intent of the evaluation process. We have choices of random and nonrandom methods to do this. Once the sample is selected we then turn our attention to instrumentation. We are concerned with the reliability, validity, and usability of the tools being used to collect data to ensure a worthwhile evaluation process.

Many quantitative techniques exist to collect data, each of which has its strengths and weaknesses. Head counts and questionnaires are the two most common techniques for gathering information. Head counts do not address quality elements, and many issues need to be considered when designing written questionnaires. Qualitative techniques such as reviewing documents and records, observation, sociometry, and interviewing are used to elicit in-depth information

---

Conclusion and Recommendations

Conclusion:

Staff expected over 1,000 participants for the 5K run, yet only 58 showed up at the day of the event. After conducting a community-wide evaluation, it was determined that the target market did not know about the event.

Recommendations:

1. Staff should begin public promotion of this event at least one month earlier than this year.

2. Staff should conduct promotional efforts at a minimum of 25 different public places (e.g., schools, churches, stores, restaurants).

3. Staff should utilize at least three different types of media to promote this run.

Figure 12.13 Some recommendations are based on the conclusions.

from respondents. These tools are often used to augment quantitative data.

Finally, reducing the data gathered is necessary to make sense of all the individual answers that have been collected. With quantitative data we commonly use descriptive analysis, which includes calculating frequencies, percentages, measures of central tendency, and measures of dispersion. With qualitative data we utilize open coding, enumeration, constant comparison, and content analysis to reduce the word data we have collected. This all leads to interpreting the results, and writing the report. This final report includes several sections, each designed to bring understanding to what was learned from the evaluation.

Programming From Here to There

Moore, Cosco, and Ringaert (2005) provide an excellent example of an evaluation report they wrote titled, *Post Occupancy Evaluation (POE) of Kids Together Park*. They conducted an evaluation of a play park (Kids Together Park) for children in Cary, NC shortly after it opened. Found on the web at http://www.design.ncsu.edu/cud/about_us/docs/KTP-POE_Report_March-05.pdf, this report includes all the elements discussed in this chapter. The report is written in common language and includes pertinent background information, methodology, the types of data collection tools used, specific information about what was learned through the evaluation, and recommendations for changes. People of all ages, including those with disabilities, served as part of the convenience sample for the evaluation.

References

Bamberger, M., Rugh, J. & Mabry, L. (2006). *RealWorld evaluation*. Thousand Oaks, CA: Sage Publications.

Henderson, K. (2006). *Dimensions of choice: Qualitative approaches to parks, recreation, tourism, sport, and leisure research*. State College, PA: Venture Publishing, Inc.

Henderson, K. & Bialeschki, M. D. (2002). *Evaluating leisure services: Making enlightened decisions* (2nd ed.). State College, PA: Venture Publishing, Inc.

Moore, R., Cosco, N. & Ringaert, L. (2005). *Post occupancy evaluation (POE) of Kids Together Park*. Natural Learning Initiative in conjunction with the Center for Universal Design. North Carolina State University. Electronic version downloaded January 14, 2009, from http://www.design.ncsu.edu/cud/about_us/docs/KTP-POE_Report_March-05.pdf

Patton, M. (2008). *Utilization-focused evaluation: The new century text*. (2nd ed.) Newbury Park, CA: Sage Publications.

Patton, M. (2002). *Qualitative evaluation and research methods* (3rd ed.). Thousand Oaks, CA: Sage Publications.

Patton, M. (1990). *Qualitative evaluation and research methods* (2nd ed.). Newbury Park, CA: Sage.

Rossman, J. R. & Schlatter, B. E. (2008). *Recreation programming: Designing leisure experiences* (5th ed.). Champaign, IL: Sagamore Publishing.

Russell, R. & Jamieson, L. (2007). *Leisure program planning and delivery*. Champaign, IL: Human Kinetics.

Section 508: The road to accessibility (n.d.). Retrieved February 26, 2009, from www.section508.gov

Appendix
Tournament Scheduling | A

The following section presents information related to the construction of several different tournament formats. Tournaments are utilized for a wide range of skill-based sport, athletic, and game events. They are used to facilitate the play of a large number of teams and/or players to maximize play and even competition across contestants. Tournaments are commonly used with team sports such as softball and soccer, as well as individual sports such as golf and downhill skiing. Programmers who offer tournaments for table games such as bridge, chess, Parcheesi, and billiards use tournaments to help organize play. Further, special events such as geography and spelling bees, hot air balloon competitions, and various events at Special Olympics utilize various tournaments to facilitate play of a large number of participants.

Michele Barbin is the primary author of this section and presents clear graphics and text to aid programmers in developing events that require formal scheduling. Several models are presented and programmers are encouraged to study each one to make a determination about which format is best suited to the specific program and its goals.

Ladder Tournament

The ladder tournament is designed to encourage participants to generate their own play through a challenge system organized by the programmer. Participants or teams are ranked initially by skill level. The time and place of the actual playing is agreed upon by the two participants. Officiating is usually done on the honor system. In its simplest form, the ladder is a straight, single-unit, step-by-step listing of ranks. The challenger may contest the person in the step immediately above her or him. Failure to arrange a contest, avoiding a challenge, or not meeting a legitimate challenge within a prescribed period, such as 48 hours after its issue, can be considered a forfeit and the challenger trades places on the ladder with the player above.

Advantages to this type of tournament are that it is easy for a programmer to arrange, and encourages participants to interact. It doesn't matter how many contestants participate since "rungs" are easily added or removed (although more than 10 rungs is not recommended). Disadvantages are that participants are limited to playing those on neighboring rungs. Also, since skills and abilities can change over the course of time, a predetermined date or time of finish is required. In addition, when large numbers of participants are involved, the ladder tournament breaks down.

This type of tournament, however, can be a useful tool. When used throughout scheduled practices (e.g., youth tennis league), players can be added if they join after the start of the season. It is also handy in helping to determine the seeding for end-of-season tournaments.

Paperwork is minimal since keeping track of this tournament can be as simple as using a bulletin board and index cards with each contestant's name.

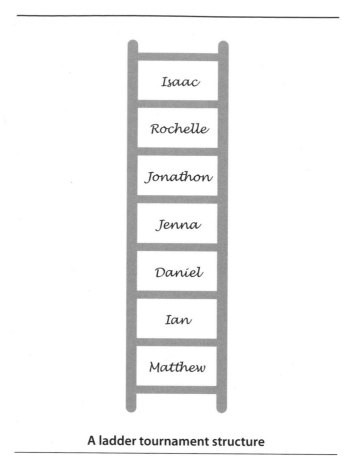

A ladder tournament structure

Pyramid Tournament

As mentioned earlier, when larger numbers of participants are involved, the ladder tournament breaks down. The solution can be to create additional subpatterns that open opportunities to play more frequently. The pyramid tournament is the next logical step as it creates a number of different opportunities for play, graduating from a broad, lower ranked base to a number one person at the peak. Any player in a lower layer may challenge anyone in the second layer, anyone in the second layer can challenge anyone in the third layer, and so on. Specific procedures must be created that identify how often a player must participate and against what level players she or he needs to participate.

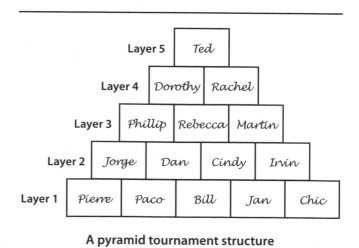

A pyramid tournament structure

Single Elimination Tournament

The single elimination tournament is efficient, but it does not maximize the play opportunities of contestants. Individuals or teams are paired randomly, asked to challenge another contestant for the initial round, or by a mechanism that assigns contestants through rankings or seeds. The system of bracketing the teams or players into paired contests is easily accomplished as long as the number of players is a power of two. Any other number means a "rigged" first round using byes until the power of 2 is reached. For example, a six or twelve team tournament requires 2 and 4 byes respectively in order to assure that four or eight teams progress to the second round. Byes can be given by random picks or through a seeded approach with the top-ranked teams receiving the byes.

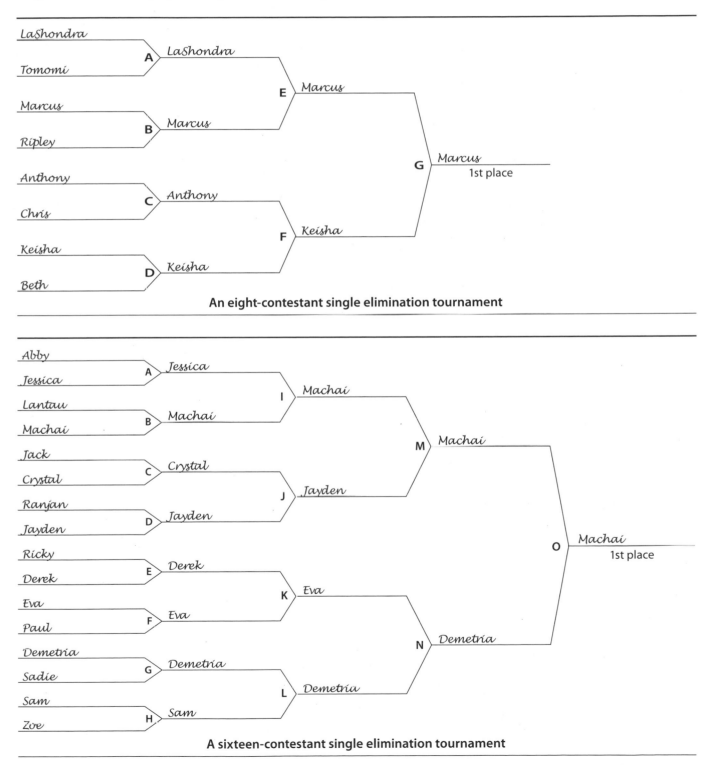

An eight-contestant single elimination tournament

A sixteen-contestant single elimination tournament

Single Elimination with Placement

Within this tournament structure, final placement (or ranking) is determined by contest. It allows for more play than the traditional single elimination structure, and may also be used to determine seeding for a future tournament. Programmers may opt to use this chart to rank the final eight teams in any size single elimination, or reduce it to determine placement for only four teams by using just the E, F and K brackets. It may be modified to determine placement of larger tournaments, also.

To do this as results come in, move the "eliminated" team to the lower brackets where indicated. For example, contest A winner moves to bracket E while the eliminated contestant takes the slot in bracket H (position A2). If the programmer wishes to heighten suspense, she or he may choose to play out the lower placement brackets first (i.e., L, J, K then G).

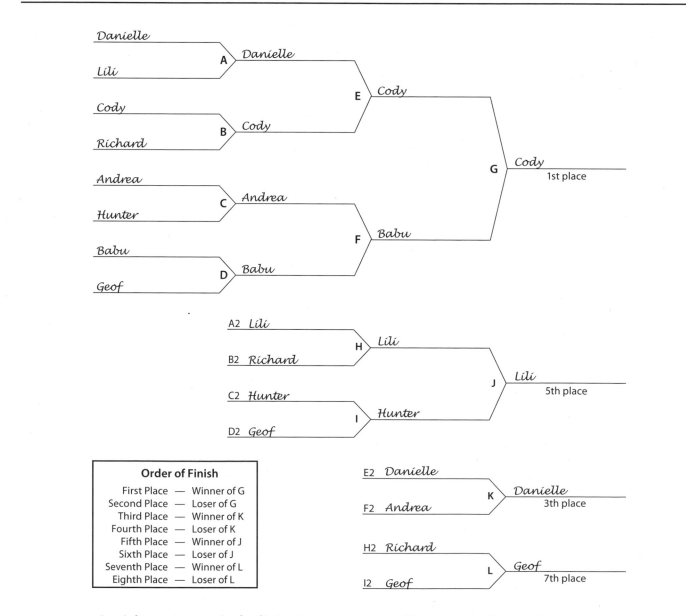

Order of Finish

First Place — Winner of G
Second Place — Loser of G
Third Place — Winner of K
Fourth Place — Loser of K
Fifth Place — Winner of J
Sixth Place — Loser of J
Seventh Place — Winner of L
Eighth Place — Loser of L

An eight-contestant single elimination tournament with placement (i.e., ranking) structure

Double Elimination Tournament

The double elimination tournament extends play of every team or individual since no one is eliminated from winning until they have lost two contests. Upon a first loss, the player moves over to the consolation bracket; a second loss eliminates them from play. If the contestant makes it through the consolation bracket without a second loss, the contestant(s) eventually play the winner of the winners' bracket for the championship.

The double elimination tournament is a popular structure since it allows more play for all players. When run well, it is a fair evaluation of skill level. However, if care is not taken during set up and while transferring contestants from the winners' bracket into the consolation bracket, contestants may feel cheated if they are defeated by the same opponent who knocked them into the consolation bracket in the first place. This occurrence can be avoided until the final rounds by using a simple crossover method.

To use this sixteen-contestant chart, place the first round players in the A–H brackets. Proceed by moving winners to the right and consolation contestants to the left. Players added to the consolation bracket in later rounds are placed in the indicated bracket (e.g., loser

of J moves to J2, top of chart). This crossover pattern within the tree avoids having players eliminated by the same team that put them into the consolation bracket until the semifinal round. In the final round, the consolation finalist needs to defeat the winners' bracket finalist twice to win the tournament since a double elimination isn't over until all contestants except one accumulate two losses.

Note in the examples on page 308, the positioning of the byes, seeding, and "crossover" pattern of the double elimination. Had the crossover pattern (indicated by the dotted arrow) not occurred, Sarah and Carter would have met a second time in bracket K as would have Tracey and Sonny (see Example 2). This would have left Sarah feeling shortchanged since not only did the same individual who knocked her into the consolation bracket eliminate her, she also played against only that individual. This crossover pattern is effective and should be used in any size double elimination tournament. Compare this sixteen-person tournament to the eight-person pattern (Example 1. p. 358). Note how the crossover happens in the nearby "branches" of the tournament tree.

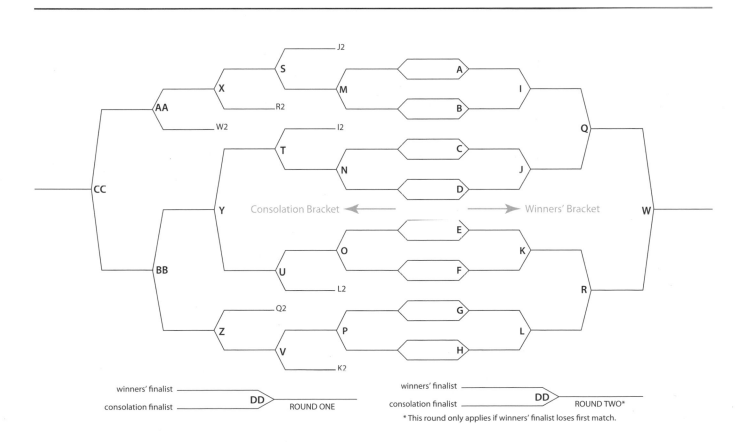

The sixteen-contestant double elimination tournament structure

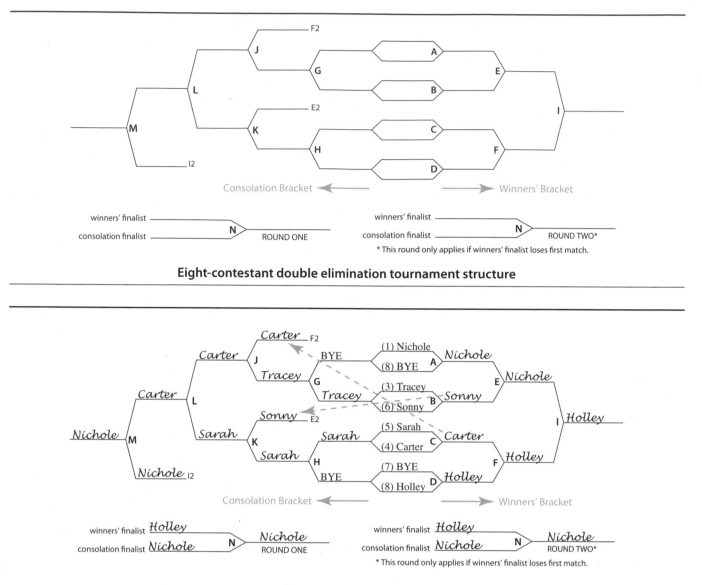

Eight-contestant double elimination tournament structure

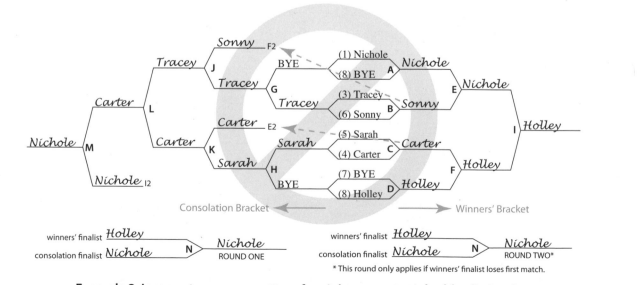

Example 1: Correct crossover pattern for eight-contestant double elimination

Example 2: Incorrect crossover pattern for eight-contestant double elimination

Double Elimination with Limited Placement

In this eight-contestant example, there is some play beyond two losses to determine overall placement (i.e., final ranking) within a tournament. Complete this as a traditional double elimination (i.e., bracket finalists play until each has accumulated two losses) with extra play for the losers of the G, H, J and K matches to determine placement. Even if the consolation bracket finalist defeats the winners' bracket finalist, it will not affect the overall placement because each of the bracket finalists would have met the third place finisher in play (see Bracket I and compare to the position of I2). If time is limited, this tournament can "give" the title to the undefeated winners' bracket finalist without necessarily meeting the consolation bracket finalist (see Order of Finish). Tournament staff should follow the alphabetical order of play for this tournament to run smoothly.

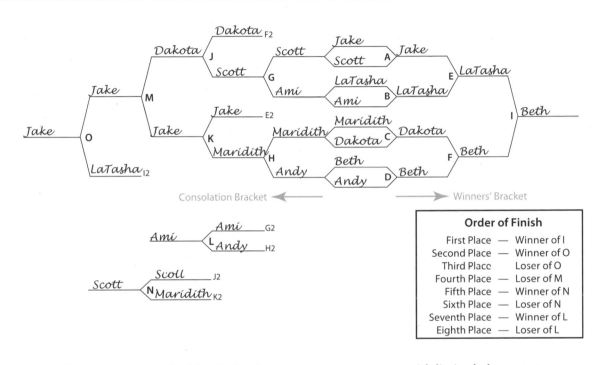

Eight-contestant double elimination tournament structure with limited placement

Order of Finish

First Place	— Winner of I
Second Place	— Winner of O
Third Place	— Loser of O
Fourth Place	— Loser of M
Fifth Place	— Winner of N
Sixth Place	— Loser of N
Seventh Place	— Winner of L
Eighth Place	— Loser of L

Setting Up Elimination Tournaments

Several common ways to set up an elimination tournament schedule include random draw, controlled draw, seeding, and challenge.

For a *random draw*, it is best to write the name of each contestant on an index card, place all the cards together, shuffle them, and then select cards randomly to determine first round pairings on the elimination tree. The advantage is that no one knows who they will meet in the first round and there is no basis on skill level or past performance. The drawback is that if you have a group of people in attendance who regularly practice together or meet each other in competition elsewhere, they may run into someone with whom they practice in the first round.

The *controlled draw* takes care of this disadvantage in the random draw. In this case, keep the contestants who play together regularly separated in the tournament tree. Whether it involves several teams that meet in league play throughout the region or a group of karate students from a particular trainer or class, these contestants can be spread through the tree first, then the other contestants can be added to the tree. The advantage is that contestants get the chance to compete against people they would seldom encounter otherwise, at least in the first round. The disadvantage is that this can be perceived by some participants (and spectators) as "stacking the deck."

A *seeded tournament* usually involves a group of contestants who compete against each other regularly, or "earned" their slots in the tournament. Whether the contestants' ranking (i.e., seed) comes from past performance, polls, intuition or statistics, seeding spreads the contestants apart by perceived abilities. For example, you are given a list of sixteen teams in the order they are expected to place at the end of the tournament according to a coaches' poll. The teams should then be paired on the tournament tree as follows:

1	v.	16
5	v.	12
3	v.	14
7	v.	10
8	v.	9
4	v.	13
6	v.	11
2	v.	15

The theory is that if teams or players are seeded appropriately, the number one and number two seeds will meet in the final round, resulting in an exciting match. Usually placement in a seeded tournament is earned through a season of play, so byes are rare. It is up to the programmer to decide how to handle "no shows" in the case of a double elimination. If a contestant drops out for any reason before a day-long tournament where contestants are required to prequalify, an alternate is usually in attendance to take their seed. This may involve shifting the seeds before the tournament begins since the alternate had not qualified for the tournament and, therefore, would have the lowest seed. For example, seed number four cannot attend due to an injury, but seed number seventeen is in attendance and ready to play. Seeds five through sixteen move up one seed and seed seventeen becomes seed sixteen.

It is also the programmer's option to set the tree and rule that if a contestant doesn't meet their challenger for any reason, it is considered a forfeit. The forfeit moves through the tree as a bye would if it occurs in the first round; the contestant who wins the forfeit advances.

A servant leader should consider all options and decide how to handle such scenarios well before the tournament. This allows potential contestants to understand the guidelines and procedures related to how the tournament is being run, and whether or not a hopeful contestant should bring any equipment or clothing. It can be a good idea to encourage hopefuls to attend; especially if you expect to use byes. Hopeful contestants are usually more than willing to play the byes just for the experience, even if regulations don't permit last-minute substitutions.

First-round challenge format allows competitors to select with whom they will compete in the first round. This, however, can be a bit tricky to set up properly on a tree. It can allow byes to occur late in the elimination tree's structure and should be avoided unless you are only a few competitors shy of a "perfect" tree. For example, twelve competitors wish to begin a tournament with a challenge-up. Fair ways of handling such a situation and eliminating byes by the end of the second round with a twelve-competitor example include

- Spread the pairs equally through the sixteen-contestant tree. You will have two branches where bye meets bye on opposite sides of the tree. Since there is no seeding in such a tournament, a random draw of cards can help determine which two of the first pairs will meet the "bye pair" in the second round. Although it may seem reasonable to allow a full challenge-up without byes to satisfy the participants, the disadvantages include additional byes required in the loser's bracket, and loss of matches that matter.

- A better alternative is to have each participant (or challenge pair) draw cards, four (or two) of which will be marked BYE. If done before challenges are made (best option), the competitors who drew byes are placed on the tree, then the remaining eight competitors challenge a non-bye opponent for their first match. If done after challenges are made, the individuals from the bye match are placed on the tree in such a manner as to give them the chance to compete later in the tree. By doing this the byes are eliminated by the end of the first consolation round, the initial matches count, and the tournament schedule will run more smoothly. See Example 3.

Each method has advantages and disadvantages and should be considered carefully with the desires of the competitors in mind.

Placement of Byes

It is rare to have an elimination tournament that doesn't involve byes, especially when preregistration for the tournament is not required. Byes can and should be played out during one-day tournaments so that all the competitors are exposed to an equal amount of physical and/or mental exertion. This can be done two ways:

(a) Ask a few experienced players to play the "byes," or

(b) Pair up the competitors who drew the byes to play a match where their results won't count (although this only works if you have an even amount of byes to start).

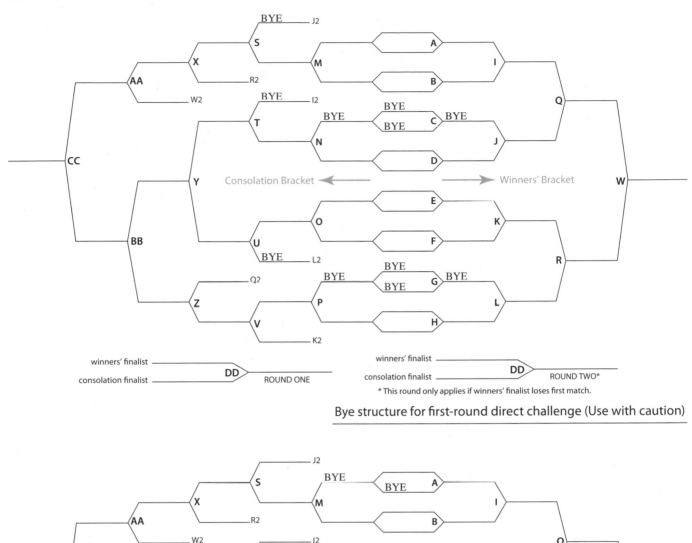

Bye structure for first-round direct challenge (Use with caution)

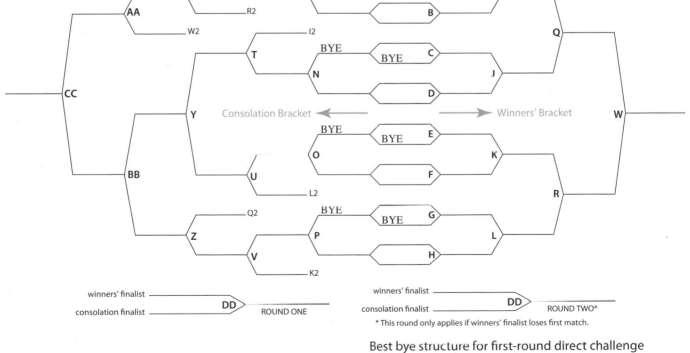

Best bye structure for first-round direct challenge

Example 3: Bye structures for a first-round challenge with twelve participants

Whether or not to "play" the byes depends upon if the organizer has enough time scheduled to complete the tournament, and what the traditional consensus of the competitors or group of competitors involves.

If using the random draw or controlled draw method of setting up the first round, space the "byes" throughout the tree first. As the names are drawn, they fall randomly down the tree giving everyone an equal chance to obtain a bye in the first round.

In the case of byes within a seeded tournament, the top ranked teams "earn" the byes and the placement shifts accordingly. For example, thirteen teams would result in this set up:

1	v.	bye
5	v.	12
3	v.	bye
7	v.	10
8	v.	9
4	v.	13
6	v.	11
2	v.	bye

Even in a situation where a league only has enough people sign up for five teams, byes, when placed in the tree correctly, are eliminated by the end of the second round. Since the "perfect" elimination tournament occurs at four and eight contestants, five teams bumps the tree structure to eight, leaving three byes in the first round and three byes in the consolation bracket of the second round. After that there should be no byes, and the tournament is played out until a winner prevails. For example

Correct Set Up			Incorrect Set Up		
1	v.	bye	1	v.	bye
3	v.	bye	2	v.	5
4	v.	5	3	v.	4
2	v.	bye	bye	v.	bye

Elimination Tournaments and Servant Leadership

A successfully run elimination tournament:

1. rids itself of all byes as soon as possible;

2. avoids contestants meeting twice in double eliminations (until the final round); and

3. keeps competitors and spectators informed.

Competitors will always be curious and ask who or what team they will meet up with next. To avoid this and keep the central coordination area clear, place a sign (or use a poster-size copy of the tournament tree) in a public area where it is updated regularly. In a fast-paced, day-long tournament, it is especially helpful to have a volunteer keep this sign up-to-date for both spectators and competitors so that curious individuals are not tempted to bother the tournament coordinators. This way the coordinators can concentrate on the organization of the tournament tree, inform participants of their next match quickly, confirm results when needed, and keep communications open to officials and staff resulting in a successful and pleasant tournament experience for everyone.

Round Robin Tournaments

The round robin tournament enables all individuals or teams to play every other individual or team. It can be used in a day-long competition, or over a longer time period. The advantage of this format is that no team or individual is eliminated, so everyone plays an equal number of games. Sometimes, three-way ties occur in a round robin tournament (e.g., players 1, 3, and 4 all won three matches, 1 beat 3, 3 beat 4, and 4 beat 1), so procedures (i.e., if or what kind of tie-breaker should occur) need to be settled on in advance if prizes or trophies are being awarded. The disadvantage of a round robin tournament is the amount of time it takes to run.

The round robin is a very versatile tournament, since it can be run with or without a formal structure. For a self-directed approach, make a grid with the contestant's names in the rows and columns. When each game is complete, the winner's name is written in the box along with each individual or team representative's initials. An example of a six-contestant, self-directed round robin grid appears below. Note that the black squares are where players would meet themselves, and that the lower half of the grid (with the optional schedule) is shaded. Competitors meet each other once in a round robin so if using a self-directed method, players can note the results in the white boxes. Time and place of the meetings may be placed on the shaded grid. Tally results by counting how many times each competitor's name is indicated as a winner on the grid.

	Roberto	Don	Deb	Kathy	Sherril	Lynne
Roberto		Don	Deb	Kathy	Roberto	Maya
Don	Court A 1 p.m. 2/14		Deb	Don	Ossie	Don
Deb	Court A 7 p.m. 2/16	Court C 1 p.m. 2/21		Deb	Ossie	Maya
Kathy	Court C 7 p.m. 2/23	Court B 7 p.m. 2/18	Court B 1 p.m. 2/14		Ossie	Kathy
Sherril	Court C 7 p.m. 2/18	Court B 7 p.m. 2/16	Court 7 p.m. 2/23	Court A 1 p.m. 2/21		Ossie
Lynne	Court B 1 p.m. 2/21	Court A 7 p.m. 2/23	Court A 7 p.m. 2/18	Court C 7 p.m. 2/16	Court C 1 p.m. 2/14	

Round robin tournament with scheduling grid

When a more structured approach is preferred, such as when facility time is limited, the tournament organizer should direct the play. In this case, using a numbers table may be a better option especially when the time to complete a round of play is short (e.g., less than 15 minutes) and if the organizers are using more than one play area (e.g., racquetball courts). In this case, the competitors or an official should approach the person handling the results; she or he will record the results, then inform the players who they will meet next. The list is ordered so that games are spaced out to provide equal rest time for each competitor as much as possible. Here is an sample table for a six competitor round robin using a structured number table.

Assign each competitor a number

1. Christopher // ⑤
2. Nicole /// ②
3. Carter // ④
4. Holley /// ③
⋆5. Matthew //// ①
6. Sarah / ⑥

Direct competitors to play in this order and circle winner's number:

R-1	R-2	R-3	R-4	R-5
①–2	1–③	1–⑤	①–6	1–④
3–④	②–5	3–⑥	4–⑤	②–6
⑤–6	④–6	②–4	2–③	3–⑤

Circle Winner's Number

	1	2	3	4	5	6
1	—	①–2	1–③	1–④	1–⑤	①–6
2		—	2–③	②–4	②–5	②–6
3			—	3–④	3–⑤	3–⑥
4				—	4–⑤	④–6
5					—	⑤–6
6						—

To Tally Results

Follow rows and columns to count circled wins for each player (e.g., shading for player 3). Usually when ties occur, two-way ties can be broken by referring to who won the contest where the "tied" players met.

Round robin tournament: Number chart structure

Index

Other Books by Venture Publishing, Inc.

21st Century Leisure: Current Issues, Second Edition
    by Valeria J. Freysinger and John R. Kelly
The A•B•Cs of Behavior Change: Skills for Working With Behavior Problems in Nursing Homes
    by Margaret D. Cohn, Michael A. Smyer, and Ann L. Horgas
Activity Experiences and Programming within Long-Term Care
    by Ted Tedrick and Elaine R. Green
The Activity Gourmet
    by Peggy Powers
Advanced Concepts for Geriatric Nursing Assistants
    by Carolyn A. McDonald
Adventure Programming
    edited by John C. Miles and Simon Priest
Assessment: The Cornerstone of Activity Programs
    by Ruth Perschbacher
Behavior Modification in Therapeutic Recreation: An Introductory Manual
    by John Datillo and William D. Murphy
Benefits of Leisure
    edited by B.L. Driver, Perry J. Brown, and George L. Peterson
Benefits of Recreation Research Update
    by Judy M. Sefton and W. Kerry Mummery
Beyond Baskets and Beads: Activities for Older Adults with Functional Impairments
    by Mary Hart, Karen Primm, and Kathy Cranisky
Beyond Bingo: Innovative Programs for the New Senior
    by Sal Arrigo, Jr., Ann Lewis, and Hank Mattimore
Beyond Bingo 2: More Innovative Programs for the New Senior
    by Sal Arrigo, Jr.
Boredom Busters: Themed Special Events to Dazzle and Delight Your Group
    by Annette C. Moore
Both Gains and Gaps: Feminist Perspectives on Women's Leisure
    by Karla Henderson, M. Deborah Bialeschki, Susan M. Shaw, and Valeria J. Freysinger
Brain Fitness
    by Suzanne Fitzsimmons
Client Assessment in Therapeutic Recreation Services
    by Norma J. Stumbo
Client Outcomes in Therapeutic Recreation Services
    by Norma J. Stumbo
Conceptual Foundations for Therapeutic Recreation
    edited by David R. Austin, John Dattilo, and Bryan P. McCormick
Constraints to Leisure
    edited by Edgar L. Jackson
Dementia Care Programming: An Identity-Focused Approach
    by Rosemary Dunne
Dimensions of Choice: Qualitative Approaches to Parks, Recreation, Tourism, Sport, and Leisure Research, Second Edition
    by Karla A. Henderson
Diversity and the Recreation Profession: Organizational Perspectives (Revised Edition)
    edited by Maria T. Allison and Ingrid E. Schneider
Effective Management in Therapeutic Recreation Service, Second Edition
    by Marcia Jean Carter and Gerald S. O'Morrow
Evaluating Leisure Services: Making Enlightened Decisions, Third Edition
    by Karla A. Henderson and M. Deborah Bialeschki
Everything from A to Y: The Zest Is up to You! Older Adult Activities for Every Day of the Year
    by Nancy R. Cheshire and Martha L. Kenney
The Evolution of Leisure: Historical and Philosophical Perspectives
    by Thomas Goodale and Geoffrey Godbey
Experience Marketing: Strategies for the New Millennium
    by Ellen L. O'Sullivan and Kathy J. Spangler

Facilitation Techniques in Therapeutic Recreation
    by John Dattilo
File o' Fun: A Recreation Planner for Games & Activities, Third Edition
    by Jane Harris Ericson and Diane Ruth Albright
Functional Interdisciplinary-Transdisciplinary Therapy (FITT) Manual
    by Deborah M. Schott, Judy D. Burdett, Beverly J. Cook, Karren S. Ford, and Kathleen M. Orban
The Game and Play Leader's Handbook: Facilitating Fun and Positive Interaction, Revised Edition
    by Bill Michaelis and John M. O'Connell
The Game Finder—A Leader's Guide to Great Activities
    by Annette C. Moore
Getting People Involved in Life and Activities: Effective Motivating Techniques
    by Jeanne Adams
Group Games & Activity Leadership
    by Kenneth J. Bulik
Growing With Care: Using Greenery, Gardens, and Nature With Aging and Special Populations
    by Betsy Kreidler
Hands On! Children's Activities for Fairs, Festivals, and Special Events
    by Karen L. Ramey
Health Promotion for Mind, Body, and Spirit
    by Suzanne Fitzsimmons and Linda L. Buettner
In Search of the Starfish: Creating a Caring Environment
    by Mary Hart, Karen Primm, and Kathy Cranisky
Inclusion: Including People With Disabilities in Parks and Recreation Opportunities
    by Lynn Anderson and Carla Brown Kress
Inclusive Leisure Services: Responding to the Rights of People with Disabilities, Second Edition
    by John Dattilo
Innovations: A Recreation Therapy Approach to Restorative Programs
    by Dawn R. De Vries and Julie M. Lake
Internships in Recreation and Leisure Services: A Practical Guide for Students, Fourth Edition
    by Edward E. Seagle, Jr. and Ralph W. Smith
Interpretation of Cultural and Natural Resources, Second Edition
    by Douglas M. Knudson, Ted T. Cable, and Larry Beck
Intervention Activities for At-Risk Youth
    by Norma J. Stumbo
Introduction to Outdoor Recreation: Providing and Managing Resource Based Opportunities
    by Roger L. Moore and B.L. Driver
Introduction to Recreation and Leisure Services, Eighth Edition
    by Karla A. Henderson, M. Deborah Bialeschki, John L. Hemingway, Jan S. Hodges, Beth D. Kivel, and
    H. Douglas Sessoms
Introduction to Therapeutic Recreation: U.S. and Canadian Perspectives
    by Kenneth Mobily and Lisa Ostiguy
Introduction to Writing Goals and Objectives: A Manual for Recreation Therapy Students and Entry-Level Professionals
    by Suzanne Melcher
Leadership and Administration of Outdoor Pursuits, Third Edition
    by James Blanchard, Michael Strong, and Phyllis Ford
Leadership in Leisure Services: Making a Difference, Third Edition
    by Debra J. Jordan
Leisure and Leisure Services in the 21st Century: Toward Mid Century
    by Geoffrey Godbey
The Leisure Diagnostic Battery Computer Software (CD)
    by Peter A. Witt, Gary Ellis, and Mark A. Widmer
Leisure Education I: A Manual of Activities and Resources, Second Edition
    by Norma J. Stumbo
Leisure Education II: More Activities and Resources, Second Edition
    by Norma J. Stumbo
Leisure Education III: More Goal-Oriented Activities
    by Norma J. Stumbo